Auditing and Accounting Studies

Markus P. Urban

The Influence of Blockholders on Agency Costs and Firm Value

An Empirical Examination of Blockholder Characteristics and Interrelationships for German Listed Firms

Foreword by Prof. Dr. Annette G. Köhler

Springer Gabler

Acknowledgements

The present work was written during my doctoral studies at the Chair of Accounting and Auditing at the Mercator School of Management, University of Duisburg-Essen. It was accepted as a dissertation by the Mercator School of Management - Faculty of Business Administration – in May 2015.

I am pleased to have the opportunity to express my thanks to all those who have supported me during the last three years. I would like to express my gratitude to my supervisor Prof. Dr. Annette G. Köhler for the opportunity to work and study at her chair. The outstanding working conditions at her chair as well as her academic and personal support throughout my doctoral studies were key success factors for the successful completion of the present work. I further want to express my gratitude to Prof. Dr. Prinz for being my second examiner. Moreover, I would like to thank Prof. Dr. Rolfes and Prof. Dr. Seidel for their participation in my examination committee as well as the interesting discussion during my dissertation defense. I also want to express my gratitude to PD Dr. Nicole V. S. Ratzinger-Sakel for her valuable assistance with regard to statistical problems.

During my doctoral studies, I was fortunate enough to work as part of a great team. The support I experienced from each member as well as the insight and expertise greatly assisted the research and contributed to the successful finalization of my thesis. In particular, I want to thank Jun. Prof. Dr. Marc Eulerich, Andrea Gantzhorn, Kirsten Gehring, StB Christian Hanke, Dr. Thilo Helpenstein, Meike Herbers, Dr. Katharina Köhler-Braun, Yu-Hui Liu, Jan Michael, Dr. Johanna Souad Qandil, Tatjana Schittko, Monika Schmock, Dr. Jochen Theis, Tatjana Wirt, Dr. Kristina Yankova as well as the student assistants at the Chair of Accounting and Auditing for the extraordinary working environment. It has been a great pleasure to work with you!

My biggest thanks, however, go to my private surroundings. I would like to express my sincere thanks to my girlfriend Tatjana Schittko for her constant readiness for professional discussions as well as her critical remarks – both greatly improved my manuscript and significantly helped me in completion of this research project. Besides her professional expertise, her outstanding patience and tolerance constituted an invaluable support, in particular during the final months of my thesis.

Finally, I would like to express my heart-felt gratitude to my parents Christel and Peter Urban. Throughout my life, they supported me in all my pursuits in any and every possible way. Their dedication and the many years of encouragement during my whole educational career provided the foundation for this work. I never could have accomplished this thesis without their unwavering, unconditional support, which is very much appreciated. I dedicate this work to my parents.

Markus Urban

Acknowledgements

Summary of the Contents

Table of Contents

List of Tables

List of Figures

List of Abbreviations

2SLS	Two-stage least squares
A	Agent
AAR	Average Abnormal Return
AEA	American Economic Association
AG	Joint stock company (German “Aktiengesellschaft”)
AGM	Annual General Meeting
AIF	Alternative Investment Fund
AIFM	Alternative Investment Fund Manager
AIFMD	Directive on Alternative Investment Fund Manager
AktG	Stock Corporation Act
AMEX	American Stock Exchange
AnlSVG	Investor Protection and Capital Markets Improvement Act
AnSVG	Investor Protection Improvement Act
ARUG	Shareholders’ Rights Directive Implementation Act
b.v.	besloten vennootschap (Dutch limited liability company)
BaFin	Federal Financial Supervisory Authority
BGBl.	Federal Law Gazette
BGH	Federal Court of Justice (Bundesgerichtshof)
BH	Blockholder
BICS	Bloomberg Industry Classification System
BilKoG	Financial Reporting Compliance Act
BilMoG	Accounting Law Modernization Act
BilReG	Accounting Law Reform Act
BMW	Bayerische Motoren Werke
bn	billion
BörsG	Stock Exchange Act
BT	British Telecommunications
BV	Book Value

KfW	Kreditanstalt für Wiederaufbau
KonTraG	Corporate Sector Supervision and Transparency Act
KStG	Corporate Income Tax Law
KWG	Banking Act
L1	Level 1
L2	Level 2
L3	Level 3
L4	Level 4
LBBW	Landesbank Baden-Württemberg
LM	Lagrange Multiplier
LSDV	Least Squares Dummy Variable
Ltd.	Limited
m	million
M.Sc.	Master of Science
M&A	Mergers & Acquisitions
Max	Maximum
MDAX	Mid Cap German Stock Index
MFI	Monetary Financial Institution
Min	Minimum
MIT	Massachusetts Institute of Technology
MitbestG	Codetermination Act
Montan-MitbestG	Mining, Iron and Steel Industry Codetermination Act
MV	Market Value
N	Quantity
No.	Number
NPV	Net Present Value
Nr.	Number (Nummer)
NYSE	New York Stock Exchange

obs.	observations
oec	oeconomicarum
OECD	Organisation for Economic Co-operation and Development
OLS	Ordinary Least Squares
Own.	(Equity) Ownership
P	Principal
pdf	portable document format
PE	Private Equity
PIPE	Private Investment in Public Equity
PP&E	Property Plant & Equipment
Prof.	Professor
R&D	Research & Development
RE	Reinsurance
Rer.	Rerum
RGBl.	Reich Law Gazette
RL	Directive (Richtlinie)
ROA	Return On Assets
S.a.r.l.	Société à responsabilité limitée
S&P	Standard & Poor's
SAP	Systemanalyse und Programmentwicklung
SD	Standard Deviation
SDAX	Small Cap German Stock Index
SE	Societas Europaea
SEAG	SE Implementation Act
SEBG	SE Employee Participation Act
SG&A	Selling, General & Administrative
SIC	Standard Industrial Classification

TecDax	Technology German Stock Index
TransPuG	Transparency and Disclosure Act
TU	Technische Universität
UCITS	Undertakings for Collective Investments in Transferable Securities
UCLA	University of California, Los Angeles
UK	United Kingdom
UMAG	Law on Corporate Integrity and Modernization of the Right of Avoidance
URL	Uniform Resource Locator
US	United States
USA	United States of America
US-GAAP	United States Generally Accepted Accounting Principles
VC	Venture Capital
VIF	Variance Inflation Factor
Vol.	Volume
VorstAG	Act on the Appropriateness of Management Board Remuneration
VorstOG	Act on the Disclosure of Management Board Remuneration
vs.	versus
w.r.t.	with respect to
WGZ Bank	Central bank for cooperative banks in Germany's Rhineland and Westphalia regions
WpHG	Securities Trading Act
WpÜG	Securities Acquisition and Takeover Act
www	world wide web
Xetra	Exchange Electronic Trading
ZR	Civil law (Zivilrecht)

List of Symbols

*	10% significance level
**	5% significance level
***	1% significance level
%	percent
~	approximately
&	and
§	paragraph
§§	paragraphs
€	Euro
$	Dollar
>	greater than
<	smaller than
Σ	sum
α	constant in a regression model
β	regression coefficient of the respective regression parameters
λ	the portion of the mean to be subtracted from the variables in the random effects model
μ_i	unobserved effect (also fixed effect) of individual i
v_{it}	idiosyncratic error term of individual i at time t
$\bar{v}_i$	v_{it} averaged over the t time periods
$\ddot{v}_{it}$	demeaned v_{it}
σ_μ^2	individual specific variance
χ^2	chi-square (test) statistic
age	difference between the respective sample year and a firm's year of incorporation
bank	presence of a bank that owns at least 5% of a firm's shares
beta	a firm's three year beta

bh_count	number of blockholders that have at least a 5% stake in the firm
BH1	largest blockholder
bh1_5to25	presence of a largest blockholder with equity ownership between 5 and 25%
bh1_25to50	presence of a largest blockholder with equity ownership between 25 and 50%
bh1_50to75	presence of a largest blockholder with equity ownership between 50 and 75%
bh1_75to100	presence of a largest blockholder with equity ownership between 75 and 100%
bh1_cont	percentage ownership of the largest blockholder, given it owns at least 5% of the firm's shares
$\widehat{\text{bh1\_cont}}$	predicted values of bh1_cont used in the 2SLS procedure
bh1_cont_sq	squared bh1_cont
bh1_dummy	presence of a blockholder which owns at least 5% of the firm's shares
bh1_fam_cont	percentage ownership of the largest blockholder, given it is a family and owns at least 5% of the firm's shares
bh1_fam_cont_sq	squared bh1_fam_cont
bh1_fam_cont*bh1_supb	interaction between bh1_fam_cont and bh1_supb
bh1_fam_cont*bh1_mgmtb	interaction between bh1_fam_cont and bh1_mgmtb
bh1_fam_cont*bh2_cont	interaction between bh1_fam_cont and bh2_cont
bh1_fam_cont*bh2_fam_cont	interaction between bh1_fam_cont and bh2_fam_cont
bh1_fam_cont*incont	interaction between bh1_fam_cont and each of the four incontestability variables, respectively
bh1_insti_cont	percentage ownership of the largest blockholder, given it is an institutional investor and owns at least 5% of the firm's shares
bh1_insti_cont_sq	squared bh1_insti_cont
bh1_insti_cont*bh2_cont	interaction between bh1_insti_cont and bh2_cont
bh1_insti_cont*bh2_insti_cont	interaction between bh1_insti_cont and bh2_insti_cont
bh1_insti_cont*incont	interaction between bh1_insti_cont and each of the four incontestability variables, respectively

bh1_majority	simultaneous presence of a largest blockholder which owns at least 50% of the firm's shares and of a second largest blockholder which owns less than 25% of the firm's shares
bh1_mgmtb	presence of the largest blockholder on its portfolio firm's management board
bh1_pe_cont	percentage ownership of the largest blockholder, given it is a private equity investor and owns at least 5% of the firm's shares
bh1_pe_cont_sq	squared bh1_pe_cont
bh1_pe_cont*bh1_supb	interaction between bh1_pe_cont and bh1_supb
bh1_pe_cont*bh1_mgmtb	interaction between bh1_pe_cont and bh1_mgmtb
bh1_pe_cont*bh2_cont	interaction between bh1_pe_cont and bh2_cont
bh1_pe_cont*bh2_pe_cont	interaction between bh1_pe_cont and bh2_pe_cont
bh1_pe_cont*incont	interaction between bh1_pe_cont and each of the four incontestability variables, respectively
bh1_si_cont	percentage ownership of the largest blockholder, given it is a strategic investor and owns at least 5% of the firm's shares
bh1_si_cont_sq	squared bh1_si_cont
bh1_si_cont*bh1_supb	interaction between bh1_si_cont and bh1_supb
bh1_si_cont*bh1_mgmtb	interaction between bh1_si_cont and bh1_mgmtb
bh1_si_cont*bh2_cont	interaction between bh1_si_cont and bh2_cont
bh1_si_cont*bh2_si_cont	interaction between bh1_si_cont and bh2_si_cont
bh1_si_cont*incont	interaction between bh1_si_cont and each of the four incontestability variables, respectively
bh1_supb	presence of the largest blockholder on its portfolio firm's supervisory board
bh1/bh2	ratio of the largest blockholder's ownership to the second largest blockholder's ownership
bh1/bh2_bh3	ratio of the largest blockholder's ownership to the sum of the second and third largest blockholders' ownership
BH2	second largest blockholder
bh2_cont	percentage ownership of the second largest blockholder, given it owns at least 5% of the firm's shares
bh2_fam_cont	percentage ownership of the second largest blockholder, given it is a family and owns at least 5% of the firm's shares

bh2_insti_cont	percentage ownership of the second largest blockholder, given it is an institutional investor and owns at least 5% of the firm's shares
bh2_pe_cont	percentage ownership of the second largest blockholder, given it is a private equity investor and owns at least 5% of the firm's shares
bh2_si_cont	percentage ownership of the second largest blockholder, given it is a strategic investor and owns at least 5% of the firm's shares
bhtypes_count	the number of blockholder types that have at least a 5% stake in the firm
bics_bm	basic materials industry
bics_comm	communications industry
bics_con_c	consumer, cyclical industry
bics_con_nonc	consumer, non-cyclical industry
bics_div	diversified industry
bics_enrgy	energy industry
bics_ind	industrial industry
bics_tec	technology industry
bics_ut	utilities industry
capex	ratio of capital expenditures to total assets
cash_assets	cash and marketable securities scaled by total assets
codet_par	dummy variable that equals one if a firm has more than 2,000 employees and zero otherwise
codet_third	dummy variable that equals one if a firm has more than 500 but less than 2,000 employees and zero otherwise
$CONTROL'_{it}$	the observation for the ith firm at the tth time period on the set of control variables
$\overline{CONTROL}'_{i}$	$CONTROL'_{it}$ averaged over the t time periods
$\ddot{CONTROL}_{it}$	demeaned $CONTROL'_{it}$
Cov(OWN,v)	covariance between an ownership variable and the idiosyncratic error term

cum_own	cumulative ownership size of all blockholders that own at least 5% of a particular firm's shares
debt	short- and long-term debt over total assets
diff_bh12345	sum of the squared differences between the ownership of the five largest blockholders, given they own at least 5% of the firm's shares
discr_assets	discretionary assets; measure of agency costs of debt
div_payout	regular cash dividend as a percentage of annual sales; measure of principal-principal agency costs
div_payout_a	regular cash dividend as a percentage of the firm's cash flows; alternative measure of principal-principal agency costs
div_prevy	dummy variable that equals one if the particular firm paid dividends in the previous year and zero otherwise
F	F (test) statistic
govt	presence of a governmental blockholder that owns at least 5% of the firm's shares
growth	percentage change in sales year-on-year
h_index	Herfindahl index; the sum of the squared individual ownership stakes of investors, given their individual stake is at least equal to 5% of the firm's shares
H_0	null hypothesis
i	indicator for individual (firm)
incont	term for the four incontestability variables
$INDUSTRY_i$	industry fixed effect that accounts for the industry of each individual i
insd_own	cumulative ownership of insiders, given their respective individual ownership stake is at least equal to 5% of the firm's shares
insolv	dummy variable that equals one if the firm went bankrupt and zero otherwise

K	number of (independent) regressors in a regression model
liq	presence of a firm in one of the major indices DAX, MDAX, SDAX, TecDax
ln_assets	logarithm of a firm's total assets
ln_bh_count	logarithm of the number of blockholders that have at least a 5% stake in the firm
ln_bhtypes_count	logarithm of the number of blockholder types that have at least a 5% stake in the firm
opex_sales	operating expenses scaled by annual sales; measure of managerial agency costs
OWN_{it}	the observation for the ith firm at the tth time period on the set of primary explanatory variables
$\overline{OWN}_i'$	OWN_{it} averaged over the t time periods
$\ddot{OWN}_{it}$	demeaned OWN_{it}
own_shares	dummy variable that equals one if the firm holds on shares and zero otherwise
pfd	presence of preferred stock
ppe_assets	ratio of net fixed assets to total assets
prof	net income (loss) scaled by total assets
R^2	coefficient of determination
resid	estimated residuals of a regression
RSS_{Post}	residual sum of squares for the post-crisis sample, comprising the years 2008-2012; used in the Chow test
RSS_{Pre}	residual sum of squares for the pre-crisis sample, comprising the years 2005-2007; used in the Chow test
RSS_w	residual sum of squares for the whole sample; used in the Chow test
SE_dummy	dummy variable that equals one if the firm is an SE

segm_chng	dummy variable that equals one if the firm changed the stock market segment and zero otherwise
stdev_ni	standard deviation of a firm's net income over the three years prior to the respective sample year
t	indicator for time period
t-1	indicator for a one-period time lag of the respective variable
t-2	indicator for a two-period time lag of the respective variable
T	number of observations of the whole sample; used in the Chow test
takeover	dummy variable that equals one if the firm was involved in a takeover, merger or squeeze-out and zero otherwise
tobinq	market value of a firm's assets divided by the replacement costs of the assets; measure of firm value
tobinq_3y_avg	tobinq averaged over the years t, t+1 and t+2
u_{it}	composite error term
$\bar{u}_i$	u_{it} averaged over the t time periods
X'_{it}	observation for the ith firm at the tth time period on a set of explanatory variables
$\bar{X}'_i$	X'_{it} averaged over the t time periods
y_{it}	observation for the ith firm at the tth time period on a dependent variable
$\bar{y}_i$	y_{it} averaged over the t time periods
$\ddot{y}_{it}$	demeaned y_{it}
$YEAR_t$	year fixed effect that comprises the year dummies of the t time periods
year_06	dummy variable for the year 2006
year_07	dummy variable for the year 2007
year_08	dummy variable for the year 2008
year_09	dummy variable for the year 2009

year_10	dummy variable for the year 2010
year_11	dummy variable for the year 2011
year_12	dummy variable for the year 2012
z	instrumental variable for bh1_cont

1 Introduction

The research at hand was given direction by a number of contemporary regulatory developments within the European Union as well as by some research gaps within the existing literature on shareholder monitoring. Section 1.1 highlights the regulatory developments, the purpose and main research questions of the present thesis resulting therefrom as well as the research gaps the present thesis intends to fill. The course of the present thesis is outlined in section 1.2.

1.1 Motivation and Purpose

> "Shareholders do not seem to have fulfilled their role of 'responsible owners', which entails actively monitoring companies and using shareholder rights to ensure long-term viability of companies and improve their corporate governance and strategy."[1]

This quote comes from the European Commission's staff working document accompanying the Green Paper on corporate governance in financial institutions published in June 2010. This Green Paper constitutes a response of the European Commission to the global financial crisis and aimed to review existing governance rules and practices in financial institutions, to make recommendations, and to remedy potential weaknesses.[2] Following the 2010 Green Paper, the Commission launched a broader review of the effectiveness of the existing corporate governance within publicly-traded firms in general. The findings were summarized in the Green Paper on the EU corporate governance framework, which was published in November 2011.[3] In both Green Papers, the Commission attaches great attention to shareholder monitoring and shareholder engagement as well as to the general role of shareholders within the governance system of companies.[4] However, as implied by the above mentioned quote, both papers criticize the role played by shareholders in the governance of their portfolio firms[5]. The Commission criticizes that shareholders, inter alia, (1) are disinterested and passive,[6] (2) frequently fail to identify and respond to weaknesses in supervisory or management boards[7] and (3) are short-term oriented.[8] Overall, the Commission states that "the financial crisis has shown that confidence in the model of the shareholder-owner who contributes to the compa-

---

1 European Commission (2010a): 23f.

2 See Commission of the European Communities (2009) for further details.

3 See European Commission (2011a): 2f.

4 The European Commission (2011a): 11 defines shareholder engagement as "actively monitoring companies, engaging in a dialogue with the company's board, and using shareholder rights, including voting and cooperation with other shareholders, if need be to improve the governance of the investee company in the interests of long-term value creation." The definition of shareholder monitoring used in the present thesis is outlined in detail in chapter 3.

5 Throughout this study, the term "firm" refers to a publicly-held entity which is meant to describe "economic organizations in which (i) management and residual claimant status (shareholding) are separable and separated functions; (ii) the residual claims (shares) are held by a number of persons; and (iii) the residual claims are freely transferable and neither entry to nor exit from the firm is restricted." Dooley (1992): 463, FN 9. The terms "firm", "corporation" and "company" are used interchangeably.

6 See European Commission (2010b): 8.

7 See European Commission (2010a): 24.

8 See European Commission (2011a): 11.

ny's long-term viability has been severely shaken"[9] which "raises questions about the effectiveness of corporate governance rules based on the presumption of effective control by shareholders"[10]. Due to these findings, the 2011 Green Paper raised a number of questions focusing, inter alia, on means to encourage shareholder monitoring and to facilitate shareholder cooperation, the necessity of shareholder identification, and the monitoring ability and protection of minority shareholders.[11] Based on the results of the public consultation with regard to the two Green Papers, the European Commission addressed these aspects also in the 2012 Action Plan on European company law and corporate governance. With regard to shareholders, it aims to improve the visibility of shareholders, the identification of the different shareholder types, the simplification of shareholder cooperation, and the general facilitation of shareholder engagement in the governance of their investee firms.[12]

As a more specific response to the financial crisis, the European Commission developed the directive on alternative investment fund managers (AIFMD)[13], which was published in 2011 and had to be transposed into national law of the member states by July 2013.[14] The Commission argued that the crisis highlighted the need to extend the existing regulation to all actors and activities that have been shown to embed significant risks to the financial markets.[15] The new regulation affects, inter alia, hedge funds, private equity funds, real estate, commodity and infrastructure funds.[16] With specific regard to private equity funds, the regulation envisages the AIFs making substantial disclosures upon the acquisition of a controlling interest, such as its intended future strategy and the effects on the firm's workforce.[17] Moreover, to limit asset stripping[18], it constrains the AIFs' ability to request any distribution (dividends or interest), capital reduction or acquisition of own shares by the respective investee firms within a period of two years following the acquisition.[19]

At least since the global financial crisis, shareholder engagement is also high on the agenda of policymakers on a global level. In light of and as a response to the crisis, the OECD's corporate governance steering group reviewed its corporate governance principles[20] and stressed the

---

9 European Commission (2010b): 8.

10 European Commission (2010b): 8. See also European Commission (2012): 8. This, in particular, refers to institutional investors. See European Commission (2010a): 24.

11 See European Commission (2011a): 3f, 15-17.

12 See European Commission (2012): 7-9; 11. These regulatory developments are outlined in greater detail in section 2.3.1.

13 The definition of AIFs encompasses investment funds that are not already regulated on a European level by the Directive on Undertakings for Collective Investment in Transferable Securities (UCITS Directive). For details on the definition of investment funds, see European Commission (2011b): Article 4 (1) a). For details on the UCITS Directive, please see European Commission (2009a).

14 See European Commission (2011b): Article 66 (1) and (2) as well as Article 70. In Germany, this Directive has been implemented with the Capital Investment Code (KAGB) in July 2013.

15 See Kramer (2011): 2077; Viciano-Gofferje (2013): 2506.

16 See European Commission (2009b): 2; European Commission (2009c): 4.

17 See § 290 (4) KAGB. See also Kramer (2011): 2083.

18 Asset stripping typically involves the acquisition of an undervalued firm with the goal of selling the components of the firm for a profit. See Berglöf (1994): 248f.

19 See § 292 (1) KAGB. See also Kramer (2011): 2083; Wollenhaupt/Beck (2013): 1955. For further details on this directive, please see section 2.3.2.

20 See also Kirkpatrick (2009).

encouragement and effective implementation of these principles.[21] Similar to the European Commission, the OECD steering group also regards the exercise of voting rights as one factor closely linked to company failures.[22] It argues, inter alia, that the interests of some shareholders and management were aligned during the past bull market, which resulted in the shareholders' neglect of the effect of excessive risk taking policies.[23] Moreover, the steering group states that shareholders tended to be reactive rather than proactive and only infrequently challenged a firm's management. In particular institutional investors are also subject to interest conflicts[24], which restrain them from playing an active, informed role. In general, in line with the European Commission, the steering group recognizes that institutional (and other) shareholders should not be discouraged from acting in concert at AGMs[25] and stresses the importance of encouraging shareholder engagement and of identifying shareholders.[26]

As becomes evident from this delineation, shareholder monitoring is currently at the heart of the corporate governance debate in an international context. Key issues constitute, but are not limited to: (1) the encouragement of shareholder engagement/monitoring, (2) minority shareholder protection, (3) means to facilitate and simplify shareholder cooperation, (4) the importance of improving the visibility and identification of shareholders, (5) the role of institutional investors, and (6) the regulation of private equity funds and other AIFMs. These issues require a clearer theoretical and empirical understanding of the nature and effect of shareholder monitoring. In particular, it is necessary to clarify if shareholder monitoring is effective in improving firm value[27] and/or performance in the first place and to determine if the effectiveness and intensity of shareholder monitoring depend on certain shareholder characteristics. Moreover, any assessment of the need for minority shareholder protection requires empirical evidence that provides proof of an exploitation of minority shareholders by larger shareholders in the European Union. In addition, the facilitation of shareholder cooperation calls for an investigation of the theoretical costs and benefits of shareholder cooperation, the performance impact of shareholder cooperation, and the ownership structures that may facilitate shareholder cooperation. With regard to shareholder identification, the resulting effort and costs can only be warranted if distinctions in the monitoring effectiveness or intensity exerted by different shareholder types can be observed. Furthermore, it is essential to empirically assess if institutional shareholders are indeed subject to interest conflicts and hence less effective monitors

---

21 See OECD (2009): 7.

22 In particular, it states that "shareholders have contributed importantly to failures of boards and companies by being too passive and reactive." OECD (2009): 53. The remaining factors linked to company failures constitute remuneration and incentive systems, risk management practices and the performance of supervisory boards. See OECD (2009) for details. Note that these factors primarily refer to financial institutions.

23 See OECD (2009): 53.

24 In this thesis, interest conflicts are expected to arise if a shareholder, alongside its equity investment, has direct or indirect interconnections with and is dependent on the investee firm for existing or future business. In this case, the interests with regard to its role as a shareholder and its role as a business partner might be in conflict. This is not to be confused with the expression conflicts of interest used in an agency theoretic context. Please see section 2.1.1.2.

25 See OECD (2009): 10f.

26 See OECD (2009): 49.

27 In the present study, the term "firm value" refers to the market value of the firm, i.e. the value that equals the market capitalization of a firm in an efficient market. For a definition of an efficient market in this study, please see section 5.1.2.

relative to other types of shareholders. Finally, the disclosure regulation constitutes a substantial burden on and higher costs for private equity firms. Besides, the constraints concerning distributions made by their portfolio firms may be regarded as a substantial qualification and restriction of a private equity firm's shareholder rights.[28] In order to justify this strict regulation,[29] it is important to empirically assess and compare monitoring performed by private equity firms with the influence of other shareholder types.[30]

Focusing on German firms, the present thesis addresses these aspects and provides a clearer understanding of the nature and effect of shareholder monitoring. Therefore, it uses the agency theory and its propositions to develop a theoretical model of blockholder[31] monitoring. The governance literature typically presumes that the significant ownership[32] of the blockholder provides it with the incentive to monitor the firm and its management which reduces managerial agency costs and ultimately increases firm value.[33] This (traditional) understanding of blockholder monitoring is extended in the present thesis which presumes that the blockholder's monitoring not only affects managerial agency costs but has a simultaneous influence on additional agency conflicts within its portfolio firm.[34] As a consequence, the blockholder's impact on firm value does not only depend on the effect on the managerial agency conflict but on the net effect of the blockholder's monitoring on *all* agency conflicts inherent in the portfolio firm. The effect of blockholder monitoring on a firm's agency costs and firm value is examined in separate analyses which enables an assessment of whether or not an effect on a firm's agency costs is indeed reflected in firm value as suggested by the traditional understanding of blockholder monitoring. Overall, the purpose of the present thesis is *to determine the influence of blockholders on agency costs and firm value.* Therefore, it investigates three research questions which gradually increase in the attention to detail paid to characteristics of the blockholders and to the firms' ownership structure. The first research question is based on blockholder homogeneity and does not account for any blockholder characteristic that might affect blockholder monitoring. It primarily serves as a base case for the two remaining research questions:

Does concentrated ownership affect agency costs and firm value?

---

28 See Wollenhaupt/Beck (2013): 1955.

29 Also the OECD realizes that the role of alternative investors, such as private equity and hedge funds, which engaged in active monitoring in recent years, "should not be hampered as a side-effect of regulatory reforms". OECD (2009): 54.

30 This assessment is of further relevance since the political debate in Europe and especially in Germany is largely skeptical of alternative investment funds, especially with regard to private equity firms and other institutional investors. See e.g. Kengelbach/Roos (2006): 12; Watt (2008): 548; Kroker/Rapp/Wolff (2010): 21; Stadler (2010): 8. These investors are criticized for a focus on profits and their perceived short-termism which impairs "stakeholders' interests and the long-term prospects of target firms." Achleitner/Betzer/Gider (2010): 806. Short-termism in this thesis refers to "actions that are profitable in the short term but value-decreasing in the long term". Bebchuk (2013): 1638f.

31 In the present thesis, a blockholder is defined as a shareholder owning at least 5% of the firm's equity.

32 Unless stated otherwise, (share) ownership refers to an equal number of cash flow and voting rights held by a particular shareholder.

33 See e.g. Shleifer/Vishny (1986): 463; Zeckhauser/Pound (1990): 149; Black (1992a): 823; Jensen (1993): 867; Shleifer/Vishny (1997): 753f; Becht/Bolton/Röell (2005): 17.

34 Dependent on the firm's capital structure and ownership structure, these additional agency conflicts comprise shareholder-debtholder agency conflicts, minority shareholder-blockholder agency conflicts, and blockholder-blockholder agency conflicts.

The second research question is based on blockholder heterogeneity and explicitly includes blockholder characteristics that may influence the intensity and effectiveness of blockholder monitoring:

Do the characteristics of the largest blockholder affect agency costs and firm value?

These characteristics refer to the size of the ownership, the blockholder's presence on either the supervisory board or management board,[35] and the blockholder's identity. The identities accounted for comprise (founding) families, strategic, institutional and private equity investors. The second research question allows conclusions with regard to the determinants of blockholder monitoring and a comparison of the effectiveness and intensity of monitoring across the different blockholder identities. Such a comparison helps to assess if institutional investors are indeed less effective monitors relative to other blockholder types and if an adverse impact of private equity firms on agency costs and firm value is observable that justifies their strict regulation.[36]

The third research question additionally incorporates blockholder interrelationships that result from ownership structures with multiple blockholders:

Do blockholder interrelationships affect agency costs and firm value as well as the relationship between the four blockholder types and agency costs and firm value?

The investigation of blockholder interrelationships focuses on the effect of a heterogenous ownership structure, the largest blockholder's incontestability, and the presence of a second blockholder. The latter aspect, especially, is expected to provide insights on the (empirical) effect of shareholder cooperation and the ownership structures that may facilitate shareholder cooperation.

Since the research, inter alia, focuses on the impact of blockholder monitoring on the minority shareholder-blockholder agency conflict, it also allows conclusions with regard to the necessity of minority shareholder protection that is proposed by the European Commission. Moreover, due to its focus on the years 2005-2012, the research further enables an investigation of blockholder monitoring during the financial crisis and thus provides evidence on whether blockholder monitoring, at least in Germany, was indeed ineffective during the crisis. Overall, the research is expected to provide meaningful evidence relevant to the issues raised by (European) regulators.

Furthermore, the research plays a part in contributing to an advancement of the current state of academic knowledge with regard to the influence of blockholders on firm-level variables and in filling the existing research gaps. More recent studies criticize the dichotomous focus of the corporate governance theory on widely dispersed ownership and the presence of a sin-

35 In this thesis, the terms "presence" and "representation" in this context are used interchangeably. In both cases, they should not be understood as the mere passive presence on the respective board but as a sign of an active involvement in the monitoring of the firm.

36 Bonini/Alkan/Salvi (2012): 21 argue that with specific regard to private equity and venture capital firms, there still exists a research gap comprising the impact of these investors on the governance structures within the firms as well as the impact of the investment size.

gle, large shareholder.[37] This traditional view of corporate governance regards other shareholders as passive observers in the control processes of a firm and fails to recognize the role played by blockholders beyond the largest blockholder despite their pervasiveness particularly within the continental European context.[38] Due to this, researchers began to extend their focus beyond the largest blockholder to incorporate the presence of additional blockholders.[39] These studies substantially differ in the extent to which additional blockholders are incorporated. For instance, *Konijn et al.* (2011) account for blockholder dispersion,[40] *Attig et al.* (2009) focus on the number of large shareholders[41] and *Renneboog/Trojanowski* (2007) measure the relative voting power.[42] While these studies represent a major advancement in the governance literature, their analyses are still aggregate and fail to account for the different identities of both the largest blockholder and the remaining blockholders.[43] However, the identities of the blockholders within a single firm might have significant impact on the likelihood of principal-principal agency conflicts. Moreover, these studies focus on the effect of the additional blockholders on, for instance, firm value; they do not provide insights on how the presence of additional blockholders affects the relationship between the largest blockholder and firm value relative to firms without additional blockholders. Finally, the studies lack sound theoretical reasoning to serve as a foundation of their proposed relationships. Overall, despite major advancements within the past years, there is still a research gap with regard to the effect of blockholder interrelationships on firm-level variables.

Disregarding potential blockholder interrelationships, most empirical studies focus on the direct effect of blockholder monitoring on some measures of firm value or performance.[44] In contrast, "only very few studies directly tackle the measurement issue of the principal variable of interest, namely agency costs."[45] To the best of the author's knowledge, no research exists

[37] See e.g. Attig/Guedhami/Mishra (2008): 721; Laeven/Levine (2008): 579; Attig/El Ghoul/Guedhami (2009): 396; Konijn/Kräussl/Lucas (2011): 1330f; Hamzah/Zulkafli (2014): 107f. Cronqvist/Fahlenbrach (2008): 3949 view the disregard of other shareholders within their sample firms' ownership structure to be a limitation of their study. Moreover, Renneboog/Trojanowski (2007): 50 argue that ownership stakes alone represent only a crude proxy for the power of a particular blockholder, since the disregard of the stakes owned by other shareholders does not enable the measurement of the largest blockholder's relative power.

[38] See e.g. the study of Laeven/Levine (2008): 586f. The authors find that 50.1% of the firms have a shareholder with more than 10% ownership and 34% of the firms have multiple large shareholders. Their sample includes 1,657 firms from Austria, Belgium, Finland, France, Germany, Ireland, Italy, Norway, Portugal, Spain, Sweden, Switzerland, and the United Kingdom.

[39] See e.g. Maury/Pajuste (2005); Attig et al. (2008); Laeven/Levine (2008); Jara-Bertin/López-Iturriaga/López-de-Foronda (2008); Attig et al. (2009); Konijn et al. (2011); Hamzah/Zulkafli (2014). Gutiérrez/Tribó (2004) focus on closely-held corporations. The role of multiple shareholders has already been described theoretically by Zwiebel (1995) and Bennedsen/Wolfenzon (2000).

[40] See Konijn et al. (2011): 1331f.

[41] See Attig et al. (2009): 397.

[42] See Renneboog/Trojanowski (2007): 49-51.

[43] Exceptions are Maury/Pajuste (2005); Attig et al. (2008); Laeven/Levine (2008); Konijn et al. (2011) and Ruiz-Mallorquí/Santana-Martín (2011). However, these studies are limited in that they analyze the effect of multiple blockholders only for a single type of dominant shareholder. E.g. Attig et al. (2008): 734 state that "it would be interesting to compare the ownership and control incentives and entrenchment effects of multiple blockholders." Jara-Bertin et al. (2008): 155 suggest that "a more detailed description of the types of shareholders and the interactions among them could provide interesting insights."

[44] See e.g. Thomsen/Pedersen (2000); Cronqvist/Nilsson (2003); Bhagat/Black/Blair (2004); Thomsen/Pedersen/Kvist (2006); Andres (2008); Setia-Atmaja (2009); Renders/Gaeremynck (2012).

[45] Florackis (2008): 38. Studies that focus on managerial agency costs include Ang/Cole/Lin (2000); Cronqvist/Nilsson (2003); Fleming/Heaney/McCosker (2005) and Sánchez-Ballesta/García-Meca (2011).

that simultaneously investigates the impact of blockholder monitoring on all types of agency costs and firm value. This is surprising, given that the traditional corporate governance perspective presumes the increase in firm value to be a result of the reduction in (managerial) agency costs stemming from the blockholder's monitoring. Due to this, it appears obvious to subject this theoretical presumption to an empirical assessment. Also *David/Hitt/Gimeno* (2001) criticize the focus of the existing literature on the direct effect of monitoring on firm performance, as "the causal chain leading from activism to performance may include several intermediate links."[46] They further argue that researchers need to pay attention to the mediators between monitoring and performance for a full understanding of the effect of blockholder monitoring.[47] In contrast to existing studies, the thesis at hand combines the measurements of agency costs and firm value into a single study and examines if the effect of blockholder monitoring on firm value is indeed attributable to its effect on a firm's agency costs. Thereby, it provides new evidence on the influence and functioning of blockholder monitoring.

Starting in the late-1990s and early-2000s, the German financial system underwent some major changes.[48] As a result of these changes, the financial system has been moving away from a bank-based model which, inter alia, significantly affected German corporate ownership patterns. According to *Ringe* (2014), the changed ownership pattern manifests itself in three aspects: a decreasing ownership concentration, a reduction of bank ownership in non-financial companies, and a rise of international, institutional investors.[49] These changes necessitate an examination of the evolution of the ownership structure of German publicly-traded firms in order to highlight the changes in German corporate ownership patterns and to provide an up-to-date description of the ownership structure that is able to map the newly formed ownership patterns on a sufficient level of detail. Moreover, these changes illustrate the need for an investigation of the influence of blockholder monitoring on German firms in the context of the changed ownership patterns and legal environment. This is achieved by the study at hand, which investigates the influence of blockholders on agency costs and firm value for the period of 2005-2012 and simultaneously accounts for two peculiarities of the German environment, namely the (still) strong role of banks as well as the legally mandated employee codetermination on supervisory boards.[50] Overall, the present thesis provides new evidence on the influ-

---

Anderson/Mansi/Reeb (2003) focus on agency costs of debt. Gugler/Yurtoglu (2003): 733 and Truong/Heaney (2007) focus on principal-principal agency costs.

46 David/Hitt/Gimeno (2001): 154.

47 Edwards/Weichenrieder (2004): 146, for example, are unable to specify if the presence of a second blockholder positively affects firm value due to its monitoring of management (i.e. due to a reduction of managerial agency costs) or due to its monitoring of the major blockholder (i.e. due to a reduction of principal-principal agency costs).

48 These changes, inter alia, refer to the regulatory framework, the role of capital markets, and banks.

49 For details, please see Ringe (2014): 11-19. Further details on the changes in the ownership structure are also provided in section 2.2.4 and 6.2.2-6.2.4 of this thesis.

50 A number of researchers argue that predictions based on a single corporate governance mechanism do not necessarily capture its real effect until other mechanisms are simultaneously controlled for, since certain governance mechanisms constitute complements or substitutes. See e.g. Bhagat/Jefferis Jr. (2002): 25; Börsch-Supan/Köke (2002): 297; Beiner et al. (2006): 252; Kaserer/Moldenhauer (2008): 9. Therefore, by controlling for bank presence and codetermination (as well as for the level of leverage and insider ownership), the present thesis at least partially addresses this criticism.

ence and functioning of blockholder monitoring as well as new evidence on corporate ownership patterns relative to existing studies[51] in the German environment.

As previously stated, the purpose of the present thesis is to determine the influence of blockholders on agency costs and firm value which it aims to achieve by investigating three research questions. In answering these research questions and to meet the purpose of the present research, the thesis at hand adopts a *positive* scientific approach, which primarily focuses on drawing theoretically-guided causal inferences.[52] According to *Creswell* (2009), problems studied by the positive approach "reflect the need to identify and assess the causes that influence outcomes"[53]. In achieving its purpose, the present research uses an approach which can be classified as *deductive*.[54] In particular, it builds on and extends the agency theory and its propositions in order to derive hypotheses on the relationship between blockholder characteristics or interrelationships and agency costs and firm value. Thereby, an essential quality of the hypotheses is their falsifiability or refutability.[55] The causal relationships specified within the hypotheses are subsequently tested (and falsified) in an empirical analysis. The results obtained in the empirical analysis have implications for the aforementioned key issues raised within the current corporate governance debate. Thus, although not being an explicit objective of the present thesis, its results – i.e. the identified cause-and-effect-relationships – can be used to address these key issues and formulate recommendations or suggestions. Thereby, the present thesis goes beyond the discovery of causal relationships, which constitutes the goal of a purely positive approach, and adopts a *normative* scientific approach.[56]

1.2 Structure

The thesis at hand is divided into a theoretical and empirical part and comprises seven chapters. Following this introductory chapter, *chapter 2* begins with the theoretical foundation and the institutional environment. Section 2.1 focuses on the agency theory which constitutes the foundation for the development of the theoretical model and the formulation of the corresponding hypotheses to be investigated empirically. The goal is to define agency theory, introduce the types of agency conflicts and the associated agency costs relevant in the present thesis as well as to outline corporate governance and its mechanisms as a potential solution to these agency conflicts. Since the relevance of the agency conflicts described in section 2.1 depends on the institutional environment in which the respective parties interact, section 2.2 provides a detailed overview and analysis of the institutional environment in which the sam-

---

51 See e.g. Edwards/Nibler (2000); Lehmann/Weigand (2000); Köke (2001); Bott (2002); Ruhwedel (2003); Kehren (2006); Groß (2007); Andres (2008), to name a few.

52 See Hussey/Hussey (1997): 52; Kornmeier (2007): 25-28, 30; Creswell (2009): 6f. The positive approach is to be distinguished from the normative approach. The latter approach focuses on the derivation of suggestions or recommendations and makes statements about things as they ought to be. See also Kornmeier (2007): 25-28, 30.

53 Creswell (2009): 7. For some key assumptions of the (post)positivist worldview, see Creswell (2009): 7.

54 See Hussey/Hussey (1997): 13. See also Creswell (2009): 55-57. The former authors state that since it uses a broad theory to deduct particular instances, deductive research can also be said to move from the general to the specific.

55 See Kornmeier (2007): 40-42. Loosely speaking, the hypotheses have to be empirically testable.

56 In particular, it uses the identified cause-and-effect relationships to develop possibilities for problem solving which in German terminology refers to an approach called "Wirtschaftstechnologie". See Kornmeier (2007): 24f. See also Theis (2014): 5.

ple firms and their blockholders operate. Thereby, this overview begins with a general description of the German financial system and the changes it has been subject to (section 2.2.1). Subsequently, it elaborates on more specific aspects of the institutional environment, in particular, the corporate governance system (section 2.2.2), the rights and obligations of shareholders (section 2.2.3), and the ownership structure (section 2.2.4). Given the description of the characteristics of the German institutional environment most important for the purpose of this thesis, section 2.2.5 clarifies the relevance of the agency conflicts in the German environment. Section 2.3 then focuses on two contemporary regulatory developments within the European Union and points out a number of issues arising from these developments that gave direction to the topic of the present thesis. Chapter 2 concludes with a brief résumé in section 2.4.

Chapter 3 is devoted to the key object of research and enlarges upon monitoring by a blockholder. The traditional corporate governance perspective expects that a blockholder with sufficient and constant equity ownership has both the incentive and power to effectively monitor firm management to the benefit of the remaining shareholders. This traditional definition of blockholder monitoring is covered in section 3.1, which highlights the functioning of blockholder monitoring (section 3.1.1), monitoring mechanisms (section 3.1.2) as well as some costs and benefits of blockholder monitoring (section 3.1.3). As the traditional definition of blockholder monitoring suffers from a number of deficiencies, section 3.2 presents these deficiencies (section 3.2.1) and introduces a revised definition of blockholder monitoring (section 3.2.2) which amends the deficiencies and is therefore better suited for the purpose of this thesis. In order to highlight problems of the existing studies that fail to account for blockholder heterogeneity, blockholder interrelationships or other determinants potentially affecting the blockholder's monitoring, section 3.3 summarizes empirical evidence on the influence of blockholder monitoring on several firm-level variables that treats blockholders as a homogenous group. Moreover, it illustrates the implications of this evidence for the present study. A short résumé is provided in section 3.4.

Building on the implications illustrated in chapter 3, *chapter 4* presents possible determinants of blockholder monitoring frequently disregarded in existing empirical evidence. Section 4.1 concentrates on blockholder characteristics which constitute the size of the blockholder's equity ownership (section 4.1.1), the blockholder's management or supervisory board presence (section 4.1.2), and the blockholder's identity (section 4.1.3). Section 4.2 focuses on blockholder interrelationships that may arise from the presence of multiple blockholders within a single investee firm. Finally, section 4.3 comprises some determinants that do not constitute key aspects within the present research, namely the legal environment (section 4.3.1), the presence of alternative governance mechanisms (section 4.3.2) as well as portfolio firm characteristics (section 4.3.3). For each determinant of blockholder monitoring, the respective section summarizes the theory as well as the empirical evidence with regard to the determinant's impact on blockholder monitoring. This approach is summarized in section 4.4.

Chapter 5 combines the preceding analyses of the theoretical background and institutional environment, the revised definition of blockholder monitoring, and the determinants of blockholder monitoring. The goal is to introduce the theoretical model of blockholder monitoring and the corresponding hypotheses to be empirically investigated as well as the operationalization of the model. Section 5.1 begins with an explanation of the model of blockholder monitoring (section 5.1.1) and highlights the assumptions underlying this model (section 5.1.2). Based on agency theoretic propositions, section 5.2 then derives the hypotheses to be investigated. After a short description of the reasoning underlying the hypotheses development, the sections 5.2.2-5.2.4 outline the hypotheses based on arguments provided in chapter 3 and 4. Thereby, they are grouped according to the three research questions the thesis aims to address. Having outlined the theoretical model and the corresponding hypotheses, section 5.3 is concerned with the operationalization of the components of the model. Section 5.3.1 focuses on the operationalization of the (dependent) agency cost and firm value variables. Section 5.3.2 and 5.3.3 focus on the key explanatory variables. Due to the complexity of their definition, section 5.3.2 is devoted to the blockholder identities. The remaining ownership structure variables are introduced in section 5.3.3 which is also structured in line with the three research questions. Relevant control variables are defined in section 5.3.4. Section 5.4 contains a short résumé.

The empirical analysis used to investigate the three research questions constitutes the focus of *chapter 6*. Prior to the empirical analysis, however, section 6.1 outlines the reasoning underlying the sample selection and construction as well as the data sources. Section 6.2 then provides a descriptive analysis of the sample. Subsequent to some summary statistics (section 6.2.1), the descriptive analysis reflects the three research questions and is based on the assumption of blockholder homogeneity (section 6.2.2), blockholder heterogeneity (section 6.2.3), and blockholder interrelationships (section 6.2.4). The goal is to provide an up-to-date description of the ownership structure of German publicly-held firms that goes beyond the level of the largest blockholder and to present evidence for the existence of ownership patterns with multiple blockholders that necessitate an empirical analysis. The descriptive analysis is followed by a regression analysis in section 6.3. Subsequent to a description and justification of the chosen methodology in section 6.3.1, each of the three research questions and the corresponding hypotheses are investigated separately in the sections 6.3.2-6.3.4. In order to verify the robustness of the results, a number of robustness tests are conducted in section 6.3.5. Chapter 6 concludes with a discussion of some limitations of the study.

Finally, *chapter 7* presents the conclusion. Therefore, it summarizes the selected approach as well as the key findings. Moreover, it uses these findings to address the key issues raised by the current debate on blockholder monitoring and formulates recommendations and suggestions. The chapter closes with a presentation of some opportunities for future research.

2 Theoretical Foundation and Institutional Environment

This thesis examines the influence of blockholders on agency costs and firm value of German listed firms from an agency theoretic perspective. As a result, the following basic questions arise: 1) What is meant by the term "agency theory" and what are its propositions? 2) How do agency costs arise and what different types of agency costs exist in listed firms? 3) Are there any mechanisms that can be used to mitigate agency costs? 4) What is the role of the German institutional environment within this analysis? The sections that follow are organized around these questions germane to the present research. Section 2.1 provides a definition of agency theory and introduces different types of agency conflicts and the resulting agency costs. Moreover, it elucidates corporate governance and its mechanisms as instruments to mitigate agency costs. Section 2.2 then provides an analysis of the institutional environment in which the firms and their blockholders operate. Finally, section 2.3 covers the institutional environment in the EU, in particular two contemporary regulatory developments that had an impact on the research design of this thesis. Section 2.4 provides a résumé.

2.1 Agency Theory

The corporate form, characterized by a separation of ownership and control, has consistently proven to constitute a superior business organization.[57] However, the corporation has not existed and functioned without deficiencies. The numerous problems arising from the agency nature of the different relationships within the corporate form have continuously constrained its economic effectiveness. The goal of this part is to provide a basic understanding of these relationships and the resulting problems.

Therefore, section 2.1.1 first introduces the agency theory, its definitions, and key elements. Sections 2.1.2-2.1.4 present the different types of agency conflicts and the resulting agency problems inherent in the corporate form and relevant in the context of this thesis. While the presence of agency problems is considered a fact by classic agency theory, it remains vague regarding the nature of the problems.[58] Therefore, the sections provide examples of the manifestation of the respective agency conflicts. Although the agency theory is "the dominant theme of empirical examinations of the relationship between equity ownership and financial performance"[59], its adequacy and applicability in the present context should still be illustrated. Hence, these sections also aim to clarify whether one can reasonably presume the presence of agency conflicts within the respective relationships altogether. Section 2.1.5 then introduces the concept of agency costs as a direct result of the agency problems. In the presence of these agency theoretic relationships and the problems and costs they bring along, the question is how to ensure an effective and efficient operation of the corporate form. Corporate governance, regarded as an instrument to ensure this effective and efficient operation, is covered in section 2.1.6.

57 See also Bhagat/Jefferis Jr. (2002): 13.
58 See Shapiro (2005): 279.
59 Dalton et al. (2003): 13.

2.1.1 Foundations of Agency Theory

The agency theory, together with the property rights and transaction cost theory, constitutes the theoretical structure of the new institutional economics.[60] Therefore, it makes sense to shortly introduce and demarcate the new institutional economics as well as the property rights and transaction cost theory in section 2.1.1.1 before probing into the agency theory within section 2.1.1.2.

2.1.1.1 New Institutional Economics

The new institutional economics sets itself the goal of explicating the reasons for the existence of (economic) institutions[61], their purpose, and to "demonstrate that institutions are susceptible to analysis."[62] It traces back to the seminal paper "The Nature of the Firm" by *Coase* (1937). Within this paper, he raises the question of why firms[63] exist, given that "if production is regulated by price movements, production could be carried on without any organization at all."[64] He proposes that the major reasons for the establishment of a firm are the costs of using the price mechanism of the external market,[65] i.e. transaction costs. He argues that by the establishment of an organization, transaction costs can be lowered.[66] These thoughts have been neglected until the early seventies.[67] At this time, researchers were taking up the thoughts of Coase, forming the foundation for the new institutional economics.[68] For example, *Williamson* (1971) proposes that internal organizations offer advantages relative to the market due to a number of beneficial internal properties and "transactional failures"[69] in the operation of external markets. With regard to the former, internal organization mitigates aggressive bargaining, possesses efficient conflict resolution mechanisms and offers informational advantages[70]. In addition, internal organization attenuates failures of the external market that result in transaction costs, such as contractual incompleteness and a defective specification of property rights.[71] Hence, organizations are regarded as "a means of achieving the benefits of collective action in situations in which the price system fails."[72]

---

60 See Witt (2001): 85. See also Ampenberger (2010): 37.

61 North (1991): 97 defines institutions as "the humanly devised constraints that structure political, economic and social interaction. They consist of both informal constraints (sanctions, taboos, customs, traditions, and codes of conduct), and formal rules (constitutions, laws, property rights)."

62 Williamson (1998): 25. See also Richter (1994): 3.

63 While Coase (1937) does not provide an exact definition of the firm, Williamson (2000): 602 states that within new institutional economics, it is necessary "to consider the firm as a governance structure (which is an organizational construction) in which internal structure has economic purpose and effect."

64 Coase (1937): 388.

65 With this assumption, the new institutional economics abandoned the proposition of perfect markets, being the cornerstone of the neoclassic financial theory. See Wolf (1999): 7f.

66 See Coase (1937): 392. Later, authors realized that there is a replacement of the transaction costs existing on the market by the costs of intra-firm transfers. See Arrow (1969): 1. See also Williamson (1971).

67 See also Williamson (1971): 122.

68 Prominent contributions are e.g. Alchian/Demsetz (1972); Arrow (1974); Williamson (1976); Klein/Crawford/Alchian (1978).

69 Williamson (1971): 112.

70 Informational advantages refer to the capacity of intra-organizational information channels to bundle and code information for retransmission, thereby lowering information costs. See Arrow (1974): 37, 53-55.

71 See Williamson (1971): 113f and Williamson (1981): 559.

72 Arrow (1974): 33.

Within the context of new institutional economics, *Williamson* (1998, 2000) distinguishes four levels of social analysis as depicted in figure 15 (appendix 1). Level one represents the social embeddedness level, constituting norms, customs, traditions and culture, and is generally taken as given by most researchers. Level two represents the institutional environment and provides the "rules of the game"[73] wherein economic activity occurs. Within this level, the theory of property rights is the most important analytic tool. The institutions of governance are situated within level three which deals with the "play of the game" [74] and strives to set up efficient governance structures. Transaction cost economics operate within this level. Finally, level four deals with resource allocations and the optimization of marginal conditions. Agency theory is concerned with this level.[75]

As shown in figure 15, new institutional economics is concerned with an analysis and efficient set-up of the institutional environment. The **property rights theory** investigates the relationship between institutions and property rights in search for potential welfare gains.[76] Property rights theorists stress that a certain good should be defined according to its associated property rights.[77] They further posit that "it is the ownership of the rights associated with the resources which constitutes the economic value of the resources."[78] Property rights are regarded "as the means by which to realize superior economic performance"[79]. In this context, property rights are not defined as the ownership of a resource but rather as the right to use a resource.[80] Hence, the owner of a property right does not own the resource itself, but rather a bundle or a part of the rights to use a particular resource.[81] Since this bundle of rights is divisible, more than a single individual can own some rights in a particular resource.[82] In order to explain the behavior of the firm[83], the property rights theory focuses on the effort of individuals within the organization to maximize their utility.[84] Individual utility maximization is thus one characteristic feature of the property rights theory. Transaction costs represent another characteristic feature. If property rights could be freely exchanged or transferred, i.e. in the absence of transaction costs, the identity of the owner and thus the distribution of property

73 Williamson (1998): 27.

74 Williamson (1998): 29.

75 For more details on the figure, see Williamson (1998): 25-29 and Williamson (2000): 596-600.

76 See also Furubotn/Richter (1991): 2. According to de Alessi (1991): 47, the distribution of property rights can have significant welfare implications.

77 This is also pointed out by Furubotn/Richter (1991): 5.

78 Kaulmann (1987): 443. See also Furubotn/Pejovich (1972): 1139.

79 Williamson (1998): 28. See also Furubotn/Pejovich (1972): 1141; Neus (1989): 9.

80 According to Furubotn/Pejovich (1972): 1140, the right of ownership entails "the right to use it, to change its form and substance, and to transfer all rights in the asset".

81 More specifically, property rights can be divided into three categories: usus – the right to use the property; abusus – the right to change, modify or destroy the property; and fructus – the right to enjoy benefits arising from the property. See Gedajlovic (1993): 733.

82 See Demsetz (1967): 347; Furubotn/Pejovich (1972): 1140; Alchian/Demsetz (1973): 17f. However, the value and the efficient use of a resource decrease with the number of individuals among which the property rights are distributed. See Kaulmann (1987): 444.

83 Within the theory of property rights, the firm is defined as a "set of contracts among factors of production, with each factor motivated by its self-interest." Fama (1980): 289.

84 The theory accounts for the fact that also nonpecuniary goods constitute elements in managers' utility functions. See Furubotn/Pejovich (1972): 1137f, 1147. Hence, it rejects profit maximization as the primary explanation of decision makers' actions and thereby contributes to explaining why firms frequently abandon the traditional goal of profit maximization. See Furubotn/Pejovich (1972): 1149.

rights would be irrelevant:[85] Those who can put the resource to its most effective use can easily negotiate with those currently in possession of the property rights. However, if the exchange causes costs, "then an alteration in the identity of the ownership rights' possessor can have allocative effects."[86] That is, in the presence of transaction costs, the organization and distribution of a resource's property rights influence the behavior of individuals interacting with this resource.[87]

Due to the importance of transaction costs, **transaction cost theory** studies their effect on economic relations.[88] It focuses on efficiency improvements by making the transactions the focus of analysis, which are defined as negotiated transfers of property rights.[89] Because any transaction causes costs, the effectiveness of organizations and mechanisms should be assessed based on their respective transaction costs.[90] These comprise all costs related to (1) "the creation or change of an institution or organization"[91] and (2) "the use of the institution or organization"[92]. The second type of costs consists of "the costs of arranging a contract ex ante and monitoring and enforcing it ex post".[93] Specific investments or sunk costs arising as a result of the establishment of an institutional framework comprise the fixed component of transaction costs. The variable component contains the costs associated with the use of the institution: (1) the costs of initiating the contract (information costs and search costs),[94] (2) the costs of completing the contract (negotiation and decision costs)[95] and (3) monitoring and enforcement costs.[96] The size of transaction costs is affected by bounded rationality,[97] opportunism[98] and a set of transaction characteristics[99]: the transaction's frequency, its uncertainty, information asymmetries and asset specificity.[100] Transactions, differing with regard to these dimensions, can be adjusted through governance structures[101] to favorably affect transaction costs.[102] Accordingly, *Williamson* (1998) describes the major problem of organizations as "aligning transactions with governance structures in order to generate a high performance re-

85 See Alchian/Demsetz (1973): 22. See also Coase (1960) and Demsetz (1967): 349.

86 Alchian/Demsetz (1973): 22.

87 See Kaulmann (1987): 444.

88 See Wolf (1999): 9. In the terminology used above, transaction costs theory deals with the play of the game.

89 See Seger (1997): 18.

90 See Seger (1997): 20.

91 Furubotn/Richter (1991): 8f.

92 Furubotn/Richter (1991): 8f. According to the authors, the focus of existing literature so far has been primarily on the second type of costs.

93 Matthews (1986): 906. This view is shared by Furubotn/Richter (1991): 9.

94 See Richter (1994): 6. See also Furubotn/Richter (1991): 9. Search costs refer, for example, to the costs associated with the search for potential managerial candidates.

95 The costs involve direct costs (e.g. lawyer), or indirect costs (e.g. opportunity costs). See Richter (1994): 7.

96 See Richter (1994): 7.

97 Bounded rationality refers to "behavior that is intendedly rational but only limitedly so." Williamson (1998): 30.

98 For a definition of opportunism, see FN 178 below.

99 See Williamson (1973): 317f.

100 See Williamson (1973): 318; Williamson (1998): 36. See also Richter (1994): 6; Wolf (1999): 10. Asset specificity refers to "the degree to which durable, transaction-specific investments are required to realize least cost supply." Williamson (1981): 555.

101 Of all governance structures, firms and markets are the primary alternatives. See Williamson (1981): 549.

102 See Williamson (1998): 37.

sult."[103] Transaction cost theory addresses this problem and examines governance structures with regard to their capability to diminish transaction costs and matches these structures with transactions in a transaction cost minimizing way.[104]

2.1.1.2 Definitions and Elements of Agency Theory

In analyzing the behavior of individuals that enter a relationship, agency theory takes up a number of issues raised within the property rights and transaction cost theory. Although it still regards an organization as a "nexus of contracts"[105], it extends this definition and views the organization "as a team whose members act from self-interest but realize that their destinies depend to some extent on the survival of the team in its competition with other teams."[106] While the agent personifies both the firm's manager and the bearer of the residual risk within the property rights theory,[107] agency theory separates these concepts and observes that the underlying ownership rights (e.g. control and income) within the modern organization are partitioned and distributed among different individuals.[108] The primary advantage of distinguishing management and risk bearing is the recognition that each is "faced with a market for its services that provides alternative opportunities and, in the case of management, motivation toward performance."[109] According to the property rights theory, the distribution and specification of property rights determine the allocation of costs and benefits across individuals. As the specification of these property rights is done via contracting, the behavior of the involved parties will depend on these contracts. The agency theory takes up these contracts and focuses on their behavioral implications for the interaction between principal and agent.[110] Agency theory also finds the presence of transaction costs to significantly impede the design of effective contractual provisions governing the interaction between principal and agent.[111] Moreover, agency costs[112] constitute a form of transaction costs, as they are a direct result of the use of an institution.[113]

In general terms, agency theory describes and explains the behavior of individuals that enter into a relationship in an environment characterized by the presence of external influences, divergent interests and asymmetric information.[114] Specifically, the object of study constitutes the situation where one player, the principal, delegates tasks to another player, the agent, in

103 Williamson (1998): 40.
104 See Williamson (1981): 549, 553.
105 Fama (1980): 290. See also Jensen/Meckling (1976): 310.
106 Fama (1980): 289.
107 In property rights theory, this person is also called entrepreneur or employer. See Fama (1980): 289.
108 See also Jensen/Meckling (1976): 311; Fama (1980): 289, 291; Furubotn/Richter (1991): 10. Fama (1980): 289 suggests that the disregard of ownership and control by the property rights theory constitutes the explanation for the failure of this literature to explain the large modern corporation.
109 Fama (1980): 291. He states that the market faced by risk bearers is the capital market, enabling them to shift among different firms (teams) and to hedge against failure of any firm (team) through diversification.
110 See also Jensen/Meckling (1976): 308.
111 See also Furubotn/Richter (1991): 10.
112 Please see section 2.1.5 for an explanation of agency costs.
113 See also Molho (1997): 120.
114 See Grossmann/Hart (1983): 9; Spremann (1987): 3; Saam (2002): 2f.

order for the agent to complete these tasks for him.[115] Given certain assumptions about people, organizations and information distribution, agency theory examines the contractual provisions governing the interaction between principal and agent,[116] analyzes typical problems[117] within the relationship, and debates mechanisms to anticipate and mitigate problems to ensure that the agent effectively and efficiently works on behalf of the principal.[118] The resulting solution is said to be Pareto-optimal in the sense that no other contract design can increase the welfare of one player without decreasing the welfare of the other.[119]

Within the agency theory, one can distinguish between two branches of research, the positivist and the normative agency theory.[120] While both branches focus on the contract between the principal and the agent and share the underlying assumptions, they differ with regard to their research approach.[121] The **positivist agency theory** is largely descriptive and empirically oriented. It tries to detect principal-agent relationships within organizations and describes and analyzes solutions for the resulting agency problems.[122] Thereby, it typically uses empirical analyses to provide evidence of its descriptive assumptions. In contrast, the **normative agency theory** uses mathematical models and derivations to abstractedly model agency problems and focuses on the description of how the principal's and agent's preferences, the type of uncertainty and the information available to both parties affect the development of an efficient contract.[123] The study at hand focuses on the positivist agency theory.

The use of agency theoretic propositions to describe interactions between individuals depends on the presence of an agency relationship between these individuals. However, theorists disagree on how the delegation of control within the relationship is to be interpreted. While some authors require control to be formally delegated, others regard the informal delegation of control as a sufficient requirement for an agency relationship to arise. Thus, definitions of agency relationships can best be differentiated along the dimension of a formal delegation (narrow definition) and an informal delegation (broad definition) of control. The **narrow definition** implies an explicit delegation of authority from the principal to the agent via a contract. *Jost* (2001) regards the contract as a key component of the principal-agent relationship which he defines as an explicit bilateral agreement between the principal and the agent, specifying con-

---

115 See Saam (2002): 8. See also Thomsen/Pedersen (2000): 690.

116 See Eisenhardt (1989): 58. See also Meinhövel (1999): 7.

117 These problems are so-called agency problems which may be defined as "productive inefficiencies" resulting from conflicting interests among parties within a firm. See Barnea/Haugen/Senbet (1985): Preface.

118 See Rees (1985a): 3; Eisenhardt (1989): 58; Pratt/Zeckhauser (1991): Preface; Sappington (1991): 45; Saam (2002): 2f, 6, 9. In the words of Rees (1985a): 3, the main purpose of the principal agent theory is "to characterize the optimal forms of such contracts under various assumptions about the information P (author's note: the principal) and A (author's note: the agent) possess or can acquire and thereby, hopefully, to explain the characteristics of such contracts which are actually observed."

119 See Barnea et al. (1985): 26; Molho (1997): 5. As the first-best solution to the agency problem can only be achieved in an unrealistic world with costless information, the outcome is called second-best. See Holmström (1979): 74; Pratt/Zeckhauser (1991): 3; Wolf (1999): 19.

120 For a more detailed analysis of the two branches, please see Jensen (1983) or Meinhövel (1999): 323.

121 See also Eisenhardt (1989): 59.

122 See e.g. Eisenhardt (1989): 58; Neus (1989): 14; Saam (2002): 9f. Seminal papers belonging to this branch include Jensen/Meckling (1976), Fama (1980), Fama/Jensen (1983a), Fama/Jensen (1983b), to name a few.

123 See e.g. Eisenhardt (1989): 60; Neus (1989): 12; Meinhövel (1999): 24; Saam (2002): 10. Seminal papers include Ross (1973); Holmström (1979); Shavell (1979); Holmstrom (1982); Arrow (1985). Both Holmstrom (1982) and Arrow (1985) apply agency theory to the work in teams.

tingencies likely to occur during their relationship.[124] According to *Sappington* (1991), for an agency relationship to arise, "the 'principal' is obliged to hire an 'agent' with specialized skills or knowledge to perform the task in question"[125]. Based on *Barnea/Haugen/Senbet* (1981), agency problems "exist when a principal, or a group of principals, employs an agent to perform a service which necessitates delegating decision making authority to the agent."[126] *Perrow* (1986) defines an agency relationship as a contract between a principal and an agent. The latter contracts to perform certain activities for the principal, who in turn contracts to reward the agent for performing the activities.[127] *Meinhövel* (1999) argues that an agency relationship only arises if a specific contract has been signed between the involved parties.[128] *Jensen/Meckling* (1976) define the agency relationship as "a contract under which one or more persons (the principal(s)) engage another person (the agent) to perform some service on their behalf which involves delegating some decision making authority to the agent."[129] However, they point to "the generality of the agency problem", arguing that "agency costs arise in any situation involving cooperative effort [...] by two or more people even though there is no clear cut principal-agent relationship."[130]

This view is shared by proponents of the **broad definition** of agency relationships which does not require an explicit, contractual delegation of authority but focuses on the existence of interdependencies between the involved parties. For example, *Schmidt* (1987) views an agency situation as the result of an interaction between people with different information, different options to choose from, and some shared or distinct goals. Within this interaction, one party (the principal) is affected by the behavior of the other party (the agent).[131] According to *Blickle* (1987), agency theory applies to "any situation in which the outcome of the cooperation of principal and agent depends both on the random state of nature and on the action or effort chosen by the agent which is unknown to the principal."[132] Also *Spremann* (1987) describes the agency relationship as cooperation between two individuals in which "one of them, the agent, is decision making. He is thus affecting his own welfare and, in addition, that of the other individual called principal."[133] Similar to *Spremann* (1987), *Arrow* (1991) regards the presence of two individuals as a typical element of a principal-agent relation: "One (the agent) must choose an action from a number of alternative possibilities. The action affects the welfare of both the agent and another person, the principal."[134] Based on *Eisenhardt* (1989), agency theory describes relationships "that mirror the basic agency structure of a principal and an agent who are engaged in cooperative behavior, but have differing goals and differing

124 See Jost (2001): 13.
125 Sappington (1991): 45.
126 Barnea/Haugen/Senbet (1981): 8.
127 See Perrow (1986): 12.
128 See Meinhövel (1999): 28, 30. See also Hartmann-Wendels (1991): 145.
129 Jensen/Meckling (1976): 308.
130 Jensen/Meckling (1976): 309.
131 See Schmidt (1987): 500f.
132 Blickle (1987): 93.
133 Spremann (1987): 3. For a similar definition, see also Wilhelm (1987): 180.
134 Arrow (1991): 37.

attitudes toward risk."[135] A very broad definition is used by *Pratt/Zeckhauser* (1991) who state that "whenever one individual depends on the action of another, an agency relationship arises. The individual taking the action is called the agent. The affected party is the principal."[136] In line with *Ross* (1973) and consistent with the broad definition, this thesis defines an agency relationship as an interaction between two or more parties in which "one, designated as the agent, acts for, on behalf of, or as representative for the other, designated the principal, in a particular domain of decision problems."[137]

Independent of the definition of an agency relationship, an analysis of the latter is theoretically trivial if information is distributed symmetrically[138] and/or is freely available[139] and contracts can be drawn up and enforced at no cost. In this case, any agency problem arising within the agency relationship can be easily eliminated through the design of a contract that specifies the agent's exact tasks and responsibilities for every state of nature.[140] However, this does not provide an accurate description of the reality. Therefore, agency theory formulates the following propositions that represent the major elements of agency theory.

In their analyses, agency theorists presuppose **rational behavior** of all parties involved. Rational behavior refers to actions with the goal to improve the players' current personal situation and at the same time recognizing these motivations in the behavior of others and taking them into account when making decisions.[141] When confronted with a number of alternatives, a rational player within the agency relationship is able to form expectations concerning the impact of agency problems on his personal wealth and chooses the alternative that provides him with the greatest utility, given the respective circumstances and constraints.[142] In the context of the positivist agency theory, researchers assume bounded rationality. This concept accounts for the limited human ability to process information and explains why contracts between principals and agents are unavoidably incomplete.[143]

A pivotal assumption of agency theory is the presence of **information asymmetries** between principal and agent. Due to the presence of transaction costs, information does not flow costlessly and is rarely freely available to all parties within the agency relationship.[144] As a result, the principal either is not able or incurs tremendous costs to monitor the characteristics, actions, information (knowledge) and intentions of the agent.[145] Thus, information asymmetries arise between the informed agent and the uninformed principal with regard to these four as-

135 Eisenhardt (1989): 59.

136 Pratt/Zeckhauser (1991): 2.

137 Ross (1973): 134. See also Levinthal (1988): 155.

138 See Meinhövel (1999): 15. Arrow (1969): 7 states that "the critical impact of information on the optimal allocation of risk bearing is not merely its presence or absence but its inequality among economic agents."

139 See Sappington (1991): 49.

140 See also Schmidt (1987): 501; Shleifer/Vishny (1997): 741.

141 See Barnea et al. (1985): 26; Saam (2002): 11.

142 See Barnea et al. (1985): 26.

143 See Williamson (1973): 317; Perrow (1986): 14; Williamson (1998): 30f; Opper (2001): 603; Saam (2002): 11f. In fact, if all players exhibited unbounded rationality, contracts between the parties were complete, leaving no room for agency problems. For a description of contracts, please see further below.

144 See Pratt/Zeckhauser (1991): 2.

145 See also Meinhövel (1999): 22f; Saam (2002): 19.

pects which can be distinguished into information asymmetry before (ex ante) and after entering the agency relationship (ex post).[146]

The problem of hidden characteristics arises ex ante and describes the principal's problem to identify the best-qualified agent from a pool of potential agents which is heterogenous with respect to their qualification, ability or characteristics. While the agent knows its true qualifications, the principal does not have this information or can only acquire the information by incurring tremendous costs.[147] Thus, ex ante, the agent possesses private information[148] about his eligibility for the tasks to be performed on behalf of the principal. He can exploit this information asymmetry by projecting a false image of his qualifications by imitating highly qualified agents.[149] As a result, the principal faces the problem of uncertainty regarding the agent's true applicability, as he will learn the actual qualification of the agent only after the contractual agreement.[150] Therefore, hidden characteristics can result in the problem of adverse selection,[151] also referred to as the lemon's problem[152]. The problem of adverse selection results in an inefficiency detrimental to both the principals and the highly qualified agents. Therefore, both parties are strongly incentivized to take measures in order to reduce these inefficiencies.[153] This involves screening by the principal and bonding by the agent.[154]

The problem of hidden action arises after the contractual agreement. Having contracted the agent, the principal is unable to monitor the behavior and actions of the agent.[155] In addition, principals are not as well informed as agents with regard to what actions should best be taken.[156] As a result, the agent has an incentive to maximize his individual utility. The information asymmetry enables the agent to make any promise regarding his behavior and to later deviate from it without being penalized.[157] For example, he may reduce his effort while at the

146 See also Stadler (2010): 74. In its later analysis, this thesis focuses on ex post information asymmetry.

147 See Jost (2001): 28; Stadler (2010): 75.

148 Private information relate to information about certain facts; the information can be privately observed by those who have access to it and is unobservable to those without access. See also Molho (1997): 1.

149 See Jost (2001): 28.

150 See also Saam (2002): 29; Stadler (2010): 75.

151 See Jost (2001): 28; Bhagat/Jefferis Jr. (2002): 10. Adverse selection refers to the problem that private information provide individuals with the opportunities and incentives to lie prior to the set-up of the contract. This can also be called "precontractual opportunism". Molho (1997): 8. See Holmstrom (1982): 324 and Levinthal (1988): 177 for alternative definitions of adverse selection.

152 Akerlof (1970): 489f describes a market for used cars in which the car's owner is usually better informed about the car's quality than the buyer. Hence, buyers are unable to judge the true quality of the used car prior to the purchase. The respective seller is aware of the car's quality, however, has no possibility to reliably signal the quality of the car. As a result, sellers of good quality cars will withdraw from the market. Consequently, only the cars of the poorest quality (lemons) are traded.

153 See also Stadler (2010): 76.

154 See Jost (2001): 28f. See also Jensen/Meckling (1976): 308.

155 See Meinhövel (1999): 15; Witt (2001): 87. The resulting information asymmetry primarily refers to the agent's expended effort. See Arrow (1991): 38. Note that if the actions of the agent were observable for the principal, they would be included in the contract.

156 See Levinthal (1988): 155.

157 See also Spremann (1987): 6; See Jost (2001): 26.

same time pretending high effort.[158] With the agent's effort being unobservable, the problems faced by the principal are to provide incentives to and adequately share risk with the agent.[159]

The problem of hidden action is augmented by the problem of hidden intention. This arises after the contractual agreement as a result of information asymmetries between the principal and the agent concerning the latter's intentions.[160] Given the principal's lack of knowledge with regard to the agent's intentions, the agent can secretly pursue its individual goals. Even if the principal learns about the agent's intentions, he may not always be able to cancel the agreement due to the costs he incurred during the contracting process (hold-up).[161]

After the contractual agreement, information regarding the nature of the external environment is not distributed symmetrically, resulting in hidden information (knowledge).[162] Hence, even if the principal is able to observe the actions of the agent, he cannot assess his performance as he does not have information regarding the external environment within which the agent operates.[163] This is because the performance of the agent consists of two components:[164] (1) the agent's individual achievements and (2) random environmental influences that can either positively or negatively affect the agent's performance.[165] Assuming the agent is aware of the type of environmental influence, he will use this information against the interest of the poorly informed principal who may observe the actions of the agent, however, cannot differentiate between bad luck[166] and low effort.[167] This problem can be aggravated if the agent consciously withholds information.[168] A possible solution to the hidden information problem constitutes signaling, which can be regarded as a knowledge transfer from the agent to the principal, and screening, which refers to the generation of knowledge by the principal.[169]

Incomplete contracts constitute the direct result of information asymmetries. Due to asymmetric information, individual actions and intentions of the agent cannot be monitored and the nature of the external environment cannot be observed. Hence, the principal cannot design a complete contract specifying the actions of the agent under each state of nature.[170] Moreover,

---

158 See also Saam (2002): 29.

159 See Rees (1985b): 83f.

160 See Stadler (2010): 78.

161 See Saam (2002): 29.

162 See Witt (2001): 87. The concepts of hidden action and information can also be combined, resulting in only three manifestations of information asymmetry. See e.g. Leiber (2008): 78. Hidden action and hidden information are regarded as giving rise to moral hazard. Moral hazard occurs when "one agent can observe the joint effects of the unknown state of the world and of decisions by another economic agent, but not the state or the decision separately." Arrow (1969): 7. This can also be called "postcontractual opportunism". See Molho (1997): 8. See Holmstrom (1982): 324 for an alternative definition of moral hazard.

163 See Stadler (2010): 77f.

164 See also Milde (1987): 40.

165 Spremann (1987): 11f calls this environmental influence an "exogenous risk the probability of which neither principal nor agent can control."

166 Bad luck can be defined as unfavorable, observable shocks to firm performance beyond the agent's control. See Bertrand/Mullainathan (2001): 901.

167 See e.g. Spremann (1987): 10, 12; Levinthal (1988): 156; Molho (1997): 119f; Jost (2001): 30.

168 See Neus (1989): 17.

169 See Meinhövel (1999): 15. Both solutions imply costs, which are described in section 2.1.5.

170 See Holmström (1979): 74, 89; Scharfstein (1988): 186. However, "essentially any imperfect information about actions or states of nature can be used to improve contracts". Scharfstein (1988): 186.

because the principal is unable to directly observe the agent's behavior, contracts cannot be costlessly enforced and hence cannot preclude adverse behavior by the agent.[171]

If both principal and agent were pursuing the same goal, the information asymmetries and incomplete contracts would be irrelevant, as the principals could rely on the agent to act in their best interest.[172] However, agency theory presumes **differential utility functions**, since goal equality between the two parties is unlikely: While the work performed by the agent on behalf of the principal creates disutility to the agent, it has a utility-enhancing effect for the principal.[173] As a result, the agent tries to generate his agreed compensation with the lowest possible effort, while the principal wants to maximize his utility through maximum effort of the agent.[174]

Given differential utility functions, agency theory assumes that both players maximize their personal utility[175] based on their individual preferences.[176] This maximization of personal utility is regarded as the ultimate goal of all players.[177] In order to achieve this goal, agency theory presupposes the display of **opportunism**[178] by the agent. According to this concept, the agent uses broad scopes of actions, such as incomplete contracts, to opportunistically pursue its individual goals at the expense of the principals.[179] According to *Jensen/Meckling* (1976) "if both parties to the relationship are utility maximizers there is good reason to believe that the agent will not always act in the best interests of the principal."[180] While *Williamson* (1998) states that it might be unnecessary to presume opportunism by all human individuals, he argues that "it is truly utopian to presume unfailing stewardship."[181]

The final assumption made by agency theory refers to **differential risk preferences** between the principal and the agent.[182] In combination with information asymmetries, differential risk preferences typically belong to the basic elements of most deliberations on agency theory.[183] The major implication of this assumption is that the players within the agency relationship differ in the extent they are willing to take on risk for the achievement of their goals.[184] Thereby, it is typically assumed that the principal is risk neutral and well diversified, whereas the agent is unable to diversify and therefore risk averse.[185] As mentioned previously, differ-

171 See Bhagat/Jefferis Jr. (2002): 9. See also Schmidt (1987): 501; Drukarczyk (1993): 305.
172 This is also stressed by Levinthal (1988): 156.
173 See Meinhövel (1999): 15f.
174 See also Saam (2002): 20. Differential utility functions may also arise from the principal's and agent's diverging preferences regarding the risk they are willing to take on.
175 The utility can be derived from both tangible goods and intangible goods. See Saam (2002): 10.
176 It is worth mentioning that the theory, in doing so, does not question the content of the individual goals. See Barnea et al. (1985): 25; Perrow (1986): 12; Saam (2002): 10.
177 See Ross (1973): 134.
178 The term "opportunism" goes back to Williamson (1973): 317, who defines it as an "effort to realize individual gains through a lack of candor or honesty in transactions."
179 See Opper (2001): 603; Saam (2002): 12.
180 Jensen/Meckling (1976): 308.
181 Williamson (1998): 31.
182 See Eisenhardt (1989): 58; Saam (2002): 8.
183 See Jost (2001): 22.
184 See also Saam (2002): 19.
185 See Ampenberger (2010): 41.

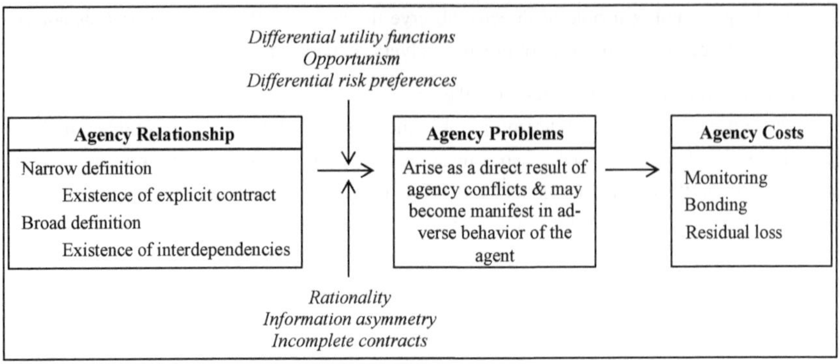

Figure 1: Agency theory

ential risk attitudes may result in differential preferences between the principal and the agent as to the best course of action.[186]

As shown in figure 1, whenever an agency relationship is characterized by the above-mentioned assumptions, the relationship is subject to agency problems.[187] These problems arise as a direct result of agency conflicts, understood as conflicts of interest between the respective parties within the agency relationship, and may become manifest in adverse behavior of the agent.[188] The agency problems bring about agency costs, which comprise monitoring and bonding expenditures and a residual loss.[189] Depending on the parties within the agency relationship, one can distinguish a number of agency conflicts. The sections that follow focus on the agency conflicts relevant in the present thesis.

2.1.2 Manager-Shareholder Agency Conflict

Although the separation of ownership[190] and control in joint-stock companies and the resulting agency relationship provides substantial benefits,[191] it also gives rise to a significant conflict of interest. Already in 1776, the "original agency theorist"[192] *Adam Smith* observed that "the directors of such companies, however, being the managers rather of other people's mon-

186 See also Eisenhardt (1989): 58.

187 See Saam (2002): 28-31. The term "agency problem" is also used by Fama (1980): 288; Fama/Jensen (1983a): 344; Agrawal/Knoeber (1996): 376; Lane/Cannella/Lubatkin (1998): 573; La Porta et al. (2000a): 2. Note that this term only refers to problems faced by the principal(s).

188 The term "agency conflict" is widely used to describe conflicts of interest between the parties involved in an agency relationship. See e.g. Burkart/Panunzi/Shleifer (2003): 2179; Renneboog/Simons/Wright (2007); 592; Guedhami/Mishra (2009): 492; Barnea/Rubin (2010): 74; Renders/Gaeremynck (2012): 125. The terms "agency conflicts" and "conflicts of interest" are used interchangeably in this thesis.

189 Please see section 2.1.5 for a detailed description of agency costs.

190 Note that agency theory argues that "ownership of the firm is an irrelevant concept" and hence dispels the "tenacious notion that a firm is owned by its security holders". Fama (1980): 290. Nevertheless, the present study puts aside the nexus-of-contracts-perspective of the firm and treats the shareholders as the owners (of the residual claims) of the firm to simplify and facilitate the discussion on their monitoring role.

191 Fama/Jensen (1983b): 301f, 305-308, argue that agency relationships stem from the benefits of a specialization of risk-bearing and decision making: while the simultaneous allocation of decision control and residual claims to management would control agency problems, it would also sacrifice "the benefits of unrestricted risk sharing and specialization of decision functions." Fama/Jensen (1983b): 306.

192 Jensen (1994): 11.

ey than of their own, it cannot well be expected, that they should watch over it with the same anxious vigilance with which the partners in a private copartnery frequently watch over their own".[193] Some 150 years later, *Berle/Means* (1932) find a separation of ownership and control within the modern US corporation,[194] and therefore question whether it is still appropriate to assume that the management of these firms operates the firms in the shareholders' interest.[195] As indicated by *Smith* and *Berle/Means*, the separation of ownership and control gives rise to an agency conflict between managers and shareholders,[196] which today is regarded as the classical agency conflict.[197] The goal of this section is to compare the two parties across the main elements of agency theory.[198] Thereby, it aims to clarify whether one can reasonably presume the presence of an agency conflict within the agency relationship between managers and shareholders.[199] Having illustrated the likely presence of an agency conflict, this section lists certain types of adverse behavior arising from this conflict.[200]

With regard to **utility functions**, *Marris* (1967) states that some individuals regard the firm as a vehicle for the satisfaction of personal needs, whereas others personally identify themselves with the firm to an extent that its economic vitality exceeds the importance of any personal considerations.[201] In this context, a shareholder can be viewed as falling in the former category, since he is generally considered as an informed and rational financial investor, "pursuing with great singleness of purpose his personal financial gain via dividends and/or capital gains."[202] Hence, the utility function of shareholders envisages the maximization of shareholder value,[203] which occurs when the value of the firm's stock, or the present value of the

193 Smith (1789): 108f (Book V, Chapter I Part III).

194 La Porta/Silanes/Shleifer (1999): 471f, 498 question the Berle and Means' picture of the modern corporation. The authors investigate the ownership structure of the 20 largest public firms across the 27 richest economies and find that relatively few of these firms are widely held as proposed by Berle and Means. They conclude that the Berle and Means statement only holds for US firms.

195 See Berle/Means (2010): 112-114. The authors were the first to study the consequences of the separation of ownership and control. Focusing on US firms, they observe two newly created groups: "the owners without appreciable control and the control without appreciable ownership". Berle/Means (2010): 113.

196 In the language of property rights theorists, the agency conflict between managers and shareholders is the result of a misallocation of the property rights usus and abusus. As a result of the modern corporation, firm shareholders have relinquished all their property rights apart from fructus – their entitlement to a share of the firm's residual profit stream. See also Gedajlovic (1993): 733.

197 See, among others, Shapiro (2005): 268; Maury (2006): 322; Guedhami/Mishra (2009): 492.

198 These comprise differential utility functions, risk preferences as well as information asymmetries.

199 Note that the relationship between shareholders and managers represents an agency relationship also based on the narrow definition: shareholders enter a contractual relationship with the manager with the acceptance of the firm's articles of association that is implied by the acquisition of shares. See Meinhövel (1999): 32. In addition, the manager signs an explicit contract with the firm, the owners of which are the shareholders. Therefore, the relationship between shareholder and manager constitutes an important example of an agency relationship. See among others Blickle (1987): 94; Spremann (1987): 9; Richter (1994): 17.

200 The analysis that follows applies to publicly-traded firms with a widely-held ownership structure and in the absence of any governance mechanism that effectively aligns managerial interests with those of shareholders. Consistent with Wolf (1999): 16 it also assumes that it is impossible or too expensive for the owners of the firm to monitor the management's actions.

201 See Marris (1967): 15.

202 Donaldson (1963): 118.

203 See e.g. Hartmann-Wendels (1991): 140; Molho (1997): 118f; Seger (1997): 128. The concept of shareholder value goes back to Rappaport (1981) and states that the fiduciary responsibility of corporate managers is the creation of economic value for shareholders. Therefore, it argues for a replacement of accounting ratios by a shareholder value approach. For details, please see Rappaport (1981): 139, 148. The maximiza-

expected future cash flows to shareholders,[204] is maximized at a given level of risk.[205] While literature views the maximization of shareholder value as the shareholders' overriding goal, there is disagreement on which financial and investment policies best serve the attainment of this goal.[206] Despite this disagreement, the financial policy of firms is always "seen through the unemotional eyes of a mobile, diversified investor seeking to maximize his personal financial objectives via ownership of common stock."[207]

The utility function of shareholders is likely to conflict with the utility function of management. Ceteris paribus, both the manager and the shareholders prefer a higher market value of the firm to a lower market value.[208] However, while shareholder value is the single source of shareholders' utility, a manager's utility function is complemented by a number of additional interests that may also conflict with the goal of shareholder value maximization:[209] monetary compensation, security, independence, professional excellence and job-specific non-pecuniary benefits inextricably linked with the firm, such as status, power and prestige.[210] With regard to independence, managers try to increase their discretionary scope of action. Since this depends on the firm's financial flexibility, management derives utility from high retained earnings rather than high payouts.[211] With regard to prestige, management generates utility from the maximization of sales which ranks ahead of profits as the main object of concern.[212] To maximize this utility, management appeases its shareholders with minimum acceptable profits adequate to secure the financing and growth of the firm. Beyond that point, however, it focuses its efforts on the enlargement of sales, i.e. its personal utility.[213] Managerial utility is also affected by the amount of effort a manager invests in the firm.[214] While the effort expended by managers positively impacts the likelihood of a favorable outcome for shareholders and thus generates value to the principal, it generates disutility to the agent. Consequently, the manager favors a low level of effort expended during the management of the firm.[215] Con-

tion of shareholder value and firm value may not always be consistent goals. The distribution of wealth to shareholders not necessarily results in greater firm value. See Walsh/Seward (1990): 423.

204 Similarly, firm value can be defined as the sum of the value of the firm's positive NPV investment opportunities and the present value of its cash flows. See Stulz (1990): 16f.

205 The maximization of shareholder value must not necessarily be the primary goal of all shareholder types. At this stage, however, the discussion does not differentiate between types of shareholders. For details regarding the differences between various shareholder types, please see section 4.1.3.

206 See also Donaldson (1963): 118. Typically, however, a firm that maximizes shareholder value invests in projects with positive net present value as long as the returns exceed the returns shareholders could realize by investing the funds on the capital markets. If this is not the case, the funds need to be paid out to shareholders as dividends. See e.g. Donaldson (1963): 125; Seger (1997): 128f.

207 Donaldson (1963): 118.

208 Even if the management does not own shares, it is reasonable to assume that it will indirectly benefit from higher share prices, for example through increased reputation.

209 See also Gordon (1961): 305f, 310; Marris (1967): 2; Baumol (1967): 46-49; Wilhelm (1987): 195. A manager thus faces a trade-off between a higher share price and higher non-monetary benefits.

210 See e.g. Williamson (1974): 32; Barnea et al. (1981): 10; Ewert (1987): 285; Stadler (2010): 80.

211 See Donaldson (1963): 121. See also Seger (1997): 131, 136.

212 See Baumol (1967): 46. The author argues that even if size did not promote profits, managers would still selfishly maximize sales due to the corresponding increases in salary, reputation and power.

213 See Baumol (1967): 48f. See also Williamson (1974): 79-81. However, Williamson (1974): 36 also argues that profits in excess of the minimum level accepted by shareholders may be desired also by managers to the extent that profits affect managerial discretion, self-fulfillment and organizational achievements.

214 See Barnea et al. (1985): 28; Hartmann-Wendels (1991): 145.

215 For a similar reasoning, see Arrow (1991): 38; Richter (1994): 17; Molho (1997): 137.

sistent with this assumption, *Baumol* (1967) argues that managers have a "desire for the quiet life"[216] and therefore avoid "the rough and tumble"[217]. While this behavior significantly simplifies the life of managers, it also results in forgone opportunities to raise share price and generate value for shareholders.

With regard to **risk preferences**, the existing literature typically assumes the manager of the firm to be risk averse.[218] This risk aversion stems from two major factors. First, managers can be regarded as "overinvested in the firms they serve"[219] in both monetary and non-monetary terms. A manager usually is employed by only one firm at a time. Regardless of whether his allegiance to his employer is larger than his drive for the attainment of personal interest, he devotes his entire energy and knowledge to the firm.[220] During his employment, the manager acquires firm-specific human capital, such as specialized training or knowledge,[221] whose use is limited to the scope of the firm. Due to this, the mobility of executives may be limited.[222] Managers have also frequently tied up a substantial portion of their personal wealth within their firms,[223] since their compensation is frequently based on stock options and other profit-sharing schemes. Hence, the manager's income is, to a significant extent, linked to the firm's performance which increases the manager's exposure to firm-specific risk and provides him with an undiversified portfolio.[224] As a result, a manager's present and future well-being is bound up with that of the firm. Second, managers have responsibility for potential mistakes and are personally liable. In case of a failure, they lose their job as well as the personal wealth related to the firm. As becomes clear, a manager is economically wedded with the firm he serves[225] and hence highly concerned about the total risk of the firm.[226]

While the manager cannot diversify his human capital and is fully exposed to firm-specific risk, it is assumed that shareholders can reduce their risk by holding a diversified portfolio of stocks.[227] As a result, shareholders are concerned only about the non-diversifiable risk inherent in the firm's stock and view increases in the firm's bankruptcy risk with equanimity.[228] In particular, shareholders are able to balance investments in cyclical businesses through a position in other non-cyclical or counter-cyclical firms.[229] Hence, shareholders may prefer a high-

216 Baumol (1967): 31.

217 Baumol (1967): 31. Also Molho (1997): 121 argues that "all other things being equal (pay etc.) they are likely to shirk".

218 See e.g. Easterbrook (1984): 653; Hartmann-Wendels (1991): 147; Wolf (1999): 77.

219 Coffee (1986): 17.

220 See Donaldson (1963): 120.

221 See Coffee (1986): 74.

222 See Coffee (1986): 17. Both the active market for executives and the resulting success of executive search firms question that the immobility of today's executives is still limited. See also Coffee (1986): 38.

223 See Amihud/Lev (1981): 606; Easterbrook (1984): 653; Coffee (1986): 18; Molho (1997): 121, 135.

224 See Amihud/Lev (1981): 606; Coffee (1986): 18.

225 See Coffee (1986): 19.

226 See Easterbrook (1984): 653.

227 See Drukarczyk (1993): 418; Jost (2001): 22. Although it has been found that individual investors do not hold well diversified portfolios, this conjecture can easily be made for professional investors that dominate the stock markets. See Coffee (1986): 17.

228 See Easterbrook (1984): 653; Coffee (1986): 18.

229 Given a diversified portfolio, drops in the share price of one firm are thus compensated by increases in the price of another firm's shares. See also Molho (1997): 121.

ly specialized and focused firm strategy, as it simplifies their diversification.[230] Differences in risk preferences between managers and shareholders may also be observed in terms of the firm's capital structure. Overall, "the rational manager has good reason to be risk averse, while the fully diversified shareholder has every reason to be risk neutral."[231]

As required for a conflict of interest to arise, the relationship between a firm's management and its shareholders is also characterized by **information asymmetries**. Ex ante, a firm's management typically has better knowledge on the possible future states of the external environment as well as on the alternatives from which the firm can choose. Ex post, the management has better knowledge of the actual state of the external environment that occurred, the alternative the firm has chosen and the corresponding outcomes.[232] In contrast, shareholders can neither observe the alternatives from which the manager has chosen a particular action nor are they in possession of information sufficient to judge on what actions should best be taken.[233] Finally, shareholders cannot judge on the manager's performance, since they face problems in observing the external environment and the competition.[234]

Based on the comparison of shareholders and managers along the three elements of agency theory, there are grounds to believe in the presence of an agency conflict between shareholders and managers.[235] This conflict of interest manifests itself through certain types of **adverse managerial behavior**, colliding with the shareholders' goal of value maximization.[236] Adverse managerial behavior is based on the following reasoning.[237] If the manager is the sole owner of the firm, he receives the full benefits and bears the full costs of both his efforts to enhance profits and his activities that increase his personal wealth at the expense of the firm. If the manager now sells some shares which have the same characteristics as his,[238] this has two effects. First, the manager no longer captures the entire gain from his profit maximization activities but still bears the entire costs of his efforts. Second, the manager still receives the full benefits of any activities increasing his personal wealth but only bears a fraction of the associated costs.[239] Hence, gains from any adverse behavior exceed the loss in value resulting from a reduction of the market value of the manager's shares.[240] As a result, with less than 100% ownership, the manager spends fewer resources on profit maximization but rather focuses on activities that increase his personal wealth. This is detrimental for firm value and ul-

230 See also Donaldson (1963): 128.
231 Coffee (1986): 13.
232 See Swoboda (1987): 168.
233 See Levinthal (1988): 155.
234 See Hartmann-Wendels (1991): 147. See also Ampenberger (2010): 31.
235 This is also assumed by Drukarczyk (1993): 81, who states that the manager will act against the interest of shareholders as long as he is not prevented from realizing such strategies. For a similar argument, see also Jensen/Meckling (1976): 308; Fama/Jensen (1983b): 304.
236 See Bott (2002): 10.
237 This reasoning goes back to the seminal paper of Jensen/Meckling (1976). The interested reader may refer to their paper for a more detailed description.
238 These characteristics refer to the cash flow rights and limited liability. See Jensen/Meckling (1976): 312.
239 These costs comprise only his proportional ownership share of the resulting reduction in the value of the firm's shares. Barnea et al. (1981): 11.
240 See Halpern (1999): 18.

timately shareholders.[241] Inter alia, the adverse managerial behavior can take the following forms.[242]

(1) Perquisites (perks) consumption[243] by managers is defined as "short-run cost-augmenting activities designed to enhance their nonsalary income, or to provide other forms of on-the-job consumption" which "reduces corporate profits by increasing costs"[244]. A manager that consumes perks spends the firm's money on items that largely serve his own interests, such as a luxury company car or office. While these expenditures generate utility to the agent, they reduce the net payoff to shareholders.[245] In addition, management has a tendency to build up organizational slack due to a preference for expenditures on staff, resulting in excessive personnel expenditures.[246] The consumption of perks constitutes a consequence of managerial aspirations for status and prestige.[247]

(2) Due to their risk aversion[248] and endeavor to diversify their employment risk, managers have a preference for diversification which smoothens fluctuations in sales and profits.[249] This is achieved through value-reducing diversification strategies which frequently result in excessive diversification,[250] which refers to "long-run strategic choices designed to maximize corporate size and growth rather than corporate profits."[251] Through the diversification into unrelated businesses, management aims at building its own diversified portfolio. Hence, it is a rational strategy from a managerial perspective.[252] In addition, diversification and the resulting

241 See e.g. Jensen/Meckling (1976): 313; Fama (1980): 295f; Easterbrook/Fischel (1981): 1170; Harris/Raviv (1991): 300; Ang et al. (2000): 84; Leiber (2008): 51-54. Ang et al. (2000): 87 state this reasoning as follows: for an owner-manager with low shareholdings, the incentives to engage in adverse behavior decline with growing personal share ownership: his share of the firm's profits increase (and hence also his exposure to losses resulting from his adverse behavior), while the gains from his adverse behavior remain constant.

242 In contrast to the agency theory, the stewardship theory assumes that managers work in the best interest of the firm and its shareholders. It conceives managers as individuals being motivated by non-financial factors and by the satisfaction from the successful accomplishment of challenging tasks. See Davis/Schoorman/Donaldson (1997): 20. It proposes that an identification of a manager with the firm "promotes a merging of individual ego and the corporation, thus melding individual self-esteem with corporate prestige". Donaldson/Davis (1991): 51. The corporate manager is intrinsically motivated to be a good steward of his firm and to do a good job and is thus "far from being an opportunistic shirker". Donaldson/Davis (1991): 51. The literature on stewardship theory examines the degree to which managers are able to achieve the level of performance they desire. Thereby, it assumes that any effect on performance depends on whether or not the structural environment facilitates effective managerial decision making rather than on the significance of agency conflicts. See Donaldson/Davis (1991): 51f.

243 Please note that also debtholders are negatively affected by managerial incentives for the consumption of perks, given that the probability of default might increase and the assets to be liquidated are reduced.

244 Gedajlovic/Shapiro (1998): 534.

245 See also Molho (1997): 120; Bott (2002): 10; Ampenberger (2010): 44.

246 See Hansch (2012): 22.

247 See also Williamson (1974): 34.

248 Due to its greater risk aversion, a firm's management might also choose projects that have low risk but offer a lower expected return. However, a low-risk investment policy is contrary to the interests of shareholders, who benefit from riskier investment policies. See Easterbrook (1984): 653; Molho (1997): 121.

249 See Amihud/Lev (1981): 606; Thomsen/Pedersen (2000): 690. Amihud/Lev (1981): 613 find that manager-controlled firms more frequently engage in mergers motivated by diversification considerations than shareholder-controlled firms.

250 See Denis/Denis/Sarin (1997): 136. Excessive diversification is also termed empire building. See e.g. Gordon (1961): 306; Amihud/Lev (1981): 606; Thomsen/Pedersen (2000): 690.

251 Gedajlovic/Shapiro (1998): 535.

252 See Coffee (1986): 20.

growth in firm size provides managers with personal benefits of control.[253] Growing firm size also satisfies the managers' need for power "by increasing the resources under their control."[254] As *Gordon* (1961) puts it, "expansion is desired for the enhancement of personal power and also because of the satisfaction of being associated with a powerful organization."[255] As a result, management invests as much as possible, provided its shareholders are unable to observe either the cash flow or management's actions.[256] Thereby, management also pursues acquisitions whose returns are below the cost of capital.[257] While managers are compensated for the negative impact of excessive diversification via risk reductions and increases in personal power, (dispersed) shareholders are adversely affected since they can achieve their desired level of risk through constructing their portfolio accordingly.[258]

(3) Since corporate managers derive utility from a low level of effort expended during the management of the firm,[259] they may engage in shirking, which is captured by the quiet-life hypothesis.[260] According to this hypothesis, management seeks to avoid cognitively difficult tasks, such as bargaining with suppliers, customers or labor unions.[261] In addition, corporate management will be unwilling to take unpleasant tasks, such as announcing necessary layoffs.[262] In general, if not effectively monitored, management will exert reduced effort,[263] which results in higher costs and bigger overheads.[264] *Bertrand/Mullainathan* (2003) examine the impact of reduced monitoring of management on managerial behavior and document increasing workers' wages as well as decreased levels of plant construction and destruction. Moreover, the total productivity and profitability decline. The authors conclude that weakly-governed managers put emphasis on enjoying the quiet life.[265]

(4) To preserve their independence, managers try to favorably influence their discretionary scope of action. Capital budgeting theory suggests that managers should accept projects offering a positive NPV and refuse projects with a negative NPV. A positive NPV project increases firm value and benefits shareholders which therefore support the NPV rule.[266] If there are

253 See also La Porta et al. (2000a): 3; Ampenberger (2010): 44.

254 Jensen (1986): 323.

255 Gordon (1961): 306. Also Gedajlovic/Shapiro (1998): 535 state that "managers indulge their needs for power, prestige, and status […] by making long-run strategic choices designed to maximize corporate size and growth rather than corporate profits."

256 However, this behavior results in a dilemma for the management: as it will always claim that cash flows are too low to finance all positive NPV projects and dividend payments simultaneously, this claim will not be credible in cases of truly low cash flows. Hence, management chooses to underinvest if cash flows are low and to overinvest if cash flows are high. See Stulz (1990): 3f.

257 See Drukarczyk (1993): 419.

258 See Amihud/Lev (1981): 605f; Höpner (2003): 103.

259 See also Arrow (1991): 38; Richter (1994): 17; Molho (1997): 137. See also Barnea et al. (1985): 28.

260 See e.g. Baumol (1967): 31; Giroud/Mueller (2010): 314.

261 See Giroud/Mueller (2010): 314.

262 See Pratt/Zeckhauser (1991): Preface.

263 See also Bott (2002): 11.

264 See Giroud/Mueller (2010): 314.

265 See Bertrand/Mullainathan (2003): 1044-1047, 1053, 1072. Their evidence is based on a large sample of plant-year observations during 1976 and 1995.

266 See also Narayanaswamy/Shukla (2001): 35f. However, the NPV rule may not hold when the firm is financed by both debt and equity. In this case, gains and losses are shared by shareholders and debtholders. Please see section 2.1.3 for details.

no positive NPV projects and firm's resources cannot be invested more profitable by the firm than by its shareholders, cash should be paid out to shareholders.[267] However, "payouts to shareholders reduce the resources under managers' control, thereby reducing managers' power, and making it more likely they will incur the monitoring of the capital markets"[268]. Because high retained earnings increase the managers' power and enables them to avoid external capital markets,[269] management derives utility from high retained earnings rather than high payouts.[270] As a result, shareholders face the problem of how to convince managers to pay out excess cash rather than waste it on inefficient projects[271] or retain it.

(5) Because current results are easier to observe than the firm's future prospects, they are frequently overemphasized by management worried about its job security.[272] As investors use the firm's earnings today to forecast firm value in the future, the manager is provided with the incentive to boost current earnings to raise the firm's value.[273] In addition, the managerial compensation systems based on profit sharing[274] often result in short-term oriented managers.[275] Since the compensation is frequently based on (short-term) outcome measures, the manager can affect his compensation by choosing projects yielding higher short-term profits. However, if the manager forgoes profitable long-term projects in order to boost profits in the short-term, this may have detrimental effects for the firm's long-term performance.[276] While the benefit to the manager might outweigh potential negative firm performance in the long-term,[277] short-termism is detrimental for the long-term oriented shareholders.

2.1.3 Shareholder-Debtholder Agency Conflict

The interest rate providers of debt capital require from firms seeking external financing is essentially driven by the degree of protection the firm grants to the providers of debt capital[278] and the firm's likelihood of default. Apart from financial risk characteristics, also the extent of a firm's shareholder-debtholder agency conflict affects the interest rate required by providers of debt capital.[279] This section aims at providing an understanding of the manifestations of this agency conflict. To do so, one first needs to illustrate that the shareholder-debtholder relationship represents an agency relationship according to the definitions provided in section

267 See Drukarczyk (1993): 421.
268 Jensen (1986): 323.
269 See also Bott (2002): 11.
270 See Donaldson (1963): 121. See also Seger (1997): 131, 136.
271 See also Jensen (1986): 323. This free cash flow hypothesis is also related to excessive diversification outlined above.
272 See Zeckhauser/Pound (1990): 150.
273 This is contrary to the tenet of capital market efficiency. Since an efficient capital market cannot be fooled, it conjectures an inflation of earnings and hence takes this into account when making valuations. However, Stein (1989): 668 argues that managers behave myopic "even when stock market participants are rational."
274 Section 2.1.6.2 defines these types of compensation systems in greater detail.
275 See e.g. Narayanan (1985): 1469.
276 See Black (1992a): 865. According to the author, this problem is especially relevant when the CEO is near retirement and does not care about long-term projects for which his successor will take the credit.
277 See Narayanan (1985): 1470.
278 Popular protection mechanisms constitute for example covenants or collaterals. These mechanisms are described in section 2.1.5.
279 For a similar argument, please see Bhojraj/Sengupta (2003): 455f.

2.1.1.2. Besides, one needs to prove the existence of an agency conflict between shareholders and debtholders. This is done based on a juxtaposition of the parties' respective utility functions, risk preferences, and information.[280] Only then, this section lists certain types of adverse behavior arising from the shareholder-debtholder agency conflict.

Meinhövel (1999) questions the applicability of the agency theory to the relationship between shareholders and debtholders, because the firm's management rather than its shareholders negotiates the terms of the contract. In this case, the parties in the (assumed) agency relationship have not directly negotiated the design of the contract governing their relationship,[281] which is required by the narrow definition of an agency relationship.[282] The existing literature addresses this problem by assuming that the firm's managers are perfectly aligned with the shareholders and therefore act as their perfect agents, so that agency costs of equity can be disregarded.[283] Given the contractual delegation of authority from the provider of debt capital (principal) to the managers of the firm (agent),[284] this assumption ensures that there is a contractual relationship between shareholders (being represented by the management) and debtholders as required by *Meinhövel* (1999). Consequently, the narrow agency relationship definition is fulfilled. Consistent with this argumentation, also existing literature characterizes the relationship between debtholders and shareholders as an agency relationship.[285]

Having clarified the existence of an agency relationship, any analysis of the shareholder-debtholder agency conflict has to be grounded on a model characterized by differential utility functions, risk preferences and asymmetric information.[286] With regard to the parties' **utility functions**, section 2.1.2 already highlighted that shareholders' utility function is limited to the maximization of shareholder value and to the maximization of the financial payoffs provided by the firm, given a certain level of risk.[287] To capture their desired payoffs, the shareholders demand this maximization irrespective of the value of the firm's debt.[288] In contrast, the market value of the firm's debt represents the primary source of utility for the debtholders, which therefore demand its maximization.[289] They are further interested in the regular payment of interest and timely repayment of the loan.[290] As a result, they derive utility from stable cash flows that enable the payment of interest. In general, debtholders want to maximize the probability that they are repaid in full.[291]

---

280 As in section 2.1.2, the remaining elements outlined in section 2.1.1.2 are assumed as given.

281 See Meinhövel (1999): 30.

282 See also the examples of the narrow definition of an agency relationship in section 2.1.1.2.

283 A similar assumption has been made by Smith Jr./Warner (1979): 118; Ewert (1987): 285; Swoboda (1987): 169; Hartmann-Wendels (1991): 270; Wolf (1999): 16; Myers (2001): 96; Bress (2008): 24.

284 More specifically, the lender (principal) delegates control over financial resources to the borrower (agent). See Walsh (2010): 489.

285 See for example Hartmann-Wendels (1991): 270; Myers (2001): 96-98; Anderson et al. (2003): 266.

286 See also Fohlin (1998): 1738. For the following discussion, one should recall that shareholders' claim is residual in property, i.e. only to whatever is left after all superior claims by e.g. debtholders or suppliers are paid. Hence, their claim does not come in a fixed or guaranteed amount. See Baums/Scott (2005): 35.

287 See also Hartmann-Wendels (1991): 271.

288 See Prowse (1994): 11.

289 See Hartmann-Wendels (1991): 271.

290 See Witt (2003): 8.

291 See Prowse (1994): 11.

The differential utility functions also affect the parties' **risk preferences**. *Mülbert* (1996) states that, "the relationship between shareholders and lenders is characterized by a conflict of interests pertaining to the riskiness of the company's business strategy"[292]. Facilitated by their limited personal liability,[293] shareholders are willing to take high risks to maximize the value of the firm. If the high risk strategy pays off and results in higher share prices, shareholders fully capture this upside while debtholders are unable to benefit from these gains. If the high risk strategy does not pay off and results in the firm's liquidation, the losses are carried by both shareholders and debtholders.[294] Hence, while shareholders are subject to both losses and benefits resulting from a risky investment policy, debtholders are subject to the losses but not to the benefits of such a policy.[295] As a result, shareholders favor a high risk strategy relative to debtholders.[296] Hence, agency problems arise whenever management, given a certain debt level, has to make a decision on the optimal use of the funds.[297]

The existence of the shareholder-debtholder agency conflict is dependent on the presence of **information asymmetries**. Given debtholders' ability to observe the external environment as well as the actions of management – acting on behalf of shareholders – they could design contracts restricting particular types of actions. However, severe information asymmetries, both ex ante and ex post, characterize the relationship between debtholders and shareholders. Prior to signing the contract, the lender tries to evaluate the quality of the borrower's promise of repayment, which is dependent on the characteristics and the behavior of the borrower. As the lender cannot directly and costlessly observe these aspects, he cannot estimate the creditworthiness of the borrower with sufficient certainty,[298] making him subject to an "information risk"[299]: The better informed borrower may withhold private information on the prospects of the firm, the risks he is willing to take, the effort he is willing to invest into the firm as well as other private information that affect the default risk and hence increase the interest payments.[300] Provided the debtholders have to formulate their required return solely based on information released by management, the information risk poses a significant threat for debtholders.[301] As a result, providers of debt capital assume that a firm raises capital whenever the superior informed management perceives the interest rate to be too low given the firm's risk characteristics.[302] Even if the debtholders face no information asymmetries ex ante, ex post they can neither control nor monitor how their funds are being used by the owners of the

292 Mülbert (1996): 462.

293 See Hartmann-Wendels (1991): 272. The shareholders' liability is limited to the share (issue) price they paid upon their investment in the firm. Please see § 54 AktG.

294 For the shareholders, their losses are limited to their initial investment. For debtholders, their losses are equal to the remaining outstanding loan balance.

295 See Long/Malitz (1985): 331; Drukarczyk (1993): 308; Bott (2002): 12; Witt (2003): 8f. If a firm takes on debt to finance a specific investment project, the interest rate should adequately reflect the project's risk.

296 See Prowse (1994): 11.

297 See also Wilhelm (1987): 190. For an illustration of these problems, please see further below.

298 See Bress (2008): 24.

299 Bhojraj/Sengupta (2003): 456.

300 For a similar argumentation, see Bester/Hellwig (1987): 137; Bhojraj/Sengupta (2003): 456.

301 See Wolf (1999): 77.

302 See Hartmann-Wendels (2001): 119f. As a result, they will demand higher interest rates than under the condition of symmetrically distributed information.

firm.[303] The borrower can typically choose between projects with differing risk characteristics. Because these characteristics cannot be observed by the lender, owners of the firm are better informed about the risk-return trade-off of possible investment opportunities than the debtholders,[304] which gives rise to the moral hazard problem.[305]

Due to these differences, management is cajoled into the transfer of value from the debtholders to the shareholders.[306] The management can carry out these transfers, inter alia, in the following ways.[307]

(1) Due to their utility function and risk preferences, holders of equity have the incentive to change the firm's investment program by substituting low risk projects for high risk projects.[308] Thereby, they urge the management to use the proceeds from debt financing to invest in projects promising very high returns if successful, even though their probability of success is low. If these projects turn out successful, the shareholders will completely capture the gains. If the projects fail, the debtholders will bear the full costs.[309] As a result of this financing, the shareholders are able to increase their upside at the expense of the debtholders.[310] The risk shifting problem might be especially relevant in the (rare) event of a possible liquidation.[311] In this case, the value of outstanding debt typically exceeds firm value and shareholders would go away empty-handed. Consequently, they demand the firm to take on high risk projects. If the project is successful, some of its gains will accrue to shareholders, increasing the value of their shares. If the project is unsuccessful, shareholders are not affected, as the firm's equity has already been lost prior to pursuing the project.[312] From the debtholders point of view, project failure directly reduces their cash flows while success provides them with gains only to the extent of the debt's value. Hence, debtholders favor a low risk strategy with a small NPV.[313]

---

303 See Hartmann-Wendels (1991): 270.

304 See Hartmann-Wendels (1991): 270.

305 See Walsh (2010): 483.

306 See Myers (2001): 96. This transfer of value may occur upon deciding on the intended use of the (raised) capital or whenever the goal of shareholder value maximization conflicts with the maximization of the market value of debt. See Wilhelm (1987): 191; Hartmann-Wendels (1991): 270.

307 In line with existing research, the following analysis assumes a risk of default on the outstanding debt. See also Jensen/Meckling (1976): 342; Myers (2001): 96. If debt has no risk of default, there is no reason for interest conflicts with shareholders, as the debtholders are not interested in the firm's risk or income.

308 See Hartmann-Wendels (1991): 278-284; Drukarczyk (1993): 307-309; Hartmann-Wendels (2001): 120; Witt (2003): 8f. This is also referred to as risk shifting or asset substitution. See Smith Jr./Warner (1979): 118f.

309 See also Jensen/Meckling (1976): 334; Easterbrook (1984): 653; Hansmann (1988): 282; Harris/Raviv (1991): 301. As the firm's equity can be considered a European-type call option on its assets, its value increases with the variance of the underlying, i.e. the firm's cash flows. Hence, by increasing the variance of the firm through a more risky investment policy, shareholders can increase the value of their option. For further details see Barnea et al. (1981): 9; Barnea et al. (1985): 33-35; Hartmann-Wendels (2001): 131; Anderson et al. (2003): 264; Nash/Netter/Poulsen (2003): 203f.

310 See Bott (2002): 13. This strategy can also involve the financing of the investment with both debt and equity capital. In this case, the shareholders are exposed to some risk as well. See Drukarczyk (1993): 311.

311 See Hartmann-Wendels (1991): 142, 284.

312 In the case of an unsuccessful project, the liquidation value of the firm declines. As the shareholders' portion of the liquidation value has been zero before, only the debtholders face the risk of losses from this strategy. For a similar argumentation, see Swoboda (1987): 169f.

313 See also Narayanaswamy/Shukla (2001): 35f.

(2) In contrast to asset substitution, the underinvestment problem[314] postulates that, in certain states of nature, a firm with outstanding debt will forego profitable investment opportunities.[315] If a firm has debt outstanding, shareholders accept an investment in a positive-NPV project only if its payoffs exceed the face value of the debt:[316] Suppose the shareholders raised new funds to finance a positive NPV project and that the firm's debt has a risk of default. In this case, the payoffs from the investment in the project first accrue to the debtholders in the form of a reduced probability of default.[317] The residual value from the investment due to shareholders may thus be smaller than their initial investment. Therefore, shareholders have no interest in the investment and abstain from it.[318] As a result, the existence of risky debt reduces the market value of the firm:[319] In general, the greater the risk of default, the greater the incentive of management to forego the investment opportunity and pay out the cash to shareholders.[320]

(3) Another strategy involves debt financed dividend payments, also called additional borrowing.[321] In this case, the shareholders demand that the firm's management borrows additional money and pays out the raised cash to shareholders.[322] Provided their claims are subordinate relative to those of the new debtholders, this strategy is detrimental for the firm's existing debtholders, as it increases the bankruptcy risk they face.[323] Hence, the existing debtholders receive a lower interest rate than would be required given the increased bankruptcy risk after the newly raised debt.[324] In addition to the capital paid out to them, shareholders also benefit from the difference in the interest rate the firm actually pays to the old debtholders and the rate it should pay based on the increased bankruptcy risk.[325]

Rational creditors recognize the potential expropriation by shareholders and try to prevent and account for any possible wealth transfer to shareholders in advance.[326] As a result, they incorporate the expected agency costs into the demand for financial assets, raising the cost of debt capital.[327] In addition, debtholders can make use of contractual changes, for example by de-

314 See Hartmann-Wendels (1991): 285-295; Drukarczyk (1993): 309f; Hartmann-Wendels (2001): 123-125.

315 See Myers (1977): 149. See also Myers (2001): 97.

316 See Barnea et al. (1981): 10.

317 See also Barnea et al. (1985): 37.

318 See e.g. Myers (1977): 153f; Smith Jr./Warner (1979): 119; Drukarczyk (1993): 3110.

319 See Myers (1977): 150, 155. The reduced firm value is thus borne by shareholders. The costs arising from the underinvestment problem constitute agency costs of debt. See Mello/Parsons (1992): 1890, 1895.

320 See also Swoboda (1987): 169; Nash et al. (2003): 204.

321 See Hartmann-Wendels (1991): 296-300.

322 See Drukarczyk (1993): 305-307; Myers (2001): 96f.

323 See Drukarczyk (1993): 305; Bott (2002): 12.

324 Note that this strategy only pays off if the market prices bonds under the assumption that the firm will issue no additional bonds. See Smith Jr./Warner (1979): 118; Nash et al. (2003): 204.

325 See Hartmann-Wendels (1991): 297; Drukarczyk (1993): 306.

326 See Hartmann-Wendels (1991): 142, 272. Thereby, it is irrelevant whether or not management actually aims to expropriate debtholders on behalf of shareholders.

327 See also Smith Jr./Warner (1979): 119; Barnea et al. (1981): 9; Easterbrook (1984): 653; Hartmann-Wendels (1987): 243; Myers (2001): 97; Anderson et al. (2003): 266; Nash et al. (2003): 203; Ellul/Guntay/Lel (2007): 9. Due to the higher costs of debt capital, it is the shareholders who ultimately have to bear the consequences of any potential expropriation of creditors. They accept these costs either because the payoffs from any expropriation of creditors exceed these monitoring costs or because these costs are offset by a higher firm value due to a lower incidence of agency costs.

manding covenants or collaterals.[328] These mechanisms are described in greater detail in section 2.1.5.

2.1.4 Principal-Principal Agency Conflicts

Researchers in the late 1990s and early 2000s began to realize that the widely dispersed ownership structure described by *Berle/Means* does not provide a universal image of ownership structures around the world. Rather, they state that, except for countries offering very good shareholder protection, "widely held firms become an exception."[329] Therefore, in those countries, the traditional manager-shareholder agency conflict is supplemented by agency conflicts occurring between two categories of principals.[330] These principal-principal agency conflicts, comprising minority shareholder-blockholder and blockholder-blockholder agency conflicts, constitute the topic of the following three sections. Section 2.1.4.1 first clarifies whether the relationships between minority shareholders and blockholders as well as between multiple blockholders represent agency relationships as required by the narrow and broad definition outlined in section 2.1.1.2. In addition, it illustrates the need for an extension of the traditional agency theory. Section 2.1.4.2 and 2.1.4.3 then focus on agency conflicts between minority shareholders and blockholders as well as between multiple blockholders, respectively. Similar to the previous sections, they first outline differences in the parties' utility functions, risk preferences and information to generally clarify the existence of agency conflicts within the agency relationships. This is then followed by a description of possible manifestations of these conflicts.

2.1.4.1 Applicability and Extension of Agency Theory

As outlined above, more recent literature has focused attention on the relationship between different shareholders.[331] This relationship has frequently been characterized as an agency relationship, usually without exposing the problems of such a generalization. Therefore, this section first clarifies that relationships between shareholders represent agency relationships before quoting two major points of criticism that necessitate the extension of the agency theory.

With regard to the **applicability of the agency theory**, the broad definition requires an agency relationship to be based on an informal, implicit delegation of authority.[332] The presence of such an implicit, intrinsic delegation can be attested to both the minority shareholder-blockholder and the blockholder-blockholder relationship. An intrinsic relationship "arises when an individual is 'naturally' endowed with the right to make a particular decision affecting other parties, who may in turn attempt to influence that decision."[333] The natural endow-

328 Alternative mechanisms constitute for example convertibles, adaptations in the bond maturity or debt priority. For details on their respective costs and benefits, please see Nash et al. (2003): 206-208.

329 La Porta et al. (1999): 498. See also Claessens/Djankov/Lang (2000): 99-104; Faccio/Lang (2002): 378.

330 See also La Porta et al. (1999): 511; La Porta et al. (2000a): 15.

331 See for example Bennedsen/Wolfenzon (2000): 116; Faccio/Lang/Young (2001): 66; Maury/Pajuste (2005); Attig et al. (2008); Dalziel/White/Arthurs (2011).

332 For the exact definition of an agency relationship, please see section 2.1.1.2.

333 Bernheim/Whinston (1986): 924.

ment of the blockholder to make a particular decision results from its large share ownership. The blockholder's decision affects the remaining shareholders of the particular firm who may influence the blockholder's decision via meetings, proposals or cooperation. An implicit delegation of control also arises if shareholders stay away from their firm's AGMs. In this case, they implicitly delegate their control to the shareholders present at the AGM. Consequently, conflicts between principals can be characterized as an agency relationship according to the broad definition.[334]

The narrow definition requires a formal, explicit contractual delegation of authority from the principal to the agent.[335] However, a number of authors propose to interpret the required contractual delegation broadly. For example, whereas *Richter* (1994) submits that an explicit contractual relationship and financial compensation is not required within the contractual idea,[336] *Eisenhardt* (1989) proposes to regard the term contract as a metaphor.[337] Hence, the contractual idea can be applied also to cases with no explicit contract between the involved parties.[338] With regard to the formal delegation, *Schanze* (1987) concludes that agency relationships are not necessarily founded on a formal contractual basis.[339] According to *Rees* (1985a) the structure of agency theory is applicable to a broad range of problems which do not necessarily involve a formal delegation.[340] Also *Rees* (1985a) states that the agency relationship can be applied to a broader class of problems "where no formal delegation relationship is explicitly involved."[341] Moreover, *Swoboda* (1987) states that "in many cases there are no contracts. Principals then are protected by law or generally accepted rules of behavior."[342] In the German context, the duty of loyalty constitutes such an accepted rule of behavior. The duty of loyalty is an obligation of a firm's shareholder(s) to be considerate of and not to damage other shareholders.[343] Furthermore, it mandates the use of the voting rights for the benefit of the firm. In case of a violation of this duty, the respective shareholder is liable to legal prosecution.[344] Hence, the duty of loyalty can be viewed as an explicit contractual relationship between the shareholders of a particular firm: Although the involved parties do not sign an explicit contract, with the investment in the stock of a particular firm, the shareholders enter the contractual relationship by consciously subjecting themselves to the restrictions implied by the duty

334 The individuals within the relationship depend on the particular principal-principal conflict. Within the minority shareholder-blockholder conflict the minority shareholders depend on the actions of the largest blockholder. Within the blockholder-blockholder conflict, the other blockholder(s) depend(s) on the actions of the largest blockholder.

335 For the exact definition of an agency relationship, please see section 2.1.1.2.

336 See Richter (1994): 16.

337 See Eisenhardt (1989): 58.

338 See Saam (2002): 7.

339 See Schanze (1987): 468; Rieckers/Spindler (2004): 358.

340 See Rees (1985a): 3.

341 Rees (1985a): 3.

342 Swoboda (1987): 167.

343 See Jilg (1996): 79.

344 See Jilg (1996): 97. For more details on the duty of loyalty, please see section 2.2.3.1.

of loyalty.[345] Hence, with few qualifications, the principal-principal relationship is also consistent with the narrow definition of agency relationships.[346]

The **criticism of the agency theory** refers to its dyadic nature and bias towards principals.[347] The central statement of the former argument constitutes its disregard of the existence of groups of principals (agents). Thus, the interdependencies resulting from the interaction between multiple agents or multiple principals are neglected. This narrow focus is indeed questionable, given the agency theory's image of the firm as a team working together to survive in the competition with other teams.[348] A similar argument is made by *Saam* (2002) who argues that if firms are viewed as networks of explicit and implicit contracts, the focus of the agency theory should not be only on dyads but also on groups.[349] Also *Pratt/Zeckhauser* (1991) criticize that the existing literature only focuses on a simple two-party relationship. However, the challenges of real work frequently involve more than one agent or principal. Hence, they argue that relationships with multiple agents or multiple principals constitute "major additional challenges, both conceptually and in the real world."[350] *Bernheim/Whinston* (1986) argue that in many cases, "the action chosen by a particular individual (the agent) affects not just one, but several other parties (the principals)"[351] which might have conflicting preferences regarding the possible actions of the agent.[352] Therefore, agency theory fails to incorporate interactions and competition between multiple agents or multiple principals.[353] In addition, *Shapiro* (2005) writes that "looking beyond the abstract, cloistered dyad also reveals that actors are not just principals or agents, but often both at the same time."[354] In the case of principal-principal conflicts, a blockholder may act as an agent to the other shareholders and simultaneously as principal to the management of the firm.

In addition, the existing literature criticizes that the traditional agency theory is biased towards the principal and explicitly assumes opportunism only by the agent.[355] However, one cannot rule out the possibility of opportunism also on the part of the principal, who might as well have an information advantage over the agent.[356] *Connelly et al.* (2010) proceed on the assumption that opportunism by principals will be a more important topic in the future. They

345 For a similar argumentation, please see Meinhövel (1999): 32.

346 Halpern (1999): 35f even regards the situation between a blockholder and the minority shareholders as being identical to the principal-agent problem described by Berle and Means.

347 For a more detailed description and additional criticism regarding the agency theory, please see Saam (2002): 50-56.

348 Please see also section 2.1.1.2 for the definition of an organization (firm) as used by agency theory.

349 See also Saam (2002): 50.

350 Pratt/Zeckhauser (1991): Preface.

351 Bernheim/Whinston (1986): 923.

352 See Bernheim/Whinston (1986): 923. The authors extend the bilateral model to include multiple risk-neutral principals. See also Dixit/Grossman/Helpman (1997): 752 and Meinhövel (1999): 93 for details.

353 See Barnea et al. (1985): 8, 28. The authors explicitly recognize problems that may arise from conflicts of interest among principals themselves. Also Shapiro (2005): 267 extends the assumption of a single principal and agent to include multiple principals and agents.

354 Shapiro (2005): 267.

355 See Perrow (1986): 14; Saam (2002): 54; Shapiro (2005): 268; Dalziel et al. (2011): 1358. Also Donaldson (1963): 117 recognizes that "most of the writers on the subject are on the side of the stockholder."

356 The possibility of an information advantage of the principal is also recognized by Sappington (1991): 54. Examples of studies that analyze principal-agent relationships with an informed principal include Maskin/Tirole (1990) and Jost (1996).

argue that more proactive owners may be inclined to "undertake actions that benefit themselves at the expense of managers and the long-term health of the firm."[357] With regard to agency relationships within firms, *Thomsen/Pedersen* (2000) point out that the agency literature does not consider the possibility that the goals of principals themselves might differ from the maximization of shareholder value. According to them, the assumption of value maximization is only "an approximation of the more general idea that owners (like managers) may be expected to maximize their utility, which may depend on other factors."[358] The absence of a uniform goal could lead to conflicts between principals. Even if blockholders strive for the maximization of firm value, they may disagree on how to maximize the value of the firm, provided they have different preferences with regard to risk and cash flows.[359] Introducing self-interested, heterogenous blockholders and the presence of multiple blockholders, the thesis at hand incorporates these points of criticism and contributes to an advancement of the traditional agency theory.

2.1.4.2 Minority Shareholder-Blockholder Agency Conflict

Empirical studies on the agency conflict between minority shareholders and blockholders have traditionally been focused on emerging economies.[360] However, due to the concentrated ownership of continental European firms, these conflicts are also relevant in developed countries.[361] Agency conflicts within the minority shareholder-blockholder relationship[362] may arise whenever both parties differ in their respective utility functions, risk preferences and information.[363]

There are two potential factors that might determine a shareholder's **risk preference:** the size of the shareholder's ownership and the level of its diversification. With regard to the first factor, the risk preferences of a particular shareholder depend on the fraction of shares it owns.[364] The larger the fraction of its shares, the more the shareholder benefits from the increased stock price resulting from a successful high-risk project. However, the shareholder is also exposed to a greater proportion of the losses in case of an unsuccessful project. The extent to which the high exposure to both profits and losses matters to a shareholder depends on the second measure of risk preference – the shareholder's level of diversification. The central scheme of this argument is that if a shareholder's investment is large *and* concentrated within a single firm, it is highly exposed to firm-specific risk. Similar to a firm's manager, a firm's blockholder – if poorly diversified – typically has a substantial portion of its wealth tied up

357 Connelly et al. (2010): 1580. Dalziel et al. (2011): 1347 denote the evidence of expropriation also by principals as "quandary for classic agency theory" which so far has treated agents rather than principals as the key source of agency conflicts.

358 Thomsen/Pedersen (2000): 692.

359 See Thomsen/Pedersen (2000): 690, 692.

360 See e.g. Young et al. (2003): 28. For a review of recent research on principal-principal agency conflicts see Young et al. (2008).

361 See Young et al. (2008): 200; Renders/Gaeremynck (2012): 126.

362 While the following description assumes a single blockholder, it is also likely that multiple blockholders collude in order to expropriate the remaining minority shareholders.

363 Within the analysis of the minority shareholder-blockholder conflict, it is assumed that management acts on behalf of the largest blockholder.

364 See also Dhillon/Rossetto (2009): 4.

within its portfolio firm.[365] As a result, it is reasonable to assume that a poorly diversified shareholder with a significant stake in a particular firm tries to avoid as much risk as possible while maintaining an adequate return on its investment. Applied to the two parties at hand, one can assume that a blockholder is more risk averse than a minority shareholder. Even if the former is a major investment firm, it should be more risk averse than the average minority shareholder that typically has invested a small amount of its personal wealth in a portfolio of stocks.

As suggested in section 2.1.2, the shareholders' **utility function** envisages the maximization of shareholder value. However, the greater risk aversion of the blockholder may cause a disagreement on which financial and investment policies best serve the attainment of shareholder value maximization. In general, the expected utility of a risk-averse shareholder decreases with increases in the variance of the shareholder's wealth. Hence, if a blockholder is risk-averse, any increase in firm-specific risk decreases his personal utility. In contrast, the utility of an individual minority shareholder will be largely unaffected by firm-specific risk, either because of its marginal investment or because the risk has been diversified away.[366] As a result, the blockholder may wish to pursue investment strategies with a lower risk, while minority shareholders may favor a high-risk strategy. Moreover, while both the blockholder and the minority shareholders always choose a high stock price over a low stock price, the blockholder's utility function may be complemented by additional utility sources. If the private utility derived from these sources is large enough, the blockholder may forego higher stock prices in order to generate this private utility to the detriment of minority shareholders.

The blockholder's pursuance of its individual utility depends on the presence of **information asymmetries** within the agency relationship. Due to their miniscule fraction of the firm's shares, minority shareholders have little incentives to incur the costs of collecting information about the external environment and the actions of the largest blockholder.[367] In contrast, the large ownership provides the blockholder with a strong incentive to collect information, as it internalizes a greater portion of the benefits arising from its information collection. Moreover, it might also receive access to information not accessible to small shareholders, e.g. via a direct provision of information by the firm's management.[368] Overall, the blockholder should have a substantial information advantage.

Based on the preceding discussion, there are grounds to believe in the presence of an agency conflict between the two parties. As shown in figure 2, the blockholder exploits its strong influence on the firm's management while simultaneously benefitting from the minority shareholders' inability to limit its discretion and control management. This uneven distribution of power can have detrimental effects for minority shareholders:[369] the blockholder may use its power to set its preferred investment policy or divert resources to itself at the expense of mi-

365 See Faccio/Marchica/Mura (2011): 3602.
366 See Faccio et al. (2011): 3602.
367 Please see also section 3.1.1 for more details.
368 Please note that this, however, is illegal, as pursuant to § 53a AktG, all shareholders shall be treated equally. § 131 (4) AktG prescribes that this information is to be provided also to minority shareholders if requested.
369 See Bress (2008): 24.

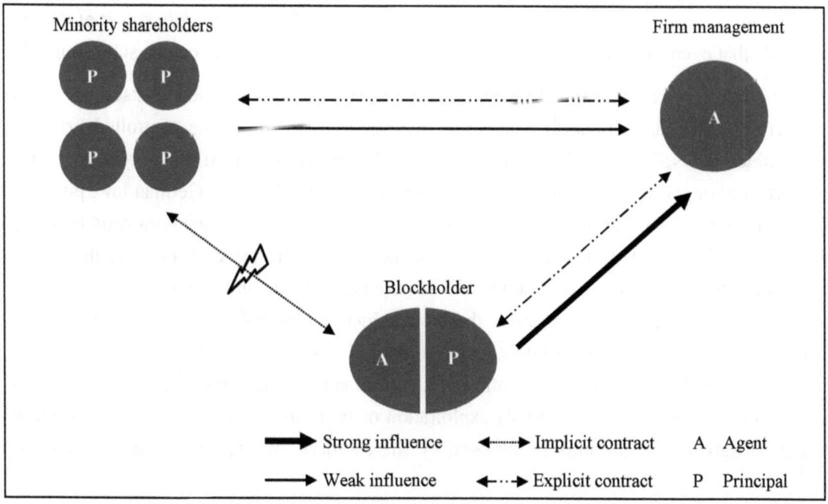

Figure 2: Minority shareholder-blockholder agency conflict

nority shareholders.[370] In this case, the blockholder exchanges firm profits for private benefits of control.[371] In the context of this study, private benefits of control are defined as "the proportion of a company's shares that does not accrue to all shareholders on a per share basis, but is instead captured by inside shareholders who control and sometimes manage the firm."[372] Private benefits may not necessarily be derived from the firm's cash flows, but can also be non-pecuniary.[373] The vehicles that may be used by the blockholder to benefit from its control position can take many forms and may be legal, illegal or located within grey areas.[374]

(1) A blockholder pursuing private benefits of control can engage in tunneling, which is defined as "the transfer of assets and profits out of firms for the benefit of those who control them."[375] Tunneling can occur in two forms. First, a blockholder can shift resources from its portfolio firm for its own benefit via self-dealing. From the perspective of the blockholder, this self-dealing can involve asset sales at favorable prices to itself or other firms under its control,[376] related party transactions,[377] loan guarantees or expropriation of the firm's opportunities.[378] Second, the blockholder can use financial transactions in order to increase its share

370 See Black (1992a): 815.

371 In line with Bennedsen/Wolfenzon (2000): 114, the present thesis generally assumes that private benefits are inefficient to extract and come at the expense of the remaining shareholders.

372 Dyck/Zingales (2004a): 51. See also Dyck/Zingales (2004b): 541. For a similar definition of private benefits, please see Baums/Scott (2005): 35; Morck/Wolfenzon/Yeung (2005): 676; Edmans (2014): 16.

373 See Barclay/Holderness (1989): 374.

374 See La Porta et al. (2000b): 4. Please note that the detrimental effects for minority shareholders not necessarily have to be caused intentionally by the blockholder.

375 Johnson et al. (2000): 22. For more details on tunneling, please see Morck et al. (2005): 678f.

376 See Halpern (1999): 32; La Porta et al. (2000a): 3; Dyck/Zingales (2004b): 541; Edmans (2014): 16.

377 In related party transactions, "the dominant shareholder arranges a deal between two companies in which he holds a controlling interest. He arranges the deal so as to provide favorable terms to the firm in which he has a larger percentage equity ownership and disadvantageous terms to the firm in which he holds a smaller ownership position." Dahya/Dimitrov/McConnell (2008): 77.

378 See also Shleifer/Vishny (1997): 758f; La Porta et al. (2000b): 4.

in the firm, e.g. through a dilutive share issuance.[379] Despite legal rules, *Johnson et al.* (2000) conclude that even in developed countries, tunneling by the blockholder can be substantial.[380]

(2) A blockholder can also transfer wealth from the minority shareholders to itself via profit transfer or control agreements.[381] Subject to ensuring the survival of the controlled firm, the blockholder may sell the firm's assets and transfer the proceeds to itself. Alternatively, it may buy assets of or sell assets to the firm at advantageous prices.[382] While German law, pursuant to § 304 AktG, obligates a blockholder to provide for adequate compensation of minority shareholders this compensation is not related to the firm's share price or the price the blockholder paid for the acquisition of control.[383] Moreover, although shareholders are able to appeal against the level of compensation, the blockholder has the right to cancel the agreement if the court – as a result of the shareholders' complaint – sets a new compensation.[384] In general, the right to block the implementation of a control agreement or profit transfer agreement is essential in preventing a (potential) exploitation of minority shareholders. However, these enterprise agreements can only be blocked by shareholders owning 25% of the share capital.[385]

(3) Due to the differential risk preferences, the pursuance of a risk averse investment policy also constitutes a problem of the minority shareholder-blockholder relationship.[386] As previously mentioned, minority shareholders and blockholders should have divergent preferences with regard to the risk and return characteristics of the firm and the investment projects it pursues. While a larger blockholder is likely to prefer a low risk project at the expense of higher profits, smaller shareholders prefer high risk-high return projects.[387] Due to the blockholder's greater power, it will enforce a risk-averse investment policy to the detriment of minority shareholders.[388] Because of its desire to preserve its private benefits, the blockholder undertakes a more risky project only if the expected benefits arising from the project sufficiently compensate for the forgone private benefits.[389] Alternatively, it could use the available re-

379 See Johnson et al. (2000): 22f. See also van der Elst/Vermeulen (2011): 7.

380 See Johnson et al. (2000): 26.

381 The maximum amount of profit transferred is equal to the annual net profit after deducting any loss carried forward from the previous year, the amount to be transferred to the legal reserves and the undistributable, restricted amount pursuant to § 268 (8) HGB. See § 301 AktG.

382 See also Jenkinson/Ljungqvist (2001): 403.

383 See Jenkinson/Ljungqvist (2001): 403.

384 See § 304 (3) and (4) AktG.

385 These transactions are also regarded as inadequately regulated by Baums/Scott (2005): 70.

386 See Edmans (2014): 16.

387 This problem is also pointed out by Dhillon/Rossetto (2009): 4.

388 Faccio et al. (2011): 3601f investigate the impact of blockholder diversification on corporate risk taking and find that firms controlled by a non-diversified and thus risk averse investor invest more conservatively. Hence, a risk averse investor will decrease firm-specific risk at the expense of small shareholders' interests.

389 See John/Litov/Yeung (2008): 1682. The authors argue that because the insiders' equity ownership and private benefits of control "are inevitably concentrated within the firms they control, that is, because of their large exposure to these firms, these dominant insiders are likely to direct the corporations they control to invest more conservatively than they would if they held a diversified portfolio of firms." While they primarily focus on shareholdings by managers, these characteristics also hold for external blockholders.

sources to invest in projects with low returns but offering the blockholder a personal benefit, for example through increasing the firm's diversification.[390]

(4) A blockholder may also affect a firm's payout policy to match its personal interest to the detriment of remaining shareholders.[391] With regard to the size of the payouts, German corporate law includes provisions that formally define the minimum and maximum amounts in terms of net income to be distributed to shareholders as dividends.[392] Pursuant to § 58 (2) Sentence 1 AktG, the management and supervisory board are allowed to transfer an amount up to 50 % of the annual net profits[393] to retained earnings without explicit consent by shareholders.[394] According to § 58 (4) AktG, the AGM shall be entitled to decide on the remaining distributable profit.[395] However, the management shall submit a proposal for the appropriation of distributable profits to the supervisory board, to be presented to the AGM;[396] if this proposal is reasonable, it is typically accepted by shareholders.[397] Overall, while the German corporate law generally requires a minimum distribution of 50 % of net profits, the existing regulation still provides a blockholder with a number of ways to affect the payout policy. First, within the limits prescribed by § 58 AktG, it can influence the exact amount within the 50% of annual net profits boundary to be retained. Within this limit, the blockholder can arbitrarily reduce the amount to be distributed to the shareholders. Second, if the blockholder has a super-majority, it can change the firm's articles and pay out or retain more of the net profits as long as the retained earnings do not exceed 50% of the share capital.[398] Finally, the blockholder can pressure management to design a proposal for the appropriation of the remaining distributable profits that matches its interests.[399] *Zeckhauser/Pound* (1990) term this form of activism "agenda control"[400]: in this case, management and its supporting blockholder(s) for-

390 See Halpern (1999): 32. Note that this might also be dependent on the identity of the blockholder.

391 See also Drukarczyk (1993): 439.

392 See Pellens et al. (2003): 309.

393 According to § 150 (1) and (2) AktG, every firm shall build up a legal reserve. The amount to be transferred to this reserve shall equal 5% of annual net profits (after the deduction of any previous year's loss carried forward) until the sum of legal reserve and capital reserves equals 10% of the share capital (or any higher percentage as set out in the firm's articles). Hence, the profits net of the amount used for the legal cash reserve constitute the basis for the distribution. See also Andres et al. (2009): 176f.

394 This can be seen as an instrument for the protection of creditors. See Pellens et al. (2003): 325. Note that this provision does not imply a binding lower bound. See Andres et al. (2009): 176f. In addition, the firm's articles may allow the management and supervisory board to retain larger or smaller amounts, as long as the retained earnings do not exceed half of the share capital. See § 58 (2) Sentence 2 and 3 AktG. See also Ellermann (2003): 23; Correia da Silva/Georgen/Renneboog (2004): 68; Ernst/Gassen/Pellens (2005): 26f; Goergen/Renneboog/Correia da Silva (2005): 381; Prokot (2006): 128.

395 This provision aims to protect minority shareholders' interests. See Pellens et al. (2003): 325.

396 See § 170 (2) AktG.

397 See Marsch (1974): 76; Ellermann (2003): 23.

398 See Pellens et al. (2003): 311. In doing so, the blockholder has to keep in mind that shareholders have a right to a dividend equal to 4% of the share capital if the retention of earnings is not required according to reasonable business judgment to ensure the viability of the firm. Otherwise, the decision on the appropriation of net profits can be contested. See § 254 (1) AktG.

399 Pellens et al. (2003): 309f, 326 find that firm executives do not regard the role of the AGM as crucial for the determination of dividend payouts.

400 See Zeckhauser/Pound (1990): 159.

mulate the proposals, while the remaining shareholders have no possibility to coordinate an opposition.[401]

Additional manifestations of the agency conflict between the two parties involves the blockholder's appointment of under-qualified persons such as family members or friends for top management positions instead of better qualified external candidates.[402] In addition, if a blockholder derives utility from an existing or potential business relationship with the particular firm, its voting decisions may be conflicted. The blockholder may therefore side with management in order to protect these business relationships.[403] In general, minority shareholder-blockholder conflicts frequently affect a firm's strategy and therefore the overall competitiveness of the firm in question.[404]

2.1.4.3 Blockholder-Blockholder Agency Conflict

In the presence of a blockholder, the previous section has highlighted the existence of a minority shareholder-blockholder agency conflict and the possible manifestations of this conflict. The differences in risk preferences, utility functions, and information have thereby largely been motivated and justified by the different sized shareholdings of the respective parties. In contrast, in the case of multiple blockholders, the differences in the size of the blockholders' share holdings may not be as substantial. Although these differences may still be large enough to cause agency conflicts, blockholder-blockholder agency conflicts are more likely to stem from the simultaneous presence of different blockholder types within a single investee firm.

With regard to **risk preferences**, different types of blockholders will differ in the degree to which they diversify their portfolio. Hence, the value of the respective stake in the firm most likely also represents a different proportion of the blockholder's total portfolio value.[405] Overall, these factors have an effect on the blockholders' tendency to accept firm-specific risk.[406]

The blockholders' types also impact their **utility functions**. First, different types vary in extent of business relationships with the investee firm.[407] If a blockholder maintains a contractual relationship with the focal firm, firm value might not constitute its primary utility source. Rather, the blockholder might accept a value-reducing decision if the benefits it receives from its business relationship outweigh the losses it bears as a shareholder. This gives rise to a con-

---

401 In line with this, Pérez-González (2003): 1 suggests that "firms with large controlling or simply influential stockholders may follow the preferences of these investors, and in consequence, they would induce the clientele the firm caters to."

402 See La Porta et al. (2000b): 4.

403 See Edmans (2014): 16.

404 With regard to the outcomes of principal-principal problems, Young et al. (2003): 31 state that firms subject to these problems "are likely to embrace strategies that benefit the majority shareholders with relatively little regard for overall firm competitiveness."

405 For example, the investment of an institutional investor in a particular firm will represent only a small fraction of its overall portfolio value, whereas the founding family might have invested all personal wealth in the firm, therefore being fully exposed to firm-specific risk.

406 See Faccio et al. (2011): 3601f. See also Dalziel et al. (2011): 1348.

407 See also Dalziel et al. (2011): 1348.

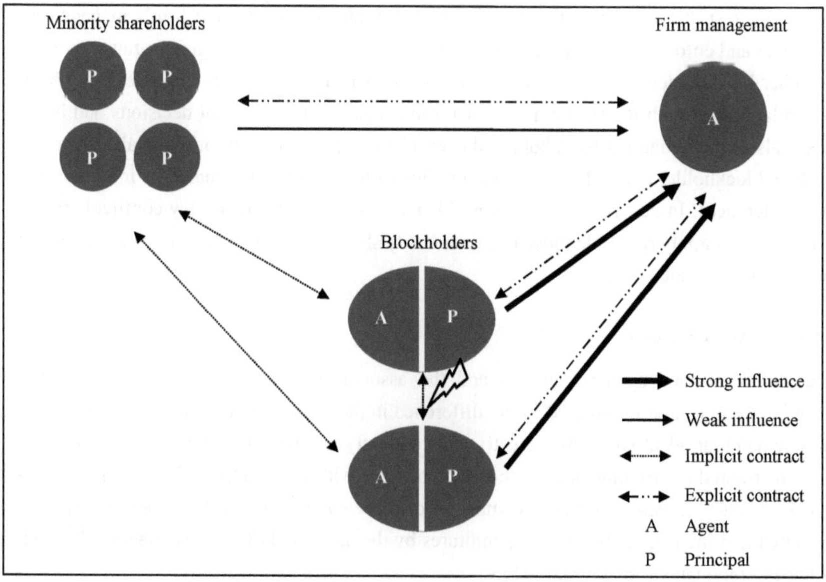

Figure 3: Blockholder-blockholder agency conflict

flict with other blockholders that do not receive compensation for the lost firm value.[408] Second, different blockholders might vary regarding their preferred investment horizon.[409] Some blockholders may focus on short-term value improvements whereas others may have a long-term view and are thus negatively affected by an excessive short-term focus. Moreover, while retaining or increasing an equity stake may be beneficial for one type of blockholder, the disposal of its stake may be beneficial for another blockholder.[410] Hence, "what serves the interests of one principal may conflict with the interests of others."[411]

In general, a blockholder has only limited possibilities to withhold information from another blockholder. However, there may still exist **information asymmetries** for the following reasons. A blockholder that maintains a business relationship with the focal firm may be able to acquire private information as a result of this business relationship. Similarly, a blockholder with an informal, personal relationship with the firm may be in possession of superior private information. Finally, a blockholder may consciously accept an informational disadvantage if its investment strategy does not provide it with the ability or the motivation to incur the costs of information collection.

Overall, the analysis shows that there are grounds to believe in the presence of a blockholder-blockholder agency conflict in case of a simultaneous presence of different blockholder types. As illustrated in figure 3, in the presence of heterogenous blockholders and the resultant con-

408 See also Bott (2002): 9.
409 See also Dalziel et al. (2011): 1348.
410 See also Dalziel et al. (2011): 1348f.
411 Dalziel et al. (2011): 1349. In line with this, Rees (1985b): 92 suggests the essential problem in case of several shareholders to be one of reconciling the divergent interests among the principals.

flict of interest, the self-interested blockholders individually monitor the firm's management to protect and enforce their self-interest either intentionally or unintentionally against those of the other blockholder(s).[412] For example, a blockholder that aims to protect its existing business relationship with the firm may side with management in important decisions and block proposals of the remaining blockholder(s) even if those are beneficial for firm value. Alternatively, a blockholder may affect the payout policy of the firm so as to match its individual return preferences. In general, the agency problems resulting from the agency conflict between blockholders largely resemble those of the minority shareholder-blockholders conflict and are therefore not repeated here.

2.1.5 Agency Costs

The aforementioned agency conflicts and the associated agency problems create agency costs.[413] These can be interpreted as the difference in the maximum welfare achievable in, on the one hand, an ideal world of perfectly and costlessly enforceable contracts and symmetrically distributed information and, on the other, a world with asymmetric information and costly contracting.[414] Agency costs are comprised of three components: (1) monitoring expenditures by the principal, (2) bonding expenditures by the agent and (3) the residual loss.[415] Each of these components is delineated below.

(1) Independent of the type of agency conflict, the principal may decide to monitor the actions of the agent and enforce its interests to mitigate the problems arising from the conflict. The use of such measures causes monitoring costs or expenditures.[416] In setting the level of monitoring, the principals balance the marginal costs of an extra unit of monitoring with the resultant marginal savings from the prevention of adverse managerial behavior.[417] As regards the *manager-shareholder conflict*, monitoring expenditures embrace all costs incurred by the shareholders while monitoring management and preventing aberrant behavior.[418] These costs involve, inter alia, the costs of becoming informed about the operations of the agent and the external environment, and the costs of communicating with the remaining shareholders to exchange information and make decisions. Moreover, they comprise costs from specific control activities that can include contracting costs, incentive and bonus compensation systems or auditing costs.[419] As regards the *shareholder-debtholder conflict*, debtholders can prevent ex-

412 See also Dalziel et al. (2011): 1349.

413 See also Barnea et al. (1981): 8 and figure 1.

414 For a similar interpretation, see Jensen/Meckling (1976): 327 and Schmidt (1987): 501. See also Jost (2001): 23; Köhler (2005): 234; Ampenberger (2010): 45. Rozeff (1982): 250 measures agency cost as "the discrepancy between the value of the 100 percent owner-managed and less than 100 percent owner-managed firm".

415 See Jensen/Meckling (1976): 308. Fama/Jensen (1983a): 327 define agency costs as "the costs of structuring, monitoring, and bonding a set of contracts among agents with conflicting interests, plus the residual loss".

416 Jensen/Meckling (1976): 308 clarify that monitoring does not only comprise the measurement or observation of the agent's behavior. Rather, it also includes the principal's effort to control the agent's behavior through budgetary restrictions, compensation schemes or operating rules.

417 See Wolf (1999): 19.

418 See Jensen/Meckling (1976): 308.

419 See e.g. Jensen/Meckling (1976): 323; Saam (2002): 23.

ploitation through contractual changes such as covenants or collaterals. Covenants constitute contractual clauses that limit the shareholders' ability to engage in value transfer strategies or enable the debtholders to influence the firm's investment strategy.[420] Collaterals constitute the right to access certain tangible assets in case of an inability of the borrower to meet its interest payments.[421] Hence, the debt is secured with tangible assets,[422] which enables the lender to avoid credit risk and monitoring costs, apart from those that accrue from monitoring the collaterals' value.[423] Since both *minority shareholder-blockholder and blockholder-blockholder conflicts* are characterized by implicit contracts, monitoring does not involve specific contractual changes. Rather, monitoring costs arise as a result of the endeavor to reduce potential information asymmetries between the respective parties and from communicating with the remaining shareholders to exchange information and make collective decisions on the firm's AGM. These costs can be substantial if firm ownership is shared among a number of principals that have divergent interests with regard to the conduct of a firm's operations, i.e. its heterogeneity.[424]

(2) The monitoring costs incurred by the principal(s) also affect the respective agent.[425] Therefore, it is in the agent's interest to ensure that the principals' monitoring is performed in the lowest cost way. Whenever the agent can produce information on his characteristics or the correctness of his decisions to the principals at lower cost than they, it pays the agent to contractually promise this information to the principals in advance. Moreover, the agent may engage in actions by which he attempts to demonstrate his intention of maximizing the principals' utility and not his.[426] Alternatively, the agent may use mechanisms that guarantee a compensation of principals in an event of adverse behavior.[427] The costs resulting from these endeavors are called bonding costs.[428] *Prior to entering an agency relationship*, the principal is unable to judge on the productive capabilities of the agent,[429] but can observe the information provided by the agent on his characteristics and attributes. These attributes can be used as signals of productive capabilities by the agent,[430] provided the transmission of these signals is too costly for a poorly qualified agent.[431] As a result of this signaling, the principal's perception of the agent's capability is adjusted. *After entering an agency relationship*, the

420 See e.g. Swoboda (1987): 170; Drukarczyk (1993): 328; Myers (2001): 97; Nash et al. (2003): 202.

421 Drukarczyk (1993): 336. This is also called secured debt. See Nash et al. (2003): 207.

422 See Nash et al. (2003): 207. See also Hansmann (1988): 282.

423 See Drukarczyk (1993): 337.

424 See Hansmann (1988): 278. The impact of heterogeneity is investigated in the empirical analysis.

425 With regard to the shareholder-debtholder agency conflict, Smith Jr./Warner (1979): 121 argue that on the one hand, covenants mitigate the agency conflict; on the other hand, they reduce management's flexibility regarding investment and financing decisions. See also Nash et al. (2003): 202f.

426 Bonding expenditures by the agent are only incurred to the extent that the resulting benefits exceed those from the pursuance of private benefits.

427 See e.g. Jensen/Meckling (1976): 308; Wolf (1999): 20; Saam (2002): 23.

428 See Jensen/Meckling (1976): 338f.

429 In fact, the information may also not become immediately available *after* entering the relationship, as the job may take time to learn or due to unobservable external states of the world. See Spence (1973): 356.

430 See also Spence (1973): 357f. The costs resulting from an alteration of these signals are called "signaling costs" and can include both psychic costs, monetary costs as well as opportunity costs.

431 Hence, signaling by the agent will only be effective in dissociating from less productive agents if the signaling costs are negatively correlated with the agent's productive capability. See also Spence (1973): 358.

agent's efforts focus on demonstrating that he is acting in the principals' interest.[432] For example, a blockholder may signal its unwillingness to exploit the remaining shareholders through the payment of dividends. As dividends guarantee a pro-rata pay out for all shareholders, they are an ideal device for limiting rent extraction of blockholders.[433] Also the management, on behalf of a blockholder, may voluntarily offer collaterals, in the form of fixed assets, to prospective debtholders to signal an unwillingness to exploit the debtholders once they have provided their funds.

(3) The monitoring and bonding costs are incurred as a result of an endeavor to minimize the **residual loss**.[434] Thereby, both parties are willing to bear monitoring and bonding costs, respectively, as long as these costs do not exceed the resultant reduction of the residual loss.[435] Generally, the residual loss can be described as the loss incurred due to the divergence of interest between principal and agent.[436] Given a world characterized by asymmetric information and costly contracting, it is the difference between the maximum welfare and the actual welfare of the principal realized by the agent for an optimal level of monitoring and bonding activities. The residual loss thus measures the reduction in welfare caused by the remaining divergence between the agent's actions and those preferred by the principal(s).[437] Alternatively, it can also be thought of as the costs arising from imperfect monitoring and bonding activities.[438] In the case of the previously described agency conflicts, the residual loss is comprised of the costs eventuating from the manifestations of the agency problems that cannot be mitigated by monitoring or bonding mechanisms. For instance, the residual loss may comprise inflated interest payments (shareholder-debtholder conflict), increased operating expenses (manager-shareholder conflict), the retention of capital (principal-principal conflicts), and a depressed share price.

As neither the principal nor the agent can ensure at zero cost that the agent will act in the interest of the principal, agency costs can never be zero.[439] However, the magnitude of agency costs varies from firm to firm, depending on the agent's taste, the effort he has to expend to exercise his self-interest and on the relative monitoring and bonding costs within the respective firms.[440] Moreover, a firm's agency costs also depend on its capital and ownership structure. A publicly-traded firm with a dispersed ownership structure is subject to the traditional agency conflict between managers and shareholders. If this firm has raised external debt, the traditional agency conflict is supplemented with a shareholder-debtholder agency conflict. While the presence of a blockholder represents a possible solution to the traditional agency

432 Moreover, he may implement systems or processes that are able to generate reliable performance information and use these as a signal to the principal. See Köhler (2005): 235.

433 Please see section 5.3.1.3 for further details on the use of dividends as a signal by blockholders.

434 See Drukarczyk (1993): 622. Schneider (1987): 483 states that agency costs aim to "minimize the difference between the realized money equivalent of the principal's welfare and that money equivalent of the principal's maximum welfare, which could be achieved by actions of the agent." In order to minimize this difference, monitoring costs will be incurred by the principal and bonding costs by the agent.

435 See Rozeff (1982): 250. See also Epstein (1991): 130.

436 See Jensen/Meckling (1976): 308. See also Hartmann-Wendels (1991): 152; Meinhövel (1999): 42.

437 See Jensen/Meckling (1976): 308; Saam (2002): 55.

438 Dalziel et al. (2011): 1349 call these "the costs of failing to control agents".

439 See Jensen/Meckling (1976): 308.

440 See Jensen/Meckling (1976): 328. See section 5.2 for hypotheses on the determinants of agency costs.

Table 1
This table shows the components of a firm's overall agency costs which vary depending on the firm's capital and ownership structure.

	Overall agency costs			
	Agency costs from manager-shareholder agency conflict	Agency costs from shareholder-debtholder agency conflict	Agency costs from minority shareholder-blockholder agency conflict	Agency costs from blockholder-blockholder agency conflict
Dispersed ownership	X			
Dispersed ownership & debt financing	X	X		
Single blockholder & debt financing	X	X	X	
Multiple blockholders & debt financing	X	X	X	X

Table 1: Overall agency costs

conflict, it sets the stage for an agency conflict between small and large shareholders.[441] Finally, the presence of multiple blockholders gives rise to an agency conflict between these blockholders. In order to account for the agency costs resulting from these four different types of agency conflicts, the present thesis introduces the concept of a firm's *overall agency costs* which is depicted in table 1. The overall agency costs are defined as the sum of the agency costs a firm, dependent on its capital and ownership structure, can be subject to.[442] In light of these agency costs, there is the need for instruments that can be used to mitigate some of these costs. Corporate governance is regarded as such an instrument and is therefore covered in the following.

2.1.6 Corporate Governance

Any financial system can fulfill its primary role of channeling capital from individual savers to investors only if it offers an adequate guarantee to the providers of capital that they will earn the return they have been promised. To minimize the risk emanating from incomplete contracts and information asymmetries,[443] the providers of capital require the existence of individuals or mechanisms with the ability to influence the activities of management in the interest of the capital providers, if necessary.[444] If these mechanisms did not exist or function effectively, the providers of capital would not be willing to lend to firms or buy the firm's eq-

441 This has also been pointed out by Young et al. (2003): 25.

442 Schneider (1987): 482-485 regards the concept of agency costs as metaphorical and calls it a "flop". He argues that for agency costs to be subsumed as costs, they have to be quantitative and observable. However, the residual loss is impossible to determine since it is unknown under which condition the principals' welfare would be maximized. In a reply, Schmidt (1987): 499 states that the concept of agency costs "directs attention to the problem of taking into account and assessing the consequences which an asymmetrical distribution of information can have for the way people organize their cooperation." In addition, he argues that the lacking observability of agency costs does neither imply an inability to clearly define agency costs in theoretical models nor to approximate agency costs in empirical studies. Moreover, the solution of the agency problem "does not require an exact quantification of the residual loss or of total agency costs." He concludes that it is "unfounded and unfair" to call agency costs a flop. Schmidt (1987): 502, 508

443 These problems have been described in section 2.1.

444 Schmidt (2004): 390 analyzes this from a more systemic perspective and states that "firms are pools of resources", generating rents for the resource providers. As the size and distribution of the rents depends on decisions made within the firm, the providers of resources have their investment at stake, providing them with a natural interest to monitor and influence managerial decision making.

uity.[445] Due to this, corporate governance plays a decisive role within the financial system,[446] affecting the profitability and growth of firms as well as their access to and costs of capital.[447] Despite this important role, researchers and regulators alike have not yet agreed upon a single corporate governance definition. Therefore, section 2.1.6.1 provides an overview of the common corporate governance definitions. Section 2.1.6.2 and 2.1.6.3 outline internal and external governance mechanisms used to ameliorate agency conflicts.[448]

2.1.6.1 Definition of Corporate Governance

In Germany the debate on corporate governance had been considered to be only of academic interest until the 1990s.[449] The globalization of capital markets and the rise of institutional investors led to an increased focus of firms on their corporate governance activities and illustrated the need for corporate governance regulation to legislators.[450] The demand for corporate governance regulation was further augmented by a number of (inter)national corporate scandals and failures.[451] These developments have brought the corporate governance discussion under increasing public scrutiny.

In the context of this discussion, there is a wealth of corporate governance definitions which depend on the respective "view of the world"[452]. They can best be grouped into shareholder- and stakeholder-oriented definitions. The narrow, **shareholder-oriented definition** is primarily used in an Anglo-Saxon context. According to this definition, "corporate governance deals with how companies are managed in the long-term interest of their shareholders."[453] *Shleifer/Vishny* (1997) define corporate governance as "the ways in which suppliers of finance to corporations assure themselves of getting a return on their investment."[454] Based on *Lehmann/Weigand* (2000), the major element of corporate governance is "the alignment of shareholders' interests with the interests of managers hired to run the firm."[455] More broadly, *Berle* (1931) takes the view that the firm has primary liability towards its shareholders. Consequently, any business decision has to be judged on whether its result protects the interest of shareholders.[456] In line with these statements, the corporate decision maker, according to *Wilhelm*

445 See Emmons/Schmid (1998): 19.

446 See Edwards/Nibler (2000): 239; Schmidt (2004): 386. For details on the German financial system, see section 2.2.1.

447 See Halpern (1999): 2. For a similar argumentation, see also La Porta et al. (2002): 1147.

448 For details on governance mechanisms and the corresponding literature, please see Gillan (2006): 385-395.

449 See du Plessis et al. (2012): 24. According to Gräwe (2013): 24 the legal term "corporate governance" was adopted in the legal terminology only 30 years ago.

450 See Becht et al. (2005): 5 for a similar argument and section 2.2.1 for further details on these developments.

451 See e.g. Jahn et al. (2002): 64; Vitols (2005): 389. Among others, these corporate scandals and failures included Enron and WorldCom in the US as well as Philipp Holzmann AG and Metallgesellschaft in Germany. For details on these scandals, please see Ballwieser/Dobler (2003) and Peemöller/Hofmann (2005): 29-36, 39-43, 87-90, 108-110.

452 Gillan (2006): 382.

453 Faccio/Lasfer (2000): 75.

454 Shleifer/Vishny (1997): 737.

455 Lehmann/Weigand (2000): 159.

456 See Berle (1931): 1074. In particular, he argues that "all powers granted to a corporation or to the management of a corporation, or to any group within the corporation, whether derived from statute or charter or both, are necessarily and at all times exercisable only for the ratable benefit of all the shareholders as their interest appears." Berle (1931): 1049.

(1987), should only care about issues having an impact on the shareholders' sphere of interest. Hence, the interests of other non-owners should only be relevant to the extent that they might restrict the decision maker's opportunity set or have another direct or indirect impact on the owners' interests.[457] Justifying the focus on shareholders, *Halpern* (1999) argues that "other suppliers of capital (both human and financial) have mechanisms through which they can protect their interests after having committed their capital."[458] In contrast, shareholders provide capital on vague terms and conditions and can easily become subject to abuses through opportunistic managerial behavior.

The broader **stakeholder-oriented definition** is primarily used in Germany and other continental European countries and accounts for the importance of a firm's stakeholders[459]. The stakeholder-oriented definition posits that all individuals with a legitimate interest in the firm should be incorporated in the firm's decision making process.[460] Hence, the stakeholder-oriented definition goes beyond shareholder protection and applies also to other stakeholders having invested their resources in a firm and whose return depends on decisions made within the individual firm which are not easily contractually agreed or monitored.[461] Hence, corporate governance is understood as "the amalgam of the firm's control concentration and structure, capital structure (including the role of banks as major creditors), and their interactions with product market competition and corporate performance."[462] Similarly, *Correia da Silva et al.* (2004) regard corporate governance as a set of mechanisms "that ensure that the agent (the management of a corporation) runs the firm for the benefit of one or multiple principals (shareholders, creditors, suppliers, clients, employees, and other parties with whom the firm conducts its business)."[463] *Hellwig* (2000) recognizes that the integration of stakeholder interest involves a valid point. However, he argues that stakeholders are frequently protected by local governments while shareholders are the least protected of all parties within the firm. According to him, among all stakeholders, shareholders therefore have the greatest need for protection.[464]

The OECD defines corporate governance as "a set of relationships between a company's management, its board, its shareholders and other stakeholders. Corporate governance also provides the structure through which the objectives of the company are set, and the means of attaining those objectives and monitoring performance are determined."[465] Although the OECD considers the relationship between shareholders and managers to be the central ele-

---

457 See Wilhelm (1987): 180.

458 Halpern (1999): 5.

459 Here, a stakeholder is defined as "any group or individual who can affect or is affected by the achievement of the organization's objectives." Freeman (2010): 46.

460 See Molz (1995): 791.

461 See Schmidt/Tyrell (2004): 50; Schmidt (2004): 386. Examples of these stakeholders include employees, creditors, suppliers, and the consumers of the firm's products.

462 Köke/Renneboog (2005): 476.

463 Correia da Silva et al. (2004): 7.

464 See Hellwig (2000): 124f. He argues that the advantage of stakeholders is their easy identifiability relative to outside shareholders, which are dispersed and therefore hard to consider as actual individuals. Due to this, "politicians, in particular local politicians, tend to align with stakeholders rather than shareholders."

465 OECD (2004): 11. The OECD's definition of corporate governance is also used by the European Commission. See European Commission (2010b): 3; European Commission (2011a): 2.

ment of corporate governance, it explicitly recognizes the conflict between shareholders as well as the interests and role of creditors.[466] This makes the OECD's definition well suited for the purpose of the present thesis.

Irrespective of the corporate governance definition, researchers agree that corporate governance mechanisms can be classified into one of two groups: mechanisms internal and external to firms. The most important of these mechanisms will be described in the following sections.[467]

2.1.6.2 Internal Corporate Governance Mechanisms

Corporate governance mechanisms are regarded as being internal if they originate and are being operated from inside the firm. The internal mechanisms covered in this section include the supervisory board and executive compensation.[468]

The **supervisory board** acts as a counterbalance to the management board. The goal is to mitigate manager-shareholder conflicts by providing shareholders, subject to the collective action problem,[469] with a representative to monitor the actions of the management on their behalf.[470] Hence, the primary responsibility of the supervisory board is monitoring of whether or not the management acts in accordance with the shareholders' interests.[471] According to *Fama/Jensen* (1983a), the board has ultimate control over agents.[472] Indeed, the supervisory board is armed with a number of monitoring instruments and has important responsibilities.[473] However, *Jensen* (1993) observes an infrequency with which firms restructure or redirect themselves as a result of internal control mechanisms. He therefore criticizes internal control systems such as supervisory boards for reacting too late and taking too long to bring about important changes in the absence of a major crisis.[474]

Executive compensation aligns managerial interest with the interest of shareholders by making the agent bear more fully the consequences of any (adverse) action.[475] Moreover, it aims to enhance the management's motivation and to overcome its inclination to shirk.[476] An efficient compensation system ties the agent's compensation to some performance outcome of the firm and provides the agent with a share of the principal's income upon reaching a certain target.[477] As a result, the costs from the generation of non-monetary benefits are partly defrayed

466 See OECD (2004): 12.

467 Since most literature focuses on an Anglo-American context, these mechanisms primarily address the manager-shareholder conflict and disregard additional stakeholders of the firm.

468 As they are not relevant in the present thesis, alternative controls such as the internal audit function are not covered here.

469 The collective action problem is described extensively in section 3.1.1.

470 See Baums (2002): 5. Note that, in the German stakeholder view, the responsibility is broader. In this environment, the supervisory board has to act to the benefit of the corporation. See section 2.2.2.1 for details.

471 See Witt (2003): 30.

472 See Fama/Jensen (1983b): 313.

473 For a more detailed description of its roles and responsibilities, see section 2.2.2.1.

474 See Jensen (1993): 852-854. See Jensen (1993): 854-862 for proof of his criticism.

475 See Becht et al. (2005): 24-26. See also Molho (1997): 122.

476 See Baums/Scott (2005): 67.

477 See Saam (2002): 31.

by management.[478] Although shareholders cannot directly observe the actions of the manager, they can observe the outcome of managerial actions. Since the design of a contract prescribing managerial actions for each state of the world is too costly,[479] a contract on the outcome is regarded as an (inferior) substitute.[480] The more precise management's effort is reflected in this outcome and the lower the agent's risk aversion, the smaller the fixed compensation component.[481] The design of a contract can also be used to induce self-selection. In this case, the principals offer a number of contracts with different characteristics and the agent self-selects into its favorable contract, thereby signaling its hidden characteristics.[482] However, this mechanism is subject to a number of problems. First, managerial compensation can only be a function of those factors that are available to shareholders and management. Due to the limited information of shareholders, they utilize coarse measures as a basis for managerial compensation,[483] which impose risks on both the shareholders and managers if they reflect factors beyond the manager's control.[484] Second, stock option plans may induce management to excessively focus on short-term performance.[485] Third, incentive pay schemes may lead to a suboptimal allocation and sharing of risk between managers and shareholders.[486] Fourth, compensation systems typically do not provide a downside for management, as it faces no cost for poor performance apart from being fired in extreme cases.[487] Finally, incentive contracts provide significant opportunities for self-dealing if negotiated with a poorly motivated or inexperienced supervisory board.[488]

2.1.6.3 External Corporate Governance Mechanisms

A corporate governance mechanism is regarded as being external if it originates from outside the firm and functions independently from the firm's influence.[489] The following section describes four of these mechanisms, the market for managers, the market for corporate control, product market competition, and monitoring by a blockholder.[490]

---

478 See Seger (1997): 38.

479 According to Goergen/Manjon/Renneboog (2008): 184, compensation contracts constitute "perhaps the simplest economic device to align managers' actions with the interests of shareholders (or more generally, stakeholders)".

480 See also Grossmann/Hart (1983): 9; Levinthal (1988): 155; Molho (1997): 122. Contracts on outcomes of managerial behavior represent inferior substitutes, as the action of the manager will not be perfectly correlated to the outcome, due to external influences that simultaneously affect the outcome.

481 See Blickle (1987): 98.

482 See also Molho (1997): 89. For example, a manager that opts for a contract offering a high fixed salary may be less likely to exert effort than a manager choosing a contract with a significant variable component.

483 See Levinthal (1988): 167.

484 See Baums/Scott (2005): 67. For the manager, the risk is that an unfavorable external environment could diminish profits (and therefore his wage) although his decisions were in shareholders' interest and to the best of the firm. The risk for the shareholders constitutes the fact that they might reward a manager whose success has only been due to a favorable external environment rather than due to his managerial skills.

485 See Molho (1997): 123; Halpern (1999): 19; Becht et al. (2005): 25.

486 See also Molho (1997): 123. According to Coffee (1986): 18, granting options to management may even worsen the asymmetric risk preferences of management and shareholders.

487 See Halpern (1999): 19; Myers (2001): 96; Baums/Scott (2005): 67.

488 See Shleifer/Vishny (1997): 745.

489 See Wolf (1999): 26.

490 Since it is not relevant in the present thesis, the external auditor is not covered here.

In a well-functioning **market for managers**, management pays for adverse behavior in the form of a lower present value of future wages.[491] Therefore, the pursuance of personal benefits by the management is constrained by its estimate of the potential costs of such actions:[492] if their firm, as a result of their adverse behavior, performs poorly, this reflects badly on the managers' abilities, lowers their prospects elsewhere and decreases the present value of their future wage.[493] Provided the existing management is continuously in competition with external managerial candidates, any adverse behavior of the existing management may not only lower its future prospects elsewhere but immediately leads to a replacement by a competitor. Both effects have a strong disciplinary effect on management.[494] Due to career competition and succession planning, this effect can also be observed within the firm:[495] As managers realize that their productivity is dependent on that of their peers, they have incentives to monitor their peers' efficiency. Also *Furubotn/Pejovich* (1972) suppose that one can expect managers to compete for higher positions and to have incentives to eliminate inefficient behavior of other managers for their own personal advancement. This type of competition would then be beneficial for shareholders.[496] Unfortunately, the market for managers is unlikely to operate efficiently, as information required for an accurate performance assessment does not flow freely.[497] As a result, the managerial behavior might not be effectively priced into present and future managerial compensation which is crucial for the functioning of the managerial labor market.[498] Moreover, an effective pricing of future managerial compensation rests on the assumption that the market is able to accurately process and understand the information.[499] This not necessarily suggests pricing is ineffective, but might be a warning against the acceptation of the contrary. Besides, *Fama* (1980) argues that the manager's perceived benefit from adverse behavior may be larger than the wealth change he actually experiences.[500] Moreover, the highly limited supply of talented managers may result in managerial competition that is less severe than required.[501] Finally, top-level managers may decide that collusion is a more profitable alternative than internal competition among themselves.[502]

Especially in Anglo-Saxon countries, the **market for corporate control** is regarded as an important disciplinary mechanism.[503] Its functioning is based on the assumption that managerial

491 See e.g. Jensen/Meckling (1976): 328f; Amihud/Lev (1981): 606, 608; Barnea et al. (1981): 12; Barnea et al. (1985): 76; Halpern (1999): 11f.

492 See Furubotn/Pejovich (1972): 1150.

493 See e.g. Fama (1980): 292; Molho (1997): 131; Stadler (2010): 83. See also Wolf (1999): 36.

494 See Seger (1997): 42.

495 Sappington (1991): 57f proposes that the threat of competition can be actively used as a disciplinary force and that it is therefore valuable for the principal to have alternatives available. Also Fama (1980): 293; Hellwig (2000): 120 state that the management's actions are actively checked by rivals within the firm.

496 See Furubotn/Pejovich (1972): 1151. This is also called bottom-up monitoring. See Wolf (1999): 32

497 See Barnea et al. (1985): 78.

498 See Molho (1997): 132.

499 See Fama (1980): 297.

500 See Fama (1980): 298. This problem is also pointed out by Amihud/Lev (1981): 608, who argue that in these cases, the adverse managerial behavior cannot be eliminated by wealth reductions.

501 See Barnea et al. (1985): 78.

502 See Fama (1980): 293.

503 See, among others, Marris (1967): 30f; Jensen/Meckling (1976): 329; Easterbrook/Fischel (1981): 1169; Fama/Jensen (1983b): 313; Scharfstein (1988): 186; Halpern (1999): 11.

misbehavior causes the firm's shares to trade at a discount relative to the price achieved given no misbehavior.[504] As a result, the firm's shares are undervalued relative to the value that could be achieved under an efficient management.[505] This price differential constitutes the incentive for a hostile acquisition.[506] A prospective bidder monitors a firm's existing management by comparing the firm's potential value with its value under current management. If this difference becomes large enough, the prospective bidder can profit from buying the firm and replacing its management, thereby restoring maximum profits.[507] Due to the management changes following a takeover, the possibility of a hostile acquisition represents a continuous threat to management which is incentivized to act in the interest of shareholders and maximize firm value.[508] This incentive, however, may be weakened by a number of factors. First, high takeover activity can trigger the installment of takeover defenses by incumbent management anxious to remain in control.[509] These mechanisms substantially increase the costs of the takeover for the acquirer and may therefore act as a deterrent.[510] Second, takeovers are highly disruptive and costly[511] and occur only infrequently.[512] Third, takeovers are cyclical in nature. During market downturns, when financing is hard to obtain, the takeover threat is not credible to corporate management and hence does not serve as an effective mechanism to discipline management.[513] Finally, the hostile takeover market is virtually non-existent in Germany and so far has played no disciplinary role.[514] Although the market for full control is non-existent, the market for partial control is very active[515] and may act as a substitute.[516] Within the market for partial control, dissatisfied investors accumulate (hostile) share blocks through private negotiations in an attempt to affect corporate decision making.[517] However, according to

504 See Easterbrook/Fischel (1981): 1170; Molho (1997): 126.

505 Scharfstein (1988): 186 notes that takeovers are also effective when shareholders cannot determine the cause for a low firm value, because the raider is better informed than dispersed shareholders.

506 See Seger (1997): 41.

507 See Molho (1997): 126. The premium paid by the bidder should equal the agency cost reduction within the target firm. See Easterbrook/Fischel (1981): 1173.

508 See also Easterbrook/Fischel (1981): 1174; Coffee (1986): 15; Seger (1997): 41.

509 See also Bebchuk/Kahan (1990): 1079.

510 For a detailed overview of the takeover defenses and managerial entrenchment strategies please see Walsh/Seward (1990): 437-441. In Germany, the management of the (potential) target firm has to refrain from any action that might prevent the success of a takeover offer during the period between the publication of the takeover decision and the publication of the result. See § 33 (1) Sentence 1 WpÜG and Baums/Scott (2005): 67; Detzer et al. (2013): 208. However, § 33 (2) Sentence 1 WpÜG states that the AGM may authorize the management to take certain actions to prevent the success of the takeover bid; this requires the majority of 75% of the voting rights. For more details, please see Arnold/Wenninger (2010): 79-89.

511 See Bebchuk/Kahan (1990): 1078; Becht et al. (2005): 13.

512 See Prowse (1994): 64.

513 See Prowse (1994): 65.

514 See e.g. Kaplan (1994): 142; Prowse (1994): 46, 50; Jenkinson/Ljungqvist (2001): 398; Witt (2003): 82; Baums/Scott (2005): 66; Hackethal/Schmidt/Tyrell (2005): 401; Chirinko/Elston (2006): 77. Prowse (1994) argues that the corporate ownership structure in Germany mitigates many of the agency problems an active takeover market is supposed to resolve, lowering the need for an active takeover market. See also Allen/Gale (1995): 203f; Emmons/Schmid (1998): 32. In addition, concentrated ownership structures increase the difficulty of successful takeovers. See Drukarczyk (1993): 646.

515 See Franks/Mayer (2001): 944; Jenkinson/Ljungqvist (2001): 398; Correia da Silva et al. (2004): 29; Baums/Scott (2005): 66; Bessler/Drobetz/Holler (2008): 6.

516 See Franks/Mayer (2001): 955.

517 Thereby, the investor does not attempt to acquire a majority stake but rather a stake large enough to exert influence on the incumbent management. See Jenkinson/Ljungqvist (2001): 401.

Goergen et al. (2008), it is "less clear whether this market for share blocks is really acting as a substitute for a market for corporate control"[518].

A firm's management is also disciplined by **product market competition**.[519] First, the more competitive the product market, the more transparent the market prices which makes it "more difficult for a controlling shareholder to tunnel out resources using manipulated transfer prices without incurring legal or reputational costs"[520]. Second, competitive markets render a constant deviation from a value-maximizing strategy impossible, since the firm in this case will succumb to the competition.[521] Third, higher costs arising from inefficient expenditures of resources on perks cannot be passed onto customers.[522] Overall, highly competitive markets will align management with the goal of an efficient production.[523] The disciplinary effect, however, is ineffective if more managers try to maximize their own utility which allows lower firm values even in a highly competitive market environment.[524] In addition, product market competition does not deter management from expropriating shareholders, since this need not affect the quality of the products or the operating costs of the firm. Rather, it affects how the value generated by the firm is distributed among the stakeholders. Unless this distribution affects product quality or cost, the product market competition is ineffective in disciplining corporate management.[525] Moreover, product market competition loses its force if a firm is able to differentiate its products in a way that customers are willing to pay higher prices.[526]

The final governance mechanism constitutes **monitoring by a blockholder**,[527] which refers to the prevalence of a concentrated ownership structure with at least one blockholder with both an interest in monitoring management and the power to credibly threaten management.[528] In contrast to dispersed shareholders, a blockholder has greater incentives to monitor management since it receives a greater portion of the increased firm value that results from its monitoring. As a result, the opportunism by the management is restricted, as it recognizes its inability to unnoticeably betray the shareholder.[529] According to *Williamson* (1974) "to the extent that stockholders are knowledgeable, powerful, and active, the capital market may indeed impose a moderately severe constraint on the behavior of the firm"[530]. However, there are also

---

518 Goergen et al. (2008): 187.

519 See Fama (1980): 289.

520 Dyck/Zingales (2004a): 64. See also Dyck/Zingales (2004b): 576f.

521 See Williamson (1974): 2; Jensen (1993): 850; Seger (1997): 43; Halpern (1999): 12; Witt (2003): 26f; Dyck/Zingales (2004a): 64; Dyck/Zingales (2004b): 576f.

522 See Molho (1997): 131.

523 See Januszewski/Köke/Winter (2002): 302. See also Drees/Mietzner/Schiereck (2013): 280. In their empirical analysis, Giroud/Mueller (2010): 313 find that product market competition mitigates managerial slack and thus prevents management from wasting corporate resources.

524 See also Seger (1997): 43. This is also added for consideration by Molho (1997): 131, who recognizes that all firms within the industry face the same agency problem.

525 See Bebchuk/Roe (1999): 152. See also Prowse (1994): 14.

526 See Prowse (1994): 68; Molho (1997): 131.

527 See also Witt (2003): 22-24. Since the concept of blockholder monitoring represents the focus of attention within the present thesis, an entire chapter (chapter 3) deals with blockholder monitoring and its costs and benefits. Thus, the following deliberations only provide a very brief introduction.

528 See Becht et al. (2005): 17. See also Jensen (1993): 867.

529 See Eisenhardt (1989): 60.

530 Williamson (1974): 25.

critics on the use of concentrated ownership. Most criticism regards blockholdings as an euphemism for a detrimental, short-term oriented disruption of firm operations. Another criticism assumes that dissatisfied blockholders abstain from exercising their voting rights and sell their stakes rather than vote against management.[531] Finally, the partial concentration of ownership meets the opposition of insulation advocates. According to them, shareholder power and the corresponding influence on firms is destructive, as it produces the problem of short-termism[532]. They therefore propose that insulating firms' supervisory boards from shareholder pressure better serves the long-term interests of these firms and their shareholders.[533]

2.2 Institutional Environment in Germany

The relevance of the previously described agency problems and corporate governance mechanisms depend on the institutional environment in which they operate.[534] First, a country's institutional environment determines the *need* for blockholder monitoring; countries with a strong legal protection and governance legislation obviate blockholder monitoring as adverse managerial actions are constrained and the interests of investors are well-protected. Second, a country's institutional environment determines the *feasibility* of engaging in monitoring. This is a function of the shareholder rights which determine the legal scope shareholders have to monitor firm management. Due to these interdependencies, the following parts provide an overview of the German institutional environment. Section 2.2.1 describes the financial system which constitutes the playing field on which the monitoring blockholders need to operate. Section 2.2.2 provides an overview of the German governance system which may act as a substitute to blockholder monitoring. Section 2.2.3 picks up on a partial aspect of the governance system particularly relevant in the present thesis, namely the shareholders' rights. Effective blockholder monitoring is a function of share ownership. Therefore, section 2.2.4 focuses on the level of ownership concentration in Germany. As a study on the influence of blockholders on agency costs would be of no academic interest in the absence of agency conflicts, section 2.2.5 evaluates the relevance of agency conflicts within the German institutional environment.

2.2.1 Financial System

In order to provide an overview of the German institutional environment, this section starts with a description of the German financial system[535] on an aggregated level, thereby highlighting a number of changes in the recent years as well as the causes and consequences of these changes.

---

531 See Pound (1988): 242.

532 For a definition of short-termism, please see FN 30 section 1.1.

533 For a detailed and critical discussion on the view of insulation advocates, please see Bebchuk (2013).

534 Since the present thesis focuses only on a single corporate governance mechanism – monitoring through a blockholder – the following sections address this mechanism exclusively.

535 Schmidt/Tyrell (2004): 21f define a financial system broadly as "the interaction between the supply of and the demand for the provision of capital and other finance-related services" that also comprises the corporate governance system. Nevertheless, due to the importance of corporate governance in this study, the German corporate governance system is elucidated separately in section 2.2.2.

In an international context, the literature differentiates between two prototypes of financial systems which mark the endpoints of a continuum of financial systems: on the one end of the continuum, there is the market-based financial system common in the US and the UK; on the other end, there is the bank-based financial system common in Germany and Japan.[536] The characteristics of *market-based financial systems* are (1) well-developed and highly liquid capital markets,[537] (2) a strong and effective protection of capital market participants,[538] (3) highly dispersed and atomized ownership structures,[539] (4) a shareholder-oriented definition of corporate governance,[540] (5) a reliance on external governance mechanisms, and (6) a one-tier board structure[541]. The characteristics of *bank-based financial systems* are (1) a strong role of banks in the provision of corporate finance and a simultaneous minor role of capital markets,[542] (2) a less effective investor protection, focused on the protection of debtholders,[543] (3) highly concentrated ownership structures,[544] (4) a stakeholder-oriented governance definition,[545] (5) a reliance on internal governance mechanisms,[546] and (6) a two-tier board model.[547]

Until the late 1990s, Germany represented a typical example of a bank-based financial system.[548] Due to the complexity of its banking system and the power of its banks, the German economy was regarded as "one of the most heavily banked economies in the world"[549]. The complexity results from its three-pillar model,[550] which still exists and consists of savings banks, cooperative banks and private commercial banks. The latter dominate the securities trading, custody and investment banking business.[551] Savings banks operate only in their respective region and provide local private and commercial customers with a wide range of services.[552] They are structured as three layers, with local savings banks being the bottom layer, a number of regional-level banks (Landesbanks) as the middle-layer and an institution at the top of the system (DekaBank).[553] Cooperative banks are member-owned and therefore serve

536 See e.g. La Porta et al. (2000b): 17; Hackethal et al. (2005): 404; Seifert/Gonenc/Wright (2005): 176; Vitols (2005): 386; Thomsen et al. (2006): 247f; Kim/Kitsabunnarat-Chatjuthamard/Nofsinger (2007): 867. Market-based systems are frequently called "outsider-systems" whereas bank-based systems are called "insider-systems". See e.g. Franks/Mayer (2001): 943f; Schmidt (2004): 397; Hackethal et al. (2005): 402.

537 See Witt (2003): 72. See also See La Porta et al. (2000b): 17.

538 See Ampenberger (2010): 81.

539 See Witt (2003): 71; Ampenberger (2010): 81.

540 Examples of shareholder-oriented corporate governance definitions have been provided in section 2.1.6.1.

541 See Witt (2003): 71; du Plessis et al. (2012): 9.

542 See La Porta et al. (2000b): 17; Mietzner/Schweizer/Tyrell (2011): 152.

543 See La Porta et al. (2000b): 19; Mietzner et al. (2011): 152.

544 See Thomsen et al. (2006): 247f.

545 See Ampenberger (2010): 85; Mietzner et al. (2011): 152. Various stakeholder-oriented definitions of corporate governance have been provided in section 2.1.6.1.

546 See also Gedajlovic/Shapiro (1998): 539; Schmidt (2004): 397; Lehmann/Frick (2005): 123.

547 See Rieckers/Spindler (2004): 354; du Plessis et al. (2012): 9.

548 See Vitols (2005): 386; Detzer et al. (2013): 19. Black/Moersch (1998): 1 regard the German financial system as the "prototype of bank-based finance".

549 Schmidt/Tyrell (2004): 31.

550 See Dietrich (2009): 49.

551 See Schmidt/Tyrell (2004): 32.

552 See Allen/Gale (1995): 183; Hackethal (2004): 79f; Schmidt/Tyrell (2004): 33; Detzer et al. (2013): 79f.

553 See Hackethal (2004): 78-82; Vitols (2005): 388.

the primary purpose of supporting the businesses of their members[554] and hence, similar to savings banks, have not primarily profit-maximizing incentives.[555] The power of German banks stemmed from a number of reasons[556]. First, private investors invested their funds primarily with banks. As a result, banks played the dominant role in channeling funds from households to firms.[557] Second, firms, if they used external financing, relied to a great extent on bank-intermediated financing and primarily took on bank credit.[558] Third, banks built and maintained close relationships with their corporate customers. Apart from being the major provider of external finance, they frequently took direct equity stakes in their customers and were represented on the firms' supervisory boards.[559] This relationship banking enabled banks to play an important role in the firms' internal affairs[560] and is referred to as "Hausbank" model.[561] Fourth, the role of banks was not contested by alternative financial intermediaries which played no role until the late 1990s.[562] The final reason constitutes the low importance of financial markets,[563] which were regarded as underdeveloped in terms of volume, organization, efficiency, liquidity, and transaction costs.[564]

The late-1990s and early-2000s were characterized by a liberalization of capital markets and advancing globalization of economies and competition, which resulted in significant changes in the German financial system. Among these changes were the following.[565]

The larger **German banks** relinquished their commercial banking business in favor of more capital-market oriented services such as asset management or investment banking.[566] Therefore, banks promoted the development of security markets to earn fees from investment banking services.[567] This shift resulted from a lower profitability of monitoring relative to fee-based services,[568] more efficient capital markets, and competitive pressure from specialized

554 See Schmidt/Tyrell (2004): 33.

555 Similar to the Landesbanks, two central institutions serve as clearing houses and central banks of the cooperative banks, namely the WGZ Bank and the DZ Bank. See Hackethal (2004): 83.

556 This list is not intended to be exhaustive; some of these aspects are taken up later.

557 See Schmidt/Tyrell (2004): 42.

558 See Black/Moersch (1998): 1; Schmidt/Tyrell (2004): 42.

559 See Elsas/Krahnen (2004): 199; Vitols (2005): 386. In 1990, a bank owned shares in approximately 25% of publicly listed German industrial companies and had at least one representative on the supervisory board in 70% of the industrial companies. See Seger (1997): 183f.

560 See du Plessis et al. (2012): 332.

561 See Schmidt/Tyrell (2004): 54; Detzer et al. (2013): 77. According to Hackethal (2004): 71, the relationship of a firm with its Hausbank is "typically more information-intensive and longer-term oriented, and thus closer than any other of the firm`s bank relationships."

562 See Maurer (2004): 125f.

563 Schmidt/Tyrell (2004): 54. In the case at hand, the financial markets refer to the primary and organized secondary markets for securities and other tradable financial instruments, primarily the organized markets for stocks and bonds. See also Schmidt/Tyrell (2004): 36.

564 See also Seger (1997): 51; La Porta et al. (2000b): 4; Schmidt/Tyrell (2004): 36; Theissen (2004): 139. La Porta et al. (1997): 1146 justify the small size of the German debt and equity markets with the weak legal protection and law enforcement of (minority) shareholders' rights.

565 See also Cromme (2005): 362. Two dimensions most significant for the thesis at hand, corporate governance and ownership structure, are further delineated in section 2.2.2 and 2.2.4, respectively.

566 See Höpner (2003): 135; Streeck/Hassel (2003): 75; Hackethal (2004): 95; Hackethal et al. (2005): 402; Vitols (2005): 387; Faust/Bahnmüller/Fisecker (2011): 12. The shift in focus applies only to the large private banks as well as to the Landesbanks.

567 See Detzer et al. (2013): 77.

568 See Kengelbach/Roos (2006): 13. See also Coffee (1991): 1306, 1312.

non-bank financial institutions.[569] The shift away from banks' commercial business is illustrated by focusing on their lending to non-banks: while lending by big banks accounted for roughly 65% of banks' assets until 1997, it fell to 46% until mid-2007, when the financial crisis began, and was further hit by the European sovereign debt crisis, resulting in a drop to 23% in the beginning of 2012.[570] Due to the banks' changed business model, links with German firms through share ownership or supervisory board presence became a disadvantage as they gave rise to interest conflicts. Thus, banks sought to reduce these links through the sale of shares and the relinquishment of their seats on supervisory boards.[571] These developments resulted in a three-fold decline in the importance of banks within the German financial system: (1) a drop of the number of bank representatives on firms' supervisory boards, (2) a decline in the share ownership in (large) German firms and (3) a reduction in the use of proxy voting.[572]

In addition, the **German capital markets** started a significant catching-up-process in the late-1990s, which is still ongoing.[573] This was supported by the German Government through a number of legislative changes[574] and the entrance of multinational (institutional) investors.[575] Figure 18 (appendix 2) shows that the stock market capitalization as percentage of GDP increased from 19% in 1992 to 37% in 2011. Focusing on the activity of the stock market, figure 19 (appendix 2) shows that the total value traded on the German stock market to GDP also increased from 21% in 1992 to 45% in 2011. However, while the importance of the German stock market increased in absolute terms, it is still small relative to other developed nations.[576] Since November 2007, there are two ways to access the German stock market, the EU-regulated market (regulated market) and the exchange-regulated unofficial market (open market).[577] The regulated market is governed by the WpHG and consists of the prime and general standard, which differ regarding their transparency levels. Whereas the general standard represents the minimum transparency requirements of the EU-regulated market,[578] firms in the prime standard comply with high international transparency standards.[579] The open market is not an official market segment but regulated by the Deutsche Börse itself.[580] Trading takes

---

569 See Hackethal (2004): 71. Through their holdings of investment funds, German banks were (and still are) among the largest players within the investment fund industry and therefore able to compensate decreasing interest revenue with increasing revenue from asset management businesses. See Hackethal (2004): 93.

570 Please see figure 16 (appendix 2). As shown in figure 17 (appendix 2), also the number of banks declined.

571 See Coffee (1991): 1306, 1312; Höpner (2003): 135; Vitols (2005): 387; Detzer et al. (2013): 79.

572 See Detzer et al. (2013): 22. See also Bessler et al. (2008): 2; du Plessis et al. (2012): 338f.

573 See Dietrich (2009): 47f. See also Faust et al. (2011): 12.

574 See Detzer et al. (2013): 22. Please see further below for details.

575 See also Baums (2002): 2.

576 A similar conclusion is reached by Detzer et al. (2013): 53.

577 See Deutsche Börse AG (2010): 5. The stock exchange system has been traditionally comprised of three market segments: (1) the official market (amtlicher Markt) which listed the most liquid stocks, (2) the semi-official market (geregelter Markt) which listed small- and mid-sized firms, and (3) the over-the-counter (unofficial) market (Freiverkehr) which was the least regulated.

578 See Deutsche Börse AG (2010): 6; Deutsche Börse AG (2012a): 1.

579 See Deutsche Börse AG (2010): 7; Deutsche Börse AG (2012a): 1. A listing in the prime standard is a prerequisite for the inclusion in one of the Deutsche Börse's main indices DAX, MDAX, SDAX, TecDax.

580 See Deutsche Börse AG (2010): 5; Deutsche Börse AG (2012b): 1.

place on seven exchanges and an electronic trading system called Xetra. Of these exchanges, the Frankfurt stock exchange is the largest and therefore most important exchange.[581]

The developments were also manifested in a shift in the wealth holdings of **German households**. In the past, nearly half of the portfolio was directed to deposit and savings accounts of banks (48% in 1991) as well as to policies with private insurance and, to a lesser degree, with pension funds (27% in 1991). Only 15% of the portfolio was invested directly or indirectly in equities. In 2007, just prior to the global financial crisis, direct or indirect investments of households in shares or investment funds equaled 23% of their portfolio.[582] Hence, although direct equity investments are still relatively small,[583] the portfolios of households today include a greater share of risky assets.[584]

Starting in the mid-1990s, **German firms** adopted a capital market orientation focusing more and more on shareholder value as the overriding management target.[585] The foray of these firms into the global product and capital markets and the consequentially increased competition also led these firms to focus on corporate governance.[586] In addition, especially larger German firms have become increasingly independent from bank financing[587] as they were beginning to also use international capital markets for funding.[588] Figure 20 (appendix 2) shows the external financing of non-financial firms. In the 1990s, the most important source of external financing had been loans. During the period of the New Economy and stock market boom, the importance of shares (and other equity) significantly increased.[589] After this boom, shares constitute an important source of external financing, although non-financial firms' reliance on external financing has been reduced as a consequence of the market turmoil of the financial and European sovereign debt crisis.[590]

The German Government responded to the internationalization of the supply and demand for capital and the claims of German firms by adapting the **regulatory framework**.[591] Starting in the 1990s, efforts were being made to move the German financial system towards a more market-oriented system by increasing the role of the German capital markets.[592] Thereby, the government attempted to strengthen the position of Germany as a host for international financial markets.[593] In addition, it started a serious debate on corporate governance which was closely linked to relatively difficult economic conditions and problems within a number of German industries that have been blamed on managerial problems and weaknesses in the su-

581 See Theissen (2004): 145; Detzer et al. (2013): 83. The remaining exchanges are located in Berlin, Bremen, Dusseldorf, Hamburg, Hannover, Munich, and Stuttgart.
582 See Detzer et al. (2013): 27, 65, 183f.
583 See Detzer et al. (2013): 183.
584 See Detzer et al. (2013): 65.
585 For details, please see Seifert et al. (2002): 38-40. See also Höpner (2003): 82; Streeck/Hassel (2003): 75.
586 See Baums (2002): 2.
587 See Hackethal et al. (2005): 402.
588 See Coffee (1991): 1306, 1312.
589 Other equity in this case refers to the equity of firms that are not joint-stock firms, e.g. limited liability firms. See also Detzer et al. (2013): 61.
590 See also Detzer et al. (2013): 61f.
591 An overview of the recent corporate governance changes is provided in section 2.2.2.2.
592 See Vitols (2005): 386; Detzer et al. (2013): 22.
593 See Detzer et al. (2013): 22.

pervision of companies. Moreover, increasing involvement of shareholders required effective regulatory safeguards to secure investor protection and confidence,[594] resulting in a development of a shareholder-friendly corporate governance legislation.[595] Finally, tax incentives promoted divestures of major shareholders which induced banks (and other blockholders) to sell their shares.[596]

The fiscal reforms, inter alia, had a significant impact on the **ownership structure** of German publicly-traded firms.[597] While German banks have disposed of nearly one-third of their shareholdings, foreign (institutional) investors have increased their share purchases.[598] These changes have led to a reduction of the banks' importance within the German financial system. In addition, also non-financial firms disposed of a large part of their shareholdings in other firms, resulting in a decline of cross-holdings[599] and the unbundling of the "Deutschland AG".[600] These changes have been most pronounced for the largest firms within the German capital markets.[601]

As pointed out previously, the emergence of **new (international) investor types** had an important impact on the German financial system. In the late-1990s, foreign investors such as investment banks, pension funds, hedge funds or private equity investors entered the German capital markets and experienced impressive growth.[602] Figure 21 (appendix 2) illustrates this growth by depicting the number and assets under management of open-end investment funds in Germany. While there were 1,970 investment funds in Germany in 1990, this number increases to 11,448 in 2012. During the same time period, the assets under management increased by a factor of 16. Figure 22 (appendix 2) graphs the yearly private equity investments in Germany by private equity firms based in Germany. While these investments exhibit a strong sensitivity to the overall economic environment, illustrated by the drops after the dot-com bubble (2002 and 2003) and the financial crisis (2009), the overall trend is highly positive. Since 1990, the investments increased from €481.1m to €5,119.4m. Overall, the entrance

594 See du Plessis et al. (2012): 16.

595 See Faust et al. (2011): 12; Detzer et al. (2013): 21, 123.

596 Tax incentives eliminated one of the reasons why large shareholders had retained their equity stakes, namely the taxation of capital gains at the full corporate tax rate. See e.g. Höpner (2003): 137; Schmid/Wahrenburg (2004): 275; Maisch (2005); Vitols (2005): 390. With the abolishment of the capital gains tax in January 2002, the liquidation of stakes held in other companies has been tax-exempt. See e.g. Nowak (2004): 438; Achleitner et al. (2010): 815; Dittmann/Maug/Schneider (2010): 36. As the markets recovered from the dot-com bubble, the major players, among others the Deutsche Bank AG, Allianz AG and Munich RE, started to liquidate significant amounts of their shareholdings. See Maisch (2005). See also Kengelbach/Roos (2006): 18. Streeck/Höpner (2003) provide a number of case studies.

597 Due to its importance for the thesis at hand, a separate section (2.2.4) is devoted to the ownership structure.

598 See also Detzer et al. (2013): 25; 186. See also Ringe (2014): 16-18.

599 See Detzer et al. (2013): 25.

600 See Seifert et al. (2002): 56f; Baums/Scott (2005): 58; Achleitner et al. (2010): 815; Dittmann et al. (2010): 36; Faust et al. (2011): 12; Detzer et al. (2013): 122; Ringe (2014): 12f. The term "Deutschland AG" is frequently used to describe the cross-holdings between industrial firms, banks, and insurance firms. See e.g. Streeck/Hassel (2003): 72; Streeck/Höpner (2003): 16; Kengelbach/Roos (2006): 12; Prokot (2006): 19, 24.

601 See Vitols (2005): 387.

602 See e.g. Hackethal (2004): 93; Maurer (2004): 136; Faust et al. (2011): 12, 34; du Plessis et al. (2012): 338f.

of multinational investors brought international market expectations to the German capital markets resulting in a greater concern with regard to the firms' governance.[603]

To recapitulate, during the last 15 years, the German financial system has been moving away from a bank-based model and pushed more towards an Anglo-Saxon model, primarily in the areas of transparency, stock markets, and voting structures.[604] The influence of banks, blockholders and cross-shareholdings in general is not a hallmark of the German financial system as was the case 15 years ago. While some of them are still key players, they today represent one of several important players within the financial system.[605] However, fundamental differences compared to market-based systems are still significant.[606] Therefore, the recent changes can best be regarded as a modification of the German financial system.[607] These changes also impinge on the corporate governance and capital market legislation, which is described in the following.

2.2.2 Corporate Governance System

As aforementioned, a country's corporate governance system may act as a substitute for blockholder monitoring and determine the potential for the pursuance of governance improvement strategies by the blockholder. Therefore, any investigation of the effect of blockholder monitoring requires an understanding of the prevalent governance system. Section 2.2.2.1 provides this understanding through a description of the most important characteristics and elements of Germany's corporate governance system. Section 2.2.2.2 then highlights a number of legislative modifications during recent years.

2.2.2.1 Characteristics and Elements

To describe and characterize the German corporate governance system, three questions should be answered. First, how is corporate governance defined in Germany, second, what are the relevant stakeholder groups and third, which governance instruments exist for each stakeholder group? With regard to the first question, the German definition of corporate governance includes the relationship between the firm, its stakeholders, and relationships between the stakeholders themselves.[608] It further accounts for the pluralism of interests and tries to balance the interest of all stakeholders, thereby explicitly striving for a maximization of stakeholder value.[609] With regard to the second question, there are at least three powerful groups of stakeholders: large shareholders, employee and/or union representatives, and banks. An addi-

603 See also Baums (2002): 2.

604 See also Bessler et al. (2008): 7; Goergen et al. (2008): 191; Ringe (2014):1f.

605 See du Plessis et al. (2012): 356. In contrast, Detzer et al. (2013): 20 argue that banks still occupy the most important position in the financial system.

606 See Detzer et al. (2013): 22.

607 See Vitols (2005): 387.

608 See du Plessis et al. (2012): 18. However, German corporate governance traditionally focuses on the protection of creditors. See Rieckers/Spindler (2004): 355.

609 See Schmidt (2004): 397; Goergen et al. (2008): 175. This maximization of stakeholder value resembles the concept of management trusteeship introduced by Donaldson (1963). This concept recognizes the plurality of interests in modern organizations and treats shareholders' interests as one of several coequal vested interests to account for when making decisions. Donaldson (1963): 118f.

tional stakeholder group might comprise the firm's management which is being represented by an increasing number of former top managers within the supervisory boards.[610] With regard to the third question, the following deliberations provide an overview of the key elements of the German governance system designed to ensure the incorporation of the stakeholders' interests. The German legislation distinguishes three interrelated organs within the internal structure of the corporation: the management board, the supervisory board and the AGM.[611]

The **management board** constitutes the firm's primary operative organ.[612] Its most important responsibility constitutes the management of the company.[613] In addition to the responsibility for internal corporate activities, the management board shall jointly represent the company externally.[614] As stated in § 76 (1) AktG, the management board manages and directs the firm under its sole responsibility. This power is inherent in the management board and cannot be delegated.[615] As a result, the AGM is not authorized to decide on matters pertaining to the management of the firm unless explicitly required by the management board.[616] Due to its exclusive right to manage the firm, *Schmidt* (2004) attributes the management board "considerable power"[617].

There are several qualifications to the power of the management board. First, there is substantial scope for indirect control over the management board by the supervisory board if the latter itself insists, or the firm's articles prescribe, that specific types of transactions can only be entered into with the supervisory board's consent.[618] Furthermore, § 90 AktG specifies significant information obligations of the management towards the supervisory board.[619] Besides, the supervisory board may request information regarding particular aspects of the firm's business.[620] In addition, the management board has a duty of care and responsibility.[621] In case of a breach of their duties, the members of the management board are jointly liable to the firm for any resulting damage.[622] In the event of a dispute on whether or not they have acted in line with the care of a diligent and conscious manager, the burden of proof lies at the management board.[623] Members of the management board can also be held liable for damages if they make

610 See Schmidt (2004): 395f. See also Höpner (2003): 139 and Hackethal et al. (2005): 398.

611 See e.g. Schröder/Schrader (1998): 21; Rieckers/Spindler (2004): 356; du Plessis et al. (2012): 55.

612 The management board is governed by §§ 76-94 AktG. The following description only provides a summary of the – subjectively – perceived most important aspects.

613 See § 76 (1) and § 77 (1) AktG. See also Schmid/Kretschmer (2004): 2; Schmidt/Tyrell (2004): 51. It was considered appropriate to translate the German phrases "Leitung" and "Geschäftsführung" with the (Anglo-American) terminology "management", which is also chosen by the GCGC (2013): 1.

614 See § 78 (1) Sentence 1 and § 78 (2) Sentence 1 AktG.

615 See § 111 (4) AktG. See also du Plessis et al. (2012): 73.

616 See § 119 (2) AktG.

617 Schmidt (2004): 393.

618 See § 111 (4) Sentence 2 AktG. See also du Plessis et al. (2012): 75.

619 See § 90 (1) and § 90 (2) AktG.

620 See § 90 (3) AktG.

621 See § 93 (1) AktG.

622 According to § 93 (1) Sentence 2, the members shall not be deemed to have violated their duties if, at the time of taking the decision, they could reasonably believe that they were acting based on adequate information and in the best interest of the firm. This business judgment rule has been introduced by the UMAG (please see section 2.2.2.2) and is also specified in Article 3.8 of the GCGC.

623 See § 92 (2) AktG. See also du Plessis et al. (2012): 81.

payments to the firm's stakeholders without the proper authorization to do so, for example contributions repaid and interest or dividends paid to shareholders.[624] Any such breach of duty also constitutes a compelling reason for the dismissal of the management board member pursuant to § 84 (3) Sentence 2 AktG. The claim for damages is not only asserted to the firm's shareholders but also to its creditors if they are unable to obtain satisfaction from the firm.[625] Due to these qualifications, "the potential of liability of management board members is in fact huge."[626]

The management board can consist of one or more members. However, if a firm has a share capital of €3m or more, the management board shall be comprised of not less than two members, unless the firm's articles provide otherwise.[627] In addition, according to § 33 (1) MitbestG and § 13 (1) Montan-MitbestG, firms with more than 2,000 employees are required to appoint a personnel director as a fully-fledged member to the management board.[628] Several conditions regulate the appointment of members of the management board, among others, a person cannot be member of the management board if it is also member of the same firm's supervisory board.[629] Usually, the management board is presided over by a chairperson (CEO) which is elected by the supervisory board.[630] In contrast to its counterpart in the United States, the chairperson has considerably less power and influence within the management and supervisory board.[631] He is therefore regarded as primus inter pares.[632] Although the members of the management board are usually specialized according to functions or areas, any decision has to be taken by the board and not by its individual members.[633]

The appointment, removal and compensation of the management board's members are in the hands of the supervisory board.[634] Members of the management board are appointed for a maximum tenure of five years, after which the contract can be renewed for additional periods of five years. Members of the management board are to be dismissed by the supervisory board. However, the dismissal needs to be well-founded; according to § 84 (3) AktG, examples include a gross breach of duties, an inability to properly manage the company or a vote of non-confidence by the AGM.[635] In such a case, the termination is immediately effective. The compensation of each member of the management board is assigned to the supervisory board and cannot be delegated to a committee.[636] The compensation shall maintain a reasonable re-

624 See § 92 (3) AktG.

625 See § 93 (5) Sentence 1 AktG.

626 du Plessis et al. (2012): 82.

627 See § 76 (2) AktG.

628 This provision cannot be affected by the firm's articles. See § 76 (2) Sentence 3 AktG.

629 See § 105 (1) AktG. For the remaining conditions, see § 76 (3) AktG and § 76 (3) Sentence 2 No. 3 AktG.

630 See § 84 (2) AktG.

631 For example, he is neither allowed to hold a seat in the supervisory board nor is he able to carry through his opinion against the majority of the remaining managers. See § 77 (1) Sentence 2 AktG.

632 However, Bernhardt (2002): 1843f observes a departure from the balance of power within the management board and a stronger focus on the Anglo-Saxon model of the CEO.

633 See § 77 (1) Sentence 2 AktG. See also Schmid/Kretschmer (2004): 4.

634 See du Plessis et al. (2012): 61.

635 See also du Plessis et al. (2012): 65f. The authors state that it is possible for the supervisory board to remove the management board if there are irreconcilable differences between management and supervisory board, for example with regard to the firm policy or future strategy.

636 See § 107 (3) Sentence 3 AktG.

lationship to the duties and performance of such members and to the financial position of the firm.[637] In addition, § 87 (2) Sentence 1 AktG enables the reduction and retroactive decrease of remuneration in response to deteriorations of the firm's financial position.

As a counterbalance to the management board, the one-tier board system was abandoned in favor of a two-tier board system consisting of a management board and a **supervisory board**[638] as long ago as 1870. The underlying rationale was to mitigate potential conflicts of interest between shareholders and managers by providing shareholders with a representative to monitor the actions of the management on their behalf.[639] Later, the composition of the supervisory board was adapted to include another stakeholder group, the firm's employees.[640] Today, typically each group of stakeholders mentioned in the beginning of this section is represented in the firm's supervisory board,[641] which might therefore be regarded as the key instrument for the governance of German firms, with the primary goal of promoting the "interests of the firm"[642].

Pursuant to § 101 (1) AktG, the members of the supervisory board are appointed by the AGM. Due to different manifestations of the codetermination, there are several systems through which the members of the supervisory board are appointed. For certain types of firms, two-thirds of the supervisory board, for other types half of the supervisory board are appointed by the AGM.[643] In addition, within certain limits, members may be appointed to the supervisory board by specific shareholders or holders of specific shares if granted by the firm's articles.[644] Typically, members of the supervisory board are elected for a period of five years.[645] The right to remove members of the supervisory board is vested in the group who appointed these members. As regards shareholder representatives, their dismissal requires a 75% majority of the votes cast in the AGM and does not depend on a compelling reason.[646]

§ 100 AktG requires a number of personal qualifications by members of the supervisory board. Among others, a person may not be member of a supervisory board if it is serving on the management board of the same firm[647] and is a member of a management board of another firm whose supervisory board includes a member of the management board of that particular company.[648] In addition, § 100 (2) Sentence 1 No. 4 AktG requires a two-year cooling-off pe-

637 See § 87 (1) AktG.

638 The supervisory board is governed by §§ 95-116 AktG. The following description only provides a summary of the – subjectively – perceived most important aspects.

639 See Baums (2002): 5.

640 The employee-representation on the supervisory board level (codetermination) is treated as a separate characteristic and will be described further below.

641 Hackethal et al. (2005): 398 refers to the stakeholders on the board as "governing coalition".

642 Baums/Scott (2005): 32.

643 Please see the discussion on the codetermination below for details.

644 See § 101 (2) AktG. For instance, the Alfried Krupp von Bohlen und Halbach Foundation, holding 23.03% of the shares in the ThyssenKrupp AG, has designated three out of ten shareholder representatives sitting on ThyssenKrupp's supervisory board. See ThyssenKrupp AG (2014).

645 See § 102 (1) AktG.

646 However, the firm's articles may provide for a different majority or additional requirements. See § 103 (1) AktG. See also Rieckers/Spindler (2004): 360; du Plessis et al. (2012): 111f.

647 See § 105 (1) AktG.

648 The latter requirement aims at preventing interlocking supervisory and management boards that had been common in the past. See also du Plessis et al. (2012): 97.

riod stating that former management board members should not be appointed to the supervisory board of the same firm within two years.[649] The German legislation does not stipulate any provisions pertaining to the professional qualifications of supervisory board members; an exception constitutes § 100 (5) AktG, which requires one independent member to have expertise knowledge in the fields of accounting or auditing. However, legislation provides rules on the size of the supervisory board. Pursuant to § 95 (1) Sentence 1 AktG, the supervisory board should consist of at least three members. The firm's articles may provide for a larger number of members, provided the number is divisible by three.[650] For firms with a share capital of €1.5m, nine members are allowed, whereas fifteen members (twenty-one members) are allowed for firms with a share capital of more than €1.5m (€10m).[651]

Important tasks of the supervisory board constitute the appointment, dismissal, supervision, and compensation of the management board.[652] As regards the appointment, the supervisory board appoints the members for a period of up to five years.[653] In addition, it names the CEO.[654] During the appointment process, informal meetings between the shareholders and the supervisory board ensure that no manager unacceptable to the blockholder is appointed.[655] The supervisory board may also revoke the appointment of management board members, provided it is well-founded.[656] Based on § 111 (1) AktG, the supervisory board is also provided with the statutory duty to supervise and oversee the actions of the firm's management in order to prevent managerial self-dealing and other forms of private benefits.[657] While § 111 (4) AktG prohibits the assumption of any management tasks,[658] the supervisory board or the firm's articles may require the management to consult the supervisory board and obtain its approval with regard to specific matters.[659] Thus, the scope of the supervisory board, to some extent, goes beyond the role of a pure monitor.[660] As regards the compensation, the supervisory board has to ensure that the aggregate remuneration level maintains a reasonable relationship to the duties and performance of the members and to the financial condition of the firm.[661] In case of extraordinary developments, it shall agree on limits to the compensation.[662] The decision on the level of compensation cannot be delegated to the compensation commit-

[649] This is still possible if the member is elected by shareholders holding more than 25% of the voting rights.
[650] See § 95 (1) Sentence 3 AktG.
[651] See § 95 (1) Sentence 4 AktG and Witt (2003): 87; Rieckers/Spindler (2004): 360; du Plessis et al. (2012): 97. These requirements do not affect the requirements set under the legislation concerning codetermination.
[652] See Rieckers/Spindler (2004): 359; Schmid/Kretschmer (2004): 6; Schmidt/Tyrell (2004): 51; du Plessis et al. (2012): 117. The supervisory board's rights and responsibilities are exclusive and not transferrable to other persons. See § 111 (5) AktG.
[653] See § 84 (1) AktG.
[654] See § 84 (2) AktG.
[655] See Rieckers/Spindler (2004): 363.
[656] See § 84 (3) AktG. For details, please see the part on the management board further above.
[657] See Baums/Scott (2005): 54.
[658] See Schröder/Schrader (1998): 21.
[659] See also du Plessis et al. (2012): 123. In fact, the supervisory board has a veto over these particular matters as the management board cannot proceed until the supervisory board signals consent.
[660] See Seger (1997): 70; Rieckers/Spindler (2004): 359; Schmidt (2004): 393; du Plessis et al. (2012): 137.
[661] See § 87 (1) AktG.
[662] See § 87 (2) Sentence 1 AktG.

tee[663] and the supervisory board is liable for any damage resulting from an unreasonable level of compensation.[664] Due to these competencies, "it can be safely assumed that in its decisions the management board will tend to give due consideration to what the supervisory board and its members think."[665]

To perform its task of supervising management, the supervisory board possesses a number of mechanisms. Each member may, upon stating the reasons, request a meeting of the supervisory board.[666] According to § 111 (2) AktG, the supervisory board may inspect the books and records of the firm and may also delegate this inspection to a committee.[667] Furthermore, the supervisory board may call for an extraordinary AGM whenever this is required by the firm's interests.[668] To ensure a free information flow between the management and supervisory board, the latter has significant information-collection and intervention powers available.[669] § 90 AktG specifies the reports to be made to the supervisory board. Inter alia, the management shall provide information on the intended business policy and other fundamental matters regarding the future conduct of the firm's business, profitability, state of business as well as material transactions. Moreover, the supervisory board may request at any time information regarding particular aspects of the firm's business.[670]

The supervisory board has been subject to criticism. First, it is regarded as being dependent on the management board concerning the quality and relevance of this information.[671] Second, the management board has frequently influenced the choice of supervisory board members, whose independency is therefore questionable.[672] Third, the legislation permits supervisory boards to be very large. However, the size of the boards results in an unproductive working atmosphere, causing a shift of the actual work to the respective committees.[673] Due to the inefficiencies resulting from the size of the supervisory board, critical topics might have already been clarified in private meetings between the management and representatives of larger shareholders without considering the members of the supervisory board.[674] Fourth, "genuine shareholder representatives are a minority on the board of almost every big German corporation"[675] as many board members represent blockholders, come from the management of other corporations or are former members of the firm's management.

---

663 See § 107 (3) AktG. These changes were the result of the VorstAG. For details, please see section 2.2.2.2.
664 See § 116 Sentence 3 AktG.
665 Schmidt (2004): 393.
666 See § 110 (1) Sentence 1 AktG. In general, the supervisory boards of listed firms shall meet at least twice per half calendar year. See § 110 (3) Sentence 1 AktG.
667 The delegation of tasks into committees is regulated in § 107 (3) AktG.
668 See § 111 (3) AktG. This requires a simple majority. See also Schmid/Wahrenburg (2004): 277.
669 See Baums/Scott (2005): 54.
670 See § 90 (3) AktG. The information cannot be distributed to particular members of the supervisory board. Pursuant to § 90 (5) AktG, all members of the board have an equal right to information.
671 See du Plessis et al. (2012): 9.
672 See du Plessis et al. (2012): 94f.
673 See Rieckers/Spindler (2004): 360f.
674 See Seger (1997): 72 for a similar argumentation.
675 Schmidt/Tyrell (2004): 51.

The legally mandated employee **codetermination** on the supervisory board level represents "one of the most remarkable peculiarities of German corporate governance"[676] and is based on the assumption that an explicit focus on shareholder value does not necessarily incorporate employees' interests.[677] Hence, the firm is understood as an organization in which employees, management, and shareholders work together with a common goal.[678] Employees therefore are entitled to play a key role in the German corporate governance system through works councils as well as employee representation on the boards of companies of specific size.[679] Today, three different codetermination models exist.[680]

The first model goes back to the Works Council Constitution Act of 1952 which has been replaced by the One-Third Participation Act (DrittelbG) in 2004. The one-third codetermination applies to stock corporations, co-operative firms and private limited firms with more than 500 but less than 2,000 employees not operating in the coal, iron or steel industry.[681] Pursuant to § 4 (1) DrittelbG, the firm's employees have to appoint at least one-third of the supervisory board members. The shareholders elect the remaining members of the supervisory board in the AGM.[682]

The second model is the parity codetermination which constitutes the most prevalent and therefore the most important case of codetermination. It is based on the Codetermination Act (MitbestG) of 1976 and applies to stock corporations, co-operative firms and private limited firms with more than 2,000 employees that are not operating in the coal, iron or steel industry.[683] The MitbestG stipulates that half of the supervisory board members has to be employee representatives while the other half has to be shareholder representatives.[684] The former is elected by the firm's employees or their delegates pursuant to § 9 MitbestG.[685] The latter are elected by the shareholders in the AGM.[686] Among the employee representatives, there have to be two representatives of the relevant trade unions.[687] Pursuant to § 27 MitbestG, the chairman of the board cannot be elected against the wishes of the shareholder representatives and can therefore be regarded as a representative of the shareholders.[688] This chairman as-

676 Hackethal et al. (2005): 401. See also Mintz (2005): 590.

677 See Witt (2001): 95.

678 See Kommission zur Modernisierung der deutschen Unternehmensmitbestimmung (2006): 9. See also Hans-Böckler-Stiftung (2007): 3.

679 See Lehmann/Frick (2005): 144.

680 See also § 96 (1) AktG.

681 See § 1 (1) DrittelbG. Exempt from this codetermination are press-related firms. See § 1 (2) DrittelbG and Schmid/Kretschmer (2004): 12; du Plessis et al. (2012): 159f.

682 See e.g. Schmid/Wahrenburg (2004): 277; Goergen et al. (2008): 184; Edwards/Weichenrieder (2009): 496. This model is also called "non-parity codetermination". Gorton/Schmid (2002): 1.

683 See § 1 (1) MitbestG. Exempt from this codetermination are press-related firms that enjoy the freedom information and opinion. See § 1 (4) No. 2 MitbestG.

684 See § 7 (1) MitbestG. In firms with less than 10,000 but more than 2,000 employees the board is to be composed of six employee and six shareholder representatives, in firms with more than 10,000 but less than 20,000 employees it is to be composed of eight employee and eight shareholder representatives and in firms with more than 20,000 employees, it is to be composed of ten employee and ten shareholder representatives.

685 See Kommission zur Modernisierung der deutschen Unternehmensmitbestimmung (2006): 10. According to § 15 (1) MitbestG, one employee representative has to be an executive manager.

686 See § 8 MitbestG.

687 See § 7 (2) MitbestG. In firms with more than 20,000 employees, three union representatives are required.

688 Employee representatives are allowed to appoint the vice-chairperson. See § 27 (2) Sentence 2 MitbestG.

sumes a peculiar role, as he is provided with a deciding vote in the event of a tie.[689] As a result, the power within the supervisory board lies with the shareholders.[690] In addition to the employee representation on the supervisory board, § 33 (1) MitbestG mandates the appointment of a personnel director as a fully-fledged member of the management board. He is responsible for all issues regarding labor relations but also backs the decisions regarding the overall management of the firm.[691]

The third model represents the strongest form of codetermination and applies only to firms subject to Montan codetermination. Going back to the Mining, Iron, and Steel Industry Codetermination Act (Montan-MitbestG) of 1951, a system of parity codetermination at the supervisory board level was made compulsory for all firms within mining, coal, iron and steel industries.[692] Within this model, employees and shareholders send an equal number of representatives to the supervisory board.[693] The members then jointly propose a neutral person which is then appointed by the AGM.[694] This neutral person has a tie-breaking vote.[695] Due to this procedure, under the Montan codetermination, shareholders cannot form the majority on the supervisory board.[696] In addition, the firm has to appoint a personnel director to serve on the management board.[697] He is responsible for all issues relating to human resources.[698] As the number of firms within the respective industries has significantly decreased, the Montan codetermination is of minor importance in the case at hand.[699]

Employee codetermination is exposed to substantial criticism. *Schröder/Schrader* (1998) argue that codetermination on the supervisory board reduces the effectiveness of corporate control exercised by the supervisory board.[700] In addition, codetermination is criticized as destroying the aim of making the supervisory board an independent body.[701] Employee representatives may also lack the professional qualification required to effectively supervise the actions of management. *Baums/Scott* (2005) criticize the current system of codetermination as it does not incorporate the interest of foreign employees. Hence, international investors may fear that decisions made within the supervisory board are made to serve the interests of local

689 See § 29 (2) MitbestG. Due to this, the system is also called "quasi-parity-codetermination". Gorton/Schmid (2002): 1; du Plessis et al. (2012): 158.

690 This is also observed by Rieckers/Spindler (2004): 361; du Plessis et al. (2012): 158. Also Dittmann et al. (2010): 41 state that "shareholders of the company retain control of the supervisory board".

691 See § 33 (2) MitbestG. See also du Plessis et al. (2012): 191.

692 See § 1 (1) Montan-MitbestG. See also Schmid/Kretschmer (2004): 12; du Plessis et al. (2012): 155f.

693 See § 4 (1) Montan-MitbestG. The Act distinguishes three types of companies based on their size. Pursuant to § 9 Montan-MitbestG, the supervisory board can be composed of up to 21 members provided they have a share capital of more than €25m.

694 See § 8 (1) Montan-MitbestG. See also du Plessis et al. (2012): 156.

695 See Emmons/Schmid (1998): 21; Schmid/Wahrenburg (2004): 277; Edwards/Weichenrieder (2009): 496; Ampenberger (2010): 63. This person is usually a prominent political or cultural figure.

696 See Rieckers/Spindler (2004): 361.

697 See § 13 (1) Montan-MitbestG. This director cannot be elected against the wishes of the employees.

698 See Emmons/Schmid (1998): 21; Schmid/Kretschmer (2004): 12.

699 See also du Plessis et al. (2012): 157.

700 See Schröder/Schrader (1998): 24. According to Wenger/Kaserer (1998): 50, the supervisory boards of German firms are "dominated by a small, and conspiratorial circle of top managers and unionists."

701 See du Plessis et al. (2012): 104f.

labor unions[702] and view the concept of codetermination as an impediment for necessary changes within German firms.[703] Overall, codetermination represents a contentious issue and is therefore regularly excluded from deliberations of politicians.[704]

The **annual general meeting**[705] is the organ where the firm's shareholders shall exercise their rights unless stated otherwise in the AktG.[706] The AGM's competency is restricted to decisions regarding issues specified in § 119 (1) AktG and can only decide on matters concerning the management of the firm if required by the management board.[707] Unless the members are elected as employee representatives pursuant to the codetermination act, the AGM is responsible for the appointment of members to the supervisory board.[708] As a result, the number of supervisory board members to be elected by the AGM, i.e. of the shareholder representatives, differs between two-thirds and one-half of the members of the supervisory board, depending on the size of the firm (presuming it has more than 500 employees) and the industry in which it operates. Based on § 103 (1) AktG, members of the supervisory board appointed by the AGM can be removed without cause by a three-quarter majority of the AGM.[709] Pursuant to § 127 AktG, shareholders can also nominate an own candidate for the election of the supervisory board. According to § 137 AktG, if the shareholder moves for the election of the person nominated by it, such motions shall be resolved prior to the proposal of the supervisory board if requested by shareholders whose holdings in aggregate exceed 10% of the share capital represented at the AGM. The appointment and removal of supervisory board members can be regarded as the most important function of the AGM.[710]

In addition, the AGM is responsible for the appropriation of distributable profits, deciding on the use of the net income earned during the year and the distribution of dividends.[711] The AGM is also in charge of the ratification of the acts of the members of the management and the supervisory board and the appointment of the auditor. Moreover, it decides about amendments to the firm's articles of incorporation, measures to increase or reduce the share capital,[712] and the appointment of auditors for the examination of matters in connection with the formation or the management of the firm as well as about the dissolution of the company.[713] Pursuant to § 147 (1) AktG, the AGM is also responsible for instituting action against management or supervisory board members for breaches of their duties.[714] The AGM may further resolve on the approval of the managerial compensation system as implied by the VorstAG,

---

702 See Baums/Scott (2005): 72. See also du Plessis et al. (2012): 170.
703 See Rieckers/Spindler (2004): 350.
704 See Bernhardt (2002): 1842. Schröder/Schrader (1998): 24 call this a "sacred cow".
705 The AGM is governed by §§ 118-149 AktG. The following description only provides a summary of the – subjectively – perceived most important aspects.
706 See § 118 (1) Sentence 1 AktG. See also du Plessis et al. (2012): 56.
707 See § 111 (4) Sentence 3 and § 119 (2) AktG.
708 See § 101 (1) AktG and § 119 (1) Sentence 1 No. 1 AktG.
709 The firm's articles may require another majority or additional requirements. See § 103 (1) Sentence 3 AktG.
710 See du Plessis et al. (2012): 88.
711 See Rieckers/Spindler (2004): 358; du Plessis et al. (2012): 58.
712 See Rieckers/Spindler (2004): 358.
713 See § 119 (1) AktG.
714 This requires a simple majority of the votes. See § 147 (1) Sentence 1 AktG.

providing them with a strong message in case they are dissatisfied.[715] According to § 133 (1) AktG, the decisions made during the AGM require a simple majority of the votes cast, as long as the firm's articles do not state otherwise. For a number of critical decisions, such as the removal of supervisory board members,[716] amendments of the firm's articles,[717] or capital increases,[718] a majority of three-fourths of the share capital represented at the AGM is required.

Pursuant to § 120 (1) Sentence 1 AktG, the AGM shall take place once a year. It is generally called by the management board which resolves thereon by a simple majority.[719] In addition, an AGM shall be called whenever required by the interests of the firm.[720] Besides, extraordinary shareholders' meetings can be requested by a (group of) shareholder(s) owning more than 5% of the firm's share capital.[721] The firm's articles may provide that the right to demand an extraordinary meeting shall require a lower level of ownership.[722] Also the supervisory board may call for an extraordinary AGM, whenever this is required by the firm's interests.[723] Based on § 118 (1) Sentence 2 AktG, the shareholders may participate in the AGM without being present and may exercise their voting rights by way of electronic communication, if allowed by the firm's articles. In contrast, members of the management and supervisory board shall be present at the AGM. However, the firm's articles may provide for cases where the attendance of supervisory board members may be via audio-visual transmission.[724]

The **German Corporate Governance Code** addresses a number of weaknesses of the governance system which also (indirectly) affects Germany's key stakeholder groups. There were two principal drivers that necessitated an elimination of these weaknesses. First, the growing importance of international shareholders was putting pressure on the investee firms to adopt internationally accepted governance standards.[725] Second, to be able to compete for capital with other foreign firms in the international capital markets, firms themselves realized the importance of adhering to governance standards.[726] Also the German Government realized that any endeavor to strengthen the German capital market requires the harmonization of existing (privately) established guidelines regarding corporate governance,[727] the creation of transparency, and the provision of a clearer understanding of the GCGC by foreign investors.[728] According to the chairman of the governance commission, the code "serves as a guideline to both German and international investors, clearly setting out the particularities of the German

715 See § 120 (4) AktG. See also du Plessis et al. (2012): 58. However, the result of the vote is non-binding. See section 2.2.2.2 for more details on the VorstAG.
716 See § 103 (1) Sentence 2 AktG.
717 See § 179 (2) Sentence 1 AktG.
718 See § 182 (1) Sentence 1 AktG.
719 See § 121 (2) Sentence 1 AktG.
720 See § 121 (1) AktG.
721 See § 122 (1) Sentence 1 AktG. See also Schmid/Kretschmer (2004): 3. See section 2.2.3.2 for an overview of shareholders' rights associated with important ownership thresholds.
722 See § 122 (1) Sentence 2 AktG.
723 See § 111 (3) AktG. This requires a simple majority. See also Schmid/Wahrenburg (2004): 277.
724 See § 118 (3) AktG.
725 See Drobetz/Schillhofer/Zimmermann (2004): 268.
726 See Drobetz et al. (2004): 268.
727 For details regarding the development of the GCGC, please see section 2.2.2.2.
728 See Rieckers/Spindler (2004): 382; Schmid/Kretschmer (2004): 17; Cromme (2005): 362; Nowak/Rott/Mahr (2005): 256; Goncharov/Werner/Zimmermann (2006): 433; Vesper-Gräske (2013): 751.

business world in the language of the capital market and matching them to international standards."[729] Its key objective is to "boost confidence in the management of German companies"[730].

The GCGC contains essential statutory regulations as well as internationally and nationally recognized standards on the management and supervision of publicly-traded companies and companies with access to capital markets.[731] It consists of seven parts, including the foreword, and covers six topics.[732] Part two deals with shareholders and the AGM, part three with the cooperation between the management board and supervisory board, part four with the management board, part five with the supervisory board, part six with transparency and disclosure issues and part seven with accounting topics such as reporting and audit of financial statements.[733] One can distinguish between three types of regulations within the code; compulsory statutory regulations, recommendations, and suggestions.[734] Compulsory statutory regulations, in most cases marked by the word "must", constitute descriptions and explanations of existing law and are thus legally binding. The goal is to present codes of conduct with regard to the management and supervision of German companies in a way understandable to foreign investors.[735] Recommendations are marked by the word "shall" and constitute the code's core recommendations. While firms can deviate from them, any divergence from the recommendations has to be made public annually.[736] Finally, the code contains suggestions, marked by the words "can" or "should". They constitute principles of good corporate governance and firms are encouraged to follow them;[737] however, a deviation from suggestions is possible without the need for an explanation.[738]

The code has been implemented as a soft law, as it was assumed that a voluntary governance system would enable the quick and effective reaction to changing needs which would not be possible if the code was legally binding.[739] However, through the declaration of conformity pursuant to § 161 AktG, the governance code has a legal basis and statutory backing.[740] According to this paragraph, apart from its statutory provisions, the code is based on a comply-or-explain approach.[741] The management and supervisory board of publicly listed firms are

729 Cromme (2005): 364. See also GCGC (2013): 1.

730 Cromme (2005): 364. See also GCGC (2013): 1.

731 See § 161 (1) Sentence 2 AktG. However, the GCGC (2013): 2 recommends the application also to non-public companies.

732 See du Plessis et al. (2012): 40; Nix/Chen (2013): 39.

733 See GCGC (2013): 3-15. A detailed description is provided by Ringleb et al. (2008).

734 See Ihrig/Wagner (2002): 790; Strunk et al. (2003): 6; Drobetz et al. (2004): 271; Nowak et al. (2005): 254; Goncharov et al. (2006): 433; Talaulicar/v. Werder (2008): 256.

735 See Ihrig/Wagner (2002): 789. This was essential, given that especially Anglo-Saxon investors did not realize that the most important governance elements were mandatory under German law, resulting in a misconception of German corporate governance. See Bernhardt (2002): 1841.

736 See Nowak et al. (2005): 254. This is also referred to as comply-or-explain approach. According to GCGC (2013): 2, this enables firms to reflect industry- and firm-specific characteristics.

737 See du Plessis et al. (2012): 40.

738 See Drobetz et al. (2004): 272; Nowak et al. (2005): 254; Vesper-Gräske (2013): 752. See also GCGC (2013): 2

739 See du Plessis et al. (2012): 31.

740 See Strunk et al. (2003): 1; Bernhardt (2008): 1686; du Plessis et al. (2012): 33; Nix/Chen (2013): 39.

741 See Cromme (2005): 364; Nowak et al. (2005): 253; du Plessis et al. (2012): 31f. The latter state that originally, it has been termed comply-or-disclose and only been changed to conform to European Law.

obliged to annually publish a declaration of conformity[742] which documents the compliance and non-compliance with the recommendations of the code.[743] In case management and/or supervisory board refuse to accept the recommendations of the GCGC, they are required to disclose this non-compliance,[744] together with the reasons for the past and future non-compliance.[745] § 161 (2) AktG further obliges that the disclosure has to be made available to shareholders continuously. This disclosure ensures that a firm's shareholders become aware of these deviations and subject the particular firm to pressure in case the explanation is not plausible.[746]

Since its implementation, the GCGC has been researched by a number of academics, focusing on its acceptance as well as on the effects of a firm's compliance to the code.[747] On behalf of the corporate governance commission, the Berlin Center of Corporate Governance regularly reviews the compliance of German firms with the corporate governance code. The most recent report, published in 2013, shows that the rate of compliance increases with the size of the firms, ranging from 71.2% (48.3%) for recommendations (suggestions) in the General Standard to 95.8% (76.7%) in the DAX. On average, the rate of compliance with recommendations equals 81.9% across all firms of the general and prime standard, which is slightly lower than the respective rate in 2010 (85.8%).[748]

2.2.2.2 Overview of Recent Corporate Governance Legislation

The changes within the German financial system outlined in section 2.2.1 manifested itself in a number of regulatory improvements. Therefore, the following part provides an overview of recent changes in the German governance legislation that helped bring about these improvements. A complete overview of the developments and evolution of the legislative changes is beyond the scope of this paper. Due to this, the subsequent part aims at providing only a short description of the most recent and relevant developments. Thereby, the emphasis is laid on legislative changes that affect the level of investor protection and/or impact the feasibility of monitoring.[749]

The first law explicitly covering corporate governance issues constituted the **Corporate Sector Supervision and Transparency Act** (KonTraG)[750], which became effective in May 1998

742 This declaration of conformity, however, is not audited or monitored in any way by an independent party. See Goncharov et al. (2006): 434.

743 See Strunk et al. (2003): 2f; Goncharov et al. (2006): 433; Nix/Chen (2013): 39.

744 See also Ihrig/Wagner (2002): 790; Vesper-Gräske (2013): 752.

745 See § 161 Sentence 1 AktG. See also du Plessis et al. (2012): 33-35. According to the author, this declaration ensures the liability of the management and supervisory board in case their firm's actual governance principles deviate from those declared.

746 See Drobetz et al. (2004): 272; Rieckers/Spindler (2004): 381; Mintz (2005): 590; Nowak et al. (2005): 253; Talaulicar/v. Werder (2008): 255.

747 A limited selection of these studies constitute Bernhardt (2002); Drobetz et al. (2004); Nowak et al. (2005); Goncharov et al. (2006); Bernhardt (2008); Talaulicar/v. Werder (2008).

748 See also table 40 in appendix 3. According to v. Werder/Bartz (2013): 887, only 17 firms comply with all provisions of the GCGC.

749 Therefore, this section also comprises the GCGC, although it has been implemented as a soft law only.

750 Also called the "Act on Control and Transparency of Enterprises" or "Corporation Control and Transparency Act". See Rieckers/Spindler (2004): 359 and Nowak (2001): 45, respectively.

and can be regarded as a "starting point for a more capital market-oriented legislation."[751] With the enactment of the KonTraG, the German legislature aimed at improving the existing control mechanisms. With regard to the management board, the newly framed § 90 (1) No. 1 AktG now clarifies the responsibility of the management board to provide future oriented information to the supervisory board.[752] Besides, the novel § 91 (2) AktG now mandates the implementation of surveillance measures by the management to ensure the early detection of developments threatening the continuation of the firm.[753] In addition, the KonTraG led to a shift of power to the supervisory board to strengthen its role as a monitor.[754] The provision affected, inter alia, the maximum number of supervisory board memberships an individual is allowed to hold,[755] increased the number of supervisory board meetings[756] and ensured that the auditor is chosen by and reports directly to the supervisory board.[757] The KonTraG also entailed a number of amendments with regard to the role and responsibility of the auditor.[758] Inter alia, it provided for an increased liability of the auditor,[759] fostered the independence of the audit firm[760] and ensured the auditor's presence on the supervisory board's or audit committee's meetings dealing with the consolidated financial statements and annual reports.[761] Another goal of the KonTraG was a reduction in the frequency of the divergence of cash flow and voting rights.[762] Therefore, the KonTraG abandoned the use of multiple vote shares[763] as of June 2003 as well as of voting rights restrictions[764] as of June 2000. Moreover, the provision aimed to reduce the power of banks to better align the proxy voting with the interests of shareholders.[765] According to § 135 (2) Sentence 2 AktG, a credit institution that wishes to exercise the voting rights on the basis of a proxy now shall bear in mind the shareholders' interests and shall ensure that its own interests do not interfere or affect the voting proposal. Furthermore the credit institution now has to point out any potential conflict of interest.[766]

---

751 Nix/Chen (2013): 38. See also Böcking/Orth (1998a): 354; Kirsch (2002): 746; Cromme (2005): 364.

752 See Claussen (1998): 180f; Seibert (1999): 10.

753 See also Claussen (1998): 181; Geib (1999): 22; Seibert (1999): 9f; Kirsch (2002): 746. For details, please see Lück (1999).

754 See Nowak (2001): 45; Schmidt (2004): 408; Hackethal et al. (2005): 401; Goergen et al. (2008): 188.

755 See § 100 (1) AktG. See also Claussen (1998): 181f; Seibert (1999): 11; Theisen (1999): 238-241; Nowak (2004): 436. However, no account shall be taken of up to five seats a representative of the parent company holds in supervisory boards of commercial enterprises, which are member firms of the group.

756 See § 110 (3) AktG. See also Claussen (1998): 182; Seibert (1999): 12f; Theisen (1999): 236-238.

757 See 111 (2) AktG. See also Böcking/Orth (1998a): 360; Claussen (1998): 182; Seibert (1999): 13f; Theisen (1999): 224-226; Nowak (2004): 436.

758 See e.g. Böcking/Orth (1998a): 356; Geib (1999): 44; Seibert (1999): 23f.

759 See Böcking/Orth (1998a): 357; Seibert (1999): 24; Nowak (2001): 45.

760 See Böcking/Orth (1998a): 357; Seibert (1999): 23.

761 See § 171 (1) AktG. See also Böcking/Orth (1998a): 360; Seibert (1999): 14; Nowak (2004): 436.

762 See Marsch-Barner (1999): 285. Please see section 4.3.3.1 for an overview of the theory and empirical evidence on a divergence of cash flow and voting rights.

763 See § 12 (2) AktG and Seibert (1999): 17; Höpner (2003): 169; Braendle (2006): 266.

764 See § 134 (1) AktG. See Claussen (1998): 181f; Marsch-Barner (1999): 287, 296; Seibert (1999): 17; Höpner (2003): 111. An exception constitutes the Volkswagen law.

765 See Böcking/Orth (1998b): 1241; Claussen (1998): 183-185; Seibert (1999): 16f.

766 See § 135 (2) Sentence 4 and 5 AktG. See also Claussen (1998): 184f. In addition, the KonTraG prohibited the use of proxy voting by credit institutions owning more than 5% of the company's share capital unless the individual shareholder has provided explicit voting instructions.

Closely related to the KonTraG is the **Raising of Equity Relief Act** (KapAEG) that became effective in April 1998.[767] Due to the globalization of capital markets, a number of German publicly-listed companies started to prepare their financial statements pursuant to internationally accepted accounting principles in addition to their mandatory statements based on German accounting principles.[768] As a response to this development and to save German companies the trouble and costs of preparing two financial statements, German legislature allowed to choose either German or internationally-accepted (US-GAAP or IAS) accounting principles for the preparation of the consolidated financial statements of publicly-listed parent companies.[769]

The **Fourth Financial Market Promotion Act** (FMFG) became effective in July 2002 and constitutes the latest of a number of acts aimed at modernizing and promoting the German financial market by adapting to the structural changes taking place globally.[770] The act contains changes in a number of laws relevant for the financial markets, among others the Stock Exchange Act (BörsG), the Securities Trading Act (WpHG), the Banking Act (KWG) as well as the Investment Companies Act (KAGG).[771] The specific objectives of these acts include (1) reinforcing the protection of investors by enhancing the transparency of capital markets and prohibiting price manipulation,[772] (2) providing market participants, especially investment companies, with a broader scope of action,[773] (3) enhancing the legal certainty, and (4) augmenting the efficiency of the supervision of credit institutions and reinsurers.[774] As regards investor protection, the centralized investigative power at the BaFin[775] allows for more effective supervision of capital markets.[776] According to § 20a (1) WpHG, it is now forbidden to make incorrect or misleading statements with regard to factors relevant for the valuation of securities or to withhold information by failing to meet compulsory notifications.[777] Furthermore, it is now forbidden to spread rumors or to engage in transactions to influence the exchange prices of securities.[778] In addition, § 15a WpHG now mandates the disclosure of director dealings without delay to increase the transparency and market efficiency by enabling the

767 See Böcking/Orth (1998b): 1241; Busse v. Colbe (1999): 403.

768 See also Geib (1999): 20; Goergen et al. (2008): 189.

769 See Böcking/Orth (1998b): 1241; Förschle/Glaum/Mandler (1998): 2281; Busse v. Colbe (1999): 403f; Geib (1999): 35; Kirsch (2002): 746. However, this provision was only applicable until the enactment of the Accounting Law Modernization Act in 2005. Please see below for further information.

770 See Kugler (2002): 1001; Park (2003): 1513; Tielmann/Heppe (2003): 191; Detzer et al. (2013): 120.

771 See Rudolph (2002): 1036; Tielmann/Heppe (2003): 191.

772 While price manipulation has been prohibited before (§ 88 BörsG), the provision had been effectively meaningless. Further, the previous provision protected the reliability and verity of the market pricing, whereas the new provision explicitly focuses on investor protection. See Altenhain (2002): 1874f.

773 For details on the effect of the new legislation on investment companies, please see Kugler (2002).

774 See Rudolph (2002): 1037; Park (2003): 1513. See also Tielmann/Heppe (2003): 191.

775 The Federal Financial Supervisory Authority (BaFin) has been founded in 2002 with the implementation of the Law on Integrated Financial Services Supervision (FinDAG). It supervises banks, financial services and insurance companies across the entire German financial markets and embodies the key functions regarding investor protection and solvency supervision. See § 4 (1) FinDAG. See Nowak (2001): 45; Tielmann/Heppe (2003): 194; Haas (2010): 60, 65; Detzer et al. (2013): 120.

776 See Park (2003): 1513; Tielmann/Heppe (2003): 194. This has previously been the responsibility of the public prosecution department. See Altenhain (2002): 1876.

777 See also § 37b (1) WpHG and Altenhain (2002): 1875, 1877; Park (2003): 1514.

778 See also Rudolph (2002): 1040. For a critical review of the provision on the manipulation of exchange and market prices, see Park (2003): 1514-1517.

market to incorporate the executives' assessment of the future performance of their firms.[779] Finally, the act addressed potential interest conflicts faced by analysts and obliges securities service companies to disclose relationships with the company in question that might result in interest conflicts.[780]

As essential governance elements were mandatory under German law, a **German Corporate Governance Code** has been regarded as unnecessary for a long period of time.[781] However, international investors did not understand the codification of essential governance elements which led to a misconception of the German corporate governance system.[782] Therefore, the German Minister of Justice in 2000 engaged a commission[783] with the goal of developing new proposals with regard to the stock corporation and securities law and to harmonize the existing governance guidelines.[784] In July 2001, the Commission submitted its findings to the government, containing a number of recommendations on the improvement of the German corporate governance system and company law, among these the proposition to develop a German Corporate Governance Code.[785] As a result of this recommendation, the Federal Ministry of Justice mandated a second commission in 2001 to develop a German Corporate Governance Code[786]. The code[787] was implemented in February 2002[788] and since then is reviewed and adjusted on a regular basis to incorporate national and international developments.[789] Since its publication and enactment in February 2002, the Corporate Governance Code has been revised every year (except for 2004 and 2011) to respond to national and international developments on corporate governance that may necessitate adjustments in the GCGC.[790] During this period, the number of recommendations and suggestions increased continuously.[791]

Following the results of the Commission, the German legislature developed the **Transparency and Disclosure Act (TransPuG)**[792] which came into effect in July 2002.[793] The TransPuG consisted of two elements. First, it addressed a range of recommendations provided by the

779 See also Rudolph (2002): 1040; Tielmann/Heppe (2003): 199.

780 See § 34b WpHG. See also Rudolph (2002): 1039; Tielmann/Heppe (2003): 196.

781 See also Talaulicar/v. Werder (2008): 256.

782 See Bernhardt (2002): 1841.

783 This commission was called Baums Commission, named after its chairperson Prof. Dr. Theodor Baums.

784 See Baums (2001): 1; Baums (2002): 2; Bernhardt (2002): 1841; Ihrig/Wagner (2002): 789; Nowak et al. (2005): 254; Bress (2008): 5; Talaulicar/v. Werder (2008): 256; Drobetz/Gugler/Hirschvogl (2009): 367.

785 See Baums (2001): 49-52; Baums (2002): 3; Rieckers/Spindler (2004): 381; Cromme (2005): 364; Köhler (2005): 229. For the complete report, please see Baums (2001).

786 As it was chaired by Dr. Gerhard Cromme (at that time chairperson of the supervisory board of ThyssenKrupp AG), the second commission was called the Cromme Commission. It consisted of 13 members, most of them highly-ranked company executives from a number of industries: Due to the strong presence of company executives, Bernhardt (2002): 1842f criticizes that agents have been selected in order to solve the principal-agent problem. See also Bernhardt (2008): 1691.

787 The GCGC has already been outlined in section 2.2.2.1.

788 See Baums (2002): 3; Ihrig/Wagner (2002): 789; Vesper-Gräske (2013): 751.

789 See Rieckers/Spindler (2004): 382; Bress (2008): 36.

790 See Goncharov et al. (2006): 433.

791 Due to the numerous recommendations and suggestions, Gräwe (2013): 29 speaks of an over-regulation.

792 Also "Law for Further Reform of Corporation Law, Accounting Law, and of Transparency and Publicity". Baums (2002): 4.

793 See Baums (2002): 4; Hirte et al. (2003): 1.

Baums Commission.[794] Second, it provided a legal basis for the GCGC through the implementation of a comply or explain principle.[795] As regards the first element, § 25 AktG now mandates that announcements by firms which by law or by the firm's articles require the publication in the firm's journals, shall be published in the Electronic Federal Gazette.[796] Furthermore, through § 126 (1) AktG, the TransPuG reduced the costs and difficulty of countermotions by shareholders.[797] In addition, according to § 118 (4) AktG, audio-visual transmission of the AGM is now admitted, provided it is authorized by the articles or the bylaws.[798] As regards the second element, the TransPuG required the declaration of conformity with the recommendations of the GCGC. This involves the annual publication of which GCGC recommendations have been or will be applied and which recommendations have not been and will not be applied, as well as reasons for the non-compliance.[799] Deviations from suggestions of the GCGC do not require the disclosure of explicit reasons.[800]

In a comprehensive package, the German legislature approved three acts to improve the existing financial market legislation, the Financial Reporting Compliance Act (BilKoG), the **Investor Protection Improvement Act** (AnSVG) and the **Accounting Law Reform Act** (BilReG).[801] The AnSVG became effective in October 2004 and, among others, implemented the market abuse directive by the European Commission in German law and extended the insider tradings legislation, the ad-hoc disclosure rules, and the publication of director's dealings.[802] For instance, the act broadened the definition of insider securities,[803] introduced a new stricter definition of insider information[804] and extended the insider definition. Moreover, the AnSVG broadened the notification and publication of inside information. The AnSVG also modified the publication of director's dealings in § 15a (2) and (3) WpHG. The BilReG came into force in December 2004. The key aspect of the BilReg constituted the implementation of the IAS/IFRS accounting principles mandated by the EU regulation.[805] Pursuant to § 315a (1) and (2) HGB, capital market-oriented firms now shall prepare their consolidated financial statements in accordance with the IFRS for financial years commencing on or after 1st January

---

794 See e.g. Baums (2002): 4; Kirsch (2002): 748; Koch (2006): 770; Drobetz et al. (2009): 367.

795 See e.g. Baums (2002): 4; Bernhardt (2002): 1841; Noack (2002): 620; Nix/Chen (2013): 39.

796 Earlier, the publication was made in paper form, which exacerbated the information collection by investors. See Ihrig/Wagner (2002): 792; Noack (2002): 620f; Hirte et al. (2003): 48; Strunk et al. (2003): 44-46.

797 See Strunk et al. (2003): 43.

798 See Ihrig/Wagner (2002): 795; Noack (2002): 623; Hirte et al. (2003): 29-31; Strunk et al. (2003): 47f. For details on additional changes, please see Strunk et al. (2003).

799 See § 161 (1) AktG. See also Ihrig/Wagner (2002): 790f; Noack (2002): 620; Strunk et al. (2003): 1; Vesper-Gräske (2013): 752.

800 See Strunk et al. (2003): 8; Drobetz et al. (2004): 272; Vesper-Gräske (2013): 752. For a more extensive description of the declaration of conformity, see Hirte et al. (2003): 5-24.

801 Due to their importance for investors, the following part will only focus on the latter two acts.

802 See Koch (2005): 267; Pluskat (2005): 1097f; Steck/Schmitz (2005): 187; Detzer et al. (2013): 121. Steck/Schmitz (2005) provide a summary of the most important changes resulting from the AnSVG.

803 According to the newly developed § 12 Sentence 1 No. 3 WpHG, insider securities now also comprise securities not directly traded on an exchange but the prices of which depend directly or indirectly on financial instruments admitted to trading. See also Koch (2005): 267.

804 In accordance with § 13 (1) Sentence 1 WpHG, inside information is defined as any specific information about circumstances which are not publicly available and relate to one or more issuers of insider securities, or to the insider securities themselves, which, if it became publicly known, would significantly affect the market price of the insider security. See also Koch (2005): 267; Steck/Schmitz (2005): 288.

805 See Kirsch (2002): 749.

2005.[806] In addition, according to § 325 (2a) HGB, capital market-oriented firms now have the option to publish their individual financial statements in conformity with IFRS.[807] In general, the BilReG increased the attractiveness of German firms for international investors.

Since German companies did not voluntarily disclose the executive compensation on an individual basis,[808] the German legislature enacted the **Act on the Disclosure of Management Board Remuneration** (VorstOG) in August 2005. This mandated the disclosure of executive remuneration for each member of the management board,[809] for every publicly-traded firm as of 31 December, 2005.[810] This disclosure was (and still is) intended to enable existing and prospective shareholders to judge on the supervisory board's effectiveness in setting executive remuneration.[811] Thereby, the German legislature made use of the threat of monitoring mechanisms at the disposal of shareholders to discipline both the management and supervisory board.[812] As a side effect, the legislature also aimed at lowering the overall level of executive compensation.[813]

The **German Law on Corporate Integrity and Modernization of the Right of Avoidance** (UMAG) became effective in November 2005 and entailed three scopes.[814] First, it introduced the shareholders' ability to take legal action to enforce liability against members of the management and/or the supervisory board.[815] The new regulation aimed at increasing the attractiveness of monitoring by shareholders while at the same time ensuring that neither management nor supervisory board become subject to an excessive flood of lawsuits that may limit managerial initiative.[816] Therefore, it linked shareholders' ability to take legal action to an ownership threshold, equaling 1% of share capital or €0.1m.[817] In addition, it required a number of conditions that have to be fulfilled for the court to give leave to file an action for damages.[818] Moreover, the UMAG aimed at a reformation of the action for annulment against resolutions of the AGM, which ought to prevent their abusive use.[819] Finally, the UMAG specified rules regarding a more effective preparation and conduct of the AGM. For instance, § 131 (2) Sentence 2 AktG states that the article or the rules of procedure according to § 129

806 This applies also to all parent firms which have applied for admission of their securities for trading on an organized German exchange up to the respective balance sheet date. Moreover, firms have to apply a number of regulations according to the HGB in addition to the IFRS requirements. See § 315a (1) HGB.

807 Based on § 315 (3) HGB *non*-capital market oriented firms have the option to prepare their *consolidated* financial statements in conformity with IFRS.

808 See Fleischer (2005): 1611; Koch/Stadtmann (2010): 2.

809 Previous legislation required only the publication of the compensation on an aggregate level for the members of the management board. See Fallgatter (2006): 207.

810 See § 285 No. 9 a) and § 314 (1) No. 6 a) HGB. See also Detzer et al. (2013): 121; Vesper-Gräske (2013): 757. However, based on § 286 (5) Sentence 1, the disclosure can be omitted by the AGM with a qualified majority. This is also called opting-out decision. See Fleischer (2005): 1614; Fallgatter (2006): 207.

811 See also Fallgatter (2006): 207.

812 See Vesper-Gräske (2013): 758.

813 See Fleischer (2005): 1612. See also Fallgatter (2006): 208.

814 See Gantenberg (2005): 207.

815 See Cromme (2005): 365. This is specified in §§ 147-149 AktG.

816 See Koch (2006): 772; Schwintowski (2007): 2696. Reduced managerial initiative is frequently regarded as a negative aspect of monitoring. Please see section 3.1.3 for further details.

817 See § 148 (1) AktG and Koch (2006): 772.

818 For details on these conditions, see § 148 (1) AktG, § 148 (3) AktG and Koch (2006): 773-800.

819 See Koch (2006): 800. Thereby, the key reform constituted § 246a AktG.

AktG may authorize the chairperson of the AGM to appropriately limit the number of questions as well as the speaking time of shareholders.[820]

In 2005, the German Government set up the **Governmental Commission for the Modernization of the German Codetermination**[821] which ought to identify the strengths and weaknesses of the German codetermination and to develop a proposal on possible ways to adapt the existing legislation on the codetermination of large German companies.[822] However, no agreement between employee and employer representatives could be reached which resulted in a report of proposals by the commission's independent members, including the statements of both employee and employer representatives separately.[823] This report did not see any need for a fundamental revision of the German codetermination system but confirmed that the system of codetermination does neither constitute a competitive disadvantage nor results in a price discount.[824] However, the commission identified three areas with the greatest need for change, namely (1) the extent of codetermination within the group structure, (2) the size of the supervisory board, and (3) the involvement of employees from outside Germany in the supervisory board.[825] Overall, the German Government did not aim to tackle the issue of codetermination, primarily due to political concerns.[826]

The major goal of the **Shareholders' Rights Directive Implementation Act** (ARUG), which came into effect in September 2009, was the facilitation of the use of voting rights by individual shareholders.[827] This entailed better access to information regarding the AGM[828] and a simplification of the use of voting rights.[829] The UMAG also deregulated the proxy voting abilities by credit institutions.[830] The amended § 135 AktG now enables four different ways through which individual shareholders can be represented at the AGM: (1) the individual can be represented by its credit institution that has been given instructions on the exercise of the voting rights; if the individual shareholder has not provided explicit instructions (but has authorized the use of the voting rights) the institution (2) can exercise the voting rights according to its own proposals or (3) can vote according to the supervisory board's proposals; (4) the

[820] See also Gantenberg (2005): 211. This rule is criticized for its vague definition of an appropriate number of questions and speaking time. See also Koch (2006): 792f. Further, Gantenberg (2005): 211f argues that a reduced speaking time may limit the shareholder's right to information.

[821] The commission was chaired by Kurt Biedenkopf and comprised three independent academics, three employee representatives as well as three employer representatives. See Kommission zur Modernisierung der deutschen Unternehmensmitbestimmung (2006): 5f. See also Hans-Böckler-Stiftung (2007): 2.

[822] See Kommission zur Modernisierung der deutschen Unternehmensmitbestimmung (2006): 6; du Plessis et al. (2012): 187. See also Hans-Böckler-Stiftung (2007): 1.

[823] See also Bernhardt (2007): 381. See Kommission zur Modernisierung der deutschen Unternehmensmitbestimmung (2006): 57-68 and 69-80 for the statement of the employer representatives and employee representatives, respectively.

[824] See Hans-Böckler-Stiftung (2007): 3. See also Bernhardt (2007): 381.

[825] For more details, please see Kommission zur Modernisierung der deutschen Unternehmensmitbestimmung (2006): 13-48 as well as Hans-Böckler-Stiftung (2007): 4f for a summary.

[826] See Bernhardt (2007): 381, 383.

[827] See Simon/Zetzsche (2010): 919f. In addition, it implemented an EU regulation and aimed at a further reformation and supplementation of the action for annulment against resolutions of the AGM that has already been the focus of the UMAG.

[828] See § 124a AktG. See also Sauter (2008): 2.

[829] See § 118 (1) and (2) AktG. See also Sauter (2008): 3f.

[830] See also Sauter (2008): 1.

individual can forward the relevant authorization to a proxy different from its credit institution, such as an association of shareholders.[831] The KonTraG had prohibited the use of proxy voting by credit institutions owning more than 5% of the company's share capital unless the individual shareholder provides explicit voting instructions. As a result of these strict restrictions, the use of proxy voting by credit institutions had come to a standstill.[832] With the ARUG, the 5% threshold was therefore increased to 20%.[833] Through this deregulation, the German legislature aimed to rekindle the use of proxy voting, thereby preventing random majorities and increasing the reliability and representativeness of decisions made at the AGM.[834]

In May 2009, the German legislature adopted the **Accounting Law Modernization Act** (BilMoG), which resulted in far-reaching changes to the German accounting principles.[835] The reform's two major objectives were a closer alignment between commercial-law accounting principles and IFRS and an improvement of the informational function of the financial statements prepared under German GAAP.[836] The changes implied by BilMoG primarily affected private small- or medium-sized firms that apply German GAAP. As the present thesis focuses on publicly-traded firms with an obligation to use IFRS for the preparation of their (consolidated) financial statements, the changes implied by BilMoG are of lower relevance. However, the BilMoG also introduced some relevant internal corporate governance rules.[837] According to the newly developed § 100 (5) AktG, at least one independent member of a firm's supervisory board now has to have experience in accounting and/or auditing.[838] In addition, the BilMoG emphasized the role of the audit committee within the supervisory board.[839] Specifically, a firm may appoint an audit committee to deal with the supervision of the accounting process, the efficiency of the internal control, risk management and revision system as well as with the external auditing.[840] Furthermore, at least one audit committee member is required to be a financial expert in the sense of § 100 (5) AktG.[841] On the whole, these changes aimed to increase the effectiveness and efficiency of monitoring exerted by the supervisory board.[842]

---

831 See § 135 (1) AktG. See also Sauter (2008): 4f; Simon/Zetzsche (2010): 919 and 932-934 in greater detail.

832 See Simon/Zetzsche (2010): 924.

833 See § 135 (3) Sentence 4 AktG. See also Sauter (2008): 5.

834 See Simon/Zetzsche (2010): 955f. However, the authors cast doubt on the effectiveness.

835 See Zülch/Hoffmann (2009): 745. BilMoG was mandatory for full-year financial statements prepared for fiscal years beginning after 31 December 2009. The new rules were voluntary for the previous year. See Lopatta et al. (2013): 236. For a short summary of the major accounting changes, please see Künkele/Zwirner (2009); Zülch/Hoffmann (2009).

836 See Lopatta et al. (2013): 234.

837 See Widmann (2009): 2602. The changes in the internal governance were primarily responses to EU legislation. See also Schichold/Kruse (2011): 2

838 See also Eggers/Reiß/Schichold (2009): 157; Widmann (2009): 2602; Schichold/Kruse (2011): 2. This person is also called a financial expert and is frequently a CFO or auditor. See Eggers et al. (2009): 157; Schichold/Kruse (2011): 2.

839 See Nonnenmacher/Pohle/v. Werder (2009): 1447.

840 See § 107 (3) Sentence 2 AktG. See also Velte (2010): 429f.

841 See § 107 (4) AktG. This is the case for capital market-oriented companies pursuant to § 264d HGB. See also Nonnenmacher/Pohle/v. Werder (2009): 1447f.

842 See also Velte (2010): 429.

In light of the global financial crisis, the German legislature published the **Act on the Appropriateness of Management Board Remuneration** (VorstAG). Becoming effective in August 2009, the VorstAG aimed at a modification and extension of the VorstOG.[843] The act entailed, inter alia, the following changes. First, according to the newly added § 87 (1) Sentence 2 AktG, the remuneration system of publicly-traded firms shall be aimed at the company's sustainable development.[844] In addition, the edited § 87 (2) Sentence 1 AktG aimed at simplifying the reduction and retroactive decrease of remuneration.[845] Second, the newly created § 100 (4) AktG states that a person who was a member of a firm's management board during the past two years is not allowed to become a member of the same firm's supervisory board (cooling-off period). Exceptions are only permissible if the respective person is elected by shareholders owning more than 25% of the firm's voting rights.[846] Finally, § 120 (4) Sentence 1 AktG now entitles the AGM to vote on the approval of the remuneration scheme.[847] However, the outcome of the shareholder vote is non-binding.[848] In addition, the act neither formulates a guideline with regard to the information on the compensation schemes provided to shareholders nor with regard to the frequency of the resolution.[849] While the new provision is equivalent to a soft law,[850] proponents argue that the denial of the remuneration scheme produces publicity which creates pressure on the supervisory board.[851]

To recapitulate, the previously described changes illustrate the willingness and political determination for reforms with regard to the modernization and internationalization of the German legislature.[852] The aforementioned changes led to, inter alia, an improved transparency and protection of smaller shareholders, who did not have any meaningful influence in the traditional German system of corporate governance.[853] This, in particular, refers to the aban-

843 See Döll (2009): 1f; Thüsing (2009): 517; Louven/Ingwersen (2013): 1222; Vesper-Gräske (2013): 759.

844 See also Thüsing (2009): 519; Louven/Ingwersen (2013): 1219; Vesper-Gräske (2013): 762. Louven/Ingwersen (2013): 1220 note that the term sustainable development is rather broad, providing the supervisory board with ample leeway in the specification of the exact goals.

845 Specifically, it states that if a firm's situation deteriorates after the determination of the remuneration, so that a continued payment under § 87 (1) AktG would be unreasonable, the supervisory board shall reduce the remuneration to a reasonable level. See § 87 (2) Sentence 1 AktG. In case of § 85 (3) AktG, the court, upon petition of the supervisory board, shall reduce executive remuneration. See also Thüsing (2009): 522f; Koch/Stadtmann (2010): 4; Vesper-Gräske (2013): 762.

846 See § 100 (4) AktG. See also Thüsing (2009): 528. According to the latter, this exception takes account of family firms, allowing the move of the founder from the management to the supervisory board. See also Vesper-Gräske (2013): 764.

847 This is also called "Say on Pay". Deilmann/Otte (2010): 545; Eulerich/Rapp/Wolff (2012): 69; Vesper-Gräske (2013): 749. Koch/Stadtmann (2010): 3 use the term "Advisory Vote".

848 This reflects the basic idea of the act: it should not infringe on the competency of the supervisory board while at the same time create justification pressure. See also Döll (2009): 20f.

849 See Deilmann/Otte (2010): 546; Vesper-Gräske (2013): 772-775. As another point of criticism, a shareholder vote on the remuneration scheme requires that the item has been duly published in advance of the AGM. As this is done by management, it is the management board that decides on the ability of shareholders to cast their votes on executive remuneration. See Döll (2009): 15. However, Vesper-Gräske (2013): 768, 785 finds that all DAX 30 firms had conducted at least one "say on pay" voting by 2011.

850 See also Deilmann/Otte (2010): 547; Eulerich et al. (2012): 69; Vesper-Gräske (2013): 765.

851 See Vesper-Gräske (2013): 765f. Investigating the approval rates of shareholders of the DAX 30 firms, Vesper-Gräske (2013): 794f finds that the high approval rates suggest that shareholders regard the remuneration as efficiently balancing compensation level and managerial performance.

852 See also Claussen (1998): 177.

853 See Goncharov et al. (2006): 432.

donment of multiple vote shares and voting rights restrictions through the KonTraG[854] as well as to the stricter and extended rules governing insider trading. In addition, the changes enhanced the rights and duties of the supervisory board which now is the key supervisory and monitoring body on behalf of shareholders, creditors, and employees.[855] Moreover, the new regulation significantly improves the information availability for international investors.[856] Finally, German legislation ensured that several modern and international best practices with regard to corporate governance are adhered to.[857] As a result of these changes, "German corporate and capital market law has been elevated to international standards"[858] and has been transformed towards a more capital market-oriented corporate legislation.[859] However, to what extent these regulations contribute to the improvement of corporate governance on the firm-level is ambiguous: a firm's corporate governance is only as effective as desired by the firm's management, supervisory board and, being the focus of this thesis, by its blockholder(s).[860]

2.2.3 Rights and Obligations of Shareholders

It has been stated above that the feasibility of engaging in monitoring and the intensity of monitoring are linked with the intervention options and shareholder rights open to the blockholder at critical thresholds of share ownership. In addition, these rights determine the severity of conflicts between principals. Thus, one needs to develop an understanding of the rights accruing to shareholders with different levels of ownership. Therefore, section 2.2.3.1 focuses on the general rights and obligations that accrue to shareholders independent of the size of their ownership. Section 2.2.3.2 then analyzes the shareholder rights that come with certain levels of ownership.

2.2.3.1 General Rights and Obligations

The general rights of shareholders can be distinguished between administrative rights and property rights.[861] As all shareholders shall be treated equally,[862] these rights accrue to all shareholders of a particular firm. The most important **administrative right** constitutes the voting right exercised in the AGM. Voting rights are to be exercised in proportion to the par value of shares and arise as from the date on which the capital contribution has been made in full.[863] The voting right also implies the right to participate in the AGM, provided shareholders have fulfilled the requirements regarding the notice of attendance and the proof to attend

[854] See also Rieckers/Spindler (2004): 379.
[855] See du Plessis et al. (2012): 53.
[856] See also Noack (2002): 621. While existing large shareholders will most likely receive their information directly from the supervisory board, this change has importance for prospective international shareholders.
[857] See du Plessis et al. (2012): 53.
[858] Nowak (2001): 48.
[859] See Rieckers/Spindler (2004): 385.
[860] This view is shared by Boecker (2010): 308.
[861] See Assmann/Lange/Sethe (2005): 152.
[862] See § 53a AktG.
[863] See § 134 (1) and (2) AktG.

the meeting.[864] Each shareholder of a firm is allowed to post (materially relevant) questions[865] and to rise to speak on issues written on the agenda.[866] In order for shareholders to have a solid basis for their decisions, they are provided with the right to information. Upon request, each shareholder shall be provided with information on the firm's AGM regarding the firm's affairs, given this information is necessary to guarantee an understanding of the items on the agenda.[867] Finally, shareholders have the right to contesting action in case a resolution of the AGM violates law or the firm's articles, or in case a shareholder, through the exercise of voting rights, has attempted to secure special benefits for itself or another person to the detriment of the firm or its shareholders. A shareholder may also institute a contesting action on the basis of incorrect, incomplete or refused information, provided that a rational shareholder would have regarded the provision of the information as essential for its ability to duly exercise its participation and membership rights.[868]

The **property rights**, among others, include the following. First, the shareholders shall be entitled to receive the firm's distributable profit, unless this profit is not to be distributed to shareholders by law, the firm's articles or by a resolution of the AGM.[869] Second, the shareholders shall have a share in the firm's distributable profits in proportion to their share in the firm's equity.[870] Third, in case of a capital increase, each shareholder shall be entitled to subscribe to new shares in proportion to its holdings in the existing share capital.[871] Finally, in case of a liquidation, the shareholders own the residual rights – that is the right to all assets of the firm remaining after fulfillment of all liabilities. These assets are to be distributed in proportion to the shares in the firm's equity.[872]

Based on § 54 AktG, the principal **obligation of shareholders** is the capital contribution which is limited to the share (issue) price and ensures that shareholders are not personally liable.[873] Another essential obligation of shareholders constitutes the publication of voting rights. Since the implementation of the InvÄndG in 2007, any party whose shareholdings reach, exceed or fall below 3%, 5%, 10%, 15%, 20%, 25%, 30%, 50% or 75% shall provide this information to the issuer of the shares and the BaFin without undue delay.[874] With the exception of the 3% threshold, the same notification requirements apply to holdings in financial instruments that result in an entitlement to acquire shares of a firm.[875] These requirements al-

864 See § 123 (2) and (3) AktG.
865 See § 126 (1) AktG.
866 See Rieckers/Spindler (2004): 357.
867 See § 131 (1) AktG. See also Rieckers/Spindler (2004): 358. However, in case the information requested might harm the company, the management board is allowed to refuse this information. See § 131 (3) AktG.
868 See § 243 (1), (2) and (4) AktG. § 245 AktG outlines preconditions for the institution of a contesting action.
869 See § 58 (4) AktG.
870 See § 60 (1) AktG.
871 See § 186 (1) AktG.
872 See § 271 (1) and (2) AktG.
873 See also Assmann et al. (2005): 153.
874 See § 21 (1) WpHG. See also Bessler et al. (2008): 7; Thamm/Schiereck (2014): 20. Voting rights do not need to be published if their holder provides investment services, holds or intends to hold the shares in question in its trading portfolio, provided this holding does not exceed 5% and if the holder ensures that the voting rights are not exercised or otherwise used to exert influence on the firm. See § 23 WpHG.
875 See § 25 WpHG. With the Investor Protection and Capital Markets Improvement Act (AnlSVG) a new reporting duty was introduced. § 25a WpHG now covers also instruments not covered under § 25 WpHG

so apply to firms acting in concert. The notification requirements are more detailed for parties whose holdings reach or exceed 10%. These must notify their goals, their interest to increase their ownership or to exchange executives as well as whether they intend to change the issuing firm's capital structure and dividend policy.[876] Finally, shareholders are subject to the duty of loyalty which describes the allegiance of a shareholder towards its firm which manifests itself as an obligation of the shareholder(s) to make use of the voting rights for the benefit of the firm. The duty of loyalty further mandates the shareholder(s) to be considerate of and not to damage other shareholders. A shareholder will be held liable for any violation of the duty which can be viewed as an unwritten stipulation of the AktG, solving internal conflicts that go beyond the company law.[877] The reason for its development is the shareholders' ability to detrimentally affect the interest of other shareholders, calling for a counterbalance in the form of mutual consideration. The existence of a duty of loyalty in the context of public firms has been neglected until 1988, when the Federal Supreme Court adjudged duties of loyalty between majority and minority shareholders.[878] While the Federal Supreme Court's decision in 1988 focused only on the duty of loyalty of majority towards minority shareholders, in 1995 the court decided that also minority shareholders have a duty of loyalty towards the other shareholders[879] and gave the duty of loyalty legal effect.[880]

2.2.3.2 Rights Associated With Certain Block Sizes

Table 2 summarizes the seven most important ownership thresholds that determine the rights accruing to shareholders of different levels of ownership.[881] The first threshold constitutes **holdings of at least 1%**, which enables shareholders to make a motion regarding a number of decisions. Among others, it enables shareholders to request a special audit if they suspect that balance sheet items are materially undervalued, or, in the case of enterprise agreements,[882] if they suspect that their firm has suffered an undue disadvantage from an unfavorable contract.[883] The next threshold occurs with **holdings of 5% or more**, which provides the respective shareholders with the right to call an extraordinary AGM. In addition, the shareholders may demand that certain items are put on the agenda of the AGM or may make a motion to the court to appoint a different auditor if there is doubt with regard to the auditor's independence. **Ownership of at least 10%** enables shareholders to make a motion to the court to remove a member of the supervisory board, provided this member has been appointed to the su-

which may enable their holder or a third party to acquire shares of a firm that have already been issued. The purpose was to prevent stealth takeover strategies aimed at listed companies. See Clifford Chance (2011): 1.

876 See § 27a WpHG. See also Thamm/Schiereck (2014): 20. Exempt from this publication are asset management firms, investment stock companies and foreign management and investment firms.

877 See Jilg (1996): 79, 97, 183. See also Ringe (2014): 8.

878 This has been a result of the so-called Linotype decision. For more details, see BGH (1988): 1579-1583.

879 This has been a result of the so-called Girmes decision. See BGH (1995): 1793-1750 for more details.

880 See Stelzig (2000): 1. This decision has been justified with the § 53a AktG, which demands the equal treatment of shareholders.

881 Note that most ownership levels refer to the share capital represented at the AGM. Table 41 (appendix 4) provides a more detailed list of the ownership rights from the perspective of minority shareholders as well as the corresponding paragraphs, which are therefore omitted in the following.

882 An enterprise agreement constitutes a control agreement or a profit transfer agreement (§ 291 (1) AktG).

883 See §§ 311-318 AktG for details on the compensation for unfavorable contracts resulting from enterprise agreements in case of no control agreement.

Table 2
This table depicts the control rights accruing to shareholders holding or exceeding certain ownership thresholds. The firms' articles of incorporation may provide for different ownership levels in certain cases.

Threshold	Control rights
≥ 1%	Right to make motion to the court for a special audit based on the suspicion that items on the balance sheet are materially undervalued, to make motion to the court for a special audit or for the substitution of a special auditor in order to audit processes of founding and managing the company and to make motion to audit business relations of the firm with its controlling enterprise.
≥ 5%	Right to call an (extraordinary) AGM, to decide on items on the agenda of the AGM and to make a motion to the court to appoint a different auditor for important reasons.
≥ 10%	Right to make a motion to the court to remove an appointed (not elected) member of the supervisory board, to vote on the ratification of the acts of an individual member of the management or supervisory board, to vote on a nomination for the election of members of the supervisory board made by a shareholder prior to acting on the proposal of the supervisory board.
≥ 25%	Blocking minority control. Right to block a number of decisions, among others, the issuance of preferred stock, capital increases, the resolution of the AGM to dissolve the company, the conclusion of an enterprise agreement, the amendment of the firm's articles of incorporation, and the removal of supervisory board members.
≥ 50%	Simple majority. Provides control over all resolutions at the AGM, among others, the appointment of supervisory board members, the appropriation of distributable income, and the ratification of the acts of the members of the management and the supervisory board. However, the presence of another shareholder (or a group of shareholders) owning more than 25% would significantly limit the discretion of the blockholder as critical decisions require a qualified majority.
≥ 75%	Super-majority control. Provides the shareholder with the power to make changes in the composition of the supervisory board, to amend the firm's articles of incorporation, to increase or reduce the share capital, to dissolve the firm, and to approve specific types of transactions.
≥ 95%	Enables the mandatory squeeze-out of minority shareholders.

Table 2: Ownership thresholds and control rights

pervisory board pursuant to the firm's articles. Moreover, this ownership level confers the right to vote on the ratification of the acts of an individual member of the management or supervisory board. Finally, it enables its owners to block the waiver or compromise of any right of indemnity against members of the management or supervisory board resulting from professional negligence and against third parties resulting from improper exertion of their influence.[884]

Ownership of 25% provides the owner(s) with a blocking minority and veto powers regarding important corporate decisions that require a qualified majority. Inter alia, it confers veto powers with regard to the issuance of preference shares, capital increases, and amendments of the firm's articles of incorporation. Moreover, the shareholders may block the removal of supervisory board members, the dissolution of the company, and the conclusion of an enterprise agreement. **Shareholdings of 50%** or more constitute the simple majority, which enable its owners to decide on all resolutions at the AGM, such as the appointment of supervisory board members, the appropriation of distributable income, and the ratification of the acts of the members of the management and the supervisory board. However, the discretion that comes with the simple majority is limited in the presence of a shareholder (group) which owns at least 25% of the firm's equity and can block decisions that require a qualified majority. Due to this, the next important control threshold occurs with **shareholdings of 75%** or more. This ownership level provides the shareholders with super-majority control and complete discretion on most important decisions. In particular, it confers the power to make changes in the

884 For additional rights, please see table 41 (appendix 4).

composition of the supervisory board, to amend the firm's articles of incorporation, to increase or reduce the share capital, to dissolve the firm, to approve specific types of transactions as well as to implement enterprise agreements. **Ownership of 95%** of a firm's equity constitutes the final control threshold and enables the mandatory squeeze-out of minority shareholders.

In conclusion, formal mechanisms granted by law provide shareholders with sufficient ability to monitor the firm's management. Hence, blockholder monitoring of management is feasible, in particular if there is a blockholder that owns at least 25% of a firm's shares. However, with regard to potential principal-principal conflicts, the preceding discussion suggests that smaller shareholders receive little protection against expropriation from large shareholders.[885] Up to the threshold of 10%, some argue even up to 25%,[886] the legislation stipulates no rights to small shareholders that enable an (effective) protection against a blockholder. Given that smaller shareholders might not necessarily hold 10%, let alone 25%, of the firm's shares and have weak incentives to collaborate, they might not be able to effectively protect themselves from the potential expropriation by a larger blockholder.[887] However, if there is a second blockholder owning 25% of the shares, it has a significant ability to limit expropriation. This conclusion illustrates the importance of the ownership sizes and the ownership structure in general when determining the relevance of agency conflicts.

2.2.4 Ownership Structure

Due to the importance of a shareholder's ownership size and a firm's ownership structure highlighted above, the next step constitutes an investigation of whether shareholders in Germany are able to reach the ownership thresholds that confer them the respective rights. As the ownership structure of German publicly-traded firms has undergone some changes, this part also highlights the evolution of the ownership structure and the potential consequences of this evolution.

Consistent with a bank-based financial system, the German corporate landscape, for decades, has been characterized by a highly concentrated ownership structure and the frequent occurrence of extensive cross-holdings and multiple control chains[888] between banks, industrial and insurance firms.[889] However, beginning in the late-1990s, the ownership structure of publicly-listed firms in Germany underwent significant changes.[890] Based on data collected by *Ampen-*

885 See also Jenkinson/Ljungqvist (2001): 402.

886 See Jenkinson/Ljungqvist (2001): 402f.

887 These inferences qualify the conclusions of section 2.2.2.2. While the abandonment of multiple vote shares and voting rights restrictions as well as the stricter rules on insider trading have increased investor protection, the legislator did not provide small shareholders with rights to actively protect themselves.

888 These structures are also called pyramid shareholder structures, defined as "multiple layers of financial holding shells that are sandwiched between an investor and a company the investor wishes to control". Schmid/Wahrenburg (2004): 283.

889 See Detzer et al. (2013): 209. For an analysis of the historical ownership concentration see e.g. Boehmer (1998); Edwards/Nibler (2000); Köke (2001); Bott (2002); Faccio/Lang (2002); Becht/Boehmer (2003).

890 These developments have been highlighted in section 2.2.1.

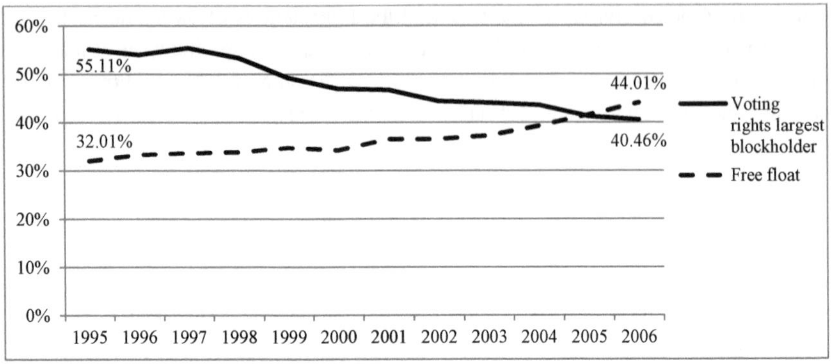

Figure 4: Evolution of the largest blockholder's voting rights in non-financial CDAX firms [source: own illustration based on Ampenberger (2010): 215]

berger (2010) figures 4-6 highlight these changes for a sample of all non-financial CDAX[891] firms.[892] Figure 4 first depicts the evolution of the voting rights of the largest blockholder as well as the dispersed ownership[893]. The results document a significant reduction of the largest blockholder's average voting rights, which decreased from 55.11% in 1995[894] to 40.46% in 2006. At the same time, the average proportion of free float increased from 32.0% in 1995 to 44.0% in 2006. The gradually decrease (increase) of the voting rights (free float) illustrates the decrement of shareholdings by the major players.

Figure 5 outlines the evolution of the number of blockholders and depicts the percentage of firms having zero, one, two, three, four, five, and more than five blockholders.[895] In 1995, 51.30%, 24.35% and 12.17% of these firms had one, two and three blockholder(s), respectively; only 0.87% of the firms did not have any blockholder. In general, most firms had a single blockholder and roughly three-quarters of the firms had either one or two blockholders. This picture has changed during the following years: The percentage of firms with a single blockholder decreased substantially to 28.14% in 2006. A the same time, the percentage of firms with two and three blockholders increased to 29.76% and 17.81%, respectively. Thus, in 2006, there were more firms with two blockholders than firms with a single blockholder. Moreover, the percentage of firms having more than one blockholder increased during the time period from previously 47.83% to 68.42% in 2006. Hence, the number of firms with multiple blockholders has increased significantly.[896] Apparently, with the sale of the stakes by

891 The CDAX is a broad stock market index and incorporates all German firms that comply to the general and prime standard. See section 6.1.1 for further details.

892 See Ampenberger (2010): 215-230. The data extends only until 2006. However, to the author's knowledge, there is no comparable data on CDAX firms available which is characterized by a similar level of detail. This data limitation is to be closed by a more detailed analysis of ownership structures in section 6.2.

893 In this case, dispersed ownership refers to shareholdings of less than 5%. See Ampenberger (2010): 200.

894 These results are roughly consistent with Bott (2002) and Ruhwedel (2003). For a sample of 425 publicly-listed German firms, Bott (2002): 252 finds the voting rights of the largest blockholder to amount to 56.7% and 55.8% in 1997 and 1999, respectively. For a sample of 238 CDAX firms in 2000, Ruhwedel (2003): 204 finds the average voting rights of the largest blockholder to equal 51.6%.

895 A blockholder is defined as a shareholder with more than 5% ownership. See Ampenberger (2010): 217.

896 These results at least illustrate the presence of a second blockholder. However, they are limited by the fact that there is no data on the voting rights of a second (or third) blockholder. For 1999, Bott (2002): 252 finds

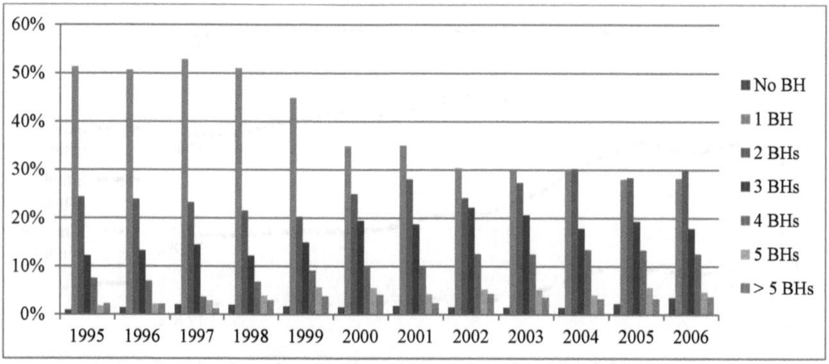

Figure 5: Percentage of non-financial CDAX firms with no, one, or multiple blockholders [source: own illustration based on Ampenberger (2010): 218]

the largest blockholders, more smaller blockholders acquired stakes in the firms. In line with this, *Achleitner et al.* (2010) observe that the withdrawal from significant shareholdings by banks and other firms resulted in a control vacuum that emerging institutional (and other) investors aimed to exploit.[897] Overall, the increase in the number of firms with multiple blockholders illustrates the need for an investigation of the effect of blockholder interrelationships – a goal of the study at hand.

In light of the important ownership thresholds outlined in section 2.2.3.2, it is necessary to investigate if shareholders in Germany are able to reach these thresholds. At least from a legal perspective, this determines the ability of blockholders to monitor managers and the relevance of principal-principal conflicts. For the years 1995-2006, Figure 6 provides this analysis by depicting the percentage of firms having a blockholder with an ownership above the respective threshold.[898] As already illustrated by the previous figure 5, 99.13% of the firms in 1995 have a blockholder. This percentage stays rather constant – in 2006 still 96.56% of the firms have such a blockholder. The highly concentrated ownership structure in 1995 is illustrated by the fact that 88.26% of the firms have a blockholder with a blocking minority and by far more than half of the firms (65.22%) have a blockholder with a simple majority.[899] About one-fourth of the firms have a blockholder with a super majority. The concentration of ownership declines in the subsequent years. In 2006, the percentage of firms with a simple majority-blockholder (super majority-blockholder) drops by roughly 30 (10) percentage points to 37.85% (17.81%). While the drop in firms with a blocking minority shareholder is substantial (20 percentage points), still two-thirds of all firms have a shareholder with the ability to block major decisions at the AGM. From a legal perspective, these results suggest that the average

the average voting rights of the second and third largest blockholder to equal 17.0% and 6.3%, respectively. For 2000, Ruhwedel (2003): 204 finds the average voting right of the second-largest blockholder to equal 16.8%. More up-to-date data will be provided in section 6.2.4.

897 See Achleitner et al. (2010): 815. See also Bessler et al. (2008): 1, 7; Faust et al. (2011): 31.

898 Unfortunately, it does not differentiate between the largest, second- or third-largest blockholder. This data limitation will be overcome in section 6.2.4.

899 These results are roughly consistent with those of Ruhwedel (2003): 209, who finds blockholders with a simple majority in 50.5% of her sample firms in 2000. The deviation might result from the different sample sizes, with 238 firms and 566 firms in Ruhwedel (2003) and Ampenberger (2010), respectively.

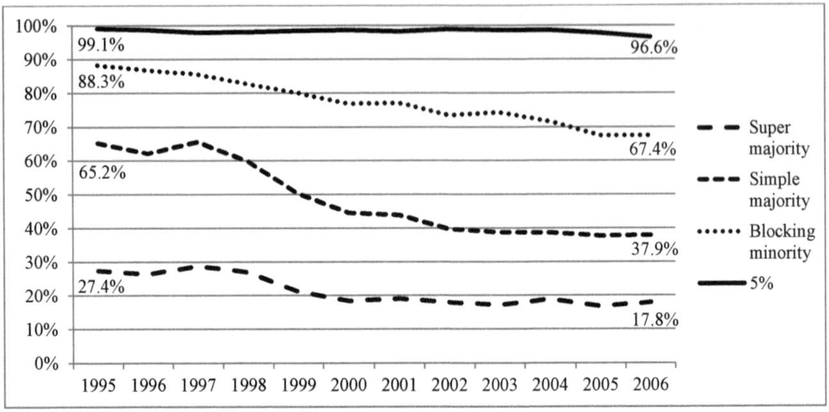

Figure 6: Percentage of non-financial CDAX firms having a blockholder that exceeds important control thresholds [source: own illustration based on Ampenberger (2010): 220]

blockholder should still be powerful enough to effectively monitor managerial decisions. However, as the data does not provide the ownership of a second or third blockholder, it is difficult to judge on the relevance of principal-principal conflicts. On the one hand, the ownership structure in 2006 is still highly concentrated, providing the largest blockholder with substantial discretion. On the other hand, the decline might also indicate that a great number of blockholders can no longer rely on their control rights safeguarded by law and now has to deal with additional blockholders that invest in their portfolio firms. The resulting blockholder interrelationships might have positive or negative effects for the remaining shareholders. This constitutes an empirical question this study aims to address.

All in all, the preceding analysis highlighted important changes with regard to the general concentration of ownership, the number of blockholders, and the important ownership thresholds. These developments and their likely consequences as well as the lack of recent data with a sufficient level of detail highlight the need for further analysis, which is provided by the thesis at hand.

2.2.5 Relevant Agency Conflicts

A prerequisite for the study of blockholders' influence on agency costs is the existence of agency conflicts. Given the findings of the previous sections, the goal of this part is to examine which of the agency conflicts introduced in section 2.1 are relevant in the German institutional environment.

An analysis of the existing literature suggests a general agreement among the corporate governance researchers with regard to the relevant agency conflicts. Due to its concentrated ownership structure, they do not regard the traditional conflict of interest between shareholders and managers as the predominant agency conflict in the German environment. Rather, conflicts between the different shareholder groups are assumed to dominate agency conflicts.[900]

[900] See Dharwadkar/George/Brandes (2000): 1999f; Edwards/Nibler (2000): 242; Bott (2002): 85; Claessens/Fan (2002): 75f; Crespi-Cladera/Renneboog (2003): 3; Gugler/Yurtoglu (2003): 732;

Particularly smaller shareholders face the risk of expropriation by larger shareholders.[901] Therefore, corporate governance research should focus on the blockholders' incentives to both benefit and expropriate smaller shareholders.[902]

The existing literature highlighted the ownership concentration as an important factor with regard to the relevance of the different types of agency conflicts.[903] Section 2.2.4 illustrated that the ownership structure in Germany is still highly concentrated. As a blocking minority already ensures significant veto rights on important corporate decisions,[904] the average percentage of voting rights of 40.46% in 2006 should ensure an effective monitoring of managerial actions by the largest blockholder at least from a legal perspective.[905] Moreover, since two-thirds of the non-financial CDAX firms have a blockholder with (at least) a blocking minority, sufficiently sized blockholders are common in the corporate environment. Therefore, relative to dispersed ownership structures, managerial agency conflicts should be of lower importance under the prevailing concentrated ownership structure.

However, concentrated ownership structures can be regarded as a double-edged sword, since the significant ownership also provides the largest blockholders with substantial discretion which they might use for the exploitation of the remaining stakeholders. Investor protection represents an important mechanism through which small shareholders can be protected against opportunistic behavior of large shareholders.[906] While section 2.2.2.2 concluded that the recent changes led to an improved transparency and investor protection, particularly with regard to small shareholders, this has been qualified in section 2.2.3.2. Also *Rieckers/Spindler* (2004) criticize that despite the requirement of a super majority for important decisions, the demand for a blocking minority present at the firm's AGM "usually leaves shareholders with smaller holdings unprotected."[907] In addition, *Bott* (2002) objects to the too broad notification intervals with regard to significant shareholdings. A shareholder, who announces its share of 25% and subsequently increases its stake to 45% will hold the super majority, given a shareholder presence on the AGMs of 60%,[908] without the need to announce this publicly.[909]

The blockholder's discretion is supported by low attendance rates of (small) shareholders at the AGMs of the firms they have invested in. Since most decisions are based on the percentage of share capital present at the AGM, the less share capital is present at the AGM, the less

Edwards/Weichenrieder (2004): 144; Achleitner et al. (2009): 19; Achleitner et al. (2010): 807. Referring to the ownership structures of Western European firms, Faccio et al. (2001): 55 state that "the salient agency problem in these economies is expropriation of outside shareholders by the controlling shareholder." See also Pagano/Röell (1998): 188.

901 See Drobetz et al. (2004): 270.

902 See La Porta et al. (1999): 474.

903 According to Gillan/Starks (2003): 6, the ownership structure has a direct impact on the magnitude as well as the nature of agency problems within a firm.

904 Please see section 2.2.3.2 for a description of the rights accruing to shareholders with different levels of voting rights.

905 Note that next to the monitoring instruments granted by legislation, a blockholder has a number of different monitoring mechanisms at its disposal. Section 3.1.2 provides an overview of these mechanism.

906 See also Ampenberger (2010): 77.

907 Rieckers/Spindler (2004): 355.

908 Please see figure 7.

909 See Bott (2002): 213f.

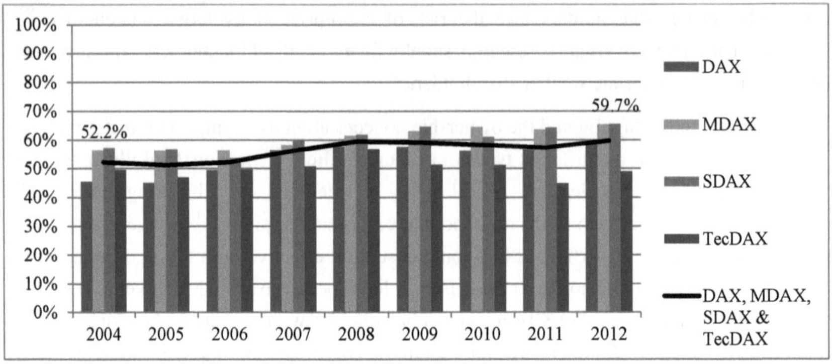

Figure 7: Average shareholders' presence at their firms' AGMs [source: Schutzgemeinschaft der Kapitalanleger e.V. (2012a-d)].

ownership is required for a blockholder to control a firm. Figure 7 depicts the average presence of shareholders at their firms' AGMs. As can be seen, the average presence across all four indices does not exceed 60% for the nine-year period; in 2006, the presence equaled a mere 52.29%.[910] Thus, with its average ownership of 40.46%, the largest blockholder in 2006 had a super majority at the firms' AGM and hence ultimate discretion with regard to the firms' decisions. Moreover, assuming the average presence of 60% at the firms' AGM, the relevant control thresholds are 15% (blocking minority), 30% (simple majority), and 45% (super majority). As a result, smaller levels of ownership are sufficient for blockholders to get their demands accepted,[911] which may be detrimental for the remaining shareholders.[912]

The discretion of blockholders – whether this has positive or negative impacts for the remaining shareholders – might be constrained by the supervisory board. First, supervisory board members are typically appointed for a period of five years. Unless a blockholder owns the super majority, it cannot affect the composition of the board to install representatives.[913] Rather, it has to wait until the next regular election of supervisory board members.[914] This regulation impedes at least the immediate influence of a blockholder on the supervisory board. In addition, codetermination within the supervisory board may limit the influence of blockholders.[915] Therefore, *Emmons/Schmid* (1998) view codetermination as inimical to shareholders' rights

---

910 Ernst et al. (2005): 9 find that more than 30% of individual shareholders do not plan to make use of their voting rights. The authors criticize this behavior as irrational, as investors at the same time fear expropriation. However, according to van der Elst (2011): 2, 11, the absence of small atomistic shareholders at the AGM is due to their rational apathy (please see section 3.1.1 for details). These shareholders are likely to free ride on the monitoring exercised by large blockholders and recognize the low probability of holding the decisive vote. Consistent with his theory, he finds that small shareholders are less willing to participate in AGMs if they are confronted with significant blockholders in the investee firm.

911 See also Prokot (2006): 130. Thamm/Schiereck (2014): 27 find that the number and intensity of activism events increased significantly during 1999-2011.

912 See also Becht/Boehmer (2003): 24; Bessler et al. (2008): 3. The low attendance rates also increase the voting power of additional smaller blockholders which might thus also have an improved ability to prevent an expropriation by the largest blockholder.

913 Please see section 2.2.2.1 for more details on the regulations regarding the supervisory board.

914 Consistent with this, Thamm/Schiereck (2014): 23 find that the closer the next election of supervisory board members, the greater the number of equity purchases by activist investors.

915 Please see section 2.2.2.1 for more details on the regulations regarding employee codetermination.

as it partially unbundles residual control rights from residual cash flow rights by allowing employees to influence corporate decision making.[916]

Despite possible constraints resulting from the composition of the supervisory board, both the prevailing ownership structure and existing legislation provide the largest blockholders with sufficient influence on a number of corporate decisions. Due to this, the manager-shareholder conflict is regarded as less important in firms with a sufficiently sized blockholder. However, the discretion of the largest blockholder, fostered by a low presence at the AGMs, carries the risk that alternative agency conflicts arise. In particular, principal-principal agency conflicts are highly relevant in the German institutional environment. Moreover, a firm's existing debtholders may be exposed to the decisions of a powerful blockholder. The significance of these agency conflicts is further enhanced if one recognizes that the impact of a blockholder goes beyond the monitoring instruments granted by legislation. Next to these instruments, a blockholder has a number of different mechanisms at its disposal, whose importance in the monitoring context are stressed by a number of authors.[917] Overall, while the managerial agency conflict may be of lower relevance in Germany, the institutional environment might constitute fertile soil for shareholder-debtholder and principal-principal conflicts.

2.3 Institutional Environment in the European Union

As mentioned in the introduction, two contemporary regulatory developments within the European Union gave direction to the topic of the present thesis. The following parts outline these regulatory developments. Section 2.3.1 deals with two Green Papers on corporate governance and section 2.3.2 with the already implemented directive on Alternative Investment Fund Managers. The goal is to delineate the content and rationale underling these developments and to highlight a number of weaknesses inherent in the propositions that demonstrate the importance of the research at hand.

2.3.1 EU Propositions on Corporate Governance

As a response to the global financial crisis, the European Commission announced the examination of governance rules and practices in financial institutions and the making of recommendations to remedy potential weaknesses.[918] The Commission followed up on this announcement with the Green Paper on corporate governance in financial institutions published in June 2010.[919] In April 2011, it published another Green Paper on the EU corporate governance framework, extending the perspective to include listed firms as a whole. Based on the findings within these Green Papers and the outcomes of the respective public consultations,

916 See Emmons/Schmid (1998): 28.

917 Please see section 3.1.2 for details.

918 Please see Commission of the European Communities (2009) for further details.

919 See European Commission (2010a): 5. The Commission also launched a public consultation. See European Commission (2010c): 3. As a result of this consultation, it committed to develop legislative proposals with regard to remuneration practices and other corporate governance issues in the financial services industry. See European Commission (2010d): 3 and European Commission (2012): 3.

the Commission published an action plan on European company law and corporate governance in 2012, comprising concrete lines of action for the upcoming years.[920]

While weaknesses of corporate governance mechanisms are not viewed as the main cause of the financial crisis, the **Green Paper on Corporate governance in financial institutions**[921] regards the lack of effective corporate governance as a significant contribution to the risk taking of financial institutions.[922] Therefore, the Green Paper lists deficiencies and weaknesses with regard to the seven components and areas of corporate governance within financial institutions.[923] As to the role of shareholders, the Commission argues that they have not fulfilled their role of responsible owners which refers to an active monitoring and use of their shareholder rights for the benefits of the firm's long-term viability.[924] In particular, the following factors are identified as driving the disinterest or passivity of shareholders of financial institutions:[925] The first factor constitutes the shareholders' business models. The possession of expansive portfolios of different shares causes a disappearance of the "concept of ownership normally associated with holding shares."[926] In addition, the short-term performance evaluation of institutional investors against peers or a benchmark index fosters a high-risk and short-term investment focus. Second, if their shareholdings are small, the monitoring costs faced by investors can dissuade shareholders from engaging in corporate governance. This is of particular relevance for foreign investors. Third, interest conflicts can limit the incentive for shareholder engagement. This is particularly relevant for institutional investors and refers to cases in which the shareholders or their parent firms maintain or expect business relationships with the firm in question. In such cases, the shareholder will be unwilling to negatively influence the commercial interests of its other business units or parent firm. Fourth, the information made available to shareholders is frequently too lengthy and/or complicated for the average shareholder to process and understand. Fifth, the Commission revealed a lack of trust between shareholders, inhibiting cooperative efforts. Finally, shareholders lack effective rights that allow the exercise of control.[927]

Overall, these factors raise questions about "the effectiveness of corporate governance rules based on the presumption of effective control by shareholders for all listed companies."[928] Therefore, the Commission calls for specific solutions to improve the existing governance

920 See European Commission (2012): 3f.

921 This refers to both the Green paper and its accompanying document, the report on "Corporate Governance in Financial Institutions: Lessons to be drawn from the current financial crisis, best practices". See European Commission (2010a).

922 See European Commission (2010b): 2, 4. See also Larosière et al. (2009): 10; du Plessis et al. (2012): 351.

923 The thesis at hand solely enlarges upon the role of shareholders. For details on the other factors, please see European Commission (2010b): 5-9 as well as European Commission (2010a): 6-35.

924 See European Commission (2010a): 23f. See also Cheffins (2009): 47-49; van der Elst (2011): 2.

925 All of the following factors can be found in European Commission (2010a): 24-26.

926 European Commission (2010b): 8.

927 See European Commission (2010b): 8; European Commission (2010a): 26. The commission notes that these problems not only affect financial institutions.

928 European Commission (2010b): 16.

mechanism in financial institutions.[929] Specific topics to be considered are the (1) strengthening of shareholder cooperation, (2) disclosure of voting practices by institutional investors, (3) adherence of institutional investors to stewardship codes of best practice, (4) identification and disclosure of potential interest conflicts faced by institutional investors, (5) disclosure of the remuneration policy for intermediaries by institutional investors, and the (6) provision of shareholders with better information on risk.[930]

Following the 2010 Green Paper on Corporate governance in financial institutions, the Commission launched a broader review on corporate governance within publicly-traded firms in general, the **EU corporate governance framework**. The purpose of this report is to provide an assessment of the effectiveness of the existing corporate governance framework and to raise a debate on the issues covered in the report.[931] While the Commission recognizes that shareholder involvement, as described in the 2010 Green Paper, matters also to EU publicly-traded firms in general, other aspects covered in the 2010 Green Paper are of only limited relevance for non-financial firms. Therefore, the 2011 Green Paper focuses on three major aspects in the center of good corporate governance: (1) the board of directors, (2) shareholders, and (3) how to apply the "comply or explain" approach.[932] With regard to shareholders, the Commission realized that the factors driving the lack of shareholder engagement in financial institutions are also relevant to shareholder behavior in non-financial institutions. Hence, this part focuses on factors that have been identified in addition to those of the 2010 Green Paper.[933] As one additional aspect, the 2011 Green Paper raises the question of shareholder identification. It argues that a better visibility might enable the issuer of the shares to engage in a dialogue with its shareholders and lead to greater involvement of the shareholders in the investee firms.[934] Moreover, the Commission is concerned about the monitoring ability and protection of minority shareholders in the presence of dominant blockholders. As regards their monitoring ability, it raises the question of whether additional rights for minority shareholders are required to provide them with the ability to better represent their interests.[935] As regards the protection of minority shareholders, the Commission is apprehensive for an extraction of private benefits by the large shareholders to the detriment of minority shareholders, specifically focusing on related-party transactions.[936] Finally, the Green Paper raises the question of employee share ownership and proposes a greater involvement of employees in the firms' governance mechanisms.[937]

929 See European Commission (2010b): 10. See also European Commission (2010a): 4. Again, this part will solely focus on propositions with regard to the role of shareholders. Please see European Commission (2010b): 11-19 for details on the remaining propositions.

930 See European Commission (2010b): 16; European Commission (2010a): 26-29.

931 The public consultation took place from April to July 2011. See European Commission (2011c): 2.

932 See European Commission (2011a): 2f. See also van der Elst/Vermeulen (2011): 2. The following part only enlarges upon the role of shareholders. For further details see European Commission (2011a): 5-10, 18-20.

933 See European Commission (2011a): 11-18 for a complete list of the factors associated with the lack of shareholder engagement.

934 See European Commission (2011a): 15f. However, the Commission also recognizes that better knowledge of its shareholders may result in managerial entrenchment and the buildup of defense mechanisms.

935 See European Commission (2011a): 16.

936 See European Commission (2011a): 17.

937 See European Commission (2011a): 17f.

Based on its reflections and the results of the public consultations as part of the two Green Papers, the European Commission identified a number of aspects in the context of corporate governance pivotal for a modern legislation of publicly-traded firms. In particular, it identified three concrete lines of action which the Commission intends to take in the coming years to modernize the existing governance framework. These are outlined in its 2012 **Action plan on European company law and corporate governance**[938] and include (1) the enhancement of transparency, (2) the engagement of shareholders, and (3) the support of firms' growth and competitiveness.[939] With regard to the first line of action, proposals include but are not limited to initiatives to improve the visibility of shareholdings and the identification of shareholders' identities. In addition, it seeks to enhance the transparency of voting policies as well as voting records by institutional investors.[940] In order to facilitate the engagement of shareholders with the investee firms, the Commission suggests an initiative aimed at improving shareholder oversight of executive remuneration policies, including a right to vote on remuneration policies and reports.[941] Moreover, it aims at strengthening shareholders' control over related party transactions and recognizes the need to provide more legal certainty on the rules of acting in concert. Finally, the Commission finds it important to further investigate obstacles to and benefits of encouraging employee share ownership.[942]

Some of the aforementioned propositions and recommendations of the Commission are questionable. These aspects constitute **issues for empirical research** and illustrate the relevance of the research at hand. First, the Commission argues that shareholders have not lived up to their role of responsible owners and rather presumes shareholders to foster excessive risk-taking. This conjecture, however, requires empirical proof. Second, to create a sense of responsibility, the Commission aims at facilitating the engagement of shareholders with the firms they invest in. However, there is no sufficient empirical basis for the presumption that active monitoring by blockholders causes performance improvements and benefits to the firm's long-term viability. This is particularly the case for institutional investors that – in the view of the European Commission – should be more actively engaged with their portfolio firms. Hence, there is a need to empirically assess if institutional shareholders provide for effective governance within firms and if this influence is special in comparison to other types of investors. This question relates to the third weakness of the propositions, namely the failure to differentiate between the diverse types of shareholders and country-level differences in the ownership structure of publicly-listed firms. This differentiation, however, is essential for a full understanding of the role and impact of shareholders, as well as for an effective and targeted regulation. For example, shareholders may not necessarily be equally suited or talented with regard to the supervision of corporate management. Hence, while the facilitation of ac-

938 The action plan is published in the context of the Commission's "Europe 2020" strategy, which, inter alia, aims at improving the business environment in Europe. See European Commission (2012): 2.

939 See European Commission (2012): 3f. As only the first two aspects are relevant for this thesis, the third aspect is not covered here. For details on this aspect, please see European Commission (2012): 12-15.

940 See European Commission (2012): 7f.

941 In Germany, the Act on the Appropriateness of Management Board Remuneration became effective in August 2009. The law has already been introduced in section 2.2.2.2.

942 See European Commission (2012): 8-11.

tive involvement may be beneficial in the case of some shareholder types, it may be detrimental in the case of other types. Fourth, the collaboration and acting in concert of shareholders is regarded as a means to encourage shareholder activism. However, so far little is known on the performance impact of shareholder collaboration. Fostering collaboration among shareholders could also have negative effects if the large blockholders collude to expropriate wealth from minority shareholders. The potential detrimental effect of shareholder collaboration relates to another concern of the Commission, namely the protection of minority shareholders. In this context, it raises the question of whether there is a need for additional rights for minority shareholders. The need for better minority shareholder protection is an empirical question which should be investigated – being conscious of different shareholder types and shareholder interrelationships.

2.3.2 EU Directive on Alternative Investment Fund Managers

According to the European Commission, the global financial crisis exposed a number of vulnerabilities in the global financial system and illustrated that stable financial systems require all significant actors on the financial markets to be subject to appropriate regulation and supervision. Therefore, the Commission initiated a program to extend the existing regulation and supervision to all actors and activities that have been shown to embed significant risks to the financial markets.[943] Actors affected by this program are entities engaged in the management of alternative investment funds (AIFM) rather than the alternative investment funds themselves (AIF).[944] The definition of AIFs encompasses investment funds[945] that are not already regulated on an European level by the Directive on Undertakings for Collective Investment in Transferable Securities (UCITS Directive).[946] These funds comprise, inter alia, hedge funds and private equity funds.[947] However, the regulation excludes AIFMs managing AIFs with total assets of less than €100m as they are not regarded as systemically relevant. For the same reason, it excludes AIFs with total assets of less than €500m, provided they are not levered.[948]

The European Commission published a proposal for a directive on AIFMs in April 2009. Following a number of amendments, the Directive on AIFMs was published in the Official Journal of the European Union in July 2011 and entered into force on the 20th day following this publication. The Directive had to be transposed into national law of the member states by July

943 See Kramer (2011): 2077; Viciano-Gofferje (2013): 2506.

944 Thereby, it is irrelevant if the AIFM is located within the EU, as long as it markets one or more AIFs within the EU. For details, please see European Commission (2011b): Article 2 (1).

945 The European Commission (2011b): Article 4 (1) a) defines investment funds as collective investment undertakings including investment compartments thereof which "raise capital from a number of investors, with a view to investing it in accordance with a defined investment policy for the benefit of those investors". Whether or not the AIF belongs to an open-end or closed-end type as well as the fund's legal structure is irrelevant. See European Commission (2011b): Article 2 (2).

946 See European Commission (2009b): 2; European Commission (2011b): Paragraph 3. For details on the UCITS Directive, please see European Commission (2009a).

947 See European Commission (2009b): 2; European Commission (2009c): 4. For further details on the affected investors, see European Commission (2011b): Article 2 (3).

948 See European Commission (2011b): Article 3 (2). See also Viciano-Gofferje (2013): 2507; Volhard/El-Qalqili (2013): 204.

2013.[949] Its primary goal is the creation of a comprehensive and secure framework for the supervision of AIFMs within the EU, taking into account their multiple types of investment strategies and techniques. In particular, the Directive aims to (1) increase the transparency of AIFMs towards their investors, supervisors and employees of the investee firms, (2) provide national- and European-level supervisors with the information and tools required for an effective monitoring of AIFMs, (3) introduce a common and robust approach with regard to the protection of investors of AIFMs, (4) strengthen the single market through fostering competition, and to (5) increase the accountability of AIFMs towards the employees of the firms they invest in and towards the public at large.[950] Among the blockholders investigated in the present thesis, private equity firms are most affected by this regulation. Hence, the following deliberations focus only on regulations affecting private equity firms.[951]

Specific arrangements for private equity funds and their managers are stated in the §§ 287-292 KAGB.[952] Upon the acquisition or disposal of shares of a non-listed firm, the AIF shall notify the BaFin of its proportion of voting rights whenever these reach, exceed or fall below the thresholds of 10%, 20%, 30%, 50%, and 75%. When an AIF acquires – individually or jointly – control over a non-listed firm, the AIFM managing the AIF shall inform the non-listed firm, the firm's shareholders (when identifiable) and the BaFin on the acquired controlling interest. This notification shall contain (1) the resulting situation with regard to voting rights, (2) the conditions subject to which the information has been acquired as well as (3) the date of the acquisition. The AIFM shall also ask the management board to inform the employee representatives, or, if there are none, the employees of the acquisition.[953] In addition, when an AIF acquires control of a non-listed or listed firm, the following information shall be made available to the particular firm, its employees or employee representatives, its shareholders (when identifiable) and the BaFin: the AIFM's identity, the policy implemented by the AIFM to prevent and manage interest conflicts between the AIFM and the firm as well as the policy for external and internal communication with the firm's employees.[954] For AIFs acquiring the majority in non-listed firms, additional disclosure requirements are mandatory, including the

[949] See European Commission (2011b): Article 66 (1) and (2) as well as Article 70. In Germany, this Directive has been implemented with the Capital Investment Code (KAGB) in July 2013. See Viciano-Gofferje (2013): 2506; Volhard/El-Qalqili (2013): 202.

[950] See European Commission (2011b): Paragraph 2-4, 27-30, 88, 90, 92, 94. The last goal explicitly refers to private equity funds.

[951] In discussing the effect of the new regulations on private equity firms, the following focuses on the paragraphs of the KAGB. The corresponding legislation by the European Commission can be found in European Commission (2011b): Article 26-30.

[952] With regard to the scope of application, the regulation differentiates between non-listed firms and listed firms. If the target firm is a listed firm, only §§ 290 (1)-(3) and 292 KAGB are to be applied. See § 287 (4) KAGB. In addition, the regulation does not apply to small- and medium-sized firms and special purpose vehicles with the purpose of purchasing, holding or administrating real estate. See § 287 (2) KAGB and Viciano-Gofferje (2013): 2507; Volhard/El-Qalqili (2013): 205. In case the AIFM acquires a non-controlling share in a non-listed firm, only the notification on the acquisition of major holdings pursuant to § 289 (1) KAGB applies. See § 287 (3) KAGB and Volhard/El-Qalqili (2013): 205. Based on § 288 (1) KAGB, control is defined as more than 50% of the voting rights of non-listed firms. With regard to listed firms, § 29 (2) WpÜG defines control as an ownership of 30% of a firm's voting capital.

[953] See § 289 (1)-(4) KAGB. See also Kramer (2011): 2083; Viciano-Gofferje (2013): 2507f; Volhard/El-Qalqili (2013): 206.

[954] See § 290 (1)-(3) KAGB. See also Kramer (2011): 2083; Viciano-Gofferje (2013): 2509; Volhard/El-Qalqili (2013): 206.

AIFs intentions with regard to the future strategy and business of the firm as well as the resulting effects on the firm's workforce.[955] AIFs that acquire control of non-listed firms are also subject to specific provisions regarding the annual report of the firm, which, inter alia, has to be provided to the firm's employee representatives or employees themselves.[956] The most far-reaching provisions, however, are established in § 292 KAGB which aims to limit asset stripping by AIFs that acquired a controlling interest in a non-listed or listed firm. Specifically, for a period of two years following the acquisition, it prohibits the AIF from facilitating, supporting or requesting any distribution (dividends or interest), capital reduction or acquisition of own shares by the firm. Moreover, the AIF is not allowed to vote in favor of these activities on the firm's AGM but shall rather use its best efforts to prevent these activities.[957] § 292 (2) KAGB includes complementary provisions designed to ensure that the distributions are exclusively financed with net (distributable) profit.[958]

The above mentioned regulations constitute a substantial burden on and higher costs for private equity firms. The disclosure requirements specified in §§ 289f KAGB in large part resemble already introduced regulations in Germany.[959] However, this regulation previously applied only to listed firms, whose number is small relative to non-listed firms. Therefore, the newly introduced requirements in the KAGB will result in a breadth of duties which may no longer be regarded as appropriate.[960] In addition, the extensive portfolio firm disclosures may constitute a disadvantage in competitive situations relative to firms that do not need to comply with these disclosure requirements. As the disclosure requirements for private equity firm's portfolio companies occasion significant costs on the parties concerned, the impact of private equity investments on their portfolio firms should be tested for to work out if these costs are justified. Furthermore, § 292 KAGB aims at protecting portfolio companies by limiting asset stripping. While this goal is certainly reasonable, it can be criticized for its one-size-fits-all approach. First, stripping assets may not always be value reducing but can help firms in financial difficulties to refocus on a core business. Therefore, the new regulation may be detrimental particularly for distressed firms that require a quick turnaround. Second, § 292 KAGB constitutes a substantial qualification and restriction of the private equity firm's shareholder rights.[961] This is reasonable only if private equity firms indeed have a detrimental effect on their portfolio companies and stakeholders. This necessitates an empirical examination of the influence of private equity firms on their portfolio companies. As a final criticism, the §§ 282-292 KAGB exclusively focus on private equity firms. Hence, it subjects these firms to stricter treatment relative to other investor types.[962] In order to substantiate this conclusion, one needs to empirically assess and compare the influence of private equity firms with the influence of other investor types.

955 See § 290 (4) KAGB. See also Kramer (2011): 2083.
956 See § 291 KAGB. See also Viciano-Gofferje (2013): 2509; Volhard/El-Qalqili (2013): 206.
957 See § 292 (1) KAGB. See also Kramer (2011): 2083; Wollenhaupt/Beck (2013): 1955.
958 See also Viciano-Gofferje (2013): 2519; Volhard/El-Qalqili (2013): 206.
959 See § 27a (1) WpHG. See also Kramer (2011): 2083.
960 See Viciano-Gofferje (2013): 2510.
961 See Wollenhaupt/Beck (2013): 1955.
962 See also Volhard/El-Qalqili (2013): 205.

2.4 Résumé

The beginning of this chapter listed a number of questions regarded as germane to the present research focus. The aim of chapter 2 was to answer these questions and to provide a background sufficient for an understanding of the analyses that follow.

In most general terms, agency theory describes and explains the behavior of individuals that enter into an agency relationship. Consistent with the broad definition, an agency relationship between two parties arises whenever one party, the agent, acts for, on behalf of, or as a representative for another party, the principal. Whenever this agency relationship is characterized by rationality, information asymmetries, incomplete contracts, differential utility functions and risk preferences as well as opportunism, it is subject to agency problems. These problems arise as a direct result of agency conflicts, understood as conflicts of interest between the respective parties within the agency relationship, and may become manifest in adverse behavior of the agent. The agency problems bring about agency costs which consist of monitoring expenditures by the principal, bonding expenditures by the agent, and the residual loss. Depending on its ownership and capital structure, a firm can be subject to up to four agency conflicts. While the manager-shareholder and shareholder-debtholder conflicts are frequently observed in the existing literature, there may be two additional conflicts that have been shown to classify as agency conflicts: (1) in the presence of a single blockholder, a firm may be subject to a minority shareholder-blockholder conflict; (2) in the presence of multiple blockholders, a firm may be faced with a blockholder-blockholder agency conflict. To account for the agency costs resulting from these four different types of agency conflicts, the present thesis introduces the concept of a firm's overall agency costs, defined as the sum of the agency costs inherent in a firm.

Corporate governance and its mechanisms are regarded as instruments to mitigate agency costs. There exist two types of corporate governance definitions, a narrow shareholder-oriented and a broad stakeholder-oriented definition. In line with the latter, the present thesis defines corporate governance as all mechanisms ensuring that, given a particular agency relationship, the agent's actions and decisions are driven by the goal of maximizing the benefit of one or more principals. Governance mechanisms can be distinguished into internal and external mechanisms. As regards the former, the present thesis exemplifies the supervisory board and executive compensation; as regards the latter, it mentions the market for managers, the market for corporate control, the product market competition, and monitoring by a blockholder which constitutes the focus of attention within the present thesis.

With regard to the institutional environment, it has been illustrated that the traditionally bank-based German financial system experienced a move towards a market-oriented financial system. This move affected the German corporate governance and investor protection legislation as well as the ownership structure. Overall, the prevailing ownership structure and the (newly implemented) legislation provide the largest blockholders with sufficient ability to engage in monitoring. This ability, however, may be constrained by the firms' supervisory board, in particular by codetermination on the supervisory board level. As a result of the blockholder's ability to monitor the firm, the managerial agency conflict may be regarded as less important in firms with a sufficiently sized blockholder. However, despite the newly introduced improvements in minority shareholder protection, the rights associated with certain block sizes, the concentrated ownership, and the low presence at the AGMs provide the largest blockholder with significant discretion. This may give rise to principal-principal agency conflicts and may expose a firm's debtholders to the decisions of an entrenched blockholder (shareholder-debtholder conflict). At the same time, the analysis highlighted an increase in the number of blockholders within a single firm. These blockholders may have an incentive to limit any expropriation by the largest blockholder. Thus, an extension of the research focus to incorporate blockholder interrelationship may be important for a complete understanding of blockholder monitoring and further illustrates the relevance of the present research.

Next to the German institutional environment, some of the blockholders studied in the present thesis are also affected by two contemporary regulatory developments within the European Union. The first development refers to two Green Papers and an action plan published by the European Commission on corporate governance. The second refers to the already implemented directive on AIFMs. Both regulatory developments have been shown to be subject to some questionable aspects and propositions. These constitute issues for empirical research which the present thesis aims to address.

3 Monitoring by a Blockholder

This chapter enlarges upon monitoring by a blockholder. Since its feasibility and relevance in the German context have already been clarified above, this chapter aims to investigate the functioning of blockholder monitoring. Therefore, section 3.1 covers the traditional definition of blockholder monitoring. As this definition suffers from a number of deficiencies, section 3.2 introduces a new, revised definition of monitoring. Section 3.3 contains a survey of the empirical evidence on monitoring by a blockholder which is followed by a résumé in section 3.4.

3.1 Traditional Definition of Monitoring

Section 3.1.1 begins with a description of the general functioning of monitoring according to the traditional corporate governance perspective.[963] Next to the monitoring instruments granted by legislation,[964] a blockholder has a number of informal mechanisms at its disposal to monitor corporate management. These mechanisms are described in section 3.1.2. Leaving opportunism by the shareholder(s) aside, monitoring comes with a number of costs. These costs of monitoring, together with its benefits, are presented in section 3.1.3.

3.1.1 General Functioning of Monitoring

Any description of the functioning of blockholder monitoring should start with a clarification of why monitoring is necessary in the first place. As explained in section 2.1.2, the separation of ownership and control within publicly-traded firms gives rise to an agency conflict within the relationship between managers and shareholders. In particular, a manager owning less than 100% of the firm's share capital has the incentive to pursue his self-interest. Thereby, he will consciously accept that his decisions are in conflict with the interest of and thus detrimental to shareholders.

The manager's pursuance of private benefits at the expense of shareholders is made possible by the preponderance of dispersed ownership.[965] In this case, each shareholder owns only a miniscule share of the voting and cash flow rights. Due to their tiny ownership, shareholders have little incentives to devote their time and effort to monitor and take actions against firm management. Since the benefits from monitoring are proportionate to the shareholdings, a small monitoring shareholder receives only a small portion of the benefits arising from its monitoring efforts. In contrast, it defrays all monitoring costs, resulting in an unfavorable cost-benefit ratio. Moreover, since the benefits from their monitoring are non-excludable,[966] these benefits are enjoyed also by the non-monitoring shareholders that can free-ride on the

[963] The traditional governance perspective focuses on the mitigation of the manager-shareholder agency conflict and is based on the corresponding assumptions of agency theory. See sections 2.1.1 and 2.1.2.

[964] See section 2.2.3.2 for an overview of the rights provided to shareholders with different ownership levels.

[965] For the sake of the argument, the following presumes a model of the firm as being owned by a large number of shareholders, each owning a tiny fraction of the firm's stock. According to Becht et al. (2005): 11, there are three reasons for dispersed ownership. First, the personal wealth of individual investors might be small relative to the required ownership. Second, investors may want to diversify their risk. Third, the investor might have liquidity concerns: a larger share might be more difficult to sell on the secondary market.

[966] See e.g. Allen/Gale (1995): 2511; Molho (1997): 124; Douma/George/Kabir (2006): 639.

efforts of the monitoring shareholder.[967] Consequently, for a small shareholder it is rational to not vote at all, thereby forgoing the opportunity to monitor firm management.[968] This results in an "under-provisioning of monitoring activities".[969] Therefore, firms with a dispersed ownership structure are said to be subject to the free-rider problem[970] or collective action problem[971]. Even if the benefits from monitoring would be sufficient to provide adequate incentives, small atomistic shareholders rationally recognize their inability to affect the outcome of the firm's voting processes.[972] Due to this futility of monitoring, "passivity serves each shareholder's self-interest, even if monitoring promises gains to shareholders as a group."[973] Consequently, a firm's shareholders choose rational apathy in the case of dispersed ownership.[974]

Hence, the separation of ownership and control does not represent the sole cause of managerial agency problems. Another reason constitutes an atomistic ownership structure and the resulting free-rider problem, which allows the managers to opportunistically pursue a firm strategy detrimental to shareholders without the risk of being punished.[975] Large shareholders with a significant and constant level of ownership are regarded as being able to solve both problems underlying rational apathy, namely the lack of incentive and the lack of power.[976]

The **incentive** to engage in monitoring depends on the outcome of a cost-benefit analysis.[977] A rational shareholder is willing to expend the effort necessary to monitor firm management only if the expected benefits of doing so outweigh the costs.[978] Ceteris paribus, the expected benefits from monitoring are a function of the probability of success and the particular issue at hand.[979] Most important, the benefits depend on the shareholder's cash flow rights which determine the extent to which the shareholder benefits from increased firm performance and stock prices that result from monitoring. In contrast to dispersed shareholders, shareholders

---

967 See e.g. Easterbrook (1984): 653; Admati/Pfleiderer/Zechner (1994): 1100; Halpern (1999): 18; Ang et al. (2000): 84; Noe (2002): 289; Gillan/Starks (2003): 6.

968 Rather, shareholders may adopt a simple rule of thumb such as "always vote with management". See Black (1990): 527; Black (1992b): 21.

969 Konijn et al. (2011): 1330f.

970 The term "free-rider problem" was coined by Grossman/Hart (1980): 43.

971 See for example Easterbrook (1984): 653; Brickley/Lease/Smith Jr. (1988): 268; Pound (1988): 242; Allen/Gale (1995): 2511; Molho (1997): 123; Seger (1997): 38; Witt (2003): 23; van der Elst (2011): 9.

972 See Brickley et al. (1988): 268; Pound (1988): 242; Bebchuk/Kahan (1990): 1080; Zeckhauser/Pound (1990): 149.

973 Black (1992b): 19. See also Black (1992a): 813; Shleifer/Vishny (1997): 764.

974 See Black (1992a): 821; Black (1992b): 21; Simon/Zetzsche (2010): 921. This problem has also been realized within the property rights theory. The "attenuation of the stockholders' property rights" (Furubotn/Pejovich (1972): 1149) is assumed to originate from the shareholders' costs of detecting and policing adverse managerial behavior as well as from an inability to enforce wealth maximization.

975 See Seger (1997): 38; van der Elst/Vermeulen (2011): 9. Due to this, an opportunistic management of firms with a dispersed ownership structure has an incentive to ensure that the voting rights associated with the shares remain dispersed and hence ineffective. See Hellwig (2000): 109.

976 See e.g. Shleifer/Vishny (1986): 463; Zeckhauser/Pound (1990): 149; Black (1992a): 823; Shleifer/Vishny (1997): 753f; Thomsen/Pedersen (2000): 691; Yafeh/Yosha (2003): 128; Kim et al. (2007): 862; Ruiz-Mallorquí/Santana-Martín (2011): 119.

977 Admati et al. (1994): 1101f note that a blockholder, through its monitoring, provides a public good, as it cannot exclude other shareholders from taking a pro rate share. However, it incurs private costs in the provision of this good. Hence, the blockholder chooses a level of monitoring dependent on the costs and benefits of the respective type of monitoring. See also Bainbridge (2012): 245.

978 See Pozen (1994): 140f; Smith (1996): 229; Gompers/Metrick (1998): 20; Bainbridge (2012): 238.

979 See Pozen (1994): 141.

with a larger stake in the firm internalize more of the resultant benefits and are therefore better able to offset the monitoring costs.[980] These costs vary with the availability of information, the costs of collecting information, and with the type of monitoring mechanism used. With regard to the availability and costs of collecting information, a large shareholder may have access to information not accessible to small shareholders, which it receives through a direct transmission from the firm's management.[981] Moreover, larger shareholders have incentives to develop specialized expertise in making investments and in monitoring their success.[982] Furthermore, once the shareholder is actively involved, the resulting detailed knowledge of managerial activities significantly reduces the monitoring costs arising from the evaluation of managerial performance relative to the monitoring costs within a widely-held firm.[983] Finally, the ownership size may affect the type of monitoring mechanism used: the management's willingness to directly negotiate with a shareholder should rise with growing ownership of the shareholder.

Similar to the incentive, also the **power** necessary to effectively and intensely monitor firm management increases with growing ownership. First, larger ownership raises the probability that the blockholder has a decisive vote on the firm's AGM, by reaching the necessary control thresholds.[984] Second, larger ownership also constitutes a more credible threat to a firm's management and therefore enables the larger shareholder to complement the monitoring mechanisms provided by law with alternative monitoring mechanisms.[985] Armed with these two mechanisms, a large shareholder is provided with sufficient power to monitor management and gain its attention.

Consequently, a large shareholder may be able to overcome the problem of rational apathy by virtue of the size of its ownership.[986] With growing ownership, both the shareholder's gains from and the probability of a favored voting outcome increase, which raises its incentive to actively monitor firm management. Corporate governance research defines this monitoring as *"any activity undertaken by the principal(s) to limit the actions of the agent that diverge from the principal's interests"*[987]. This definition has three implications. First, monitoring does not necessarily have to be performed by a single principal (shareholder), but can also be done by multiple principals (shareholders). Second, the definition does not specify a certain type of monitoring but regards monitoring as "any activity" used to limit the actions of the agent (management). Third, by using the singular form "principal's interest", the definition implicitly treats the principals (shareholders) as a homogenous group and assumes goal congruence within this group.[988] Taking the agency-theoretic assumption as a basis, this goal constitutes

980 See Gillan/Starks (2000): 279; Edwards/Weichenrieder (2004): 144.
981 See DeMott (1998): 328. As noted before, the favorable treatment of some shareholders is illegal by law.
982 See Bainbridge (2005): 10.
983 See Amihud/Lev (1981): 609f.
984 See Black (1992a): 822. These thresholds are outlined in section 2.2.3.2.
985 Please see section 3.1.2 for details on the alternative monitoring mechanisms. The mechanisms granted by law have been described in section 2.2.3.2.
986 See Emmons/Schmid (1998): 30; Gorton/Schmid (2000): 48.
987 Brickley et al. (1988): 285.
988 This goal congruence is also assumed in cases where multiple principals engage in monitoring.

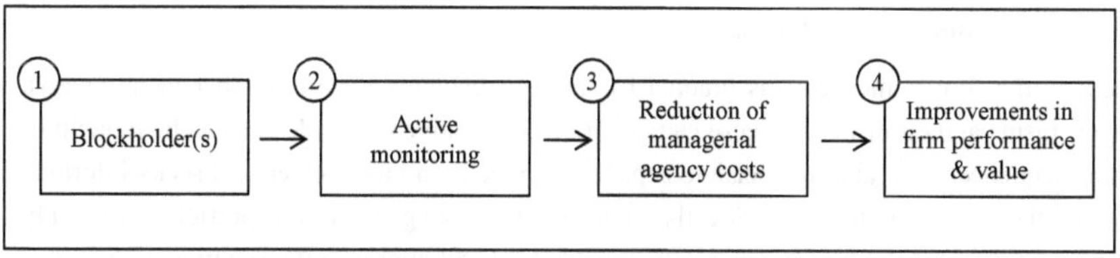

Figure 8: Functioning of blockholder monitoring

the maximization of shareholder value.[989] Thus, the definition stipulates shareholder value as the principals' single interest and consequently also as the ultimate managerial goal.[990] Presuming goal congruence, the definition further implies that the monitoring principal(s) (shareholder(s)) always monitor in the interest of the remaining principals (shareholders).

Next to this broad monitoring definition, a number of more narrow definitions exist. For example, *Rose/Sharfman* (2013) define shareholder activism as "any action(s) of any shareholder or shareholder group with the purpose of bringing about change within a public company without trying to gain control."[991] More specifically, *Sunder/Sunder/Wongsunwai* (2011) define activism as "an exercise of control rights by equity investors, aimed at effecting change in the targeted firm in order to address an underlying problem within the firm which has resulted in an undervalued firm."[992] *Edmans* (2014) recognizes that intervention results in costs for the activist shareholder. According to the author, "intervention encompasses any action that an investor can undertake, that improves firm value but is personally costly to the investor."[993] The European Commission defines shareholder engagement as "actively monitoring companies, engaging in a dialogue with the company's board, and using shareholder rights, including voting and cooperation with other shareholders, if need be to improve the governance of the investee company in the interests of long-term value creation."[994]

The general functioning of blockholder monitoring is summarized in figure 8. The large ownership provides a blockholder (1) with the incentive and power to monitor (2). The presence of a monitoring blockholder constrains the opportunistic manager's discretion and increases the risk of being detected. The higher probability of being detected translates into higher costs of opportunistic managerial behavior which reduces the general attractiveness of such behavior and thereby mitigates managerial agency problems and the resulting agency costs (3).[995] As a consequence, the presence of a monitoring blockholder is assumed to positively affect firm performance and value (4).[996] The monitoring mechanisms used to constrain managerial discretion are described in the following section.

989 Please see section 2.1.2 for details on the utility function of shareholders.
990 Also Maug (1998): 66 regards monitoring as "a comprehensive label for all value-enhancing activities".
991 Rose/Sharfman (2013): 3.
992 Sunder/Sunder/Wongsunwai (2011): 25.
993 Edmans (2014): 4. Further definitions are provided by Black (1990): 522; Smith (1996): 227; Ryan/Schneider (2002): 555; Stadler (2010): 12.
994 European Commission (2011a): 11.
995 Note that effective monitoring by the principal(s) does not affect the utility functions of management. Therefore, the incentives of the agent are only aligned with those of the principal(s) to the extent that any non-obedience by the agent will result in the agent's punishment by the principal(s). See Wolf (1999): 39.
996 For a detailed description of the benefits (and costs) of blockholder monitoring, please see section 3.1.3.

3.1.2 Monitoring Mechanisms

Next to the formal mechanisms granted by law, shareholders have a number of alternative mechanisms at their disposal. These can either be cooperative or hostile and can be thought of as a "sequence of escalating decision steps"[997]: Typically, a blockholder first seeks informal, behind-the-scenes influence via directly contacting the management of its portfolio firm. Only if management resists the agreement, the blockholder will approach the supervisory board or use other (public) voice options.[998] However, public voice options are considered to be "a last resort"[999], as they may result in entrenched positions and damage the relationship between blockholder and management.[1000] In addition to the voice option, a blockholder also has an exit option. Both options are described in the following.[1001]

The first **voice option** constitutes informal influences, also called "informal jawboning"[1002]. In this case, the monitoring blockholder directly and informally contacts firm management to obtain financial information, communicate its dissatisfaction with decisions taken by the management, propose improvements, and negotiate compromises with the management.[1003] Alternatively, a management that is aware of the substantial power of its blockholder frequently informs this blockholder on business issues and takes actions that comply with the expectations of the blockholder.[1004] The use of informal influences is especially common when long-term relationships exist between the blockholder and its portfolio firm.[1005] This monitoring mechanism also provides an advantage for management. If management adapts its decisions to the interest of the blockholder, it does not lose its face and avoids public criticism.[1006] *Becht et al.* (2008) conduct a clinical study of active monitoring by the Hermes UK Fund and find that private and informal influences are most predominantly used for active monitoring, which involves multiple meetings and phone calls with members of the firms' management and supervisory boards. The fund also privately contacts other shareholders to communicate their monitoring objectives and generate support for these objectives.[1007] The effectiveness of such influences depends on the blockholder's power, the credibility of the threat and on the discernment of management.[1008] Only if activism via informal influences fails, public initiatives will be taken by the monitoring shareholder.[1009] In line with this,

[997] Gantchev (2013): 611.

[998] See Black (1998): 6; Ryan/Schneider (2002): 555.

[999] Ryan/Schneider (2002): 555.

[1000] Public voice options also cause more costs for the blockholder. See also Armour/Cheffins (2009): 6.

[1001] A blockholder dissatisfied with a firm's performance has a third option, namely to hold its shares and do nothing. As this behavior is not consistent with blockholder monitoring, it is not covered in this thesis.

[1002] Pozen (1994): 146; Edmans (2014): 6. Based on a survey of ten supervisory board members and ten investor relation officers, this is the most frequently used measure. See Nix/Chen (2013): 140f, 193f.

[1003] See Black (1992a): 817, 847; Allen/Bernardo/Welch (2000): 2511; MacNeil (2010): 426; van der Elst/Vermeulen (2011): 2. This can be done, inter alia, via one-on-one meetings, investor relation conferences, and road shows.

[1004] See Connelly et al. (2010): 1562, 1573. Note that the transfer of private information is illegal. See §§ 12-14 WpHG.

[1005] See Seger (1997): 76.

[1006] See also Gottschlich (1996): 276.

[1007] See Becht et al. (2008): 3095f.

[1008] See Gottschlich (1996): 276.

[1009] See MacNeil (2010): 426.

Thamm/Schiereck (2014) find that in more than 75% of the cases, the activist investor remains unnoticed by the capital markets and the general public.[1010] Similarly, *Gillan/Starks* (2003) argue that much activism will be conducted in private meetings of blockholder representatives and management. Hence, conflicts that are decided in public may be only those for which no solution has been found in prior informal meetings.[1011]

If monitoring through informal influences has been ineffective, it can hint at problems or managerial inefficiencies through its influence on the supervisory board. [1012] This can be done either straightforwardly during a meeting of the supervisory board or inconspicuously. In the latter case, a blockholder representative on the supervisory board may approach management to express concern or show displeasure about certain decisions. In the former case, the representative secures support of the remaining supervisory board members to increase the pressure on firm management. Even if the blockholder is not directly or indirectly represented on the firm's supervisory board, it can contact one of the shareholder representatives within the board and vent its displeasure.

In addition, the blockholder can exercise its legal rights provided by law. In particular, this refers to the shareholders' right to vote on the firm's AGM, to decide on items on the agenda of the AGM or to call an extraordinary AGM. As illustrated in section 2.2.3.2, depending on the size of its ownership, the blockholder can also refuse to ratify the acts of an individual member of the management or supervisory board, block important decisions or change the composition of the supervisory board.

The activism exerted on the firm's AGM may be complemented by activism via media. This involves hostile media campaigns[1013] to publicly denounce managerial behavior and/or decisions or to lobby other shareholders and the public interest prior to an AGM. The increased public attention significantly increases the pressure on management if it cannot provide a convincing reason for a particular type of behavior or decision. A hostile media campaign also simultaneously acts as a strong signal of management's unwillingness to accept cooperative attempts of the monitoring blockholder.[1014]

Next to the voice option, a blockholder may also choose the **exit option.**[1015] The threat to exit is interdependent with and enhances the effectiveness of other forms of monitoring, as it constitutes an implicit, continuous disciplinary threat to the firm's management.[1016] Moreover, through the implicit threat to exit, a blockholder might be able to induce efficient investments and to improve firm value even if it is unable to directly intervene with the firm's manage-

---

1010 See Thamm/Schiereck (2014): 21, 24. Similarly, Connelly et al. (2010): 1562, 1573 state that investor activism is not always instantaneously apparent.

1011 See Gillan/Starks (2003): 11f. See also Gillan/Starks (1998): 20.

1012 See Allen et al. (2000): 2511; du Plessis et al. (2012): 336f.

1013 See Connelly et al. (2010): 1571.

1014 See Prevost/Rao (2000): 177f.

1015 The disposal of shares by dissatisfied investors is also called "vote with their feet" or "Wall Street Rule". For the former, see e.g. Wahal (1996): 20; Gillan/Starks (2003): 5; Parrino/Sias/Starks (2003): 4. For the latter, see e.g. Brickley et al. (1988): 268; Black (1990): 573; Kahn/Winton (1998): 100; Connelly et al. (2010): 1569; Bainbridge (2012): 238.

1016 See Admati/Pfleiderer (2009): 2646, 2676.

ment. In this case, it adds value by an expression of loyalty for fundamentally sound firms that exhibit weak short-term results.[1017] In contrast to a myopic (short-sighted) investor, a blockholder has the incentive to gather information about the firm's fundamental value to understand whether disappointing short-term results stem from mismanagement or long-term investments that pay off in the future. In case of the former, the blockholder benefits from selling its stake, thereby depressing the share price. In case of the latter, the blockholder does not sell its stake, which acts as a signal to other shareholders and mitigates a drop in share price caused by the disappointing results. Thereby, the blockholder incentivizes the management to pursue long-term strategies and prevents an excessive focus on short-term results.[1018]

Even the actual exit of a blockholder might induce significant changes, since it causes selling price pressure and concerns for negative signals conveyed to other investors.[1019] Particularly the negative signal may pose a threat to the firm's management ex post, as it may result in a chain reaction and the divesture by other shareholders. Consequently, the firm will be undervalued and a potential takeover target. Although this mechanism is only conceivable as a last resort, its mere existence increases the blockholder's power ex ante and may obviate an actual disposal of shares.[1020]

In general, the power and effectiveness of using the threat to exit as a form of monitoring relies on the costs to management resulting from the blockholder's potential exit and the credibility of the threat. The former depends on whether managerial compensation is tied to firm's stock price and whether the exit of a blockholder has a negative price impact.[1021] The latter depends on liquid stock markets,[1022] which enable the investor to sell its stake without suffering a substantial drop in share price. The threat to sell shares will be particularly effective if the blockholder menaces to sell its shares to potential raiders.[1023] However, critics question the credibility of the threat to exit. First, assuming an efficient market, the firm's results are immediately incorporated into its stock price. Hence, the blockholder cannot profit from selling as it will fully bear the costs of the depressed share price,[1024] which would not only hurt the firm's management, but also the blockholder itself.[1025] Second, upon the sale of their stakes, blockholders lose their monitoring device.[1026] Finally, *Drukarczyk* (1993) argues that although the sale admittedly depresses the share price, this does not affect the management as long as it does not plan to raise capital externally via the issuance of shares.[1027]

1017 See Edmans (2009): 2485. This loyalty presupposes a long-term oriented investor.

1018 See Edmans (2009): 2481-2483.

1019 Parrino et al. (2003): 37, 42 find that an outsider is more likely to replace the CEO following divestures of institutional investors, which provides evidence that this divesture impacts corporate decision making.

1020 See also Seger (1997): 78 and Edmans (2014): 3f. The latter states that "the threat of intervening or selling may be sufficient to induce managers to maximize value, so that the actual act is not necessary."

1021 See also Admati/Pfleiderer (2009): 2646.

1022 For details on the impact of liquidity on blockholder monitoring, please see section 4.3.3.2.

1023 Shleifer/Vishny (1986): 470f accentuate the role blockholders can play in the facilitation of takeovers. See also Allen et al. (2000): 2511; Bott (2002): 17.

1024 This argument has been brought forward by Edmans (2009): 2497. See also Gillan/Starks (2000): 278.

1025 Therefore, Admati/Pfleiderer (2009): 2677 also require the blockholder to be better informed than other investors, so that the (potential) sale of its shares has a price impact not experienced otherwise.

1026 According to Coffee (1991): 1289, "'exit' may mean less 'voice'."

1027 See Drukarczyk (1993): 442, 625.

3.1.3 Costs and Benefits of Monitoring

Since monitoring by a blockholder provides a number of costs and benefits to the firm's shareholders, the goal of this section is to provide an overview of the monitoring costs and benefits from the perspective of a firm's shareholders.[1028] At the end of this section, some monitoring costs and benefits that accrue exclusively to the monitoring blockholder are presented.

The primary **benefit** [1029] from the blockholder's monitoring constitutes the removal of information asymmetries between the management and the shareholders.[1030] This removal significantly limits the manager's discretion in decision making and increases the possibility of being detected and punished for opportunistic behavior. Thus, managers faced with active monitoring by one or multiple blockholders must confront the possibility of being replaced and thus of losing their private benefits of control. This outlook will create incentives for the management to engage in activities that reduce the probability of being replaced which will be preventive in nature and entail endeavors to generate shareholder support.[1031] This support depends on the shareholders' perceived quality of the existing management which in turn depends on the degree to which it is able to generate value for the shareholders, ceteris paribus. Therefore, management will focus its efforts on the maximization of shareholder value in the hope that it can decrease the probability of being replaced.[1032]

The removal of information asymmetries and the resulting managerial focus on the maximization of shareholder value should ultimately be reflected in a mitigation of adverse managerial behavior. Even if this is not the case, the blockholder is able to scrutinize and effectively assess the decisions of the firm's management. For example, if the management unjustifiably retains cash, the blockholder, being sufficiently informed to assess the firm's cash needs, requests the pay out of any excess cash to shareholders.[1033] This leads to a reduction of the agency costs of free cash flow and raises firm value through greater cash flows that accrue to shareholders.[1034] Similarly, the well-informed blockholder encourages a focused strategy and resists a diversification strategy that is usually favored by management.[1035] In addition, the presence of an informed blockholder benefits the firm's investment program by acting as a signal of managerial quality. Due to its superior information, a blockholder can better judge on the investment program of its portfolio firm than small, uninformed shareholders. If the blockholder recognizes that the current program forgoes short-term results in favor of signifi-

---

1028 Since this discussion is still based on the traditional agency theoretic definition of monitoring, it assumes opportunism only by the agent (the management). Consequently, this section does not incorporate any adverse behavior by the principal. This is accounted for in section 3.2.

1029 The benefits of monitoring may depend on the competencies of the blockholder: in particular, the blockholder's knowledge on how to best maximize firm value needs to be at least as good as the managers'.

1030 See Bhagat et al. (2004): 4.

1031 See also Bebchuk/Kahan (1990): 1101.

1032 However, the firm's management may also be inclined to myopically focus on short-term performance increases to manipulate shareholders' perceptions of its quality. See also Bebchuk/Kahan (1990): 1102f. For more details on the costs of monitoring, please see further below.

1033 See Black (1992a): 838.

1034 See Beiner et al. (2006): 250.

1035 See Amihud/Lev (1981): 615; Black (1992a): 837.

cant long-term payoffs, it will support management in its decision.[1036] This signals the suitability of the investment program and the managerial quality to the remaining shareholders and provides incentives for management to create long-term value also at the expense of short-term payoffs.

A blockholder may also foster improvements in the firm's governance structures which complement its external monitoring and further contribute to greater transparency and a removal of information asymmetries. For example, a blockholder may demand improvements in the supervisory board structure with regard to its independence or qualification, thereby strengthening the supervisory board. The blockholder may also place representatives on the supervisory board.[1037] Moreover, a blockholder has sufficient power and expertise to promote managerial compensation systems that better relate managerial income to long-term performance measures.[1038]

A blockholder's presence may result in additional benefits not directly associated with a reduction of managerial agency costs. For instance, the presence of a particular blockholder may provide a certification effect to the investee firm which might benefit from the blockholder's reputation and the signaling effect associated with the blockholder's equity investment.[1039] Moreover, a sufficiently-sized blockholder frequently contributes strategic or operational know-how, technologies and other resources to its portfolio firms. These resources should enable the portfolio firm to make more informed and therefore better decisions which should be reflected in a higher firm value.[1040]

In general, effective monitoring efforts "forestall managerial opportunism while not inhibiting entrepreneurship in the day-to-day management of the firm."[1041] The reduction of managerial opportunism and inefficiencies is ultimately reflected in a higher firm value. The size of the value increase resulting from monitoring should depend on the extent of managerial mismanagement, ceteris paribus.[1042] Moreover, it should depend on the extent of additional benefits not directly related to an agency cost reduction, such as certification or the provision of resources to the portfolio firm.

As to the **monitoring costs**, the major argument against monitoring focuses on the trade-off between accountability and authority. It is argued that the firms' managers cannot be held accountable without undermining their discretionary authority. The separation of ownership and control is essential as the firm requires a central, autonomous decision-making authority vested with the power of fiat. The corporate form, characterized by this separation of ownership, succeeds because it provides a decision making structure well-suited to manage and operate large businesses. If managerial actions were subject to frequent shareholder review and partic-

---

1036 See Kaplan (1994): 143.
1037 See Black (1992a): 836, 839, 842.
1038 See Black (1992a): 837.
1039 See Claessens/Fan (2002): 80 for a similar argument.
1040 See Seifert et al. (2002): 130f.
1041 Lane et al. (1998): 574.
1042 In addition, the size of the benefits depends on the monitoring intensity and effectiveness. See section 5.2 for hypotheses on factors that have an impact on the intensity and effectiveness of blockholder monitoring.

ipation in decision making, the time and attention of management would shift away from the pursuance of economic benefit for the firm. Even more important, greater shareholder monitoring (accountability) would relocate the authority from the managers to the shareholders which results in the original problem the separation of ownership and control aimed to reduce and sacrifices "the benefits of unrestricted risk sharing and specialization of decision functions."[1043] Thus, the separation of ownership and control has strong efficiency justifications.[1044]

A related cost may result from an over-monitoring of management by the blockholder. In particular, a firm's management, if provided with decision making autonomy, is induced to show initiative, such as searching for new investment opportunities. This managerial initiative is diminished if the ownership structure is concentrated and blockholders are likely to interfere, thereby reducing managerial autonomy.[1045] In addition, concentrated ownership and the resulting continuous threat of intervention creates uncertainty for the manager,[1046] which may lead to a further erosion of managerial initiative.[1047]

As stated above, in the presence of a monitoring blockholder, firm management is incentivized to enhance its perceived quality so as to generate shareholder support and reduce the probability of being replaced. However, if management, as a response to active monitoring and the threat of being replaced, decides to increase its perceived rather than its actual performance, it may excessively focus on short-term results. This can have particular high costs if management forgoes profitable long-term investments to myopically boost short-term performance.[1048]

An additional cost constitutes the reduced liquidity of the firm's shares which does not stem from the blockholder's monitoring itself but rather from the blockholder's large equity investment in the particular firm.[1049] When an investor decides to acquire a large equity stake in a target firm, it thereby reduces the number of shareholders that can engage in the trading of the particular stock, effectively reducing its liquidity.[1050] Since lower liquidity of a stock decreases the price informativeness of equity, it also reduces managerial incentives to maximize firm value.[1051] Thus, blockholder monitoring comes at the expense of a lower price informativeness.

Having described the costs and benefits from the perspective of a firm's remaining shareholders, the following part focuses on monitoring **costs and benefits exclusive to the blockholder**. With regard to the benefits, the blockholder itself profits from an enhanced reputation,

1043 Fama/Jensen (1983b): 306.

1044 For the entire paragraph, see Bainbridge (2012): 238-241. See also Seger (1997): 37.

1045 See Burkart/Gromb/Panunzi (1997): 693f.

1046 See Bebchuk/Kahan (1990): 1104f.

1047 See Edmans (2014): 3.

1048 See Bebchuk/Kahan (1990): 1103. Note that an excessive managerial focus on short-term profits requires the blockholder to have imperfect information about the firm's prospects and investment opportunities. Otherwise, an informed blockholder would prevent an excessive short-term focus.

1049 See Correia da Silva et al. (2004): 15.

1050 See Bolton/Von Thadden (1998): 3.

1051 See Edmans (2014): 12

provided its monitoring indeed results in an improved value of its portfolio firm. Depending on the type of the blockholder, this can have several positive side effects, for example increased capital inflows in the case of an investment firm. With regard to the costs,[1052] a blockholder first suffers from illiquidity, which does not allow the blockholder to quickly buy or sell shares,[1053] or inhibits the efficient incorporation of the value of the blockholder's monitoring into the share price.[1054] Second, through holding a significant stake in a single firm rather than smaller stakes in multiple firms, the blockholder forgoes the benefits of a more diversified portfolio and is significantly exposed to firm-specific risk. Provided the blockholder is not diversified otherwise, it therefore incurs costs of under-diversification.[1055] Third, the blockholder incurs costs that arise during its evaluation of the firm's management and performance and involve the search for the causes of poor performance and possible alternative strategies to the one followed by the underperforming firm. The final costs constitute the costs resulting from the actual blockholder activism. These depend on the monitoring mechanism used and might include the costs associated with the communication with and the vote recruitment of the remaining shareholders, costs of lawyers and consultants or media costs.[1056]

These monitoring costs are private and fully internalized by the blockholder, whereas the aforementioned benefits are shared with the remaining (free-riding) shareholders proportionally.[1057] As a result, the blockholder may use its monitoring for private benefits to offset parts of the free-riding effect of the other shareholders and to ensure an adequate compensation for its costs. Since such a behavior is not considered in the traditional blockholder monitoring definition, it appears to be necessary to develop a revised definition of monitoring. Section 3.2 attempts to provide such a definition.

3.2 Revised Definition of Monitoring

The traditional monitoring definition is based on the classic manager-shareholder agency conflict and the corresponding agency theoretic assumptions. However, some of the assumptions underlying this conflict may not be applicable in the case of a single (or multiple) blockholder(s). As a result, the traditional monitoring definition needs to be adapted to be applicable in the case at hand as well as to incorporate the shareholder-debtholder and principal-principal agency conflicts. Section 3.2.1 begins with a description of the deficiencies of the traditional monitoring definition. Section 3.2.2 then proposes a revised definition of monitoring which remedies these deficiencies and is therefore better suited for the purpose of the thesis at hand.

1052 These costs do not comprise the actual acquisition price of the share block, since it is assumed that the same amount of capital would have been invested by the investor anyway.

1053 See Gompers/Metrick (1998): 30.

1054 For details on the effect of liquidity on blockholder monitoring, please see section 4.3.3.2.

1055 See Gompers/Metrick (1998): 30; Kim et al. (2007): 862; Truong/Heaney (2007): 668. See also Dyck/Zingales (2004b): 541; Armour/Cheffins (2009): 9.

1056 See Armour/Cheffins (2009): 8.

1057 See Shleifer/Vishny (1986): 466; Huddart (1993): 1408; Gantchev (2013): 611.

3.2.1 Deficiencies of the Traditional Definition of Monitoring

The traditional monitoring definition is based on the agency theoretic assumption of differential risk preferences between the managers and the shareholders. As argued in section 2.1.2, agency theoretic literature presumes the manager to be highly risk averse due to its direct undiversified exposure to firm-specific risk. In contrast, shareholders are assumed to be well diversified and therefore less concerned about firm-specific risk. While this assumption may hold for small, individual shareholders, large shareholders might exhibit a similar aversion towards risk as managers. The blockholder's risk aversion can be described as a function of three aspects: the level of its portfolio diversification, the size of its stake in the respective firm, and the level of private benefits it is able to extract from the firm.[1058] In combination, these factors may reduce the blockholders' risk appetite. As a result, one cannot necessarily presume that monitoring by a risk averse blockholder is in the interest of the remaining small, well-diversified and risk neutral shareholders.

The agency literature on the manager-shareholder conflict unanimously regards the maximization of shareholder value as the shareholders' overriding goal and insinuates that blockholder monitoring is driven by "shareholder wealth maximizing goals"[1059]. The assumption that the maximization of firm value constitutes the single goal of shareholders, irrespective of their characteristics or interrelationships might be doubtful, since it presumes that shareholders' interests are exclusively tangible and independent of any environmental circumstances. However, in some situations, a blockholder may derive benefits from goals although they decrease shareholder value.[1060] In fact, large blockholdings might not be motivated by the endeavor to maximize shareholder value but rather by the ability to generate private benefits of control.[1061] Hence, with sufficient ownership, private benefits complement shareholder value as determinants of shareholders' utility function. The blockholder may thus be faced with a choice between the maximization of the value of its (and the remaining shareholders') equity ownership and the pursuance of private benefits.

Based on the assumption of homogenous risk preferences and utility functions, the traditional definition assumes that blockholder monitoring is in the interest of all shareholders. However, given the two previous arguments, this assumption is not a fait accompli. The other side of the coin is that a significant and constant level of ownership indeed provides a blockholder with the incentive and ability to monitor management; this monitoring, however, does not necessarily have to be in the interest of the remaining shareholders.[1062] If one expands the concept of opportunism and also allows for opportunistic behavior by the shareholder(s), a blockholder may indulge the desire to use its superior power and the passivity of the small sharehold-

1058 See John et al. (2008): 1682; Faccio et al. (2011): 3602 and section 2.1.4.2 and 2.1.4.3 for further details.

1059 Smith (1996): 227.

1060 See Anderson/Reeb (2003): 1304. See also Gottschlich (1996): 51-53. The existence of different goals is even more likely when allowing for different types of blockholder.

1061 See also Prowse (1994): 59; Connelly et al. (2010): 1566. The generation of private benefits is attractive, since they do not have to be shared with the remaining shareholders. See also Armour/Cheffins (2009): 10.

1062 This problem has also been recognized by Coffee (1991): 1281; Shleifer/Vishny (1997): 758; Lane et al. (1998): 560f.

ers[1063] to press management to focus on the pursuance of private benefits.[1064] Thereby, the blockholder also accepts potential negative effects for the remaining shareholders resulting from its monitoring.[1065] Even in the absence of opportunism, the monitoring blockholder may regard the generation of private benefits as a compensation for the costs it is exposed to as a result of its readiness to monitor the firm. While the other shareholders do not bear any of these costs, they capture a proportionate part of the gain, for the blockholder is unable to charge.[1066] To ensure an adequate compensation for the costs and risks it faces, the blockholder may therefore engage in the generation of private benefits,[1067] which may negatively affect firm performance and/or shareholder value.[1068] A blockholder's incentive to pursue private benefits depends on the outcome of a cost-benefit analysis, whereby it compares the expected private benefits with the expected costs that result from these private benefits. Thus, whether or not blockholder monitoring is in the interest of the remaining shareholders solely depends on the outcome of this cost-benefit analysis, the blockholder's power, and on the congruence of the blockholder's utility function and risk preferences with those of the other shareholders.

Since the traditional monitoring definition is based on the classic manager-shareholder agency conflict, it naturally disregards the additional agency relationships within the firm that have been described in section 2.1.3 and 2.1.4. Whereas effective monitoring by blockholders may reduce agency costs between management and the monitoring blockholders, it may simultaneously give rise to additional agency conflicts,[1069] because the benefits accruing to the monitoring blockholders may come at the expense of other stakeholders within the firm.[1070] In this case, the negative consequences to other stakeholders are caused unintentionally. However, the concentrated ownership of the monitoring blockholder(s) may also create the incentive to exercise improper influence on the firm's management to intentionally extract benefits at the expense of the remaining stakeholders.[1071] Thus, if the monitoring blockholder's self-interest differs from the interest of the remaining stakeholders, agency conflicts between the parties might arise.[1072] Although there may be more parties affected by the blockholder's monitoring,[1073] the study at hand limits its focus to conflicts of the (monitoring) blockholders with debtholders and with the remaining shareholders. To incorporate these additional agency conflicts, the traditional monitoring definition needs to be adjusted.

1063 See Bhagat/Jefferis Jr. (2002): 24. See also Dahya et al. (2008): 74.

1064 See also Black (1992a): 855; Bebchuk/Roe (1999): 145; Gugler/Yurtoglu (2003): 733; Dahya et al. (2008): 74. The pursuance of private benefits depends on the blockholder's share ownership and the likelihood of the blockholder getting caught and punished. See Morck et al. (2005): 676.

1065 See Andres (2008): 432. See also Lehmann/Frick (2005): 128.

1066 See Zeckhauser/Pound (1990): 156. Therefore, Huddart (1993): 1407 asks: "why would anyone become a large shareholder when small shareholders earn identical returns, need not monitor, and can diversify?"

1067 See Admati et al. (1994): 1125; DeMott (1998): 337. Also Huddart (1993): 1418 states that private returns as a side product of monitoring compensate the blockholder for the free-riding of minority shareholders.

1068 Hence, blockholder monitoring not per se results in the improvements suggested in step 4 of figure 8.

1069 See Anderson et al. (2003): 267; Witt (2003): 35; Kim et al. (2007): 862; Edmans (2014): 3.

1070 See Goergen et al. (2008): 179. Kim et al. (2007): 862 state that "while large owners take governance into their own hands, their governance may not benefit minority shareholders".

1071 The expropriation by blockholders is also referred to as the entrenchment effect of large ownership. See e.g. Claessens/Fan (2002): 76; Edwards/Weichenrieder (2004): 143; Ernst et al. (2005): 30 to name a few.

1072 See Dalziel et al. (2011): 1352.

1073 Other parties include for example the firm's employees, suppliers or consumers.

To conclude, a definition of monitoring for the purpose of the present thesis needs to incorporate the following aspects: (1) with regard to the monitoring blockholder's utility function, the maximization of shareholder value as the general goal of all shareholders is complemented by private benefits of control; (2) opportunistic behavior may be exerted also by shareholder(s) which implies that a monitoring blockholder may force management to focus on the pursuance of the blockholder's self-interest also at the expense of the remaining shareholders; (3) due to the adapted utility function and the allowance for opportunism, the effect of monitoring by the blockholder may also be value deteriorating; and (4) the monitoring blockholder may either consciously or unconsciously affect other parties within the firm and may therefore exacerbate the agency conflict within the respective relationship. The following section presents a revised definition that incorporates these aspects.

3.2.2 Revised Definition of Monitoring

Having clarified the traditional, somewhat idealistic, definition of monitoring and its deficiencies, this section introduces the understanding of (blockholder) monitoring used within the present thesis.

In the existing literature, shareholder monitoring in general can be described as a continuum of response alternatives to firm performance (figure 9).[1074] At the one end, individual shareholders buy and sell shares, thereby actively expressing their opinion on the future prospects of the firm. At the other end, shareholders buy into the firm by means of a (hostile) takeover and initiate substantial changes in the firm's structure. Monitoring by a blockholder lies between these two extremes and can be further distinguished into "defensive" or "offensive" monitoring.[1075] Defensive monitoring occurs when a blockholder with a pre-existing stake continuously monitors the firm's management.[1076] In this case, the key feature is the ownership of a stake in the firm before the blockholder engages in monitoring.[1077] In contrast, offensive monitoring is temporary and occurs when a blockholder purchases a significant stake in a firm with the intention of urging for quick, short-term changes in firm value. The blockholder then sells its shares and benefits from the price differential between the price of the shares before and after its activism.[1078] On the continuum, offensive monitoring can be placed between defensive monitoring and a takeover.

The study at hand examines the effect of defensive, continuous blockholder monitoring,[1079] which – as shown in figure 9 – not only comprises the *supervision* of the firm's processes but also the *active exercise of influence* on firm management. The *supervision* is expected to be continuous and to make managers more sensitive of and responsive to the needs and goals of the monitoring blockholder. The *active exercise of influence* is temporary and occurs only if

1074 See also Gillan/Starks (1998): 2.

1075 See Armour/Cheffins (2009): 2. See also Black (1992b): 21; MacNeil (2010): 224f.

1076 See Armour/Cheffins (2009): 2f.

1077 See MacNeil (2010): 225.

1078 For a similar argumentation, please see Armour/Cheffins (2009): 3; MacNeil (2010): 225.

1079 An effective examination of offensive blockholder monitoring requires an event study methodology and is therefore not part of the empirical research.

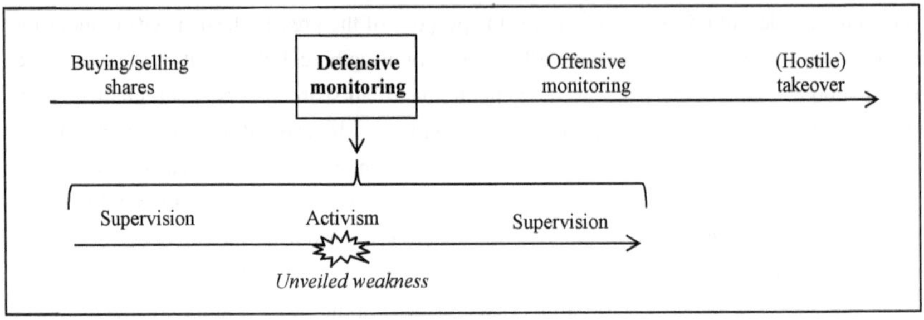

Figure 9: Understanding of blockholder monitoring

the supervision unveils weaknesses that make activism necessary. Thus, blockholder monitoring in this thesis is regarded as an umbrella term, comprising both supervision and activism.

In particular, blockholder monitoring comprises *any activity undertaken by the blockholder(s) to limit actions of the managers that diverge from the self-interest of the monitoring blockholder(s) which may simultaneously influence other agency relationships within the firm.* This definition has a number of implications.

(1) While the revised definition replaces the term "principal(s)" used in the traditional definition by the term "*blockholder(s)*" for illustrative purposes, it retains the (possible) plural form in order to imply that monitoring can be performed by either a single blockholder or a group of blockholders.

(2) Similar to the traditional definition, also the revised definition does not specify a certain type of monitoring. Instead, it regards monitoring as "*any activity*" undertaken by the blockholder to limit the actions of the managers. Within this thesis, these activities can address the following four aspects:[1080] financial aspects, which might involve changes in the capital structure or changes in the level of payouts,[1081] strategic aspects, such as acquisitions or carve-outs of business units, operating aspects, such as operational planning or cost reductions, and governance aspects, such as executive compensation or board composition.[1082]

(3) The use of the notion of "*self-interest*" mirrors the previously mentioned concerns that monitoring by a single blockholder or a group of blockholders does not necessarily have to be in the interest of the remaining stakeholders and "reflects the reality that effective control of a corporation confers the opportunity not only to improve performance and increase value, but also to divert wealth away from shareholders and other groups"[1083]. The conjecture of self-interest as the goal of a monitoring blockholder reflects the altered utility function and illustrates that the ultimate goal of a blockholder does not per se constitute shareholder value max-

1080 Rose/Sharfman (2013): 4 more broadly differentiate between two areas that can become subject to shareholder influence. Performance-driven influence which addresses the firm's strategy and mode of operation and governance-driven influence which seeks changes in a firm's governance structures.

1081 See also Stadler (2010): 88.

1082 See Bebchuk (2013): 1659. See also Stadler (2010): 89. The aspects the monitoring blockholder attempts to influence most likely depend on the blockholder type and its experience and ability.

1083 Dyck/Zingales (2004a): 51.

imization. As a result, blockholder monitoring may not necessarily improve firm performance or firm value.

(4) As has been argued above, the traditional definition focuses on the alignment of managerial actions with the "*principal's interests*". Thereby, it implicitly treats the shareholders as a homogenous group with congruent utility functions and risk preferences. However, based on their different levels of ownership or different identities, shareholders may rather be heterogenous. In order to account for this heterogeneity, the revised definition uses the plural form "blockholder(s)" to clarify that if monitoring is performed by multiple blockholders, this monitoring will also be driven by different blockholder interests. Thereby, it also allows for potential blockholder-blockholder agency conflicts between the (heterogenous) monitoring blockholders.

(5) The traditional definition further implies that the blockholder(s) engaging in monitoring and incurring the resulting costs will act in the interest of the remaining free-riding shareholders. However, as previously mentioned, even in the absence of opportunism, the monitoring blockholder may regard private benefits as a compensation that offsets parts of this free-riding effect. The term "*monitoring blockholder(s)*" used in the revised definition should clarify that monitoring will only be in the (self) interest of those blockholders engaging in monitoring. Whether or not this monitoring will be in the interest of the passive shareholders only depends on the outcome of the monitoring blockholder's (blockholders') cost-benefit analysis, its (their) relative power and the congruence of the monitoring blockholder's (blockholders') goals with those of the passive shareholders.

(6) Blockholder monitoring of firm management may (either intentionally or coincidentally) affect other agency relationships within the firm, since blockholders simultaneously act as agents to the firm's debtholders and remaining shareholders. To the extent to which the monitoring blockholder's (blockholders') self-interest differs from the self-interests of the affected parties, monitoring may aggravate the problems within the remaining agency relationships inherent in a firm. These interdependencies are accounted for in the revised monitoring definition by recognizing that the activity *"may simultaneously influence other agency relationships within the firm"*.[1084]

3.3 Empirical Evidence on the Impact of Blockholder Monitoring

The preceding sections provided a general understanding of blockholder monitoring. Given this theoretical understanding, the following sections comprise a review of the existing empirical literature on the effect of blockholders or concentrated ownership on a number of dependent variables.[1085] Until the mid-1980s, a central premise of the modern financial theory was that ownership of publicly-traded US firms is dispersed. Based on the paper by *Berle/Means* (1932),[1086] the separation of ownership and control has been the dominant para-

---

[1084] It is important to stress that the factors just described constitute risks rather than certainties. Whether or not they will materialize remains to be seen in the empirical analysis of this thesis.

[1085] To highlight the weaknesses of this literature, the review focuses on studies on the effect of ownership concentration or blockholders in general, without accounting for different blockholder characteristics.

[1086] See Berle/Means (2010). It was originally published in 1932 by Harcourt, Brace & World.

digm.[1087] However, in the 1980s, research suggested that ownership in public firms was not as dispersed as had been widely suggested. As a response, researchers began to analyze the impact of concentrated ownership on corporate decisions.[1088] At the beginning, the focus of this research was on the relation between firm value and ownership of managers and non-managers[1089] as well as on the disciplinary force external blockholders and institutional investors exert on the firm's management and the resulting impact on firm value and/or performance.[1090] Since then, the empirical research on ownership concentration has broadened its scope and can today be distinguished into a number of branches. The empirical evidence reviewed in this section can be grouped into studies on the impact of ownership concentration or blockholders on performance (section 3.3.1), target firm characteristics (section 3.3.2), and executive compensation and turnover (section 3.3.3).[1091] Section 3.3.4 summarizes the implications of the empirical evidence. Overall, the goal is to map, assess, and evaluate the existing body of research on blockholder monitoring.[1092]

3.3.1 Impact on Target Firm Performance

One of the first empirical studies on the impact of ownership concentration was provided by *Holderness/Sheehan* (1988). Using a sample of 114 US firms traded on the NYSE or AMEX, they investigate the effect of majority shareholders, defined as individuals or entities owning at least half but less than all of the firm's stock, on their portfolio firms. They find evidence inconsistent with an expropriation of corporate resources by the blockholder. More specifically, they argue that the great persistence of ownership and the survival of firms majority-owned by a blockholder should not be observed in the case of expropriation by blockholders. Additionally, their results suggest no significant differences in firm characteristics (investment policies) and performance (both accounting rates and Tobin's q) between majority-owned and widely-held firms. Hence, they conclude that expropriation does not constitute a motivation for concentrated ownership.[1093] However, this evidence also provides no support for the notion that blockholder monitoring limits managerial discretion and thereby generates benefits relative to firms without a blockholder.

The ineffectiveness of blockholder monitoring is also suggested by the results of *Karpoff/Malatesta/Walkling* (1996), who utilize shareholder-initiated proxy proposals as a meas-

1087 See Bhagat/Jefferis Jr. (2002): 22f.

1088 See Barclay/Holderness (1989): 371f. In 1988, the Journal of Financial Economics published a special issue containing seventeen papers presented at the Conference on the Distribution of Power Among Corporate Managers, Shareholders and Directors. For an overview of the insights from these papers, please see Jensen/Warner (1988).

1089 Among the most popular studies are Demsetz/Lehn (1985); Morck/Shleifer/Vishny (1988); McConnell/Servaes (1990); Stulz (1990); Hermalin/Weisbach (1991).

1090 See Brickley et al. (1988); Holderness/Sheehan (1988); Pound (1988) to name a few.

1091 The perceptive reader will identify relevant papers on the effect of blockholders that are not mentioned in the following part. Therefore, it is important to note that this section only focuses on literature that investigates the effect of ownership concentration or blockholders in general, without differentiating between different types of blockholders or alternative blockholder characteristics. Anyhow, the author apologizes for not considering all relevant papers that are worth mentioning.

1092 According to Tranfield/Denyer/Smart (2003): 208 these are in fact the main goals of literature reviews in management research.

1093 See Holderness/Sheehan (1988): 344f.

ure of shareholder monitoring. For a US sample, they examine the characteristics of firms that become subject to such proposals as well as the proposals' effect on firm performance. With regard to the former, a proposal is more likely at firms with poor performance in terms of market-to-book ratio, operating return on sales and sales growth, which may signal severe managerial agency problems. However, the results provide little evidence that the proposals bring about performance improvements at the targeted firms.[1094] While these results indicate that shareholders become active when faced with poor portfolio firm performance, the effectiveness of this activism is questionable.[1095]

For a sample of US firms, *Bhagat et al.* (2004) examine the performance impact of investors that hold a large share block for a substantial time and actively monitor firm's performance.[1096] Their results are mixed. While the effect on firm performance is positive during the subsample of 1987-1990, they find no significant relationship in the remaining periods. They justify this result with an active takeover market in the period of 1987-1990 during which blockholder monitoring may have helped to prevent value-destroying acquisitions and encouraged restructurings.[1097] Similar to the findings by *Holderness/Sheehan* (1988) and *Karpoff et al.* (1996), however, they also do not find consistent evidence for a beneficial effect of blockholder ownership. Hence, they conclude that their findings "are discouraging for a simplistic theory that large-block shareholders are better monitors and therefore induce better performance"[1098].

While the previous studies fail to provide support for the benefits of blockholder monitoring, there are a number of studies that actually find the presence of blockholders to be detrimental for measures of firm performance and/or value. Using an unbalanced panel of 309 Swedish firms traded on the Stockholm Stock Exchange during 1991-1997, *Cronqvist/Nilsson* (2003) find a robust and significant negative relationship between ownership of the controlling blockholder and firm value as well as operating performance. The authors interpret this as evidence for agency costs of blockholdings.[1099] For a sample of Norwegian firms during the period of 1989-1997, *Bøhren/Ødegaard* (2006) support the negative relationship between concentrated ownership and firm value found by *Cronqvist/Nilsson* (2003). In particular, *Bøhren/Ødegaard* (2006) discover an inverse relationship between ownership concentration, measured by the Herfindahl index, and economic performance, measured by Tobin's q.[1100] According to them, the inverse relationship suggests a dominance of the costs of large owners over their benefits and conclude that these powerful shareholders either do not engage in

1094 See Karpoff/Malatesta/Walkling (1996): 366, 370, 392. Their sample consists of 866 corporate governance proposals at 317 US firms during 1987-1990.

1095 This holds for public and private institutions and individual investors. See Karpoff et al. (1996): 372.

1096 Their sample is based on more than 1,500 US firms during 1983-1995. See Bhagat et al. (2004): 8, 27.

1097 See Bhagat et al. (2004): 28.

1098 Bhagat et al. (2004): 3.

1099 See Cronqvist/Nilsson (2003): 709, 714. They define a controlling shareholder as a shareholder owning at least 25% of the firm's voting rights. Firm value is proxied by Tobin's q, operating performance by the return on assets. See Cronqvist/Nilsson (2003): 701, 704, 711.

1100 In an additional analysis, they find that the firms' market value increases by 0.4% with every percentage point reduction in the ownership concentration. See Bøhren/Ødegaard (2006): 44.

monitoring or their monitoring, if carried out, does not benefit all stakeholders.[1101] Evidence consistent with an expropriation by blockholders is also consistent with Australian evidence. In a study of 316 Australian publicly-listed firms during 2000-2005, *Setia-Atmaja* (2009) finds that closely-held firms significantly underperform widely-held firms in terms of Tobin's q.[1102]

For Germany, *Lehmann/Weigand* (2000), among others, empirically investigate how ownership concentration affects firm profitability (measured by return on total assets) for a sample of 361 firms from the German mining and manufacturing industries.[1103] The authors expect concentrated ownership to positively affect firm profitability through a reduction of information asymmetries both between management and existing shareholders as well as between the firm and external investors in general. However, contrary to this assumption, they find a negative relation between the return on total assets and ownership concentration, which they view as supportive of an inefficient ownership concentration and rent extraction of the blockholder. Hence, they argue that the presence of a blockholder does not inevitably lead to increased profitability but seems to be sub-optimal at least for German firms.[1104]

Bott (2002) uses an event study methodology to examine the stock price reactions following changes in the ownership structure based on two cross-sections of German publicly-traded firms in 1997 and 1999. She documents that the publication of an increase in the concentration of voting rights result in a negative abnormal return.[1105] This finding suggests that the market regards the benefits of blockholder monitoring to be smaller than the costs of a reduced liquidity that results from the increased ownership concentration. Alternatively, the market identifies an exploitation and self-dealing of the blockholder and immediately incorporates the expected costs into the firm's share price.

Broader and hence more representative samples are used by *Thomsen/Pedersen/Kvist* (2006) and *Cziraki/Renneboog/Szilagyi* (2010). For a sample comprised of Anglo-American and Continental European firms during 1990-1998, *Thomsen et al.* (2006) regress the fraction of closely-held shares on Tobin's q. While the relationship is insignificant for Anglo-American firms, the authors discover a negative and significant impact of ownership concentration in Continental European firms. The authors justify the insignificance for Anglo-American firms with the better investor protection in the US and the UK,[1106] which may limit any generation of private benefits by the blockholder. With regard to the European evidence, they conclude

[1101] The authors further distinguish between inside and outside investors and find that the value destruction of ownership concentration in general "may be driven by unique costs of outside as opposed to inside concentration." See Bøhren/Ødegaard (2006): 44. They conclude that shareholder identity matters. The evidence is based on pooled cross section-time series panel data from a sample of all non-financial firms listed on the Oslo Stock Exchange. In 1997, the sample consisted of 217 firms. See Bøhren/Ødegaard (2006): 36.

[1102] See Setia-Atmaja (2009): 699, 701, 706. The author classifies firms as being closely-held whenever a single shareholder controls at least 20% of the voting rights.

[1103] Of the 361 firms, only 183 were officially listed. The remaining firms include non-traded stock corporations as well as limited liability firms and limited commercial partnerships. See Lehmann/Weigand (2000): 165.

[1104] See Lehmann/Weigand (2000): 174, 181, 189f.

[1105] See Bott (2002): 395. In 1997 (1999) the sample comprised 432 (443) firms.

[1106] The results are based on 587 Anglo-American firms (489 from the US, 109 from the UK) and 276 firms from Continental Europe (among these firms are 78 from France and 74 from Germany). See Thomsen et al. (2006): 254, 264.

that firm value rises in response to decreases in ownership because of an "improved liquidity, or weaker entrenchment and fewer private benefits at the expense of minority shareholders."[1107]

Cziraki et al. (2010) examine shareholder proposals as a tool for shareholders to express their dissent and to discipline corporate management for a sample of nine European countries during 1998 and 2008.[1108] Their results reveal that the target firms typically underperform and have low leverage which the authors regard as evidence of the activists being valuable monitors. However, shareholders' proposals that are put to vote at the firms' AGMs cause significantly negative market reactions which are strongest if the target firms have already underperformed previously. These results illustrate that the market does not regard proposals as a valuable control mechanism but rather views it as a negative signal with regard to the firms' governance. Consequently, the authors conclude that shareholder proposals, at least in Europe, are used as "emergency break rather than steering wheel"[1109]. This is consistent with the presumption that public voice options are considered to be a last resort only to be used if management resists an informal agreement.[1110]

3.3.2 Impact on Target Firm Characteristics

Empirical studies on the effect of ownership concentration or blockholders on target firm characteristics can be further distinguished into studies on agency cost proxies and payout policy. This part first reviews studies on agency costs before focusing on the blockholder's impact on payouts.

Denis et al. (1997) provide evidence on the impact of ownership concentration on **agency costs**. They examine the agency cost hypothesis of an excessive corporate diversification based on a cross-sectional sample of 933 US firms in 1984. According to this hypothesis, managers have a preference for diversification as they want to reduce the firm's risk and enhance their power, prestige and status.[1111] The results reveal a strong negative relationship between the level of diversification and ownership of blockholders.[1112] Thus, monitoring through a blockholder appears to be effective in the prevention of value-reducing diversification by the firm's management.

In contrast, concentrated ownership is found to be ineffective in reducing managerial agency problems by *Singh/Davidson III* (2003). Using a sample of 118 US firms in 1992 and 1994, they study the relationship between the ownership structure and agency costs. The authors do not find that the ownership of at least 5% of the firm's equity by outside blockholders in-

1107 Thomsen et al. (2006): 262.

1108 Their sample is based on 290 proposals. Thereof, 195 were submitted in the UK and 95 in Austria, France, Germany, the Netherlands, Norway, Portugal, Russia, and Switzerland. See Cziraki/Renneboog/Szilagyi (2010): 750.

1109 Cziraki et al. (2010): 740f, 772.

1110 See section 3.1.2.

1111 For further details, please see section 2.1.2.

1112 See Denis et al. (1997): 136, 158.

creases the firm's asset utilization or lowers discretionary managerial expenses.[1113] These results are contrary to those found by *Florackis* (2008). Based on a sample of 897 publicly-traded UK firms over the period 1999-2003, he aims to investigate the effectiveness of corporate governance mechanisms in the alleviation of two proxies for agency costs – the asset turnover and the SG&A to sales ratio. The results suggest that the concentration of corporate ownership[1114] is significantly associated with higher asset turnover and lower discretionary spending by management.[1115]

Further evidence on the impact of ownership concentration on (managerial) agency problems is provided by the studies of *Leech/Leahy* (1991), *David et al.* (2001), *Brailsford/Oliver/Pua* (2002) and *Yafeh/Yosha* (2003). *Leech/Leahy* (1991) use a sample of 470 UK-listed firms during 1983-1985 to test the effect of ownership structure on firm behavior. They use various measures of ownership structure and find these measures to be associated with higher sales growth and profit margins.[1116] *David et al.* (2001) assume that activism by blockholders reduces excessive short-termism by management and is associated with a greater focus on the long-term viability of target firms. They investigate their hypothesis using a sample of 73 US firms during 1987-1993. In line with their hypothesis, the authors find that activism is positively associated with R&D spending. This relationship is strongest in firms with favorable growth opportunities, in which increases in R&D spending are most beneficial for firm value. They conclude that the exercise of influence through activism successfully pressures management to focus on the firm's long-term viability.[1117] *Brailsford et al.* (2002) investigate the ability of a firm's ownership structure to explain the cross-sectional variation in its capital structure. They hypothesize that management has a personal interest in low debt levels to avoid the discipline that comes with regular interest payments. However, an effectively monitoring blockholder might use the debt level as a complementary monitoring device. Based on a sample of Australian firms, the authors find a positive impact of blockholdings on the level of debt, suggesting an active monitoring role by the blockholder.[1118] For a sample of 180 listed Japanese firms in 1990, *Yafeh/Yosha* (2003) find that firms with a concentrated ownership structure have lower expenditures on activities offering scope for managerial self dealing, such as advertising, general sales and administrative expenses. They substantiate their findings with an effective monitoring and the resulting limitation of managerial discretion provided by the concentrated ownership structure.[1119]

1113 See Singh/Davidson III (2003): 814. The authors measure asset utilization as the ratio of annual sales to total assets and discretionary managerial expenses as the level of SG&A expenses scaled by assets. See Singh/Davidson III (2003): 798f.

1114 The ownership concentration is measured as the sum of the equity stakes of shareholders greater than 3%. See Florackis (2008): 42.

1115 See Florackis (2008): 48, 53.

1116 See Leech/Leahy (1991): 1434f.

1117 See David et al. (2001): 148, 152f. However, they find that the sole ownership of a stake has no influence on R&D spending, suggesting that passive ownership might not put sufficient pressure on management.

1118 See Brailsford/Oliver/Pua (2002): 3f, 6f, 17, 23. The evidence is based on 49 listed firms during 1989-1995.

1119 See Yafeh/Yosha (2003): 132, 134. The authors measure concentrated ownership as the cumulative percentage held by a firm's ten largest shareholders.

Using a sample of 1,000 US firms during 1974-1980, the study of *Rozeff* (1982) is one of the first to empirically investigate the **payout policy** also from an agency perspective. The author hypothesizes that increased dividends reduce the free cash flow problem and hence managerial agency costs. The results provide evidence consistent with the hypothesis that shareholders call for higher dividends when they own larger stakes in the firm. According to the author, the evidence is in support of the argument that dividends constitute an element of a firm's optimal monitoring package, thereby helping to reduce agency costs.[1120] *Rozeff's* (1982) results are supported by *Renneboog/Szilagyi* (2006). Based on the Dutch stakeholder-oriented governance regime, they use a sample of 150 listed firms during the years 1996-2004 to provide evidence on the substitutability of dividends and shareholder control.[1121] They find no evidence suggesting that dividends and concentrated ownership structures constitute substitutes but argue that dividends are used as complements by blockholders in their effort to reduce agency problems within the firm, being consistent with the study of *Rozeff* (1982).[1122]

Using a sample of 985 UK firms between 1992-1998, *Renneboog/Trojanowski* (2007) examine the relationship between a firm's dividend policy and the voting power enjoyed by its blockholders. They find that the presence of strong blockholders always negatively impacts the payout ratios and weakens the relationship between earnings and dividend payouts. The authors conclude that blockholders "appear to realize that overly generous payout may render the company to be liquidity constrained, and consequently, result in suboptimal investment policy."[1123] Therefore, they forgo dividend payments and allow their portfolio firms to build up financial slack.[1124] From an agency perspective, however, the results of *Renneboog/Trojanowski* (2007) could also be interpreted differently: a powerful blockholder pursues it self-interest and curtails the dividend payments to use the retained earnings for its own private benefits, to the detriment of minority shareholders.

Khan (2006) recognizes the probability that the payout policy can be abused by a blockholder to exploit minority shareholders and provides a different explanation for the detected negative relationship. In particular, she regresses ownership concentration, measured as the sum of the five largest shareholders' ownership, on the level of dividend payments for 330 UK firms in the period of 1985-1997.[1125] She finds a concave relationship turning negative when the ownership concentration exceeds 9.6% and concludes that there is a nonlinear, negative relationship between ownership concentration and dividend payments. According to *Khan* (2006), the findings are consistent with two explanations.[1126] On the one hand, the negative relationship can be supportive of models in which dividends represent a substitute for monitoring by blockholders. On the other hand, it can be supportive of powerful blockholders that engage in

[1120] See Rozeff (1982): 250, 256-258.

[1121] Thereby, the authors control for shareholder power restrictions common in the Dutch governance system. For details, please see Renneboog/Szilagyi (2006): 5f.

[1122] The authors argue for an application of their results also to other stakeholder-oriented governance systems. See Renneboog/Szilagyi (2006): 8, 17.

[1123] Renneboog/Trojanowski (2007): 58. The authors submit that only 6% of the analyzed firms have a majority owner. See Renneboog/Trojanowski (2007): 47f, 57.

[1124] See Renneboog/Trojanowski (2007): 55.

[1125] See Khan (2006): 176, 182.

[1126] See Khan (2006): 173, 186.

self-dealing and use the earnings for their own private benefits rather than distribute them to shareholders.

In contrast to the concave relationship found by *Khan* (2006), *Truong/Heaney* (2007) find a convex relation between the largest shareholdings and dividend payout ratios. Their results suggest that for low ownership, the largest shareholder is negatively related to the dividend payouts; as the ownership increases, the relationship turns positive. According to *Truong/Heaney* (2007), their results reflect the substitution hypothesis: whereas an investor with low ownership engages in active monitoring, reducing the need for additional control mechanism via dividends, an investor with larger ownership and a position to exploit minority shareholders is required to subject itself to additional control via dividend payments.[1127] The evidence of *Truong/Heaney* (2007) supports the finding of *Faccio at al.* (2001). Using a sample of firms from 14 countries for the years 1992-1996, they find that the level of dividend payouts is positively related to the presence of a blockholder. They interpret these results as evidence of blockholders being required to pay higher dividends in order to "offset greater investor concerns about expropriation"[1128].

Further evidence on the use of dividends as a signal by blockholders to minority shareholders is provided by an investigation of the highly concentrated ownership structure of Italian firms. For the period 1999-2004, *De Cesari* (2012) examines whether the payout policy of Italian firms is affected by agency conflicts between the blockholder and the minority shareholders. The author finds that a firm's likelihood of paying dividends decreases with the cash flow stake of the firm's controlling blockholder but increases with the divergence of the blockholder's cash flow and voting rights. In addition, the share of dividend payouts in total payouts – that is dividends and repurchases – is negatively related to the ownership size of the blockholder and positively related to the divergence of cash flow and voting rights. According to the author, this evidence is consistent with a substitution effect. In the presence of a strong monitor whose interests are aligned with minority shareholders, dividends as monitoring mechanism are less important. In contrast, when there is a blockholder with a strong incentive to expropriate minority shareholders, firms tend to pay dividends and prefer dividends over repurchases in order to signal the general unwillingness to expropriate minority shareholders.[1129]

3.3.3 Impact on Executive Compensation and Executive Turnover

As mentioned in section 3.1.3, a blockholder with sufficient power and expertise may promote managerial compensation systems that better relate managerial income to performance measures. This section deals with a few empirical studies that investigate this theoretical relationship.

1127 See Truong/Heaney (2007): 668f. Their evidence is based on a cross-sectional dataset comprising 8,279 firms from 37 countries in 2004.

1128 Faccio et al. (2001): 64. The cross-sectional regressions are based on a sample of 5,897 firms from France, Germany, Hong Kong, Indonesia, Italy, Japan, Malaysia, Philippines, Singapore, South Korea, Spain, Taiwan, Thailand, and the UK. See Faccio et al. (2001): 57f.

1129 See De Cesari (2012): 207f, 210, 215. The evidence is based on a sample of 176 firms listed on the Milan stock exchange during 1999-2004.

Werner/Tosi/Gomez-Mejia (2005) study the effect of ownership structure on the criteria used to determine compensation based on a sample of US firms. Their results reveal that manager-controlled firms decouple incentive compensation from firm performance and focus on a greater linkage of compensation to firm growth. In contrast, in shareholder-controlled firms, compensation is closely tied to measures of firm performance. Hence, when firm management enjoys much discretion, it sets the compensation policy according to its own preferences which constitute a reduction of employment and compensation risk as well as the creation of a harmonious work environment. The authors argue that in the presence of blockholder monitoring, managerial discretion is limited and compensation is set to align management with the goal of maximizing shareholder value.[1130]

Armstrong/Gow/Larcker (2013) examine whether shareholder votes for or against equity pay plans of corporate executives affect firms' future compensation policies. To the authors' surprise, the results provide little evidence that shareholders' voting behavior affects the level and composition of future executive incentive compensation plans. Additional analyses collectively indicate that shareholder voting on equity compensation plans is an ineffective mechanism to influence a firm's incentive compensation policy.[1131]

For Germany, both *Kaplan* (1994) and *Franks/Mayer* (2001) study the effect of blockholdings on the relationship between executive turnover and firm performance. *Kaplan* (1994) investigates the relationship between top executive turnover and firm performance in 42 firms in the 1980s. He finds that turnover of the management board increases significantly with poor stock price performance and earnings losses. In contrast, supervisory board turnover is only significantly related to poor stock price performance. *Kaplan* (1994) also examines whether the turnover differs for firms controlled by large blockholders. He finds insignificant results, indicating that large blockholders do not protect existing management in cases of poor performance. However, the results also provide no support for an effective monitoring by blockholders; in this case, turnover would be more strongly related to firm performance in firms with a large blockholder.[1132] *Franks/Mayer* (2001) study the effect of ownership concentration on the relationship between board turnover and firm performance for a sample of 75 firms during 1989-1994. In general, they find board turnover to be closely related to poor firm performance. The authors suggest that this relationship is likely to be stronger for firms with a concentrated ownership structure, provided concentrated ownership overcomes the free-rider problem.[1133] However, the relationship between turnover and performance is not found to be stronger for firms with concentrated ownership.[1134] Overall, the result of the studies question the added value of concentrated ownership in Germany with regard to an effective managerial compensation.

1130 See Werner/Tosi/Gomez-Mejia (2005): 378-380, 382. The sample constitutes 407 firms during 1997-1998.

1131 See Armstrong/Gow/Larcker (2013): 910-913, 948. The evidence is based on sample of 9,420 votes over the period of 2001-2010.

1132 See Kaplan (1994): 145, 154f.

1133 The free-rider problem, has been described in section 3.1.1.

1134 See Franks/Mayer (2001): 944, 959, 965-968. The relationship is not found to be stronger when control is exerted via a control pyramid or when controlling for family and bank ownership.

3.3.4 Implications of the Empirical Evidence

With regard to the effect of concentrated (blockholder) ownership on firm performance and/or value, the studies reviewed fail to provide support for the presumption that blockholder monitoring is beneficial. Instead, a number of studies find the presence of a blockholder or concentrated ownership to be detrimental for measures of firm performance and/or value. The authors generally regard this evidence as being supportive of an inefficient ownership concentration and rent extraction of a blockholder. In contrast, however, the majority of empirical studies finds concentrated ownership or the presence of a blockholder to be effective in the limitation of managerial discretion as reflected in (1) a prevention of value-reducing diversification, (2) higher asset turnover, and (3) reduced discretionary spending. However, if the presence of a blockholder indeed results in effective monitoring and a reduction in managerial discretion, this should also be reflected in the firm's performance and/or firm value.

Furthermore, studies on the effect of blockholder monitoring on executive compensation and turnover provide evidence inconsistent with effective blockholder monitoring. Most studies find little evidence that shareholders' voting behavior affects the level and composition of future executive incentive compensation plans. In addition, the relationship between executive turnover and firm performance is not stronger for firms with concentrated ownership. However, in case of effective blockholder monitoring, executive turnover should be more strongly related to firm performance in firms with concentrated ownership.

With regard to the evidence on the impact of blockholders on the payout ratio, some studies find a positive effect of blockholders on the dividend payout ratio. The authors argue that dividends are used by effectively monitoring blockholders to reduce managerial agency problems, paying out excess cash to shareholders to constrain managerial discretion and reduce the free cash flow problem. Other studies, however, find that blockholdings are negatively related to the payments of dividends. This might support the hypothesis that a blockholder with sufficient power might use the earnings for its own private benefits, to the detriment of minority shareholders. However, the negative relationship may also be a result of a substitution effect which presumes that dividends are redundant in the presence of an effectively monitoring blockholder.

The review of this literature has two implications. First, given the inconsistent findings, it appears to be necessary to combine measures of agency costs and firm performance and/or value into a single study. Consistent with the theoretical functionality of monitoring highlighted in figure 8, such a study would first clarify the impact of blockholder monitoring on proxies of agency costs within a firm. In a second step, it would investigate whether or not the effect on the agency cost proxies translates into enhanced firm performance and/or value. For example, such a research set-up could clarify if the reductions in managerial discretion and the associated agency costs are not associated with higher firm value because of simultaneous negative effects of blockholder monitoring on other agency conflicts. Moreover, it could provide insight on the value effect of dividend payments by blockholders' portfolio firms to better understand the motives underlying dividend payments. Due to the new insights that could be gained, the study at hand utilizes such a research approach and investigates the impact of blockholders on agency costs and ultimately firm value. The theoretical model is outlined in chapter 5.

The second implication is a direct result of the type of studies reviewed and therefore has been expected. As previously mentioned, the review focused on literature that investigates the effect of ownership concentration or blockholders in general, without differentiating between different types of blockholders or alternative characteristics. Such a lack of differentiation leads to inconsistent results which have also been found by existing literature reviews.[1135] In general, any review on the influence of blockholdings or concentrated ownership does not seem to provide consensus support for an influence of concentrated shareholdings on firm characteristics and firm value. This mixed evidence might be a result of a preponderance of existing empirical studies that amalgamate different forms of blockholder types despite potential differences with regard to their incentives, goals and abilities.[1136] The analysis above illustrates the difficulty of detecting evidence of monitoring when blockholders are treated as a homogenous group of investors – total shareholdings of investors seem to be uninformative.[1137] Thus, any interpretation of the existing evidence on the effect of blockholders on firm characteristics should be made cognizant of the potential weaknesses inherent in large parts of the existing research. Therefore, a more comprehensive perception of the factors that shape blockholders' propensity towards monitoring might enable the refinement of existing studies and help to arrive at more conclusive findings on the impact of blockholders on their portfolio firms.[1138] Due to this, the study at hand accounts for a number of factors that may affect blockholders' monitoring. These factors go beyond the characteristics of the blockholders and generally incorporate potential determinants that are in most cases disregarded within existing empirical studies. They are introduced in chapter 4.

3.4 Résumé

The goal of this chapter was to describe and investigate the functioning of blockholder monitoring. Based on the classic agency theory, section 3.1 showed that a blockholder with sufficient and constant equity ownership has both the incentive and power to effectively monitor firm management and thus overcomes the free-rider problem faced by small shareholders. The mechanisms used to monitor firm management can be thought of as a sequence of decision steps, ranging from informal meetings with firm executives to public voice and exit options. An effective use of these mechanisms by the blockholder constrains managerial discretion, mitigates managerial agency problems and the resulting costs and thereby increases firm value and performance. However, blockholder monitoring comes with a number of costs. Critics argue that a greater shareholder involvement relocates the decision making authority from the managers to the shareholders and therefore creates the original problem the separation of

1135 See e.g. Walsh/Seward (1990): 434; Gillan/Starks (1998): 31; Bhagat/Jefferis Jr. (2002): 20, 28; Dalton et al. (2003): 13f; Beiner et al. (2006): 255; Alonso-Bonis/de Andrés-Alonso (2007): 209; Konijn et al. (2011): 1331. Crespi-Cladera/Renneboog (2003): 18 state that "mere ownership structure does not matter."

1136 See also Bhagat/Jefferis Jr. (2002): 29; Connelly et al. (2010): 1573.

1137 See also Cronqvist/Fahlenbrach (2008): 3973.

1138 This view is also shared by Ryan/Schneider (2002): 554.

ownership and control aimed to reduce. In addition, it has been criticized for eroding managerial initiative and reducing the liquidity of a firm's stock.

Since the traditional definition of blockholder monitoring outlined in section 3.1 is based on the classic agency conflict and the corresponding agency theoretic assumptions, section 3.2 extended this monitoring definition. Based on the weaknesses of the traditional understanding of blockholder monitoring highlighted in section 3.2.1, section 3.2.2 developed a revised definition of blockholder monitoring, that – among others – accounts for possible private benefits of control and opportunism by the blockholder and recognizes a possible effect of blockholder monitoring also on the remaining agency conflicts within the firm.

In order to assess and evaluate the existing body of empirical research on blockholder monitoring in general, section 3.3 summarized the existing empirical literature on the effect of blockholders or concentrated ownership on a number of dependent variables. This review highlighted two implications for the study at hand whose consideration is imperative when examining the influence of blockholders on their portfolio firms. First, it may be necessary to combine measures of agency costs and firm performance and/or value into a single study in order to better understand possible interactions between different agency costs and their impact on firm value. Second, inconsistent evidence provided by studies that focus on blockholders in general might result from their presumption of blockholder homogeneity despite potential differences with regard to their incentives, goals and abilities. Therefore, a more comprehensive recognition of the determinants of blockholder monitoring may provide more conclusive evidence with regard to the impact of blockholders on their portfolio firms.

4 Determinants of Blockholder Monitoring

Following the arguments provided in the résumé of chapter 3, this chapter introduces possible determinants of blockholder monitoring that have frequently been disregarded in existing empirical studies. In general terms, a blockholder's monitoring can be affected by the following factors: blockholder characteristics, blockholders interrelationships, the legal environment, the presence of alternative governance mechanisms, and the characteristics of the respective blockholder's portfolio firm. The goal of the subsequent sections is to provide an overview of these factors. For each factor, the respective section summarizes the theory as well as the empirical evidence with regard to the impact of the factors on blockholder monitoring. These analyses serve as a basis for the construction of the theoretical model and the hypotheses to be developed in chapter 5. Section 4.1 focuses on the blockholder characteristics and section 4.2 on blockholder interrelationships. Since the legal environment, the presence of alternative governance mechanisms, and the firm characteristics do not constitute the focus of the present thesis, the respective factors are pooled in section 4.3. Section 4.4 constitutes the résumé.

4.1 Blockholder Characteristics

A blockholder's monitoring is likely to depend on its individual characteristics which, inter alia, constitute the blockholder's resource endowments and experience in monitoring as well as its ability to exert pressure on firm management. Moreover, they comprise the blockholder's time horizon and the absence of any significant agency conflicts which enables the blockholder to provide a judgment of managerial performance unbiased by present or future business relationships. These characteristics are highly dependent on the size of the blockholder's ownership (section 4.1.1), its presence on the firm's management or supervisory board (section 4.1.2), and its identity (section 4.1.3).

4.1.1 Ownership Size

Among others, larger shareholders should be better able to exert pressure on a firm's management but are also provided with substantial discretion in decision-making. Therefore, the size of the blockholder's equity ownership should constitute an important determinant of blockholder monitoring and represents a distinctive feature of shareholders.[1139]

4.1.1.1 Theory

The size of a blockholder's equity ownership affects both the monitoring feasibility and the blockholder's incentive. A blockholder's incentive to engage in monitoring depends on the outcome of a cost-benefit analysis, involving a comparison of the expected benefits with the costs that result from active monitoring. The monitoring costs are primarily fixed and hence do not increase with growing ownership.[1140] While the net benefit of monitoring is negative for smaller holdings, the monitoring costs can be better distributed with growing ownership,

---

1139 See also Bott (2002): 20.

1140 See also Brennan/Thakor (1990): 995; Bott (2002): 85.

increasing the net benefit of monitoring.[1141] In general, the larger the shareholdings of an investor, the larger will be its financial benefit from any increase in share prices and the smaller are the proportional monitoring costs.[1142] Consequently, above a certain threshold amount of stock, the benefits accruing to the blockholder exceed the costs from its monitoring.[1143] Due to lower relative monitoring costs, shareholders with larger stakes in a firm should in general have a greater incentive to engage in monitoring.[1144]

A blockholder's incentive to engage in monitoring may also stem from the greater exposure to firm-specific risk and a reduced liquidity of its share block. With regard to the former, since the blockholder relinquishes its diversification, it compensates this reduced diversification through an active monitoring of its portfolio firm. With regard to the latter, greater ownership aggravates the sale of the share block, as the blockholder also has to acquiesce greater depreciations in the share price following the announcement of the disposal.[1145] As a result, a dissatisfied blockholder is strongly incentivized to monitor the firm's management, as the alternative of selling the block is not available.[1146]

Next to the incentives, the size of the blockholder's equity share also determines its power and the feasibility of effective managerial monitoring. Since the effectivity of monitoring depends on the blockholder's ability to credibly threaten management, the probability of successful monitoring of the portfolio firm increases with a larger share ownership.[1147] Directly, the larger ownership provides the blockholder with greater voting power on a firm's AGM and hence with a veto right on important corporate decisions.[1148] This direct power translates into an indirect, implicit threat to management which therefore may be more willing to cooperate with the blockholder in private negotiations.[1149]

While the blockholder's equity share and the resulting power increases the feasibility of managerial monitoring in the interest of all shareholders, it also increases its discretion and thus the ability to generate private benefits of control. The large ownership insulates the blockholder from any monitoring by other (larger) shareholders and thereby makes the blockholder incontestable.[1150] The generation of private benefits by a larger blockholder is also called entrenchment hypothesis.[1151] The incentive to pursue private benefits depends on a trade-off between the blockholder's utility associated with self-dealing and the blockholder's loss of wealth associated with the misallocation of resources resulting from the self-dealing. While greater ownership provides the blockholder with the power to generate private benefits in the

1141 See also Kahan/Rock (2007): 1048.
1142 See also Edwards/Weichenrieder (2004): 149; Chen/Harford/Li (2007): 283.
1143 See Huddart (1993): 1412, 1417f.
1144 See Gottschlich (1996): 298; Kahn/Winton (1998): 100; Chen et al. (2007): 283.
1145 See Gottschlich (1996): 90.
1146 For further details on the effect of liquidity on blockholder monitoring, please see section 4.3.3.2.
1147 See Edwards/Weichenrieder (2004): 149.
1148 Please see section 2.2.3.2 for an analysis of the voting rights associated with certain block sizes.
1149 See Ryan/Schneider (2002): 561.
1150 For instance, a blockholder with the supermajority of the shares present at a firm's AGM may decide on important corporate decisions without the possibility of a veto by small shareholders.
1151 See Thomsen/Pedersen (2000): 691; Brailsford et al. (2002): 23; Claessens et al. (2002): 2741; Maury/Pajuste (2005): 1821; Ruiz-Mallorquí/Santana-Martín (2009): 242, to name a few.

first place, it simultaneously increases its exposure to the losses resulting from the generation of private benefits.[1152] In contrast, the gains from the blockholder's adverse behavior remain constant.[1153] Hence, the blockholder's incentive to generate private benefits at the expense of firm value should be lower, the larger the size of its blockholdings.[1154] Consequently, high levels of blockholder ownership improve the alignment of interests between the blockholder and the smaller shareholders and reduce the former's incentives to expropriate the latter.[1155] This is also referred to as convergence-of-interest hypothesis.[1156] To sum up, it may be possible that the blockholder's incentive structure changes as its equity holdings increase,[1157] which is indicative of a non-linear relationship.

4.1.1.2 Empirical Evidence

Existing studies commonly employ a linear specification of blockholder ownership despite little knowledge about the exact functional form of the relationship which might lead to biased estimated coefficients.[1158] Moreover, few studies research the impact of ownership size on the firm independent from blockholder types. Hence, there is no avoiding the fact that this section mixes ownership size with blockholder identities which are described separately in section 4.1.3.

As early as in 1989, *Wruck* analyzed the effect of private equity sales to a single investor or a group of investors. She found the announcement of such a private equity sale to increase shareholder wealth by 4.5%. This increase is positively associated with the change in ownership concentration when the resulting concentration is either high or low. For intermediate levels, the effect is negative.[1159] Consistent with the theory above, *Wruck* (1989) argues that within the intermediate ownership range, the ability of the blockholder to become entrenched possibly outweighs any benefits resulting from the presence of a blockholder. In particular, within this range, it is rational for the blockholder to pursue private benefits of control. *Thomsen/Pedersen* (2000) as well as *Gugler/Yurtoglu* (2003) are unable to detect an intermediate range but find a bell-shaped or inverted u-shaped relationship. *Thomsen/Pedersen* (2000) find a bell-shaped effect of ownership concentration on firm performance and state that greater ownership increases firm performance up to the point of minority control; greater ownership beyond that point has little effect.[1160] *Gugler/Yurtoglu* (2003) investigate the impact of own-

1152 See also Barnea et al. (1985): 75f.
1153 See Ang et al. (2000): 87.
1154 See also Bott (2002): 71.
1155 See Claessens/Fan (2002): 76. Strictly speaking, a larger cash flow ownership does not necessarily align the interests of the blockholder with those of the shareholders. Instead, it increases the costs a blockholder will be exposed to if it engages in expropriation activities that negatively affect firm value.
1156 See, among others, Brailsford et al. (2002): 23; Claessens et al. (2002): 2741; Maury/Pajuste (2005): 1821; Ruiz-Mallorquí/Santana-Martín (2009): 251; Ruiz-Mallorquí/Santana-Martín (2011): 121.
1157 See Bhagat/Jefferis Jr. (2002): 24f; Anderson/Reeb (2003): 1321.
1158 This is also pointed out by Bott (2002): 160. See also Börsch-Supan/Köke (2002): 311f, 315. The authors criticize that quadratic and higher order terms are typically not considered by existing research.
1159 See Wruck (1989): 3-5, 23. The evidence is based on 128 private equity sales during 1979-1985 in the US.
1160 See Thomsen/Pedersen (2000): 699. The authors measure firm performance as the market-to-book value of equity and use a 1990-sample of 435 firms from Austria, Belgium, Denmark, Finland, France, Germany, the United Kingdom, Italy, the Netherlands, Norway, Spain, and Sweden. See Thomsen/Pedersen (2000): 695.

ership on the dividend payout ratio as a proxy for small-large shareholder agency conflicts[1161] and find an inverted u-shaped relationship: The payouts increase with increasing voting rights of the largest blockholder. At a certain size of voting rights, however, the relationship turns negative. The authors argue that the initial positive relationship stems from the rising monitoring ability of the blockholder, limiting the discretion of firm management. As the voting rights increase further, the incentives and ability for self-dealing increase, negatively affecting the small-large shareholder conflict.[1162]

For German publicly-traded firms, *Bott* (2002) conducts an event study to examine the stock price reactions following changes in the ownership structure. She finds that the exceeding of a low ownership threshold of 10% is associated with more positive stock price reactions than the exceeding of a high threshold value (75%). She argues that the market associates small blockholdings with the monitoring hypothesis and large blockholdings with the self-dealing hypothesis.[1163] This evidence is inconsistent with the findings by *Drobetz et al.* (2009). They investigate the determinants of good corporate governance in Germany as measured by a corporate governance index.[1164] Due to the highly concentrated ownership structure in Germany, the authors hypothesize that the ownership structure will have an effect on the adoption of corporate governance rules. Their results document a non-linear relationship between ownership concentration and the corporate governance rating: for an equity ownership below 50%, the impact on the governance rating is negative while it is positive for ownership levels beyond 50% of a firm's equity. The authors regard this as evidence consistent with an entrenchment of blockholders at low to intermediate levels of ownership and with greater blockholder monitoring incentives for high ownership levels.[1165]

Leiber (2008) studies the effect of family ownership on the performance of German firms. Overall, her results illustrate that the higher the family's ownership, the greater the increase in firm performance.[1166] Focusing on a sample of Western European family firms, *Maury* (2006) examines the impact of family ownership and/or control on the performance of their firms. In contrast to *Leiber* (2008), the author finds evidence consistent with a non-monotonic relationship: the positive effect of family involvement tapers off at higher levels of ownership; the effect on firm value is strongest for non-majority family firms. This indicates that the benefits from family entrenchment increase with greater ownership, suggesting a conflict between the family and the remaining shareholders.[1167] This evidence is consistent with the findings of *Anderson/Reeb* (2003). For US family firms, they examine, inter alia, the possibility of nonlinearities between firm performance and the level of family ownership. Their results indeed indicate a non-linear relation between firm performance and family ownership. Specifically,

---

1161 See Gugler/Yurtoglu (2003): 733.

1162 See Gugler/Yurtoglu (2003): 739.

1163 See Bott (2002): 397, 403.

1164 This index is largely based on the components of the German Corporate Governance Code.

1165 See Drobetz et al. (2009): 372f, 378.

1166 See Leiber (2008): 129, 200. The sample used in the analysis comprises both private and public German firms in 1999 (336 firms) and 2004 (558 firms).

1167 See Maury (2006): 322, 324, 333, 339f. The sample comprises 1,672 firms from Austria, Belgium, Finland, France, Germany, Ireland, Italy, Norway, Portugal, Spain, Sweden, Switzerland, and the UK.

using ROA (Tobin's q), family ownership is associated with superior performance relative to non-family firms up to an ownership level of about 60% (31%).[1168]

Focusing on the impact of insider share ownership on the value of the firm, *Morck et al.* (1988) study the effect of shareholdings of the firms' board of directors. Their results are consistent with a non-linear relationship: whereas they find a positive relationship for ownership within the range of 0% and 5%, there is a negative relationship between 5% and 25%. The relationship turns positive again for an ownership beyond the level of 25%. They conclude that the insiders' incentive to maximize firm value versus their own benefits depends on the size of their ownership.[1169] Using a similar methodology, *McConnell/Servaes* (1990) apply quadratic ownership terms and a piece-wise regression approach to determine the relationship between insider ownership and equity value. Their results indicate increases in firm value for ownership levels of up to 40-50% and decreases beyond this level. Hence, these results support both the convergence-of-interest and the entrenchment hypothesis.[1170] Similar results are found by *Hermalin/Weisbach* (1991). Also focusing on the impact of insider ownership on firm performance, the authors find that Tobin's q increases with greater insider ownership for lower ownership levels. However, at levels beyond 20%, insider ownership negatively affects Tobin's q.[1171] These results convey that the insiders' utility function and thus their incentive structure changes with the level of ownership: at higher levels, insiders may become too entrenched and less interested in the goals of the remaining shareholders.

In general, this evidence illustrates the necessity to account for the size of the blockholder's ownership and potential non-linearities. Such an analysis is provided by the present thesis, which accounts for non-linearities through the use of different ownership intervals and quadratic ownership terms.

4.1.2 Management/Supervisory Board Presence

The roles and responsibilities of the management and supervisory board have been extensively outlined in section 2.2.2.1. The representation of a blockholder on either board provides the blockholder with a legitimate influence on the firm and its management. Therefore, the impact of blockholder monitoring on agency costs and firm value may depend on its presence on these boards.[1172]

4.1.2.1 Theory

An involvement of the blockholder in the management board or supervisory board can have three different manifestations.[1173] First, a blockholder can simply influence the criteria a management or supervisory board member should fulfill. For example, it may require more ex-

[1168] See Anderson/Reeb (2003): 1321.
[1169] See Morck et al. (1988): 294-296, 300f, 311f. The authors use a sample of 371 Fortune 500 firms in 1980.
[1170] See McConnell/Servaes (1990): 596, 601, 610.
[1171] See Hermalin/Weisbach (1991): 105f, 111. The authors' evidence is based on a sample of 142 NYSE firms in 1971, 1974, 1977, 1980, and 1983.
[1172] Here, the presence should not be understood as the mere passive presence on the respective board. Rather, it is expected that a blockholder present on the board takes an active role in the monitoring of the firm.
[1173] See also Nix/Chen (2013): 200 for a similar reasoning.

perts or more independent members on the supervisory board. Second, the blockholder can send a representative to the management or supervisory board. This representative is loyal to the blockholder and hence represents the blockholder's interests on the management or supervisory board. Third, the blockholder itself may take a seat on the management or supervisory board. In this case, the blockholder will place one of its employees on the respective board. Such a direct representation may provide the blockholder with the greatest access to information and the strongest influence on corporate decision making.

While a blockholder's presence on its portfolio firm's management board should be less common, supervisory board presence is more frequently used by blockholders to increase their power and ensure that their interests are preserved.[1174] This is due to the fact that the formal influence on management, in particular its appointment and dismissal, is not exercised on the firms' AGMs but assumed by the supervisory board. In addition, the supervisory board sets the compensation of the management board.[1175] Although a blockholder may be able to influence the supervisory board's decisions also without a representation on the board, for example through informal meetings with the shareholder representatives, its presence on the supervisory board may be crucial for a blockholder that aims at credibly threatening the firm's management. Since it provides the blockholder with a legitimate influence on the firm, this may be a valuable complement to informal influences via private meetings. This view is also shared by *Bertrand/Mullainathan* (2001), who argue that a blockholder sitting on the supervisory board can exert control not only via implicit pressure or voting behavior but also with a direct voice in the supervisory board.[1176] In addition, the representation of a blockholder on the supervisory board constitutes "an important source of privileged and valuable information"[1177] and a strong channel for information flow not only from the management to shareholders but also vice versa, which may enable the resolution of conflicts before they actually occur.[1178]

Due to the benefits that come with an involvement of the blockholder in the firm's bodies, *Gottschlich* (1996) argues that activism with the goal of value maximization requires the presence on the supervisory board or at least the involvement in the selection process of supervisory board members.[1179] Based on the same reasoning, *Kehren* (2006) regards the (non-)presence of a blockholder in the firm's bodies as a signal of the activism displayed by this blockholder.[1180] For a blockholder that aims to have an influence on firm decisions, a presence on the firm's boards is indispensable. Hence, all active investors should have an incentive to place a representative on either the management or the supervisory board. Thereby, the

---

1174 Please see section 6.2.3.1 for details.
1175 See also section 2.2.2.1 for further details.
1176 See Bertrand/Mullainathan (2001): 921.
1177 Schmidt (2004): 396.
1178 See Agarwal/Elston (2001): 226.
1179 See Gottschlich (1996): 320. Also Kim et al. (2007): 865 argue that blockholders might place independent directors on the board in order to increase firm value.
1180 See Kehren (2006): 156. Therefore, a representation should be more common in firms with a greater need for oversight, i.e. with larger expected agency costs. See also Bonini et al. (2012): 23.

value of a representative in the supervisory board can be realized with a minority representation only; frequently, it is sufficient to ask the right questions.[1181]

However, from the perspective of the remaining stakeholders, blockholder representation on the firm's bodies may also be disadvantageous, since the blockholder does not necessarily place a representative on the supervisory or management board to more effectively monitor the firm in the interest of all shareholders. A strong supervisory board, endowed with a mandate to monitor the blockholder on behalf of the remaining shareholders, might raise the likelihood of a self-dealing blockholder getting caught and punished and thereby increases the costs of any profit diversion.[1182] Therefore, blockholders seeking private benefits of control may use their power to appoint supervisory or management board members aligned with them.[1183] In addition, the presence on the supervisory or management board and the frequent interaction between the management and the blockholder as a consequence thereof, increases the risk of collusion between the blockholder and the firm's management.[1184]

4.1.2.2 Empirical Evidence

Consistent with superior access to privileged and valuable information resulting from a presence on the firm's bodies, active investors are found to be insensitive to the disclosure quality[1185] of potential portfolio firms. According to *Bushee* (2004), this insensitivity results from the fact that these investors frequently supplement the firm's disclosure with their individual research and are often entitled to a seat on the supervisory board.[1186] For German publicly-traded firms in 2001, *Kehren* (2006) finds this presence on the firm's bodies to depend on the ownership size of the respective blockholder. Blockholders that are present neither in the supervisory nor in the management board have on average the smallest ownership. In addition, nearly 70% of the largest blockholders hold more than one seat in the supervisory or the management board; only 10% of the largest blockholders are not present on their portfolio firm's bodies. Moreover, in univariate regression models of various shareholder power variables on the shareholder's presence on the management or supervisory board, he finds that the voting rights have the largest explanatory power.[1187] These results suggest that blockholders try to complement the power provided by their ownership with a presence on the firm's bodies. Whether this is beneficial for the remaining stakeholders is answered based on a number of different studies.

Bertand/Mullainathan (2001) investigate the pay-performance relationship based on a sample of 792 US firms during 1984-1991. The results indicate that the average firm pays a CEO as

1181 See also Black (1992a): 843.

1182 For a similar argumentation, please see Dahya et al. (2008): 76.

1183 See Kim et al. (2007): 865; Setia-Atmaja (2009): 697. This argument might be of particular relevance in the German context of codetermination: as a self-dealing blockholder cannot replace the employee representatives, it will have a greater incentive to place representatives on the remaining portion of the board.

1184 Although Seger (1997): 108 focuses only on banks, he also states that their presence on the firm's boards fosters collusion between the bank and the firm.

1185 The disclosure quality is measured by the security analysts' ratings from the Association for Investment Management and Research (AIMR). For more details, please see Bushee (2004): 33.

1186 See Bushee (2004): 33.

1187 See Kehren (2006): 158f, 162.

much for observable luck[1188] as it does for an overall movement in performance. The authors hypothesize that firms with better governance structures pay less for observable luck relative to the total compensation. This is corroborated by the results which document that the pay for luck significantly decreases in the presence of a blockholder. This effect is amplified by the blockholder's presence on the board, suggesting an enhanced monitoring ability as a result of board representation.[1189]

However, board representation may lower the blockholder's monitoring incentive if it results in a collusion with the firm's management. *Gordon/Pound* (1993) use the 1990 proxy season in the US to explore the impact of the information and ownership structure on voting outcomes on shareholder-sponsored proposals to change a firm's governance structure. Their results depict, inter alia, a negative relation between the percentage of votes in favor of the proposals and blockholder representation on the board of directors. Hence, the results support the hypothesis that blockholders with a board representation are strategically aligned with corporate management. This is confirmed by the fact that blockholders without board representation oppose the management position.[1190]

Ascribing opportunistic behavior to the blockholder, *Dahya et al.* (2008) use data on 799 firms from 22 countries to investigate the ability of an independent board to increase firm value in the presence of a dominant blockholder. They hypothesize that an independent board with sufficient power to monitor the dominant blockholder can limit its ability to divert resources from the firm, resulting in a higher firm value. Their results indicate a positive and significant relationship between firm value and the percentage of board members unaffiliated with the firm's dominant shareholder. This relationship is particularly strong in countries with weak shareholder protection. In addition, they find that a higher proportion of independent directors is associated with a reduced frequency of related party transactions.[1191] The results suggest that an independent supervisory board may be able to limit the generation of private benefits in case of an opportunistic blockholder.

These results are in line with the findings of *Kim et al.* (2007) and *Setia-Atmaja* (2009). *Kim et al.* (2007) examine the relation between minority shareholder protection laws, ownership concentration, and board of director independence for 229 firms from 14 European countries in 2000. They find board independence and ownership concentration to be negatively related, suggesting that blockholders desire inside directors. However, the authors do not explain whether this negative relation is due to blockholders' endeavor to increase the effectiveness of their monitoring or due to their eagerness for greater power and thus better ability to extract private benefits.[1192] In light of the previous findings by *Dahya et al.* (2008), the latter explanation seems to be more reasonable. *Setia-Atmaja* (2009) observes a negative relation between

1188 Bertrand/Mullainathan (2001): 901 define luck as "changes in firm performance that are beyond the CEO's control."
1189 See Bertrand/Mullainathan (2001): 903, 921f, 929.
1190 See Gordon/Pound (1993): 697f, 701f, 715. Their sample comprises 266 proposals.
1191 See Dahya et al. (2008): 73-75, 96. The evidence is based on publicly listed firms from 2002-2004. For a list of the countries used in the study, please see Dahya et al. (2008): 79.
1192 See Kim et al. (2007): 872.

board independence and ownership concentration also for a sample of 316 publicly-listed Australian firms during the period of 2000-2005. In addition, he finds closely-held firms to underperform widely-held firms. Consequently, he argues that the controlling blockholders prefer lower board independence to have more discretion when extracting private benefits. *Setia-Atmaja* (2009) therefore rejects the hypothesis of a substitution of board independence by the monitoring role of a blockholder.[1193]

Overall, the results suggest that a blockholder's presence on a firm's executive bodies may increase its discretion and therefore also its incentive to generate private benefits of control. Accounting for a blockholder's presence on the firm's bodies therefore seems to be imperative for a study on the effect of blockholder monitoring. The presence in general as well as the impact of this presence on blockholder monitoring may also depend on the identity of the blockholder. This is covered next.

4.1.3 Identity

The identity of the blockholder may constitute an important proxy for the blockholder's capability of monitoring, its incentives, and objectives.[1194] In addition, it may affect the way the blockholder engages in monitoring which is most likely reflected in the strategy of the portfolio firm, its capital structure, payouts, and performance.[1195] Moreover, a blockholder's own organizational or ownership structure may affect the intensity and effectiveness of monitoring. For a number of blockholder types, the individuals managing a blockholder might not be those who benefit from active monitoring. If the incentives of the individual that manages the largest blockholder are not linked to the value of the portfolio firm's equity, it has no motive to devote monitoring efforts.[1196] Due to these reasons, *Lehmann/Weigand* (2000) state that "the location of control rights can be a more important determinant of the degree of control exerted by owners than ownership concentration."[1197] Treating blockholders as a homogenous group may therefore miss interesting relationships.[1198] Due to this, the following sections examine four different blockholder types that are observed in German publicly-traded firms and also constitute the blockholder types investigated in the subsequent empirical research, namely families, private equity, institutional and strategic investors. The goal is to highlight each blockholder type's characteristics and their effect on the relationship with the investee firms to lay the ground for the hypotheses development in section 5.2.

1193 See Setia-Atmaja (2009): 695, 698.

1194 See Prowse (1994): 33. See also Renneboog/Trojanowski (2007): 49; Attig et al. (2009): 413; Connelly et al. (2010): 1564.

1195 See Thomsen/Pedersen (2000): 689, 703. Although all blockholders would benefit from increasing share prices, blockholders maintaining additional relationships with the portfolio firm trade off shareholder value against their other goals. Hence, the monitoring of the blockholder depends on the priority it attaches to higher share prices versus other goals, which in turn differs between blockholder types.

1196 See also Edwards/Weichenrieder (2004): 155.

1197 Lehmann/Weigand (2000): 162. Also Cronqvist/Nilsson (2003): 700 state that agency costs "may differ between different categories of controlling owners."

1198 See Edmans (2014): 4.

4.1.3.1 Family

According to *Flören* (2002) a family can be defined as "a social system consisting of individuals, related either by blood, by marriage or by legal adoption, interacting with and influencing the behavior of each other."[1199] Families are associated with unique characteristics. If these are embedded into a business context, they may provide a number of costs and benefits to a family blockholder.

4.1.3.1.1 Theory

Research on family firms is exposed to significant criticism from academics and business professionals, since, to the present day, scholars have had problems in agreeing upon a single, widely-accepted definition.[1200] Popular family firm definitions account for the different means by which a family can influence the family firm. Besides the mere ownership, this influence also comprises family representation on the firm's bodies.[1201] Most frequently, scholars define family firms as those in which a family member is either represented on the board of directors (supervisory board), the management board or in which a family owns at least 5% of the shares.[1202] Thereby, scholars combine the concept of board representation and blockholder identity which makes a separate investigation of these determinants of blockholder monitoring impossible. In contrast, the present thesis defines family firms as those in which the founding family owns at least 5% of the equity. Board presence is controlled for using a separate variable.[1203]

The intertwinement between family and business results in a number of unique attributes[1204] which may provide family firms with potential advantages but also disadvantages relative to nonfamily firms.[1205] The first attribute of families constitutes the provision of patient financial capital. The founder and its descendants are typically characterized by the desire to pass the firm to subsequent generations. Therefore, their primary concern is the long-term survival of their firm.[1206] As a consequence, families and the firms they own adopt a long-term focus and do not push management for short-term results.[1207] This allows the pursuit of long-term strat-

---

1199 Flören (2002): 28.

1200 See Habbershon/Williams (1999): 5. See also Chrisman/Chua/Litz (2003): 470. Common to the numerous definitions is the attempt to distinguish family firms from non-family firms. See Sharma (2004): 3f.

1201 See also Ampenberger (2010): 16.

1202 See e.g. Anderson/Reeb (2003): 1308; Villalonga/Amit (2006): 389; Andres (2008): 435. Ampenberger (2010): 24 requires a minimum ownership of 25%. See Leiber (2008): 16-20, 33-36 and Ampenberger (2010): 19f for an overview of alternative definitions used in the literature.

1203 See section 5.3.2.4 for details. Also Maury (2006): 324 separates family ownership and family representation on the firm's bodies.

1204 According to Chrisman et al. (2003): 470f, the essence of family firms consists of four aspects: (1) the intention to sustain family control, (2) unique, inseparable and synergistic resources and capabilities resulting from the integration of family and business, (3) the family's vision with regard to the generation of transgenerational value creation, and (4) the pursuance of this vision.

1205 See also Mazzi (2011): 179. The unique attributes of family firms can also be called "familiness", defined by Habbershon/Williams (1999): 11 as "the unique bundle of resources a particular firm has because of the systems interaction between the family, its individual members, and the business."

1206 See Ellul et al. (2007): 9.

1207 See Sirmon/Hitt (2003): 343. See also Anderson/Reeb (2003): 1302; Faust et al. (2011): 78; Chen/Qiang/Dai (2013): 1167.

egies that may negatively affect short-term performance but pay out in the long-term.[1208] The families' long-term investment horizon is also manifested through a presence in the firm that frequently spans different generations.[1209] Due to their concern for the survival of their firm, family members – especially the founder – are willing to provide survivability capital which refers to the families' readiness to provide additional private and personal resources[1210] to their firm if deemed necessary. This capital can be regarded as a "safety net"[1211] and might be particularly important during periods of economic downturn or firm-specific crises. It represents an advantage relative to non-family firms, where survivability capital is less likely to occur due to a lack of loyalty and/or long-term commitment with the firm in question.[1212]

The risk aversion typically associated with family firms embodies another family firm attribute and can be regarded as a direct result of the families' concern for the long-term survival of their firms. This survival and the retention of intrafamily relatedness takes precedence over other goals such as the maximization of shareholder value stressed by different shareholder types.[1213] Moreover, the reputation of a family is closely linked to the survival of the firm.[1214] Thus, a strict adherence to shareholder value maximization might not be the primary goal of family firms. They are rather concerned with a complex system of economic and noneconomic goals that transcend a focus on profitability and firm value.[1215] The risk aversion of family firms is amplified by an insufficient diversification of the family. Since it most likely has invested a significant portion of its private wealth into the firm,[1216] most of the family-wealth is tied up in the firm which exposes the members of the family to considerable firm-specific, idiosyncratic risk which other shareholders are able to diversify.[1217] This is why family firms avoid excessive risk taking[1218] and try to build their own diversified portfolio through diversification into unrelated businesses.[1219]

Unique family firm attributes also constitute superior human and social capital relative to non-family firms. With regard to human capital,[1220] their typically early and continuous involvement in the firm enables family members to develop deep, firm-specific, specialized knowledge about the firm's processes and technologies.[1221] Since this knowledge is primarily

---

1208 See Anderson/Reeb (2003): 1306; Sirmon/Hitt (2003): 345.

1209 See Ellul et al. (2007): 9. Empirical evidence on the persistence of family firms based on a comprehensive dataset of German family firms is provided by Nowak/Ehrhardt/Weber (2006): 16f.

1210 These resources could include for example free labor, additional capital or monetary loans. See Sirmon/Hitt (2003): 343.

1211 Sirmon/Hitt (2003): 343, 345.

1212 See Sirmon/Hitt (2003): 343f. However, the authors note that not all family firms have survivability capital.

1213 See Sirmon/Hitt (2003): 341; Ellul et al. (2007): 9. See also Anderson et al. (2003): 264.

1214 See Ellul et al. (2007): 9.

1215 For example, Chrisman et al. (2003): 469 draw a picture of a lifestyle family firm that diverts resources to produce noneconomic benefits.

1216 See Thomsen/Pedersen (2000): 693.

1217 See Nowak et al. (2006): 8; Ellul et al. (2007): 4.

1218 See Ellul et al. (2007): 9.

1219 See Coffee (1986): 20. This motive is similar to the managerial motive for diversification. See section 2.1.2.

1220 Coleman (1988): 100 defines human capital as skills, knowledge, and capabilities acquired by an individual that enable the individual to act in new ways.

1221 See Anderson/Reeb (2003): 1302. See also Leiber (2008): 91.

tacit, it is difficult and costly to develop and to transfer within non-family firms.[1222] The existence of a deep understanding of the firm's processes and technologies is especially pronounced for the founder of the firm. Social capital[1223] refers to the families' own emotional attachment and strong commitment to the firm which enables the families to establish a warm and friendly working environment. As a consequence, families might be better able to stimulate commitment and determination of management and employees relative to non-family firms.[1224] In addition, their long-term involvement enables family firms to better understand, interpret, and assess the actions of management.[1225] The social capital also refers to a family's superior ability to establish valuable business relationships with the various external stakeholders through gaining a good reputation.[1226] This reputation, as well as the long-term involvement of the family may result in superior relationships with external parties such as local governments, suppliers, customers, and capital providers who might therefore be willing to provide special conditions for a family firm.[1227]

Another unique characteristic of family firms constitutes the presence of altruism,[1228] which can have both negative and positive effects.[1229] With regard to the latter, members of the family subordinate their self-interests for the collective good of the family.[1230] In addition, altruism promotes and sustains the family bond and fosters loyalty as well as commitment within the family.[1231] With regard to the former, a family's altruism may cause the family members to be too generous.[1232] This can result in an employment of unqualified family members instead of better qualified external management which limits the scope and effectiveness of the labor market competition as an external corporate governance mechanism.[1233] Moreover, excessive altruism may lead to a decoupling of the agent's (the family member's) employment from performance,[1234] as the perception of executive competencies may be colored by emo-

1222 See Sirmon/Hitt (2003): 341f.

1223 Social capital facilitates productive actions by focusing on relationships among persons and the resources embedded therein. See Coleman (1988): 100. According to Sirmon/Hitt (2003): 342, it is composed of three dimensions: structural (network ties and configuration), cognitive (shared language and narratives) and relational (trust, norms and obligations) dimensions.

1224 See Lehmann/Weigand (2000): 162; Sirmon/Hitt (2003): 342.

1225 See Ampenberger (2010): 46. However, the family shareholder may also take on an omniscient attitude and intervene into the day-to-day decision-making, impeding the management of the firm. See also Lehmann/Weigand (2000): 162.

1226 See also Anderson et al. (2003): 267f; Ellul et al. (2007): 9.

1227 See Anderson/Reeb (2003): 1306. See also Anderson et al. (2003): 267f; Sirmon/Hitt (2003): 342; Ellul et al. (2007): 9.

1228 Altruism is a trait that relates one person's prosperity not only to his own actions but also to the prosperity of those with whom it interacts. See Bergstrom (1995): 75.

1229 See also Ampenberger (2010): 46.

1230 See Sharma (2004): 16.

1231 See Schulze et al. (2001): 102.

1232 See Schulze et al. (2001): 102f.

1233 Therefore, Gomez-Mejia/Nunez-Nickel/Gutierrez (2001): 83 argue that "emotional aspects of the relationship may neutralize mechanisms to reduce agency costs, a situation that is less likely to occur under non-family contracting."

1234 See Gomez-Mejia et al. (2001): 81.

tions.[1235] As a consequence, contracts within family firms are most likely based on emotions and sentiments and therefore depart from economic rationality.[1236]

The presence of altruism is not equally pronounced among the family firms. Rather, the ownership or organizational structure of family firms may also give rise to intra-family conflicts – conflicts between the members of the (founding) family.[1237] In general, one cannot assume that the incentives, desires and objectives of one family member are identical to those of the remaining family members. Divergent interests may be especially pronounced among the descendants of the founder. As a result, family firms may suffer from sibling rivalry and envy.[1238] These intra-family conflicts can have severe consequences on the family firm. First, the firm's governance may be concerned with the settlement of disputes between the family members,[1239] which may distract attention away from the effective and efficient management of the firm's business. Moreover, the divergent interests within the family blockholder may result in heterogenous or conflicting demands on the family firm's management.[1240]

4.1.3.1.2 Empirical Evidence

To ensure comparability with the sections on the other blockholder types, the theoretical part solely focused on the characteristics of families as blockholders and did not account for a family's direct involvement in the firm's bodies. For the same reason, the following section differentiates between three types of family owned firms: (1) founder-controlled firms, if the founder of the firm is still its CEO, (2) descendant-controlled firms, if one of the founder's descendants is the CEO and (3) professionally-managed firms, if the firm is managed by an external manager.[1241]

Anderson/Reeb (2003) were the first to provide large sample evidence on the effect of family ownership on the performance of large public firms in the US.[1242] They detect stronger accounting and market performance for firms with family ownership compared to non-family firms. They further control for the CEO status and find the market performance to be better only in family firms with either the founder or an outside professional manager as the CEO. Descendants of the founder serving as a CEO do not have an effect on market performance. Overall, their results suggest superior firm performance of family firms relative to non-family

1235 See Gomez-Mejia et al. (2001): 81, 84; Chen et al. (2013): 1167. This is also supported by empirical results. The authors find that in family firms, executives are held less accountable for observed results.

1236 See Gomez-Mejia et al. (2001): 82. Therefore, relationships within family firms tend to make interest conflicts "more difficult to resolve due to self-control and other problems engendered by altruism." Schulze et al. (2001): 102.

1237 See Chen et al. (2013): 1166.

1238 See Gomez-Mejia et al. (2001).

1239 See Schulze et al. (2001): 105.

1240 See also Leiber (2008): 82. Rydqvist (1987): 110 argues that although conflicts between family members are likely to arise, they are only seldomly solved by way of voting power or a public power struggle.

1241 For a more complete review of the existing evidence on the impact of family involvement, the interested reader may refer to Leiber (2008): 37-40.

1242 Prior to this, Ang et al. (2000): 97 have provided evidence that firms in which a family is the controlling blockholder exhibit lower managerial agency costs as proxied by the ratio of operating expenses to annual sales. The evidence is based on a sample of 1,709 small, private US family businesses in 1992.

firms if the CEO is a member of the founding family or an outside manager.[1243] In a related study, *Anderson et al.* (2003) find that founding family ownership leads to significantly lower costs of debt financing relative to non-family firms.[1244] Hence, debtholders regard family ownership as an ownership structure that better protects their interests.[1245]

Just as *Anderson/Reeb* (2003), *Villalonga/Amit* (2006) control for family representation in the firms' bodies. Their results indicate that family presence increases Tobin's q only if the founder is still active as either a CEO or chairman of the board. If a descendant of the founder serves as a CEO, the family's presence in the firm negatively affects firm value. The authors conclude that the manager-shareholder conflict in non-family firms is more costly than the conflict between family and non-family shareholders in founder-CEO firms. However, the reverse is true if a descendant serves as a CEO, suggesting an exploitation of minority shareholders by the family and/or the management.[1246]

Also for the US, *Chen et al.* (2013) study the effect of family ownership on the turnover-performance sensitivity of CEOs. They distinguish family firms being run by a member of the founding family, family firms being run by a professional CEO, and non-family firms. They find the turnover-performance sensitivity to be lower for both family firms being run by a member of the family and non-family firms, relative to family firms being run by professional CEOs. This result is consistent with the assumption that family owned firms benefit from valuable monitoring by the respective families.[1247] However, the results also imply that families are reluctant to replace family members following poor firm performance. This reluctance might be the consequence of family altruism. Alternatively, the low sensitivity may be a result of an extraction of private benefits by the CEO on behalf of the remaining family members, who are willing to accept performance declines. In both cases, the result is a conflict of interest between the family and the remaining shareholders.

Maury (2006) and *Thomsen/Pedersen* (2000) provide European evidence. Focusing on a sample of Western European family firms, *Maury* (2006) finds that family firms exhibit a better performance than firms controlled by non-family blockholders. However, this is limited to active family ownership, where the family holds at least one executive position; family ownership itself does not affect the performance relative to non-family ownership.[1248] In contrast to *Maury* (2006), *Thomsen/Pedersen* (2000) do not distinguish between family ownership and active family involvement. Based on a sample of 435 of the largest European firms, they find families to have a significant negative influence on the market-to-book value of their portfolio

[1243] See Anderson/Reeb (2003): 1303, 1308. Their sample comprises 403 S&P 500 firms during 1992-1999.

[1244] This evidence is based on a sample of 252 firms from the Lehman Brothers Index and the S&P 500 over the period of 1993 through 1998. Please see Anderson et al. (2003): 264, 269 for further details.

[1245] This is especially interesting given the fact that the impact of outside blockholders on the costs of debt financing is insignificant. See Anderson et al. (2003): 278.

[1246] See Villalonga/Amit (2006): 386-388, 414f. Their evidence is based on a sample of 508 US firms listed on the Fortune 500 during the years 1994-2000.

[1247] See Chen et al. (2013): 1166-1168, 1173, 1188f. The authors utilize a sample of 1,865 firms in the S&P 1500 Index covering the period 1996-2005.

[1248] See Maury (2006): 322, 324, 339f. The sample comprises 1,672 public firms from Austria, Belgium, Finland, France, Germany, Ireland, Italy, Norway, Portugal, Spain, Sweden, Switzerland, and the UK.

firms. According to the authors, families seem to emphasize nonprofit goals next to profit goals.[1249]

The performance of family firms is also investigated by a number of German studies. Among others, *Ehrhardt/Nowak* (2003) investigate changes in governance following 105 IPOs of German family firms. They find that families maintain a significant stake in the firms even ten years after the IPO and argue that a family's private benefits of control seem to be large enough to justify a partial sale of the firm only.[1250] Furthermore, these firms exhibit a poor post-IPO performance which is regarded as evidence for a maximization of private benefits by the family at the expense of shareholder value.[1251] Using a comprehensive dataset of German family firms extending from 1903 until 2003, *Nowak et al.* (2006) investigate the effect of family ownership on firm performance. Their results document an outperformance of family firms relative to non-family firms in terms of operating performance. However, following the transfer of control from the founding family to subsequent generations, the performance of family firms decreases.[1252] Evidence on lower performance for family firms controlled by descendants is also provided by *Andres* (2008). Based on 275 German listed firms from 1998 to 2004, he finds family ownership to cause stronger accounting-based performance and a higher Tobin's q compared to non-family firms. Moreover, founder-controlled family firms exhibit a better performance than descendant-controlled and professionally-managed firms.[1253] Comparing family blockholders with ownership of alternative blockholder types, he further finds that families add value to a firm "in a way that distinguishes them from all other types of blockholders."[1254]

Using two samples of German family firms in 1999 and 2004, *Leiber* (2008) studies the effect of family ownership and active involvement on the performance of family firms. Overall, her results illustrate a significantly higher performance for family relative to non-family firms. The most important determinant of firm performance constitutes the ownership level: the higher the family's ownership, the greater the increase in firm performance. The results also indicate a positive effect for an active involvement of the family with their firms, measured by a representation in one of the firm's bodies. However, this relationship is non-linear. Up to a certain threshold, which the author is unable to determine, the number of family members represented in the firm's bodies is positively related to performance. This relationship reverses beyond this threshold. Possible explanations may be family opportunism arising from the ex-

---

1249 See Thomsen/Pedersen (2000): 695, 699. Their 1990-1995 sample is based on non-financial firms from Austria, Belgium, Denmark, Finland, France, Germany, the United Kingdom, Italy, the Netherlands, Norway, Spain, and Sweden.

1250 See Ehrhardt/Nowak (2003): 230. Alternatively, the founding-family might be unwilling to sell its ownership completely due to strong emotional attachments to their firms.

1251 Their evidence covers the period during 1970 and 1990. See Ehrhardt/Nowak (2003): 225, 230.

1252 See Nowak et al. (2006): 22, 24. Their data is based on both publicly-traded and private family firms.

1253 See Andres (2008): 439.

1254 Andres (2008): 441. Here, the different definition of family blockholders and the alternative blockholder types should be noted. Please refer to Andres (2008): 435, 441 for details.

cessive family control or an unduly employment of low-qualified family members due to altruism.[1255]

Overall, the unique firm attributes reviewed in section 4.1.3.1.1 apparently translate into superior performance of family firms relative to non-family firms; the corresponding evidence for the US, Europe, and Germany is consistent with an outperformance of family firms. This seems to be the case primarily if a founder is represented on the firms' bodies.

4.1.3.2 Private Equity Investor

Due to their active role in the management of their portfolio firms, private equity firms have faced substantial public antagonism in the past. This active role constitutes one of several characteristics of private equity firms which are reviewed in the following. Due to their similar business models, private equity and venture capital firms are thereby treated as a single blockholder group.[1256]

4.1.3.2.1 Theory

Various types of transactions can be classified under the umbrella term private equity. Common among all these transactions is the fact that the equity capital involved in these transactions has been raised privately.[1257] In addition, it is not used for investments into publicly-traded securities such as bonds.[1258] Instead, in a typical private equity transaction, the private equity firm agrees to acquire a firm, which can be either publicly-traded or private.[1259] To finance investments, the private equity firm periodically raises capital through private equity funds which are typically closed-end funds, providing investors with no possibility to withdraw money for a certain amount of time.[1260] These funds are usually organized as limited partnerships, with the limited partner providing the capital (investors) and the general partners managing the fund (the private equity firm).[1261] In most cases, the general partners provide 1% of the fund's capital themselves. The fund has a fixed lifetime which is generally ten years.[1262] At the end of the fund's contractual lifetime, the private equity firm realizes its return through an exit.[1263] The main source of return represents the capital gain which is the difference between the acquisition price and the disposal price.[1264]

1255 See Leiber (2008): 129, 200-202. The sample used in the analysis comprises both private and public German firms in 1999 (336 firms) and 2004 (558 firms).

1256 Cheffins/Armour (2008): 8 also group venture capital under the umbrella term private equity. See also section 5.3.2.2 for a definition of this blockholder type.

1257 The investors generally comprise high net-worth individuals, investment funds, banks or insurance firms. See Bevilacqua (2006): 107, 110f; Cheffins/Armour (2008): 10; Kaplan/Strömberg (2009): 123.

1258 See Cheffins/Armour (2008): 8.

1259 See Kaplan/Strömberg (2009): 124. See also Watt (2008): 554. In the case of publicly-traded firms, the target is usually taken private and de-listed from the stock market. See Cheffins/Armour (2008): 11.

1260 See Watt (2008): 553.

1261 See Cheffins/Armour (2008): 8; Watt (2008): 549.

1262 However, this period can be extended for up to three additional years, given the consent of the partners. See Cheffins/Armour (2008): 10; Kaplan/Strömberg (2009): 123.

1263 The exit is typically done either via a secondary-sale to a strategic investor or another private equity firm or an IPO. See Watt (2008): 555; Kaplan/Strömberg (2009): 128f.

1264 See Watt (2008): 555.

Since the focus of the present thesis is placed on listed firms, there is the obvious question why private equity firms are also considered as blockholders – there are two factors that justify their inclusion. First, (minority) equity investments made by private equity firms in publicly-traded firms may become more likely, as private equity firms can also add value without having full control over their portfolio firms and might face difficulties in securing financing sources that enable the acquisition of full control.[1265] Consistent with this assumption, *Kroker et al.* (2010) observe the recent trend of investments in listed equity without taking the target firm private.[1266] Second, following the IPO of a portfolio firm, private equity firms frequently retain substantial stakes in order to benefit from further increases in share prices.[1267] As a result, private equity firms also hold stakes in publicly-listed firms.

A key characteristic of private equity investments is an active ownership.[1268] Since their main source of return constitutes the capital gain, the role of private equity firms goes beyond the provision of finance. Rather, they make modifications to their portfolio firms to improve firm operations and create value.[1269] These changes can be grouped into financial, governance, and operational changes.[1270] Among others, the private equity firm creates strong incentives for the portfolio firm's management to maximize firm value.[1271] By providing management with stock options and requiring management to make a direct investment into their firm's equity, they increase both the upside and downside for management which reduces managerial incentives to manipulate short-term performance.[1272] In addition, private equity firms increase the leverage of their portfolio firms, especially if they have used a leveraged buyout. Due to the required regular interest payments, leverage creates pressure on management to operate efficiently and reduces the available cash flow for discretionary managerial spending.[1273] However, excessive use of leverage may also result in significant financial distress costs for the portfolio firm.[1274] These can, for example, materialize in declined capital expenditures which rais-

---

1265 See Kaplan/Strömberg (2009): 143f.

1266 See Kroker et al. (2010): 2. For instance, a private equity investment in a listed German firm that attracted a great deal of attention constituted the 4.39% stake taken by the US private equity investor The Blackstone Group in Deutsche Telekom in April 2006. See Deutsche Telekom (2006): 107.

1267 See also Hochberg (2011): 430. If the particular firm has been part of the private equity firm's portfolio, the private equity firm has strong incentives to install proper governance systems to ensure the preservation of the firm's value until it disposes off all its shares in the former portfolio firm.

1268 According to Bonini et al. (2012): 22, private equity firms engage in "intense pre-investment screening, the development of accurate financing contracts, and continuous post-investment monitoring and advisory."

1269 See Bottazzi/Rin/Hellmann (2008): 489.

1270 See Kaplan/Strömberg (2009): 130. See also Bevilacqua (2006): 110.

1271 Cheffins/Armour (2008): 5 state that managers running portfolio firms of private equity firms "have robust incentives to meet prescribed financial targets".

1272 See Kaplan/Strömberg (2009): 130f, 135. Private equity firms are also actively involved in the firm's governance, typically placing well-experienced representatives on the boards. See Kaplan/Strömberg (2009): 131. Sometimes, the fund's general managers will sit on the board themselves. See Cheffins/Armour (2008): 12; Barthelmess (2010): 140. According to the former, the result is "a more dynamic and challenging boardroom style". Since the presence on the firm's bodies has been described separately in section 4.1.2, this section does not enlarge upon this topic.

1273 See Cheffins/Armour (2008): 12. See also Opler/Titman (1993): 1987f. For empirical evidence on the US, please see Travlos/Cornett (1993): 21f.

1274 See Opler/Titman (1993): 1987f.

es concerns that private equity firms focus on current cash flows at the expense of future cash flows.[1275]

As previously mentioned, private equity funds are typically closed-end funds with a fixed life time of ten years. Therefore, the fund's managers are not evaluated periodically but only at the end of the period. In addition, they are not affected by short-term share redemptions. Consequently, private equity firms are not required to focus on maintaining the liquidity of their investment and therefore assume a long-term investment horizon.[1276] Since their investment is illiquid, a premature exit is usually not possible. Hence, private equity firms are forced to take actions if they are dissatisfied with the portfolio firm's performance.[1277] In addition, their long-term investment horizon favorably affects the portfolio firm's strategy. Due to the "patient capital"[1278], the focal firm is not limited to short-term strategies but can pursue strategies that offer significant long-term benefits by foregoing short-term earnings.[1279] In contrast, *Watt* (2008) criticizes private equity as being "the opposite of 'patient capital'. Results have to be obtained quickly, and companies are not run for any ethical, emotional or other reasons apart from maximizing returns."[1280]

Private equity firms generally employ small teams of professional investment and fund managers as well as personnel with significant operational expertise.[1281] As a result, these firms are highly qualified and experienced in the management of their portfolio firms. Moreover, a private equity firm can utilize its experience gained from other investments and generate economies of scale and scope. For instance, it can transfer key executives between its portfolio firms and thus ensure a transfer of best practices between portfolio firms.[1282] The experience is further enhanced through the private equity funds' frequent specialization on certain industries which results in superior knowledge, expertise, and strong business skills in that particular sector.[1283] This qualifies private equity firms to successfully initiate change among their portfolio firms.[1284] Due to these factors, private equity firms are generally supposed to have superior capabilities with regard to understanding and evaluating their portfolio firms' business environment, the potential opportunities for the improvement of shareholder value as well as with regard to the provision of managerial support and expertise.[1285] In addition, private equity firms are experienced in the handling of other private equity firms that have also

1275 See Kaplan/Strömberg (2009): 133.
1276 See Achleitner et al. (2010): 809; Mietzner/Schweizer (2011): 5. Private equity firms are also termed dedicated institutions, which Bushee (2004): 32 defines as investors taking large, stable ownership positions in their portfolio firms.
1277 See Wright/Robbie (1998): 526.
1278 Connelly et al. (2010): 1572.
1279 See also Connelly et al. (2010): 1572.
1280 Watt (2008): 555. For an overview of the most frequent points of criticism, please see Watt (2008): 557.
1281 See Achleitner et al. (2010): 808f.
1282 See Barthelmess (2010): 153.
1283 See Mietzner/Schweizer (2011): 5.
1284 See Kroker et al. (2010): 2.
1285 See Achleitner et al. (2010): 809; Barthelmess (2010): 135.

invested in a particular portfolio firm, since they frequently combine forces in the acquisition of larger targets.[1286]

As has been outlined above, a private equity firm invests on behalf of its providers of capital. The relationship may thus be subject to agency problems between the investors (principals) and the private equity fund managers (agents)[1287] which may result in a lack of effort exerted by the fund managers and ultimately in a weak portfolio firm and fund performance. However, the existence of agency problems is unlikely. First, the fund's managers usually provide 1% of the fund's capital themselves, which aligns their interests with those of the external investors. Second, a performance-based compensation highly incentivizes fund managers to maximize the returns of their funds.[1288] This compensation consists of up to three components. First, the fund managers earn an annual management fee which equals a percentage[1289] of the capital committed to the respective fund. In addition, upon reaching a certain target, they receive a portion of the fund's profits at the end of the investment period, which typically equals 20%.[1290] Furthermore, some funds charge the investee firms a deal and monitoring fee.[1291] Since a significant portion of the fund managers' compensation depends on performance, they have a direct financial incentive to maximize the value of their portfolio firms.[1292] Moreover, private equity firms calculate their fees based on realized capital gains at the end of the investment period which provides private equity managers with a strong long-term incentive.[1293]

Venture capital represents a specific type of private equity. It may best be differentiated based on the timing of its investment. Venture capital firms primarily invest in young or emerging firms and typically do not acquire a majority stake.[1294] However, due to the convergence of both investor types, a strict differentiation between private equity and venture capital is only hardly possible.[1295] Similar to private equity firms, venture capital firms are extensively involved in the firms they fund, with the activities spanning from monitoring to providing support and governance.[1296] While this provides significant advantages to the portfolio firm, venture capital involvement can also be time consuming for the entrepreneur of the investee

1286 See Cheffins/Armour (2008): 10.

1287 See Wright/Robbie (1998): 533.

1288 See Barthelmess (2010): 121f; Mietzner et al. (2011): 156. The fund's performance is, in turn, strongly linked to the performance of the portfolio firms. See Achleitner et al. (2010): 809.

1289 This percentage typically lies within the range of 1% and 3%. See Cheffins/Armour (2008): 9.

1290 This is also called "carried interest". See Cheffins/Armour (2008): 9; Watt (2008): 553; Kaplan/Strömberg (2009): 123f; Mietzner/Schweizer (2011): 5.

1291 See Kaplan/Strömberg (2009): 123f.

1292 See Cheffins/Armour (2008): 9.

1293 See Mietzner/Schweizer (2011): 3f.

1294 See Kaplan/Strömberg (2009): 121. Wright/Robbie (1998): 521 define venture capital as "the investment by professional investors of long-term, unquoted, risk equity finance in new firms where the primary reward is an eventual capital gain, supplemented by dividend yield." Hellmann/Puri (2000): 968 define venture capitalists as "professional investors who specialize in the financing of young private companies."

1295 See Barthelmess (2010): 8. Wright/Robbie (1998): 523 observe an extension of venture capital firms into a wider range of activities, such as management buy-outs.

1296 See Hellmann/Puri (2000): 959f. See also Wright/Robbie (1998): 525; Dai (2007): 543; Bottazzi et al. (2008): 489.

firm.[1297] In addition, since they focus on young and quickly-growing firms in their start-up phase,[1298] venture capital firms frequently face severe asymmetric information due to the uncertainty with regard to their portfolio firms' business models and profitability.[1299] As a consequence, they have developed expertise and experience in dealing with information asymmetries and can leverage and expand their knowledge when conducting new investments.[1300]

4.1.3.2.2 Empirical Evidence

Empirical research on private equity can be grouped into several categories, investigating among others, (1) the pre- and post-buyout performance of the target, (2) the returns to investors of the private equity firm (i.e. the performance of the fund itself), (3) the returns to the shareholders of the target, and (4) the accounting performance of the target.[1301] Thereby, most literature focuses on pure going private buyouts, wherein the private equity firm acquires either 100% of a private or a publicly-listed target.[1302] Due to this, most of the existing empirical evidence cannot be transferred to the private equity investments the study at hand focuses on. Therefore, the empirical evidence presented in this section only focuses on studies that investigate the effect of private equity investments in listed firms, i.e. those where the targets are not taken private following the private equity investment.

Based on a review of the existing empirical literature on private equity, *Cumming et al.* (2007) conclude that the buyout returns are significantly increased through the adoption of corporate governance mechanisms such as active monitoring by the private equity firm, higher debt levels, and executive compensation based on equity ownership.[1303] Similarly, having reviewed existing evidence on the ability of private equity firms to create value, *Watt* (2008) concludes that it is both theoretically and empirically likely that private equity adds value to the portfolio firms.[1304]

Based on two German samples, *Achleitner et al.* (2010) and *Mietzner et al.* (2011) focus on the characteristics of firms targeted by private equity firms. *Achleitner et al.* (2010) analyze these characteristics to investigate private equity investment motives. They find that private equity investors invest in firms with high agency costs resulting from low managerial ownership and generate value through the alignment of incentives by providing management with greater ownership.[1305] In addition, the targets have low expected financial distress costs and hence are well-suited for leverage increases which are used to discipline corporate management. However, the authors point to potential wealth transfers from debtholders to sharehold-

1297 See Hellmann/Puri (2000): 960.
1298 See Barthelmess (2010): 8.
1299 See Wright/Robbie (1998): 521.
1300 See also Bonini et al. (2012): 22.
1301 For an overview, please see Cumming/Siegel/Wright (2007).
1302 See e.g. Kaplan (1989); Opler/Titman (1993); Cotter/Peck (2001); Renneboog et al. (2007); Kaplan/Strömberg (2009), to name a few.
1303 See Cumming et al. (2007): 445.
1304 See Watt (2008): 559. However, he argues that the sources of these gains are largely unknown.
1305 See Achleitner et al. (2010): 813, 825. The evidence is based on data on 96 hedge fund and 57 private equity targets in Germany within the time period of 1998-2007.

ers and state that this "seems to be the most likely problem"[1306] regarding private equity firms. Overall, they conclude that private equity investors create wealth in the long-run.[1307] *Mietzner et al.* (2011) confirm the finding that private equity targets are well-suited for leverage increases and find evidence that target firms also increase leverage after the private equity investment.[1308]

Evidence on the effect of private equity investments in listed firms is provided by a number of recent studies. *Klein/Zur* (2009) examine confrontational activism[1309] by, among others, private equity, venture capital, and private asset management firms based on a US sample of 154 activist campaigns between 2003 and 2005. The authors document significant abnormal stock returns upon announcement of their proposals; these are sustained in the following year. They suggest that the market expects this activism to create value. The investors are also found to be very successful in enforcing their demands, exhibiting a success rate of 65%. In their activism, the investors focus on changes in performance and significantly cut R&D expenditures relative to comparable firms.[1310]

Using an event study methodology on 48 private equity transactions in Germany from 1998 to 2007,[1311] *Achleitner et al.* (2009) find that the announcement of a private equity transaction results in significant and positive abnormal returns for target shareholders. According to the authors, this evidence is in support of the monitoring hypothesis. In addition, the abnormal return is positively related to the level of free float prior to the acquisition. Hence, in the absence of an existing blockholder, monitoring by the private equity firm is viewed more favorably. The negative relationship between the second largest shareholder's voting rights and the abnormal return further supports this theory.[1312] The monitoring hypothesis found by *Achleitner et al.* (2009) is supported by the findings of *Mietzner et al.* (2011). Based on a German sample of 171 firms in which a private equity investor acquired at least 5% of the voting rights between 1993 and 2009, they find the cumulative abnormal returns for the target firms to be significantly positive. In addition, they investigate the long run buy-and-hold abnormal returns of private equity targets after the investment. Their results document that the target firms outperform the market.[1313] This is in support of superior active monitoring by private equity firms.

The German evidence provided above, however, is not supported by *Kroker et al.* (2010), who use a broader sample of European publicly-listed firms. They also provide evidence on shareholder wealth effects of private equity investments, focusing on the abnormal returns

---

1306 See Achleitner et al. (2010): 826.

1307 See Achleitner et al. (2010): 826.

1308 See Mietzner et al. (2011): 166.

1309 Confrontational activism are instances in which a shareholder acquires at least 5% of the shares and explicitly states its intend to proactively influence the firm and its management. See Klein/Zur (2009): 225.

1310 See Klein/Zur (2009): 187-189; 226.

1311 These transactions involve at least 25% of the firm's outstanding equity. See Achleitner et al. (2009): 12.

1312 See Achleitner et al. (2009): 16f, 19f, 22. The authors also compare the returns to a control sample of 145 purchases by banks, insurance companies, and industrial firms and find that the cumulative abnormal returns for private equity transactions are significantly higher.

1313 The buy-and-hold abnormal returns represent 150-, 200-, 250-, and 300-day holding periods. The CDAX index constitutes the benchmark. See Mietzner et al. (2011): 158, 175.

around the announcement of an investment and their drivers. The authors find a significant positive abnormal return upon the announcement of the private equity investment.[1314] However, these returns are explained by the superior stock-picking rather than monitoring ability of private equity firms: their target firms are undervalued relative to a sample of control firms. Moreover, the results do not suggest that target firms exhibit superior accounting results during the three years following the initial investment. This is inconsistent with the assumption that private equity firms improve the target firm's profitability through active ownership and the provision of industry experience.[1315]

In order to explore the role of venture capital firms, *Hellmann/Puri* (2000) examine their operational impact for a dataset of 173 start-up firms in the Silicon Valley in 1996 and 1997. They find that venture capital firms, inter alia, through their superior business knowledge and monitoring, influence growing firms to bring their products to market faster.[1316] This indicates that venture capital firms also affect operational processes within the investee firms. Besides, venture capital firms are found to increase their portfolio firm's value. Based on a sample of US transactions during 1995-2003, the results of *Dai* (2007) document that venture capital firms improve firm value both in the short- and long-run. In addition, they frequently request board seats of the firms they invest in and are more interested in the firm's fundamentals rather than quick profits. This is appreciated by the capital markets, causing a positive valuation effect.[1317] Using a European sample of investments by venture capital firms during 1998-2001, *Bottazzi et al.* (2008) examine the determinants and consequences of venture capital firm activism. They find that activism by venture capital firms leads to superior exit performance, which is both statistically and economically significant.[1318]

Hochberg (2011) compares three governance-related variables for venture capital- and non-venture capital-backed firms to examine the venture capital's impact on the corporate governance structures of newly public firms in the US. The results support the hypothesis that venture capital firms set up stronger governance structures in the firms they fund. Specifically, they reduce the level of earnings management as proxied by discretionary accruals. In addition, venture capital-backed firms experience significantly higher abnormal returns following the announcement of the adoption of shareholder rights agreements relative to other firms.[1319] Finally, firms backed by venture capital have a higher proportion of outsiders on their boards and are less likely to have CEO/chairman duality, suggesting a better monitoring of management's decisions. *Hochberg* (2011) further tests whether these effects are specific to the impact of venture capital firms or can be observed in the presence of other blockholders as well.

[1314] Following the investments, the targets are not taken private. See Kroker et al. (2010): 2.

[1315] See Kroker et al. (2010): 2f, 8f, 21f. The authors employ a dataset of 377 European private equity investments in publicly-listed firms in eighteen European countries during 1997-2006.

[1316] See Hellmann/Puri (2000): 962, 966, 980.

[1317] See Dai (2007): 561f.

[1318] See Bottazzi et al. (2008): 489, 503, 511. The evidence is based on investments in 1,652 firms by 119 venture capital firms in 17 European countries.

[1319] The market's reaction to shareholder rights agreements is indicative of the market's perception of the firm's governance. If management acts on behalf of shareholders, these agreements can be used to negotiate higher premiums with a potential bidder, resulting in a higher payoff for shareholders. This is reflected in a positive market reaction upon the announcement of the agreement. See Hochberg (2011): 431.

Consistent with the special role of venture capital, the author finds insignificant impacts of strategic and angel investors[1320] on the governance of their portfolio firms.[1321]

Overall, the empirical evidence on the effect of private equity investments in listed firms provides evidence of positive abnormal stock returns for target firm shareholders. Hence, the characteristics of private equity firms reviewed in section 4.1.3.2.1 are regarded as favorable by target firm shareholders. However, the positive abnormal returns may also be based on superior stock picking abilities of private equity firms. Venture capital firms are consistently found to positively affect portfolio firms in terms of operational improvements, firm value, exit performance, and governance.

4.1.3.3 Institutional Investor

Corporate blockholdings by institutional investors are a highly controversial issue. While some regard them as beneficial, others describe them as "disruptive, opportunistic, misguided, and as best as ineffective."[1322] The discussion focuses on a number of characteristics unique to those investors and the characteristics' impact on the relationship with the portfolio firms; both are reviewed in the following.

4.1.3.3.1 Theory

Institutional investors pool large amounts of capital to invest it on behalf of their capital providers.[1323] From a macroeconomic perspective, institutional investors engage in the provision of funds for the capital market, being used by both governments and companies. From a microeconomic perspective, they offer households the possibility of a risk and fund pooling, providing them with a better payoff in terms of risk and reward than possible through a direct, individual investment. This pooling of resources also benefits the respective institutional investor as it enables the investor to enjoy economies of scale and to cover the costs of asset management. Investment vehicles frequently used by institutional investors comprise stocks, bonds, and money market instruments.[1324]

With regard to their role as blockholders, one of the key characteristics of institutional investors constitutes their significant size. Due to the large investment volumes, they are typically well-diversified, which brings the advantage of a low risk aversion.[1325] In addition, their large number of portfolio firms enables institutional investors to generate economies of scale[1326] which arise because many corporate governance topics occur in similar form in other portfolio firms of the investor. To the extent that the investor's engagement entails costs common

[1320] According to Hellmann/Puri (2000): 964, "angel investors are independently wealthy individuals who diversify part of their wealth by investing in young companies."

[1321] See Hochberg (2011): 430-434, 475. The author utilizes a dataset consisting of 2,827 IPOs during 1983-1994, of which 1,041 are venture capital-backed firms.

[1322] Becht et al. (2008): 3094.

[1323] Since July 2013, both open-end and closed-end institutional investors in Germany are governed by the newly implemented Capital Investment Code (KAGB). See section 2.3.2 for details.

[1324] See Maurer (2004): 106, 125. Note that the vehicles used also depend on the type of institutional investor.

[1325] See Thomsen/Pedersen (2000): 693.

[1326] See Black (1990): 580f; Black (1992a): 818; Thomsen/Pedersen (2000): 694.

for other portfolio firms, these costs can be distributed over a larger number of portfolio firms.[1327] Hence, the investor, offering similar proposals at its portfolio firms, may reduce its per-firm solicitation costs. At the same time, it may be able to obtain a constant per-firm benefit from a successful proposal.[1328] Diversification also increases the expertise of the money manager on some topics relative to the firm's manager. For example, the money manager can observe the effectiveness of structural rules already implemented across its other portfolio firms. Firm's management typically lacks this broader perspective.[1329]

The organizational and ownership structure constitutes another key characteristic of institutional investors. As they are fiduciaries, investing on behalf of others, institutional investors act as agents of their own investors.[1330] Given the absence of appropriate incentives,[1331] it is not guaranteed that the institutional investor chooses to exert high levels of effort as long as its management incurs the monitoring costs but does not receive a share of the monitoring benefits.[1332] Therefore, institutional investors might be subject to agency conflicts as well.[1333] Consequently, the question is how to motivate the institutional investors to exert effort for the benefits of their own investors if they do not directly benefit from their efforts.[1334] This is typically ensured through an incentive-based compensation system. However, institutional investors frequently pay the funds' managers only an asset-based fee, which provides weak incentives to exert effort and to incur the associated costs. Although superior fund performance through an active monitoring of portfolio firms might result in an increase of the fund's assets under management, this indirect increase in compensation comes with a time delay and has a negligible effect on the fund managers' incentive structure.[1335]

However, the agency relationship between the institutional investor's management and its capital providers is at the same time advantageous in the sense that the managers of investment funds also "have strong incentives not to breach fiduciary duties or other legal rules because they are agents"[1336]. As their principals will reap most of the gain from any violation of legal rules, agents will lose much more than they can potentially gain. Therefore, Black

1327 See Kahan/Rock (2007): 1048.

1328 See Black (1992a): 822; Black (1992b): 22. In fact, according to Kahan/Rock (2007): 1043, institutional investors typically target a set of portfolio firms at the same time and with the same goals. Black (1990): 580f notes that the economies of scale imply that the investor will focus on more general process and structural issues that are relevant for all its portfolio firms rather than on firm-specific issues.

1329 See Black (1992a): 853.

1330 See Black (1992b): 29. Also Admati et al. (1994): 1125 recognize agency problems between the fund's management and its shareholders.

1331 See Black (1992a): 815.

1332 See Coffee (1991): 1326. Becht et al. (2005): 21 state that a major problem of institutional investors is that fund managers themselves do not have a direct financial stake in the firms they are supposed to monitor.

1333 See Grinstein/Michaely (2005): 1393. See also Bainbridge (2005): 17.

1334 See Gottschlich (1996): 317.

1335 For a similar argumentation, please see Kahan/Rock (2007): 1050-1054. Kahan/Rock (2007): 1052 argue that "even for the funds that charge explicit performance fees, incentives are not much stronger." Managers of hedge funds constitute an exception: since they typically charge a significant performance-based fee linked to the fund's annual return, they substantially benefit from the financial success of their monitoring activities. See Brav et al. (2008): 1735; Mietzner/Schweizer (2011): 5.

1336 Black (1992b): 30.

(1992) argues that "the money manager's cost-benefit calculus overwhelmingly favors staying well within the applicable legal rules."[1337]

Another key characteristic of institutional investors constitutes a potential presence of interest conflicts. Institutional investors are frequently associated with other financial institutions, such as a bank or an insurance company. Consequently, they might either directly or indirectly have interconnections with and be dependent on the firm's managers for future business. Hence, institutional investors may face interest conflicts and may therefore be reluctant to antagonize existing or future clients when it comes to certain business decisions.[1338] Moreover, institutional investors that challenge their investee firms' management in important decisions might be refused access to privileged information in the future, as they would fall from favor with management. Hence, they would cut themselves off from the information flow, previously enabling them to profit from private information.[1339] In the worst case, these investors might lose any business they conduct with the firm in question. Institutional investors that develop a reputation for challenging management may also have problems to find future business with other firms.[1340] As a consequence, affiliated institutional investors may identify with the firm's interest for commercial reasons and side with the management also in those cases where managerial decisions are not in the shareholders' interests.[1341]

Moreover, especially open-end institutional investors are subject to severe competitive pressure.[1342] The majority of investment funds are evaluated by comparing the funds' return with a stock market index or competitors.[1343] If a fund's performance falls behind the performance of a peer, myopic investors will withdraw their money and invest it with a competitor.[1344] As a result of the intense competition for investors, institutional investors might be particularly concerned about improvements in the stock market performance of their portfolio firms. Thereby, they might focus on strategies to create wealth in the short-run and pass this performance pressure on to their portfolio firms.[1345] Moreover, open-end institutional investors need to ensure their ability to pay out funds if required by their investors. Therefore, they typically have no interest in obtaining majority control in their portfolio firms in order not to tie up capital.[1346] Rather, they most likely hold smaller stakes in a greater number of firms to avoid the markdowns associated with the sale of large stakes.[1347]

1337 Black (1992b): 30. Ellul et al. (2007): 11 argue that because private benefits have to be divided among several owners, the incentive of institutional blockholders to extract private benefits might be low.

1338 See Coffee (1991): 1321; Black (1992a): 814; Kahan/Rock (2007): 1054f.

1339 See Coffee (1991): 1324. Note that the transfer of private information is illegal. See §§ 12-14 WpHG.

1340 See Black (1992a): 827.

1341 See Borokhovich et al. (2006): 661f. See also OECD (2009): 53. Interest conflicts are especially relevant for insurance companies and banks, as they frequently have additional business relationships with the firm. See Black (1990): 600f. Hedge funds face fewer interest conflicts, as they are typically privately-owned and do not belong to other financial institutions. See Kahan/Rock (2007): 1066f; Brav et al. (2008): 1735.

1342 See Ruiz-Mallorquí/Santana-Martín (2011): 120.

1343 See Douma et al. (2006): 643.

1344 See also Coffee (1991): 1326; Mietzner/Schweizer (2011): 6.

1345 See Höpner (2003): 93; Achleitner et al. (2010): 826. According to Mietzner et al. (2011): 157 these investors exhibit a strong shareholder orientation and aggressive behavior to realize quick gains.

1346 See Armour/Cheffins (2009): 6; Mietzner/Schweizer (2011): 6.

1347 See Gottschlich (1996): 269f.

However, institutional investors are regarded as being able to compensate their smaller stock ownership through a collaboration with their peers. Institutional investors frequently hold stakes in the same portfolio firms and can combine their bargaining power. Moreover, they have a number of coordination mechanisms to enhance their effectiveness despite their smaller share blocks in the respective firm. The frequent organization in coordinating bodies provides institutional investors with access to research and inside information that might be unavailable to other investors.[1348] As a consequence, they are likely to be better informed than other investors of similar size.[1349]

4.1.3.3.2 Empirical Evidence

Due to the growing importance of institutional investors, researchers have increased their endeavors to explain their impact on their portfolio firms. Next to investigating institutional investors in general, the empirical literature explicitly focuses on the effect of pension funds and hedge funds.

The impact of **pension funds**, inter alia, is studied by *Wahal* (1996) and *Faccio/Lasfer* (2000). *Smith* (1996), *Barber* (2006), and *Becht et al.* (2008) utilize a case study design. *Wahal* (1996) investigates the efficacy of monitoring by nine major US pension funds between 1987-1993. Although these are found to be successful in implementing changes in the firms' governance structures, abnormal returns upon targeting announcements are insignificant. In addition, neither long-term stock price performance nor accounting measures of performance improve as a result of pension fund monitoring. Hence, the author casts doubt on the efficacy of pension funds as corporate monitors.[1350] This US evidence is corroborated by *Faccio/Lasfer* (2000), who analyze the impact of pension funds on 289 UK firms. They find firms owned by pension funds to not operate more efficiently or pay higher dividends than a control group. Moreover, the results do not indicate that pension funds add value for their portfolio firms. According to the authors, the results are consistent with two explanations. First, pension funds are passive investors, simply focusing on a buy-and-hold strategy. Second, pension funds refrain from any interaction in fear of negative publicity.[1351] Regardless of the explanation, the results cast doubt on whether pension funds constitute effective monitors.

Smith (1996) examines the effect of pension funds focusing on targets of CalPERS.[1352] He finds that more than 70% of the targets adopted the governance changes proposed by CalPERS or at least made changes sufficient to warrant a settlement. Upon the announcement of a successful (unsuccessful) targeting, the stock price reacts positively (negatively). However, while monitoring by CalPERS affects the stock price, it does not significantly increase op-

1348 See Grinstein/Michaely (2005): 1393.

1349 See also Grinstein/Michaely (2005): 1393. However, international foreign investors might be subject to an informational disadvantage and therefore prefer domestic investments if they want to take an active part in the governance of firms. See Brennan/Cao (1997): 1853-1855, 1876. Kang/Stulz (1997): 5 examine the distribution of foreign share ownership in Japan from 1975 to 1991 and find that foreign investors primarily invest in large firms. Consistent with an information disadvantage of foreign investors, their preference for large firms is caused by lower information collection costs relative to small foreign firms.

1350 See Wahal (1996): 2f, 6, 20.

1351 See Faccio/Lasfer (2000): 102, 105f. The evidence is based on the years 1992-1996.

1352 The study is based on 51 targets of CalPERS activism during 1987-1993. See Smith (1996): 228.

erating performance.[1353] Using a more recent sample of monitoring by CalPERS between 1992 and 2005, *Barber* (2006) also studies the gains to shareholders from CalPERS activism. In his qualitative analysis, he finds that CalPERS generally implemented reforms that led to increases in shareholder rights. During the investigated period, the total long-run gains of its activism amount to $89.5bn.[1354] *Becht et al.* (2008) conduct a clinical study of active monitoring by the Hermes UK Focus Fund over the period of 1998-2004. They find that the monitoring objectives aimed at are (1) restructuring (widely-diversified) firms, (2) replacing the CEO or the chairman of the board, and (3) increasing the cash payouts to shareholders. If these objectives are achieved, this achievement results in positive and significant abnormal returns around the announcement of these changes.[1355]

Evidence on **hedge fund** activism primarily focuses on the US. *Clifford* (2008) investigates the relationship between activist campaigns by 197 hedge funds and the corresponding value implications for the target firm during 1998-2005. His results document that hedge fund activism is associated with a positive value creation. He finds that firms targeted by activist hedge funds earn higher returns than firms targeted by passive hedge funds and are able to increase their operating efficiency in the year following the acquisition. In addition, the author finds no prove for myopic or self-oriented hedge fund behavior.[1356] Using a comparable approach, *Brav et al.* (2008) find that hedge funds tend to target cash cows having low growth opportunities, sound cash flows, and low payouts.[1357] Upon the intervention announcement, the market reacts favorably, anticipating value increases resulting from the hedge fund's activism.[1358] Ex post, target firms increase their payouts as well as operating profit ratios. The results document that hedge funds do not generate value due to superior stock-picking abilities but because of an active intervention with managerial decisions. Overall, the results are consistent with the perception that informed shareholders can reduce agency costs at the targeted firms and can act as monitor on behalf of the remaining shareholders of the investee firm and their own shareholders.[1359]

Klein/Zur (2009) examine confrontational activism[1360] by hedge funds and document significant abnormal stock returns upon announcement of hedge fund proposals; these returns are sustained in the following year. They suggest that the market expects this activism to create

1353 See Smith (1996): 228, 251.

1354 However, Barber (2006): 2, 21 qualifies his statement, as he cannot directly link the abnormal returns to CalPERS activism.

1355 See Becht et al. (2008): 3095-3097. Please note that a generalization of these results is difficult, as the results are based on a single fund only and on information voluntarily provided by the fund.

1356 See Clifford (2008): 324, 335.

1357 Also the results of Boyson/Mooradian (2011): 170, 184f, 193, 200f document that hedge fund targets are typically cash cows, exhibit poor growth prospects, and are thus likely to suffer from high agency conflicts.

1358 The size of the abnormal return depends on the types and goals of activism, with the highest returns for a focus on changes in business strategies, such as takeovers or spin-offs. See Brav et al. (2008): 1731.

1359 See Brav et al. (2008): 1730-1732, 1773. The authors stress the point that monitoring by hedge funds does not shift value from debtholders to shareholders. Their evidence is based on a US sample of 1,059 hedge fund-target pairs during the period of 2001-2006. See also the results of Boyson/Mooradian (2011): 170, 184f, 193, 200f, which focus on a sample of 418 activist events during 1994-2005.

1360 Klein/Zur (2009): 225 define confrontational activism as instances in which a shareholder acquires at least 5% of the shares and explicitly states its intent to proactively influence the firm and its management.

value.[1361] The investors are also found to be very successful in enforcing their demands, exhibiting a success rate of 60%. In their activism, hedge funds appear to address the agency costs of free cash flow[1362] and demand higher dividends, share repurchases, and debt-to-asset ratios.[1363]

Analyzing the characteristics of hedge fund targets, *Mietzner et al.* (2011) find support for the free cash flow hypothesis: relative to their peers, target firms significantly reduce cash holdings and increase the dividend payout ratio after the investment. Moreover, hedge funds tend to target firms with a high free float of shares to ensure that their decisions are not blocked. However, the ownership concentration increases over time following the hedge fund's investment. This might be interpreted as evidence of investors recognizing the positive impact of the hedge fund's active monitoring. The authors also investigate the long run buy-and-hold abnormal returns of hedge fund targets after the investment. Contrary to the positive wealth effects of the previous studies, they find these firms to underperform the market.[1364] According to them, this might result from resistance against hedge funds' short-term shareholder value maximization either from inside the firm (e.g. by debtholders) or from outside the firm (e.g. by the government).[1365]

Providing evidence for Germany, *Bessler et al.* (2008) investigate the impact of hedge fund activism based on a sample of 324 events in Germany during 2000 and 2006. Their results reveal that activism by hedge funds increases shareholder value both in the short- and long-run.[1366] The effect is more pronounced for firms being subject to greater information asymmetries as proxied by the stock's liquidity. Moreover, the reputation of the investor matters in the short-run.[1367]

Being one of the first studies on **institutional investors** in general, *Brickley et al.* (1988) investigate the relation between institutional investor ownership and votes on managerial antitakeover amendments as a proxy for shareholder monitoring activities. Their results document that institutional investors vote more actively on these amendments than non-blockholders. Furthermore, the authors document a greater likelihood to oppose management for pressure-insensitive relative to pressure-sensitive investors.[1368] They conclude that some institutions are subject to interest conflicts between the maximization of shareholder value for their own

---

1361 In contrast, Greenwood/Schor (2009): 363, 374 hypothesize that the returns to hedge fund activism are driven by investors' expectations that the firm will eventually be taken over. Based on 980 activist events during 1993-2006, they find that positive announcement returns are explained by the hedge funds' ability to force their portfolio firms into a takeover rather than governance changes.

1362 For more details on the agency costs of free cash flow, please see section 2.1.2.

1363 See Klein/Zur (2009): 187-189; 226. The evidence is based on a sample of 151 activist campaigns between 2003 and 2005.

1364 The buy-and-hold abnormal returns represent 150-, 200-, 250-, and 300-day holding periods. The CDAX index constitutes the benchmark. See Mietzner et al. (2011): 158, 161, 166, 175. The sample consisted of 78 hedge fund transactions between 2001 and 2009.

1365 See Mietzner et al. (2011): 180.

1366 However, the authors note that the long-term results depend on the methodology employed. For details, please see Bessler et al. (2008): 25-27.

1367 See Bessler et al. (2008): 4f, 29f.

1368 Pressure-insensitive investors include mutual funds, endowments, foundations, and public pension funds. Pressure-sensitive investors include banks, insurance companies and trusts. See Brickley et al. (1988): 284.

investors and the maximization of future profits accruing to themselves.[1369] Also based on anti-takeover amendments, *Agrawal/Mandelker* (1990) investigate the effect of an adoption of these amendments on shareholder wealth in the presence of institutional blockholders.[1370] The authors find a positive and significant relationship between the proportion of equity owned by institutions and the share price reactions around the announcement of such amendments. Hence, in the absence (presence) of institutional blockholders, companies propose amendments detrimental (beneficial) to shareholders.[1371] Based on the same methodology, *Borokhovich et al.* (2006) find that the holdings of affiliated investors are negatively related while the holdings of unaffiliated investors are positively related to abnormal returns resulting from the announcement of such anti-takeover amendments.[1372] The results suggest that the market regards affiliated investors as inefficient monitors.

Gillan/Starks (2000) study activism by institutional investors using the voting outcome and stock market reaction on 2,042 shareholder proposals submitted from 1987 to 1994 in the US. They find that both the voting outcome and the stock market reaction depend on the specific issue raised and on the identity of the sponsor. With regard to the latter, proposals issued by institutional investors receive more favorable votes than those of individuals, however, result in a small but negative effect on share prices. According to the authors, this negative effect might be caused by the remaining shareholders' perception of the proposal as a signal of managerial unwillingness to privately negotiate with the major blockholder.[1373] More recent evidence on the US is provided by *Cornett et al.* (2007). The authors document a significant positive relation between ownership by institutional investors and firm performance as measured by operating cash flow returns. However, when distinguishing between pressure sensitive and pressure insensitive investors, a positive relation is found only for the latter investor type.[1374] The authors conclude that pressure sensitive investors are "compromised as monitors by their interests in protecting business relations with the firm."[1375]

Institutional investors are further found to have a significant impact on their portfolio firms' characteristics. With regard to dividend payouts, *Short/Zhang/Keasey* (2002) find consistently higher dividend payout ratios for firms with more than 5% institutional ownership across all

1369 See Brickley et al. (1988): 274, 277-279, 284. The sample comprised 201 US firms that proposed 308 anti-takeover amendments in 1984.

1370 The analysis is based on the following reasoning: if monitoring of the institutional blockholder is effective, management will not propose amendments harmful to shareholders or will be discouraged from doing so.

1371 See Agrawal/Mandelker (1990): 145f, 152, 156f, 159. The evidence is based on data on 372 US firms during 1979-1985. The authors point out that their results are likely to be understated, as part of the institutional monitoring has already been incorporated in the stock price.

1372 See Borokhovich et al. (2006): 676.

1373 See Gillan/Starks (2000): 277, 301, 303.

1374 See Cornett et al. (2007): 1776f, 1787, 1792. Their evidence is based on a sample of S&P 100 firms in the 1990s. Pressure sensitive investors constitute bank trust departments and insurance firms and pressure insensitive investors constitute investment firms and independent investment advisors.

1375 Cornett et al. (2007): 1792. Focusing on institutional investors in the US, also Chen et al. (2007): 280-282 are unable to prove monitoring by these investors. However, when controlling for the ownership size, the length of the time vested as well as the investors' independence, they find that independent investors with large ownership and a long-term orientation engage in monitoring when it comes to acquisition decisions.

four models used.[1376] They argue that this relationship may indicate the institutions' effort to lower managerial access to free cash flow.[1377] With regard to bond issues, *Bhojraj/Sengupta* (2003) explore the relationship between institutional ownership and bond yields and ratings. They find that firms with greater institutional ownership enjoy higher bond ratings and lower bond yields, being consistent with the view that institutional ownership plays "an active role in reducing management opportunism and promoting firm value"[1378]. With regard to executive compensation, *Almazan/Hartzell/Starks* (2005) find a positive relation between the pay-performance sensitivity of executives and institutional investors. However, this is only the case for active institutions, defined as those having low expected monitoring costs.[1379] With regard to R&D investments by portfolio firms, *Bushee* (2004) finds those firms with greater ownership by institutions to be less likely to cut R&D investments. Apparently, due to their superior knowledge and experience, institutions are more likely to understand that short-term increases in earnings as a result of cutting R&D expenses have detrimental long-term effects.[1380]

With regard to international evidence, *Douma et al.* (2006) use a sample of Indian publicly listed firms and find that ownership of financial institutions does not have a significant impact on the return on assets but a significant and positive impact on Tobin's q. Hence, institutional investors have a greater impact on performance when measured using stock market criteria.[1381] For a sample of 1,000 proposals at about 250 Israeli firms in 2006, *Hamdani/Yafeh* (2012) are able to find consistent evidence that institutional investors with business ties to their portfolio firms are more likely to support company proposals than stand-alone investors.[1382] This result contests the effectiveness of institutional monitoring in the presence of interest conflicts. Based on a sample of 111 Spanish firms during 1996-2009, *Ruiz-Mallorquí/Santana-Martín* (2011) find significantly positive relationships between Tobin's q and the largest blockholder if this blockholder is an institutional investor.[1383] Using a survey approach,[1384] *Nix/Chen* (2013) provide an understanding of the role of institutional investors in the corporate governance of German listed firms. According to the respondents, institutional investors have a good understanding of the firm's business and are most likely to take ac-

1376 For details on the four models, please see Short/Zhang/Keasey (2002): 110-113. The sample comprises 211 firms listed on the London Stock Exchange over the period of 1988-1992. See Short et al. (2002): 113.

1377 See Short et al. (2002): 109. For a sample of US firms, however, Grinstein/Michaely (2005): 1411f, 1422f do not find a significant effect of institutional investors on the total payout ratio. These results suggest that institutional investors do not monitor through affecting firms' dividend policy.

1378 Bhojraj/Sengupta (2003): 459. The US sample comprises 1,005 industrial bond issues during 1991-1996.

1379 See Almazan/Hartzell/Starks (2005): 5-7, 31. For details on the determinants of the expected monitoring costs, please see Almazan et al. (2005): 6.

1380 See Bushee (2004): 31.

1381 See Douma et al. (2006): 646f, 651. The sample consisted of 1,005 firms listed on the Bombay Stock Exchange during 1999-2000. The authors argue that these results may indicate a superior stock-picking ability of institutional investors. However, this assumption is not explicitly tested.

1382 See Hamdani/Yafeh (2012): 693.

1383 See Ruiz-Mallorquí/Santana-Martín (2011): 121, 124.

1384 Of the 20 persons surveyed, ten were supervisory board members and ten were investor relations officers.

tion in case of an underperformance, a crisis or corporate finance issues. The most frequently used measure to prompt change by the investors constitutes direct, non-public dialogue.[1385]

Overall, the review of the existing literature suggests that there might be differences with regard to the effect on portfolio firms also within the group of institutional investors.[1386] Whereas the evidence on the role of pension funds casts doubt on their efficacy as corporate monitors, hedge funds are generally regarded as effectively monitoring on behalf of the remaining shareholders and their own investors. In general, interest conflicts that arise as a result of an existing or potential business relationship with the portfolio firm may affect the impact of institutional investors.

4.1.3.4 Strategic Investor

Next to acquiring full control via a takeover, a firm may also acquire only a stake in another firm's equity. In this case, the acquiring firm is called a strategic investor. The specific characteristics of this investor type and their effect on the relationship with the investee firm are examined in the following.

4.1.3.4.1 Theory

Investments by a strategic investor can also be called intercorporate shareholdings, which refer to equity holdings by one firm in another.[1387] Intercorporate shareholdings can exist both horizontally and vertically. In the former case, a firm owns an equity stake in one of its competitors. In the latter case, intercorporate shareholdings exist between a supplier and a customer or vice versa. The characteristics of a strategic investor and their effect on the relationship with the respective investee firm depends on the goals and investment motives of the strategic investor. Typically, acquisitions by strategic investors are motivated by strategic goals; however, due to the organizational structure of the strategic investor, acquisitions may also be pursued based on managerial goals.[1388]

With regard to strategic goals, intercorporate shareholdings may be used to secure supplier- and customer-relationships as well as other cooperative agreements with the firm in question.[1389] Moreover, block ownership may be motivated by a desire to create synergies.[1390] If both firms are involved in strategic alliances or joint ventures, intercorporate shareholdings

1385 See Nix/Chen (2013): 140f; 193f.

1386 This heterogeneity is also recognized by Grinstein/Michaely (2005): 1422, who argue that "it is also possible that there is too much heterogeneity among institutions to capture this effect when we are looking at institutions as a whole."

1387 See Bøhren/Norli (1997): 267. Interdependencies of enterprises without a control agreement are governed in § 311-318 AktG. Among others, § 312 (3) AktG requires the management of the controlled enterprise to comment on detrimental influences by the controlling enterprise and on whether or not the disadvantage has been compensated. See also Edwards/Weichenrieder (2004): 155.

1388 A firm may also invest parts of its liquidity buffer in other firms rather than keeping it as cash on hand. However, these investments most likely will be rather small, so as to enable the investing firm to sell its stakes quickly and without a discount in case of liquidity problems. Thus, this motive should not be relevant for the larger holdings of strategic investors this study deals with. See Bøhren/Norli (1997): 270

1389 See Höpner (2003): 95.

1390 See Drees et al. (2013): 278.

might cause a better alignment of interest and incentives of the firms.[1391] For instance, intercorporate ownership reduces the strategic partner's temptation to cheat, as the competitor's or supplier's profit loss will hurt the cheater through a lower payoff from the cheater's equity stake in the betrayed firm.[1392] Moreover, the block ownership constitutes a credible commitment which reduces contracting and monitoring costs faced by both parties within the relationship.[1393] This might be of particular importance in environments characterized by greater uncertainty and information asymmetries for the involved parties.[1394]

In contrast to purely financial investors, the strategic investor is likely to devote more resources to the relationship as it may want to internalize the beneficial effects resulting from the behavior and business conduct of the investee firm.[1395] Therefore, it may facilitate an exchange between the two firms, resulting in transfers of knowledge and information which may ultimately cause a reduction of information asymmetries between the investor and the investee firm.[1396] The involvement of the strategic investor with the investee firm is particularly effective due to a clearer understanding of the investee firm's business model which results from the strategic investor's superior industry knowledge and/or operating expertise.[1397] The strategic investor can leverage this industry and technology expertise as well as its existing assets which might constitute valuable complements to those of the acquired firm. As a result, their privileged knowledge in the respective business areas and the ownership of specific assets make strategic investors well-positioned to gain direct benefits from blockholdings.[1398] These direct benefits positively affect the strategic investor's incentive for an active involvement in the investee firm. Its incentive is further enhanced through continuous business relationships and the resulting long-term time horizon of both parties.[1399] As a side effect, block ownership might also help to reduce information asymmetries with regard to the availability and quality of the investee firm's investment opportunities. In the presence of information asymmetries, corporate blockholders are able to ensure the availability of external financing and significantly reduce the costs of raising external capital by acting as a validation mechanism.[1400]

However, strategically motivated intercorporate shareholdings may also have some disadvantages. First, the acquiring strategic investor may follow a hidden agenda. For example, the block ownership may be motivated by an interest in a technology of the target.[1401] To secure this technology, a strategic investor may acquire a significant share in the respective firm and

1391 The investment also helps splitting the benefits from strategic alliances. See Bøhren/Norli (1997): 267.
1392 See Bøhren/Norli (1997): 268.
1393 See Drees et al. (2013): 281.
1394 See Allen/Phillips (2000): 2792, 2794. See also Fee/Hadlock/Thomas (2006): 1219.
1395 See Fee et al. (2006): 1219.
1396 See also Thomsen/Pedersen (2000): 694; Dushnitsky/Lenox (2006): 756; Drees et al. (2013): 281.
1397 See Allen/Phillips (2000): 2792, 2796.
1398 See Dushnitsky/Lenox (2006): 754, 756f.
1399 See Bott (2002): 57.
1400 See Allen/Phillips (2000): 2792, 2796; Fee et al. (2006): 1222.
1401 See Drees et al. (2013): 278. Dushnitsky/Lenox (2006): 754 argue that investments in other firms can be an effective means to scan the environment for new technologies or business models that may either complement or threaten the firm's business.

subsequently try to transfer important assets from the target firm, such as technology, R&D, and employees. In this case, the blockholder transfers value from the target's shareholders to its own shareholders.[1402] Second, a partial acquisition by a strategic investor may be motivated by the elimination of a competitor.[1403] In this case, the acquired stake will only serve as a toehold for a complete takeover of the firm. As a result, the acquiring firm might have weak incentives to foster improvements in the target firm. Finally, although they may pursue strategic investments in other firms, large multinational enterprises might put greater emphasis on their group profitability rather than on the profitability of their portfolio firms.[1404]

Intercorporate shareholdings may also be a result of agency problems arising from the ownership structure of the investing firm. In case the investing firm is publicly-traded, it may be subject to agency problems between its management and its shareholders. As outlined in section 2.1.2, based on its risk aversion, management may have an interest in the acquisition of stakes in other firms to reduce the firm-specific risk of the firm it is employed at. In this case, the management's incentive for investments into other firms is based on own private benefits rather than based on shareholder value-maximization goals.[1405] If an investment is purely carried out by an incumbent management, e.g. to reduce risk, a weak involvement with the target firm can be expected. Even if the acquisition is motivated by strategic objectives, the organizational structure of the acquiring firm is essential: if the management of the strategic investor does not, either directly or indirectly, benefit from an accretion of the portfolio firm, the control influence of the strategic investor might fail to materialize.[1406]

4.1.3.4.2 Empirical Evidence

Empirical evidence on the effect of corporate blockholdings is rather sparse. While the literature has specifically examined the effect of institutional and other blockholders on their portfolio firms, there are only a few empirical investigations focusing specifically on corporate blockholders.[1407] The findings of these papers are presented in the following.

Bøhren/Norli (1997) explore the reasons for and determinants of intercorporate shareholdings for a sample of Norwegian firms. They find that, inter alia, governance motives and cash flow management motives are important determinants of intercorporate shareholdings. With regard to the former, they find that managers of firms with high free cash flows cross-invest in each other to protect themselves from the threat of a hostile takeover. With regard to the cash flow management, they find (short-term) investments in other firms to be an integral part of the cash management of the investing firms.[1408] These findings do not suggest any strategic motivations for an intercorporate investment and thus do not provide evidence of active monitoring by the investing firm.

1402 See Drees et al. (2013): 281f.
1403 Please note that such an acquisition might be subject to the Act against Restraints of Competition (GWB).
1404 See Thomsen/Pedersen (2000): 694.
1405 See Bøhren/Norli (1997): 268.
1406 See Bott (2002): 59.
1407 See also Allen/Phillips (2000): 2791f.
1408 See Bøhren/Norli (1997): 272, 285f. The sample comprises all firms listed on the Oslo Stock Exchange during 1980-1994.

Fee et al. (2006) use a more narrow approach and focus on the reasons for and consequences of corporate equity ownership by customers in their suppliers. Based on business relationships between US firms, their results suggest that the likelihood of corporate equity ownership is highest in environments where information asymmetries can have significant adverse effects. In particular, corporate equity ownership is significantly related to whether the supplier's operations are R&D intensive, to the fraction of sales made by the supplier to the customer, and to the presence of an alliance agreement between the two firms. In addition, corporate equity ownership is positively related to the supplier's financial constraints, indicating that the customer can serve as an informed source of capital, easing the financial constraints of the investee firm (i.e. the supplier).[1409]

Investigating the impact of strategic investors on the performance of their portfolio firms, *Douma et al.* (2006) compare the performance effects of ownership by foreign corporations and foreign financial institutions, focusing on a sample of Indian firms. Their results document a positive and significant impact of ownership by foreign corporations on both the ROA and Tobin's q.[1410] In contrast, ownership by foreign financial institutions is insignificant. The authors conclude that corporate blockholders bring benefits through superior monitoring abilities, resource endowments and skills, while also providing portfolio firms with a package of capital, management, and technology.[1411]

Barclay/Holderness/Sheehan (2009) examine the relationship between corporate stock ownership and dividend payments. Based on a sample of 376 US firms, the authors find that 68% of the firms with a corporate blockholder do not pay dividends. This is neither due to absent tax benefits nor a result of agency problems. Rather, they find that corporate blockholders use the funds for capital expenditures rather than dividend payments. Apparently, corporate blockholders obtain greater benefits from the pursuance of strategic interactions with their portfolio firms than from using their power to exploit the firm and opt for greater dividend payments at the expense of shareholders.[1412]

Moreover, two studies focus on abnormal returns to targets and strategic investors upon the announcement of the stock acquisition. In their seminal paper, *Allen/Phillips* (2000) investigate ownership by corporate blockholders and its effect on the investee firms using a sample of US equity purchases made by other firms. More specifically, they examine the abnormal returns to targets and purchasers upon the announcement of a block purchase as well as operating changes resulting from the corporate block purchase. Their results document significant increases of targets' stock prices upon the announcement of a corporate block purchase. Moreover, relative to industry peers, target firms substantially increase their investment expenditures and operating cash flows following the block purchase. These increases do not result from a reduction of liquidity constraints. Rather, further tests corroborate the hypothesis

---

[1409] See Fee et al. (2006): 1223, 1247f. The authors' evidence is based on a US sample comprising 10,493 relationships during 1988-2001.

[1410] Note that these results are not driven by subsidiaries of foreign corporations. See Douma et al. (2006): 646f.

[1411] See Douma et al. (2006): 647, 651, 654. The sample is comprised of 1,005 Indian firms and covers the years 1999-2000.

[1412] See Barclay/Holderness/Sheehan (2009): 2424f. Their research is based on a sample of 376 US publicly-listed firms in 1995, 1998, 2001 and 2004.

that corporate blockholdings substantially reduce contracting and monitoring costs. The effect of these reductions is strongest in environments characterized by greater information asymmetries and in the presence of business relationships between the firms.[1413]

Significant effects of strategic investors are also found by *Drees et al.* (2013). Focusing on 113 transactions within European countries, the authors examine the impact of corporate minority block purchases on the valuation of both target and acquirer. They find significant and positive cumulative abnormal returns for the target as well as the combined entity. The authors further investigate factors that explain the observed abnormal returns. The results reveal that the abnormal returns are significantly higher if the target exhibits agency costs that can be addressed by the new corporate shareholder, such as the mitigation of information problems and the alignment of interests. Furthermore, they find significantly positive abnormal returns for both the acquiring and the target firm in the long-run. The authors conclude that corporate shareholders are able to generate value both for their own and their target's shareholders.[1414]

Theoretically, section 4.1.3.4.1 argues that the specific characteristics of strategic investors and their relationship with the investee firms should positively affect the incentives of strategic investors to actively monitor their portfolio firms. Overall, the empirical results suggest that this is indeed the case; strategic investors, inter alia, seem to facilitate the removal of information asymmetries.

4.2 Blockholder Interrelationships

In addition to the blockholder's characteristics, the presence of additional blockholders next to the largest blockholder and the resulting interrelationships may also affect blockholder monitoring. With regard to their influence, there are two conceivable scenarios which are described in the following.

4.2.1 Theory

In situations where multiple principals (blockholders) share a common agent (management), the principals may contend about the right to use the agent's time and effort.[1415] In these situations, each blockholder requires a certain task to be performed by a common management and the attainment of this task might affect the outcome of another task. Within this framework, two different scenarios are possible. Under **cooperative monitoring**, the blockholders decide to jointly engage in monitoring of firm management so as to maximize their joint payoff. Under **independent monitoring**, the blockholders individually engage in monitoring of firm management so as to maximize their individual payoff and simultaneously engage in bi(multi)lateral monitoring to mitigate any negative effects arising from the monitoring performed by the other blockholder(s).

1413 See Allen/Phillips (2000): 2793f, 2797, 2813. The evidence is based on a US sample comprising 402 equity stake purchases during 1980-1991. Of these, 150 represented block purchases by corporations that were accompanied by product market relationships.

1414 See Drees et al. (2013): 278f, 298, 302. The authors' sample comprises 113 transactions over the 1993-2006 period in a number of European countries.

1415 See also Mezzetti (1997): 323f.

The scenario of **cooperative monitoring** by blockholders is likely to occur in case of homogenous or at least reconcilable utility functions and risk preferences of those blockholders willing to take an active role in the firm's governance. In this case, an agency conflict between the blockholders is unlikely. Since they are utility maximizers, the blockholders may engage in cooperative monitoring, as this enables them to maximize the joint payoff from their monitoring.[1416] First, by subjecting the firm's management to consistent, homogenous monitoring, the cooperating blockholders are able to extract more rent from the management.[1417] Moreover, the characteristics of blockholders may be complementary and thus result in an enhanced and more effective monitoring. Second, the monitoring costs for a group of blockholders are lower than for a single blockholder. Since these monitoring costs are primarily fixed, they can be split across a larger group of monitoring blockholders. Monitoring costs may be further reduced by the accomplishment of synergies within the group of monitoring blockholders. Consequently, also smaller blockholders may be incentivized to join the group of monitoring blockholders. This implies that the cooperative monitoring does not have to be established ex ante. For instance, monitoring exerted by one blockholder may draw the attention of other blockholders to the inadequacy of managerial decisions and may result in their support.[1418] Thus, cooperation may be established as a response to weak managerial performance ex post. The cooperation between different blockholders is also regarded as a means to foster shareholder engagement with their portfolio firms both by the European Commission and the UK government.[1419]

However, cooperative monitoring of firm management by blockholders does not necessarily have to be in the interest of the remaining stakeholders. Instead of effectively monitoring firm management in the interest of all involved parties, a blockholder might have the incentive and ability to enforce a collusive agreement with additional blockholders.[1420] In the case of a blockholder collusion, "controlling shareholders enjoy private benefits and minority shareholders can no longer count on the presence of a peer that monitors corporate decisions on their behalf."[1421] A group of cooperating blockholders may have the incentive to collude and expropriate firm resources whenever they regard this expropriation as the most profitable alternative. Hence, in the case of collusion, there is no conflict of interest between blockholders. However, in lieu thereof arises a conflict between the coalition and the affected party which may be minority shareholders or debtholders.

The scenario of **independent monitoring** is likely to occur in cases where the (monitoring) blockholders have different and irreconcilable utility functions and risk preferences. Even if blockholders have similar risk preferences and utility functions with regard to their economic interest, these do not necessarily have to be similar with regard to noneconomic prefer-

[1416] See Pagano/Röell (1998): 209. This assumes that the agreement between the blockholders can be "fully enforced and maintained under all contingencies". Bloch/Hege (2001): 22.

[1417] See Mezzetti (1997): 339. In this case, "the agent always loses", as he cannot play both ends against the middle.

[1418] See also David et al. (2001): 146.

[1419] For details, please see MacNeil (2010): 431-435 and European Commission (2012): 8-11.

[1420] See Pagano/Röell (1998): 209f.

[1421] Gomes/Novaes (2005): 1.

ences.[1422] Since the blockholders, according to the agency theory, are utility maximizers and characterized by opportunism, they try to individually maximize their respective utility functions. Thus, the blockholders independently monitor firm management. Thereby, the independently monitoring blockholders are heedless of any negative consequences of their monitoring for the additional blockholder(s). As outlined in section 2.1.4.3, the blockholder-blockholder agency conflict predominates in this scenario.[1423] To mitigate the negative consequences that arise from the monitoring of the other blockholder(s), the blockholders also engage in bi(multi)lateral monitoring.[1424] In this case, monitoring does not only go from the blockholders to the management but also from one blockholder to another. This bi(multi)lateral monitoring may increase the costs of the blockholders' generation of private benefits by increasing the probability of being revealed and caught. As a result, the bi(multi)lateral monitoring has the potential to reduce the generation of private benefits.[1425] This monitoring does not have to be established ex ante. For instance, monitoring exerted by blockholder A may draw the attention of blockholder B to the private benefits generated by A. As a response to the significant self dealing by A, B engages in monitoring of A, ultimately resulting in bilateral monitoring of the blockholders.

4.2.2 Empirical Evidence

Starting in the early 2000s, researchers began to account for the presence of more than one blockholder when investigating the impact of a firm's ownership structure on firm value and/or performance. Since multiple blockholders are primarily present in Western European and East Asian countries, the empirical literature focuses on these countries.

Based on a sample of firms from Western European and East Asian countries during the years 1992-1996, *Faccio et al.* (2001) examine the expropriation by corporate insiders, proxied by the level of dividends. The authors find that the level of dividend payouts is positively related to the presence of multiple blockholders which they interpret as evidence of the additional blockholder being able to mitigate expropriation by the largest blockholder.[1426] These results are corroborated based on a more extensive sample covering more than 1,100 firms from eight East Asian and thirteen Western European countries. In particular, *Attig et al.* (2008) find the firms' cost of equity capital to decrease with the presence of another blockholder, the size of the second largest blockholder, and the presence of a large number of blockholders. Consistent with the evidence by *Faccio et al.* (2001), the results indicate that the presence of additional blockholders next to the major blockholder represents an internal governance

---

[1422] See also Schulze et al. (2001): 102.

[1423] According to Hellwig (2000): 103, the conflict between blockholders is aggravated if management strives for greater independence by "playing the different classes of shareholders off against each other".

[1424] Bilateral monitoring is performed only if its benefits justify the costs associated with this form of monitoring. In line with this, Bloch/Hege (2001): 10f find that the dominant strategy of smaller blockholders is to not participate in the AGM when (1) their preferences are in line with those of the largest blockholder or (2) the costs arising from a deviation from their preferences by the blockholder do not exceed the voting cost.

[1425] See also Edwards/Nibler (2000): 243.

[1426] See Faccio et al. (2001): 57f, 66.

mechanism that can mitigate a firm's agency costs.[1427] In addition, a greater parity in the blockholders' ownership and hence a greater control contestability of the largest blockholder leads to more effective monitoring and a lower cost of equity capital.[1428]

Bhojraj/Sengupta (2003) focus on potential conflicts between a group of blockholders and the firm's debtholders. Based on 1,005 bond issues of US firms during 1991-1996, the authors find that firms with greater institutional ownership enjoy higher bond ratings and lower bond yields. However, using the total percentage of a firm's stock held by institutions, they find an adverse effect on bond ratings,[1429] being consistent with a collusion of the institutions in order to extract private benefits.

Gutiérrez/Tribó (2004) examine the impact of multiple large shareholders on a sample of 5,288 Spanish firms during 1996 and 2000. Consistent with a collusion of multiple blockholders, they find evidence of a private benefit extraction for blockholder groups possessing an intermediate size of ownership. They propose that in this case, the colluding blockholders' ownership is large enough to ensure control over the firm while still being small enough not to expose the blockholders to the costs of any expropriation. In addition, their results indicate that the contestability of both the largest blockholder and the blockholder group has a positive effect on performance and thus limits any extraction of private benefits.[1430] This is in line with the findings of *Attig et al.* (2008). The importance of the contestability of the largest blockholder is also affirmed by the results of *Maury/Pajuste* (2005). Based on a sample of 136 Finnish firms, the authors find that the contestability of the largest blockholder has a positive effect on firm value. This evidence is consistent with a multilateral monitoring of the blockholders which is particularly effective if the control rights are more equally distributed among the blockholders.[1431]

With regard to German evidence, *Edwards/Nibler* (2000) investigate the role of the ownership concentration within the German system of corporate governance. Their results indicate that minority shareholders benefit from ownership concentration, depending on the respective blockholder type. Moreover, they find that the voting rights of the second largest blockholder are positively related to the firms' market-to-book ratios.[1432] Consistent with the theoretical reasoning in the previous section, these results indicate that the presence of additional blockholders results in the monitoring of the largest blockholder's behavior.[1433] This evidence is confirmed by the results of *Lehmann/Weigand* (2000). Based on 316 firms during 1991-1996,

---

[1427] See Attig et al. (2008): 730. The Asian sample was estimated in 1996 and the European sample between 1996 and 1999. See Attig et al. (2008): 723.

[1428] See Attig et al. (2008): 730.

[1429] See Bhojraj/Sengupta (2003): 464.

[1430] See Gutiérrez/Tribó (2004): 4, 16, 22f.

[1431] See Maury/Pajuste (2005): 1813-1815.

[1432] However, this result is only significant if the second largest blockholder is not a non-bank firm. See Edwards/Nibler (2000): 256f.

[1433] See Edwards/Nibler (2000): 256f, 259f. The authors' evidence is based on a sample comprising the 156 largest German non-financial firms in 1992 and includes both listed an unlisted firms.

they report that the presence of a second blockholder significantly improves the relationship between the largest blockholder and firm profitability.[1434]

Similar to *Faccio et al.* (2001), also *Gugler/Yurtoglu* (2003) use the dividend payout ratio as a proxy for the minority shareholder-blockholder agency conflict and investigate the impact of ownership concentration on the dividend payout ratio. They find the voting rights of the largest shareholder to have a significantly negative influence. In contrast, the voting rights of the second largest blockholder are positively related to the payout ratio, pointing to a monitoring function of the second largest blockholder.[1435] The authors complement this evidence with an event study on dividend change announcements. Consistent with the results of the regression analysis, they find that the CAARs and AARs of majority-controlled firms and firms without a second blockholder are significantly negative for the subsample of dividend decreases. In contrast, firms having another large blockholder do not exhibit negative CAARs or AARs following dividend decreases.[1436] Hence, the results support the view that a second large blockholder acts as a "countervailing balance"[1437] to the largest blockholder, provided it is endowed with sufficient power and incentives.

Overall, the empirical results to a large part suggest that the presence of one (or more) additional blockholder(s) is able to limit the exploitation of private benefits by the largest blockholder. However, the results also provide some evidence of the collusion of blockholders that occurs when their utility functions and risk preferences are reconcilable.

4.3 Other Determinants of Blockholder Monitoring

Since the legal environment, the presence of alternative governance mechanisms, and the firm characteristics may also affect the blockholder's monitoring but do not constitute model variables, they are described more briefly within the following sections.

4.3.1 Legal Environment

Blockholder monitoring may depend on the interrelationship between blockholder monitoring and the legal environment in which the blockholder operates. The design and execution of a country's legislation, e.g. with regard to shareholder rights, affect the need for and the scope of blockholder monitoring. Furthermore, an effective legislation reduces the discretionary scope of a monitoring blockholder and thus its incentive to pursue private benefits. The corresponding theory is described in section 4.3.1.1. The theoretical arguments are complemented by empirical evidence in section 4.3.1.2.

1434 See Lehmann/Weigand (2000): 165, 185.

1435 See Gugler/Yurtoglu (2003): 736f, 739. The authors employ a sample of 266 firms during 1992-1998.

1436 The evidence is based on 510 dividend increases and 226 dividend decreases over 1992-1998. See Gugler/Yurtoglu (2003): 742-744.

1437 Gugler/Yurtoglu (2003): 744.

4.3.1.1 Theory

The legal environment is likely to determine the blockholder's monitoring in three major ways. First, a country's legal environment affects the need for blockholder monitoring. Second, it sets the legal scope of a (monitoring) blockholder to exert influence on the firms' management. Third, it affects the extent to which the blockholder pursues its self-interest to the detriment of remaining stakeholders.

The **need for blockholder monitoring** depends on the degree of legal protection of (minority) shareholders provided by a country's legal environment. In countries exhibiting a strong legal protection of shareholders, blockholder monitoring may be less important as shareholders are more effective in advocating and protecting their interests.[1438] These shareholders also have less fear of being expropriated by firm management or a blockholder and are thus willing to hold smaller stakes and be passive investors.[1439] In contrast, if a country's investor protection rights are weak, shareholders need substitute mechanisms to enhance the firm-level governance. In this case, concentrated ownership may provide an important control device as it enables blockholders to monitor and exert pressure on managers.[1440] Therefore, in countries with poor minority shareholder protection, shareholders want to retain a sizeable stake in the firm to prevent expropriation by firm management or larger shareholders.[1441] Thus, in case of weak investor protection, the benefits of being a large shareholder outweigh the costs.[1442]

The **legal scope** of a blockholder willing to engage in monitoring is a function of the rights provided to shareholders of different levels of ownership in the particular country which determine the blockholder's ability to affect firm policy and governance decisions.[1443] Moreover, as the blockholder might engage in the monitoring of a firm through the exercise of its voting rights, the monitoring feasibility depends on the degree of legal protection of these voting rights. Especially if the blockholder does not hold the majority of the shares, blockholdings may constitute an effective monitoring device only in countries having sophisticated legal systems that both provide the respective ownership rights and ensure their enforcement and protection. Due to this, the legal protection of shareholder rights and their enforcement on the one hand and blockholder monitoring on the other hand are complementary in a country with an effectively installed corporate governance regulation.[1444]

The legal environment further affects the **extent to which the blockholder pursues its self-interest** to the detriment of remaining stakeholders. As has been argued in section 3.2, this depends, inter alia, on the outcome of a cost-benefit analysis in which the blockholder compares the benefits from the pursuance of private benefits with the resulting costs. A country's legal environment constitutes an important determinant of the costs resulting from the genera-

[1438] See Truong/Heaney (2007): 671.
[1439] See La Porta et al. (1999): 473, 512.
[1440] See Truong/Heaney (2007): 671.
[1441] See La Porta et al. (1999): 473, 512. Consequently, the authors argue that the ownership structure can be viewed as a response to the domestic legal environment a firm operates in.
[1442] See Kim et al. (2007): 864. For a description of the costs and benefits of monitoring, see section 3.1.3.
[1443] See also Armour/Cheffins (2009): 12.
[1444] See Shleifer/Vishny (1997): 755, 769.

tion of private benefits. By affecting the probability of being sued, the legal environment and the speed of enforcement determine the costs of private benefits to the blockholder and hence its incentive to generate private benefits of control.[1445] Moreover, disclosure and transparency standards determine the information available to minority shareholders. The more accurate the information provided and the more substantial the transparency, the higher are the odds of the discovery of an improper diversion of firm resources by the blockholder.[1446] As a consequence, the blockholder faces greater difficulties to expropriate value without facing legal penalties or reputational costs.[1447] In contrast, within a system of poor corporate governance, the costs from a diversion of firm resources are likely to be small.[1448] Finally, an effective legal environment hinders collusive agreements between the blockholder and potential additional blockholders that may come at the expense of the remaining capital providers.[1449]

4.3.1.2 Empirical Evidence

Among the first to empirically investigate country effects in the relationship between ownership concentration and firm performance, *Gedajlovic/Shapiro* (1998) find that the institutional context constitutes a strong moderator of corporate governance and firm behavior. According to the authors, their results indicate differences in the mechanisms constraining corporate managers' discretion across institutional contexts.[1450] Differences across institutional contexts are also reflected in the dividend policies of firms. In their study of the dividend payout ratio for more than 4,000 firms from 33 countries, *La Porta et al.* (2000a) find that firms in common law countries and in countries with good shareholder protection have higher dividend payouts relative to firms in civil law countries. They argue that the well-protected minority shareholders in the common law countries use their legal rights to force firms to pay out dividends.[1451] Two years later, the same authors find that higher cash flow ownership improves Tobin's q particularly in countries with poor investor protection. *La Porta et al.* (2002) regard these findings as indirect evidence of an expropriation of minority shareholders by the blockholder when investor protection is poor and the blockholder is weakly exposed to the costs of its expropriation.[1452] Further evidence consistent with an effect of the legal environment on the relationship between ownership concentration and firm variables is provided by *Thomsen et al.* (2006), *Kim et al.* (2007), and *Laeven/Levine* (2008).[1453]

1445 See Dyck/Zingales (2004b): 576.

1446 See Cheffins (2006): 1279f. With high quality disclosure rules in place, investors also face less difficulties in distinguishing good firms from bad firms.

1447 See Dyck/Zingales (2004a): 64; Dyck/Zingales (2004b): 576.

1448 See Bloch/Hege (2001): 32. Therefore, La Porta et al. (2000a): 4, 15 argue that investor protection determines the extent of minority shareholder and creditor expropriation by blockholders. The legal environment also indirectly affects firms' ownership structures: while investors, aware of the fact that high quality corporate law limits expropriation by blockholders, are willing to purchase shares, blockholders have reduced incentives to hold larger share blocks. For details, see Cheffins (2006): 1279.

1449 See Pagano/Röell (1998): 210. See also Gomes/Novaes (2005): 2.

1450 See Gedajlovic/Shapiro (1998): 543, 549f. The sample includes 1,030 firms during the years 1986-91 from Canada, France, Germany, the UK, and the US.

1451 See La Porta et al. (2000a): 17f, 21-23. For a list of the countries, please see La Porta et al. (2000a): 14.

1452 See La Porta et al. (2002): 1154, 1163, 1168f. The results are based on a 539-firm sample of the 20 largest firms of the 27 richest economies during 1995 and 1996. See Braendle (2006) for some criticism.

1453 See Thomsen et al. (2006): 254, 264, 266; Kim et al. (2007): 870, 878; Laeven/Levine (2008): 581f.

The impact of country-level differences is also studied by focusing on the level of the control premium. In theory, the size of the control premium blockholders are willing to pay for a majority ownership in a firm is indicative of the blockholder's intention to utilize its acquired position of power for its personal benefit. *Dyck/Zingales* (2004b) find the control premium paid to be greatest in countries that offer less investor protection,[1454] arguing that private benefits of control can be reduced by better legal protection of minority shareholders and better law enforcement.[1455] Using a dataset from Bulgarian privatization auctions, *Atanasov* (2005) investigates the role of blockholders in a country with weak legal protection of minority shareholders. He finds that the blockholders pay significant control premiums for a majority ownership in a firm. Subsequent to the auction, the market value of the acquired firms is 40-60% below the value of comparable firms without a blockholder. He concludes that in a weak legal environment, unconstrained blockholders apparently choose the easier and less costly option of expropriating minority shareholders to generate private benefits.[1456]

Differences in the relationship between ownership concentration and firm characteristics variables are also found for specific blockholder types. With regard to insider ownership, *Seifert et al.* (2005) investigate the relation between firm performance and equity ownership for the US, England, Germany, and Japan. They find the relationship between insider ownership and firm performance to differ across these countries.[1457] With regard to family firms, *Maury* (2006) finds that active family involvement leads to a better performance relative to firms controlled by non-family blockholders. However, while family ownership and control is beneficial for the remaining shareholders in countries with effective minority shareholder protection, the value benefits from family involvement disappear in countries with lower legal protection.[1458] *Ellul et al.* (2007) examine the impact of family firms on the agency costs of debt under different debtholder protection environments.[1459] Their results suggest that family firms suffer from high agency costs of debt when the protection is weak and benefit from low agency costs of debt when the protection is strong.[1460] Hence, families apparently focus on the generation of private benefits in an environment where they can hardly be challenged.

The studies reviewed in this section indeed find the blockholder's monitoring to differ across legal environments, as suggested by the theoretical arguments listed in section 4.3.1.1. The primary reason for this is the blockholder's increased incentive to pursue private benefits of control when minority shareholders are weakly protected.[1461]

1454 See Dyck/Zingales (2004b): 538.

1455 See Dyck/Zingales (2004b): 538, 589f. The sample comprises 393 control transactions in 39 countries during 1990-2000. For the measurement of the private benefits of control see Dyck/Zingales (2004b): 547.

1456 See Atanasov (2005): 200, 227f.

1457 See Seifert et al. (2005): 188f.

1458 See Maury (2006): 322, 424, 339f. The sample comprises 1,672 firms from Austria, Belgium, Finland, France, Germany, Ireland, Italy, Norway, Portugal, Spain, Sweden, Switzerland, and the UK.

1459 Their sample is based on international bond issues from 1995-2000 including 1,072 firms from 24 different countries. See Ellul et al. (2007): 2.

1460 See Ellul et al. (2007): 37f.

1461 The impact of the legal environment is not investigated empirically due to a focus on the German market.

4.3.2 Presence of Alternative Governance Mechanisms

The blockholder's potential to ameliorate agency costs may depend on the presence and effectiveness of alternative governance mechanisms within the portfolio firm. The following sections outline the theory with regard to this dependency and summarize the corresponding empirical evidence.

4.3.2.1 Theory

Due to the broad menu of corporate governance mechanisms at the disposal of firms' decision makers,[1462] the use of one mechanism may either depend upon the use of an another mechanism (complementary effect) or substitute for the use of another mechanism (substitution effect).[1463]

With regard to the **complementary effect**, a monitoring blockholder may install corporate governance mechanisms in order for those mechanisms to complete its own monitoring. For example, through the placement of representatives on the management or supervisory board, the blockholder increases its access to information and significantly lowers its monitoring costs.[1464] Moreover, a blockholder may complement its monitoring by providing a firm's management or supervisory board members with significant equity ownership or by increasing the firm's level of debt. A blockholder may also choose a higher quality of the internal corporate governance of its portfolio firm if it wants to overcome the loss in value resulting from the market anticipating a diversion of corporate resources by the blockholder. This constitutes a credible signal of the blockholder's unwillingness to divert corporate resources, since effective governance mechanisms increase the costs of any diversion by the blockholder and result in less diversion and an increased firm value.[1465] In the case of a complementary effect, the blockholder's monitoring might not have a direct effect on agency costs and firm value but would be moderated through the governance mechanisms installed by the blockholder.

With regard to the **substitution effect**, a firm's ownership structure might only constitute "one governance mechanism to be considered among a range of governance mechanisms."[1466] Since their results of a meta-analysis of the existing literature on the relationship between share ownership and firm performance do not consistently support the predictions of agency theory, *Dalton et al.* (2003) criticize the agency theory for regarding governance mechanisms as independently mitigating agency problems. Instead, they propose the incorporation of potential interdependencies among alternative governance mechanisms.[1467] In particular, the blockholder's incentive to engage in monitoring may be reduced in firms which have already

[1462] Please see section 2.1.6.2 and 2.1.6.3 for a description of the most important internal and external governance mechanisms, respectively.

[1463] See also Bhagat/Jefferis Jr. (2002): 25; Bott (2002): 165; Witt (2003): 32f; Bhagat et al. (2004): 5; Beiner et al. (2006): 252; Kaserer/Moldenhauer (2008): 9, to name a few.

[1464] Please see section 4.1.2 for the impact of management and/or supervisory board presence.

[1465] See Dahya et al. (2008): 76.

[1466] Dalton et al. (2003): 20f.

[1467] See Dalton et al. (2003): 20f. See also Beiner et al. (2006): 251f.

strong governance mechanisms in place. The presence of these mechanisms offers less potential for the pursuance of governance improvement strategies and therefore reduces the net payoffs from monitoring. As a consequence, alternative governance mechanisms, either individually or in combination, might substitute for monitoring by a blockholder. In this case, blockholder monitoring would not have an effect on performance in the presence of alternative governance mechanisms.[1468]

Bhagat/Jefferis Jr. (2002) observe that – to a great extent – the existing literature only considers the effect of a single governance mechanism on firm performance.[1469] However, regressions using only a single governance mechanism might result in spurious and misleading findings.[1470] *Börsch-Supan/Köke* (2002) term the problem of a potential interaction of different governance mechanisms as "missing variables"[1471] and argue that the measurement of the effect of a particular corporate governance mechanism might not be correct if these mechanisms are omitted.[1472] Thus, "researchers must take great care in isolating the impact of individual governance characteristics"[1473].

4.3.2.2 Empirical Evidence

The majority of empirical studies that control for possible interrelationships between measures of ownership concentration and alternative governance mechanisms provide results largely in support of the existence of interrelationships.

Allowing for the interdependence between insider ownership, debt, and dividend levels, *Jensen/Solberg/Zorn* (1992) find that financial decisions and the ownership by insiders are interdependent. Insider ownership has a negative impact on a firm's level of leverage and dividend payments, being supportive of a substitution of these governance mechanisms.[1474] In addition, *Agrawal/Knoeber* (1996) investigate the effectiveness of seven different corporate governance mechanisms in reducing managerial agency problems.[1475] When examining their impact on firm performance separately, four mechanisms are significant. However, when examining all mechanisms in a single regression, only three mechanisms remain significant. Using a simultaneous equations approach to account for interdependency, only one mechanism remains significant,[1476] being consistent with an interdependency of these mechanisms. Focusing on blockholder types, *Chirinko/Elston* (2006) find evidence that the effect of bank ownership can be substituted by ownership concentration and hence may constitute only one of several available control mechanisms.[1477] Focusing on ownership by insiders, *Kaserer/Moldenhauer*

[1468] See Bhagat et al. (2004): 5. This problem is also pointed out by Bott (2002): 165; Witt (2003): 32f; Kaserer/Moldenhauer (2008): 9.
[1469] See Bhagat/Jefferis Jr. (2002): 3.
[1470] See Agrawal/Knoeber (1996): 378.
[1471] Börsch-Supan/Köke (2002): 297.
[1472] See Börsch-Supan/Köke (2002): 315.
[1473] Denis/Sarin (1999): 214.
[1474] See Jensen/Solberg/Zorn (1992): 261.
[1475] For a description of these mechanisms, please see Agrawal/Knoeber (1996): 379.
[1476] See Agrawal/Knoeber (1996): 379. For details on the methodology, see Agrawal/Knoeber (1996): 391-393.
[1477] See Chirinko/Elston (2006): 71f, 80, 83. Their sample comprises 91 German firms between 1965-1990.

(2008) find that this governance mechanism acts as a substitute for monitoring by external blockholders.[1478]

For Germany, *Januszewski et al.* (2002) analyze the interaction of product market competition and ownership concentration as determinants of firm performance. Consistent with a complementary effect, the disciplinary role of concentrated ownership is strengthened by more severe product market competition.[1479] Further evidence consistent with a complementary effect is provided by *Cornett et al.* (2007). The authors document a significant positive relation between ownership by institutional investors and firm performance as measured by operating cash flow returns. To test for an interrelationship of monitoring by institutional investors and other governance variables, the authors control for insider ownership, board of director characteristics, age and tenure of the CEO as well as CEO's pay-performance sensitivity. The results indicate positive interactions of institutional ownership and the governance variables. Apparently, monitoring by an institutional blockholder is more effective when it is complemented by additional mechanisms.[1480]

Only few studies do not find interrelationships between governance mechanisms to be significant. *Hermalin/Weisbach* (1991) attempt to measure the effect of board composition and insider ownership on firm performance individually and simultaneously. In separate regressions, the authors find that the board composition does not significantly affect Tobin's q. In contrast, for lower (higher) ownership levels, insider ownership positively (negatively) affects Tobin's q. When combining the two governance mechanisms, the authors do not find changes in the signs or significance of these variables.[1481] These results convey that insider ownership and board composition affect Tobin's q independently. Focusing on the impact of the quality of a firm's corporate governance on firm value, *Beiner et al.* (2006) find a positive relationship between the firm-specific governance and Tobin's q. To test for possible substitution effects, the authors control for five additional governance mechanisms.[1482] In regressions allowing for the simultaneous adoption of these governance mechanisms, the authors find that this adoption does not affect the results obtained from regressions of the governance index and the five governance mechanisms individually.[1483]

Although the review of the empirical evidence does not allow a conclusion on whether blockholder monitoring and alternative governance mechanisms act as substitutes or complements, the existing empirical evidence has still highlighted the need to control for potential interrelationships when examining the impact of blockholder monitoring.

1478 See Kaserer/Moldenhauer (2008): 1, 23. Their evidence is based on a German sample of CDAX firms, resulting in 648 firm year observations for the years 1998 and 2003.

1479 See Januszewski et al. (2002): 301f, 304, 322, 325f. The evidence is based on a sample of 491 German manufacturing firms during 1986-1994.

1480 See Cornett et al. (2007): 1774f, 1791f. Their sample comprises firms in the S&P 100 in the 1990s.

1481 See Hermalin/Weisbach (1991): 101f, 106, 109. The authors' evidence is based on a sample of 142 NYSE firms in 1971, 1974, 1977, 1980 and 1983.

1482 See Beiner et al. (2006): 277.

1483 See Beiner et al. (2006): 259, 267-271. The evidence is based on a sample of 109 firms listed on the Swiss Stock Exchange by the end of 2002 and is robust to endogeneity.

4.3.3 Firm Characteristics

A number of firm characteristics potentially affect the blockholder's incentive to engage in monitoring. Since most of these characteristics are controlled for in existing empirical evidence, the following sections review only two determinants which might impact a blockholder's incentive to monitor.

4.3.3.1 Divergence of Cash Flow and Voting Rights

Thus far, the analysis presumed that blockholders' equity ownership or shareholdings are characterized by an equality of cash flow and voting rights. However, there may be instances in which there is a divergence of cash flow and voting rights. The following sections outline the possible consequences of such divergences for the blockholders' monitoring both theoretically and empirically.

4.3.3.1.1 Theory

In general, a divergence of cash flow and voting rights and the resulting violation of the one-share-one-vote rule can have substantial consequences for the monitoring of a blockholder. As has been argued in section 3.2, a rational blockholder pursues and extracts private benefits of control as long as the benefits exceed the costs resulting from their extraction. These costs primarily refer to forgone appreciations or drops in the firm's share prices. With regard to this cost-benefit analysis, a divergence of cash flow and voting rights has two simultaneous effects. First, while the blockholder still holds voting rights sufficient to effectively monitor firm management, the lower cash flow rights decrease the blockholder's benefits from its monitoring; the costs of monitoring, however, remain constant. Second, due to the lower cash flow rights, a self-dealing blockholder internalizes a smaller fraction of the costs resulting from the extraction of private benefits but fully enjoys the benefits.[1484] In addition, the greater voting rights still provide the blockholder with sufficient discretion for the extraction of private benefits. As a consequence, if a blockholder owns significantly more voting than cash flow rights, its incentives to pursue its self-interest to the detriment of the remaining shareholders increase.[1485] Hence, a blockholder may be more interested in the extraction of private benefits relative to improving firm value due to its relatively smaller claim to the firm's cash flows.[1486] In general, the conflicts of interest between different shareholders, described in section 2.1.4, might be augmented when there is a divergence of cash flow and voting rights.[1487]

Within the German institutional context, there may be two reasons for a divergence of cash flow and voting rights.[1488] First, a firm may have issued share classes that differ with regard to their relative proportion of voting rights and dividend entitlements.[1489] According to § 12

1484 See also Cronqvist/Nilsson (2003): 696; Laeven/Levine (2008): 585.
1485 See also Claessens et al. (2002): 2754.
1486 See Gorton/Schmid (2000): 33.
1487 See Edwards/Weichenrieder (2004): 144; Becht et al. (2005): 19; Edwards/Weichenrieder (2009): 490.
1488 Since the implementation of the KonTraG, multiple vote shares have been abandoned (see § 12 (2) AktG). In addition, also voting rights restrictions have been prohibited. See § 134 (1) AktG.
1489 See Edwards/Weichenrieder (2009): 490. See also Edwards/Nibler (2000): 242.

AktG, the German stock corporation act allows a firm to issue preferred shares that confer no voting rights.[1490] Based on § 139 (2) AktG, up to 50% of the firm's total equity can be issued as preferred stock. If a firm has issued preferred stock, a blockholder may expropriate the holders of preferred stock by opting for a retention of corporate profits for its own benefit. Since they have no voting rights on the firm's AGM, the holders of preferred stock are unable to prevent their exploitation. However, this form of exploitation is limited by law: § 140 (2) AktG provides holders of preferred stock with voting rights if the preferred dividend is not paid in any given year and if the amounts in arrear are not paid in the next following year, together with the full preferred dividend for the respective year. While the exploitation via a retention of profits may be mitigated, it is unlikely that the compelling law eliminates all possibilities of an expropriation of holders of preferred stock by a blockholder.[1491] Second, a blockholder may exercise control through a chain of other firms; this is called a control pyramid.[1492] Suppose a blockholder owns 70% of the voting rights in firm A, which in turn owns 51% of the voting rights in firm B. This pyramid structure provides the blockholder with majority control over firm B although it owns only 35.7% (the product of 70% and 51%) of the cash flow rights. Hence, in the case of pyramiding, a particular firm is controlled by a shareholder indirectly through another firm that it does not fully control, resulting in a divergence of the cash flow and voting rights.[1493]

4.3.3.1.2 Empirical Evidence

The impact of a divergence of cash flow and voting rights on the relationship between blockholder ownership and portfolio firms has been researched by studies in an international and German context.

With regard to the international context, *Claessens et al.* (2002) investigate the relationship between ownership stakes by a blockholder and firm valuation based on a sample of publicly-listed firms from nine East Asian countries. They document that firm value increases with greater cash flow ownership of the blockholder. In contrast, they find a negative effect of control rights on firm value, which is particularly severe for larger deviations of cash flow and voting rights.[1494] This evidence is consistent with a pursuance of private benefits at the expense of firm value by the blockholder and is corroborated by a number of additional international studies. Using data on Finnish listed firms, *Maury/Pajuste* (2005) find that the separation of voting and cash flow rights facilitates the extraction of private benefits relative to firms with one-share-one-vote policies.[1495] For a sample of publicly-traded Norwegian firms, *Bøhren/Ødegaard* (2006) find an inverse relationship between the fraction of non-voting

[1490] Preferred shares are governed within the §§ 139-141 AktG. See also Schmid/Wahrenburg (2004): 280. Examples of firms that make use of dual class stock include BMW AG, being controlled by the Quandt family as well as Porsche AG, being controlled by the Porsche and Piech families.

[1491] See also Bak (2002): 282f.

[1492] See Edwards/Weichenrieder (2009): 490. See also Edwards/Nibler (2000): 242.

[1493] See Faccio/Lang (2002): 372. See also Goergen et al. (2008): 178.

[1494] See Claessens et al. (2002): 2769f. The countries investigated include Hong Kong, Indonesia, South Korea, Malaysia, the Philippines, Singapore, Taiwan, and Thailand.

[1495] See Maury/Pajuste (2005): 1827.

shares outstanding and performance. The authors conclude that the issuance of non-voting shares enables the largest blockholder to extract wealth from other shareholders.[1496]

The exploitation of minority shareholders by the blockholder in the case of a divergence of cash flow and voting rights is also supported when considering cross-country samples. Using a sample of more than 1,600 firms from thirteen Western European countries, *Laeven/Levine* (2008) also find that the difference between control and cash flow rights has a negative impact on firm value as measured by Tobin's q.[1497] Based on a sample of eight East Asian and thirteen Western European countries, *Attig et al.* (2008) find that the separation of voting and cash flow rights of the largest blockholder increases the costs of equity capital. Apparently, firms with multiple share classes need to compensate investors for the potential extraction of private benefits.[1498]

With regard to the German context, *Gugler/Yurtoglu* (2003) investigate the impact of ownership on the dividend payout ratio as a proxy for small-large shareholder agency conflicts based on data of 266 firms during the period of 1992-1998. They find that a deviation from the one-share-one-vote principle reduces the payout ratio and hence increases the small-large shareholder conflict. According to the authors, blockholders in this case have a greater incentive to seek private benefits.[1499] Based on a sample of 105 IPOs of founding-family owned firms during 1970-1990, *Ehrhardt/Nowak* (2003) investigate changes in governance following IPOs of these family firms. They find that founding families issue non-voting preferred stock to keep their private benefits of control in the long-run.[1500] Using data on 97 publicly-listed firms in 1991, the results of *Edwards/Weichenrieder* (2004) indicate that increases in the largest blockholder's cash flow (voting) rights are associated with a larger (lower) market-to-book-ratio.[1501] These results are also consistent with the pursuance of private benefits by a blockholder whose voting rights exceed its cash flow rights. Similar results are provided by *Edwards/Weichenrieder* (2009). Based on data for 207 listed German firms during 1991-1993, they also find that share value negatively (positively) depends on the voting rights (cash flow rights) of the largest blockholder. Moreover, the magnitude of the private benefits depends on the extent of the divergence between the largest blockholder's voting and cash flow rights.[1502] In contrast to the previous studies, *Kehren* (2006) finds evidence contrary to the expectation that a divergence of cash flow and voting rights results in self-dealing or opportunistic behavior by the largest blockholder. For a sample of publicly-traded firms in 2001, his re-

1496 See Bøhren/Ødegaard (2006): 36, 44f. The evidence is based on a sample of all non-financial firms listed on the Oslo Stock Exchange and comprises the period of 1989 to 1997.

1497 See Laeven/Levine (2008): 595.

1498 See Attig et al. (2008): 723, 729. The evidence is based on 1,165 firms from eight East Asian and 13 Western European countries.

1499 See Gugler/Yurtoglu (2003): 736f, 739.

1500 See Ehrhardt/Nowak (2003): 225.

1501 See Edwards/Weichenrieder (2004): 160. The evidence is based on data on 97 German publicly listed firms with voting rights taken from the 1991 shareholders' general meeting. Edwards/Weichenrieder (2004): 151.

1502 See Edwards/Weichenrieder (2009): 506.

gression of the ratio of voting rights to cash flow rights on firm performance yields insignificant results.[1503]

Overall, the studies provide strong support for the blockholders' incentive to pursue private benefits in case of diverging cash flow and voting rights. However, it should be noted that the studies based on German evidence, with the exception of *Kehren* (2006), use outdated samples which do not account for the prohibition of multiple vote shares and voting rights restrictions in 1998. Yet, this prohibition represented a major reinforcement of minority shareholders' rights and hence might have contributed to a reduction in self-dealing by blockholders.

4.3.3.2 Liquidity of a Firm's Stock

In general, liquidity refers to "the ability to buy or sell an asset quickly and at a known price – that is, a price not substantially different from the prices for prior transactions, assuming no new information is available."[1504] The liquidity of a firm's stock may influence the propensity of blockholder monitoring. However, with regard to the direction of this influence, the existing literature provides conflicting predictions;[1505] these are reviewed in the following.

4.3.3.2.1 Theory

On the one hand, researchers argue that greater liquidity reduces a blockholder's incentive to engage in monitoring. This is based on the following reasoning. In the presence of illiquidity, a blockholder faces difficulties to find a counterparty for the trade of its ownership stake and therefore suffers a substantial drop in share price upon selling its stake. Given a blockholder is dissatisfied with the existing management and/or firm performance, illiquidity therefore forces the particular blockholder to incur the costs of monitoring the firm's management as the alternative of selling the stock is more costly or not available at all.[1506] In contrast, liquidity enables the blockholder to sell its stake without suffering a substantial drop in the value of its stake. As a result, liquid stocks enable a blockholder to dispose of its shares and leave rather than engage in more costly monitoring in case it is dissatisfied with the performance of the firm and/or its management.[1507] Hence, liquidity is regarded as detrimental to shareholder monitoring.[1508] Although increased liquidity may enable takeover specialists to accumulate share blocks more cheaply, the threat of a takeover should be unable to provide the same level of monitoring as blockholder ownership.[1509]

On the other hand, it is argued that liquidity improves the credibility of a blockholder's monitoring mechanisms and provides a blockholder with the ability and the incentive to monitor firm management. With regard to the first point, high liquidity increases the credibility of the

---

1503 See Kehren (2006): 204
1504 Reilly/Brown (2011): 96f.
1505 See Edmans/Fang/Zur (2013): 1443f.
1506 See also Gorton/Schmid (2000): 54.
1507 See Maug (1998): 66. See also Edmans et al. (2013): 1443f.
1508 See also Bhide (1993): 43.
1509 See Bhide (1993): 44.

blockholder's threat to exit. Thereby, a blockholder might be able to improve firm value even if it is unable or unwilling to directly intervene with the firm's management.[1510] The disposal of the shares drives down the firm's stock price and may simultaneously act as a signal to other investors.[1511] If they also decide to dispose of their stakes, the drop in share price is amplified. This hurts managers ex post as it increases the potential of becoming a takeover target and negatively affects their compensation if it is equity aligned.[1512] Ex ante, the manager will thus be anxious to maximize firm value.[1513] Moreover, *Edmans* (2009) argues that the blockholder, aware of and better informed about the long-term prospects of a firm, can show loyalty to firms that pursue beneficial long-term investments but suffer from weak short-term earnings.[1514] However, the signal of loyalty would not be credible if the stock were illiquid, thereby preventing the blockholder from selling its stake anyway.[1515] With regard to the second point, liquid shares facilitate monitoring by blockholders as they enable a potential blockholder to buy into firms potentially being subject to managerial mismanagement in the first place.[1516] The liquidity of the target firm's stock also provides the blockholder with greater incentives to engage in monitoring. Since the firm's stock price better reflects the value of the blockholder's monitoring, liquidity significantly increases the monitoring blockholder's benefits. In addition, liquidity allows the blockholder to benefit from its monitoring by further increasing its ownership which enables it to internalize a greater portion of its monitoring benefits.[1517]

The liquidity of a firm's stock may also determine the type of blockholder that engages in monitoring. Upon the acquisition of an equity stake, the future blockholder faces a trade-off between monitoring control and liquidity: the large stake necessary to obtain sufficient monitoring influence on a firm is less liquid than smaller stakes without any significant influence.[1518] The importance of liquidity within this trade-off may vary depending on the type of investor. For example, mutual funds, banks or insurance firms – in general all open-end funds – allow their respective investors to withdraw their money upon short notice. These investors therefore have to keep parts of their funds in liquid investments to be able to meet redemptions.[1519] Moreover, these investors avoid the markdowns associated with the sale of large stakes.[1520] Hence, for open and short-term investors, a large ownership and the resulting monitoring role is unacceptable if it negatively impacts the liquidity of their stake.[1521]

1510 See Edmans (2009): 2485; Edmans et al. (2013): 1476.

1511 See Parrino et al. (2003): 37, 42.

1512 See Seger (1997): 78; Edmans et al. (2013): 1443f.

1513 Please see also the description of the governance mechanisms in section 3.1.2 for details on the exit option.

1514 See section 3.1.2 for more details on these mechanisms.

1515 See Edmans (2009): 2484f. Also Admati/Pfleiderer (2009): 2678 argue that "liquidity need not interfere with, and in fact may enhance, corporate governance."

1516 See Maug (1998): 66. See also Edmans et al. (2013): 1443f.

1517 Yet if the stock market is illiquid, the blockholder chooses the least costly monitoring alternative, as it cannot easily buy more stakes to increase the benefits it internalizes as a result of its monitoring.

1518 See also Black (1992a): 874.

1519 See Coffee (1991): 1318.

1520 See Gottschlich (1996): 269f. See also Gompers/Metrick (1998): 10f.

1521 See Coffee (1991): 1318.

4.3.3.2.2 Empirical Evidence

Empirical evidence that explicitly accounts for the impact of liquidity is sparse. Focusing on the US, *Gompers/Metrick* (1998) use the fraction of a firm's stock held by its five largest institutional investors to analyze how the preferences of these investors differ from other investors. Their results show a strong and consistent preference of institutional investors for liquidity.[1522] *Almazan et al.* (2005) find that the influence of institutional investors on the managers' pay-performance sensitivity and compensation level is lower when the firm's shares are less liquid. This can be regarded as an indication of either higher firm-specific monitoring costs[1523] or lower firm-specific monitoring benefits that reduce the investor's incentive to engage in monitoring in the case of low liquidity.

Recent studies investigate the impact of liquidity on blockholder monitoring by using evidence on hedge funds. *Back/Li/Ljungqvist* (2013) investigate whether greater liquidity harms governance by enabling the blockholder to sell its stake when dissatisfied with managerial performance or whether it improves governance by enabling blockholders to acquire significant ownership and become active. Using a theoretical model, they find a lower probability of blockholder activism in the presence of greater liquidity. In empirical models that measure the effect of liquidity shocks on shareholder activism, the authors are able to bear out the findings of the theoretical model. Using hedge fund activism as a proxy for general shareholder activism, the results indicate that higher trading liquidity discourages hedge fund blockholders from actively engaging in their portfolio firm's governance.[1524]

Edmans et al. (2013) explore the effect of stock liquidity on hedge funds' decisions to invest into a firm and hedge funds' choice of governance mechanism once they become a blockholder. Their results show that greater liquidity enables the hedge fund to acquire a stake in a particular firm. Given the hedge fund has acquired a block, liquidity negatively impacts the likelihood of an active monitoring by the hedge fund. However, this negative impact does not result from an abstention from governance altogether but rather from the selection of an alternative governance mechanism, i.e. exit. Consistent with the theoretical argumentation above, *Edmans et al.* (2013) find the threat of exit to represent an effective governance mechanism, resulting in positive announcement returns and operating performance improvements.[1525] The authors conclude that although liquidity curtails active monitoring, "this effect is outweighed by the greater probability of block formation in the first place"[1526].

Overall, both the theoretical arguments provided in section 4.3.3.2.1 as well as the empirical evidence above illustrate the need to control for the effect of liquidity on a blockholder's monitoring. The incorporation of liquidity may be of particular relevance in the thesis at hand, since it investigates multiple blockholder types which may be affected by stock liquidity to varying degrees.

1522 See Gompers/Metrick (1998): 1f, 16. Their evidence is based on the years 1980-1996.

1523 See Almazan et al. (2005): 7, 13. The authors use a sample of 1,914 US firms from 1992-1997.

1524 See Back/Li/Ljungqvist (2013): 1f, 25f.

1525 The evidence is based on a sample of 1,821 Schedule 13 filings by 101 hedge funds during 1995 and 2010. See Edmans et al. (2013): 1452.

1526 Edmans et al. (2013): 1476.

4.4 Résumé

Chapter 3 has concluded that a decent, relevant analysis of the influence of blockholders on their portfolio firms requires the incorporation of possible determinants of the blockholder's monitoring. The goal of this chapter was to present an overview of these determinants by highlighting the respective theoretical reasoning and the empirical evidence. Thereby, it focused on those determinants that have not been consistently incorporated by existing empirical studies, namely blockholder characteristics, blockholder interrelationships, the legal environment, the presence of alternative governance mechanisms, and two characteristics of the respective blockholder's portfolio firm. For each of the possible determinants of blockholder monitoring, the theoretical and empirical arguments highlighted the need to incorporate these determinants when aiming at the provision of more conclusive evidence with regard to the impact of blockholders on agency costs and firm value.

The following chapter 5 draws on the analysis of the determinants of blockholder monitoring and incorporates these determinants into a theoretical model of blockholder monitoring. Thereby, the model focuses on blockholder characteristics (i.e. ownership size, management/supervisory board presence, and identity) and blockholder interrelationships. The firm characteristics and alternative governance mechanisms do not constitute model variables but serve as control variables that are also incorporated in the model of blockholder monitoring. The impact of the legal environment is not examined at all, since the present thesis focuses on the German environment only. Next to the model of blockholder monitoring, also the agency theoretic derivation of the hypotheses on blockholder monitoring in section 5.2 is based on the determinants outlined in the preceding sections.

5 Theoretical Model, Hypotheses, and Operationalization

Chapter 5 lays the ground for and introduces the theoretical reasoning underlying the empirical analysis. Therefore, it combines the analysis on the theoretical background and institutional environment of chapter 2, the explanation of the mechanism "blockholder monitoring" in chapter 3 as well as the possible determinants of blockholder monitoring introduced in chapter 4. Section 5.1 explains the model of blockholder monitoring that constitutes the basis for the empirical investigation. Building on the broad explanation of the model, section 5.2 enlarges upon the particular relationships within the model to develop hypotheses to be investigated in the empirical analysis. Section 5.3 focuses on the operationalization of the model's components. Section 5.4 provides the résumé.

5.1 Theoretical Model

The following sections introduce the model that constitutes the basis for the empirical investigation. Therefore, section 5.1.1 provides an explanation of this model whereas section 5.1.2 points to some important assumptions that have been made in the development of the model.

5.1.1 Explanation of the Model

Section 3.1.1 outlined the functioning of blockholder monitoring from the traditional governance perspective. According to this perspective, the blockholder is able to overcome the problems underlying rational apathy and engages in the monitoring of firm management in the interest of the remaining shareholders. Figure 8 illustrates that the monitoring of firm management by the blockholder constrains managerial discretion in decision-making and thereby brings about reductions in managerial agency costs which result in improved performance and firm value. However, this traditional understanding of blockholder monitoring and its implications may be subject to some deficiencies.

First, section 3.2.1 argued that some of the assumptions made by the traditional perspective might not be applicable in the presence of one or more blockholders. Therefore, the revised definition of blockholder monitoring accounts for the fact that the goal of shareholder value maximization may be complemented or replaced by private benefits of control the monitoring blockholder(s) can generate and thus implies that monitoring may not necessarily be beneficial to the remaining shareholders. Moreover, it recognizes that monitoring, even if it successfully reduces managerial agency costs, may simultaneously give rise to and affect additional agency conflicts within the firm. Second, the analysis of empirical studies in section 3.3 failed to provide support for the presumption that blockholder monitoring is beneficial to the remaining shareholders. Instead, a number of studies find the presence of concentrated (blockholder) ownership to be detrimental for measures of firm performance and/or value. In contrast, a majority of empirical studies regard concentrated (blockholder) ownership to be effective in reducing managerial agency costs. This reduction is reflected in a prevention of value-reducing diversification, higher asset turnover, and lower discretionary spending. However, if the presence of a blockholder indeed results in lower managerial agency costs, then, according to the traditional monitoring definition, this should be reflected in firm performance and/or value. Consistent with the revised monitoring definition, the insignificant or negative impact of monitoring may be the result of a simultaneous effect of monitoring on the remaining agency conflicts within a firm which may outweigh any reductions in managerial agency costs.

The inconsistent empirical results in section 3.3 may also be a result of problems that arise when focusing on the effect of ownership concentration or blockholders in general, i.e. when blockholders are treated as a homogenous group. In this case, one loses important information on the blockholder that may affect both its incentive to monitor and the nature of its monitoring. Moreover, also the characteristics of the portfolio firm, the legal environment, alternative governance mechanisms, and blockholder interrelationships may affect the monitoring by a blockholder. Chapter 4 presented an overview of the factors that should be incorporated in a model of blockholder monitoring.

The theoretical model that is to be examined in the empirical analysis of this thesis extends the model of blockholder monitoring presented in section 3.1.1 in order to account for the adaptations of the traditional definition of blockholder monitoring. Moreover, it incorporates likely determinants of blockholder monitoring which frequently have been neglected – or at least have not been considered simultaneously – in existing empirical investigations. This model is depicted in figure 10.

Due to its significant ownership of a firm's equity, a blockholder[1527] has both the incentive and the power to use its ownership as a basis for an active and continuous monitoring of the firm and its management (path 1).[1528] In line with the revised definition in section 3.2.2, this active monitoring involves both the continuous supervision of the firm's processes and the active exercise of influence on firm management in case the supervision unveils a weakness. The active monitoring is directed at a limitation of managerial actions that diverge from the self-interest of the monitoring blockholder.[1529] The blockholder's monitoring can be aimed at financial, operating, strategic, and governance issues.

Although blockholder monitoring, per definition, is focused on the actions of the management, it may simultaneously give rise to new or compound existing agency conflicts within the firm whenever the interests of the monitoring blockholder are in conflict with those of other stakeholders. These simultaneous effects cannot be captured by a sole focus on managerial agency costs as implied by the traditional perspective of blockholder monitoring. In order to capture these effects, the model investigates the blockholder's effect on managerial agency costs, agency costs of debt, and principal-principal agency costs, the latter measuring both the minority shareholder-blockholder and the blockholder-blockholder agency costs (path 2). The impact of blockholder monitoring on each of the components of a firm's overall agency costs is examined in three separate regression models.

1527 While the explanation of the model uses the singular form only, the monitoring can also be performed by a group of blockholders cooperatively or by multiple blockholders independently.

1528 This study does not focus on ex ante target characteristics but on the ex post effect of a blockholder investment on its portfolio firm. See Achleitner et al. (2010) for a study on the ex ante target characteristics.

1529 For greater details with regard to the definition of monitoring, please see section 3.2.2.

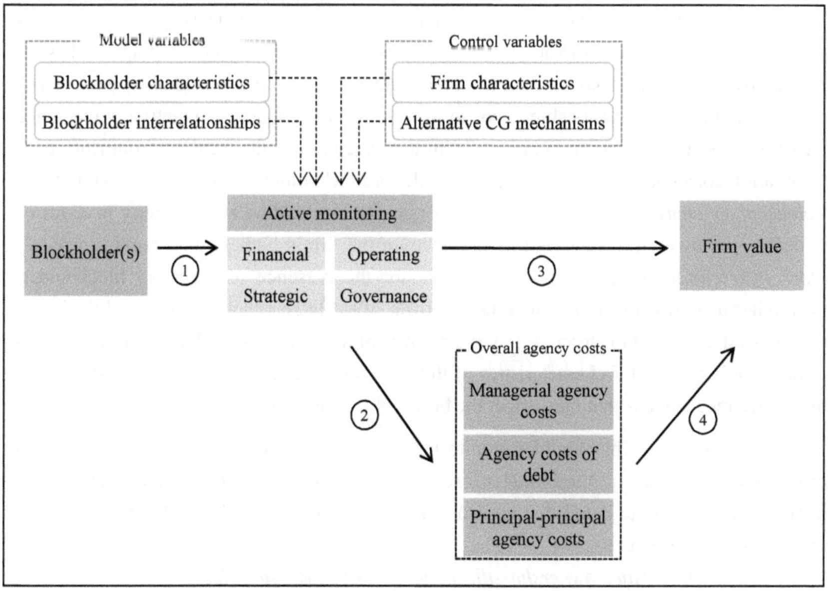

Figure 10: Theoretical model of blockholder monitoring

While path 2 measures the effect of blockholder monitoring on the firm's inherent agency costs, path 3 directly measures the effect of blockholder monitoring on firm value. In general, blockholder monitoring will only increase firm value if it reduces a firm's overall agency costs. Therefore, the direct focus on the relationship between blockholder monitoring and firm value provides an understanding of the simultaneous effects of blockholder monitoring on the components of a firm's overall agency costs and their possible interplay. Consequently, it enables a judgment on the net effect of blockholder monitoring on the overall agency costs which is not possible based on the results of the separate investigation of each agency cost type in path 2.

As explained in section 3.1.1, the theory of blockholder monitoring assumes that the impact of blockholder monitoring on agency costs is ultimately reflected in the firm's value. However, existing empirical studies focus on the relationship either between blockholder monitoring and agency costs or between blockholder monitoring and firm value; they do not test if the impact of blockholder monitoring on firm value is a result of or mediated by its effect on agency costs. In contrast to existing studies, the present study therefore combines the measures of agency costs and firm value and empirically investigates if the three agency cost types have an effect on firm value in the first place (path 4).[1530] Moreover, to examine if the effect of blockholder monitoring on firm value exclusively stems from a reduction of a firm's overall agency costs, the analysis investigates if blockholders have an effect on firm value also when controlling for a firm's agency costs.

[1530] The combination of agency cost measures and firm value also constitutes an implication of the empirical evidence that has been pointed out in section 3.3.

The blockholder monitoring and hence its impact on the three components of a firm's overall agency costs (path 2) and firm value (path 3) is unlikely to be homogenous. Chapter 4 has introduced five factors that may determine a blockholder's monitoring: blockholder characteristics, blockholder interrelationships, portfolio firm characteristics, alternative governance mechanisms, and the legal environment. With the exception of the legal environment, these factors are incorporated into the theoretical model of blockholder monitoring.[1531] With regard to *blockholder characteristics*, the model accounts for blockholder heterogeneity in terms of its identity, its ownership size, and its presence on the firm's bodies. With regard to *blockholder interrelationships*, the model accounts for the presence of a second blockholder, blockholder incontestability (i.e. the relative power of the largest blockholder), and the heterogeneity of the ownership structure (i.e. the number of different blockholders). Simultaneously, the model controls for characteristics of the portfolio firm and the presence of alternative governance mechanisms that may affect the blockholder's monitoring.

Based on this model of blockholder monitoring, three research questions are investigated *to determine the influence of blockholders on agency costs and firm value.* These gradually increase in the attention to detail that is paid to characteristics of the blockholder(s) and to the firms' ownership structure:

1. Does concentrated ownership affect agency costs and firm value?

Apart from firm characteristics and the presence of alternative governance mechanisms, the model at this stage disregards any factor that might affect blockholder monitoring and treats blockholders as a homogenous group.

2. Do the characteristics of the largest blockholder affect agency costs and firm value?

The second research question is based on blockholder heterogeneity and explicitly accounts for blockholder characteristics in terms of the blockholder's ownership size, the blockholder's presence on either the supervisory board or management board, and the blockholder's identity.

3. Do blockholder interrelationships affect agency costs and firm value as well as the relationship between the four blockholder types and agency costs and firm value?

The third stage is based on the assumption of blockholder interrelationships; while still accounting for blockholder heterogeneity, this stage also incorporates blockholder interrelationships which comprise the effect of a heterogenous ownership structure, the largest blockholder's incontestability, and the presence of a second blockholder.

As a result of the stagewise approach, the model is able to provide a complete understanding of the mechanism of blockholder monitoring while controlling for the effect of portfolio firm characteristics and alternative governance mechanisms.

5.1.2 Model Assumptions

The model explained previously is based on a number of assumptions. The first of these refers to the use of firm value as the dependent variable. In line with existing theory, this thesis as-

[1531] Due to a focus on the German market, an analysis of the impact of the legal environment on the blockholder's monitoring is not possible.

sumes that the value of the firm is the ultimate variable of interest for the remaining shareholders.[1532] However, the maximization of firm value may not always be consistent with the maximization of shareholder value which has been regarded as the key source of utility for shareholders in section 2.1.2.

The second implicit assumption is that the share price correctly "reflects the value of corporate benefits that accrue to all shareholders in proportion to their fractional ownership"[1533]. There can be two streams of corporate benefits arising from share ownership. First, the share price captures the present value of the expected payment of dividends and other cash flows generated by the firm and accruing to shareholders. Second, the share price reflects any private benefit the shareholder either can secure itself or is exposed to by another shareholder.[1534] The return to a marginal shareholder will consist of the pro rata share of the firm's total cash flows less the costs arising from agency conflicts, such as private benefits of control. If the marginal shareholder correctly anticipates these returns, the value of the share is determined by the present value of these expected returns.[1535] In order to correctly anticipate these returns, the study at hand assumes that existing or potential investors formulate rational expectations, are knowledgeable about and able to provide estimates of agency costs possibly inherent in publicly-traded firms.[1536] It further presumes that the investors are able to properly recognize that the blockholder's monitoring affects these agency costs and assess that the monitoring effectiveness depends on the determinants of blockholder monitoring.[1537] If existing or potential future investors were unaware of the agency costs arising from poor governance, or did not understand the effect of blockholder monitoring and its determinants on agency costs (and firm value), differences in the ownership structure would not affect firm value.[1538] For instance, a fundamental assumption of the model is a strong positive correlation between managerial performance, managerial efficiency, and the market value of the firm. This implies that a firm being managed poorly, in the sense of not offering a return as great as could be achieved with a more efficient management, has a lower market value than comparable firms.[1539] Hence, agency conflicts and the resulting agency costs reduce what minority shareholders are willing to pay for a firm's shares, lowering the value of all firms where the existence of agency costs represents a real possibility.[1540]

The theoretical model also depends on the assumption of capital market efficiency.[1541] According to Fama (1970), one can distinguish between three forms of market efficiency. With regard to the weak form efficiency, the share price reflects all information on historical prices

1532 See also Kehren (2006): 22.

1533 Barclay/Holderness (1989): 373. See also Börsch-Supan/Köke (2002): 318.

1534 See Barclay/Holderness (1989): 373f.

1535 See Edwards/Nibler (2000): 251.

1536 This is similar to the assumption of rationality by the agency theory. See Jensen/Meckling (1976): 318; Barnea et al. (1985): 33.

1537 See also Edwards/Weichenrieder (2009): 499.

1538 For a similar discussion, please see Core/Guay/Rusticus (2006): 659, 684f.

1539 See Manne (1965): 112. While Manne (1965) focuses on the market for corporate control, the implications of this assumption are also relevant in the case at hand. See the following discussion in the text.

1540 See Dyck/Zingales (2004a): 52. Please note that also a firm's debtholders are presumed to be aware of potential transfers of wealth by the blockholder(s).

1541 See also Stadler (2010): 170.

and returns. With regard to the semi-strong form efficiency, share prices fully reflect all obviously publicly available information. In contrast, the strong form market efficiency requires the share price to fully reflect all available information, including inside information relevant for price formation.[1542] In order for the blockholder monitoring to be incorporated into a firm's share price, the study at hand presupposes the market to be semi-strong form efficient. As long as the capital markets are efficient and characterized by rational expectations of investors, a firm's share price will reflect the existing and potential investors' unbiased estimates of the inherent agency costs, the blockholder's monitoring as well as the monitoring costs and benefits.[1543] As a result, any impact on the value of the firm does not necessarily imply a real economic effect but rather mirrors the expectation of investors with regard to the significance of agency costs and the effect of blockholder monitoring.[1544]

Since the model examines the relationship between blockholder monitoring, agency costs, and firm value using the agency theory as the theoretical basis, it assumes that the reduction of the types of agency costs as a result of blockholder monitoring is the sole driver of firm value. However, the effect of the blockholder on firm value may not exclusively stem from agency cost reductions. For example, the presence of a blockholder with a favorable reputation may simply provide certification for the portfolio firms.[1545] If the blockholders indeed have a certification effect, their presence should have a significant impact on firm value but an insignificant impact on agency costs.

5.2 Hypotheses

Having introduced the model of blockholder monitoring, the following hypotheses sections zero in on particular relationships within the model. For each relationship, the following sections develop a number of hypotheses; the corresponding theoretical reasoning is based on arguments provided in the chapters three and four. In line with the empirical approach, the hypotheses are grouped according to those under the assumption of blockholder homogeneity (section 5.2.2), blockholder heterogeneity (section 5.2.3), and blockholder interrelationships (section 5.2.4). However, the hypotheses sections start with a description of the reasoning underlying the development of the hypotheses.

5.2.1 Reasoning Underlying the Hypotheses Development

The hypotheses formulated in the following are in part based on theoretical reasoning and in part based on the results of existing empirical studies. In the case of theoretical reasoning, the hypotheses are primarily derived from agency theoretic propositions.[1546]

1542 See Fama (1970): 383, 388, 414f.

1543 For a similar argumentation, please see Jensen/Meckling (1976): 345. Note that in this case, the price of a firm's equity measures its value for (remaining) shareholders and reflects the costs and benefits of blockholder monitoring from their perspective. See also Thomsen et al. (2006): 248, 266.

1544 See also Höpner (2003): 159.

1545 See Claessens/Fan (2002): 80 and section 3.1.3.

1546 Whereas the following deliberations focus on a single blockholder only, please note that the "blockholder" can also be a group of blockholders.

With regard to the **manager-shareholder agency conflict**, the inherent agency costs depend on differential utility functions and risk preferences between the firm's management and its shareholders. The agency costs are further amplified by the presence of information asymmetries between the better-informed management and the weakly informed shareholders.[1547] The presence of a blockholder is regarded as being able to mitigate these agency costs. This mitigation depends on the monitoring intensity and its effectiveness in constraining managerial discretion; both intensity and effectiveness are a function of (1) the feasibility of monitoring, (2) the blockholder's capability, and (3) the blockholder's incentive to engage in monitoring. The feasibility may depend on the power of the blockholder, the capability on the experience of the blockholder, and the incentive on a trade-off which involves the comparison of the costs and benefits of effective managerial monitoring. Consequently, the corresponding hypotheses on the manager-shareholder agency conflict focus on how the blockholder characteristics and interrelationships affect the utility functions and risk preferences as well as the information asymmetries between the manager and the shareholders. Moreover, they focus on how the blockholder characteristics and interrelationships affect the feasibility of monitoring, the blockholder's capability, and the blockholder's incentive to engage in monitoring.

As implied by the revised definition of monitoring,[1548] the blockholder may coincidentally influence other agency relationships within the firm, because it simultaneously acts as an agent of a firm's debtholders and remaining shareholders. Since the agent (i.e. the blockholder) is assumed to pursue its self-interest, the effect of its monitoring on the respective agency relationship depends on the presence of information asymmetries as well as on the degree to which its utility function and risk preferences differ from those of the respective principal.[1549] The extent to which the blockholder pursues its self-interest to the detriment of the principal(s) further depends on the outcome of a cost-benefit analysis in which the blockholder compares the expected costs and benefits from the exploitation to those from an effective monitoring of the management. Moreover, any pursuance of its self-interest to the detriment of the principal(s) is contingent on the (relative) power of the blockholder.

With regard to the **shareholder-debtholder conflict**, the hypotheses therefore focus on how the blockholder characteristics and interrelationships affect the utility functions and risk preferences as well as the information asymmetries between the debtholders and the blockholder. In addition, they focus on how the blockholder characteristics and interrelationships affect the blockholder's power as well as the costs and benefits arising from a transfer of value from the debtholders to the blockholder (i.e. the blockholder's incentive). With regard to the **principal-principal conflict**, the hypotheses focus on how the blockholder characteristics and interrelationships give rise to divergent utility functions and risk preferences as well as to information asymmetries between the small and large shareholders and between multiple blockholders. Moreover, the hypotheses focus on how the blockholder characteristics and interrelationships

[1547] Differential utility functions, risk preferences, and information asymmetries can also be regarded as sources of agency costs.

[1548] Please see section 3.2.2 for further details.

[1549] Here, the effect of the blockholder's monitoring on the respective agency relationship should be understood as the blockholder's incentive to effectively monitor the firm and its management versus its incentive to exploit the remaining capital providers through its monitoring.

affect the blockholder's power, give rise to and affect the private benefits of control as well as the resulting costs defrayed by the monitoring blockholder which determine its incentive to exploit the remaining shareholders.

Firm value can be regarded as reflecting the net effect of the blockholder characteristics and interrelationships on a firm's overall agency costs. Consequently, the blockholder characteristics and interrelationships only raise firm value if they decrease a firm's overall agency costs. Therefore, the hypotheses on firm value are solely based on the expected net effect that results from aggregating the hypotheses on managerial agency costs, agency costs of debt, and principal-principal agency costs.[1550]

To reduce their complexity, some hypotheses in the subsequent sections introduce the term "*ownership size effect*" which refers to the relationship between the largest blockholder's ownership and any type of agency cost or firm value.[1551] If a higher ownership size of the largest blockholder results in *lower agency costs* or *lower firm value*, there is a *negative ownership size effect.* If a higher ownership size of the largest blockholder results in *higher agency costs* or *higher firm value*, there is a *positive ownership size effect.*

5.2.2 Hypotheses under the Assumption of Blockholder Homogeneity

As explained in section 5.1.1, the empirical analysis in stage 1 involves the estimation of a base case to highlight the importance of incorporating blockholder characteristics and interrelationships in the stages 2 and 3, respectively. Apart from the variables that control for firm characteristics and alternative governance mechanisms, it disregards any factor that might affect blockholder monitoring and focuses on aggregate measures of ownership concentration and the presence of a blockholder.

A key deficiency of measures presuming blockholder homogeneity is the fact that they are uninformative in relation to the effect of blockholder monitoring, since they do not allow any inference with regard to the drivers of the agency costs mentioned in section 5.2.1. Generally, the feasibility of monitoring firm management (e.g. manager-shareholder conflict) as well as the pursuance of self-interest to the detriment of debtholders (e.g. shareholder-debtholder conflict) and the remaining shareholders (e.g. principal-principal conflict) depends on the power of the (monitoring) blockholder. However, aggregate measures of ownership concentration do not allow any prediction regarding the blockholder's power. For instance, a cumulative ownership of 56% may result from an ownership structure in which there is a largest blockholder owning 6% of the shares and ten additional blockholders owning 5% of the shares. However,

1550 In calculating the net effect, each agency cost component is weighted equally. It should be noted that the effect on firm value exerted by the blockholder characteristics and interrelationship may stem from additional effects not incorporated in the hypotheses development (see also section 3.1.3 and 5.1.2). First, the presence of a blockholder may provide a certification effect for its portfolio firm which can, for instance, benefit from the blockholder's reputation. See also Claessens/Fan (2002): 80. Second, the blockholder might also provide its portfolio firms with know-how, technologies or expertise. While such a transfer of resources in general has no effect on agency costs, rational shareholders are able to account for these factors and incorporate them when valuing the firm's shares.

1551 There are thus four ownership size effects: (1) an ownership size effect on managerial agency costs, (2) an ownership size effect on agency costs of debt, (3) an ownership size effect on principal-principal agency costs, and (4) an ownership size effect on firm value.

it may also result from a largest blockholder owning 51% of the shares and a second blockholder owning 5% of the shares. In the latter case, the blockholder's power is sufficient to effectively monitor management and to exploit the remaining capital providers. In the former case, none of the blockholders might have sufficient power to directly influence management or exploit the remaining capital providers. However, based on aggregate measures, this cannot be differentiated, making predictions hardly possible.

Moreover, the severity of conflicts between the parties of the respective agency relationship depends on the degree to which the utility function and risk preferences of the blockholder match those of the management, debtholders or remaining shareholders. The utility function and risk preferences of the blockholder in turn are expected to depend on its ownership size and identity. Since aggregate ownership measures do not account for the size or type of blockholder, this information cannot be used to explain the variation in agency costs or firm value. Finally, because aggregate ownership measures amalgamate different blockholder identities and variations in the ownership structure, they only measure their net effect. Given the various potential blockholder identities and interrelationships, a theoretically guided formulation of a relationship is impossible.

The difficulty of detecting evidence of monitoring in case blockholders are treated homogenously is also the result of an analysis of the existing literature. As pointed out in section 3.3, any review of the influence of blockholdings or concentrated ownership does not seem to provide consensus support with regard to an impact of concentrated shareholdings on firm characteristics and firm value.

In light of these arguments, stage 1 refrains from a hypothesis-based investigation. Instead, the empirical investigation of stage 1 is guided by the corresponding research question: Does concentrated ownership affect agency costs and firm value?

5.2.3 Hypotheses under the Assumption of Blockholder Heterogeneity

As argued above, the assumption of blockholder homogeneity does not allow any inference with regard to the drivers of agency costs mentioned in section 5.2.1. In contrast, the incorporation of blockholder characteristics enables predictions with regard to the effect of the blockholder's (1) size, (2) presence on the firm's most important bodies, and (3) type on these drivers and hence the level of agency costs. Therefore, the following parts formulate hypotheses based on the following research question: Do the characteristics of the largest blockholder affect agency costs and firm value?

5.2.3.1 Impact on Managerial Agency Costs

The following section formulates expectations regarding the effect of the largest blockholder's characteristics on managerial agency costs.

Ownership Size of the Largest Blockholder

In terms of the agency cost drivers, the ownership size of the largest blockholder is likely to affect both the feasibility of monitoring and the incentive to engage in monitoring. With regard to the **blockholder's incentive**, the size of the equity ownership determines the extent to which the monitoring blockholder benefits from the increase in the portfolio firm's stock price that comes with effective monitoring. Thus, the greater the ownership, the more benefits the monitoring blockholder can internalize.[1552] The largest blockholder may derive further benefit from the reduction of its exposure to firm-specific risk that results from its poor diversification. It is therefore more likely to limit managerial actions that would further increase its risk exposure. Next to the benefits, also the largest blockholder's monitoring costs should be favorably affected by its level of ownership. First, these costs are fixed in the sense that they do not increase with growing ownership.[1553] A larger ownership stake hence enables the blockholder to better distribute monitoring costs and lowers the proportional monitoring costs. Second, the monitoring costs vary with the availability of information and the costs of collecting information. Both availability and costs of collecting information should be affected by growing ownership since management may provide a large blockholder with access to information a smaller blockholder may not be provided with. Finally, a blockholder with sufficient ownership does not require the support of other shareholders. As a result, it saves the costs associated with communication and negotiation between multiple blockholders.[1554] In general, due to lower relative costs and higher benefits, a larger ownership should provide a blockholder with a greater incentive to engage in monitoring.

With regard to the **feasibility of monitoring**, a greater ownership should increase the blockholder's power and hence its ability to exert credible pressure on corporate management. Directly, the larger ownership provides the blockholder with a number of formal rights granted by law which should significantly increase the feasibility of monitoring.[1555] Investors that ascribe importance to the formal rights that come with certain ownership levels should try to exceed the necessary ownership thresholds.[1556] The direct power that comes with greater ownership is complemented by an indirect, implicit threat to management which ensures that a larger blockholder gets a better hearing from corporate management which should also be more willing to cooperate with the blockholder. Thus, by providing the blockholder with sufficient power to credibly threaten management, the ownership size should favorably affect the monitoring feasibility.[1557] Overall, increasing ownership is associated with a greater incentive to engage in monitoring and a greater feasibility of monitoring which in turn enhance the monitoring intensity and effectiveness c.p.

The monitoring intensity and effectiveness also depend on the **sources of agency conflicts**. Since the ownership of the largest blockholder measures the aggregated effect of all types of largest blockholders, expectations in terms of the blockholder's utility function are difficult to formulate. Nevertheless, it is reasonable to expect that the majority of blockholder types de-

---

1552 Also Bainbridge (2012): 253 argues that it makes no sense for a blockholder to engage in "altruistic public service" unless it captures a substantial portion of the benefits.

1553 See also section 4.1.1.1.

1554 See also Bainbridge (2005): 12.

1555 The rights granted to shareholders of different size have been covered in section 2.2.3.2.

1556 Thereby, the blockholders aim to exceed the desired threshold with the minimum possible ownership so as to reduce their capital investment.

1557 See also Rozeff (1982): 254f.

rives utility from the minimization of managerial agency costs. With regard to the presence of information asymmetries, larger ownership should contribute to the reduction of information asymmetries between management and the blockholder (and the remaining shareholders) since management either voluntarily provides additional information or the blockholder uses its influence in order to request additional information.

In light of the greater monitoring intensity and effectiveness as well as the reduction of information asymmetries, the largest blockholder's ownership should be associated with lower managerial agency costs of the portfolio firm.[1558] Hence, the following hypothesis is formulated:[1559]

H1.1$_a$: The larger the ownership size of the largest blockholder, the lower a firm's managerial agency costs c.p.

However, increasing ownership may eventuate in a convergence of the blockholder's risk preferences with those of management, since greater ownership increases the blockholder's risk exposure, c.p. While this may result in greater managerial monitoring as argued above, it may also result in a homogenization of utility functions and ultimately in a collusion or siding with the management and thus ineffective monitoring. Moreover, while greater levels of ownership increase the feasibility of monitoring, they also increase the blockholder's discretion and hence its power to generate private benefits. To generate these benefits, the largest blockholder may require the cooperation of the firm's management which should adversely affect the intensity and effectiveness of its monitoring. Therefore, *Dalziel et al.* (2011) argue that when the blockholder monitors for its self-interest rather than for the benefits of all involved parties, the reduction in agency costs will be lower relative to cases in which the blockholder monitors in the interest of all stakeholders. The blockholder in this case "deprives the firm of some of the benefits of control."[1560] Based on these arguments, the largest blockholder's ownership may cause increases in managerial agency costs for higher levels of ownership. On the other hand, greater ownership also increases the costs of generating private benefits. Since these most likely come at the expense of firm value, a greater ownership of the largest blockholder results in a greater exposure to these costs and a lower net benefit of private benefits relative to the net benefit from effective managerial monitoring. This suggests that with increasing ownership levels, the largest blockholder's ownership may result in reduced managerial agency costs.[1561] Due to these conflicting theories, theoretical arguments alone cannot unambiguously predict the relationship:

H1.1$_b$: The ownership size effect[1562] on a firm's managerial agency costs is non-linear c.p.

[1558] This is supported by Ang et al. (2000): 102, who find that agency costs, as measured by the sales-to-assets ratio, decrease for increases in ownership of the primary blockholder. The evidence is based on data comprising 1,708 small privately-held US firms in 1992. See Ang et al. (2000): 85.

[1559] Please note that all hypotheses presented below constitute alternative hypotheses. The subject of the empirical investigation therefore does not constitute the hypotheses presented below but the corresponding null hypotheses. If the respective null hypothesis can be rejected, the alternative hypothesis is accepted.

[1560] Dalziel et al. (2011): 1351.

[1561] Smaller levels of ownership, in contrast, may be associated with higher managerial agency costs.

[1562] For an explanation of the ownership size effect, see the last paragraph of section 5.2.1.

Presence on the Firm's Most Important Bodies

With regard to a presence on the firm's supervisory board, the resulting direct voice should significantly increase the **feasibility of monitoring**. A blockholder represented on the board has a legitimate influence on a number of important decisions that should be more difficult to affect simply by virtue of its ownership.[1563] Direct access to the other supervisory board members might further enable the blockholder to draw the attention of these members to the inadequacy of managerial decisions and may result in their support which increases the pressure on management. However, critics argue that inefficiencies and codetermination[1564] on the supervisory board level may cause the management and the blockholder to clarify critical topics in private meetings without considering the members of the supervisory board. Thus, supervisory board presence might be superfluous.[1565]

Furthermore, the representation on the supervisory board affects the **sources of the agency conflict**. First, it contributes to a reduction of information asymmetries between the management and the blockholder.[1566] Members of the supervisory board are provided with information on the intended business policy and other fundamental matters regarding the future conduct of the firm's business and are also able to request information regarding particular aspects of the firm's business. This direct access to information may go beyond the level of information management provides to a blockholder without board representation and may substantially limit management's discretion.[1567] However, supervisory board presence and the frequent interaction between the management and the blockholder as a consequence thereof, may also result in a convergence of interest and compatible utility functions of management and blockholder. As a result, the monitoring intensity may be negatively affected.

Finally, the board representation most likely affects the **blockholder's incentive** to engage in active monitoring. Disregarding the additional costs that are associated with the process of installing a representative, the greater and continuous access to information and the more direct involvement in the firm's processes should result in decreased monitoring costs.[1568] However, the blockholder should also face greater costs of effective monitoring due to opportunity costs arising from the foregone private benefits whose extraction would be facilitated by the blockholder's greater power.[1569] Since the generation of private benefits may require managerial support, the blockholder may secure this support through some kind of incentive compensa-

[1563] For instance, it can affect the appointment and dismissal of members of the firm's management board as well as its compensation. The responsibilities have been presented in greater detail in section 2.2.2.1.

[1564] Since codetermination may affect the blockholder's power in the supervisory board, the extent of codetermination is controlled for in the regression analysis. See section 5.3.4.2 for the reasoning.

[1565] See also section 2.2.2.1. Note that if a supervisory board presence is considered superfluous, blockholders should not be frequently represented on the board.

[1566] See Leiber (2008): 201 for a similar reasoning focusing on family firms.

[1567] Please note that the transfer of private information is illegal. See §§ 12-14 WpHG.

[1568] See also DeMott (1998): 328; Leiber (2008): 201. Gantchev (2013): 612 finds supervisory board representation to be the least expensive monitoring alternative compared to proxy contests and negotiations.

[1569] Also the empirical evidence provided in section 4.1.2.2 suggests that blockholder presence on a firm's bodies may increase its discretion and therefore its incentive to generate private benefits of control.

tion that allows management to realize some private benefits at the expense of managerial agency costs.[1570]

Overall, while board representation should increase the feasibility of monitoring and lower information asymmetries, it may also result in a convergence of interest between management and blockholder. Moreover, the greater power might be used by the blockholder to pursue private benefits which it tries to generate by securing managerial support. Due to these countervailing effects, a non-directional hypothesis is formulated:

> *H1.1$_c$: The representation of the largest blockholder on a firm's supervisory board has an effect on a firm's managerial agency costs c.p.*

If the blockholder is represented on the management board, this board representation should affect the **sources of the agency conflict**. Assuming the representative is accepted by the remaining members and able to generate support within the board, one may regard this situation as one where ownership and control are united. As a consequence, the interests of management and the blockholder should be naturally aligned which reduces managerial incentives to be opportunistic.[1571] Moreover, since the blockholder, via its representative, is directly involved in the decision processes, information asymmetries between management and blockholder should be virtually absent. Furthermore, the board presence affects the **feasibility of monitoring**: Independent of the blockholder's interest, it is provided with an influence on the firm that goes beyond the supervision of corporate management. In fact, the blockholder, in this case, is directly involved in the decision making process of the management and can therefore influence the decisions already at an early stage. In addition, the board presence affects a **blockholder's incentives** by reducing the costs of monitoring. However, a representation on the management board simultaneously increases the monitoring costs due to its ability to generate private benefits and the resulting opportunity costs. Similar to a supervisory board representation, private benefits may come at the expense of lower managerial agency costs. Hence, also the relationship between management board representation and managerial agency costs is theoretically ambiguous:

> *H1.1$_d$: The representation of the largest blockholder on a firm's management board has an effect on a firm's managerial agency costs c.p.*

Blockholder Identity

The identity of the blockholder is expected to affect the sources of the agency conflict, the blockholder's capability and its incentive to engage in the monitoring of corporate management.

As regards the **sources of the agency conflict**, the *information asymmetries* between management and blockholder should be less pronounced for private equity firms and strategic investors. Both types have extensive business knowledge and operating expertise and thus supe-

[1570] According to Bainbridge (2012): 247, also management might be willing to pay private benefits to the blockholder in exchange for its abandonment of monitoring.

[1571] Even if the remaining members do not explicitly support the blockholder representative, the mere presence of the representative increases the costs of adverse actions through a greater risk of being revealed.

rior capabilities in understanding and evaluating their portfolio firms' business environment. However, the information asymmetries should be lowest for family blockholders, as their long-term involvement provides them with deep firm- and industry-specific knowledge. In contrast, institutional investors should have less extensive business and industry knowledge, since they are typically diversified and not focused on a particular industry. While *utility functions* should differ between private equity investors and management, the former typically provide management with incentives to operate efficiently. Consequently, the management's utility functions should be aligned with those of the private equity firm. Due to the continuous and long-term interaction of families with the firm's management, they may be able to align the interest of the management with their own interest which over time results in similar utility functions. Since institutional investors are strongly focused on the maximization of shareholder value, their utility functions should differ from those of management. With regard to *risk preferences*, institutional investors exhibit a low risk aversion relative to the undiversified and hence highly risk averse management. Although private equity investors are less diversified and own larger stakes than institutional investors, they should also be less risk averse than management. Based on the arguments provided in section 4.1.3.1.1, family blockholders should exhibit a high risk aversion and focus on the avoidance of excessive risk taking. Compared to the other investor types, their risk preferences should therefore roughly match those of corporate management.

With regard to the **blockholder's incentive**, the performance-based compensation common in private equity firms ensures that their investment professionals receive a substantial share in the profits and thus gain substantial *monitoring benefits*. The long-term commitment of family blockholders, their concern about the survival of their firm as well as their desire to enhance family reputation should also provide the family with significant benefits from their monitoring.[1572] Presuming a purely strategically motivated acquisition, the strategic investor benefits from its monitoring due to improved business relationships and reduced contracting costs.[1573] However, in contrast to private equity firms, the organizational structure of strategic investors provides weak incentives for those actually involved in the monitoring, since their compensation is not tied to the performance of their portfolio firms. A similar argument applies to institutional investors. Moreover, due to their rather short-term focus, institutional investors bear the direct costs of any activism, however, are unable to capture some of the long-term benefits. With regard to *monitoring costs*, private equity and institutional investors can utilize their experience gained from other investments and distribute monitoring costs across a larger number of firms and are further able to generate economies of scale and scope, reducing the monitoring costs per firm. Moreover, both investors typically establish private, direct monitoring and coordination mechanisms to reduce the costs of monitoring. However, the cooperation with other shareholders, required due to their smaller ownership stakes, may create additional expenditures by institutional investors.[1574] Since institutional investors are frequently

1572 See also Thomsen/Pedersen (2000): 693.

1573 An acquisition may also be motivated by an interest in the resources of the target firm. In this case, the investor should receive no additional benefit from monitoring.

1574 See also Bainbridge (2012): 244.

dependent on firm management, they face additional costs of lost future business in case they engage in active monitoring.[1575] Finally, they may have higher monitoring costs relative to domestic investors (e.g. families or strategic investors) because they are frequently located abroad.[1576] Strategic investors may be able to reduce their monitoring expenditures through a facilitation of employee and/or knowledge transfers. Also families face low monitoring costs due to their already existing understanding of firm processes.

In terms of the general **capability** to monitor, based on their business models, institutional investors and private equity firms should be highly qualified and experienced in the management and supervision of their portfolio firms. In contrast, strategic investors in general should be less experienced monitors, since this is not part of their business model. To the extent that monitoring requires detailed knowledge about the firm's technologies and processes, families should be highly effective monitors,[1577] since they are better able to understand, interpret, and assess the actions of management.

Concluding, the four blockholder types differ in a number of aspects that determine the sources of the agency conflict, their incentive to engage in monitoring, and their capability to monitor corporate management. These differences may translate in a heterogenous impact on managerial agency costs. Consequently, the following hypothesis is formulated:

> *H1.1$_e$: The ownership size effect on a firm's managerial agency costs differs between the four blockholder types c.p.*

In contrast to the other types, families should be most effective in reducing managerial agency costs: they are likely to face the lowest information asymmetries, to have the strongest incentive and a strong capability to engage in monitoring. These aspects result in the following hypothesis:

> *H1.1$_f$: If the largest blockholder is a family, then the negative ownership size effect on a firm's managerial agency costs is strongest c.p.*

Institutional investors have been found to select the size of their ownership based on two considerations: their desired level of diversification and their desired level of influence on the firm. As a consequence, an institutional investor with a larger stake in its portfolio firm should have a higher desired level of influence which translates into a more intense and effective monitoring and a stronger influence of the blockholder on managerial agency costs.[1578] This reasoning is intuitive since, as argued above, the institutional investor faces high monitoring costs. Hence, its incentive to engage in intense and effective monitoring should be stronger for higher levels of ownership than for lower levels of ownership.[1579] Thus, a non-linear relationship is expected. A non-linear relationship may also arise for families, since the incentive structure may differ between families with low to moderate and those with high

---

[1575] See also Gottschlich (1996): 317; Chen et al. (2007): 283. In fact, the OECD (2009): 53 views interest conflicts of institutional investors as one reason for shareholder passivity during the financial crisis.

[1576] For a similar argumentation, please see Brennan/Cao (1997): 1853.

[1577] See also Anderson/Reeb (2003): 1305; Ampenberger (2010): 46.

[1578] For a similar reasoning see Bonini et al. (2012): 23.

[1579] Moreover, institutional investors with higher levels of ownership are more likely to be long-term oriented.

ownership. Large family ownership may potentially lead to entrenchment which most likely causes higher managerial agency costs. Moreover, the retention of intrafamily relatedness may take precedence over other goals. A family's altruism may cause family members to be too generous, to employ unqualified family members or to decouple the existing management's employment from performance. As a consequence, managerial inefficiencies, either intentionally or unintentionally, increase. A non-linear relationship as a result of excessive family control or an unduly employment of low-qualified family members due to altruism is also found by *Leiber* (2008).[1580] As a result, the following hypothesis with regard to families and institutional investors is formulated:

> *H1.1$_g$: If the largest blockholder is either a family or an institutional investor, then the ownership size effect on a firm's managerial agency costs is non-linear c.p.*[1581]

The empirical evidence reviewed in section 4.1.3.1.2 suggests the importance of controlling for supervisory or management board presence when investigating the effect of families. On the one hand, family presence on the firm's boards provides a superior ability to align the management's and supervisory board's interests with those of the family.[1582] Moreover, due to family altruism, a family-CEO may act as a steward, with a strong identification with the firm and the collective good of the family.[1583] Hence, a representation of a family member may eliminate or at least substantially reduce the conflict between the family blockholder and management as it unites ownership, control and/or management.[1584] On the other hand, a representation of the family in the firm's bodies may also facilitate the entrenchment of families and/or result in heightened managerial inefficiencies. For instance, family representatives may not be selected based on objective performance criteria which results in an employment of unqualified family members rather than better qualified external managers.[1585] Moreover, having selected a family representative, its performance may not be as strictly supervised as the performance of an external manager, which facilitates managerial inefficiencies. While these problems should not exist for the remaining blockholder types, board representation may also increase the feasibility of monitoring and the incentive to monitor and thus the monitoring intensity and effectiveness. Hence, board presence may not be of importance for family blockholders exclusively. To investigate whether blockholder representation on the firm's bodies has a greater effect on agency costs for families relative to the remaining blockholder types, the following hypothesis is formulated:

> *H1.1$_h$: If the largest blockholder is a family, then the effect of the largest blockholder's representation on a firm's management or supervisory board on the ownership size effect on a firm's managerial agency costs is strongest c.p.*[1586]

1580 See Leiber (2008): 129, 200-202.

1581 This effect is tested for each of the four blockholder types individually. However, no hypothesis is formulated regarding private equity and strategic investors due to an absence of a sound theoretical reasoning.

1582 See Anderson/Reeb (2003): 1306; Ampenberger (2010): 46.

1583 See Anderson/Reeb (2003): 1307. For more details on the stewardship theory, please see section 2.1.2.

1584 See Schulze et al. (2001): 99; Villalonga/Amit (2006): 387; Leiber (2008): 55. This applies only to firms not subject to intra-family agency conflicts.

1585 See Anderson/Reeb (2003): 1301f, 1306f; Leiber (2008): 57.

1586 This hypothesis is tested for management and supervisory board representation individually.

5.2.3.2 Impact on Agency Costs of Debt

The following section formulates expectations regarding the effect of the largest blockholder's characteristics on agency costs of debt.

Ownership Size of the Largest Blockholder

Referring back to section 2.1.3, there likely is a conflict of interest between the shareholders and debtholders of a firm which primarily stems from significant differences in terms of risk preferences and utility functions. Shareholders are generally said to focus on the maximization of shareholder value and are willing to take substantial amounts of risk in order to achieve this goal. In contrast, debtholders are interested in stable cash flows that enable the firm to make regular interest payments and therefore favor a low risk strategy. In the presence of a blockholder, the conflict of interest between both parties may be exacerbated. As a result of the blockholder's presence, there is a shareholder with sufficient incentives and power to use its monitoring to push through strategies that favor shareholders' rather than debtholders' interests. Consequently, the largest blockholder's ownership should increase agency costs of debt.

However, it has been argued previously that the definition of monitoring employed in the present thesis presumes the blockholder to pursue its own self-interest. As a consequence, the size of agency costs of debt depends on the **sources of the agency costs**, i.e. the extent to which its individual risk preferences and utility functions differ from the interest of debtholders. In contrast to small, individual shareholders, the significant ownership of the largest blockholder reduces its diversification and most likely increases its risk aversion; a failure of a high-risk project would only have a minor effect on small shareholders but would result in major losses for both the blockholder and the debtholders.[1587] Hence, one may argue that the risk preferences of large blockholders and debtholders are more compatible relative to those of small shareholders and debtholders.[1588]

With regard to the **blockholder's incentive**, one can reasonably assume that the largest blockholder takes a long-term investment horizon. However, the expropriation of debtholders should be profitable for shareholders only in the short-run. In the longer run, shareholders will bear the costs of a value transfer either through a reduced access to debt capital or through the costs of monitoring and enforcing the contracts by debtholders – that is, higher interest payments.[1589] Hence, blockholders with large share ownership and a long-term, strategic goal should be confronted with significant costs arising from a value transfer. They therefore have low incentives to expropriate debtholders and are rather incentivized to mitigate shareholder-

[1587] The loss on the side of the blockholder not only stems from its financial loss, but also from a significant reputational loss.

[1588] Filatotchev/Mickiewicz (2006): 159 argue that the blockholder might even collude with financial institutions and other fixed-claim holders, e.g. in order to expropriate minority shareholders.

[1589] See also the discussion in section 2.1.3.

debtholder agency conflicts and to develop a reputation for being an honest borrower, as they realize that their portfolio firm might need to raise debt capital more than a single time.[1590]

Based on **empirical evidence**, *Bhojraj/Sengupta* (2003) conclude that blockholders do not aggravate the agency problem between debtholders and shareholders; rather, debtholders consider the presence of a blockholder to be beneficial since they reduce what the authors call "agency and information risk"[1591]: through the monitoring of managerial performance, the reduction of a misallocation of funds, and by improving disclosures, blockholders lessen information asymmetries between the firm and its providers of debt capital.[1592] Also *Sunder et al.* (2011) provide evidence that blockholder monitoring does not uniformly result in heightened agency costs of debt. Although they find that shareholder activism in relation to mergers and capital structure changes leads to higher costs of debt, activism used to resolve managerial entrenchment problems causes lower costs of debt.[1593]

Based on the agency theoretic arguments and the findings of existing literature, agency conflicts between shareholders and debtholders may be attenuated through greater ownership of the largest blockholder. Consequently, the following hypothesis is formulated:

> *H1.2$_a$: The larger the ownership size of the largest blockholder, the lower a firm's agency costs of debt c.p.*

If the blockholder utilizes its monitoring to shift value from the debtholders to itself and the remaining shareholders, its incentive to do so should be greatest at lower levels of ownership. In this case, (1) its risk preferences are similar to those of small shareholders, (2) its exposure to any costs resulting from the value shift is bearable, and (3) the blockholder might not necessarily have a long-term strategic interest in the firm. In contrast, the incentive to signal the absence of agency conflicts with debtholders should be strongest for blockholders with relatively larger ownership levels. Hence, the largest blockholder's ownership may increase agency costs of debt at lower levels but may decrease agency costs of debt for larger levels of ownership. As a result, one may expect a non-linear relationship between the largest blockholder's ownership and agency costs of debt.

> *H1.2$_b$: The ownership size effect on a firm's agency costs of debt is non-linear c.p.*

Presence on the Firm's Most Important Bodies

It is argued above that both agency theoretic arguments and findings of existing literature suggest that greater ownership of the largest blockholder attenuates agency conflicts between shareholders and debtholders. In particular, since the largest blockholder most likely has a long-term investment horizon, it will face the costs of a transfer of wealth either through reduced access to debt capital or through higher interest payments; both factors reduce the **blockholder's incentive** to engage in a transfer of wealth. This argumentation is also valid

---

1590 See also Anderson et al. (2003): 264. For a similar argument, see Myers (1977): 161. Even if the blockholder does not require additional debt capital in one portfolio firm, it may require a good reputation among creditors for future investments.

1591 Bhojraj/Sengupta (2003): 459.

1592 See Bhojraj/Sengupta (2003): 472.

1593 See Sunder et al. (2011): 1, 5, 7.

with regard to the largest blockholder's presence on the firm's supervisory board. Acquiring a board representation constitutes a tedious task and entails additional costs for a blockholder. Consequently, only long-term blockholders should aspire after a board representation. Since these blockholders, however, face the greatest exposure to the costs from any transfer of wealth, they should have a low incentive to expropriate debtholders. Hence, the following hypothesis regarding supervisory board representation is formulated:

H1.2$_c$: The representation of the largest blockholder on a firm's supervisory board has a negative effect on a firm's agency costs of debt c.p.

If the largest blockholder aims at a transfer of value from the debtholders to the shareholders despite the costs involved, it most likely strives for management board representation, since it provides the blockholder with an influence on the firm that goes beyond the supervision of corporate management. First, it increases the **feasibility** to transfer value from debtholders. Since board representation provides the blockholder with direct access to the management and the decision making process, it should increase the blockholder's power relative to the debtholders. In addition, its influence is not limited by employee representatives that may vote in favor of debtholders.[1594] Moreover, management board representation affects the **sources of the agency conflict**. Due to better access to information, the information asymmetries between the blockholder and the debtholders should be exacerbated. Hence, the blockholder may be able to conceal wealth transfer strategies. Provided debtholders do not account for potential transfers of wealth ex ante, a blockholder with management board representation may face lower costs resulting from its transfer of wealth which increases a **blockholder's incentive** to exploit debtholders. Overall, a blockholder on the management board is provided with additional power and discretion which may limit its exposure to the costs from a transfer of value from the debtholders. Consequently, the incentive and power to shift value from the debtholders is greatest for blockholders with a management board representation. In line with this, management board presence should be associated with greater agency costs of debt:

H1.2$_d$: The representation of the largest blockholder on a firm's management board has a positive effect on a firm's agency costs of debt c.p.

Blockholder Identity

The blockholder identity is likely to affect the blockholder's incentive to engage in a wealth transfer at the expense of debtholders and the extent to which the blockholder differs from the debtholders in terms of its utility function and risk preference.

With regard to the **blockholder types' incentive**, the expected costs from a value transfer for family blockholders are likely to be high. First, since they are characterized by a long-term commitment and involvement in their portfolio firms, they would be significantly affected by a denied access to debt capital or increased interest payments. Second, families would risk the valuable business relationships they have established between their portfolio firms and the respective bank(s) which may provide the firms with access to capital at special conditions.

[1594] For further information on employee representation, please see section 2.2.2.1.

Relative to families, institutional investors are usually regarded as short-term investors. Due to their short-term focus, they should also be largely unaffected by their portfolio firm's reduced access to debt capital or other costs resulting from their value transfer. However, since the institutional investors' money managers act as agents to their own investors, they do not directly benefit from any value transfer that results from their monitoring and should consequently have a lower incentive to monitor. Moreover, banks also invest in the funds of institutional investors and may be unwilling to invest into another fund once they become aware of value transfers by the institutional investor. This argument also applies to private equity firms, whose incentive to transfer value from debtholders should also be low because they frequently use large amounts of bank debt when acquiring stakes in their portfolio firms. Any transfer of value would therefore impose high costs on the private equity investor, since it may face difficulties to take on loans for subsequent transactions. Similar to private equity firms, strategic investors would also be confronted with the costs arising from a value transfer and are thus discouraged to act against the debtholders' interests. Since they most likely require debt financing for their own business, they should have no interest in a negative reputation among debtholders.[1595]

In terms of the **sources of agency conflicts**, differential utility functions and risk preferences between a family blockholder and debtholders are unlikely, since a family blockholder also exhibits a high risk aversion and focuses on the avoidance of excessive risk taking. In contrast, institutional investors can be classified as risk prone investors and hence should have risk preferences that substantially differ from those of debtholders. Moreover, they should be strongly focused on improvements in the stock market performance of their portfolio firms. Thus, they are more likely to focus on equity value maximization rather than on firm value maximization.[1596] Similar to institutional investors, private equity investors also have a strong focus on the maximization of equity value and hence a different utility function compared to the debtholders. However, since their risk aversion is not as low as the risk aversion of institutional investors, their risk preferences should be more compatible with those of debtholders. As a result, shareholder-debtholder conflicts should be less distinct.

Empirical evidence on institutional investors implies that the changes in the firms' financial and accounting policy resulting from hedge fund activism on average benefit shareholders but are harmful for bondholders. Thus, the presence of an activist hedge fund is associated with the expropriation of bondholder wealth.[1597] Moreover, bondholder activism is found to be more likely in firms owned by institutional investors relative to other firms. Hence, bondhold-

[1595] If the acquisition of the portfolio firm is motivated by an interest in the resources of the target firm, the utility function of debtholders and the strategic investor should differ. While the former is interested in the firm's ability to pay stable interest, the latter tries to transfer important assets. This is tantamount to a transfer of value, since it should negatively affect the portfolio firm's ability to make interest payments.

[1596] See also Anderson et al. (2003): 265.

[1597] See Klein/Zur (2011): 1735, 1737, 1761, 1764. The finding could also be consistent with the hypothesis that hedge funds target firms in financial difficulties to initiate a turnaround. If they fail, this also reduces bondholder wealth. However, this interpretation is regarded as unlikely. See Klein/Zur (2011): 1736.

ers appear to regard the costs of expropriation by institutional shareholders as greater relative to other blockholders.[1598]

Overall, of the four blockholder types, institutional investors have the greatest incentive to shift wealth from debtholders to themselves. Due to their long-term interests and continuous interaction with debtholders, the remaining blockholders should abstain from a transfer of wealth and rather have an impetus to mitigate agency conflicts. Consequently, the following hypotheses are formulated:

> *H1.2$_e$: If the largest blockholder is an institutional investor, then the larger the ownership size of the largest blockholder, the higher a firm's agency costs of debt c.p.*
>
> *H1.2$_f$: If the largest blockholder is either a family, private equity or strategic investor, then the relation between the ownership size of the largest blockholder and a firm's agency costs of debt is non-positive c.p.*[1599]

Anderson et al. (2003) argue that families with greater ownership possess both the voice and the power to force their portfolio firms to meet their demands. Among others, large family ownership may therefore lead to family entrenchment at the expense of other claimants and to wealth expropriation from bondholders. In order to investigate a potential non-linear relation between family ownership and the agency costs of debt, they regress the costs of debt on family ownership and a squared family ownership term. In line with an entrenchment at higher ownership levels, their results indicate a u-shaped relationship, suggesting that family firms with larger family ownership face higher costs of debt financing.[1600] In order to investigate if a non-linear relationship can also be found in the present study, the following hypothesis is formulated:[1601]

> *H1.2$_g$: If the largest blockholder is a family, then the ownership size effect on a firm's agency costs of debt is non-linear c.p.*

If the size of the ownership and the greater power that comes with this ownership results in an entrenchment of the family, a similar entrenchment should be observed if the family is represented on the supervisory or management board which provides the family with greater discretion in decision making. In line with this, *Anderson et al.* (2003) find that firms in which a family member is the CEO face higher costs of debt financing.[1602] In order to investigate if the entrenchment effect is a phenomenon only observed for family firms, the following hypothesis is formulated:

> *H1.2$_h$: If the largest blockholder is a family, then the effect of the largest blockholder's representation on a firm's management or supervisory board on the ownership size effect on a firm's agency costs of debt is strongest c.p.*[1603]

1598 See Gao/Gao/Smith (2009): 2.

1599 This effect is tested for each of the blockholder types individually.

1600 See Anderson et al. (2003): 279-281.

1601 While a non-linear relationship is investigated for all four blockholder types, no hypothesis is formulated regarding the remaining types due to an absence of a sound theoretical reasoning.

1602 Their result is driven by firms which have founder descendants as CEO. See Anderson et al. (2003): 278.

1603 This hypothesis is tested for management and supervisory board representation individually.

5.2.3.3 Impact on Principal-Principal Agency Costs

The following section formulates expectations regarding the effect of the largest blockholder's characteristics on principal-principal agency costs.

Ownership Size of the Largest Blockholder

Based on agency theoretic propositions, the ownership of the largest blockholder should be associated with a widening gap between the risk preferences, utility functions, and information of the largest blockholder and the remaining shareholders.[1604] Hence, in terms of the **sources of the agency conflict**, the ownership of the largest blockholder should raise principal-principal agency costs, since the self-interest of the blockholder does not match the interest of the remaining shareholders. However, any pursuance of a blockholder's self-interest is contingent on the power of the blockholder and its incentive which depends on the outcome of a cost-benefit analysis.[1605] With regard to the **blockholder's power**, a blockholder with a small stake does not possess sufficient power to pursue its self-interest against the interest of the remaining shareholders.[1606] A large blockholder, however, should be able to use its superior power to monitor corporate management in its self-interest and generate private benefits of control (entrenchment hypothesis). The large ownership insulates the blockholder from any monitoring by the remaining shareholders and provides it with greater power to push through personal interests which results in a "discretion in private benefit extraction"[1607].

With regard to the **blockholder's incentive**, when deciding on the pursuance of private benefits, the largest blockholder trades off its private benefits against its loss of wealth associated with the decrease in firm value that most likely results from the presence of a principal-principal agency conflict. As argued in section 4.1.1.1, while greater ownership provides the blockholder with the power to generate private benefits, it simultaneously increases its exposure to the losses resulting from the generation of private benefits. The convergence-of-interest hypothesis therefore states that higher levels of ownership improve the blockholder's alignment of interest with those of the remaining shareholders. In order to attract minority shareholders, blockholders credibly signal the absence of expropriation.[1608]

To recapitulate, given differential utility functions and risk preferences, large ownership increases the blockholder's power and hence the feasibility of generating private benefits. However, it also increases the blockholder's exposure to the costs from these private benefits and hence lowers its incentive to pursue private benefits. Due to these opposite effects, no exact prediction is possible. The direction of the relationship is thus an empirical question:

> *H1.3$_a$: The ownership size of the largest blockholder has an effect on a firm's principal-principal agency costs c.p.*

1604 For details, please see section 2.1.4.

1605 See also the argumentation in section 3.2.2.

1606 If the position of the largest blockholder is not large enough to be the dominant shareholder, the blockholder is reliant upon the collaboration of other larger shareholders or minority shareholders in order to reach the majority of the votes and, thus, to influence firm strategy and managerial actions. This dependence constrains the blockholder's discretion and limits private benefits. See also Jara-Bertin et al. (2008): 148.

1607 Maury/Pajuste (2005): 1818.

1608 See Young et al. (2008): 208.

The previous argumentation suggests that it is possible for a blockholder's incentive structure to change as its equity holdings increase.[1609] In particular, there might be a range in which the blockholder's level of ownership simultaneously makes it indefeasible and limits its exposure to the costs resulting from expropriation.[1610] For these levels, the ownership may result in blockholder entrenchment and in a greater incentive to engage in expropriation. Above this level, the blockholder is exposed to a greater portion of the costs resulting from its private benefit generation; consequently, the cost-benefit analysis results in a reduced incentive to exploit minority shareholders and in a lower level of principal-principal agency costs.[1611] As a result, one should expect a non-linear relationship between the largest blockholder's ownership and principal-principal agency costs:

> *H1.3$_b$: The ownership size effect on a firm's principal-principal agency costs is non-linear c.p.*

Presence on the Firm's Most Important Bodies

With regard to <u>supervisory board</u> presence, it may be possible that the frequent interaction with management over time affects the **sources of the agency conflict**. In particular, the interaction may result in a convergence of interest between the blockholder and firm management which may subsequently collude and use their combined influence against the interest of the remaining shareholders. Putting aside a potential collusion, the presence may affect the information asymmetries existing between the largest blockholder and the remaining shareholders. Members of the supervisory board are provided with detailed information on fundamental matters regarding the firm's business and are able to request information from management. The presence on the board therefore constitutes an important source of privileged and valuable information that is not possessed by remaining shareholders, provided they have no board representation. As a consequence, the largest blockholder has substantial discretion and may affect decisions unobservable for the remaining shareholders.[1612]

Board representation may also affect the **blockholder's incentive**. While the size of the private benefits should stay constant, the costs of these private benefits should be lower relative to blockholders without board representation. First, the blockholder representative within the supervisory board should reduce the extent to which the supervisory board engages in the monitoring of the blockholder and hence lower the blockholder's likelihood of being caught and punished. Second, a blockholder representative has a better ability to develop trust which may result in a lower probability of facing resistance in the supervisory board. Third, its increased discretion may enable the blockholder to conceal its exploitation and hence further lower the costs of private benefits. As a result, the net benefit of private benefits is higher for blockholders with a board representation.

Finally, board representation increases the **blockholder's power**. The direct access to the management, the privileged access to information, and the influence on a number of im-

---

1609 See also Bhagat/Jefferis Jr. (2002): 24f; Anderson/Reeb (2003): 1321 and section 4.1.1.2.
1610 See also Gugler/Yurtoglu (2003): 733.
1611 See also La Porta et al. (2002): 1151; Farinha (2003): 1176.
1612 This may e.g. involve some form of agenda control which has been explained in section 2.1.4.2.

portant decisions increase the blockholder's power relative to blockholders without board representation.

To sum up, under the assumption of differential utility functions and risk preferences and holding constant the blockholder's ownership level, the largest blockholder's representation on the firm's bodies should increase principal-principal agency costs. Consistent with this, *Cronqvist/Nilsson* (2003) state that "direct involvement facilitates expropriation, and may thus result in larger agency costs" [1613].

H1.3$_c$: The representation of the largest blockholder on a firm's supervisory board has a positive effect on a firm's principal-principal agency costs c.p.

Most of the arguments above also apply to a representation on the management board. However, one may argue that the discretion of the blockholder in this case is greater, since the blockholder is more directly involved in the decision processes of the management which are not observable for shareholder representatives in the supervisory board. This may further increase information asymmetries and enable the blockholder to push through its interests before the respective topic is presented to the supervisory board. Nevertheless, the ability of the blockholder to pursue private benefits should depend on the strength of the supervisory board and the board's incentive to supervise managerial decisions in the presence of a blockholder. Overall, the following hypothesis is formulated:

H1.3$_d$: The representation of the largest blockholder on a firm's management board has a positive effect on a firm's principal-principal agency costs c.p.

Blockholder Identity

The severity of the principal-principal conflict in the portfolio firms of the four blockholder identities depends on the identities' impact on the sources of the agency conflict and the incentive of the respective type to pursue its self-interest against the interest of the remaining shareholders.

With regard to the **sources of the agency conflict**, the equity stake of a family blockholder, which frequently constitutes a major portion of the family's personal wealth, is likely to be large and concentrated within a single firm, which strongly exposes the family to firm-specific risk. Due to their financial and emotional ties to their firms, families may follow risk reduction strategies to secure firm survival which result in unnecessary costs for the diversified minority shareholders.[1614] In contrast, institutional investors typically hold well diversified portfolios and therefore exhibit risk preferences similar to those of smaller shareholders. Compared to these investors, private equity firms are likely to own larger stakes and to hold a smaller number of portfolio firms which should increase their risk aversion. Similarly, strategic investors own large stakes in their portfolio firms, however, are unlikely to hold multiple

---

1613 Cronqvist/Nilsson (2003): 700. Also the empirical evidence provided in section 4.1.2.2 suggests that blockholder presence on a firm's bodies may increase its discretion and therefore its incentive to generate private benefits of control. In fact, blockholders may aim for board representation just to ensure their ability to expropriate the remaining shareholders.

1614 See also Andres (2008): 434.

portfolio firms. Consequently, apart from institutional investors, the blockholder types should be more risk averse than the remaining smaller shareholders – the difference should be most pronounced for families and least pronounced for private equity firms.

Due to their extensive industry knowledge, strategic and private equity investors should have better information regarding the external environment than the remaining shareholders. Moreover, strategic investors are typically engaged in a business relationship with their portfolio firms which provides them with an inconspicuous and hence advantageous channel for diverting profits.[1615] Their privileged knowledge in the respective business areas as well as the creative leeway in the contractual design makes strategic investors well-positioned for the extraction of private benefits.[1616] Although institutional investors have less extensive industry knowledge, they are generally successful in gaining access to inside information and hence have an informational advantage over smaller shareholders. The information asymmetries relative to the remaining shareholders should be greatest for family blockholders, as they possess deep, tacit firm- and industry-specific knowledge.

Private equity and institutional investors most likely have purely financial goals and are focused on the maximization of shareholder value. Consequently, their utility functions should match those of the remaining shareholders. However, institutional investors are typically regarded as being short-term oriented and may pursue short-term improvements in the focal firm's stock price at the expense of long-term performance.[1617] As the remaining shareholders have a long-term view, they are negatively affected by a potential focus on short-term performance. In contrast to these investors, families and strategic investors typically have additional (business) relationships with their portfolio firms. Hence, their goal is to maximize their utility across the entire range of relationships, complementing (or even replacing) the shareholder value goal.[1618] Due to their preference for the retention of intrafamily relatedness and firm survival, family blockholders may forego higher stock prices in order to generate these private benefits to the detriment of minority shareholders. Moreover, family ownership may cause conflicts between the family (who might regard the firm as its private possession) and outside shareholders (who view the firm as a joint possession of all shareholders).[1619] Strategic investors may derive utility from an existing or potential business relationship with their portfolio firm and may therefore side with management in order to protect these business relationships.[1620] Thereby, they might be willing to accept value drops if the benefits they receive from their business relationships outweigh the losses they bear as shareholders. Since the re-

1615 See also section 4.1.3.4.1.

1616 For instance, strategic investors may be able to make favorable deals with their portfolio firms regarding transfer prices, patents or technologies. See also Cronqvist/Nilsson (2003): 700.

1617 With regard to empirical evidence, Kahan/Rock (2007): 1087, 1092 find that institutional investor activism is "designed to achieve short-term payoff at the expense of long-term profitability." However, based on a literature review, Bebchuk (2013): 1672f does not find support for the claim that institutional investors are short-term oriented and exhibit myopic activism.

1618 See Thomsen/Pedersen (2000): 694.

1619 See Young et al. (2003): 28. The authors call this an "us versus them" mentality of the firm.

1620 See Bott (2002): 57. Note that this may, to a lesser extent, also be the case for institutional investors. See Pound (1988): 242.

maining shareholders do not receive compensation for the loss in firm value, this gives rise to a conflict with other shareholders.[1621]

With regard to the **blockholder's incentive**, institutional investors are frequently located abroad and exposed to less pressure from politicians and unions relative to domestic blockholders (e.g. strategic investors or families) which may lower their costs of private benefits. However, since they frequently hold stakes in the same portfolio firms and depend on their mutual cooperation, a generation of private benefits against the interests of other shareholders should severely damage the investor's reputation and would be associated with significant costs.[1622] The gains of any private benefit extraction by the manager of an institutional or strategic investor largely accrue to the institution that employs the manager. However, when extracting private benefits, the manager risks personal liability. As a result, he might not find private benefits to be worth the risk.[1623] If the private benefits realized by a private equity firm increase the return for its investors, the private equity manager has a strong incentive to pursue private benefits, since its compensation is strongly tied to the return realized for the investors. However, the size of the benefits should be greatest for family blockholders. In contrast to the aforementioned types of investors, the private benefits arising from any self-interested behavior by the family do not have to be shared with several owners.[1624] This should provide the family with greater incentives to extract private benefits relative to other investor types.[1625]

To recapitulate, all types should have superior information relative to the remaining shareholders. Of the four types, institutional and private equity investors should have utility functions and risk preferences that are most compatible to those of the remaining shareholders, suggesting that their self-interest might be similar to the interest of the remaining shareholders. In contrast, the utility functions and risk preferences of families and strategic investors should diverge from those of smaller shareholders. Moreover, strategic investors are regarded as being well-positioned to extract private benefits. Relative to other investors, families should have the greatest incentive to extract private benefits. As a consequence, the following hypotheses are formulated:

> *H1.3$_e$: If the largest blockholder is either a private equity or an institutional investor, then the larger the ownership size of the largest blockholder, the lower a firm's principal-principal agency costs c.p.*[1626]

> *H1.3$_f$: If the largest blockholder is either a family or strategic investor, then the larger the ownership size of the largest blockholder, the higher a firm's principal-principal agency costs c.p.*[1627]

1621 If the strategic investor's acquisition is motivated by an interest in the resources of the target firm, the utility function of the remaining shareholders and the investor are even more likely to differ. While the former is interested in the firm's long-term survival, the latter tries to transfer important assets. Since this negatively affects a firm's expected cash flows, the remaining shareholders are adversely affected.

1622 This argument is also supported by Seger (1997): 119.

1623 See also Black (1992a): 857.

1624 See also Ellul et al. (2007): 11.

1625 See Villalonga/Amit (2006): 387.

1626 This effect is tested for each of the blockholder types individually.

Provided that families or strategic investors increase principal-principal agency costs via an extraction of private benefits, their power to do so should be greater with higher levels of ownership and the legal rights that come with higher ownership levels. Hence, one may reasonably expect that the private benefits should be greater for higher than for lower levels of ownership. This expectation results in the following hypothesis:

H1.3$_g$: If the largest blockholder is either a family or strategic investor, then the ownership size effect on a firm's principal-principal agency costs is non-linear c.p.[1628]

Arguments mentioned earlier as well as existing literature suggests that the "us versus them" mentality of family blockholders is more pronounced if they are present on the management or supervisory board. They may consequently treat other investors as being inferior and find the presence of external shareholders disturbing.[1629] This may result in a situation, "where non-family members (...) are excluded from major top-level decisions and minority shareholders' interests are neglected."[1630] Hence, the unity of ownership and control may ultimately result in family entrenchment and the exercise of managerial prerogatives.[1631] Overall, families may intentionally use their power for the generation of private benefits to the detriment of the remaining shareholders.[1632]

However, board representation and the resulting easier access to information and the direct involvement in the firm's decision making also provides the other three blockholder types with greater power and discretion which they can use either for an improved monitoring in the interest of the remaining shareholders or for a generation of private benefits. Therefore, the following hypothesis is formulated:

H1.3$_h$: The largest blockholder's representation on a firm's management or supervisory board has an effect on the ownership size effect on a firm's principal-principal agency costs c.p.[1633]

5.2.3.4 Impact on Firm Value

The following section formulates expectations regarding the effect of the largest blockholder's characteristics on firm value.

Ownership Size of the Largest Blockholder

As argued in section 5.2.1, the influence of the largest blockholder's ownership on the value of its portfolio firm should stem from its net impact on the overall agency costs. With regard

1627 This effect is tested for each of the blockholder types individually.

1628 This effect is tested for each of the blockholder types individually. However, no hypothesis is formulated regarding private equity and institutional investors due to an absence of a sound theoretical reasoning.

1629 This problem may be further increased if one acknowledges that families are generally reluctant to dilute their ownership in order to finance growth and thus will eschew to include nonfamily investors unless they are in dire need to do so. See Sirmon/Hitt (2003): 341.

1630 Young et al. (2003): 28.

1631 See also Cheffins (2006): 1319; Chen et al. (2013): 1166.

1632 See also Leiber (2008): 62f; Chen et al. (2013): 1171. Also Maury/Pajuste (2005): 1815 find that families with board representation are more prone to the extraction of private benefits.

1633 This hypothesis is tested for each blockholder type and for management and supervisory board representation individually.

to the components of the overall agency costs, the largest blockholder's ownership is expected to lower both managerial agency costs and agency costs of debt. Due to potential opposite effects, no directional hypothesis on the effect of the largest blockholder's ownership on principal-principal agency costs is formulated. Nevertheless, the expected net effect on overall agency costs should lead to a higher firm value. Hence, the following hypothesis is formulated:

> *H1.4$_a$: The larger the ownership size of the largest blockholder, the higher firm value c.p.*

Since the theoretical argumentation concerning the impact of the largest blockholder's ownership size on agency costs of debt and principal-principal agency costs suggests greater agency cost reductions for larger levels of ownership, a similar non-linear relationship between the largest blockholder's ownership and firm value should be expected. The necessity to account for non-linearities has further been pointed out by the existing empirical evidence as summarized in section 4.1.1.2.

> *H1.4$_b$: The ownership size effect on firm value is non-linear c.p.*

Presence on the Firm's Most Important Bodies

Concerning the largest blockholder's presence on the bodies of its portfolio firm, the previous analyses on the components of the firm's overall agency costs yield the following results. Due to countervailing effects, both supervisory and management board representation may either increase or decrease a firm's managerial agency costs. With regard to agency costs of debt, the presence of the largest blockholder on a firm's supervisory board (management board) is expected to decrease (increase) a firm's agency costs of debt. Finally, the blockholder's presence on both management and supervisory board is expected to increase principal-principal agency costs.

The analysis based on the blockholder's presence on the supervisory board therefore yields ambiguous results: while it is expected to increase principal-principal agency costs, it is expected to decrease agency costs of debt. With regard to managerial agency costs, agency theoretic propositions suggest that board representation can be associated with both increased and decreased agency costs. Overall, these results do not provide sufficient confidence to formulate a directional hypothesis:

> *H1.4$_c$: The representation of the largest blockholder on a firm's supervisory board has an effect on firm value c.p.*

In contrast, based on the expectations above, the blockholder's presence on the management board has an increasing net effect on the overall agency costs. As a result, it should decrease firm value.

> *H1.4$_d$: The representation of the largest blockholder on a firm's management board has a negative effect on firm value c.p.*

Blockholder Identity

Agency theoretic propositions suggest the following influence of the four blockholder types on the components of a firm's overall agency costs.

Of all blockholder types, family blockholders are expected to result in the strongest decrease in managerial agency costs. Moreover, their ownership should not result in higher agency costs of debt. However, family ownership is expected to be associated with higher principal-principal agency costs. In total, family ownership is expected to decrease the overall agency costs of its portfolio firms.[1634]

> *H1.4$_e$: If the largest blockholder is a family, then the larger the ownership size of the largest blockholder, the higher firm value c.p.*

While no directional expectation regarding the effect of private equity blockholders on managerial agency costs is formulated, private equity investors are expected to decrease principal-principal agency costs. Moreover, private equity investors should not engage in a transfer of wealth from debtholders and hence are not expected to increase agency costs of debt. In summary, private equity firms are expected to decrease a firm's overall agency costs and increase firm value.

> *H1.4$_f$: If the largest blockholder is a private equity investor, then the larger the ownership size of the largest blockholder, the higher firm value c.p.*

Institutional investors are expected to increase a firm's agency costs of debt and to decrease a firm's principal-principal agency costs; with regard to managerial agency costs, a non-directional hypothesis is formulated. Similar to institutional investors, no directional hypothesis with regard to the effect of strategic investors on managerial agency costs is postulated. Concerning agency costs of debt, strategic investor should have a low incentive to shift value from debtholders and should not be associated with higher agency costs of debt. However, strategic investors should be associated with higher principal-principal agency costs. As a result, the impact of both institutional investors and strategic investors is unknown, resulting in a non-directional hypothesis for both blockholder types:

> *H1.4$_g$: If the largest blockholder is an institutional investor, then the ownership size of the largest blockholder has an effect on firm value c.p.*
>
> *H1.4$_h$: If the largest blockholder is a strategic investor, then the ownership size of the largest blockholder has an effect on firm value c.p.*

Since the theoretical argumentation suggests a non-linear relationship between family ownership and all components of agency costs, a non-linear relationship is also expected between family ownership and firm value:

> *H1.4$_i$: If the largest blockholder is a family, then the ownership size effect on firm value is non-linear c.p.*

1634 This is in line with existing evidence which finds that "families successfully balance the two agency problems that minority shareholders are exposed to (owner-manager conflicts on the one hand and minority shareholder expropriation by a controlling shareholder on the other hand)." Andres (2008): 439f and 444. The evidence is based on 275 German listed companies from 1998 to 2004. See Andres (2008): 431.

To the extent to which existing and prospective shareholders account for the non-linearities hypothesized concerning the impact of institutional investors on managerial agency costs and of strategic investors on principal-principal agency costs, a non-linear relationship should also be observed for the relationship between these investors and firm value:

> *H1.4$_j$: If the largest blockholder is an institutional investor, then the ownership size effect on firm value is non-linear c.p.*

> *H1.4$_k$: If the largest blockholder is a strategic investor, then the ownership size effect on firm value is non-linear c.p.*

Finally, existing empirical evidence and agency theoretic propositions highlighted the importance of management or supervisory board presence for family blockholders. However, the impact of the remaining blockholder types on the components of the overall agency costs may depend on board presence as well. In line with the hypothesis on principal-principal agency costs, the following hypothesis is formulated:

> *H1.4$_l$: The largest blockholder's representation on a firm's management or supervisory board has an effect on the ownership size effect on firm value c.p.*[1635]

5.2.4 Hypotheses under the Assumption of Blockholder Interrelationships

Consistent with the empirical approach described in section 5.1.1, the deliberations in the following sections account for blockholder interrelationships. Therefore, the sections focus on (1) the ownership size of a second blockholder, (2) heterogenous ownership structures, and (3) the incontestability of the largest blockholder.[1636] The hypotheses are based on the following research question: Do blockholder interrelationships affect agency costs and firm value as well as the relationship between the four blockholder types and agency costs and firm value?

5.2.4.1 Impact on Managerial Agency Costs

The following section formulates expectations regarding the effect of blockholder interrelationships on managerial agency costs.

Ownership of a Second Blockholder

The presence of a second blockholder is likely to affect the largest blockholder's incentive to engage in monitoring as well as the feasibility of monitoring. With regard to the **feasibility of monitoring**, the presence of another blockholder may allow the monitoring of corporate management also in cases where the largest blockholder individually would not have sufficient power to do so. The combined voting rights of the cooperating blockholders may enable the blockholders to reach control thresholds that provide them with legal rights that facilitate their monitoring of corporate management.

[1635] This hypothesis is tested for each blockholder type and for management and supervisory board representation individually.

[1636] The impact of the largest blockholder's incontestability is only investigated for principal-principal agency costs and firm value. Moreover, the effect of the ownership of a second blockholder and the incontestability of the largest blockholder are examined while accounting for the blockholder identities.

With regard to the **blockholder's incentive**, a rational blockholder aims at a reduction of the monitoring costs and/or at an increase of the monitoring benefits. In the presence of a second blockholder, the largest blockholder may therefore seek to engage in cooperative monitoring. As outlined in section 4.2.1, this enables the blockholders to distribute the fixed monitoring costs and to realize monitoring synergies that lower the monitoring costs. Moreover, the blockholders may have complementary monitoring skills that enhance the monitoring effectiveness and increase the monitoring benefits that accrue to both blockholders. The largest blockholder's incentive may also be increased in case the second largest blockholder engages in bilateral monitoring. If the largest blockholder receives private benefits from the firm's management in exchange for a lax monitoring, the second largest blockholder should increase the probability of being revealed and consequently the costs of private benefits.[1637] As a result, the largest blockholder may have greater incentives to effectively monitor management. Overall, the following (conditional) hypothesis is formulated:

> *H2.1$_a$: The larger the ownership size of the second largest blockholder, the stronger the negative ownership size effect on a firm's managerial agency costs c.p.*[1638]

However, the presence of a second blockholder may also result in a collusive agreement with the largest blockholder in order to pursue private benefits contrary to the interests of the remaining shareholders.[1639] The incentive of the two blockholders to collude depends on the similarity of their utility functions and risk preferences. Therefore, a collusion should be more likely if the largest and second largest blockholder are of the same type. As argued earlier, the generation of private benefits might require managerial support; the blockholders may secure this support by reducing their monitoring intensity, thereby allowing management to realize some private benefits. Hence, in case of a collusion, the ownership of the second blockholder should result in greater managerial agency costs. Section 5.2.3.3 argues that the likelihood of a generation of private benefits is most likely if the largest blockholder is a strategic investor or a family. If the second largest blockholder is of the same type, the incentive to collude and exploit firm resources should therefore be greatest for strategic investors and families. As a result, in the presence of a second blockholder of the same type, these blockholders may reduce the intensity and effectiveness of their managerial monitoring in favor of private benefits. This expectation results in the following hypothesis:

> *H2.1$_b$: If the two largest blockholders are either members of a family or strategic investors, then the larger the ownership size of the second largest blockholder, the stronger the positive ownership size effect on a firm's managerial agency costs c.p.*[1640]

1637 As the legal rights of the second largest blockholder(s) may be limited (see section 2.2.3.2), it may rely on informal influences in order to supervise the largest blockholder.

1638 This effect is tested for the four blockholder types individually.

1639 The likelihood of collusion should be particularly high if the largest blockholder in stage 2 of the regression analysis increases managerial agency costs. However, it is also possible that the generation of private benefits is feasible not before the presence of another blockholder willing to collude. In this case, a formerly decreasing effect on managerial agency costs would turn sign.

1640 This effect is tested for each of the blockholder types individually.

Heterogenous Ownership Structure

On the one hand, a greater number of blockholders may lower the **feasibility** of engaging in monitoring, since a blockholder willing to monitor most likely has to cooperate with the remaining blockholders. Moreover, the costs of organizing a larger group of blockholders to take concerted action should increase with the number of blockholders,[1641] which may raise the costs of monitoring and negatively affect the blockholder's **incentive** to engage in monitoring.[1642] On the other hand, a heterogenous ownership structure may be regarded as a proxy for the possibility to capture complementarities in monitoring. This should enhance the **blockholder's capability** to engage in monitoring. Moreover, the complementarities should reduce the monitoring costs and hence increase the **blockholder's incentive** to engage in monitoring.[1643] The largest blockholder's incentive to effectively monitor corporate management should further increase due to a supervision of the blockholder's monitoring activities by the additional blockholders. Overall, a heterogenous ownership structure should increase the effectiveness of monitoring.[1644]

To conclude, a heterogenous ownership structure raises the blockholders' capability to engage in monitoring. While the costs of cooperation between blockholders should increase the costs of monitoring, these costs should be outweighed by complementarities and an increased effectiveness of monitoring. Finally, the presence of additional blockholders results in a multilateral monitoring and a supervision of blockholders' actions. Due to this, the following hypothesis is formulated:

> *H2.1$_c$: The more heterogenous a firm's ownership structure, the lower its managerial agency costs c.p.*

5.2.4.2 Impact on Agency Costs of Debt

The following section formulates expectations regarding the effect of blockholder interrelationships on agency costs of debt.

Ownership of a Second Blockholder

Section 5.2.3.2 argues that the expropriation of debtholders should be profitable for blockholders only in the short-run. In the long-run, their portfolio firms suffer from a reduced access to debt capital or higher interest payments which both negatively affect firm value and hence increase the costs of expropriating debtholders for the blockholder. As a result, the ownership of the largest blockholder should generally be associated with lower agency costs of debt for blockholder types with a long-term horizon. These types should have low incen-

---

1641 See Hansmann (1988): 278; Leech/Leahy (1991): 1423f for a similar argument.

1642 The blockholder's incentive should be more negatively affected if the multiple blockholders engage in independent monitoring, which may result in blockholder-blockholder agency conflicts.

1643 The lower costs might outweigh the lower portion of the benefits from monitoring the largest blockholder receives due to its (potentially) smaller share ownership.

1644 See also Bloch/Hege (2001): 32. The authors also state that a blockholder may voluntarily give control of the firm to another blockholder, if the difference in capability between the two blockholders is significant. In this case, the inefficient blockholder will have a greater benefit from relinquishing monitoring to the other blockholder, which should positively affect the monitoring effectiveness. See Bloch/Hege (2001): 9.

tives to expropriate debtholders but are rather incentivized to develop a reputation for being an honest borrower through effective monitoring and the signaling of low shareholder-debtholder conflicts. Based on this assumption, the **blockholder's incentive** to develop a reputation for being an honest borrower (rather than to transfer value from debtholders) should be augmented by the ownership of a second blockholder in two ways. First, the ownership of a second blockholder lowers the monitoring (or signaling) costs, respectively. Second, it may increase the largest blockholder's incentive to develop a good reputation among debtholders via a supervision of the largest blockholder's behavior which makes transfers of value less attractive. The latter aspect may be of particular relevance for those blockholders that are more short-term interested and hence more likely to shift value from debtholders. Hence, the second blockholder's effect should be most significant for institutional investors, which are expected to be most likely to transfer value from debtholders.[1645] This expectation translates into the following hypothesis:

> *H2.2$_a$: If the largest blockholder is an institutional investor, then the larger the ownership size of the second largest blockholder, the stronger the negative ownership size effect on a firm's agency costs of debt.*

While a second blockholder in general should have the incentive to engage in the monitoring of the largest blockholder, the incentive to do so depends on the inconsistency of the interests between the largest and second largest blockholder. If the two blockholders share reconcilable interests, independent and bilateral monitoring is unnecessary. Rather, they have an incentive to engage in a cooperative monitoring, as this increases their power and lowers their costs of monitoring. A cooperation is beneficial for the debtholders only if the (joint) interest of the two blockholders is similar to the interest of the debtholders. As the blockholders' self-interests should not be affected by a second blockholder, the ownership of a second blockholder should amplify the relationship between the largest blockholder's ownership and agency costs of debt detected in stage 2. Therefore, across all four blockholder types, the following relationship is hypothesized:

> *H2.2$_b$: If the two largest blockholders are of the same type, then the larger the ownership size of the second largest blockholder, the stronger the ownership size effect on a firm's agency costs of debt c.p.*

Heterogenous Ownership Structure

As argued earlier, a blockholder's incentive to engage in a wealth transfer at the expense of debtholders should depend on its time horizon; a long-term oriented blockholder should be exposed to the costs from any transfer of wealth and should therefore have a weak incentive to transfer wealth. Presuming the presence of a large blockholder that is short-term oriented and hence aims to exploit a firm's debtholders, more heterogenous ownership structures should reduce the **blockholder's incentive** to do so. A more heterogenous ownership structure increases the probability that at least one of the remaining blockholders is long-term oriented and therefore unwilling to shift value from debtholders. This blockholder should conse-

1645 In this case, the monitoring results in the greatest benefits for the second largest blockholder.

quently engage in independent monitoring and supervise the largest blockholder to limit its discretion.[1646] As a result of this monitoring, the probability of being revealed is significantly higher which increases the downside of any transfer of wealth for the largest blockholder. All in all, a heterogenous ownership structure increases the probability that there is a blockholder whose self-interest is in line with the interest of the debtholders or whose exposure to the costs resulting from an exploitation of debtholders is sufficiently high to provide it with a stimulus to limit such an exploitation. This assumption translates into the following hypothesis:

> *H2.2$_c$: The more heterogenous a firm's ownership structure, the lower its agency costs of debt c.p.*

5.2.4.3 Impact on Principal-Principal Agency Costs

The following section formulates expectations regarding the effect of blockholder interrelationships on principal-principal agency costs.

Ownership of a Second Blockholder

As pointed out in section 3.2.1, a rational blockholder whose self-interest differs from the interest of the remaining shareholders balances private benefits against the resulting costs that are defrayed by the monitoring blockholder. However, to pursue private benefits in the first place, the blockholder needs to be equipped with sufficient power. Under the assumption of blockholder interrelationships, the benefits, costs, and power of the largest blockholder may depend on the presence of additional blockholders. Therefore, the blockholder is able to use its position for the maximization of its self-interest only in the "absence of a countervailing force"[1647].[1648] First, the ownership of a second blockholder naturally has a negative effect on the ownership of the largest blockholder, which reduces the largest **blockholder's power**. Second, if the second largest blockholder has utility functions and risk preferences irreconcilable with those of the largest blockholder, it should engage in bilateral monitoring to mitigate any negative consequences arising from each others monitoring of firm management.[1649] By increasing the probability of being revealed and caught, this bilateral monitoring should increase the costs and hence reduce the **blockholder's incentive** to generate private benefits.

Overall, by increasing the costs of private benefits and decreasing the power of the largest blockholder, the ownership of a second largest blockholder is expected to decrease the self dealing of the largest blockholder.[1650] However, if the largest blockholder's ownership is not associated with higher principal-principal agency costs, the second largest blockholder is un-

---

1646 As the legal rights of the second largest blockholder(s) may be limited (see section 2.2.3.2), it may rely on informal influences in order to supervise the largest blockholder.

1647 Dahya et al. (2008): 74.

1648 See also Bainbridge (2012): 246.

1649 See also section 4.2.1.

1650 Dhillon/Rossetto (2009): 4 propose that, depending on their ownership stake, investors have different preferences for a project's risk and return characteristics. While a large blockholder favors a low risk strategy, well diversified minority shareholders favor a high risk strategy. Due to its greater power, the blockholder wins this conflict of interest. However, the presence of a second blockholder can mitigate this conflict of interest and shift the investment decision to an outcome offering higher return for the minority shareholders.

likely to engage in the costly monitoring of the largest blockholder. Since the probability of a generation of private benefits should be highest if the largest blockholder is a strategic investor or a family,[1651] the second largest blockholder's ownership should therefore have the greatest effect on the relationship between these investors and principal-principal agency costs. Consequently, the following hypothesis is formulated:

H2.3$_a$: If the largest blockholder is either a family or strategic investor, then the larger the ownership size of the second largest blockholder, the stronger the negative ownership size effect on a firm's principal-principal agency costs c.p.[1652]

As pointed out above, the influence of the second largest blockholder on the relationship between the largest blockholder's ownership and principal-principal agency costs depends on the inconsistency of the interests between the largest and second largest blockholder. In case the two blockholders share reconcilable utility functions and risk preferences, bilateral monitoring is improbable. Since their interests are similar, it is less costly to engage in cooperative monitoring which increases the blockholders' power and incentive to monitor corporate management. As the blockholders' self-interests are unlikely to be affected, the ownership of a second blockholder should therefore amplify the relationship between the largest blockholders' ownership and principal-principal agency costs detected in stage 2. This assumption results in the formulation of the following hypothesis across all four blockholder types:

H2.3$_b$: If the two largest blockholders are of the same type, then the larger the ownership size of the second largest blockholder, the stronger the ownership size effect on a firm's principal-principal agency costs c.p.

Heterogenous Ownership Structure

A heterogenous ownership structure should reduce the largest **blockholder's power** and hence the feasibility of diverting corporate resources. A larger number of blockholders should result in independent monitoring and increase the likelihood that one of these blockholders challenges the largest blockholder in order to prevent the diversion of resources. As a result, in case the largest blockholder aims at a collusion with one or more blockholders, heterogenous ownership structures increase the probability that there is a blockholder that cannot be convinced to collude and subsequently tries to challenge the coalition.[1653] Even if the blockholders could be convinced to cooperate, the number of blockholders makes bargaining more expensive and increases coordination costs, since every decision made requires the consent from other blockholders.[1654] Moreover, excessive bargaining between the blockholders may prevent business decisions that would benefit the blockholders but harm minority shareholders.[1655] Overall, a heterogenous ownership structure raises the costs involved in the generation

1651 See also section 5.2.3.3 and 5.2.4.1.

1652 This effect is tested for each of the blockholder types individually. If families and strategic investors are not associated with greater principal-principal agency costs in stage 2, the supervision by a second largest blockholder might not be necessary and hence be insignificant.

1653 See also Attig et al. (2009): 409.

1654 See Bennedsen/Wolfenzon (2000): 114. This presupposes that no individual blockholder owns more than 50% of the stock.

1655 See Gomes/Novaes (2005): 1f. The authors call this the "bargaining effect".

of private benefits and consequently lowers the **blockholder's incentive** to generate private benefits. Therefore, the presence of additional blockholders should lead to improvements in the firm's governance as independent monitoring among a large number of blockholders prevents investments against minority shareholder's interest.[1656] Rather than pursuing private benefits, the blockholders may compete for the votes of small shareholders on a firm's AGM by acting in line with small shareholders' interest. However, while a heterogenous ownership structure avoids principal-principal agency costs stemming from the conflicts between minority shareholders and blockholders, it may simultaneously give rise to blockholder-blockholder agency conflicts which increase a firm's principal-principal agency costs. Since the strength of the two crosscurrent effects is unknown, the following undirectional hypothesis is formulated:

> *$H2.3_C$: The heterogeneity of a firm's ownership structure has an effect on its principal-principal agency costs c.p.*

Blockholder Incontestability

Section 5.2.3.3 argues that large ownership increases the blockholder's power and hence the feasibility of generating private benefits. While the absolute size of the largest blockholder, as stressed under the assumption of blockholder heterogeneity, may be a proxy for its power, a more sophisticated proposition on the power of the blockholder requires the focus on the largest blockholder's ownership relative to other blockholders that could potentially engage in monitoring and challenge the largest blockholder. In this regard, higher incontestability of the largest blockholder should increase the **blockholder's power** and hence the feasibility of generating private benefits. In particular, greater incontestability reduces the largest blockholder's dependence on the remaining shareholders in order to reach the necessary control thresholds. In addition, greater incontestability is associated with a reduced ability of additional blockholders to challenge the largest blockholder on a firm's AGM, e.g. by blocking important decisions.[1657] Moreover, since greater incontestability measures the relative power of the blockholder, it does not necessarily increase the blockholder's exposure to the costs from private benefits – in fact, greater incontestability may arise from low share ownership of the second and third largest blockholder rather than from a supermajority of the largest blockholder.

In contrast, greater incontestability is unlikely to affect the **sources of agency conflicts**, i.e. the blockholder's self-interest. Hence, a blockholder's incontestability should have an increasing effect only for those blockholders that are likely to differ from the remaining shareholders in terms of their self-interest. As argued previously, the probability of a generation of private benefits should be highest if the largest blockholder is a strategic investor or a family. Therefore, the incontestability of the largest blockholder should have an increasing effect if the

[1656] For a similar argument see also Attig et al. (2008): 724.

[1657] Note that the remaining blockholders can still use the media to generate awareness for self dealing by the largest blockholder. However, greater incontestability of the largest blockholder limits the effectiveness of those mechanisms that accrue to the blockholders by nature of their ownership. See also section 2.2.3.2.

largest blockholder is either a family or a strategic investor.[1658] In contrast, greater incontestability should either have no or a decreasing effect on the relationship between the ownership of private equity or institutional investors and principal-principal agency costs.[1659] Consequently, the following hypotheses are formulated:

H2.3$_d$: If the largest blockholder is either a family or strategic investor, then the larger the incontestability of the largest blockholder, the stronger the positive ownership size effect on a firm's principal-principal agency costs c.p.[1660]

H2.3$_e$: If the largest blockholder is either a private equity or an institutional investor, then the relation between the incontestability of the largest blockholder and the ownership size effect on a firm's principal-principal agency costs is non-positive c.p.[1661]

5.2.4.4 Impact on Firm Value

The following section formulates expectations regarding the effect of blockholder interrelationships on firm value.

Ownership of a Second Blockholder

Overall, the previous discussion suggests that the ownership of a second largest blockholder should contribute to a reduction of the components of the overall agency costs within the firm. First, it increases the largest blockholder's power and its incentive to engage in monitoring. Second, under the presumption of differential interests of the two largest blockholders, the second largest blockholder raises the costs of any adverse behavior of the largest blockholder by limiting its discretion, increasing its likelihood of being revealed and thereby lowering the largest blockholder's incentive to generate private benefits. Hence, existing and prospective shareholders should generally regard the presence of a second blockholder to be beneficial. As a result, the following hypothesis is formulated:

H2.4$_a$: The larger the ownership size of the second largest blockholder, the stronger the positive ownership size effect on firm value c.p.[1662]

The presence of a second blockholder that is of the same type as the largest blockholder should also increase the largest blockholder's power and incentive to engage in monitoring. However, since the two blockholders should have similar interests, the second blockholder is unlikely to engage in monitoring of the largest blockholder. Rather, both blockholders will engage in a cooperative monitoring with its effect being dependent on the self-interest of the blockholder type. In line with the previous discussions, the ownership of the second blockholder is expected to amplify the effect of the largest blockholder which should be accounted for by the remaining shareholders.

1658 Also Maury/Pajuste (2005): 1828f hypothesize that the contestability of control is more important in family owned firms.

1659 A decreasing effect may stem from a greater power or incentive to engage in effective monitoring.

1660 This effect is tested for each of the blockholder types individually.

1661 This effect is tested for each of the blockholder types individually.

1662 This effect is tested for the four blockholder types individually.

$H2.4_b$: If the two largest blockholders are of the same type, then the larger the ownership size of the second largest blockholder, the stronger the ownership size effect on firm value c.p.

Heterogenous Ownership Structure

The expectations with regard to a heterogenous ownership structure formulated in the preceding sections suggest a unidirectional relationship: It is expected to decrease a firm's managerial agency costs and agency costs of debt either through an increased supervision of the largest blockholder's monitoring activities or through an enhanced effectiveness and lower costs of blockholder monitoring. With regard to principal-principal agency costs, it can either have an increasing or decreasing effect. Since the effect of a heterogenous ownership structure in general should be favorable from the shareholders' perspective, rational shareholders should account for this favorable effect and incorporate the lower overall agency costs into the firm's value. Thus, the following hypothesis is formulated:

$H2.4_c$: The more heterogenous a firm's ownership structure, the higher firm value c.p.

Blockholder Incontestability

As argued in section 5.2.4.3, increases in the incontestability of the largest blockholder result in a greater discretion and substantial power of the blockholder. Provided the particular blockholder's interest differs from the interest of the remaining shareholders, as is the case for families and strategic investors, the incontestability should be associated with higher principal-principal agency costs. These costs should be incorporated in the valuation of the firm's shares, thereby depressing firm value.

This assumption is supported by preliminary empirical evidence. *Maury/Pajuste* (2005) find that the largest blockholder's inability to form the simple majority through collusion is value enhancing.[1663] *Attig et al.* (2009) observe that multiple blockholders of comparable size are more efficient monitors and increase firm value.[1664] They conclude that the difference between the ownership of the largest and second largest blockholder is significantly negatively related to firm value.[1665] In light of these findings and the theoretical arguments, the following hypotheses are formulated:

$H2.4_d$: If the largest blockholder is either a family or strategic investor, then the larger the incontestability of the largest blockholder, the stronger the negative ownership size effect on firm value c.p.[1666]

1663 See Maury/Pajuste (2005): 1825-1827. The evidence is based on data of 136 non-financial Finnish listed firms over the period of 1993-2000. See Maury/Pajuste (2005): 1819f.

1664 See Attig et al. (2009): 397f. The evidence is based on a 1996-sample of 1,252 publicly-traded firms from Hong Kong, Indonesia, Japan, Korea, Malaysia, Philippines, Singapore, Taiwan, and Thailand.

1665 See Laeven/Levine (2008): 595. Their sample comprises cross-sectional data on 1,657 firms from 13 Western European companies collected at some point during 1996-1999.

1666 This effect is tested for each of the blockholder types individually.

H2.4$_e$: If the largest blockholder is either a private equity or an institutional investor, then the relation between the incontestability of the largest blockholder and the ownership size effect on firm value is non-negative c.p.[1667]

5.3 Operationalization

Having outlined the model of blockholder monitoring and the hypotheses to be investigated, the next step involves the explanation of how the components within the model are operationalized. Therefore, section 5.3.1 focuses on the measurement of the three agency cost types and firm value. Section 5.3.2 contains the measurement of the blockholder identities.[1668] In line with the stagewise empirical approach, section 5.3.3 provides a definition of the explanatory variables presuming blockholder homogeneity (section 5.3.3.1), heterogeneity (section 5.3.3.2), and interrelationships (section 5.3.3.3). Finally, section 5.3.4 introduces the control variables to be used in the regression analysis.

5.3.1 Agency Costs and Firm Value

When measuring agency costs, one has to keep in mind that the three components of agency costs contained in the model cannot be identified and measured directly.[1669] Rather, they can only be indirectly approximated by (1) variables that represent circumstances that most likely lead to agency problems and the associated costs as well as by (2) aggregate outcome measures that proxy for specific components of agency costs.[1670] Being aware of this limitation, the operationalization of managerial agency costs constitutes the focus of section 5.3.1.1. Section 5.3.1.2 deals with the measurement of agency costs of debt whereas section 5.3.1.3 outlines the proxy for principal-principal agency costs.[1671] In addition to the individual measurement of the components of a firm's overall agency costs, the present study also incorporates a measure of firm value (section 5.3.1.4).[1672]

5.3.1.1 Managerial Agency Costs

The assumption that better corporate governance – or blockholder monitoring in the case of the present study – reduces managerial agency costs is admittedly vague. *Bertrand/Mullainathan* (2003) argue that for researchers, it is virtually impossible to translate the hypothesis into predictions regarding specific and observable managerial behavior due to data limitations that constrain the specific outcomes to be studied.[1673] Therefore, the study at hand

---

1667 This effect is tested for each of the blockholder types individually.

1668 Although the blockholder identities constitute a blockholder characteristic and thus a measure of blockholder heterogeneity, the complexity of the definition necessitates a separate explanation.

1669 This problem has also been noticed by Villalonga/Amit (2006): 401.

1670 While this is a problem faced by all empirical studies focusing on agency costs, it is usually not addressed in these studies. Wolf (1999): 47f represents an exception.

1671 Since the proxies do not directly measure monitoring or bonding expenditures, they may understate total agency costs. See also Ang et al. (2000): 86, FN 4. In contrast, the measure of firm value incorporates all components of agency costs.

1672 Please note that, for the sake of simplicity, the explanations below use the singular form of blockholder only. However, these deliberations also apply to a group of blockholders.

1673 See Bertrand/Mullainathan (2003): 1044.

follows existing studies and uses an aggregate outcome measure as a proxy for managerial behavior.

In order to measure managerial agency costs, the present thesis employs an efficiency ratio that is frequently used in accounting and financial economics research. This ratio constitutes the **expense ratio** *[opex_sales]* which is defined as a firm's operating expenses[1674] scaled by annual sales.[1675] This measure captures managerial cost discipline, that is the extent to which a firm's management controls operating costs.[1676] Since managerial expenses on perks and other non-essentials should be reflected in the expense ratio, it also captures excessive perquisite consumption.[1677] In general, it measures the costs arising from shirking and perquisite consumption by the corporate management.[1678] However, the expense ratio neither measures indirect agency costs arising from a distortion of decision making nor agency costs not reflected in the income-statement, such as monitoring expenses by shareholders or bonding expenditures by the management.[1679] Nevertheless, *Ang et al.* (2000) conclude that the expense ratio constitutes a satisfactory measure of managerial agency costs, as it provides "results consistent with the predictions of agency theory for a wide range of potentially high to low agency cost organizational and management structures."[1680]

With regard to the interpretation in the empirical analysis, a higher expense ratio indicates greater managerial agency costs.

5.3.1.2 Agency Costs of Debt

According to *Prowse* (1990), the potential for shareholders to engage in wealth-transferring strategies detrimental to debtholders depends on three characteristics: (1) the degree to which the assets of the firm can be put to multiple uses, (2) the costs of the debtholders to monitor and control the use of the assets, and (3) whether or not the shareholders can gain from shifting the use of assets.[1681]

The present thesis utilizes a variable that measures the degree to which the blockholders are able to engage in wealth-transfer strategies (characteristic 1) and the costs of the debtholder to monitor and control the use of the firm's resources (characteristic 2).[1682] In particular, it measures the potential for blockholders to engage in wealth transfer strategies by the amount

---

1674 Operating expenses include SG&A expenses and other operating expenses after CoGS. One-time gains or losses are excluded.

1675 The expense ratio is also used e.g. by Ang et al. (2000): 85f; Fleming et al. (2005): 34f; Fauver/Fuerst (2006): 702; Dybvig/Warachka (2010): 8; Sánchez-Ballesta/García-Meca (2011): 409.

1676 See Fleming et al. (2005): 34f; Dybvig/Warachka (2010): 8, 18; Sánchez-Ballesta/García-Meca (2011): 409.

1677 See Ang et al. (2000): 86.

1678 For further details on perquisite consumption and shirking, please see section 2.1.2.

1679 See Ang et al. (2000): 86.

1680 Ang et al. (2000): 95.

1681 See Prowse (1990): 51.

1682 The study also aimed to use interest expenses as a more direct measure of agency costs of debt. However, due to poor data availability and quality, the study abstains from the use of a firm's interest expenses.

of **discretionary assets** *[discr_assets]*, calculated as $1 - \frac{Net\ fixed\ assets}{Total\ assets}$.[1683] In contrast to tangible assets, discretionary assets cannot be collateralized and therefore provide weaker protection against a possible expropriation for creditors.[1684] Discretionary assets are also more difficult to monitor. Hence, the less a firm's assets are tangible, the lower the difficulty for the blockholder to engage in wealth-transferring investment projects.[1685] In line with this, *Hwang/Kim* (1998) argue that with increasing intangible (discretionary) assets, shareholders can more easily engage in wealth-transferring activities.[1686] Also *Shome/Singh (1995)* state that the potential for wealth transfers from debtholders to shareholders increases with higher levels of discretionary assets through asset risk-shifts or asset sales.[1687] In addition, intangible assets are firm-specific and can often only be used efficiently in one particular firm. Due to this non-redeployability, agency costs of debt will be greater for firms with a high asset specificity.[1688]

It is important to note that the variable does not measure the severity of wealth transfers by the blockholder; rather, it indicates that the blockholder engages in activities that could *potentially* be used for the concealment of wealth transfer activities and hence provide *opportunities* for the blockholder to transfer wealth.[1689] Overall, firms that invested more in the preceding assets may be susceptible to the shareholder-debtholder agency conflict. In line with this, a blockholder that aims at an exploitation of debtholders should be positively related to the amount of discretionary assets. Thus, in the empirical analysis, higher discretionary assets are associated with a greater potential to engage in wealth transfer strategies by the blockholder and hence higher agency costs of debt.

5.3.1.3 Principal-Principal Agency Costs

The principal-principal conflicts are proxied by the **dividend payout ratio.**[1690] A number of conflicting theories have been proposed to explain the dividend policy of firms. Models predicting dividend payments can be classified into:[1691] (1) states characterized by information symmetry,[1692] (2) states characterized by information asymmetry, in particular the cash flow

---

1683 Net fixed assets – or PP&E – are defined as gross fixed assets less accumulated depreciation. The amount of discretionary assets has also been used by, among others, Prowse (1990): 52; Shome/Singh (1995): 9; Hwang/Kim (1998): 42.

1684 See Titman/Wessels (1988): 3. See also Sánchez-Ballesta/García-Meca (2011): 396.

1685 See also Prowse (1990): 52; Beiner et al. (2006): 253.

1686 See Hwang/Kim (1998): 49.

1687 See Shome/Singh (1995): 9. Also Kaserer/Moldenhauer (2008): 24 propose to use intangible assets as a measure for discretionary power.

1688 See Brailsford et al. (2002): 12f.

1689 See also Prowse (1990): 51. In general, these activities can also be used by management to conceal the generation of managerial private benefits. For details, please see the Yafeh/Yosha (2003).

1690 Due to severe data constraints, the present study only focuses on dividend payments. It does not examine share repurchases which should be motivated by a similar reasoning.

1691 See Frankfurter/Wood (2002): 111.

1692 Assuming information symmetry, Miller/Modigliani (1961): 425 claim in their seminal paper that the "dividend policy has no effect on the current value of the firm or its cost of capital", implying that dividend policy is irrelevant. See also Al-Malkawi/Rafferty/Pillai (2010): 174.

signaling hypothesis[1693] and models based on agency theory[1694] as well as (3) behavioral models[1695]. These models implicitly assume that managers set the level of dividends autonomously. However, this may not be applicable in the presence of one or more blockholders with sufficient ownership. In this case, one can doubt the managers' ability to decide on the level of dividends without the approval of the blockholder,[1696] which tries to adapt the payout policy to fit its personal interests.[1697] This adaptation may be detrimental to the remaining (minority) shareholders whose interests regarding dividend payouts may differ from those of the blockholder(s).[1698] Therefore, the dividend payout ratio is frequently used as a proxy for (the likelihood of) principal-principal conflicts.[1699]

The dividend payout ratio is defined as a firm's regular cash dividend as a percentage of the firm's annual sales *[div_payout]*.[1700] In contrast to the use of cash flows, sales are more difficult to manipulate or smooth via accounting practices and are less subject to theft. Note that the ratio has no economic interpretation; annual sales are used as deflator only.[1701]

Firms subject to greater principal-principal conflicts are assumed to pay lower levels of dividends, since "dividends transfer wealth from the discretion of the controlling shareholder to all shareholders on a pro rata basis."[1702] In line with this, a lower dividend payout ratio is re-

---

1693 The cash flow signaling hypothesis states that a firm's dividend policy reveals information about the firm's cash flows management expects to generate in the future. Hence, any increase in dividends is interpreted as a signal of higher future cash flow levels. Among the most important authors are Lintner (1956); Bhattacharya (1979); John/Williams (1985); Miller/Rock (1985). Support for the signaling hypothesis has been provided by Kalay (1980); Bernheim/Wanzt (1995); Yoon/Starks (1995); Gerke/Oerke/Sentner (1997); Allen et al. (2000); Cheffins (2006). For criticism, please see Easterbrook (1984); DeAngelo/DeAngelo/Skinner (1996); Benartzi/Michaely/Thaler (1997); Brav et al. (2005).

1694 Hypotheses based on agency theory argue that dividends reduce managerial agency problems by increasing the frequency of external capital raising. See e.g. Easterbrook (1984); Farinha (2003). In addition, dividends reduce the discretionary cash available to management and hence its ability to use the cash for its personal benefits. Therefore, shareholders prefer the secure income in the form of dividends as opposed to insecure capital gains. This is also called bird-in-hand-theory. See Gordon (1959); Lintner (1962); Gordon (1963). For details on the agency motive of dividends, see also Donaldson (1963); Yoon/Starks (1995); La Porta et al. (2000a); Cheffins (2006); Helwege/Pirinsky/Stulz (2007); Topalov (2011).

1695 Behavioral models neglect the presence of rational investors that focus on the maximization of their personal utility and explain dividend preferences based on socioeconomic and psychological patterns of behavior. For more details, see Frankfurter/Wood (2002): 115-117 and Topalov (2011): 46-57.

1696 This view is shared by Gugler/Yurtoglu (2003): 753. Also La Porta et al. (2000a): 3 find that "controlling shareholders can effectively determine the decisions of the managers."

1697 See also section 2.1.4.2 and 2.1.4.3. This view is also shared by Ellermann (2003): 40. See also John/Williams (1985): 1065; Al-Malkawi et al. (2010): 182. Lucas/McDonald (1998): 236 state that managers follow a payout policy with the lowest possible costs to shareholders.

1698 See also Pérez-González (2003): 7. Here, the underlying assumption is that the remaining (minority) shareholders have taste for dividends. This reasoning is conclusive, given it is these shareholders who are the victims of any adverse behavior at the firm level. See also La Porta et al. (2000a): 3. This is also supported by Ernst et al. (2005): 9 who survey 800,000 shareholders of Deutsche Post AG and find that investors have a preference for mandatory dividends.

1699 See for example Gugler/Yurtoglu (2003): 733; Pérez-González (2003): 7; Setia-Atmaja (2009): 698.

1700 This measure has also been also used by La Porta et al. (2000a): 11; Faccio et al. (2001): 60; Truong/Heaney (2007): 673.

1701 See La Porta et al. (2000a): 11. The selection of the respective variable has been subject to data availability. Alternative measures include the ratio of dividends and net earnings before extraordinary items, e.g. also used also by Zeckhauser/Pound (1990): 172; La Porta et al. (2000a): 11; Faccio et al. (2001): 60; Gugler/Yurtoglu (2003): 737; Barclay et al. (2009): 2431. Moreover, dividends can be measured as the ratio of the firm's dividends to its market capitalization. See Faccio et al. (2001): 60; De Cesari (2012): 210.

1702 Faccio et al. (2001): 59f. See also Setia-Atmaja (2009): 698.

garded as a signal of rent extraction by the monitoring blockholder.[1703] If the blockholder is willing to exploit minority shareholders, it should be interested in a retention of earnings; in this case, the firm's financial resources remain under the blockholder's control.[1704] Consequently, the blockholder maximizes its private benefits by enforcing low dividend levels which come at the expense of other shareholders.[1705] In contrast, firms exposed to low principal-principal conflicts should exhibit higher dividend payments. A blockholder which monitors in the interest of the remaining shareholders may regard large cash holdings tied up within its portfolio firm as too risky. It therefore addresses this risk by demanding dividends and reducing the level of cash holdings, thereby offering fewer opportunities for the financing of perks by management and hence mitigating the free cash flow problem outlined in section 2.1.2.[1706] Moreover, the monitoring blockholder might "demand a higher dividend as part of the optimum monitoring package"[1707] to complement its own monitoring efforts and reduce its monitoring costs.[1708] Since dividends curb any potential self-dealing of the blockholder by guaranteeing a pro-rata pay out, a blockholder may also use dividend payments to signal the absence of principal-principal conflicts. Thus, the monitoring blockholder can reduce investors' concerns about expropriation and build up a reputation for fair treatment of shareholders.[1709]

To recapitulate, dividend payments are inversely related to principal-principal agency costs. Consequently, higher dividend payments are associated with lower principal-principal agency costs.

5.3.1.4 Firm Value

As outlined in section 5.1.1, the net effect of blockholder monitoring on the overall agency costs is investigated by complementing the three agency cost proxies with a proxy of firm value.[1710]

Consistent with existing research, the present study measures firm value via **Tobin's q** *[tobinq]*[1711] which is defined as the market value of a firm's assets divided by the replacement

1703 See Gugler/Yurtoglu (2003): 733, 735.

1704 See Cheffins (2006): 1305.

1705 See Truong/Heaney (2007): 668. See also Renneboog/Szilagyi (2006): 4.

1706 See Faccio et al. (2001): 56; Farinha (2003): 1183; Young et al. (2003): 31; Truong/Heaney (2007): 668; Bøhren/Josefsen/Steen (2012): 4.

1707 Rozeff (1982): 254.

1708 See Rozeff (1982): 250; Zeckhauser/Pound (1990): 171. A blockholder's monitoring may be complemented because managers with low available retained earnings are required to raise money externally, subjecting them to the scrutiny of external capital markets. According to Easterbrook (1984): 654, this increases their incentive to act in investors' interest, as "contributors of capital are very good monitors of managers."

1709 See e.g. La Porta et al. (2000a): 7; Gugler/Yurtoglu (2003): 733; Young et al. (2003): 31; Cheffins (2006): 1305; Bøhren et al. (2012): 5; De Cesari (2012): 207.

1710 The use of stock market returns within this study design is not possible. Provided the stock market is semi-strong form efficient, any effect of the blockholder on agency costs would be directly incorporated into the firm's share price once investors learn about the change in the ownership structure. Thus, following the period of change, there should be no relationship between ownership structure and the returns even if ownership had an impact on performance. See also Boehmer (2000): 119; Bhagat/Jefferis Jr. (2002): 18.

1711 Tobin's q goes back to Tobin (1969), who argued that the principal way in which financial policies may affect demand is by changing the value of physical assets relative to the replacement costs of these assets.

costs of the assets.[1712] Here, the market value of a firm's assets is defined as the sum of the market value of equity at year-end and the market value of debt. Since the market value of debt is unavailable, it is assumed that the market value is identical to the book value of debt.[1713] Since active markets for used capital assets do not exist, the replacement costs of a firm's assets are difficult to estimate.[1714] Therefore, existing studies assume that the replacement values of a firm's assets equal their book values and therefore proxy replacement costs via the book value of assets.[1715] In particular, the present study defines Tobin's q as follows:

$$[tobinq] = \frac{MV\ Equity + BV\ Liabilities + MV\ Preferred\ stock + Minority\ interest}{BV\ Total\ assets}$$

According to *Chung/Pruitt* (1994), this definition represents "a compromise between analytical precision and computational effort."[1716] To test the applicability and accuracy of Tobin's q using book values, the authors conduct a ten-year comparison of Tobin's q values obtained from the market value and book value definition, respectively. Their results indicate strong support for the equivalence of the two definitions; at least 96.6% of the total variation in the market value-based Tobin's q is explained by the book value-based Tobin's q definition. Hence, the authors conclude that financial analysts wishing to employ the book value-based definition can do so "with considerable confidence"[1717].

In contrast to the accounting-based ratios used to proxy for the specific types of agency costs, Tobin's q is future-oriented and reflects investors' assessment of the firm's ability to generate cash flows in the future.[1718] It is based on the assumption that the replacement costs of a firm's assets constitute a measure of the alternative-use value of the particular assets. Consequently, whenever a firm fails to use its assets to create at least as much value as the alternative-use value, the assets would be better employed elsewhere. If a firm is perceived to use its assets poorly, this should be reflected in a lower share price. Moreover, the possibility of self-dealing by a blockholder reduces what prospective shareholders are willing to pay for a firm's financial securities, depressing the value of firms where such self-dealing represents a real possibility.[1719] As a result of the lower market valuation of the firm's financial assets, firms subject to greater agency costs and an ineffective asset use should have a Tobin's q of less

---

1712 Tobin's q is frequently used in similar studies. See e.g. Agrawal/Knoeber (1996): 386; Faccio/Lasfer (2000): 86; Cronqvist/Nilsson (2003): 701; Maury/Pajuste (2005): 1820; Thomsen et al. (2006): 255; Laeven/Levine (2008): 586; Attig et al. (2009): 398; Setia-Atmaja (2009): 699; Ruiz-Mallorquí/Santana-Martín (2011): 122; Renders/Gaeremynck (2012): 128.

1713 See also Hermalin/Weisbach (1991): 104; Chung/Pruitt (1994): 71; Faccio/Lasfer (2000): 86; La Porta et al. (2002): 1155; Drobetz et al. (2004): 276; Maury/Pajuste (2005): 1820; Seifert et al. (2005): 179; Douma et al. (2006): 647; Attig et al. (2009): 398. See Perfect/Wiles (1994): 317-324 for several possibilities to estimate the market value of a firm's debt.

1714 See also Perfect/Wiles (1994): 324-326.

1715 See e.g. Chung/Pruitt (1994): 71; Faccio/Lasfer (2000): 86; Claessens et al. (2002): 2751; La Porta et al. (2002): 1155; Drobetz et al. (2004): 276; Maury/Pajuste (2005): 1820; Seifert et al. (2005): 179; Douma et al. (2006): 647; Thomsen et al. (2006): 257.

1716 Chung/Pruitt (1994): 71.

1717 Chung/Pruitt (1994): 72.

1718 See Demsetz/Villalonga (2001): 213; Cornett et al. (2007): 1776; Ruiz-Mallorquí/Santana-Martín (2011): 122. According to Demsetz/Villalonga (2001): 213, Tobin's q is therefore to a great degree driven by investor psychology. For the assumptions made with regard to investor behavior, please see section 5.1.2.

1719 See Dyck/Zingales (2004a): 52.

than one.[1720] In contrast, a Tobin's q above one indicates that the capital market regards the firm's internal organization – including the blockholder's monitoring efforts – as effective with regard to the use of the existing assets and the mitigation of agency conflicts and therefore expects the agency costs within the firm to be insignificant.[1721] With regard to the empirical analysis, a higher Tobin's q therefore is associated with lower overall agency costs inherent in a particular firm.

Dybvig/Warachka (2010) point to a potential problem when using Tobin's q as a dependent variable. This problem results from the use of assets in the denominator of Tobin's q. Based on the assumption that managers may enjoy the quiet life and underinvest in growth opportunities,[1722] the authors theoretically show that underinvestment increases Tobin's q, although it reduces a firm's net present value.[1723] However, a positive effect of underinvestment on Tobin's q presumes that the firm's shareholders are unaware of managerial behavior.[1724] Otherwise, any foregone investment opportunity resulting from management enjoying the quiet life would be punished by shareholders through a depressed share price and a lower Tobin's q. In the presence of blockholders with strong incentives to engage in managerial monitoring, this assumption is at least questionable. Since Tobin's q typically uses book values, another criticism argues that this incorporates into Tobin's q a significant portion of the accounting problems typically faced only by accounting measures.[1725] Finally, as a result of its future orientation, Tobin's q is susceptible to endogeneity issues if blockholders are attracted to firms offering high future performance.[1726] Nevertheless, according to *Börsch-Supan/Köke* (2002), Tobin's q "might be the best measure available."[1727] Moreover, since Tobin's q is the most commonly used measure in the existing literature, the use of this variable facilitates a comparison of the empirical results with existing evidence.

5.3.2 Blockholder Identity

Strictly speaking, the blockholder identity also represents a characteristic of blockholders. However, due to the importance of the identity, the different blockholder identities are described separately in the following sections. Prior to this, section 5.3.2.1 summarizes three general issues with regard to the definition of the blockholder identity variables.

1720 See also Lewellen/Badrinath (1997): 78.

1721 See also Hermalin/Weisbach (1991): 104; Cronqvist/Nilsson (2003): 701. In case the value of Tobin's q is above one, a firm is perceived to own valuable (intangible) assets. These can e.g. be a monitoring blockholder providing the firm with input valuable for a successful operation of the firm's business.

1722 The quiet life hypothesis has been described in section 2.1.2.

1723 Specifically, suppose a firm has a Tobin's q of 2.0 which results from a market value of debt and equity equal to 200 and a book value of assets equal to 100. If the management invests in a project requiring 50 units of additional capital and generating benefits equal to 80 units, it decreases Tobin's q to 1.87 (200+80)/(100+50) despite having a NPV of 30 units. See Dybvig/Warachka (2010): 3.

1724 Dybvig/Warachka (2010): 10 also expect managers to have better information with regard to the demand and costs than investors.

1725 See Demsetz/Villalonga (2001): 213.

1726 See Cornett et al. (2007): 1777. The problem of endogeneity is addressed in section 6.3.5.4.

1727 Börsch-Supan/Köke (2002): 318.

5.3.2.1 General Issues

With regard to the **approaches to measure a shareholder's ownership**, one can distinguish between those focusing on the ownership of ultimate owners and those focusing on the direct ownership at the first-tier level. In addition, one can use voting power indices.

The weakest-link principle focuses on the measurement of ultimate owners within a pyramidal structure. According to this method, a firm has an ultimate owner if there is a shareholder whose ownership exceeds a certain threshold at each level of the control chain.[1728] *Edwards/Weichenrieder* (2009) fault that the weakest-link principle is not theoretically motivated and also does not recognize differences in cash flow and voting rights. Therefore, they propose an examination of the ultimate owner that recognizes potential divergences between cash flow and voting rights.[1729]

Next to the weakest-link principle, voting power indices have been used to measure the control rights of shareholders. The most widely used are the Shapley-Shubik and the Banzhaf voting power index.[1730] These measure a shareholder's ability to influence the outcome of a vote by making its power proportional to the number of times the shareholder is pivotal in a coalition of voters (Shapley-Shubik) or to the number of times the shareholders is a critical voter (Banzhaf).[1731] However, *Edwards/Weichenrieder* (2009) criticize the voting power indices, since they result in substantially different measures of voting power and do not have a theoretically clear-cut foundation. Moreover, these models require assumptions about unobserved voting rights.[1732]

Finally, one can examine the first-tier level ownership, thereby implicitly equating voting rights and cash flow rights.[1733] This method is utilized in the study at hand due to three reasons. First, a consistent identification of the ultimate owner is not possible, since it is dependent on whether all firms in the control chain are subject to the publication requirements pursuant to § 21 (1) WpHG.[1734] If a firm in the control chain is privately-held, ownership data is typically unavailable. Consequently, focusing on the first-tier owner is regarded as a more consistent alternative. Since the thesis at hand does not focus on the ultimate owner, it also does not incorporate the divergence of cash flow and voting rights that result from a pyramidal ownership structure. Instead, it controls for a divergence of cash flow and voting rights by distinguishing between firms with preferred and common stock outstanding. Second, literature that compares the effectiveness of various measures of shareholder ownership provides no direct evidence that ultimate ownership is a superior measure of ownership concentration relative to first-tier ownership. *Correia da Silva et al.* (2004) do not find that their results

---

1728 La Porta et al. (1999); Claessens et al. (2000); Faccio et al. (2001); Faccio/Lang (2002); De Cesari (2012) among others, use this definition of ownership.

1729 See Edwards/Weichenrieder (2009): 491, 496f.

1730 See e.g. Maury/Pajuste (2005): 1821; Attig et al. (2008): 724; Laeven/Levine (2008): 598.

1731 For more details, please see Shapley/Shubik (1954); Milnor/Shapley (1978); Laruelle/Valenciano (2001). See also Edwards/Weichenrieder (2009): 493.

1732 For more details, please see Edwards/Weichenrieder (2009): 493.

1733 A similar approach is chosen by Ampenberger (2010): 28.

1734 See also section 2.2.3.1.

change when using the first-tier rather than the ultimate owner.[1735] Also *Edwards/Weichenrieder* (2009) conclude that "measures that trace control through ownership chains do not outperform those that rely on immediate ownership at the first-tier level"[1736]. Third, the study does not employ voting power indices as those presume the shareholders to differ only with respect to their ownership stakes. As a primary interest of the study is the investigation of blockholder heterogeneity, voting power indices are of limited use in the case at hand.[1737] Besides, *Kehren* (2006) does not find the Shapley value to be a better indicator of blockholder power than the blockholder's ownership size.[1738]

With regard to the **ownership threshold**, a shareholder has to own at least 5% of the firm's equity[1739] to be classified as a blockholder. Existing literature assumes that in developed economies, shareholders can effectively monitor and reduce principal agent conflicts within their portfolio firms even with a small minority stake.[1740] With regard to the German environment, an ownership of 5% provides the respective blockholder with some important rights, such as the right to call an extraordinary AGM or the right to demand that certain items are put on the AGM's agenda.[1741] *Edwards/Weichenrieder* (2009) criticize the use of larger thresholds, since they find it difficult to accept that "a firm is widely held if it has a single large owner holding 19 per cent of the voting rights with the other 81 per cent being dispersed over very many small owners, as is implied by the use of a 20 per cent threshold."[1742] In contrast, *Edmans* (2014) criticizes that the typically used ownership level of 5% is rather arbitrarily chosen and not motivated by theory. Furthermore, he states that the level of ownership required to induce and enable monitoring by the blockholder might also differ from firm to firm.[1743] This is plausible, since a 5% blockholder in a widely-held large company may have a significantly greater ability to engage in monitoring than a 5% blockholder in a small company with another shareholder owning 60% of the firm's shares. Due to this, the present study accounts for variations in the blockholder's ownership size and the presence of additional blockholders. Unfortunately, however, the data does not allow for the incorporation of pooling agreements between shareholders which for example exist between the founders of SAP AG.

With regard to the **definition of the blockholder types**, one has to face a trade-off. On the one hand, a narrow differentiation between blockholder types results in a greater comparability of the blockholders within each blockholder group. On the other hand, the differentiation into shareholder groups is limited by the sample size which has to remain large enough to en-

---

1735 See Correia da Silva et al. (2004): 152.

1736 Edwards/Weichenrieder (2009): 490.

1737 Please see Gorton/Schmid (2000): 37f for a similar argumentation.

1738 See Kehren (2006): 215.

1739 If a firm has both common stock and preferred stock outstanding, the percentages are those attached to common stock.

1740 A similar threshold has been used e.g. by Agrawal/Knoeber (1996): 383; Lehmann/Weigand (2000): 166; Faccio et al. (2001): 57; Singh/Davidson III (2003): 799; Köke/Renneboog (2005): 485; Thomsen et al. (2006): 248; Borokhovich et al. (2006): 653; Chen et al. (2007): 286; Konijn et al. (2011): 1332; Mietzner et al. (2011): 152; van der Elst (2011): 17.

1741 See section 2.2.3.2 for further details.

1742 Edwards/Weichenrieder (2009): 491.

1743 See Edmans (2014): 19f.

sure statistical significance.[1744] In order for a blockholder to qualify as a particular blockholder type, the respective investor has to meet one of the following criteria: it either has to be classified as a particular type in the financial press or it has to define itself as a particular investor type on its company homepage.[1745] The four mutually exclusive blockholder categories are introduced in the following sections.

5.3.2.2 Private Equity Investor

Due to their similar business models, this group comprises the share ownership of either private equity or venture capital firms, given their respective ownership exceeds 5%.[1746] This refers to both international and German private equity/venture capital firms. Moreover, it includes holding companies (Beteiligungsgesellschaften), if they are (1) not owned by the founder of the portfolio firm and (2) engaged in an active management of their portfolio firms and thus follow a private equity investment and management approach. Not included in this group are private equity/venture capital firms that belong to the investment arm of a strategic investor. For example, Burda Digital Ventures GmbH belongs to Hubert Burda Media and therefore is not classified as a venture capital firm. This is because the behavior of such captive private equity/venture capital firms is likely to be strongly affected by the strategic goals of its parent organization.[1747] In addition, this group excludes Federal State owned private equity companies that specialize in the provision of funds for small and medium-sized firms such as the Sued Beteiligungen GmbH which is a subsidiary of LBBW.

5.3.2.3 Institutional Investor

The institutional investor group encompasses the ownership of several different types of institutional investors.[1748] These include (1) mutual funds (e.g. Jupiter Fund Management), (2) specific investment funds (e.g. Absolute Return Europe Fund) as well as (3) investment firms whose specific fund cannot be identified (e.g. Fidelity Investments). The group also comprises hedge funds or alternative asset management firms (e.g. Centaurus Capital Limited). In addition, the class of institutional investors encompasses investment banks (e.g. Goldman Sachs), pension funds (e.g. BT Pension Scheme), and insurance firms (e.g. Massachusetts Mutual Life Insurance). However, due to presumed interest conflicts, this group does not comprise investment firms if those are owned by a bank or an insurance firm (e.g. DWS Investment GmbH which is owned by Deutsche Bank).

The classification of institutional investors suffers from the weakness that it combines multiple types of institutional investors. These investors, however, are likely to differ in a number of characteristics, such as the time horizon, trading behavior, level of activism, and business

---

[1744] See also Cronqvist/Fahlenbrach (2008): 3950. This trade-off particularly applies to the definition of institutional investors.

[1745] For a similar approach see Achleitner et al. (2010): 814.

[1746] For an explanation of private equity and venture capital firms, please see section 4.1.3.2.1.

[1747] For a similar argument, see also Bottazzi et al. (2008): 495.

[1748] For an explanation of institutional investors, please see section 4.1.3.3.1.

ties with the portfolio firm.[1749] The types of investors that comprise the institutional investor group may range from low activism to high and aggressive activism. On the one hand, mutual funds, investment funds and investment firms represent a rather passive form of activism.[1750] On the other hand, hedge funds are prepared to take an active, hands-on role in order to improve the value of the firm. They consequently take initiative and accelerate necessary changes within their portfolio firms.[1751] *Sherman/Beldona/Joshi* (1998) distinguish pension funds, mutual funds, banks, and insurance companies and find the impact of these investor groups on the policies of their portfolio firms to differ.[1752] Heterogeneity of investors exists even within the group of pension funds. *Guercio/Hawkins* (1999) document significant heterogeneity in fund objectives and tactics, being driven by the funds' differing investment strategies.[1753] Due to these differences, a more sophisticated examination of the institutional investors would be appropriate. However, the study refrains from any further differentiation since this would significantly reduce the respective sample size and hence the statistical validity.

5.3.2.4 Family

The present study defines a family blockholder as a shareholder which is either the founder of the firm or a member of the founding family.[1754] Due to the absence of a universal definition of the term founder,[1755] the thesis at hand regards a person as the founder if this is explicitly stated on the firm's homepage or in alternative information sources provided by the respective firm. This definition also applies to single persons or a group of non-family-related persons (e.g. the founders of SAP). The group of family blockholders also comprises foundations, wealth management firms, and holding companies if they can be traced back to the founder of the firm.

In existing studies on family firms, the founding families are assumed to act coordinated and vote collectively.[1756] Therefore, the holdings of different family members are frequently combined. For example, Leech (2001) states that "holdings in the same firm by different members of the founding family, and other interest groups closely associated with the company, were amalgamated into a single block"[1757]. However, in the case at hand, the shareholdings of the family members are not combined into a single holding due to two reasons. First, the isolated analysis ensures the comparability with the other investor types, whose blockholdings are also

[1749] Due to these differences, Bushee (2004): 29 differentiates between three categories of institutional investors: "transient" institutions, characterized by a high portfolio turnover and low ownership; "dedicated" institutions, owning large and stable positions in individual firms; and "quasi-indexers", trading infrequently and holding small stakes, thereby replicating an index strategy.

[1750] See Kahan/Rock (2007): 1043.

[1751] See Armour/Cheffins (2009): 4. Hedge fund activism in most cases is strategic. Ex ante, the hedge fund investor ensures that a firm benefits from its activism and only then acquires a stake and becomes active. See also Kahan/Rock (2007): 1069; Sunder et al. (2011): 2.

[1752] See Sherman/Beldona/Joshi (1998): 166, 171f.

[1753] See Guercio/Hawkins (1999): 294.

[1754] Since the study focuses on the founding family, the Quandt family, being a long-term blockholder and member of the supervisory board of BMW AG, is not regarded as a family blockholder. Although the family holds the shares since the 1960s, the founder of BMW AG is Karl Rapp.

[1755] See Leiber (2008): 20f.

[1756] See e.g. Cronqvist/Nilsson (2003): 704; Maury/Pajuste (2005); Andres (2008): 435.

[1757] Leech (2001): 42. See Villalonga/Amit (2006): 392 for a similar approach.

not based on an aggregate ownership. Second, under the assumption of blockholder interrelationships, the present study separately investigates the effect of coalitions between blockholders of the same type.

5.3.2.5 Strategic Investor

The group of strategic investors comprises blockholdings of non-financial companies that are assumed to use their blockholdings for the pursuance of strategic interests. In addition, the group comprises holding companies which do not produce products or offer services themselves but only own shares in other companies. With regard to these holding companies, it is ensured that their motives as well as the financing and management of their portfolio firms differ from private equity investors. Moreover, it is assured that the ultimate owner of the holding company is not a founding family member.

5.3.3 Ownership Structure

The following sections present the ownership variables and their respective definitions grouped according to the different stages of the regression analysis. The variables are summarized in table 3 at the end of section 5.3.3.

5.3.3.1 Blockholder Homogeneity

As explained in section 5.1.1, the first stage of the regression analysis presumes blockholder homogeneity and disregards any blockholder characteristic in order to serve as a base case for the analyses that follow. The variables used in this stage measure the general level of ownership concentration as well as the presence of a blockholder.

The level of ownership concentration is proxied by two variables. The first variable measures ownership concentration as the cumulative ownership size *[cum_own]* of all investors, given these blockholders own at least 5% of the particular firm's shares.[1758] Higher values for the cumulative ownership size indicate a greater ownership concentration. The second variable constitutes the Herfindahl index *[h_index]*,[1759] which is defined as the sum of the squared individual ownership stakes of investors, given their individual stake is at least equal to 5% of the firm's shares:

$$Herfindahl\ index = (\%\ Stake_1)^2 + (\%\ Stake_2)^2 + (\%\ Stake_3)^2 + \ldots + (\%\ Stake_n)^2$$

The *[h_index]* has the valuable property that it increases if the ownership of a blockholder increases at the expense of a smaller investor's ownership. The variable takes a maximum of one if a single investor owns all shares and decreases to zero for dispersed ownership. Hence, a lower value indicates a higher ownership dispersion.

1758 A similar definition is employed by e.g. McConnell/Servaes (1990): 600; Agrawal/Knoeber (1996): 383; Demsetz/Villalonga (2001): 218.

1759 The index is used e.g. by Seger (1997): 205f; Gorton/Schmid (2000): 39; Lehmann/Weigand (2000): 166; Bøhren/Ødegaard (2006): 44; Kehren (2006): 197; Konijn et al. (2011): 1333, to name a few. The index goes back to the work of Herfindahl (1950) and was originally used to measure industrial concentration.

Besides the level of ownership concentration, stage 1 also focuses on the presence of a blockholder measured by *[bh1_dummy]* which constitutes a dummy variable equal to one if there is a blockholder which owns at least 5% of the firm's shares and zero otherwise.

5.3.3.2 Blockholder Heterogeneity

The second stage of the regression analysis accounts for blockholder heterogeneity and extends the first stage by incorporating blockholder characteristics in terms of their ownership size, their presence on the firm's bodies, and their type.[1760] In particular, the following variables are employed.

The ownership size of the largest blockholder *[bh1_cont]* is measured using a continuous variable that is equal to the percentage ownership of the largest blockholder, given it is at least equal to 5% of the firm's shares.[1761] Thereby, the variable overcomes the disadvantage of the dummy variable used in stage 1 and accounts for the fact that the incentive of a blockholder to engage in monitoring may be a function of its ownership size.

The potential non-linear effect of the largest blockholder's ownership is proxied by the squared ownership of the largest blockholder *[bh1_cont_sq]*, given it owns at least 5% of the firm's shares. In addition, the potential non-linearity is modelled using a linear model with different slopes for certain ownership ranges, thereby allowing for a potential piecewise-linear relationship.[1762] This relationship is investigated by splitting *[bh1_cont]* into four sub-variables: *[bh1_5to25]* for ownership between 5 and 25%, *[bh1_25to50]* for ownership between 25 and 50%, *[bh1_50to75]* for ownership between 50 and 75%, and *[bh1_75to100]* for ownership between 75 and 100%.

To measure the effect of a blockholder's representation on the firm's bodies, two dummy variables are defined. The first dummy variable accounts for the presence of the largest blockholder on its portfolio firm's supervisory board *[bh1_supb]* and equals one if the largest blockholder is represented on the firm's supervisory board and zero otherwise. The second dummy variable accounts for the presence of the largest blockholder on its portfolio firm's management board *[bh1_mgmtb]* and equals one if the largest blockholder is represented on the firm's management board and zero otherwise. A blockholder is considered to be present on a firm's management or supervisory board if at least one of the boards' members (1) is the blockholder itself,[1763] (2) has the same family name, is a relative or affiliate of the blockholder, or (3) is an employee of the blockholder.

In order to measure the effect of the ownership of a particular blockholder type, the analysis introduces a variable for each of the four blockholder types outlined in section 5.3.2: *[bh1_pe_cont]* for private equity investors, *[bh1_fam_cont]* for families, *[bh1_si_cont]* for

---

1760 The definition of the blockholder identities has already been covered in section 5.3.2.

1761 Gedajlovic/Shapiro (1998): 544; Thomsen/Pedersen (2000): 696; Beiner et al. (2006): 258; Maury (2006): 325; Faccio et al. (2011): 3607, among others, use a similar definition.

1762 For a similar approach, see Morck et al. (1988): 298; Kaserer/Moldenhauer (2008): 10; Drobetz et al. (2009): 371.

1763 Note that this applies to supervisory boards only. If the blockholder is a single individual, which is not the founder, and represented in the management board, it is classified as an insider.

strategic investors, and *[bh1_insti_cont]* for institutional investors. The variable for the respective blockholder type equals the percentage ownership of the largest blockholder if it is one of the respective types and its ownership is at least equal to 5% of the firm's shares. As for *[bh1_cont]*, potential non-linear effects of the largest blockholder's ownership are proxied by a variable which measures the squared ownership of the largest blockholder type, given it owns at least 5% of the firm's shares.[1764]

To examine if the ownership size effect of the largest blockholder's identity is affected by the blockholder's board representation, the two proxies for the largest blockholder's presence on its portfolio firm's supervisory board *[bh1_supb]* or its management board *[bh1_mgmtb]* are interacted with the blockholder identity variables, respectively.[1765] In this case, the interaction variables allow for different slopes (i.e. coefficients) for the ownership size of the respective blockholder given its representation on either management or supervisory board.

5.3.3.3 Blockholder Interrelationships

The third stage of the analysis finally accounts for the presence of blockholders beyond the largest blockholder and the resulting blockholder interrelationships. In particular, it focuses on the ownership of a second blockholder, the largest blockholder's incontestability, and a heterogenous ownership structure.

The ownership of a second blockholder is measured by two types of variables. First, *[bh2_cont]* equals the ownership of the second largest blockholder, given it owns at least 5% of a firm's shares. Second, the variables *[bh2_pe_cont]*, *[bh2_fam_cont]*, *[bh2_si_cont]*, and *[bh2_insti_cont]* equal the percentage ownership of the second largest blockholder if it is one of the respective types and owns at least 5% of the firm's shares. Thus, the first variable type measures the effect of the second blockholder's ownership independent of its identity, whereas the second variable type explicitly accounts for the blockholder identity. In order to investigate if the ownership of a second blockholder affects the ownership size effect of the four blockholder types on agency costs and firm value, the two variable types are interacted with the blockholder type variables introduced in the previous section. This interaction allows the ownership size effect on the dependent variable to depend on the ownership of the second largest blockholder.[1766]

The incontestability of the largest blockholder is measured by four variables. *[bh1/bh2]* measures the relative power of the largest blockholder and is calculated as the ratio of the largest blockholder's ownership to the second largest blockholder's ownership.[1767] Hence, a higher ratio indicates a greater incontestability of the largest blockholder. This variable is expanded to also incorporate the ownership of the third largest blockholder. Hence,

1764 This yields *[bh1_pe_cont_sq]*, *[bh1_fam_cont_sq]*, *[bh1_si_cont_sq]*, and *[bh1_insti_cont_sq]*.

1765 Interaction variables model situations in which the effect of a change in one of the independent variables on the dependent variable depends on the value of another independent variable. An interaction between a continuous and a binary variable allows for a difference in slopes, which depends on the value of the binary variable. For further information, please see Stock/Watson (2012): 316-328; Wooldridge (2012): 230-241.

1766 See also Stock/Watson (2012): 324.

1767 See also Attig et al. (2008): 723f; Attig et al. (2009): 399.

[bh1/bh2_bh3] measures the power of the largest blockholder relative to the second and third largest blockholder and is calculated by dividing the largest blockholder's ownership by the sum of the second and third largest blockholders' ownership.[1768] Thus, higher values indicate a lower ability of the second and third largest blockholder to challenge the largest blockholder and thus a greater incontestability. The third incontestability measure is an adaptation of the Herfindahl index used in stage 1. It is calculated as the sum of the squared differences between the ownership of the five largest blockholders, given they own at least 5% of the firm's shares:[1769]

$$[diff\_bh12345] = (bh1 - bh2)^2 + (bh2 - bh3)^2 + (bh3 - bh4)^2 + (bh4 - bh5)^2.$$

The variable proxies for the dispersion of ownership between the five largest blockholders. In general, the higher *[diff_bh12345]*, the greater the dispersion and thus the power of the largest blockholder. Although the previous variables may have more appeal due to their continuous nature, the power of the largest blockholder is also measured using a dummy variable in order to account for the important legal rights that are associated with certain levels of ownership. Therefore, *[bh1_majority]* is equal to one if the largest blockholder is equipped with the simple majority (more than 50%) and the second largest blockholder does not hold a blocking minority and thus has no veto powers regarding important corporate decisions (less than 25%). In line with the hypotheses, the incontestability variables are interacted with the blockholder type variables introduced in the previous section.

Two proxies are used to measure the heterogeneity of a firm's ownership structure. First, *[ln_bh_count]* constitutes a continuous variable and measures the *number of blockholders* that have at least a 5% stake in the firm. Second, *[ln_bhtypes_count]* measures the *number of blockholder types* that have at least a 5% stake in the firm. If blockholders of the same type are more likely to engage in cooperative rather than independent monitoring, this variable should be a more efficient measure of a heterogenous ownership structure than *[ln_bh_count]*. It is expected that the relationship between the agency cost proxies, firm value, and heterogenous ownership structures is stronger for a lower heterogeneity: the blockholder monitoring should be more affected by the presence of a second or third blockholder than by the presence of an eighth or ninth blockholder. Therefore, the natural logarithm of these variables is used.

Table 3
This table summarizes the definitions of the explanatory ownership variables used in the regression analysis.

Variable name	Variable definition
Blockholder homogeneity	
cum_own	The cumulative ownership size of all blockholders, given these blockholders own at least 5% of the particular firm's shares
h_index	The sum of the squared individual ownership stakes of investors, given their stake is at least equal to 5% of the firm's shares: $(\%\ Stake_1)^2+(\%\ Stake_2)^2+\ldots+(\%\ Stake_n)^2$

1768 See also Attig et al. (2008): 724; Jara-Bertin et al. (2008): 149.

1769 See also Maury/Pajuste (2005): 182; Jara-Bertin et al. (2008): 149; Attig et al. (2009): 399.

Table 3 cont'd

Variable name	Variable definition
bh1_dummy	Dummy variable: 1 if there is a blockholder which owns at least 5% of the firm's shares; 0 otherwise
Blockholder heterogeneity	
bh1_cont	The percentage ownership of the largest blockholder, given it is at least equal to 5% of the firm's shares
bh1_cont_sq	Squared bh1_cont
bh1_5to25	Dummy variable: 1 if the largest blockholder's ownership is between 5 and 25% of the firm's shares; 0 otherwise
bh1_25to50	Dummy variable: 1 if the largest blockholder's ownership is between 25 and 50% of the firm's shares; 0 otherwise
bh1_50to75	Dummy variable: 1 if the largest blockholder's ownership is between 50 and 75% of the firm's shares; 0 otherwise
bh1_75to100	Dummy variable: 1 if the largest blockholder's ownership is between 75 and 100% of the firm's shares; 0 otherwise
bh1_supb	Dummy variable: 1 if the largest blockholder is represented on its portfolio firm's supervisory board; 0 otherwise
bh1_mgmtb	Dummy variable: 1 if the largest blockholder is represented on its portfolio firm's management board; 0 otherwise
bh1_pe_cont	The percentage ownership of the largest blockholder if it is a private equity investor and its ownership is at least equal to 5% of the firm's shares
bh1_fam_cont	The percentage ownership of the largest blockholder if it is a family and its ownership is at least equal to 5% of the firm's shares
bh1_si_cont	The percentage ownership of the largest blockholder if it is a strategic investor and its ownership is at least equal to 5% of the firm's shares
bh1_insti_cont	The percentage ownership of the largest blockholder if it is an institutional investor and its ownership is at least equal to 5% of the firm's shares
Blockholder interrelationships	
bh2_cont	The percentage ownership of the second largest blockholder, given owns at least 5% of the firm's shares
bh2_pe_cont	The percentage ownership of the second largest blockholder if it is a private equity investor and its ownership is at least equal to 5% of the firm's shares
bh2_fam_cont	The percentage ownership of the largest blockholder if it is a family and its ownership is at least equal to 5% of the firm's shares
bh2_si_cont	The percentage ownership of the largest blockholder if it is a strategic investor and its ownership is at least equal to 5% of the firm's shares
bh2_insti_cont	The percentage ownership of the largest blockholder if it is an institutional investor and its ownership is at least equal to 5% of the firm's shares
ln_bh_count	The logarithm of the number of blockholders that have at least a 5% stake in the firm
ln_bhtypes_count	The logarithm of the number of blockholder types that have at least a 5% stake in the firm

Table 3 cont'd

Variable name	Variable definition
bh1/bh2	The ratio of the largest blockholder's ownership to the second largest blockholder's ownership
bh1/bh2_bh3	The ratio of the largest blockholder's ownership to the sum of the second and third largest blockholders' ownership
diff_bh12345	The sum of the squared differences between the ownership of the five largest blockholders, given they own at least 5% of the firm's equity: $(bh1 - bh2)^2 + (bh2 - bh3)^2 + (bh3 - bh4)^2 + (bh4 - bh5)^2$
bh1_majority	Dummy variable: 1 if the largest blockholder is equipped with the simple majority and the second largest blockholder does not hold a blocking minority; 0 otherwise

Table 3: Definition of explanatory ownership variables

5.3.4 Control Variables

The regression models also include independent (control) variables that either influence the primary explanatory variables (i.e. the ownership structure) or the dependent variables. Thereby, potential biases arising from omitted variables[1770] are mitigated.[1771] The following sections describe and define these control variables. In line with the theoretical model,[1772] the description of the variables is subdivided into those controlling for firm characteristics (section 5.3.4.1) and those controlling for the presence of alternative governance mechanisms (section 5.3.4.2). In addition, section 5.3.4.3 introduces additional control variables that belong to neither group.

5.3.4.1 Firm Characteristics

The following part primarily comprises variables that control for firm characteristics that may affect the presence of blockholders as well as the dependent variables.

Firm age *[age]*, measured as the difference between the respective sample year and the year of incorporation,[1773] is used as a control variable since the presence of blockholder types may depend on the age of the firm. For example, the founding family is likely to hold a greater portion of the shares in younger firms.[1774] In addition, venture capital firms specialize in the provision of capital for young firms and hence are more likely to be involved with younger firms. Firm age may also directly affect a number of dependent variables. With regard to the expense ratio, firm age is expected to have a decreasing effect. Due to learning curve effects, older firms can be expected to operate more efficiently relative to their younger peers.[1775]

[1770] Omitted variables can be defined as "those variables that should be included in the vector of explanatory variables, but for various reasons are not." Roberts/Whited (2013): 498.

[1771] See also Konijn et al. (2011): 1334.

[1772] Please see figure 10.

[1773] Among others, Anderson/Reeb (2003): 1315; Leiber (2008): 139; Ampenberger (2010): 206; Renders/Gaeremynck (2012): 130 use the year of establishment rather than the year of incorporation as a basis for the calculation. However, data on the year of establishment is unavailable in Bloomberg, which constitutes the data source for the (financial) firm specific data. See section 6.1.3.

[1774] See also Ampenberger (2010): 206.

[1775] See also Ang et al. (2000): 89.

With regard to Tobin's q, firm age may have a negative effect, since older firms are typically more mature and therefore grow at a slower rate. This is likely to be reflected in the firm's share price relative to high-growth firms.[1776] Firm age should result in higher dividend payments: since older firms have only few growth opportunities, they should pay out excess cash.

The regressions also use two variables to control for **firm-specific risk**. The first measure is defined as a firm's three-year beta *[beta]* which estimates the degree a stock price will fluctuate based on a given movement in the representative market index – in the case at hand, the market index is defined as the CDAX.[1777] The second measure constitutes the standard deviation of a firm's net income over the previous three years *[stdev_ni]*.[1778] It is expected that the different blockholder types have different preferences regarding the risk of their (prospective) portfolio firms. As a result, the blockholder types may not be randomly distributed across different firms but rather select a firm based on their individual risk preferences. In addition, due to greater information asymmetries, the benefits from monitoring that arise to the blockholder and hence its incentive to engage in monitoring should be larger in case of more risky business operations.[1779]

Firm size, due to its skewed distribution measured as the logarithm of total assets *[ln_assets]*,[1780] is added as control variable due to a number of reasons. First, the presence of blockholders may be negatively related to firm size, since they face greater difficulty and costs when aiming to acquire a significant stake in a firm with a large market capitalization.[1781] Second, firm size may increase the general level of agency costs within a firm due to an increasing complexity and hence difficulty of monitoring. This may either result in passivity or in an increased relative benefit of self-dealing on the part of the blockholder.[1782] Third, firm size may have a direct effect on some of the dependent variables. With regard to the expense ratio, large firms can benefit from economies of scale and scope which reduces operating costs.[1783] As a result, larger firms should have a lower expense ratio. With regard to the dividend payout ratio, larger firms should grow at a smaller rate and hence are not required to retain their earnings in order to finance their (few) growth opportunities. Consequently, larger firms should more likely pay out their earnings as dividends.[1784] With regard to Tobin's q, a negative effect is expected. This may either stem from the greater agency costs as a result of the increased complexity or from the low growth rate of large, mature firms.[1785]

1776 See also Ampenberger (2010): 206.

1777 A firm's beta has also been used by e.g. Villalonga/Amit (2006): 391; Konijn et al. (2011): 1334.

1778 For a similar definition, see Sánchez-Ballesta/García-Meca (2011): 396; Chan/Hsu (2013): 399.

1779 See also Kim et al. (2007): 868.

1780 This definition is also used by e.g. Gedajlovic/Shapiro (1998): 545; Lehmann/Weigand (2000): 172; Faccio et al. (2001): 60; Gugler/Yurtoglu (2003): 737-739; Maury/Pajuste (2005): 1821; Bress (2008): 140; Attig et al. (2009): 400. Note that the empirical results are unchanged when using the logarithm of annual sales.

1781 See Konijn et al. (2011): 1334.

1782 See also Gutiérrez/Tribó (2004): 12. Since larger firms are typically subject to greater scrutiny from the capital markets which reduces information asymmetries, firm size may also be associated with lower agency costs. See e.g. Wolf (1999): 54; Chen/Yur-Austin (2007): 592; Helwege et al. (2007): 1012.

1783 See Ang et al. (2000): 89f; Singh/Davidson III (2003): 800.

1784 See Denis/Osobov (2008): 80; Topalov (2011): 170. See also Correia da Silva et al. (2004): 78.

1785 See Maury/Pajuste (2005): 1821; Konijn et al. (2011): 1334.

As has been argued in section 4.3.3.1, a divergence of cash flow and voting rights might have significant consequences for the nature and extent of a blockholder's monitoring. Within the German institutional context, such a divergence may be a result of the issuance of preferred stock.[1786] Thus, it may be necessary to control for the **presence of preferred stock** *[pfd]* which is done by a dummy variable equal to one if a firm has issued preferred stock or both common and preferred stock. With regard to the former, a blockholder's ability to effectively monitor firm management is limited: since the blockholder only holds non-voting shares, it is cut out of its ability to vote on the firm's AGM which may reduce its power and hence credibility to threaten firm management. In case a firm issued both common and preferred stock, the conflict of interest between different shareholders may be augmented,[1787] since the blockholder has an incentive to exploit the holders of the non-voting shares.

Furthermore, all regressions control for stock **liquidity** *[liq]*, proxied by a dummy variable equal to one if the firm is listed in one of the major indices DAX, MDAX, SDAX, TecDax.[1788] It is expected that firms listed in one of these important indices receive greater public interest and are more easily accessible for investors. Consequently, stocks in these indices should be traded more frequently which in turn results in greater liquidity.[1789] As has been argued in section 4.3.3.2, the liquidity of a firm's stock may influence the inclination of blockholder monitoring. With regard to the direction of this influence, the existing literature provides conflicting predictions. While a stock's liquidity facilitates the accumulation of large equity stakes in the first place,[1790] it may also enable a blockholder to dispose of its shares and leave rather than engage in more costly monitoring in case it is dissatisfied with the firm's performance. In addition, high liquidity also increases the credibility of the blockholder's threat to exit and may thereby contribute to a more effective monitoring. Hence, no clear predictions on the effect of *[liq]* on the dependent variables can be made.

Sales growth *[growth]*, measured as the percentage change in sales year-on-year,[1791] is used to proxy for a firm's growth opportunities which are likely to affect both the dividend payouts and Tobin's q. With regard to the former, the presence of growth opportunities may call for a retention and reinvestment of earnings in order to finance these opportunities.[1792] Thus, both blockholder(s) and minority shareholders should agree on lower payouts if a firm has good investment opportunities available.[1793] Consequently, firms with higher sales growth and thus more investment opportunities should pay fewer dividends relative to their low-growth firms.[1794] With regard to the latter, Tobin's q is likely to be affected by the presence of growth

1786 Preferred shares are governed within the §§ 139-141 AktG. For details, please see also section 4.3.3.1.

1787 See Becht et al. (2005): 19.

1788 A similar definition has been employed by Drobetz et al. (2004): 289.

1789 See also Prokot (2006): 36.

1790 See Konijn et al. (2011): 1334.

1791 This definition is also applied by e.g. Seger (1997): 233; Gedajlovic/Shapiro (1998): 545; Maury/Pajuste (2005): 1822; Dittmann et al. (2010): 44. According to La Porta et al. (2000a): 11, this variable has the disadvantage that it relies on the past as proxy for the future.

1792 See Faccio et al. (2001): 62. Also Denis/Osobov (2008): 80 and La Porta et al. (2000a): 19 use investment opportunities as a control variable.

1793 See also La Porta et al. (2000a): 6.

1794 See Rozeff (1982): 249; Jensen et al. (1992): 259; Gugler (2003): 1299f; Truong/Heaney (2007): 669.

opportunities, because it reflects the market's perception of the firm's profitability in the future.[1795] Since faster growing firms have higher valuations, a positive relationship between sales growth on Tobin's q is expected.[1796]

Regressions based on a firm's dividend payout ratio also control for its profitability and lagged dividend payments. **Profitability** *[prof]* is measured as a firm's net income/loss scaled by total assets.[1797] The former is defined as the firm's profit after all expenses have been deducted and includes the effects of all one-time, non-recurring and extraordinary gains or losses. Thereby, the variable also accounts for transitory shocks that may affect a firms' dividend policies.[1798] When setting their dividend policies, firms regard their earnings as a major factor which generally dominates the decision on whether or not to change the payout ratio.[1799] Moreover, the likelihood of a dividend increase is found to be higher in the case of positive earnings in the current year.[1800] Consequently, profitability is expected to positively affect the payout ratio. **Lagged dividend payments** *[div_prevy]* constitutes a dummy variable that equals one if the particular firm paid dividends in the previous year and zero otherwise. Since dividends tend to be sticky, firms set their dividend policy with specific regard to the existing dividend rate which is considered as a central benchmark for future dividend payments.[1801] Consequently, lagged dividend payments should be positively related to the dividend payout ratio.

A firm's **capital expenditures** *[capex]*, defined as the ratio of capital expenditures to total assets,[1802] is used as control variable in regressions based on the ratio of discrete assets and Tobin's q. Due to its very nature, investments in fixed assets should be negatively related to the amount of discrete assets. Whereas the first effect is straightforward, *[capex]* have an unknown effect on Tobin's q which depends on the managerial motive underlying the investments. Ceteris paribus, if the management's investment motive is based on the FCF hypothesis or empire building, capital expenditures should be negatively related to firm value. In contrast, if management pursues investment opportunities with a positive NPV, or, more generally, invests in the interest of the shareholders, capital expenditures should result in a higher firm value.

Moreover, **asset tangibility** *[ppe_assets]* and the **level of cash** *[cash_assets]* are used as control variables in regressions based on Tobin's q. *[ppe_assets]* is defined as the ratio of net fixed assets (PP&E) to total assets.[1803] The existing literature argues that firms with a lower asset tangibility generate more cash flows from the use of intangible assets (such as human

---

1795 See Laeven/Levine (2008): 593.

1796 See Maury/Pajuste (2005): 1822.

1797 For a similar definition, please see De Cesari (2012): 212. Also Goergen et al. (2005): 383; Denis/Osobov (2008): 80 control for firms' profitability.

1798 See also Goergen et al. (2005): 383.

1799 See Lintner (1956): 102.

1800 See Goergen et al. (2005): 386.

1801 See Lintner (1956): 99.

1802 See Attig et al. (2009): 400; Konijn et al. (2011): 1334. Capital expenditures refer to the amount the firm spent on purchases of tangible fixed assets.

1803 See e.g. Dyck/Zingales (2004a): 60; Dyck/Zingales (2004b): 548; Maury/Pajuste (2005): 1822; Konijn et al. (2011): 1334; Renders/Gaeremynck (2012): 130.

capital).[1804] Consequently, a negative relation between *[ppe_assets]* and Tobin's q is expected. A firm's level of cash *[cash_assets]* is measured as cash and marketable securities scaled by total assets. On the one hand, the level of cash can serve as a cushion for hard times and unforeseen opportunities and ensures the continuance of operations also during internal or external liquidity shocks. On the other hand, the level of cash represents a good proxy for the monitoring blockholder's level of discretion.[1805] Moreover, in the presence of an ineffective monitor, management can also use the cash for the financing of perquisites or empire building.[1806] As a result, no clear prediction on the relationship can be made.

5.3.4.2 Alternative Governance Mechanisms

As has been outlined in section 4.3.2, the extent of a blockholder's monitoring as well as its potential to ameliorate agency costs may depend on the presence and effectiveness of alternative governance mechanisms within the portfolio firm. Therefore, the regressions also control for insider equity ownership and leverage. Moreover, the study incorporates two governance mechanisms that constitute special features of the German institutional environment, namely the presence of banks as well as the legally mandated employee codetermination on the supervisory board level.[1807]

Insider ownership *[insd_own]* is defined as the cumulative ownership of insiders, given their respective individual ownership stake is at least 5%.[1808] Insiders comprise members of the management and supervisory board, if they do not belong to the founding family. The group of insiders also comprises foundations, wealth management firms, and holding companies that can be traced back to a member of either the management or supervisory board. Moreover, insiders comprise former members of either the management or supervisory board.[1809] Two hypotheses formulate expectations regarding the impact of insider ownership; the entrenchment hypothesis and the convergence-of-interest hypothesis.[1810] The convergence-of-interest hypothesis states that growing managerial equity holdings increase the manager's exposure to the fraction of the costs resulting from its value reducing strategies.[1811] These higher costs re-

1804 See Laeven/Levine (2008): 596; Konijn et al. (2011): 1337.

1805 For a similar argument, please see Prowse (1990): 52.

1806 Please see section 2.1.2 for details.

1807 Note that the inclusion of additional governance variables controls for the firms' adoption of alternative governance variables at the same time, but it does not control for their interdependence with blockholder monitoring. See Beiner et al. (2006): 267.

1808 As an example: if a member of the management board holds 6% (4%) and a member of the supervisory board holds 8% (6%) of a firm's equity, *[insd_own]* would equal 14% (6%).

1809 While the incorporation of former members deviates from the definition used in other (international) studies, it is in line with Kaserer/Moldenhauer (2008): 8. They argue that this definition accounts for a peculiarity of German firms, where former board members still exert significant influence on their former firms, provided they have sufficient ownership.

1810 See e.g. Morck et al. (1988): 294; Anderson/Reeb (2003): 1304; Farinha (2003): 1173; Thomsen et al. (2006): 248; Kaserer/Moldenhauer (2008): 2; Sánchez-Ballesta/García-Meca (2011): 392. Both hypotheses have already been used in the context of ownership size in section 4.1.1. The hypotheses need not be mutually exclusive, as the relationship between insider ownership and firm performance might not be monotonic but dependent on the size of the insiders' ownership. The potential non-linearity of insider ownership has been investigated in a number studies. Please see e.g. Morck et al. (1988); McConnell/Servaes (1990); Hermalin/Weisbach (1991); Seifert et al. (2005); Beiner et al. (2006); Bøhren/Ødegaard (2006).

1811 See Denis et al. (1997): 140.

duce the attractiveness of adverse managerial actions and at the same time provide incentives to raise the firm's stock price.[1812] Hence, *[insd_own]* is assumed to align the incentives of insiders with those of the shareholders,[1813] reduce agency costs, and to result in a positive impact on firm value.[1814] As a consequence, the convergence-of-interest hypothesis implies a lower need for blockholder monitoring and thus a negligible effect of the ownership variables.[1815] The entrenchment hypothesis, on the other hand, argues that larger ownership simultaneously increases insiders' discretion and thus their ability to generate private benefits of control. Moreover, it may insulate insiders from other mechanism that reduce agency conflicts.[1816] If the entrenchment hypothesis is valid, it implies greater agency costs as well as reduced firm value. Overall, it creates the need for blockholder monitoring which acts as a valuable counterbalance and may be able to limit managerial entrenchment and the resulting negative consequences.

Leverage is defined as short- and long-term debt over total assets *[debt]*[1817] and is frequently regarded as a governance device due to the associated interest and principal payments. These payments create pressure on corporate management not to waste the firm's cash flow and are therefore said to have a disciplinary effect on management which ultimately reduces managerial agency costs.[1818] Hence, *[debt]* should be associated with lower managerial agency costs and may provide some of the managerial monitoring that, in the absence of leverage, would have been provided by the blockholder.[1819] In addition to its effect on managerial agency costs, leverage should also be negatively related to the level of discretionary assets. In contrast to tangible assets, intangible, discretionary assets are not collateralizable and are lost in the event of bankruptcy. Therefore, existing and prospective debtholders may limit investments in intangible assets and rather push for tangible assets,[1820] resulting in a negative expected relationship between leverage and the amount of discretionary assets. Second, leverage should be negatively related to the level of dividend payments since dividends are typically regarded as a substitute governance mechanism for reducing agency costs of free cash flow.[1821] In addition, actively monitoring debtholders may try to reduce dividend payments because they fear a transfer of wealth to the firm's shareholders.[1822] With regard to firm value, no clear prediction can be made. While the disciplinary effect may have an increasing effect,

1812 See Hermalin/Weisbach (1991): 104.
1813 See Seifert et al. (2005): 172.
1814 See also Morck et al. (1988): 294; Dalton et al. (2003): 14. Evidence consistent with this hypothesis is found by, among others, Denis et al. (1997): 136, 158; Ang et al. (2000): 85, 91f; Singh/Davidson III (2003): 797f, 801, 808f; Florackis (2008): 48, 53; Kaserer/Moldenhauer (2008): 1, 24, 27, 33.
1815 See Bøhren/Ødegaard (2006): 31.
1816 See Morck et al. (1988): 294; Hermalin/Weisbach (1991): 104.
1817 This measure is also used by Faccio et al. (2001): 60; Gugler/Yurtoglu (2003): 739; Chen/Yur-Austin (2007): 594; Attig et al. (2009): 400; Konijn et al. (2011): 1334.
1818 See e.g. Barnea et al. (1981): 13f; Singh/Davidson III (2003): 800; Maury/Pajuste (2005): 1821; Pindado/de la Torre (2006): 664; Konijn et al. (2011): 1334; Mietzner/Schweizer (2011): 15.
1819 See also Pindado/de la Torre (2006): 664, 674.
1820 See Hwang/Kim (1998): 42.
1821 See also Rozeff (1982): 252; Travlos/Cornett (1993): 5; Allen et al. (2000): 2520; Faccio et al. (2001): 61f; Truong/Heaney (2007): 669.
1822 See also Faccio et al. (2001): 61f.

leverage also raises a firm's riskiness and bankruptcy costs which should have a decreasing effect on Tobin's q.[1823]

As has been described in section 2.2.2.1, there are three forms of **codetermination**: (1) one-third codetermination which applies to firms with more than 500 but less than 2,000 employees; (2) parity codetermination which applies to firms with more than 2,000 employees, and (3) Montan codetermination which only applies to firms subject to Montan codetermination.[1824] Therefore, the regression models include a dummy variable that equals one if a firm has more than 500 but less than 2,000 employees *[codet_third]* and a dummy variable that equals one if a firm has more than 2,000 employees *[codet_par]*.[1825] The remaining firms serve as a base case.[1826]

Codetermination may affect blockholder monitoring in a number of ways. First, employee representation introduces a highly-informed monitor to the supervisory board. Due to the employees' detailed knowledge of the firm, their representation might enhance monitoring of managers, limit adverse managerial actions[1827] and therefore reduce the need for blockholder monitoring. Second, the detailed knowledge of the firm may allow employee representatives to evaluate and uncover decisions made by the management for the benefit of the blockholder(s) but to the detriment of the remaining stakeholders. As a result, employee representation should limit the blockholder's discretion and self dealing.[1828] Third, codetermination may increase the costs of monitoring.[1829] These costs depend on the extent to which management and/or the employee representatives resist the changes proposed by the blockholder.[1830] Furthermore, the excessive involvement of the employees may enable them to choose a particular type of action that maximizes employees' private benefits rather than the value of the firm.[1831] Moreover, the trilateral interdependence between the management, the employee representatives, and the shareholder representatives decelerates decision making and further increases the costs of monitoring for the blockholder. In a codetermination environment, it might also be more difficult for active blockholders to be heard and thus to address the agency problems inherent in the firm.[1832]

Only a few studies investigate the impact of employee representation on a firm's financial performance.[1833] *Gorton/Schmid* (2002) find an equal representation of employees to nega-

---

1823 See Barnea et al. (1981): 13f; Maury/Pajuste (2005): 1821f; Konijn et al. (2011): 1334.

1824 Due to the few firms subject to Montan codetermination, it is disregarded in the following analysis.

1825 A similar variable is used by Gorton/Schmid (2000): 44.

1826 Note that the actual level of codetermination may sometimes differ from the legally mandated level since some seats on the supervisory board may be temporarily vacant. The variables used cannot control for these cases, which, however, should occur infrequently. Moreover, the number of firms subject to Montan codetermination is negligible.

1827 See Fauver/Fuerst (2006): 674, 680f.

1828 See Fauver/Fuerst (2006): 674, 683.

1829 Jensen/Meckling (1979): 474 argue that codetermination interferes with the natural economic forces and state that "the fact that stockholders must be forced by law to accept codetermination is the best evidence we have that they are adversely affected by it."

1830 See also Bainbridge (2012): 244.

1831 See Fauver/Fuerst (2006): 679, 683. See also Gorton/Schmid (2000): 32.

1832 See Mietzner/Schweizer (2011): 2.

1833 See also Fauver/Fuerst (2006): 675.

tively affect these firms' market to book ratios relative to firms with one-third employee representation.[1834] The authors also find that equal representation results in higher wage bill to sales and employee to sales ratios. Thus, parity codetermination focuses on a maximization of employee rather than shareholder utility which shareholders incorporate into the firms' share prices.[1835] *Fauver/Fuerst* (2006) study whether codetermination protects the interests of minority shareholders and increases firm value. They find that firms with employee representation are more likely to pay dividends, being consistent with a reduced expropriation of shareholders by the blockholder. Moreover, codetermination reduces management's discretionary scope of action and thus its ability to shirk or consume perquisites. Finally, codetermination improves the Tobin's q for firms that operate in industries requiring high levels of cooperation with employees. However, if codetermination exceeds moderate levels, the employee representatives seem to focus on their own private benefits at the expense of firm value.[1836] Nevertheless, employee codetermination is expected to be an efficient additional monitoring mechanism that should decrease a firm's overall agency costs and hence increase firm value.

Despite a general decrease in importance, banks are assumed to still play a special role within the German financial system.[1837] Therefore, the present study controls for **bank presence** *[bank]* which is defined as a dummy variable equal to one if a bank owns at least 5% of a firm's shares.[1838] Banks may have versatile linkages to German non-financial firms. Next to the direct stock ownership, these linkages may arise from the provision of loans, the consulting services and from the use of proxy voting.[1839] In addition, banks frequently own investment firms which in turn own shares in a number of publicly-traded firms.[1840] As a result of the versatile linkages, the particular bank might have privileged access to information which provides the bank with detailed, private knowledge about the investee firm.[1841] This knowledge may provide banks with a competitive advantage[1842] relative to a non-bank blockholder with similar ownership. This advantage may be increased if the bank is also a lender to its portfolio firm, in which case it has an additional source of information and can generate

---

1834 Note that employees do not necessarily need to act against the interest of shareholders to cause a lower firm value. Rather, they might simply make poor decisions that are reflected in the firm's share price. See Gorton/Schmid (2000): 50.

1835 The authors' evidence is based on a sample of the largest 250 non-financial, publicly-traded firms in Germany during 1989-1993. See Gorton/Schmid (2002): 1, 3, 11, 16f. This evidence supports their earlier findings. See Gorton/Schmid (2000): 32, 62.

1836 See Fauver/Fuerst (2006): 674, 677, 702f. The results are based on all publicly-traded German firms in 2003.

1837 For further details on the role of banks in the German financial system, please see section 2.2.1.

1838 A bank is defined as a traditional bank (e.g. Deutsche Bank) and neither includes investment banks nor savings banks (Sparkassen), regional state banks (e.g. LBBW), public-law development banks (e.g. KfW) or other governmental financial institutions. However, this group includes asset management firms if those are owned by a bank (e.g. DWS Investment GmbH, owned by Deutsche Bank).

1839 See also Drukarczyk (1993): 631; Agarwal/Elston (2001): 226. However, due to more extensive regulation, increased competition and concerns expressed by institutional investors, the use of proxy voting has decreased significantly. See Noack (2002): 625; Rieckers/Spindler (2004): 378. Overall, proxy voting has been replaced by proxies nominated by the respective firms or shareholder communities. See Simon/Zetzsche (2010): 924f. For proxies nominated by the firms, please see § 134 (3) Sentence 5 AktG.

1840 See du Plessis et al. (2012): 335. See also Drukarczyk (1993): 631.

1841 See Richter (1994): 37; Thomsen/Pedersen (2000): 693; Mintz (2005): 590.

1842 In this thesis, a firm has a competitive advantage "when it is implementing a value creating strategy not simultaneously being implemented by any current or potential competitors." Barney (1991): 102.

economies of scale and scope in the use of these information.[1843] This puts banks in a good position to monitor corporate management. However, whether or not a bank's monitoring is in the interest of the remaining shareholders – and hence substitutes for blockholder monitoring – is uncertain.

Disregarding potential agency problems within the bank itself, a bank's primary goal is the maximization of profits. This can be achieved either by an appreciation of the value of its investment or by an expansion of customer relationships.[1844] In the latter case, a bank might have goals different from the maximization of shareholder value[1845] and may use its private information for its individual benefit,[1846] i.e. the acquisition of business relationships with the portfolio firm.[1847] Therefore, a bank may be regarded as a pressure sensitive investor:[1848] It maintains business relationships with the portfolio firm, supports management's decisions and, if there is an unsolvable disagreement, sells its stakes rather than challenge management to protect its business relationships.[1849] Thus, banks may hesitate to intervene and act as a "rubber stamp"[1850] for managers as long as the performance of the portfolio firm is acceptable.[1851] At worst, a bank may collude with management and contribute to its protection,[1852] provided the business relationship with the firm generates sufficient profits.[1853]

Due to the special role of banks within the German financial system, there are numerous studies that analyze the impact of banks' equity ownership on the characteristics of their portfolio firms.[1854] Overall, the results of these studies are mixed.[1855] Within the present study, it is expected that a bank blockholder, due to the above mentioned benefits, reduces managerial agency costs. Since a bank blockholder possesses superior access to information, it may also be able to monitor firm management in case of substantial discretionary assets and serve as a signal of the absence of agency conflicts. Consequently, *[discr_assets]* are expected to be higher in the presence of a bank blockholder. Given the assumption that a bank blockholder is simultaneously a creditor of its portfolio firm, it should try to reduce dividend payments be-

---

1843 See Boehmer (2000): 121. See also Black (1992a): 853; Black/Moersch (1998): 1; Elsas/Krahnen (1998): 1286; Halpern (1999): 14.

1844 See Seger (1997): 133.

1845 See Gorton/Schmid (2000): 30; Prokot (2006): 27.

1846 See Agarwal/Elston (2001): 226f.

1847 See Seger (1997): 81; Boehmer (2000): 122; Ruiz-Mallorquí/Santana-Martín (2011): 120.

1848 See Ruiz-Mallorquí/Santana-Martín (2011): 120.

1849 See Black (1992b): 23; Ruiz-Mallorquí/Santana-Martín (2011): 120. In contrast, pressure insensitive investors do not have business relationships with their portfolio firms. See also Brickley et al. (1988): 268; Cornett et al. (2007): 1772 for a similar classification.

1850 Brickley et al. (1988): 274.

1851 See Black (1990): 601; Gottschlich (1996): 153; Seger (1997): 101; Connelly et al. (2010): 1572.

1852 See Hellwig (2000): 127; Borokhovich et al. (2006): 655.

1853 See Chirinko/Elston (2006): 81.

1854 Cable (1985) was one of the first researchers to examine bank involvement. Others include Gorton/Schmid (2000); Boehmer (2000); Edwards/Nibler (2000); Agarwal/Elston (2001); Goergen et al. (2005); Chirinko/Elston (2006); Dittmann et al. (2010). Elsas/Krahnen (1998) focus on the role of Hausbanks.

1855 However, the validity of the reviewed evidence may be limited today; most studies focus on the impact of banks prior to some important changes in the role of banks and the German financial system in general. Please see section 2.2.1 for an overview of these changes.

cause it fears a transfer of wealth to the firm's shareholders.[1856] Due to their potential dual role, bank presence should result in a lower firm value.

5.3.4.3 Others

Next to the above mentioned control variables, a number of additional control variables are employed which neither classify as firm characteristics nor as governance mechanisms.

The regressions control for **firms that leave the sample** during the sample period. In particular, the models use dummy variables in order to control for (1) firms that went bankrupt *[insolv]*, (2) firms that were involved in a takeover, merger or squeeze-out *[takeover]*, and (3) firms that changed the stock market segment *[segm_chng]*. *Börsch-Supan/Köke* (2002) criticize that researchers too frequently eliminate firms with data available for only some of the sample years so as to obtain a balanced panel. This would result in a sample that contains only top- or sufficiently-performing firms, since all firms with poor performance are eliminated. However, the authors argue that a firm's exit decision may be strongly correlated with a governance failure. Therefore, "not using this information means to include it in the error term."[1857] Also *Faccio/Lasfer* (2000) are aware of this problem and argue that the deletion of firms that went bankrupt creates survivorship bias,[1858] as it results in only profitable firms being contained in the sample. In general, the complete elimination of these firms could result in overly optimistic evidence. Due to this, the empirical analysis counters this problem through the use of dummy variables. Since they may be correlated with governance failures and weak performance, it is expected that *[insolv]* and *[segm_chng]* are associated with greater agency cost and lower firm value. According to the disciplinary role of takeovers,[1859] undervalued firms become subject to takeovers; however, also successfully performing firms may be taken over. Hence, no prediction regarding the sign of the *[takeover]* coefficient can be made.

In order to control for **governmental presence** *[govt]*, the regressions include a dummy variable equal to one if the government owns at least 5% of a firm's shares. Governments tend to complement the firm's strategy with their own political interests, such as low output prices or stable employment. These goals may collude with goals of the blockholder and the remaining shareholders[1860] and may severely affect a blockholder's ability to engage in as well as the costs of effective monitoring in the interest of the remaining shareholders. Moreover, agents running public sector bodies or governmental institutes have a lower incentive to engage in monitoring of their portfolio firms as their wealth is not directly tied to the value of the firm's stock.[1861] In line with this, existing studies hypothesize that government-owned firms should

[1856] See Easterbrook (1984): 653; Amihud/Murgia (1997): 407; Seger (1997): 213; Gugler (2003): 1318; Correia da Silva et al. (2004): 140; Al-Malkawi et al. (2010): 190.

[1857] Börsch-Supan/Köke (2002): 309.

[1858] See also Faccio/Lasfer (2000): 103. In this case, a survivorship bias refers to the potential relationships among surviving firms, the relative performance of surviving and non-surviving firms, and the presence or absence of blockholders in surviving and non-surviving firms. See also Bhagat et al. (2004): 15.

[1859] Please see section 2.1.6.3.

[1860] See Seifert et al. (2002): 132.

[1861] See Edwards/Weichenrieder (2004): 160.

exhibit a weak performance in terms of conventional performance measures.[1862] This hypothesis is empirically supported: blockholdings by the government are found to have a negative influence on the firms' market-to-book ratio[1863] and profitability.[1864] Therefore, governmental presence is expected to increase agency costs and decrease firm value.

In line with existing research, the present thesis uses **industry dummies** to account for effects arising as a result of the nature of the firm's industry.[1865] Based on the BICS,[1866] the sample comprises firms from nine different industry sectors. Therefore, eight dummy variables are defined to control for industry effects;[1867] the technology sector represents the base case. Industry effects can be multifaceted. First, the general presence of a particular type of blockholder may depend on the firm's industry. Second, the nature of the respective industries may directly affect the variables used to measure the different types of agency costs. For example, intangible assets may be more important for technology based and pharmaceutical industries. Hence, these industries will have higher *[discr_assets]*. With regard to dividend payments, non-cyclical industries can more easily predict their future cash flows and hence may be more confident in setting a certain level of dividend payments.[1868] Moreover, since the value of Tobin's q depends on growth opportunities, firms operating in mature industries should have lower values for Tobin's q although they are effectively monitored by a blockholder. Finally, the intensity of the product market competition may vary depending on the industry;[1869] in industries with an intense product market competition, the importance of blockholder monitoring may be lower.[1870]

Next to industry effects, the regression models control for **time effects**[1871] by including year dummies for each year during the sample period from 2005-2012.[1872] The incorporation of year dummies is based on the assumption that the importance of and the incentive to engage in monitoring might be dependent on the external market environment. For example, *Spremann* (1987) argues that the information asymmetry between the shareholders and the man-

1862 See Thomsen/Pedersen (2000): 694.

1863 See e.g. Thomsen/Pedersen (2000): 699; Edwards/Weichenrieder (2004): 160.

1864 See Andres (2008): 441.

1865 See e.g. Maury/Pajuste (2005): 1822; Andres (2008); Jara-Bertin et al. (2008): 150; Laeven/Levine (2008): 594; Ruiz-Mallorquí/Santana-Martín (2011): 123; Renders/Gaeremynck (2012): 131; Qandil (2014): 229f.

1866 In contrast to the BICS, the SIC and the GICS offered only poor availability and were therefore of limited use in the study at hand. The poor availability might be due to the sample composition which also incorporates the General Standard which includes smaller firms that might not be relevant for global standards. When SIC and GICS industry classifications were available, these were compared with the BICS. In case of deviations between the three classifications, the industry was identified manually. This resulted in the change of "Eisen- und Hüttenwerke AG" from the "financial" to the "basic materials" industry and of "EValue Ventures AG" from the "communications" to the "financial" industry.

1867 These variables are *[bics_bm]* for basic materials; *[bics_comm]* for communications; *[bics_con_c]* for consumer, cyclical; *[bics_con_nonc]* for consumer, non-cyclical; *[bics_div]* for diversified; *[bics_enrgy]* for energy; *[bics_ind]* for industrial and *[bics_ut]* for utilities.

1868 See also Correia da Silva et al. (2004): 79.

1869 See Thomsen/Pedersen (2000): 697.

1870 See Thomsen/Pedersen (2000): 695, 697. For details on the governance role of product market competition, please refer to section 2.1.6.3.

1871 Time effects are also controlled for by Lehmann/Weigand (2000): 176; Maury/Pajuste (2005): 1822; Konijn et al. (2011): 1335; Renders/Gaeremynck (2012): 131; Qandil (2014): 229f, to name a few.

1872 The year dummies use the year 2005 as base case. Hence, the models include seven dummies: *[year_06]*, *[year_07]*, *[year_08]*, *[year_09]*, *[year_10]*, *[year_11]*, and *[year_12]*.

agement becomes more a hindrance the greater the variation of the environmental influence.[1873] In these cases, it is even more difficult for shareholders to assess managerial performance which aggravates the hidden information problem outlined in section 2.1.1.2. The variation of the environmental influence might have been particularly high during the financial and economic crisis, during which the importance of blockholder monitoring might have been significantly greater. In addition, the time period may affect the dependent variables. For example, it can be expected that the financial crisis affected the firms' Tobin's q and dividend payouts through a general drop in share prices and declining earnings, respectively.

5.4 Résumé

The goal of chapter 5 was to lay the ground for and introduce the theoretical reasoning underlying the regression analysis of chapter 6. Therefore, section 5.1 combined the analysis on the theoretical background and institutional environment, the explanation of blockholder monitoring, and the possible determinants of blockholder monitoring to develop a model of blockholder monitoring. This model accounts for four factors that may affect the blockholder's monitoring, namely blockholder characteristics (heterogeneity), blockholder interrelationships, portfolio firm characteristics, and the presence of alternative governance mechanisms. To highlight the importance of these factors, the model is estimated in stages, presuming (1) blockholder homogeneity, (2) blockholder heterogeneity, and (3) blockholder interrelationships. Grounded on agency theoretic reasoning, section 5.2 then picked up on the arguments provided in the chapters three and four and derived hypotheses with regard to the specific relationships depicted in the model for each of the three stages. Finally, the operationalization of the model's components was outlined in section 5.3.

Having provided the theoretical model, the corresponding hypotheses as well as the operationalization, chapter 6 focuses on the empirical examination of the theoretical considerations.

[1873] See Spremann (1987): 24.

6 Empirical Analysis

The empirical analysis examines the proposed theoretical relationships between blockholder monitoring and agency costs as well as between blockholder monitoring and firm value based on the assumption of blockholder homogeneity, heterogeneity, and interrelationships. However, section 6.1 first introduces the data used to examine these relationships. Section 6.2 contains the summary statistics and the descriptive analysis that is structured based on the assumption of blockholder homogeneity, heterogeneity, and interrelationships. Following this preliminary evidence, section 6.3 focuses on the regression analysis that is used to investigate the hypotheses that have been formulated in chapter 5. Finally, section 6.4 points to some limitations of the study.

6.1 Data

The following sections present the data that serves as the basis for the empirical analysis. Section 6.1.1 first explains the reasoning underlying the selection of the sample. Section 6.1.2 explains the steps involved in the construction of the sample. Since the data has been compiled from a number of sources, section 6.1.3 lists the sources of the respective data.

6.1.1 Sample Selection

Next to the determinants mentioned in chapter 4, the sample composition also constitutes a factor that might affect the relationship between blockholder monitoring and agency costs and firm value. Therefore, the reasons and motivation underlying the sample selection are described in the following to ensure transparency with regard to the sample selection.

Although most research focuses on either publicly-traded or private firms, some studies simultaneously incorporate publicly-traded and private firms.[1874] However, the listing status might significantly affect the degree of ownership concentration and other firm characteristics and hence might bias the results when investigating private and publicly-traded firms simultaneously.[1875] Moreover, the relationship between blockholder monitoring and agency costs and firm value may be affected by the time period. *Bhagat/Jefferis Jr.* (2002) criticize that the majority of extant studies gathers data only at one (or more) points in time. However, they argue that the only way to investigate the impact of blockholders on firm performance "is to consider performance over long horizons of several years."[1876] Also *Peng* (2003) argues that the results, "while valid at a given point in time, may not hold longitudinally."[1877] The study at hand addresses these concerns and employs yearly (panel) data[1878] from 2004 to 2012.[1879]

[1874] Studies that focus on public and private firms are e.g. Maury (2006); Nowak et al. (2006); Leiber (2008).

[1875] For similar arguments, see also Bott (2002): 163.

[1876] Bhagat/Jefferis Jr. (2002): 28.

[1877] Peng (2003): 283.

[1878] Because the cross-sectional by far exceeds the time series dimension, one can speak of micropanel data. See Jara-Bertin et al. (2008): 150. For the benefits and limitations of panel data, please see Baltagi (2008): 6-11.

[1879] Note, however, that the 2004 data is only used for robustness tests. Unless stated otherwise, the empirical analysis starting in section 6.2 is based on the sample from 2005-2012.

The goal of the present research is to determine the influence of blockholders on agency costs and firm value. Therefore, it is necessary to select a sample that allows for such an examination. Several characteristics of the German environment ensure its suitability for the study at hand. First, the specific components of its governance system, such as its two-tier board structure, the still strong role of banks or the legally mandated codetermination,[1880] may affect the monitoring ability as well as the need for blockholder monitoring. Second, although the German Government has taken various measures to improve transparency and ensure investor protection,[1881] the protection of minority equity investors is still regarded as rather weak.[1882] Consequently, the German environment still allows a potential blockholder to pursue governance improvement strategies.[1883] Alternatively, the private control opportunities could provide an extra incentive for blockholder ownership.[1884] Third, section 2.2.4 illustrated that the ownership structure in 2006 is still highly concentrated, providing the largest blockholder with substantial discretion.[1885] Furthermore, the percentage of firms with a single blockholder decreased substantially, whereas the percentage of firms with two and three blockholders increased. These ownership structures are well suited for an investigation of blockholder interrelationships. Fourth, the weaker protection of small shareholders, the concentrated ownership structure, and the strong role of banks suggest that agency costs may be composed not only of manager-shareholder agency costs but of all components of a firm's overall agency costs.[1886] In the light of these circumstances, the German environment is well suited for an investigation of blockholder monitoring and blockholder interrelationships and the effect on agency costs and firm value.

The focus on German publicly-traded firms is primarily motivated by more extensive disclosure requirements for publicly-traded firms relative to private firms.[1887] As a result, this focus ensures a greater availability of financial data and of information on the firms' ownership structures. For example, § 21 (1) WpHG requires the publication of shareholdings in an issuer whose home country is Germany and hence enables the collection of the ownership structure in the first place. Moreover, the severity of the four agency conflicts outlined in section 2.1 is significantly greater for publicly-listed firms than for private firms, since the latter are frequently characterized by a unity of ownership and control.[1888]

To ensure the representativeness of the conclusions drawn from the empirical analysis, the sample is chosen to be as representative of the German corporate environment as possible. However, due to the significant effort involved in the data collection and the poor data quality for firms subject to low disclosure standards, an exhaustive data collection of all publicly-listed firms is not regarded as reasonable. Rather, the study at hand focuses on all firms listed

---

1880 Please see section 2.2.2.1 for details on the characteristics and elements of the German governance system.
1881 For further details, please see section 2.2.2.2.
1882 See Achleitner et al. (2010): 806f. See also Nowak et al. (2005): 257.
1883 See Achleitner et al. (2010): 806f.
1884 See Thomsen et al. (2006): 249.
1885 For additional but less recent evidence, see e.g. La Porta et al. (1999): 492f; Becht/Röell (1999): 1053; Bott (2002): 252; Ruhwedel (2003): 204.
1886 Please see the discussion in section 2.2.5 for details. See also Achleitner et al. (2010): 806f.
1887 See also Ampenberger (2010): 186.
1888 See also Ampenberger (2010): 186f.

in the CDAX at least once during the sample period of 2004-2012. The CDAX has been introduced in 1993 and incorporates all German firms that comply to the general and prime standard. Since they are incorporated in the prime standard, the CDAX also comprises the most important selection indices DAX, MDAX, SDAX, and TecDAX which include the most liquid issues listed on the Frankfurt Stock Exchange.[1889] As has been outlined in section 2.2.1, the prime and general standard differ with regard to their transparency levels.[1890] Nevertheless, member firms of both indices have to prepare their consolidated financial statements based on the IFRS.[1891] As a result, the financial reporting is consistent across all firms in the sample. According to *Deutsche Börse* (2013), the CDAX "reflects the performance of the overall German equity market, and is consequently well suited for analytic purposes."[1892]

Due to its focus on publicly-traded firms, the sample might be subject to a sample selection bias. *Börsch-Supan/Köke* (2002) argue that publicly-traded firms should be the most profitable and largest firms in the market. If this assumption is correct and the decision to go public depends on the performance of the respective firms, also the probability to be contained in the sample is influenced by performance. In addition, firms may go public to get access to external funding which they require to finance their investment opportunities; the availability of significant investment opportunities in turn leads to rising market values. As a consequence, the impact of the ownership structure on the performance of publicly-traded firms could be biased and inconsistent, since the performance influences the probability of being in the sample.[1893] In order to reduce this selection bias, the sample used in this study is selected to be as comprehensive as possible. However, the level of comprehension depends on two important factors. First, the data has to be available. Especially the historical availability of a firm's ownership structure is difficult and time-consuming to obtain. As the ownership of private firms does not have to be disclosed, the problem of data availability is even more problematic for private firms. Therefore, a comprehensive and consistent description of the ownership structure of private firms cannot be guaranteed. Second, the income statement and balance sheet data has to be comparable across firms. This is neither the case for private firms nor for firms not listed in the CDAX. Hence, a comparison of these firms with the sample firms would be biased by differences in accounting standards. Given these restrictions, the sample used for the empirical analysis corrects for selection bias in the best possible way.[1894] Moreover, the sample construction abstains from the deletion of firms that went bankrupt during the

---

1889 See Deutsche Börse AG (2013): 7f. Thereof, the DAX comprises the largest and most actively traded firms and the SDAX the smallest and least liquid firms. The TecDax incorporates the largest firms from the technology sector.

1890 See Deutsche Börse AG (2010): 7; Deutsche Börse AG (2012a): 1.

1891 As described more detailed in section 2.2.2.2, the BilReg requires the implementation of the IAS/IFRS accounting principles since 2005. This is why the empirical analysis is based on the 2005-2012 company financial data.

1892 Deutsche Börse AG (2013): 10. For further information, please see the Guide to the Equity Indices of Deutsche Börse, currently in Version 6.19.

1893 See Börsch-Supan/Köke (2002): 305-311.

1894 As argued previously, the simultaneous investigation of publicly-listed and private firms might also lead to biased results, since the blockholder's monitoring may depend on the listing status of the respective firm.

sample period and thereby also comprises poorly performing firms which may further reduce the selection bias.[1895]

Having outlined the reasoning underlying the sample selection, the following section 6.1.2 focuses on the specific construction of the sample.

6.1.2 Sample Construction

The construction of the sample is carried out in a step-wise procedure which is summarized in Table 4. In the **first step**, all firms[1896] listed in the CDAX index at least once during the sample period of 2004 to 2012 are identified. This results in the identification of 845 firms (5,871 firm years).

The **second step** involves the exclusion of financial firms, which are subject to strict regulation, exhibit a different structure of the balance sheet, and are thus difficult to compare to non-financial firms. Moreover, their policies and performance may be determined by regulatory requirements and may therefore potentially bias the regression results. The exclusion of financial firms is consistent with various (international) studies and hence also ensures a better comparability.[1897] The exclusion of financial firms is based on the BICS. In total, 140 financial firms are excluded from the sample.

As outlined above, the number of stocks in the CDAX does not equal the number of firms. Hence, the **third step** involves the deletion of double-listed stocks from the sample.[1898] In addition, if a firm is not listed in the CDAX in a particular year, the respective firm year observation is dropped from the sample. After step three, the total number of non-financial firms in the sample equals 671 (4,747 firm years). Thereof, 620 firms issued only common stock whereas 51 firms issued only preferred stock or both common and preferred stock.

In the **fourth step**, the ownership structure and shareholder identity of these 671 firms is collected manually.[1899] For some firms, the sum of all ownership rights exceeds 100%. In most cases, this is due to a double listing of a single investor. In this case, the duplicate entry is deleted. For the remaining firms, the ownership structure is researched and adapted manually. Since the "Orbis" database in some cases provides only the name of the investment vehicle used by a particular investor, the ultimate owner of these vehicles identified. For instance, the fund Pyramus S.a.r.l. registered in Luxembourg is ultimately owned by the private equity firm Apax Partners. Hence, the fund is classified as a private equity investor. It should be noted that the data on the ownership structure provided by "Orbis" is gathered from multiple sources during a calendar year. Hence, although "Orbis" reports the ownership structure as of December 31, the respective data can be based on an earlier point in time within the same

---

1895 Please see also section 5.3.4.3.

1896 Please note that if a firm has issued both common and preferred stock, it is double-listed in the CDAX. Hence, the number of firms in step one and two overrates the actual number of firms in the sample. This problem is solved within step three.

1897 See e.g. Jensen et al. (1992): 253; Faccio/Lasfer (2000): 83; La Porta et al. (2002): 1154; Singh/Davidson III (2003): 797; Maury/Pajuste (2005): 1815; Ampenberger (2010): 192, to name a few.

1898 As a result of this exclusion, at this stage the number of stocks equals the number of firms in the sample.

1899 Please see section 6.1.3 for details on the data sources and the approach used for the classification.

Table 4
This table summarizes the step-wise procedure used for the construction of the sample.

Step	Operation		No. of firms
1	Identification of firms listed in the CDAX at least once during 2004-2012		845
2	Exclusion of financial firms	-140	
3	Deletion of double-listed stocks	-34	
4	Firms without ownership data	-14	
5	Firms that went bankrupt, were taken over, or changed their stock market segment prior to the sample period	-94	
	Firms with no financial data available	-16	
6	Collection of data on blockholder presence on supervisory or management board	-	
	Sample including year 2004		547
	Firms lost due to exclusion of observations for 2004		-16
	Primary sample excluding year 2004		**531**

Table 4: Summary of the sample construction

year. However, this should not cause a problem, since the ownership structure tends to be stable at least within this relatively short time frame.[1900] No ownership data in any year was available for 14 firms; hence, the sample firms are reduced to 657 (4,678 firm years).

For these 657 firms, the balance sheet and income statement data is collected in the **fifth step**. Financial data was unavailable for several firms. In the great majority of these cases, the unavailability results from insolvencies, takeovers, squeeze-outs, and changes of the stock market segment during the sample.[1901] Therefore, observations of firms that went bankrupt, were involved in a takeover or squeeze-out as well as firms that changed their stock market segment during the sample are excluded as of the year of the event.[1902] Following an insolvency, the shell company frequently remains listed on the CDAX. For example, Biodata Information Tech AG filed for bankruptcy in 2001, however, remained listed in the CDAX until 2010. Therefore, 77 firms that went bankrupt, 16 firms that were subject to a takeover or squeeze-out and one firm that changed the stock market segment prior to the sample period are dropped. Following step five, the sample comprises 547 firms.

In the **final step**, the data gathered in the previous steps is complemented with hand-collected data on the blockholder(s)' presence on the supervisory board and/or the management board of the respective portfolio firms.

As outlined in footnote 1879, the 2004 data is used for robustness tests only. Therefore, the respective observations are not included in the primary sample depicted in Table 5. As can be seen, the sample constitutes an unbalanced panel comprising 531 firms (3,309 firm years).[1903] Thereof, 492 firms issued only common stock whereas 39 firms issued only preferred stock or both common and preferred stock. Of all sample firms, 273 firms (~ 51%) are comprised in

[1900] Please see the results of the descriptive analysis in section 6.2.3.1.

[1901] For 16 firms, the reason for the missing data is unknown; these observations are also excluded.

[1902] Hence, an observation on a firm that declared insolvency in April 2006 is also dropped from the sample in 2006. As already outlined in section 5.3.4.3, the empirical analysis uses three dummy variables to control for firms that leave the sample.

[1903] Since the data is not available for all variables, the exact number of observations depends on the respective empirical model employed. The size of the sample is therefore provided with the respective outputs.

Table 5
This table provides an overview of the primary sample (excluding the year 2004) in terms of number of firms and number of firm years, both distinguished between firms with preferred and common stock.

No. of firms (per years in sample)				No. of firms (per year)			
Years in sample	Preferred stock	Common stock	Total	Year	Preferred stock	Common stock	Total
1	1	26	27	2005	38	397	435
2	1	26	27	2006	37	377	414
3	3	36	39	2007	36	422	458
4	1	31	32	2008	34	405	439
5	1	37	38	2009	33	378	411
6	0	56	56	2010	33	365	398
7	2	37	39	2011	33	356	389
8	30	243	273	2012	31	334	365
	39	**492**	**531**		**275**	**3,034**	**3,309**

Table 5: Overview of the primary sample

the sample for the whole time period. The average number of years a firm is represented in the data is 6.2 years. The size of the sample reaches its maximum in 2007 (458 firms) and its minimum in 2012 (365 firms). The number of firms per year overall declines from 435 in 2005 to 365 in 2012. During this period, 59 firms went bankrupt, 62 firms were taken over or subject to a squeeze-out and 26 firms changed their market segment.[1904] Of the 531 firms within the sample, there are also 23 SEs. Compared to the AG, an SE differs in a number of points which may affect a blockholder's monitoring. Among others, SEs can choose between a two-tier board model and a one-tier board model.[1905] Moreover, adapted rules with regard to the German codetermination apply to SEs.[1906] Therefore, as a robustness test, the regression analysis also includes a dummy variable to identify SEs.

6.1.3 Data Sources

The dataset underlying the empirical analysis is formed by an amalgamation of two databases and data obtained from the sample firms' annual reports.

For the most part, both dependent and control variables are based on fundamental (financial) data from the firms' annual financial statements. This data is obtained from the data provider Bloomberg. Moreover, Bloomberg provided information on the sample (CDAX) composition. The collection of data on the sample firms' ownership structure is most demanding in terms of availability and is carried out manually using Bureau van Dijk's "Orbis" database, which contains information on corporate ownership for over 30 million shareholder/subsidiary links.[1907] Thereby, the "Orbis" data for the year 2005 is complemented with data from the Hoppenstedt Aktienführer. In this way, the ownership structure for 28 additional firms in

[1904] The reasons for a firm's entry are not identified.

[1905] For further details, please see §§ 15-19 SEAG for the two-tier board model and §§ 20-49 SEAG for the one-tier board model. However, larger SEs typically choose the two-tier model; for instance, all SEs in the DAX employ a two-tier model.

[1906] Please see SEBG for further details.

[1907] Please see Bureau van Dijk (2013) for more details on the "Orbis" database.

Table 6
This table presents the type of data as well as the data source for the respective type of data.

Type of Data	Data Source
Data on the sample composition	Bloomberg
Data on the sample firms' ownership structure	Bureau van Dijk's "Orbis" database; Hoppenstedt Aktienführer; Annual reports; BaFin; Internet research
Data on the shareholder identities	Internet research; Annual reports; Ad hoc disclosures
Financial data of the sample firms	Bloomberg
Data on shareholders' presence on supervisory and/or management boards	Annual reports; Ad hoc disclosures; Internet research

Table 6: Data sources

2005 is collected.[1908] As a plausibility check, the ownership of a random sample of firms is reassessed based on the respective firms' annual reports, figures reported by the BaFin, and based on internet research.

Since the classifications of blockholder types provided by the "Orbis" database do not resemble the definitions used in the present thesis, the classification of the shareholders into the different types introduced in section 5.3.2 is done based on internet research, annual reports, and ad hoc disclosures. Unfortunately, the database is not consistent with regard to the naming of the shareholders which frequently differs across years and across firms. For instance, the ownership structure of Altana AG contains both Susanne Klatten and Skion GmbH. However, Skion GmbH is owned by Susanne Klatten. In these cases, the ownership structure exceeds 100% and is manually corrected.

The data on the blockholders' presence on the supervisory board and/or management board of the respective portfolio firms is collected based on the firms' annual reports, ad hoc disclosures, and internet research. Table 6 provides an overview of the data sources used.

6.2 Descriptive Analysis

In order to assess the characteristics of the data and to judge on the appropriateness of any generalization of the empirical results, the regression analysis is preceded by a descriptive analysis of the sample. Section 6.2.1 presents the summary statistics of the dependent variables, the primary explanatory variables, and the control variables. Consistent with the stagewise empirical approach, the remaining sections include an analysis under the assumption of blockholder homogeneity (section 6.2.2), blockholder heterogeneity (section 6.2.3), and blockholder interrelationships (section 6.2.4). Thereby, these sections extend the analysis in section 2.2.4 and focus on presenting evidence for the existence of ownership structures that necessitate an empirical analysis.

6.2.1 Summary Statistics

The following tables depict the summary statistics for the variables used in the empirical analysis. In order to minimize the impact of extreme values – outliers[1909] – the 5% and 95%

[1908] Unfortunately, the Hoppenstedt Aktienführer was only available for the year 2005.

Table 7
This table presents summary statistics for all firms in the sample during the sample period from 2005-2012, focusing on the dependent and (continuous) control variables. The number of firm years depends on the data availability of the respective variable.

Variable	Mean	Median	Max	Min	SD	N
Dependent variables						
opex_sales	0.7302	0.9111	1.4168	0.1297	0.3846	3,289
discr_assets	0.8138	0.8455	0.9988	0.4422	0.1578	3,291
div_payout	0.0021	0.0001	0.0134	0.0000	0.0040	2,643
tobinq	1.5067	1.2498	3.3633	0.7840	0.7132	3,290
Control variables						
growth	0.1002	0.0627	2.3142	-0.7264	0.3650	3,264
age	14.8115	9.0000	141.0000	0.0000	23.5163	3,177
prof	0.0071	0.0321	0.1676	-0.3340	0.1148	3,309
ppe_assets	0.1926	0.1586	0.5578	0.0101	0.1612	3,291
beta	0.8250	0.7987	1.5687	0.0211	0.3740	3,197
stdev_ni	39.1403	5.5313	366.2246	0.3727	88.4028	3,296
capex	0.0392	0.0311	0.1130	0.0037	0.0305	3,206
cash_assets	0.1645	0.1127	0.5512	0.0106	0.1516	3,308
ln_assets	5.3278	5.0482	9.7388	2.3269	1.9901	3,309
debt	0.1896	0.1596	0.5554	0.0000	0.1663	3,269
insd_own	0.0383	0.0000	1.0000	0.0000	0.1197	3,309

Table 7: Summary statistics for the dependent and continuous control variables

tails of each fundamental (financial) variable, except those of the dummy variables and firm age, are winsorized. This procedure sets any extreme values to the 5th and 95th percentile, respectively.[1910]

Table 7 focuses on the dependent and (continuous) control variables and presents summary statistics for all firms from 2005-2012. With regard to the dependent variables, a comparison of mean and median shows that the winsorizing has eliminated the most significant outliers; in most cases, both measures are approximately similar. An exception constitutes the dividend payout variable, whose mean and median differ substantially and which therefore also exhibits a greater dispersion as measured by its standard deviation. As can be seen, *[div_payout]* is also characterized by a lower data availability relative to the remaining dependent variables – data is available for only 2,643 firm year observations.[1911] Turning to the controls, the sample firms have an average age *[age]* of about 15, earn a positive net income *[prof]* and grow in terms of year-on-year sales *[growth]*.

For the dichotomous variables used as controls, table 8 depicts the frequencies for all firm year observations in the sample. As can be seen, nearly 60% of the firm year observations are subject to either one-third (25.64%) or parity (34.05%) codetermination.[1912] Moreover, in 14.72% of the firm year observations, a bank holds more than 5% of the firm's shares. These

1909 An outlier can be regarded as "an observation far away from most or all other observations." Ghosh/Vogt (2012): 3455.

1910 A first winsorization at the 1% and 99% level was not efficient in eliminating outliers. For a similar approach, please see La Porta et al. (2002): 1158; Maury/Pajuste (2005): 1820; Bøhren/Ødegaard (2006): 14; Maury (2006): 325, to name a few.

1911 As a consequence, the corresponding regressions are also based on a smaller sample.

1912 Note that in this case, the frequency refers to those firms for which data on the number of employees is available. Hence, the total frequency equals 3,260 rather than 3,309.

Table 8
This table presents the absolute and relative frequencies of the dichotomous variables to be used as control variables for all firms in the sample during the sample period from 2005-2012.

	0		1		Total	
Variable	**Freq.**	**%**	**Freq.**	**%**	**Freq.**	**%**
insolv	3,137	94.80	172	5.20	3,309	100
takeover	3,122	94.35	187	5.65	3,309	100
segm_chng	3,188	96.34	121	3.66	3,309	100
govt	3,096	93.56	213	6.44	3,309	100
liq	2,362	71.38	947	28.62	3,309	100
pfd	3,034	91.69	275	8.31	3,309	100
bank	2,822	85.28	487	14.72	3,309	100
codet_third	2,424	74.36	836	25.64	3,260	100
codet_par	2,150	65.95	1,110	34.05	3,260	100
SE_dummy	3,141	94.92	168	5.08	3,309	100

Table 8: Absolute and relative frequencies of the dichotomous control variables

numbers illustrate the importance of controlling for these mechanisms specific for the German institutional environment. The German government holds at least 5% of a particular firm's shares in more than 6% of the firm year observations. In addition, for about 30% of all firm year observations, the respective firms are listed in one of the major indices DAX, MDAX, SDAX and TecDax.

Table 9 presents the distribution of the firm year observations into the nine industry sectors to be used as control variables. Observations of firms operating in the industrial sector constitute the largest group, followed by the non-cyclical and cyclical consumer sector. Diversified and utility firms constitute the smallest groups. During the sample period, the frequency of the respective industries remains rather constant; the largest increase (from 24.60% to 28.22%) is recorded for industrial and the largest decrease (16.32% to 13.97%) for technology firms.

Summary statistics for the explanatory ownership variables are presented in table 10. Across all sample firms, the average (median) cumulative ownership of all blockholders equals 53.50% (55.64%). The average (median) ownership of the largest blockholders equals 38.44% (31.07%). Hence, the largest blockholder on average holds more than the blocking

Table 9
This table presents the distribution of the firm year observations into the nine industry sectors to be used as control variables for all firms in the sample during the sample period from 2005-2012.

	2005	**2006**	**2007**	**2008**	**2009**	**2010**	**2011**	**2012**	**Total**
Basic materials *[bics_bm]*	17	15	18	17	16	17	17	16	133
Communications *[bics_comm]*	64	57	60	59	56	54	50	48	448
Consumer, cyclical *[bics_con_c]*	78	75	76	71	65	66	68	65	564
Consumer, non-cyclical *[bics_con_nonc]*	82	81	85	83	77	74	71	64	617
Diversified *[bics_div]*	3	4	1	2	2	2	2	2	18
Energy *[bics_enrgy]*	5	5	11	11	9	10	10	9	70
Industrial *[bics_ind]*	107	101	123	119	113	109	108	103	883
Technology *[bics_tec]*	71	68	76	70	66	59	56	51	517
Utilities [*bics_ut]*	8	8	8	7	7	7	7	7	59
Total	**435**	**414**	**458**	**439**	**411**	**398**	**389**	**365**	**3,309**

Table 9: Distribution of sample firms into industry sectors

Table 10
This table presents summary statistics for all firms in the sample during the sample period from 2005-2012, focusing on the primary explanatory ownership variables.

Variable	Mean	Median	Max	Min	SD	N
cum_own	0.5350	0.5564	1	0	0.2965	3,309
h_index	0.2468	0.1508	1	0	0.2606	3,309
bh1_cont	0.3844	0.3107	1	0	0.2765	3,309
bh1_pe_cont	0.0361	0	1	0	0.1264	3,309
bh1_fam_cont	0.1279	0	1	0	0.2257	3,309
bh1_si_cont	0.1401	0	1	0	0.2828	3,309
bh1_insti_cont	0.0142	0	0.9498	0	0.0674	3,309
bh2_cont	0.0876	0.0703	0.5000	0	0.0934	3,309
bh2_pe_cont	0.0049	0	0.3773	0	0.0307	3,309
bh2_fam_cont	0.0226	0	0.5000	0	0.0657	3,309
bh2_si_cont	0.0168	0	0.4990	0	0.0567	3,309
bh2_insti_cont	0.0136	0	0.4100	0	0.0394	3,309
bhtypes_count	1.9184	2	7	0	1.2063	3,309
bh_count	2.3421	2	10	0	1.5915	3,309
ln_bhtypes_count	0.5792	0.6931	1.9459	0	0.5291	3,087
ln_bh_count	0.7432	0.6931	2.3026	0	0.5969	3,091
diff_bh12345	0.1885	0.0562	1	0	0.2599	3,309
bh1/bh2	2.2197	1.2900	17.9218	0	2.9437	3,091
bh1/bh2_bh3	1.7913	0.9653	17.9218	0	2.7347	3,091

Table 10: Summary statistics for the explanatory ownership variables

minority.[1913] Of the four largest blockholder types, strategic investors and families on average hold the largest equity stakes. The average (median) ownership of the second largest blockholder amounts to 8.76% (7.03%). Moreover, the sample firms have on average 2.34 different blockholders. Further details on the ownership structure are provided in the following sections 6.2.2-6.2.4.

6.2.2 Analysis under the Assumption of Blockholder Homogeneity

A prerequisite for a study on the influence of blockholders on agency costs and firm value is the existence of concentrated ownership structures for a sufficient number of firms within the sample. Under the assumption of blockholder homogeneity, this is to be tested in the subsequent section.

Table 11 depicts the arithmetic mean of the cumulative ownership size of all blockholders *[cum_own]* and of the Herfindahl index *[h_index]* as well as the number and percentage of firms with a blockholder owning more than 5% of the firm's voting rights *[bh1_dummy]*. Overall, the table illustrates the highly concentrated ownership structure in the German institutional environment. For each year of the sample period, the *[cum_own]* is larger than 50%. Across all years, the average cumulative ownership equals 51.74%. In other words, on average, 51.74% of a firm's voting rights are held by blockholders. Moreover, the ownership concentration is very stable; the lowest ownership concentration equals 50.42% (in 2006) whereas the highest concentration equals 55.18% (in 2010).

1913 The numbers incorporate firms whose largest shareholder does not fulfill the blockholder definition in section 5.3.2.1. Hence, average blockholder ownership in firms with a blockholder should be larger.

Table 11
This table depicts the evolution of the ownership concentration for the sample firms from 2005 to 2012. For each year, it depicts the arithmetic mean of the cumulative ownership size of all blockholders *[cum_own]* and of the Herfindahl index *[h_index]*. In addition, it depicts the number and percentage (in italics) of firms with a blockholder *[bh1_dummy]*.

	2005	2006	2007	2008	2009	2010	2011	2012
cum_own	0.5173	0.5042	0.5438	0.5333	0.5418	0.5518	0.5501	0.5404
h_index	0.2361	0.2336	0.2413	0.2414	0.2549	0.2567	0.2603	0.2537
bh1_dummy	402	370	424	410	385	375	374	351
	0.9241	*0.8937*	*0.9258*	*0.9339*	*0.9367*	*0.9422*	*0.9614*	*0.9616*
N	435	414	458	439	411	398	389	365

Table 11: Evolution of the ownership concentration

A similar picture emerges for the Herfindahl index, which also remains stable during the sample period. Since a higher value indicates a higher ownership concentration, the ownership of the sample firms is least concentrated in 2006 (23.36%) and most concentrated in 2011 (26.03%). The values for the Herfindahl index in 2005 and 2006 are comparable to those observed by *Ampenberger* (2010) who reports values of 25.82% and 24.59% in 2005 and 2006, respectively.[1914] However, he finds a strongly decreasing ownership concentration from 1995 to 2006 which may be a direct result of the tax incentives set by the German Government and other changes within the institutional environment.[1915] The rather constant concentration of ownership reported in table 11 may be an indication that the major changes in the ownership structure of German publicly-traded firms are concluded in the mid-2000s or at least do no longer affect the concentration of ownership.[1916]

With regard to the *[bh1_dummy]* variable, apart from a slight drop in 2006, the percentage of firms with a blockholder always exceeds 90%; in 2011 and 2012, more than 96% of the sample firms have a blockholder.

Overall, the results so far constitute first evidence of the concentrated ownership structures in the German corporate environment. Following significant changes and the unbundling of the Deutschland AG in the early 2000s, the ownership concentration has decreased, but remains stable during the period of 2005-2012. Despite these changes, a blockholders is present in nearly all of the sample firms covered in this study. Further, more detailed evidence is provided in the following sections.

6.2.3 Analysis under the Assumption of Blockholder Heterogeneity

The incorporation of blockholder heterogeneity can only be warranted if the characteristics of the largest blockholder are sufficiently pronounced. A large enough stake in the hands of the largest blockholder represents a necessary condition for any discussion of the potential monitoring of blockholders and shall be tested in section 6.2.3.1. In addition, this section provides an overview of the blockholder's presence on the boards of its portfolio firms. Section 6.2.3.2

1914 The slight deviations may result from his larger sample size, which equals 494 in both 2005 and 2006. For additional details, please see Ampenberger (2010): 215.

1915 See Ampenberger (2010): 216. See also the discussion in section 2.2.4.

1916 It may still be possible that some blockholders sell their stake to a different investor. This selling, however, would not affect the ownership concentration since the stake merely changes the holder.

Table 12
This table depicts the evolution of the largest blockholder's ownership *[bh1_cont]* for the sample firms from 2005 to 2012. Panel A depicts the arithmetic mean ownership of the largest blockholder. Panel B presents the number and percentage (in italics) of firms with a blockholder that has an ownership above the important control thresholds.

	2005	2006	2007	2008	2009	2010	2011	2012
Panel A								
Mean ownership	0.4061	0.4109	0.4028	0.4009	0.4174	0.4233	0.4203	0.4131
Panel B								
5%	402	370	424	410	385	375	374	351
	0.9241	*0.8937*	*0.9258*	*0.9339*	*0.9367*	*0.9422*	*0.9614*	*0.9616*
Blocking minority	269	251	275	266	257	265	260	244
	0.6184	*0.6063*	*0.6004*	*0.6059*	*0.6253*	*0.6658*	*0.6684*	*0.6685*
Simple majority	139	137	154	149	153	148	147	134
	0.3195	*0.3309*	*0.3362*	*0.3394*	*0.3723*	*0.3719*	*0.3779*	*0.3671*
Super majority	49	51	64	61	64	55	64	59
	0.1126	*0.1232*	*0.1397*	*0.1390*	*0.1557*	*0.1382*	*0.1645*	*0.1616*
N	435	414	458	439	411	398	389	365

Table 12: Evolution of the largest blockholder's ownership

then focuses on the evolution of the different blockholder types to identify if they are represented in a sufficient number of sample firms. In section 6.2.3.3, the portfolio firms of these blockholder types are compared to get a first descriptive insight on the potential impact of the blockholder types on their portfolio firms.

6.2.3.1 Evolution of the Largest Blockholder

Table 12 depicts the evolution of the largest blockholder's ownership. Similar to the overall ownership concentration examined in the previous section, the ownership of the largest blockholder presented in panel A remains stable.[1917] During the sample period, it varies within the range of 40.09% in 2008 to 42.33% in 2010.[1918] Hence, the mean ownership of the largest blockholder exceeds 40% in each year of the sample period. On average, the blockholder's ownership therefore by far exceeds the 25% threshold required for a blocking minority and should therefore provide sufficient power to effectively monitor corporate management. However, this ownership may also point to a substantial discretion of the largest blockholder. Referring to the average shareholder presence on the firms' AGMs depicted in figure 7, the average blockholder owned the simple majority at the firms' AGMs in every year of the sample and the super majority in 2005 and 2006. Further insight on the power of the largest blockholder is provided in panel B. As has already been outlined in section 6.2.2, the percentage of firms with a blockholder exceeds 90% in each year of the sample. Disregarding the low presence at the firms' AGMs, more than 60% of the sample firms have a blockholder with a blocking minority during the sample period. Still roughly one-third of the firms have a blockholder with the simple majority in every year except 2005. The super majority is held by blockholders in 11.26% of the firms in 2005; the same figure equals 16.16% in 2012. Overall,

[1917] The stable ownership provides further support for the proposition that the changes in the ownership structure of German publicly-traded firms during the early 2000s have largely been concluded.

[1918] The ownership for the years 2005 and 2006 is comparable to the figures by Ampenberger (2010): 215 who reports an ownership of 41.25% and 40.46% in 2005 and 2006, respectively.

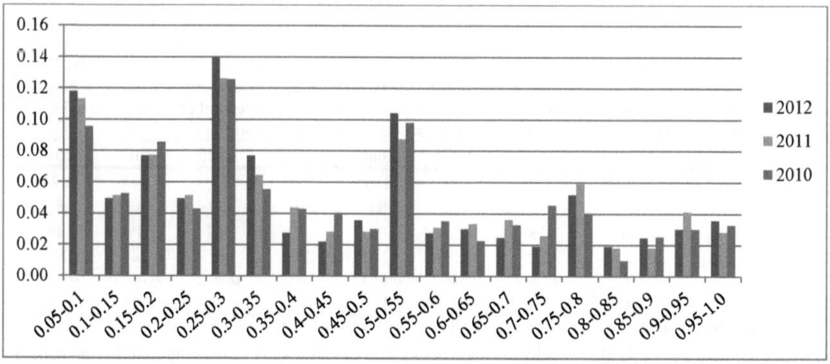

Figure 11: Distribution of the largest blockholder in different ownership intervals in 2010-2012

table 12 suggests that, at least from a legal perspective, the largest blockholder is large enough to effectively monitor corporate management, however, is also provided with substantial discretion in a significant number of firms.

Within section 2.2.3.2, it has been argued that the feasibility of engaging in monitoring as well as the level of monitoring is linked with the intervention options and shareholder rights open to the blockholder at critical ownership thresholds. To analyze if blockholders indeed consciously acquire their stakes with due regard to these ownership thresholds and the respective rights, figure 11 depicts the distribution of blockholders across a number of intervals between 5% and 100%.[1919] This figure highlights that the intervals 5-10%, 25-30%, 50%-55% and – to a lesser extent – 75-80% show strong frequencies.[1920] This points to the importance of threshold values and supports the view that blockholders consciously follow ownership thresholds in order to be provided with the rights associated with the respective ownership.[1921] In order not to needlessly tie up capital, the blockholders aim to acquire these rights with the minimum possible ownership.[1922] Thus, blockholders seem to attach importance to the formal mechanisms granted by law to enhance their monitoring ability.

An additional possibility to improve the monitoring feasibility and lower the costs is to place a representative on either the supervisory or the management board.[1923] In order to investigate the use of this mechanism, table 13 depicts the number of firms with a blockholder in which the largest blockholder is present on the supervisory board *[bh1_supb]*, the management

1919 To ensure an illustrative presentation, the figure only includes the years 2010, 2011 and 2012.

1920 This finding is consistent with earlier evidence for Germany. See Bott (2002): 257; Kehren (2006): 144f. Note that the interval 95-100% does not show a greater frequency, although an ownership of 95% enables the squeeze-out of minority shareholders. Also the intervals 15-20% as well as 30-35% show stronger frequencies. This may be explained by the fact that these ownership levels provide their holders with a blocking minority or simple majority at the firm's AGMs when considering the low presence at the AGMs. An investor cognizant of this fact may select its ownership accordingly.

1921 The interval 25-30% may be of additional importance. According to § 35 (2) WpÜG, shareholders holding more than 30% of a firm's outstanding shares (i.e. have gained control of the target pursuant to § 29 (2) WpÜG) have to announce a mandatory offer for the acquisition of all remaining outstanding shares, provided the 30% were not acquired via a takeover offer. See also Thamm/Schiereck (2014): 22. Blockholders may try to prevent such an offer by maintaining an ownership below this threshold.

1922 See also the hypothesis derivation on the effect of the size of the largest blockholder in section 5.2.3.1.

1923 See section 4.1.2 for a theoretical and empirical discussion.

Table 13
This table depicts the number of firms with a blockholder in which the largest blockholder is present on the firm's most important bodies. *[bh1_supb]* refers to the blockholder's presence on the firm's supervisory board and *[bh1_mgmtb]* refers to its presence on the firm's management board. supb & mgmtb refers to cases in which the largest blockholder is present on both boards. Total refers to the number und percentage (in italics) of firms in which a blockholder is present on either supervisory or management board.

	2005	2006	2007	2008	2009	2010	2011	2012
bh1_supb	169	163	193	198	192	195	195	185
bh1_mgmtb	100	90	103	94	93	87	85	80
supb & mgmtb	17	18	22	20	22	19	19	14
Total	252	235	274	272	263	263	261	251
	0.6269	*0.6351*	*0.6462*	*0.6634*	*0.6831*	*0.7013*	*0.6979*	*0.7151*
N	402	370	424	410	385	375	374	351

Table 13: Largest blockholder's presence on its portfolio firm's supervisory or management board

board *[bh1_mgmt]*, or both. In addition, it shows the number and percentage of firms with a blockholder in which the largest blockholder is present on either supervisory or management board (total). For each year during the sample period, the largest blockholder is represented in one of the bodies in more than 60% of the firms with a blockholder. In 2012, the largest blockholder is represented on either supervisory or management board in 71.51% of the firms. In line with the expectations, the presence of the largest blockholder on the supervisory board is more common than its presence on the management board.[1924] For a small number of firms (between 4.2% and 5.7%), the blockholder is found to be present on both management and supervisory board. Overall, the results illustrate that the largest blockholder appreciates this mechanism and frequently makes use of it to ensure access to privileged information and to augment its influence. To the extent that the presence constitutes a signal of activism, the largest blockholder appears to actively monitor corporate management in more than 60% of the cases.

6.2.3.2 Evolution of the Blockholder Types

To illustrate the evolution of the most important blockholder types, table 14 contains the identity of the largest blockholder in firms that have a blockholder. Thereby, it is limited to the four blockholder types that constitute the focus of the empirical analysis and to banks and insiders; these types together make up the largest blockholder in at least 87% of the sample firms during 2005-2012.

Families constitute the largest blockholder most frequently. In 2012 still 110 firms (31.34%) have a family as the largest blockholder, although the number of firms decreases steadily during the sample period. This highlights the importance of family firms in the German environment also in the case of publicly-traded firms.[1925] If the largest blockholder is a family, it holds between 40.62% (in 2011) and 43.97% (in 2010) of the voting rights which provides the

[1924] This is due to the fact that the blockholder will be interested in the monitoring of firm management rather than in the day-to-day management of the firm. Moreover, most blockholders may lack the resources necessary to place a representative on their portfolio firm's management.

[1925] The importance of family firms in Germany is also stressed by Franks/Mayer (2001): 947; Faccio/Lang (2002): 379; Leiber (2008): 1f; Ampenberger (2010): 5f, to name a few.

Table 14
This table depicts the types of the largest blockholder in those firms that have a blockholder during the sample period from 2005-2012. The respective first line shows the frequency of the blockholder type and the second line its arithmetic mean ownership when being the largest blockholder.

	2005	2006	2007	2008	2009	2010	2011	2012
Family	147	135	134	127	115	115	118	110
	0.4174	*0.4122*	*0.4392*	*0.4256*	*0.4342*	*0.4397*	*0.4062*	*0.4089*
Strategic	100	99	108	106	104	100	100	93
	0.5538	*0.5711*	*0.5648*	*0.5599*	*0.5823*	*0.5527*	*0.5915*	*0.6065*
Private equity	43	41	60	52	49	43	38	34
	0.3075	*0.3166*	*0.2954*	*0.3496*	*0.3248*	*0.3652*	*0.3451*	*0.3675*
Institutional	25	31	51	42	31	31	30	36
	0.1807	*0.1651*	*0.1540*	*0.1826*	*0.1524*	*0.1730*	*0.1758*	*0.1770*
Insider	37	27	29	24	28	28	30	25
	0.3171	*0.2902*	*0.3205*	*0.3149*	*0.3315*	*0.3668*	*0.3646*	*0.3242*
Bank	14	8	10	15	13	11	12	7
	0.2925	*0.2681*	*0.1937*	*0.1437*	*0.1884*	*0.1969*	*0.1813*	*0.1536*
N	402	370	424	410	385	375	374	351

Table 14: Evolution of the largest blockholder types

family with veto rights on important corporate decisions, however, does not provide the family with a simple majority.[1926]

The second largest ownership category constitutes strategic investors. Their frequency remains largely constant during the sample period, ranging from an (absolute) maximum of 108 in 2007 to an (absolute) minimum of 93 in 2012.[1927] Provided they are the largest blockholder, strategic investors hold the simple majority of the voting rights and thus the largest ownership among all investor types. This supports the presumption that they have a strategic interest in their portfolio firms and hold larger stakes to ensure their power and influence in the decision making processes of the firm.[1928]

Private equity investors are the largest blockholder in 34 of the sample firms in 2012 (9.69%) which at the same time constitutes the lowest frequency of private equity investors. The highest number of private equity owned firms is reached in 2007, where markets were flooded with liquidity and credit. In this year, a private equity investors is the largest blockholder in 60 firms (14.15%). In the wake of the financial crisis and the uncertainty as a consequence of the European sovereign debt crisis, the number of private equity owned firms steadily decreased from 2008 to 2012.[1929] When being the largest blockholder, private equity firms on average take a minority position, however, own a stake large enough to have veto rights on important corporate decisions.[1930]

Similar to private equity investors, also the ownership of institutional investors is affected by the global financial crisis. Just prior to the crisis in 2007, 51 of the sample firms (12.03%)

1926 Since the definition of a family blockholder does not combine the holdings of members of the same family, the family may reach the simple majority if it pools its voting rights and acts in concert.

1927 In relative terms, they are most common in 2009 (27.01%) and least common in 2005 (24.88%).

1928 For similar results, please see Thomsen/Pedersen (2000): 697; Bott (2002): 278-282; Kehren (2006): 155f.

1929 This is not a German phenomenon. Also the global private equity industry remained flat in the years following the financial crisis. For details, please see Bain & Company (2013).

1930 This is in line with the recent trend that private equity firms are more frequently investing into publicly-traded firms without requiring a majority stake. Please see Lazette (2013) for further details.

have an institutional investor as the largest blockholder, up from 6.22% in 2005. In the subsequent years, however, the frequency drops to about 8.02% in 2011. In 2012, 10.26% of the sample firms have an institutional investor as the largest blockholder. If institutional investors are the largest blockholder, their ownership level is the lowest of all four blockholder types studied in the empirical analysis; it ranges from a minimum level of 15.40% in 2007 to a maximum level of 18.26% in 2008. The low ownership relative to other investors is consistent with their focus on liquidity: in order not to tie up capital, institutional investors typically acquire only minority control.[1931]

Next to these four identities, table 14 also comprises two types that are used as control variables. Insiders constitute the largest blockholder in 25 sample firms (7.12%) in 2012. In case they are the largest blockholder, insiders on average hold large ownership stakes which fall between a range of 29.02% (2006) and 36.68% (2010). Banks make up the largest blockholder in only seven sample firms (1.99%) in 2012, down from 15 firms (3.66%) in 2008 and 14 firms (3.48%) in 2005. In comparison to a frequency of 6% in 1999,[1932] the 2012 figure may be regarded as evidence of a decline in the importance of banks that resulted from their endeavor to sell their stakes in other firms.[1933] This endeavor also grows apparent when focusing on the average ownership of banks in case they constitute the largest blockholder; apart from a temporary increase in the years 2009/2010, the average ownership continuously decreases from about 29.25% in 2005 to 15.36% in 2012.

Overall, the results illustrate the importance of founding family ownership and strategic investors. Although their frequency is decreasing, both types of blockholders constitute the largest blockholder in about 58% of the sample firms in 2012. Private equity and institutional investors each constitute the largest blockholder in about 10% of the sample firms in 2012. In general, all blockholder types are represented in a sufficient number of sample firms which represents a necessary condition for the proposed analysis of different blockholder types. However, in order to warrant the analysis, one needs to further demonstrate that a classification of firms into different blockholder types is indispensable. That is, one needs to investigate whether there are differences between the portfolio firms of the four blockholder types that make a separate treatment necessary. Therefore, the following section focuses on a comparison of important firm characteristics between the four blockholder types.

6.2.3.3 Comparison of Blockholder Types

Table 15 presents a comparison of the means for the dependent variables, as well as for the primary explanatory and important control variables across the four blockholder identities.[1934]

[1931] As outlined in section 4.1.3.3.1, institutional blockholders frequently cooperate to advance their interests and thereby compensate for their smaller individual stakes. Moreover, since they frequently hold stakes in very large firms, significant amounts of funds are necessary to acquire a substantial ownership in these firms. As a result, their relatively small stake might be sufficient for an influence on the firm.

[1932] See Bott (2002): 278-282. Her evidence is based on a sample of 975 published voting rights.

[1933] See section 2.2.1 for further details. This conclusion only holds for the largest blockholder; banks may still maintain (smaller) holdings in a large number of firms. See section 6.2.4.2 for the respective analysis.

[1934] Please note that this evidence is only preliminary, since it treats the variables as being independent.

As can be seen, portfolio firms of institutional investors have the lowest *[opex_sales]*, followed by portfolio firms of founding families.[1935] Surprisingly, private equity investors' portfolio firms have the highest *[opex_sales]*; due to their active involvement with their portfolio firms, these investors were expected to increase managerial cost discipline. Private equity investors' portfolio firms also exhibit the highest ratio of discretionary assets and make the largest dividend payments.[1936] Portfolio firms of strategic investors have the lowest dividend payout ratio, although the difference is only significant compared to portfolio firms of private equity investors and families. Finally, portfolio firms of private equity investors have the highest *[tobinq]*; the difference relative to the remaining types is strongly significant. While the firm values of the portfolio firms of families and strategic investors are roughly similar, the value is lowest for institutional investors' portfolio firms.

Turning to the control variables, insider ownership is greatest for firms whose largest blockholder is a private equity investor. In comparison to the remaining types, the difference is significant and in support of the presumption that private equity firms incentivize the management of their portfolio firms via equity-based compensation.[1937] Moreover, the average growth of their portfolio firms, their age as well as their size is in line with the expectation formulated in section 5.3.4.1 and suggests that private equity investors invest in firms in an earlier stage of their development.[1938] This may also explain the negative *[prof]* of their portfolio firms which may be unprofitable in early stages of their development.[1939]

In contrast to the remaining blockholder types, institutional investors target the largest and oldest firms which is consistent with the expectation and explains their low relative ownership levels found in the previous section. Moreover, their portfolio firms exhibit the greatest firm-specific risk in terms of both *[beta]* and *[stdev_ni]*. One may argue that institutional investors, due to their size and superior ability to diversify, are not as concerned about risk as families or strategic investors and hence do not shrink from an investment that is more risky. Finally, portfolio firms of institutional investors have the largest debt levels. Consistent with the disciplinary effect of higher debt levels, these blockholders may increase their portfolio firms' debt levels to discipline corporate management and substitute their own monitoring. The higher debt levels may be fostered by a high ratio of tangible assets as measured by *[ppe_assets]*. Overall, the differences in the control variables illustrate the importance of controlling for these variables in the regression analysis.

1935 The differences in *[opex_sales]* for both family and institutional investors relative to the remaining blockholder identities are statistically significant.

1936 These differences are statistically significant.

1937 See section 4.1.3.2.1.

1938 In line with the expectations stated in section 5.3.4.1, also portfolio firms of family blockholders are significantly younger than those of strategic or institutional investors.

1939 See also Hellmann/Puri (2002): 190.

Table 15
This table compares the means for the dependent variables, the most important control and explanatory variables across the four blockholder types for all firms in the sample from 2005-2012. The comparison is based on a two-sample t-test assuming equal variances; in case a Levene test indicated unequal variance of the two samples, the t-test was calculated under the assumption of unequal variance. Based on two-sided p-Values,*, **, and *** indicates statistical significance at the 10%, 5%, and 1% level, respectively.

	Private equity (1)	**Family (2)**	**Strate-gic (3)**	**Institu-tional (4)**	**(2) - (1)**	**(3) - (1)**	**(4) - (1)**	**(3) - (4)**	**(4) - (2)**	**(3) - (2)**
opex_sales	0.8061	0.6742	0.7427	0.6181	-0.1319***	-0.0634***	-0.1879***	0.1246***	-0.0561**	0.0685***
discr_assets	0.8448	0.8234	0.8016	0.7819	-0.0214**	-0.0432***	-0.0629***	0.0197*	-0.0415***	-0.0218***
div_payout	0.0028	0.0022	0.0019	0.0021	-0.0006*	-0.0009***	-0.0007*	-0.0002	-0.0002	-0.0004*
tobinq	1.7166	1.5581	1.5182	1.3802	-0.1586***	-0.1985***	-0.3364***	0.1379***	-0.1778***	-0.0399
insd_own	0.0192	0.0163	0.0091	0.0041	-0.0030	-0.0100***	-0.0151***	0.0051**	-0.0122***	-0.0071***
growth	0.1193	0.0964	0.0884	0.0956	-0.0229	-0.0309	-0.0237	-0.0072	-0.0008	-0.0080
age	10.2697	13.1802	16.0871	21.5254	2.9106***	5.8175***	11.2557***	-5.4382**	8.3451***	2.9069***
prof	-0.0257	0.0300	0.0070	0.0140	0.0558***	0.0326***	0.0397***	-0.0071	-0.016	-0.0230***
ppe_assets	0.1600	0.1789	0.2062	0.2282	0.0189**	0.0462***	0.0682***	-0.0220**	0.0493***	0.0273***
beta	0.8838	0.8348	0.7186	0.9684	-0.0490**	-0.1652***	0.0846***	-0.2498***	0.1336***	-0.1162***
stdev_ni	18.1231	32.3681	34.1211	72.8246	14.2450***	15.9980***	54.7015***	-38.7036***	40.4565***	1.7530
capex	0.0400	0.0385	0.0405	0.0426	-0.0015	0.0004	0.0026	-0.0022	0.0041**	0.002
cash_assets	0.1849	0.1801	0.1481	0.1429	-0.0048	-0.0368***	-0.0420***	0.0052	-0.0373***	-0.0320***
ln_assets	4.7887	5.2639	5.2371	6.3887	0.4752***	0.4485***	1.6000***	-1.1516***	1.1248***	-0.0267
debt	0.1761	0.1816	0.1759	0.2111	0.0054	-0.0002	0.0350***	-0.0352***	0.0296***	-0.0056
bh2_cont	0.1276	0.1035	0.0756	0.0773	-0.0240***	-0.0520***	0.0503***	-0.0017	0.0263***	0.0279***
bh_count	3.1972	2.5015	2.0383	2.6787	-0.6957***	-1.1590***	-0.5185***	-0.6404***	-0.1772*	0.4632***
diff_bh12345	0.1168	0.1777	0.3652	0.0418	0.0609***	0.2485***	-0.0750***	0.3235***	0.1359***	-0.1875***
bh1/bh2	1.9238	2.6923	2.2446	1.2927	0.7685***	0.3208*	-0.6311***	0.9519***	1.3996***	0.4477***
bh1/bh2_bh3	1.3883	2.1958	1.9219	0.9275	0.8075***	0.5336***	-0.4608***	0.9944***	1.2683***	0.2740***

Table 15: Comparison of blockholder types across continuous variables

With regard to the ownership variables, the second largest blockholder of portfolio firms of private equity investors has on average the greatest equity stakes. In addition, private equity portfolio firms have the largest number of blockholders. The smallest number of blockholders is observed for portfolio firms of strategic investors. This is plausible, since strategic investors on average hold the simple majority of the voting rights[1940] which reduces the attractiveness of a sizeable investment in those firms. The blockholder incontestability variables illustrate

1940 See section 6.2.3.2.

Table 16
This table shows the distribution of observations into the industry sectors for all firm year observations whose largest blockholders is a family, a private equity, strategic, or institutional investor. Moreover, it presents their exposure to codetermination as well as their presence on the firms' supervisory or management boards.

	Private equity	Family	Strategic	Institutional
Basic materials *[bics_bm]*	8	12	32	23
Communications *[bics_comm]*	67	152	133	15
Consumer, cyclical *[bics_con_c]*	49	171	157	53
Consumer, non-cyclical *[bics_con_nonc]*	75	192	157	37
Diversified *[bics_div]*	1	5	3	4
Energy *[bics_enrgy]*	16	26	10	8
Industrial *[bics_ind]*	83	240	192	93
Utilities *[bics_ut]*	0	0	22	3
Technology *[bics_tec]*	61	203	104	41
codet_third	107	244	226	66
codet_par	85	342	247	146
bh1_supb	203	450	508	37
bh1_mgmtb	22	550	59	7
N	360	1,001	810	277

Table 16: Comparison of blockholder types across dichotomous variables

that families have the greatest incontestability of all types and hence should best be able to generate private benefits.

Table 16 compares the blockholder types across a number of dichotomous variables. As regards the industry affiliation, the types are most common in the industrial sector. The relative frequency of institutional investors in this sector exceeds the frequency of the remaining investors by 10 percentage points. With regard to the blockholders' exposure to codetermination, about 75% of the institutional investors' portfolio firm observations are subject to either one-third or parity codetermination; the same number amounts to about 50% for the remaining types. This difference is intuitive, since institutional investors, relative to the remaining types, appear to hold stakes in larger firms. Consistent with the deliberations in section 4.1.3.2.1, private equity firms are frequently represented on the supervisory boards of their portfolio firms. This mechanism is also very frequently used by strategic investors – apparently, they try to secure their strategic interests via a direct representation in the firm's supervisory board. Consistent with a short-term interest, institutional investors are rarely represented on the board.[1941] As expected, board representation is particularly important for families: in more than half of the observations, the founding family is represented on the management board.

In conclusion, the comparison highlighted substantial differences between the portfolio firms of the four blockholder types that necessitate the separate treatment of these groups.

6.2.4 Analysis under the Assumption of Blockholder Interrelationships

The analysis of the ownership structure in section 2.2.4 highlighted the existence of a significant number of firms with multiple blockholders. However, from today's perspective, the analysis provided in section 2.2.4 is based on an outdated sample and does not contain a sufficient level of detail. These problems are overcome in the following sections. First, section

1941 Also Coffee (1991): 1330 finds that institutional investors typically do not have supervisory board presence.

6.2.4.1 focuses on the evolution of the number of blockholders that hold a stake in the sample firms from 2005-2012. Second, section 6.2.4.2 examines the types of additional blockholders and their respective frequencies. Finally, section 6.2.4.3 compares firms with a single blockholder and firms with multiple blockholders across a number of firm characteristics.

6.2.4.1 Evolution of Blockholders' Ownership

Table 17 presents the evolution of blockholders' ownership during 2005-2012, given the respective blockholder holds at least 5% of a firm's equity. For each year, it presents the number of firms that have a single blockholder, two, three, four, five or more than five blockholders, as well as the relative frequency of these firms. In order to overcome the general lack of data on the ownership of additional blockholders, the table also provides the average level of ownership of the respective additional blockholder.[1942] This allows the clarification of whether the additional blockholders are equipped with power sufficient to limit the discretion of the largest blockholder.[1943]

Of the 402 sample firms that have at least one blockholder, 154 firms (38.31%) have a single blockholder in 2005. Following a significant drop from 2005-2008, the relative frequency of firms with a single blockholder increases until 2011; nevertheless, in 2012, only 112 firms (31.91%) have a single blockholder, which constitutes a decrease in the amount of more than 6 percentage points relative to 2005.[1944] Consequently, in line with the evidence in section 2.2.4, the number of firms with more than one blockholder increases during the sample period. In 2005, 61.69% of the firms have more than one blockholder; the same number amounts to 68.09% in 2012. Apart from the year 2005, at least two-thirds of the firms have more than one blockholder during the sample period. This evidence clarifies the importance of considering these additional blockholders; any study focusing on the largest blockholder only may be biased due to the omission of potential blockholder interrelationships.

During the sample period, about one-fourth of the sample firms have two blockholders. The average ownership of the second blockholder lies between 13% and 15%. Although this level does not provide the second blockholder with a blocking minority (and the associated strong ability to limit the largest blockholder's discretion), its level exceeds the 10% threshold and thus provides the blockholder with some additional rights that may at least increase the largest blockholder's costs of self dealing.[1945]

The frequency of firms with three blockholders steadily increases from 15.67% in 2005 to 20.80% in 2012. In no year except 2005, the third blockholder's average level of voting rights exceeds 10%. Hence, at least in terms of legal rights, it should have less control ability than the second largest blockholder. Moreover, also the number of firms with four blockholders

1942 For example, % Own. for firms with two blockholders provides the average voting rights of the second blockholder, % Own. for firms with three blockholders provides the average voting rights of the third blockholder etc.

1943 The following analysis disregards the low presence at the firms' AGMs.

1944 On average, the single blockholder holds more than 50% of the firm's equity and thus possesses the simple majority in its portfolio firms.

1945 For a discussion of these rights, please see section 2.2.3.2.

Table 17
This table depicts the evolution of blockholders' ownership in those firms that have a blockholder during the sample period from 2005-2012. For each year, the table shows the number of firms (N) with a single blockholder, two, three, four, five, and more than five blockholders. In addition, it contains the relative frequency of these firms (% Freq.) as well as the arithmetic mean ownership of the additional blockholder (% Own.).

		2005	2006	2007	2008	2009	2010	2011	2012
One BH	N	154	122	119	110	119	117	126	112
	% Freq.	0.3831	0.3297	0.2807	0.2683	0.3091	0.3120	0.3369	0.3191
	% Own.	*0.5211*	*0.5455*	*0.5794*	*0.5594*	*0.5748*	*0.5721*	*0.5642*	*0.5763*
Two BH	N	108	108	122	121	107	101	88	91
	% Freq.	0.2687	0.2919	0.2877	0.2951	0.2779	0.2693	0.2353	0.2593
	% Own.	*0.1493*	*0.1387*	*0.1400*	*0.1345*	*0.1346*	*0.1373*	*0.1331*	*0.1303*
Three BH	N	63	65	66	77	61	63	77	73
	% Freq.	0.1567	0.1757	0.1557	0.1878	0.1584	0.1680	0.2059	0.2080
	% Own.	*0.1017*	*0.0959*	*0.0969*	*0.0885*	*0.0912*	*0.0945*	*0.0886*	*0.0870*
Four BH	N	38	43	49	55	50	56	49	45
	% Freq.	0.0945	0.1162	0.1156	0.1341	0.1299	0.1493	0.1310	0.1282
	% Own.	*0.0825*	*0.0753*	*0.0755*	*0.0740*	*0.0736*	*0.0730*	*0.0759*	*0.0765*
Five BH	N	24	20	29	20	37	22	22	22
	% Freq.	0.0597	0.0541	0.0684	0.0488	0.0961	0.0587	0.0588	0.0627
	% Own.	*0.0714*	*0.0694*	*0.0676*	*0.0660*	*0.0652*	*0.0654*	*0.0701*	*0.0654*
More than five BH	N	15	12	39	27	11	16	12	8
	% Freq.	0.0373	0.0324	0.0920	0.0659	0.0286	0.0427	0.0321	0.0228
	% Own.	*0.0894*	*0.0850*	*0.1125*	*0.1073*	*0.1200*	*0.0792*	*0.0751*	*0.0691*
N		402	370	424	410	385	375	374	351

Table 17: Evolution of the blockholders' ownership

increases during the sample period. In 2012, 12.82% of the sample firms have four blockholders, constituting an increase of approximately 3.4 percentage points relative to 2005. In 2012, there were half as much firms with five blockholders than firms with four blockholders. With the exception of 2009, the number of firms with five blockholders does not exceed 7% of the sample firms. Only some firms (2.28% in 2012) have more than five blockholders. The maximum number of blockholders equals ten. The average number of blockholders remains constant and equals 2.30 in 2005 and 2.43 in 2012.

Overall, the evidence summarized in table 17 highlights the importance of incorporating potential blockholder interrelationships. At least two-thirds of the sample firms with a blockholder have more than one blockholder; by far more than one-third of the sample firms have more than two blockholders. Further insight into the relative power of the blockholders is provided in figure 12 which graphically illustrates the average ownership of the largest and second largest blockholder as well as the combined ownership of (hypothetical) blockholder coalitions.

As stated previously, the largest blockholder on average holds voting rights of just above 40%. As a result, the largest blockholder possesses a blocking minority, but does not own the simple majority. However, it may still have substantial discretion if not monitored by another blockholder.[1946] By its very nature, the second largest blockholder assumes a central role in limiting the discretion of the blockholder. However, whether it can exert this control is questionable. As can be seen in figure 12, its ownership is substantially lower than the ownership

1946 Please see section 6.2.3.1 for further details regarding the largest blockholder's discretion.

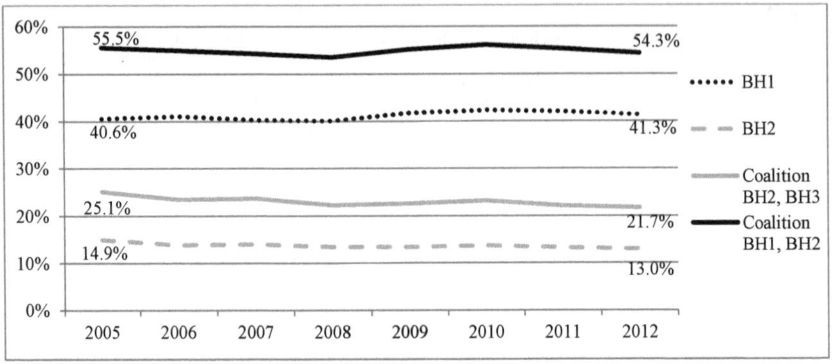

Figure 12: Average ownership of BH1, BH2, and potential blockholder coalitions

of the largest blockholder. Further details are provided by Table 42 and 43 (appendix 5). The former table shows that, on average, more than one-third of the sample firms with a blockholder have a second blockholder whose ownership exceeds the 10% threshold; in at most 11.08% of the sample firms (in the year 2007), this blockholder holds a blocking minority. Since the ability of the second largest blockholders to monitor the largest blockholder depends on their relative size, table 43 compares their respective ownership levels across the whole sample period. As can be seen, 60.23% of the firms with a blockholder owning less than 10% also have a second blockholder owning less than 10% of the voting rights. Moreover, 54.95% (18.79%) of the firms with a blockholder owning between 10 and 25% (25 and 50%) have a second blockholder owning between 10 and 25% (25 and 50%) of the voting rights. At least in these firms, the second largest blockholder should have the ability to limit the largest blockholder's discretion.

To reach the blocking minority and thus to acquire power sufficient to limit the largest blockholders' discretion, the second largest blockholder may cooperate with the third largest blockholder. However, as depicted in figure 12, the combined ownership of the second and third largest blockholder exceeds the 25% threshold only in 2005. Furthermore, the discussion in section 4.2 and 5.2.4 illustrated that the second largest blockholder may also have the incentive to collude with the largest blockholder and expropriate firm resources if both regard this expropriation as the most profitable alternative. Assuming a collusion between the largest and second largest blockholder, figure 12 shows that this coalition would hold the simple majority and would be able to control the firm, provided the remaining blockholders do not cooperate.[1947]

In conclusion, the analysis illustrated the importance of considering potential blockholder interrelationships when investigating the influence of blockholders. With regard to the ability of additional blockholders to limit the largest blockholder's discretion, the coalition of the second and third largest blockholder is unable to reach a blocking minority. At least from a legal perspective, this may increase the largest blockholder's incontestability. However, this moni-

1947 In this case, the latter would reach a blocking minority and hence a veto right on important decisions.

toring may depend on additional factors; one of these constitutes the types of the additional blockholders.

6.2.4.2 Types and Frequency of Additional Blockholders

Table 18 presents the type, the absolute number and relative frequency of the second and third largest blockholder for the whole sample period, provided the largest blockholder is a family, a strategic, private equity or institutional investor, an insider or a bank.

In general, across all firm year observations, institutional investors constitute the second or third largest blockholder most frequently (N=820). This is in line with their investment approach which involves the acquisition of smaller stakes in a greater number of firms. Furthermore, it illustrates the importance of institutional investors also within the German environment. This environment is characterized by a strong importance of family ownership and

Table 18
This table depicts the types, absolute number, and relative frequency (in italics) of the second and third largest blockholders for the whole sample period, given the largest blockholder is either a family, a strategic, private equity, or institutional investor, as well as for firm years where the largest blockholder is an insider or a bank.

Largest BH is	Family	Strategic	Private equity	Institutional	Insider	Bank	Total
second largest BH is							
Family	**254**	60	67	12	22	14	**506**
	0.2537	*0.0741*	*0.1861*	*0.0433*	*0.0965*	*0.1556*	***0.1637***
Strategic	87	**100**	44	18	30	1	**336**
	0.0869	***0.1235***	*0.1222*	*0.0650*	*0.1316*	*0.0111*	***0.1087***
Private equity	36	22	**36**	6	4	0	**110**
	0.0360	*0.0272*	***0.1000***	*0.0217*	*0.0175*	*0.0000*	***0.0356***
Institutional	117	96	57	**97**	20	23	**458**
	0.1169	*0.1185*	*0.1583*	***0.3502***	*0.0877*	*0.2556*	***0.1482***
Insider	75	33	33	6	**55**	4	**223**
	0.0749	*0.0407*	*0.0917*	*0.0217*	***0.2412***	*0.0444*	***0.0721***
Bank	48	47	22	50	12	**11**	**199**
	0.0480	*0.0580*	*0.0611*	*0.1805*	*0.0526*	***0.1222***	***0.0644***
Other	171	97	61	26	55	13	**443**
	0.1708	*0.1198*	*0.1694*	*0.0939*	*0.2412*	*0.1444*	***0.1433***
third largest BH is							
Family	**109**	27	47	15	16	5	**229**
	0.1089	*0.0333*	*0.1306*	*0.0542*	*0.0702*	*0.0556*	***0.0741***
Strategic	39	**35**	20	22	13	2	**161**
	0.0390	***0.0432***	*0.0556*	*0.0794*	*0.0570*	*0.0222*	***0.0521***
Private equity	33	7	**30**	4	6	2	**88**
	0.0330	*0.0086*	***0.0833***	*0.0144*	*0.0263*	*0.0222*	***0.0285***
Institutional	100	68	64	**50**	23	12	**362**
	0.0999	*0.0840*	*0.1778*	***0.1805***	*0.1009*	*0.1333*	***0.1171***
Insider	34	20	13	3	**44**	0	**117**
	0.0340	*0.0247*	*0.0361*	*0.0108*	***0.1930***	*0.0000*	***0.0379***
Bank	34	32	22	26	8	**3**	**136**
	0.0340	*0.0395*	*0.0611*	*0.0939*	*0.0351*	***0.0333***	***0.0440***
Other	74	24	14	19	11	1	**173**
	0.0739	*0.0296*	*0.0389*	*0.0686*	*0.0482*	*0.0111*	***0.0560***
N	1,001	810	360	277	228	90	**3,091**

Table 18: Type, number, and frequency of the second and third largest blockholder

strategic investors also with regard to the second and third largest blockholder (N=735 and N=497, respectively). The least frequent second or third largest blockholder constitute private equity investors (N=198). Hence, at least on an aggregated level, the supervision of the largest blockholder – if such a role exists in the first place – should be assumed primarily by institutional investors, families, and strategic investors which together make up the second or third largest blockholder in about two-thirds of the cases.

For each largest blockholder type except private equity and banks, the most common second largest blockholder is of the same type as the largest blockholder. The most common third largest blockholder is of the same type as the largest blockholder if families, institutional investors or insiders constitute the largest blockholder. Generally, if the first and the second or third largest blockholder are of the same type, conflicts between these blockholders should be less likely since they may at least have reconcilable utility functions and risk preferences. Consequently, they should not engage in independent, bi(multi)lateral monitoring but rather in cooperative monitoring which can either be beneficial or, in the case of a collusive agreement, detrimental for the remaining shareholders.[1948]

Since family firms frequently use private equity investors as an exit channel and to solve succession problems, it is expected that families frequently hold stakes in firms whose largest blockholder is a private equity investor. Consistent with the expectation, families constitute the most common second largest blockholder if the largest blockholder is a private equity firm (18.61%). Moreover, across all types of largest blockholders, families most frequently constitute the third largest blockholder if the largest blockholder is a private equity firm (13.06%).

As depicted in table 14, institutional investors acquire only smaller equity stakes in their portfolio firms. This investment strategy is only attractive if the size of their voting rights still enables them to gain some influence over management and corporate policy. Since their influence on the firm is limited in the presence of additional larger blockholders, institutional investors are expected to prefer investments in firms whose largest blockholder on average holds smaller stakes.[1949] Moreover, due to their small equity stake also in case they are the largest blockholder, institutional investors are assumed to partner and cooperate in order to overcome this disadvantage. Therefore, it is expected that they frequently invest in firms with other institutional blockholders.[1950] In line with the expectation, institutional investors tend to less frequently constitute the second or third largest blockholder in firm years where the largest blockholder is either a family or a strategic investor, which both, on average, hold the largest ownership stakes. Moreover, institutional investors constitute the second (third) largest blockholder in 35.02% (18.05%) of the firm years in which the largest blockholder is an institutional investor which may provide evidence for a cooperation.

In order to finance a larger deal, reduce their initial investment or risk, private equity firms may use syndicate structures, which often involve two or more private equity firms. Due to

1948 Please see section 4.2 for further details.

1949 This argument is supported by Achleitner et al. (2010): 822, who find that hedge funds prefer to invest in firms with a diverse ownership structure and without a controlling blockholder.

1950 See also Smith (1996): 228; Brav et al. (2008): 1732. With regard to hedge funds, Mietzner/Schweizer (2011): 23 find that hedge funds target firms whose shareholders are already hedge funds.

this, one may expect a greater frequency of other private equity investors in firm years in which the largest blockholder is a private equity investor. In line with this expectation, private equity firms frequently constitute the second or third largest blockholder if the largest blockholder is also a private equity investor.

Concluding, institutional and strategic investors and families constitute the most common types of second or third largest blockholders. With a few exceptions, the largest blockholder type also embodies the most common second or third largest blockholder type in the respective firm which may constitute preliminary evidence of coalition forming by blockholders of the same type.

6.2.4.3 Comparison of Single and Multiple Blockholder Firms

The mere presence of sample firms with multiple blockholders can be regarded as an essential but insufficient condition for an analysis of blockholder interrelationships. To justify the analysis of blockholder interrelationships, table 19 compares firms with a single blockholder and multiple blockholders so as to highlight differences that may require separate treatment.

With regard to the dependent variables, table 19 depicts differences between firms with a single blockholder and multiple blockholders in terms of *[opex_sales]*, *[discr_assets]*, and *[tobinq]*.[1951] However, these differences are not statistically significant.

Turning to the control variables, significant differences between the two groups of firms exist in terms of insider ownership, age, profitability, firm-specific risk as measured by both *[beta]* and *[stdev_ni]* as well as in terms of firm size. The average age, profitability, and size of firms with a single blockholder exceed the respective numbers for firms with multiple blockholders. With regard to the two proxies for portfolio firm risk, firms with multiple blockhold-

Table 19
This table compares the means for the dependent and control variables across firms with a single blockholder and multiple blockholders for all firms in the sample from 2005-2012. The comparison is based on a two-sample t-test assuming equal variances; in case a Levene test indicated unequal variance of the two samples, the t-test was calculated under the assumption of unequal variance. Based on two-sided p-Values,*, **, and *** indicates statistical significance at the 10%, 5%, and 1% level, respectively.

	Single blockholder	Multiple blockholders	Difference
opex_sales	0.7385	0.7254	0.0131
discr_assets	0.8062	0.8148	-0.0086
div_payout	0.0022	0.0022	0.0001
tobinq	1.4845	1.5273	-0.0428
insd_own	0.0240	0.0488	-0.0248***
growth	0.0924	0.0992	-0.0068
age	16.5088	14.3541	2.1547**
prof	0.0144	0.0066	0.0078*
ppe_assets	0.2003	0.1911	0.0092
beta	0.7466	0.8552	-0.1086***
stdev_ni	45.4555	35.5315	9.9239***
capex	0.0394	0.0398	-0.0004
cash_assets	0.1511	0.1706	-0.0196***
ln_assets	5.4796	5.2775	0.2021**
debt	0.1880	0.1895	-0.0015

Table 19: Comparison of firms with single and multiple blockholders

[1951] The difference in terms of dividend payouts is negligible.

ers on average have higher values for *[beta]*, whereas firms with a single blockholder have higher values for *[stdev_ni]*. Both differences are statistically significant. The difference with regard to the average amount of insider ownership is intuitive, since the average insider ownership of firms with a single blockholder is based on the ownership of the largest blockholder which only rarely constitutes an insider. In contrast, insiders more frequently constitute the second or third largest blockholder, which increases the average insider ownership of firms with multiple blockholders.[1952]

Overall, the results indicate that both groups do not significantly differ in terms of the dependent variables. However, there are significant differences between the two groups across a number of firm characteristics that are expected to affect the dependent variables. This may suggest the existence of differences between these groups also in terms of the dependent variables when accounting for interrelationships between the variables in the regression analysis conducted in the part that follows.

6.3 Regression Analysis

After the descriptive analyses provided a general understanding of the data at hand, the following sections focus on the regression analysis used to investigate the theoretical relationships proposed in chapter 5. Therefore, section 6.3.1 first delineates the applied empirical methodology. The sections 6.3.2-6.3.4 then present the results of the regressions that are estimated given the assumption of blockholder homogeneity, heterogeneity, and interrelationships.[1953] Finally, section 6.3.5 deals with a number of robustness tests used to illustrate the consistency and reliability of the results.

6.3.1 Methodological Considerations

Several techniques are available to researchers to model panel data. Therefore, the following section first provides a short description of the most important techniques (section 6.3.1.1). Subsequently, section 6.3.1.2 focuses on the applicability of these techniques in the context of the present analysis. Finally, section 6.3.1.3 contains specification and diagnostic tests for the selected regression model.

6.3.1.1 Regression Models for Panel Data

The following section surveys three of the most frequently used techniques for panel data analysis. However, it first presents the general panel data regression equation.

Panel Data Regression Equation

Before analyzing panel data estimation techniques in greater detail, it is necessary to develop a general understanding of a panel data regression equation in general. Due to the panel data set, which includes both cross-sectional and time series observations, the basic framework for

1952 See also the table 14 and 18.

1953 All regressions have been estimated using the statistical software STATA.

the empirical analysis is a regression model that has a double subscript on its variables. The model takes the following form:

$$y_{it} = \alpha + \beta_1 X_{it}^{'} + u_{it} \qquad i = 1,\ldots, N;\ t = 1, \ldots, T \qquad (6.1)$$

Here i denotes the firm being observed and t denotes the time period. Hence, the i constitutes the cross-section whereas the t constitutes the time series dimension. α represents the constant and X'_{it} is the observation for the ith firm at the tth time period on a set of explanatory variables. y_{it} measures the observation for the ith firm at the tth time period on a dependent variable. u_{it} constitutes the composite error and is defined as

$$u_{it} = \mu_i + v_{it}, \qquad (6.2)$$

where μ_i denotes the unobservable individual factors that affect y_{it}. μ_i is assumed to be time-constant and hence does not have a t subscript. In general, it accounts for any firm-specific effect that is not included in the regression model.[1954] In the present empirical setting, μ_i constitutes an unobserved firm characteristic such as managerial quality or a firm's work atmosphere which are likely to stay constant over time. v_{it} represents the unobserved factors that vary with individuals and over time and affect y_{it}. This is also called idiosyncratic error and can be compared to the errors in a time series regression.[1955] Hence, for each t, u_{it} is the sum of an unobserved effect and an idiosyncratic error.[1956]

Based on assumptions regarding the properties of the firm-specific effect μ_i, one can distinguish different panel regression techniques.

Pooled-OLS Regression

In order for an OLS regression to consistently estimate the regression parameters, u_{it} is assumed to be uncorrelated with the explanatory variables X'_{it}. Therefore, under the assumption that the idiosyncratic error term v_{it} is uncorrelated with X'_{it}, a pooled-OLS regression only yields unbiased and consistent results if μ_i is uncorrelated with X'_{it} – that is, there is no bias caused from the omission of a time-constant variable.[1957] Therefore, pooled-OLS regressions are based on the assumption that all firm-specific properties that affect y_{it} can be observed.[1958] In particular, if the control variables are able to capture all relevant firm-specific characteristics, there is no relevant unobserved firm-specific characteristic that affects y_{it}. In this case, a pooled-OLS regression can be used to fit the model.[1959]

The pooled-OLS regression treats all firm observations for all time periods as a single sample.[1960] The idea is to pool the cross-sectional and time series data, while controlling for the unobserved heterogeneity across firms. In general, the goal is to solve the impact of unobservable firm characteristics that simultaneously affect the ownership and agency costs and firm value variables through the application of a broad number of control variables to capture

1954 Since it is unobservable and fixed over time, μ_i is also called unobserved effect or fixed effect, respectively. See Wooldridge (2012): 456.

1955 See e.g. Greene (2003): 285; Dougherty (2007): 411f; Baltagi (2008): 13; Wooldridge (2012): 456f.

1956 See Wooldridge (2010): 291.

1957 See Wooldridge (2010): 283; Wooldridge (2012): 456.

1958 See Greene (2003): 285.

1959 See Dougherty (2007): 411f.

1960 See also Dougherty (2007): 411f.

as much of the error term as possible.[1961] With regard to the present thesis, the pooled-OLS methodology would involve the estimation of the following regression model:[1962]

$$y_{it}= \alpha+\beta_1 \sum_{i=1}^{N} OWN_{it}+\beta_2 \sum_{i=1}^{N} CONTROL'_{it}+\nu_{it} \quad (6.3)$$

Here, y_{it} constitutes the dependent variable for firm i at time t. In the present study, this constitutes the proxies for the three types of agency costs as well as the proxy for firm value as outlined in section 5.3.1.[1963] OWN_{it} refers to the primary explanatory variables that are used in the different stages of the regression analysis, e.g. *[cum_own]* in stage 1.[1964] $CONTROL'_{it}$ constitutes a vector of control variables, such as firm size or age that are employed depending on the dependent variable and should solve the impact of any firm characteristics that affect y_{it}.[1965] The subscripts i and t refer to the firms being observed and the year at which they are observed, respectively. ν_{it} constitutes the error term and α the intercept term.[1966]

Fixed Effects Model

The identification of firm-specific properties that affect y_{it} and hence minimize the omitted variables problem is very challenging. If μ_i is correlated with any of the explanatory variables, the OLS regression estimates are subject to unobserved heterogeneity bias and inconsistent.[1967] A solution to this problem is to allow the firm-specific effect μ_i to be (arbitrarily) correlated with the explanatory variables X'_{it}.[1968] This is achieved through the use of a fixed effects regression model. The idea for estimating the coefficients is to transform equation 6.1 so as to eliminate the unobserved effect μ_i. Thereby, the model requires strict exogeneity of the explanatory variables conditional on the unobserved effect.[1969] Moreover, the μ_i are assumed to be constant over time.[1970] Two of the possible transformations are described in the following.

The first, traditional approach regards μ_i as parameters to be estimated. This is done by defining a dummy variable for each individual in the sample and putting it into the regression equation along with the explanatory variables.[1971] Note that, in this case, the constant is dropped; by defining dummy variables for all individuals, the μ_i becomes the intercept for each of the individuals. However, the use of firm-specific dummy variables restricts the use of other dummies, as they lack time series variation and would be perfectly correlated with these

1961 See Dougherty (2007): 411f; Laeven/Levine (2008): 594; Wooldridge (2010): 282; Stock/Watson (2012): 393; Wooldridge (2012): 456.

1962 The pooled regression model is used for example by Maury/Pajuste (2005): 1824; Chen/Yur-Austin (2007): 594; Andres (2008); Kaserer/Moldenhauer (2008): 27-29; Ampenberger (2010): 183; Bøhren et al. (2012): 14; Chhaochharia/Kumar/Niessen-Ruenzi (2012): 49; Coles/Lemmon/Meschke (2012): 159.

1963 Hence, based on the four dependent variables, the study uses four separate regression specifications.

1964 For an explanation of the primary explanatory variables used in each stage of the regression analysis, please see section 5.3.2 and 5.3.3.

1965 The control variables have been described in section 5.3.4.

1966 See also Brooks (2008): 487f.

1967 See Dougherty (2007): 411f.

1968 See Greene (2003): 285; Wooldridge (2012): 457. This is one of the major reasons for the use of panel data.

1969 See Wooldridge (2010): 301.

1970 See Baltagi (2008): 14. See also Himmelberg/Hubbard/Palia (1999): 360.

1971 See Wooldridge (2010): 308; Stock/Watson (2012): 396.

variables.[1972] Due to the use of firm-specific dummies, this method is also called **least squares dummy variable** (LSDV) regression.[1973]

If the number of individuals (firms) is large, a regression based on the LSDV approach has a great number of regressors (i.e. the explanatory variables and the dummy variable for each individual) and the regression might be impossible to estimate.[1974] Therefore, most statistical packages, including Stata, use a different approach – the within transformation.[1975] The **within transformation**[1976] or within-groups regression[1977] obtains the transformation of equation 6.1 by averaging this equation over the t time periods:

$$\bar{y}_i = \alpha + \beta_1 \bar{X}_i' + \mu_i + \bar{v}_i \quad (6.4)$$

In the next step, equation 6.4 is subtracted from the original equation 6.1:

$$y_{it} - \bar{y}_i = \alpha - \alpha + \beta_1(X_{it}' - \bar{X}_i') + \mu_i - \mu_i + v_{it} - \bar{v}_i \quad (6.5)$$

$$y_{it} - \bar{y}_i = \beta_1(X_{it}' - \bar{X}_i') + v_{it} - \bar{v}_i \quad (6.6)$$

As can be seen in equation 6.6, this time demeaning of the original equation results in the removal of the time-constant, unobserved effect μ_i.[1978] As a result, equation 6.6 can be estimated by pooled-OLS, which in this case is called fixed effects estimator or within estimator.[1979] It received the latter name since it explains the variations about the mean of the respective dependent variable by using the variation about the means of the independent variables for the observations relating to a certain individual (firm).[1980] Hence, it focuses on the time variation *within* each cross section (firm).[1981] However, the time demeaning also results in a loss of the intercept α and of all explanatory variables that are constant for each individual (firm). This constitutes a major disadvantage of the fixed effects model, since it does not allow for the use of dummy variables as explanatory variables.[1982] However, dummy variables may be used indirectly, if interacted with time-varying variables.[1983]

With regard to the present thesis, the following regression equation would have to be estimated:[1984]

$$y_{it} - \bar{y}_i = \beta_1(OWN_{it}' - \overline{OWN_i'}) + \beta_2(CONTROL_{it}' - \overline{CONTROL_i'}) + v_{it} - \bar{v}_i \quad (6.7)$$

which could be written as:

1972 See e.g. Kohler/Kreuter (2005): 240; Chirinko/Elston (2006): 72; Ellul et al. (2007): 26; Andres (2008): 439; Baltagi (2008): 15; Bøhren et al. (2012): 14; Wooldridge (2012): 482.

1973 See Dougherty (2007): 414; Brooks (2008): 489.

1974 See Greene (2003): 287; Stock/Watson (2012): 398; Wooldridge (2012): 485.

1975 Note that both approaches yield exactly the same results. The only difference constitutes the degrees of freedom. For further details, please see Dougherty (2007): 415.

1976 See Wooldridge (2010): 302.

1977 See Dougherty (2007): 412.

1978 See Brooks (2008): 491f.

1979 See Stock/Watson (2012): 399; Wooldridge (2012): 482f.

1980 See Dougherty (2007): 412; Wooldridge (2012): 482.

1981 See Wooldridge (2010): 304.

1982 See e.g. Dougherty (2007): 412; Baltagi (2008): 15; Cameron/Trivedi (2009): 251; Wooldridge (2010): 302; Wooldridge (2012): 482. The dummy variables' contribution to the variation in the dependent variable in this case gets absorbed in the overall individual fixed effect.

1983 See Wooldridge (2012): 484. This approach is also used by Lehmann/Weigand (2000): 185.

1984 Fixed effects models have been used by, among others, Bertrand/Mullainathan (2001): 905; Singh/Davidson III (2003): 808; Cornett et al. (2007): 1782; Dittmann et al. (2010): 49.

$$\ddot{y}_{it} = \beta_1 \sum_{i=1}^{N} \ddot{OWN}_{it} + \beta_2 \sum_{i=1}^{N} \ddot{CONTROL}_{it} + \ddot{v}_{it} \qquad (6.8)$$

Here, $\ddot{y}_{it}$ denotes the demeaned observations for the dependent variables, i.e. the proxies for the three types of agency costs as well as the proxy for firm value. $\ddot{OWN}_{it}$ refers to the demeaned observations for the primary explanatory variables that are used in the different stages of the regression analysis.[1985] $\ddot{CONTROL}_{it}$ constitutes a vector of the demeaned observations of the control variables that are employed depending on the dependent variable, i.e. it measures observable heterogeneity.[1986] In contrast to the pooled-OLS, this regression model does not include any dummy variables.

Equation 6.8 is able to adjust for unobserved heterogeneity in the sample firms[1987] and fully accounts for all time-invariant differences in agency costs and firm value across groups of firms not accounted for by the explanatory variables.[1988] In general, it can remove the impact of omitted variables bias, as long as these variables vary across firms but are constant over time.[1989] However, next to the major disadvantage of restricting dummy variables, fixed effects regressions have a further major disadvantage with regard to the study at hand. The present study aims at explaining the influence of blockholders on agency costs and firm value by an empirical comparison of firms with different ownership structures in terms of blockholder characteristics and interrelationships. Hence, it focuses on the difference *between* firms. In contrast, the fixed effects model focuses on differences *within* firms, i.e. the time variation within each firm.[1990] However, the ownership structure of the sample firms is rather stable,[1991] offering little variation to be used in order to explain the variation of the dependent variables. As a consequence, fixed effects regression results should be less significant.[1992]

Random Effects Model

The fixed effects model aimed at eliminating μ_i, since it was assumed to be correlated with the explanatory variables X'_{it}. In contrast, the random effects model assumes that μ_i is uncorrelated with the explanatory variables across all time periods.[1993] Under this assumption, the model could be estimated via OLS. This, however, would ignore equation 6.2: Since μ_i is subsumed into the composite error term (u_{it}) in each time period, the u_{it} are serially correlated across time.[1994] Therefore, a GLS procedure is preferable over pooled-OLS. This involves the

1985 Please see section 5.3.2 and 5.3.3.

1986 The control variables have been described in section 5.3.4.

1987 See Börsch-Supan/Köke (2002): 301; Andreas/Rapp/Wolff (2010): 35.

1988 See also Lehmann/Weigand (2000): 182; Woidtke (2002): 125; Kohler/Kreuter (2005): 240; Edwards/Weichenrieder (2009): 500.

1989 See also Brooks (2008): 489; Stock/Watson (2012): 396.

1990 See also Börsch-Supan/Köke (2002): 303; Kohler/Kreuter (2005): 239; Cameron/Trivedi (2009): 260.

1991 For details, please see the descriptive analysis in section 6.2.

1992 While the ownership structure may be substantially different across firms, it changes slowly from year to year within a single firm. Since the fixed effects model removes the cross-sectional variation, one may not find any meaningful relationship even if one existed. See also Zhou (2001): 560.

1993 See e.g. Greene (2003): 293f; Brooks (2008): 498f; Wooldridge (2010): 286; Wooldridge (2012): 490f.

1994 Since μ_i constitutes the fixed unobserved characteristic of each individual, the composite error term for an individual over three periods will be: $u_{11} = \mu_1 + v_{11}, u_{12} = \mu_1 + v_{12}, u_{13} = \mu_1 + v_{13}$. As a result, they are correlated across time. See Dougherty (2007): 417.

subtraction of a weighted mean from the dependent and independent variables which results in quasi-demeaned data on each variable.[1995]

Similar to the fixed effects model, the random effects model also accounts for all unobserved characteristics at the firm level. The major advantage of the random effects model relative to the fixed effects model is the fact that it allows for the use of constant explanatory variables.[1996] In addition, it incorporates both between- and within-firm effects and hence should be more suited for the present research.[1997] Random effects also avoid the loss of degrees of freedom that result from the demeaning performed in a fixed effects model.[1998] However, the random effects model requires the observations to be a random sample from a given population.[1999] In general, its assumptions are far more stringent than those of the fixed effects model which frequently limits the application of random effects.[2000]

With regard to the present thesis, the random effects model would involve the estimation of the following regression equation:[2001]

$$\begin{aligned} y_{it} - \lambda\bar{y}_i &= \alpha(1-\lambda) + \beta_1(\mathrm{OWN}'_{it} - \lambda\overline{\mathrm{OWN}'_i}) + \beta_2(\mathrm{CONTROL}'_{it} - \lambda\overline{\mathrm{CONTROL}'_i}) \\ &\quad + (u_{it} - \lambda\bar{u}_i) \end{aligned} \tag{6.9}$$

Here, y_{it} denotes the observations for the dependent variables, i.e. the proxies for the three types of agency costs as well as the proxy for firm value. $\overline{OWN'_i}$ refers to the observations for the primary explanatory variables that are used in the different stages of the regression analysis.[2002] $\overline{CONTROL'_i}$ constitutes a vector of control variables that are employed depending on the dependent variable.[2003] Finally, the parameter λ determines the portion of the mean to be subtracted from the variables and depends on the number of time periods and the variance of μ_i and v_{it}.[2004] In contrast to the fixed effects model, this regression model allows for the use of dummy variables.

6.3.1.2 Applicability for the Present Analysis

In order to find out which of the previously described regression models should be employed, several tests are conducted that compare the models' consistency. These tests are performed for each stage and the major explanatory ownership variables and are depicted in table 44 (appendix 6).

1995 Hence, in contrast to the fixed effects model, the transformation involves the deduction of a part of the mean rather than the complete mean. For details, please see Brooks (2008): 498f; Wooldridge (2010): 292-296; Wooldridge (2012): 490f.

1996 See Brooks (2008): 500; Wooldridge (2012): 490. However, it cannot handle lagged dependent variables.

1997 See also Lins (2003): 174.

1998 See Baltagi (2008): 17.

1999 See Dougherty (2007): 420. It is questionable whether the sample at hand is truly randomly drawn from the population of publicly-traded German firms.

2000 See Brooks (2008): 500.

2001 Random effects models have been used e.g. by Köke/Renneboog (2005): 512; Barontini/Caprio (2006): 711; Thomsen et al. (2006): 261; Mínguez-Vera/Martín-Ugedo (2007): 95; Setia-Atmaja (2009): 699.

2002 Please see section 5.3.2 and 5.3.3.

2003 The control variables have been described in section 5.3.4.

2004 For further details, please see Brooks (2008): 498f; Wooldridge (2012): 490f.

The first test involves a comparison of the fixed effects model and pooled-OLS which is done via an **F-test for fixed effects**. In terms of the LSDV approach, the test has the null hypothesis that all dummy parameters are equal to zero. The alternative hypothesis states that at least one of the dummy parameters is different from zero. If the relevant test statistic is significant and the null hypothesis has to be rejected, pooled-OLS estimates which omit these dummies might be biased.[2005] In this case, fixed effects should be used. If the null hypothesis cannot be rejected, pooled-OLS yields consistent results.[2006] Across all stages and for each of the explanatory ownership variables employed, the F-test for fixed effects results in a rejection of the null hypothesis. Hence, given the data at hand, the fixed effects model appears to be more appropriate than pooled-OLS.

The **Breusch-Pagan Lagrange multiplier** (LM)[2007] test constitutes the most common test to detect the presence of random effects, i.e. whether one should prefer the random effects model over pooled-OLS.[2008] If the model is so well specified that the composite error term in equation 6.2 only consists of the idiosyncratic error term v_{it}, one should use pooled-OLS. The absence of the unobserved effect μ_i is (statistically) equivalent to $\sigma_\mu^2 = 0$. Therefore, the LM test examines the existence of individual heterogeneity by testing the variance of the μ_i under the null hypothesis that the individual specific variance is zero – that is $H_0: \sigma_\mu^2 = 0$.[2009] The relevant test statistic is based on the estimated residuals of a pooled-OLS regression and follows a chi-squared distribution with one degree of freedom.[2010] If the null hypothesis has to be rejected, there is a significant random effect and the random effects model is more appropriate than pooled-OLS. The results of the LM test indicate the presence of a significant random effect: the null hypothesis of zero individual specific variance has to be rejected across all stages and explanatory variables. Consequently, the random effects model should be preferred over pooled-OLS.

In order to choose between random or fixed effects, the **Hausman test** is employed.[2011] The key issue here is whether one can plausibly assume μ_i to be uncorrelated with all X'_{it}. Hence, the null hypothesis of this test is that the μ_i are distributed independently of all X'_{it}. If this is the case, the estimated coefficients of the random and fixed effects regression should not differ systematically. Consequently, the Hausman test is based on the difference between the estimated coefficients of the fixed and random effects model. The appropriate test statistic has a chi-squared distribution with $K - 1$ degrees of freedom.[2012] If the hypothesis cannot be rejected, both fixed and random effects are consistent. However, the fixed effects model would be inefficient since it involves a substantial loss of degrees of freedom.[2013] A rejection of the null hypothesis results in the conclusion that the unobserved effect μ_i is correlated with at least one

2005 See Baltagi (2008): 28.
2006 See Greene (2003): 287; Baltagi (2008): 15.
2007 See Breusch/Godfrey (1980).
2008 See Dougherty (2007): 420.
2009 See Wooldridge (2010): 299.
2010 For more details, see Baltagi (2008): 63-65. See also Greene (2003): 299.
2011 For three caveats of this test, please see Wooldridge (2010): 329.
2012 See Greene (2003): 301f; Baltagi (2008): 72f; Cameron/Trivedi (2009): 260f.
2013 See Dougherty (2007): 419.

of the explanatory variables. In this case, random effects are problematic and fixed effects should be used.[2014] A major shortcoming of the Hausman test is that it assumes the random effects estimator to be efficient. This assumption, however, is invalid if cluster-robust standard errors are used.[2015] In this case, a robust version of the Hausman test is performed. The results of this test lead to the rejection of the null hypothesis; since the unobserved effect μ_i seems to be correlated with at least one of the explanatory variables, fixed should be preferred over random effects.

In conclusion, the previous tests suggest that the fixed effects model is most appropriate for the data at hand. Unfortunately, its applicability for an investigation of the hypotheses formulated in section 5.2 is limited. As outlined above, the fixed effects model restricts the use of dummy variables. However, some of the dummy variables, such as codetermination or bank presence, are regarded as essential, since they either control for unique characteristics of the German institutional environment or for factors regarded as important determinants of the blockholder's monitoring. Even more important, the fixed effects model focuses on the variation *within* firms to explain the variation of the respective dependent variable. However, the goal of the present research is to use the variation *between* firms – that is differences in terms of their ownership structure – in order to explain the variation of the dependent variables. Since the descriptive analysis suggests that the ownership structure across the sample firms remains rather stable, little variation within firms is expected that can be used to explain the variation in the dependent variables. In the presence of (close to) time-invariant variables and given the goal of the present research, the fixed effects model therefore appears to be less suitable.[2016]

Due to the disadvantages of the fixed effects model for the present research, pooled-OLS is used as the primary regression model. Rather than using a simple pooled regression model, an advanced version of the pooled-OLS is used which includes industry and year fixed effects, taking into account unobserved effects across industries and time. Hence, equation 6.3 is supplemented with $\mathrm{YEAR_t}$ and $\mathrm{INDUSTRY_i}$ which control for these year and industry fixed effects, respectively. The primary regression model to be estimated is therefore specified as follows:

$$y_{it} = \alpha + \beta_1 \textstyle\sum_{i=1}^{N} \mathrm{OWN}_{it} + \beta_2 \sum_{i=1}^{N} \mathrm{CONTROL'}_{it} + \beta_3 \mathrm{YEAR}_t + \beta_4 \mathrm{INDUSTRY}_i + v_{it} \quad (6.10)$$

Here, y_{it} constitutes the dependent variable, i.e. the proxies for the three types of agency costs as well as the proxy for firm value, for firm i at time t. OWN_{it} refers to the ownership variables that are used in the different stages of the regression analysis. $\mathrm{CONTROL'}_{it}$ constitutes a vector of control variables that are used in each regression specification and includes *[age], [ln_assets], [pfd], [liq], [insd_own], [debt], [codet_third], [codet_par], [bank], [insolv],*

2014 See Wooldridge (2012): 493.

2015 See Cameron/Trivedi (2009): 261.

2016 See also the discussion in Hermalin/Weisbach (1991): 106f; Zhou (2001): 560; Ruhwedel (2003): 248f. Also Coles et al. (2012): 166 state that "the inclusion of fixed effects is useful econometrically" but obscures in the cross-sections everything that is important and interesting about firm-specific decisions. This opinion is shared by Roberts/Whited (2013): 559.

[takeover], [segm_chng], and *[govt]*. These control variables are complemented by additional control variables that are employed depending on the dependent and ownership variable. v_{it} constitutes the error term and α the intercept term.[2017] The regression model illustrates that only time constant firm-specific effects are not controlled for. In order to test for the impact of these time constant firm-specific effects, the fixed effects model is employed as a robustness test in section 6.3.5.1.

6.3.1.3 Specification and Diagnostic Tests

Having selected the regression model, it is necessary to check the assumptions underlying pooled-OLS to ensure consistent and unbiased regression results. These assumptions are tested for each of the regression specifications depicted in appendix 7. Table 45 (appendix 8) presents the results.

One of the main assumptions of OLS regressions constitutes the **assumption of homoscedasticity**. This assumes that the variance of the error term, given the independent variables, is constant and does not depend on the independent variables.[2018] While the regression estimators will not be biased in the presence of heteroscedasticity, the standard errors could be incorrect and lead to wrong inferences.[2019] As the constant variance of the error terms is an implicit assumption of OLS regressions, this assumption has to be tested to ensure correct inferences from the regression results. In order to test for homoscedasticity, two tests are employed: the White-test for heteroscedasticity[2020] as well as the Breusch-Pagan test[2021]. If the resulting p-Value is sufficiently small, the null hypothesis of homoscedasticity needs to be rejected in both tests. For all regression specifications, the results of the White-test lead to the rejection of the respective null hypothesis. Similarly, the results of the Breusch-Pagan test lead to a rejection of the null hypothesis for all specifications except those employing [opex_sales]. Overall, the results suggest the presence of heteroscedasticity. Therefore, the regression analysis employs standard error estimates that account for the presence of heteroscedasticity. These are larger than the usual standard errors, resulting in a more conservative hypotheses testing which requires greater evidence for a rejection of the null hypothesis.[2022]

OLS regression analysis further assumes that the error term is not subject to **autocorrelation** which implies that the covariance between the error terms (over time or cross-sectionally) is zero. If there is a systematic association between the values of the error term, they are said to be autocorrelated or serially correlated.[2023] In this case, the error term contains a time-constant

2017 The detailed regression specification for each of the dependent variables are depicted in appendix 7.

2018 See also Wooldridge (2010): 199f.

2019 See e.g. Greene (2003): 222; Brooks (2008): 132; Stock/Watson (2012): 396; Wooldridge (2012): 53.

2020 The White-test consists of a regression of the squared residuals on the independent variables, the squares of the independent variables, and their cross products. For details on the White-test, please see Dougherty (2007): 230f; Brooks (2008): 134f; Wooldridge (2012): 274-276.

2021 In contrast to the White-test, the Breusch-Pagan test conserves on degrees of freedom and is therefore employed as an additional test. For details, please see Wooldridge (2012): 271-273.

2022 See Brooks (2008): 138.

2023 See Dougherty (2007): 70f; Brooks (2008): 139; Wooldridge (2012): 350. According to the latter, serial correlation is of particular importance in time series and panel data analyses with longer time series.

omitted factor in each period.[2024] The consequences of ignoring autocorrelation equal those in the presence of heteroscedasticity: wrong standard errors could result in false inferences as to whether or not an independent variable is a significant determinant of the variation of the dependent variable.[2025] Since the sample of this study contains the same individuals (firms) a repeated number of times, serial correlation is likely to be a problem. Therefore, the presence of autocorrelation is tested using an approach developed in *Wooldridge (2012)* that is robust in the presence of heteroscedasticity and unbalanced data. It performs a Wald test for autocorrelation under the null hypothesis of no autocorrelation.[2026] The p-Values of the Wald test, reported in the last column of table 45 (appendix 8), provide evidence of an incorrect null hypothesis and thus point to the presence of autocorrelation. Hence, the regression specifications are estimated using clustered standard errors. These allow the regression errors to be arbitrarily correlated with a cluster (firm) but presume them to be uncorrelated across clusters (firms). Thus, standard errors clustered by firms account for both autocorrelation and heteroscedasticity.[2027]

To conduct hypotheses tests on the regression parameters, one typically assumes that the residuals have a **normal distribution**.[2028] This is justified by the central limit theorem which states that, "if a random variable is the composite result of the effects of a large number of other random variables, it will have an approximately normal distribution even if its components do not, provided that none of them is dominant."[2029] Hence, a violation of the normality assumption is inconsequential when employing a sufficiently sized sample.[2030] This typically requires observations of 30 or more.[2031] Since this threshold is by far exceeded in the present study, the normality assumption is presumed to hold.

Another implicit assumption made by OLS is that the independent variables of the regression model are not correlated with each other. If the explanatory variables are highly correlated, the regression model is subject to a problem called **multicollinearity** which is defined as "high (but not perfect) correlation between two or more of the independent variables"[2032]. Although the problem of multicollinearity cannot be clearly defined, ceteris paribus, it is better to have less correlation between the explanatory variables,[2033] since the presence of multicollinearity causes higher standard errors of the explanatory variables, which affects the sig-

---

2024 See Wooldridge (2010): 198.

2025 For example, in case of a positive autocorrelation, the standard errors will be lower than the true standard errors, increasing the likelihood to reject the null hypothesis when it actually is true (type I error). See Brooks (2008): 150.

2026 For further details, please see Drucker (2003) and Wooldridge (2012): 319-321.

2027 See Stock/Watson (2012): 406.

2028 See Brooks (2008): 161.

2029 Dougherty (2007): 71. See also Stock/Watson (2012): 92-94.

2030 See Brooks (2008): 164.

2031 See Stock/Watson (2012): 94.

2032 Wooldridge (2012): 96. See also Leiber (2008): 196.

2033 See Wooldridge (2012): 98.

nificance of the respective variables.[2034] In addition, the confidence intervals will be inflated and significance tests might yield erroneous results.

In order to investigate the presence of multicollinearity, a correlation matrix comprising all variables to be included in the regression models of the empirical analysis has been calculated.[2035] Although *Kennedy* (2008) states that a correlation coefficient of 0.8 or 0.9 indicates high correlation,[2036] the description focuses on coefficients larger than 0.5. In terms of Spearman's coefficients, a number of control variables have correlations larger than 0.5. There is an intuitive high correlation (0.58) between *[capex]* and *[ppe_assets]*.[2037] A high correlation (0.80) is also observed between *[stdev_ni]* and *[ln_assets]*. Since *[ln_assets]* is correlated with *[liq]* (0.70) and *[codet_par]* (0.77), also *[stdev_ni]* is correlated with these variables. Moreover, *[liq]* and *[codet_par]* are correlated (0.59). Finally, there is a negative correlation between *[codet_par]* and *[codet_third]* (-0.51). Since a firm cannot be subject to both parity and one-third codetermination, this negative correlation has been expected. High correlations are also observed between the ownership variables. For example, *[diff_bh12345]* is highly correlated with *[cum_own]*, *[h_index]*, *[bh1_cont]*, *[bh1_5to25]*, and *[bh1_75to100]*. However, since none of these highly correlated ownership variables are *simultaneously* used within a single regression, the high correlations do not constitute a problem.

Further evidence on multicollinearity is provided by the VIFs, which are calculated for each of the regression specifications estimated in the regression analysis. The VIF utilizes the coefficient of determination, R^2, which can be a signal of high multicollinearity. In particular, the respective independent variable is regressed on the remaining independent variables within the regression specification to obtain the R^2. This is then used to calculate the VIF of the explanatory variable i: $\mathrm{VIF_i} = \frac{1}{1-R_i^2}$.[2038] In general, a VIF larger than ten can be regarded as a sign of multicollinearity.[2039] The results of the tests are depicted in table 46 (appendix 8), with the highest VIF for each specification shaded in grey.[2040] As can be seen, the highest VIF for each specification is well below the threshold of 10. Consequently, multicollinearity does not constitute a problem in the present analysis.

2034 See Dougherty (2007): 134. This can lead to an erroneous non-rejection of the null hypothesis. See Bress (2008): 182.

2035 Since some of the variables used are dichotomous, the results of Pearson's correlation may be invalid. Therefore, the matrix also includes Spearman's rank-order correlation coefficients which are able to measure the association between two variables also for non-continuous variables. For further information, please see Schira (2005): 94-96. Due to the size of the correlation matrix, it is not presented in this thesis. Nevertheless, the key issues are mentioned in the text.

2036 See Kennedy (2008): 196.

2037 Capital expenditures represent funds used by firms to acquire physical assets and hence increase the ratio of property, plant and equipment to total assets.

2038 See Greene (2003): 57f; Wooldridge (2012): 99. See also Bress (2008): 182; Leiber (2008): 196.

2039 See Leiber (2008): 196; Wooldridge (2012): 99; Chan/Hsu (2013): 401. See also Maury (2006): 339 for the use of VIF. However, Wooldridge (2012): 99 criticizes the VIF to be "arbitrary and not especially helpful."

2040 For the sake of clarity, Table 46 (appendix 8) only depicts the VIFs of the specification (in terms of key explanatory variables) with the highest mean VIF. For example, the VIFs for the variables in column two, i.e. *[opex_sales]* in stage 1, are based on the specification using the *[h_index]* as key ownership variable. The specifications using either *[cum_own]* or *[bh1_dummy]* thus have a lower mean VIF.

Overall, the previous tests indicate the presence of heteroscedasticity and autocorrelation. However, through the use of standard errors clustered by firm, the pooled-OLS regressions are consistent in the presence of both problems. Having selected the appropriate methodology and ensured its consistency, the following sections present the results of the regression analysis.

6.3.2 Analysis under the Assumption of Blockholder Homogeneity

The following sections provide the results of stage 1, which serves as the base case of the regression analysis. The key goal of this stage is to investigate whether concentrated ownership affects the three agency cost proxies as well as firm value.

6.3.2.1 Impact on Managerial Agency Costs

Table 20 presents the pooled-OLS results of the analysis relating the two aggregate ownership measures and the presence of a blockholder to the managerial agency cost proxy, taking into account a set of control variables as well as industry and time fixed effects.[2041]

Specification 1.1.1 reports a negative but insignificant coefficient of the cumulative ownership of blockholders *[cum_own]*. Similarly, the Herfindahl index *[h_index]* used in specification 1.1.2 is insignificant. Also the presence of a blockholder *[bh1_dummy]* is unable to explain a significant portion of the variation in the managerial agency cost proxy. The insignificant coefficients are not surprising, since the review of previous studies which treat blockholders as a homogenous group already suggested the difficulty of detecting any empirical evidence of blockholder monitoring. At this stage, there may be two major reasons for the insignificance of the three ownership variables. First, there is no systematic relationship between blockholder monitoring and managerial agency costs. In this case, the blockholders either do not engage in monitoring of managerial actions or their monitoring is ineffective in reducing managerial agency costs.[2042] Second, there is a systematic relationship. However, as the effects are averaged across different blockholder characteristics and interrelationships, potential significant but opposing effects cancel out or are reduced which drives down the significance levels of the aggregate ownership variables.

The model specifications also include a set of control variables whose coefficients are interpreted in the following.[2043] Due to learning curve effects, older firms are expected to operate more efficiently than their younger peers. In contrast to this expectation, the age variable *[age]* significantly increases the managerial agency cost proxy.[2044] The firm size variable *[ln_assets]* is negatively related to the agency cost proxy and statistically significant at the 1%

2041 The regression specifications are depicted in appendix 7.

2042 Note that if there is no systematic relationship, the incorporation of blockholder heterogeneity or interrelationships would fail to yield a significant relationship as well. This is to be tested in stage 2 (section 6.3.3) and 3 (section 6.3.4) of the regression analysis.

2043 Please note that all regressions based on managerial agency costs as measured by *[opex_sales]* presented in the sections that follow include the same set of controls. For brevity, in the following analyses, the coefficients of these controls are only analyzed in detail if they change signs or are substantially affected in terms of magnitude or statistical significance.

2044 Fleming et al. (2005): 49 observe an insignificant relationship between firm age and agency costs.

level in each of the three specifications. The coefficients therefore provide evidence of economies of scale and are consistent with the findings of *Ang et al.* (2000), *Singh/Davidson III* (2003), and *Fleming et al.* (2005).[2045] If the issuance of preferred stock *[pfd]* aggravates the effective monitoring of firm management by the blockholder, this apparently does not materialize in higher managerial agency costs: the respective variable has an insignificant impact on *[opex_sales]* in all specifications. In addition, a stock's liquidity *[liq]* significantly decreases managerial agency costs, suggesting that it contributes to an effective managerial monitoring.

Of the five variables that control for the presence of alternative governance mechanisms, only the level of debt has a significant effect (at the 5% level) on managerial agency costs in each

Table 20

This table presents the stage 1 pooled-OLS results w.r.t. managerial agency costs as proxied by *[opex_sales]* (specification 1.1.1-1.1.3). The regressions include industry and year fixed effects; standard errors are clustered by firm. T-statistics are reported in parentheses. In case of a directional hypothesis, one-sided p-Values are calculated. *, **, and *** indicates statistical significance at the 10%, 5%, and 1% level, respectively.

	(1.1.1)	(1.1.2)	(1.1.3)
cum_own	**-0.0424**		
	(-0.94)		
h_index		**-0.0570**	
		(-1.03)	
bh1_dummy			**0.0393**
			(0.81)
age	0.0017***	0.0017***	0.0017***
	(2.63)	(2.67)	(2.58)
ln_assets	-0.0565***	-0.0561***	-0.0566***
	(-3.62)	(-3.60)	(-3.36)
pfd	0.0304	0.0300	0.0224
	(0.57)	(0.56)	(0.42)
liq	-0.1187***	-0.1215***	-0.1077***
	(-2.69)	(-2.78)	(-2.50)
insd_own	0.0625	0.0508	0.0451
	(0.65)	(0.54)	(0.48)
debt	0.2027***	0.2001***	0.2067***
	(2.44)	(2.40)	(2.49)
codet_third	0.0171	0.0171	0.0116
	(0.43)	(0.43)	(0.29)
codet_par	-0.0542	-0.0532	-0.0602
	(-0.91)	(-0.89)	(-1.01)
bank	-0.0375	-0.0437*	-0.0418*
	(-1.26)	(-1.47)	(-1.41)
insolv	0.1163**	0.1142**	0.1134**
	(2.11)	(2.09)	(2.10)
takeover	0.0185	0.0226	0.0185
	(0.24)	(0.29)	(0.23)
segm_chng	-0.0604	-0.0619	-0.0625
	(-0.81)	(-0.84)	(-0.85)
govt	0.0340	0.0298	0.0275
	(0.58)	(0.51)	(0.47)
Constant	0.9690***	0.9588***	0.9150***
	(13.28)	(13.57)	(10.96)
Industry dummies	Yes	Yes	Yes
Year dummies	Yes	Yes	Yes
Adjusted R^2	0.1921	0.1924	0.1918
Number of obs.	3,084	3,084	3,084
Firms	489	489	489

Table 20: Regression results of managerial agency costs under the assumption of blockholder homogeneity

[2045] See Ang et al. (2000): 100; Singh/Davidson III (2003): 809; Fleming et al. (2005): 44.

specification. Due to the disciplinary effect that is generally ascribed to debt, an inverse relationship between the level of debt and managerial agency costs has been expected. Although the existing literature also provides no evidence of this disciplinary effect,[2046] the significantly positive effect of debt in the present study is surprising; the debt level does not seem to be effective in reducing managerial shirking and perquisite consumption. Consistent with *Singh/Davidson III* (2003), there is no relation between inside ownership and managerial agency costs,[2047] which yields no support for the incentive-alignment hypothesis. Moreover, the inverse relationship between employee board representation and managerial agency costs observed by *Fauver/Fuerst* (2006)[2048] cannot be confirmed in the present study. However, the presence of a bank blockholder seems to contribute to a reduction of managerial agency costs; the coefficient is significantly smaller than zero in specification 1.1.2 and 1.1.3.

The regressions also include three dummies that control for insolvency *[insolv]*, takeover *[takeover]* or segment change *[segm_chng]* of a particular firm. While the latter two variables are insignificant, firms that went bankrupt were exposed to significantly higher managerial agency costs relative to their nonbankrupt peers. The presence of a governmental blockholder *[govt]* does not significantly affect managerial agency costs. Of the unreported industry dummies, the energy, industrial, and utilities industries have significantly higher *[opex_sales]* relative to the technology industry which underscores the importance of controlling for differences across industries.[2049] In terms of year dummies, relative to the year 2005, the year 2009 has a significant positive effect on *[opex_sales]*. This may suggest that firms during the financial crisis experienced increased operating expenses. Alternatively, this may suggest that firm management exploited their superior information and the unfavorable external environment and engaged in shirking and/or perquisite consumption while explaining any costs related to such behavior with the unfavorable external environment.

In terms of goodness-of-fit, the independent variables in all three specifications explain about 19% of the sample variation in the managerial agency cost proxy. While *Wooldridge* (2012) cautions against overemphasizing the goodness-of-fit,[2050] a comparison with existing empirical evidence illustrates that the adjusted R^2 is similar to those of *Sánchez-Ballesta/García-Meca* (2011) and *Fleming et al.* (2005): the studies report an adjusted R^2 of 18% and 20%, respectively.[2051] However, it is important to point out that the standard interpretation of the adjusted R^2 changes when the variance of the error term is not constant. Therefore, it can only be thought of as an approximation of the adjusted R^2 in case the variance of the error terms is constant.

2046 See e.g. the findings of Ang et al. (2000): 100; Singh/Davidson III (2003): 809f; Fleming et al. (2005): 44 who all find an insignificant relationship between debt and managerial agency costs.

2047 See Singh/Davidson III (2003): 809.

2048 See Fauver/Fuerst (2006): 703.

2049 See also Ang et al. (2000): 100.

2050 See Wooldridge (2012): 203-205.

2051 See Fleming et al. (2005): 44f; Sánchez-Ballesta/García-Meca (2011): 412. Focusing on a sample of small US firms, Ang et al. (2000): 98 explains 24% of the variation in managerial agency costs.

6.3.2.2 Impact on Agency Costs of Debt

Table 21 reports the pooled-OLS results using the specifications 1.2.1-1.2.3 which measure the impact of the three ownership variables *[cum_own]*, *[h_index]*, and *[bh1_dummy]*, and of a set of control variables on the potential of blockholders to transfer value from debtholders *[discr_assets]*.[2052]

The results of specification 1.2.1 indicate a negative and significant association (at a 5% level) between the blockholders' potential to engage in wealth transfer strategies and the cumulative ownership of blockholders *[cum_own]*. As shown in column two, a one unit increase in

Table 21
This table presents the stage 1 pooled-OLS results w.r.t. agency costs of debt as proxied by *[discr_assets]* (specification 1.2.1-1.2.3). The regressions include industry and year fixed effects; standard errors are clustered by firm. T-statistics are reported in parentheses. In case of a directional hypothesis, one-sided p-Values are calculated. *, **, and *** indicates statistical significance at the 10%, 5%, and 1% level, respectively.

	(1.2.1)	(1.2.2)	(1.2.3)
cum_own	**-0.0318****		
	(-2.31)		
h_index		**-0.0210**	
		(-1.24)	
bh1_dummy			**-0.0126**
			(-0.97)
capex	-2.0275***	-2.0392***	-2.0398***
	(-14.16)	(-14.20)	(-14.16)
age	-0.0007***	-0.0007***	-0.0007***
	(-3.51)	(-3.54)	(-3.62)
ln_assets	0.0048	0.0051	0.0050
	(1.09)	(1.15)	(1.13)
pfd	-0.0256	-0.0280*	-0.0295*
	(-1.20)	(-1.32)	(-1.37)
liq	0.0353***	0.0381***	0.0425***
	(3.26)	(3.49)	(3.99)
insd_own	0.0048	-0.0037	-0.0010
	(0.19)	(-0.15)	(-0.04)
debt	-0.2389***	-0.2388***	-0.2377***
	(-8.56)	(-8.48)	(-8.47)
codet_third	-0.0569***	-0.0587***	-0.0602***
	(-4.37)	(-4.50)	(-4.59)
codet_par	-0.0772***	-0.0789***	-0.0809***
	(-3.92)	(-3.98)	(-4.07)
bank	0.0112*	0.0084	0.0111*
	(1.41)	(1.05)	(1.38)
insolv	0.0156	0.0141	0.0145
	(0.83)	(0.75)	(0.77)
takeover	-0.0335	-0.0330	-0.0361
	(-1.18)	(-1.16)	(-1.26)
segm_chng	0.0022	0.0018	0.0031
	(0.12)	(0.10)	(0.18)
govt	-0.0170	-0.0198*	-0.0184
	(-1.12)	(-1.31)	(-1.21)
Constant	1.0147***	1.0042***	1.0130***
	(51.56)	(52.90)	(45.28)
Industry dummies	Yes	Yes	Yes
Year dummies	Yes	Yes	Yes
Adjusted R^2	0.5107	0.5088	0.5082
Number of obs.	3,020	3,020	3,020
Firms	487	487	487

Table 21: Regression results of agency costs of debt under the assumption of blockholder homogeneity

2052 The regression specifications are depicted in appendix 7.

the cumulative ownership results in a 0.0318 unit decrease in the ratio of discretionary assets c.p. Consequently, the cumulative ownership results in lower agency cost of debt. Turning to specifications 1.2.2 and 1.2.3, a similar effect of the respective ownership variable on the ratio of discretionary assets can be observed. However, neither *[h_index]* nor *[bh1_dummy]* unfold a significant influence. Nevertheless, in terms of the discussion in section 6.3.2.1, the significance of *[cum_own]* can be regarded as evidence of a systematic relationship between blockholder monitoring and the agency cost of debt proxy. Apparently, both *[h_index]* and *[bh1_dummy]* are unable to uncover this relationship.[2053] Overall, the results further highlight the importance of employing more advanced variables that are better able to account for the particularities of a firm's ownership structure.

As regards the control variables,[2054] in line with the expectation, there is a strongly significant inverse relationship between the amount spent on capital expenditures *[capex]* and the potential for shareholders to engage in wealth transfer strategies. Moreover, firm age *[age]* significantly reduces and the liquidity proxy *[liq]* increases *[discr_assets]*. Although larger firms should be more difficult to monitor for debtholders, *[ln_assets]* does not have a significant effect on *[discr_assets]*. Firms that issue preferred stock *[pfd]* have less discretionary assets relative to firms that issue only common stock and should therefore be exposed to lower agency costs of debt.

With regard to the presence of alternative governance mechanisms, the level of insider ownership has no significant effect on the wealth transfer opportunities offered by a firm. Hence, neither a better alignment of managerial interests with those of the shareholders nor managerial entrenchment appears to adversely affect debtholders. As expected, a firm's level of debt *[debt]* has a significantly negative effect on the shareholders' potential to engage in wealth transfer strategies at the expense of the debtholders. This suggests that existing and prospective debtholders may limit investments in intangible assets.[2055] Alternatively, the negative relationship might illustrate the difficulty of taking on debt for firms that offer potential to exploit debtholders. Relative to firms with no codetermination, both codetermination regimes *[codet_third]* and *[codet_par]* reduce the shareholders' opportunities to exploit debtholders. One may argue that their long-term concern as well as their detailed knowledge of the firm's operations provide employee representatives with both the incentive and the ability to evaluate and uncover (investment) decisions made to the benefit of the shareholder(s) only. It is expected that a bank blockholder, due to its superior access to information, is capable of monitoring firm management also in case of a high ratio of discretionary assets. Moreover, a bank blockholder might signal the firm's creditworthiness and an absence of agency costs of debt.[2056] Consistent with this argumentation, the coefficient of *[bank]* is positive and signifi-

---

2053 The insignificance of the *[h_index]* may be somewhat more unexpected, since it is highly correlated with the cumulative ownership.

2054 Please note that all regressions based on agency costs of debt as measured by *[discr_assets]* presented in the regression outputs that follow include the same set of controls. For brevity, in the following analyses, the coefficients of these controls are only analyzed in detail if they change signs or are substantially affected in terms of magnitude or statistical significance.

2055 See Hwang/Kim (1998): 42.

2056 For a similar argument, please see Chirinko/Elston (2006): 76.

cant in specification 1.2.1 and 1.2.3. Overall, firm-level governance mechanisms appear to effectively prohibit a firm from offering potential opportunities for the blockholder to transfer wealth from the debtholders.

None of the three variables that control for an insolvency *[insolv]*, takeover *[takeover]* or segment change *[segm_chng]* have a significant effect on *[discr_assets]*. However, consistent with the expectation, the presence of a governmental blockholder lowers the blockholders' opportunities to exploit debtholders (and hence agency costs of debt), albeit the coefficient is significant only in specification 1.2.2. As expected, an examination of the industry dummies indicates significant industry fixed effects; apart from the communications and diversified industries, all remaining industries have significantly less *[discr_assets]* than the technology industry. The regression results further suggest important time effects. Relative to the year 2005, the years 2006-2008 have a significantly positive effect on *[discr_assets]*. As of 2008, the effect turns insignificant. These results may suggest that the acquisition of *[discr_assets]* was easier during economic boom times. One reason may be that, in light of the financial crisis, existing and prospective debtholders may have been more rigorous in the limitation of investments in intangible assets.

With regard to the goodness-of-fit, the respective ownership variable, the set of control variables as well as the industry and year fixed effects in each specification are able to account for about 51% of the sample variation in the agency cost of debt proxy. A major portion of this variance is explained by the capital expenditures and the alternative governance mechanisms.

6.3.2.3 Impact on Principal-Principal Agency Costs

In order to investigate whether concentrated ownership affects principal-principal agency costs, table 22 shows the pooled-OLS results of specifications 1.3.1-1.3.3. In each of the specifications, the dividend payout ratio is regressed on one of the three ownership variables *[cum_own]*, *[h_index]*, and *[bh1_dummy]* along with some additional control variables and time and industry fixed effects.[2057]

Focusing on column two, the cumulative ownership of a firm's blockholders is positively related to the dividend payout of the portfolio firm: on average, a one unit increase in *[cum_own]* is associated with a 0.0010 unit increase in the dividend payout ratio c.p.; the effect is significant at the 5% level.[2058] A similar result can be observed for the Herfindahl index *[h_index]* which also has a significant (at the 5% level) and positive effect on dividend payouts. Although being of a substantially lower magnitude, the coefficient of *[bh1_dummy]* in specification 1.3.3 still is weakly significant and positively associated with dividend payouts. In particular, the dividend payments as proxied by *[div_payout]* made by firms with a blockholder exceed those made by firms without a blockholder by 0.0004 units c.p.[2059] Taken

[2057] The regression specifications are depicted in appendix 7.

[2058] Please note that the dividend payout ratio has no interpretative appeal.

[2059] It may be counterintuitive that a firm with a blockholder has a lower likelihood of principal-principal conflicts than a widely-held firm. Since principal-principal conflicts may only arise in the presence of at least one blockholder, one would expect the best possible outcome for a firm with a blockholder to be an absence of principal-principal conflicts. However, recall that the payment of dividends primarily signals that the

together, the positive coefficients of the three ownership variables illustrate that the blockholders monitor in the interest of the remaining shareholders and signal a reduced likelihood of principal-principal conflicts for concentrated ownership structures. The fact that this effect is captured (at varying magnitude) by all three aggregate ownership variables suggests that this effect predominates across the various particularities of a firm's ownership structure.

Since *[div_payout]* scales the paid dividends by annual sales, the size of the coefficients is rather small and may suggest that their effect on the dividend payouts is of miniscule magnitude. To provide some indication of the economic magnitude of the coefficients, the standardized (beta) coefficients are calculated.[2060] With regard to specification 1.3.1, a one standard deviation increase in cumulative ownership increases the dividend payout ratio by 0.07 standard deviation. While the effect of cumulative ownership is far below the standardized effect of *[div_prevy]* (0.39), it is larger than the standardized effect of a firm's growth or age.

Turning to the controls, the variables accounting for firm heterogeneity generally enter with the expected signs, given both the arguments provided in section 5.3.4 and in earlier empirical work.[2061] Consistent with the theoretical prediction, growth opportunities *[growth]* have a strongly significant (at the 1% level) negative influence on the dividend payout ratio which is also in line with existing evidence by e.g. *La Porta et al.* (2000a) and *Truong/Heaney* (2007).[2062] In contrast, the results suggest a strongly significant and positive impact of a firm's profitability *[prof]* on the dividend payments.[2063] Moreover, dividends indeed tend to be sticky; firms that paid dividends in the previous year *[div_prevy]* have a significantly greater dividend payout ratio in the current year relative to their peers.

The theoretical reasoning in section 5.3.4.1 suggests that both firm age *[age]* and firm size *[ln_assets]* have a negative relation to the dividend payout ratio since both older and larger firms tend to be more mature and have fewer growth opportunities which results in a larger payout of excess funds. However, the weak correlation between these two variables identified in the (not depicted) correlation matrix suggests that the effect of these variables cannot be explained with the same theory. Therefore, it is not surprising that the coefficient of *[age]* is significantly positive and in line with the theoretical prediction, whereas the coefficient of *[ln_assets]* is negative and significant (at the 1% level).[2064] A possible explanation of this neg-

blockholder monitors in the interest of the remaining shareholders. As a consequence, one expects a lower likelihood of principal-principal conflicts. Since there is no blockholder in widely-held firms, *[bh1_dummy]* thus measures the difference in dividend payouts for firms without a blockholder and those with a blockholder that monitors in the interest of the remaining shareholders.

2060 In the case of standardized coefficients, one measures the effect of the independent variables not in terms of the original unit of measurement but in terms of standard deviations. See Wooldridge (2012): 188.

2061 All regressions based on principal-principal agency costs as measured by *[div_payout]* presented in the subsequent tables include the same controls. For brevity, in the following analyses, the coefficients of these controls are only mentioned in case they change signs or are substantially affected in terms of magnitude or statistical significance.

2062 See La Porta et al. (2000a): 23; Truong/Heaney (2007): 679. Faccio et al. (2001): 69 and Gugler/Yurtoglu (2003): 738f find a negative but insignificant relationship.

2063 Similar results are observed by Truong/Heaney (2007): 679; Denis/Osobov (2008): 66. Also Goergen et al. (2005): 386 find the likelihood of a dividend increase to be higher in the case of positive earnings.

2064 For Germany, Gugler/Yurtoglu (2003): 738f observe a similar relationship with regard to firm size. In contrast, Faccio et al. (2001): 69 and Denis/Osobov (2008): 66 find dividend payments as well as the likelihood of paying dividends to increase with firm size.

Table 22
This table presents the stage 1 pooled-OLS results w.r.t. principal-principal agency costs as proxied by *[div_payout]* (specification 1.3.1-1.3.3). The regressions include industry and year fixed effects; standard errors are clustered by firm. T-statistics are reported in parentheses. In case of a directional hypothesis, one-sided p-Values are calculated. *, **, and *** indicates statistical significance at the 10%, 5%, and 1% level, respectively.

	(1.3.1)	(1.3.2)	(1.3.3)
cum_own	**0.0010****		
	(2.37)		
h_index		**0.0014****	
		(2.23)	
bh1_dummy			**0.0004***
			(1.69)
growth	-0.0006***	-0.0006***	-0.0006***
	(-3.10)	(-3.04)	(-3.25)
prof	0.0061***	0.0060***	0.0063***
	(4.89)	(4.82)	(5.00)
div_prevy	0.0032***	0.0032***	0.0032***
	(11.87)	(11.83)	(11.85)
age	0.0000**	0.0000**	0.0000**
	(2.16)	(2.11)	(2.29)
ln_assets	-0.0006***	-0.0007***	-0.0007***
	(-4.43)	(-4.57)	(-4.62)
pfd	-0.0001	-0.0000	0.0001
	(-0.09)	(-0.05)	(0.10)
liq	-0.0007	-0.0006	-0.0009*
	(-1.40)	(-1.31)	(-1.87)
insd_own	-0.0001	0.0002	0.0000
	(-0.08)	(0.21)	(0.04)
debt	-0.0028***	-0.0027***	-0.0028***
	(-3.34)	(-3.27)	(-3.41)
codet_third	0.0003	0.0003	0.0004
	(0.86)	(0.83)	(1.15)
codet_par	-0.0001	-0.0001	0.0000
	(-0.23)	(-0.27)	(0.02)
bank	-0.0001	0.0000	-0.0001
	(-0.30)	(0.13)	(-0.33)
insolv	0.0004	0.0004	0.0004
	(0.72)	(0.79)	(0.71)
takeover	0.0001	-0.0000	0.0002
	(0.12)	(-0.01)	(0.3)
segm_chng	-0.0011**	-0.0011**	-0.0011***
	(-2.29)	(-2.23)	(-2.40)
govt	0.0003	0.0005	0.0004
	(0.79)	(1.03)	(0.93)
Constant	0.0035***	0.0038***	0.0037***
	(4.68)	(5.40)	(4.94)
Industry dummies	Yes	Yes	Yes
Year dummies	Yes	Yes	Yes
Adjusted R^2	0.2843	0.2854	0.2803
Number of obs.	2,228	2,228	2,228
Firms	425	425	425

Table 22: Regression results of principal-principal agency costs under the assumption of blockholder homogeneity

ative coefficient might be the complexity and hence difficulty of monitoring large firms. This may facilitate an exploitation of other shareholders by the monitoring blockholder through the retention of profits and hence result in greater agency costs.

If the issuance of preferred stock *[pfd]* results in a conflict of interest between the holders of the different share classes, this apparently does not materialize in a retention of profit: *[pfd]* has an insignificant negative impact on the dividend payout ratio in all specifications. The liquidity of a firm's stock *[liq]* has a significant negative effect on the dividend payout ratio only in specification 1.3.3. Presuming that greater liquidity results in a better oversight of corporate management and the blockholder(s) by the capital market, the coefficient constitutes weak evidence of a substitution effect with regard to dividend payments and liquidity.[2065]

As regards the control variables on the presence of alternative governance mechanisms, only the level of debt *[debt]* is significant (at the 1% level). Consistent with the expectation, the level of debt negatively affects the level of dividend payouts.[2066] Hence, dividends may be regarded as a substitute for leverage in terms of limiting the firms' free cash flow which reduces the blockholder's demand for dividends as well as the necessity to grant dividends as a signal to other shareholders.[2067] Inconsistent with both the entrenchment and the convergence-of-interest hypothesis, the level of insider ownership *[insd_own]* does not significantly affect the payment of dividends.[2068] This can be reasonably substantiated with the presence of blockholders: As argued in section 5.3.1.3, in the presence of blockholders, the managers' (i.e. the insiders') ability to autonomously decide on the level of dividends can be questioned. As a consequence, also their level of ownership (and its effect on managerial incentives) should have no effect on the payment of dividends. The expected negative relationship between the presence of a bank blockholder *[bank]* and dividend payments cannot be confirmed. Finally, the extent of employee codetermination measured by *[codet_third]* and *[codet_par]* is found to have an insignificant influence on the level of dividends.

Of the three variables that control for firms that leave the sample, only *[segm_chng]* has a significant (and negative) effect on the level of dividends. Contrary to the expectation, firms that went bankrupt during the sample period do not pay significantly less dividends than their peers prior to their insolvency. Governmental presence *[govt]* has no effect on the payment of dividends which illustrates that governmental blockholders neither mitigate nor give rise to conflicts between multiple blockholders as hypothesized in section 5.3.4.3. The unreported industry dummies indicate no significant industry fixed effects. Relative to the technology industry, only the utility industry appears to pay significantly more dividends; the respective variable is significant in specification 1.3.1 and 1.3.3. The year dummies support the stickiness of dividends: none of the year dummies has a significant effect on the level of dividends, suggesting that the sample firms in general stuck with their dividends also through the market turmoil resulting from the global financial crisis.

Previous studies that use the dividend payout ratio as proxy for principal-principal agency conflicts differ in their empirical specification or do not provide a R^2. Hence a comparison of the goodness-of-fit is hardly possible. Nevertheless, the independent variables in the three specifications explain about 28% of the sample variation in the principal-principal agency

2065 Note that, a stock's liquidity is negatively correlated with the ownership concentration. As a greater ownership concentration results in higher dividend payments, greater liquidity and a consequently lower concentration of ownership thus results in lower dividend payments.

2066 Similar relationships are observed by Faccio et al. (2001): 69; Gugler/Yurtoglu (2003): 738f.

2067 See also section 5.3.1.3.

2068 Also Topalov (2011): 170 finds that management ownership has an insignificant impact on the probability of dividend payments. His evidence is based on a sample of 229 (164) German listed firms in 2000 (2006).

cost proxy, which is comparable to the 32% explained by *Truong/Heaney* (2007) who focus on dividend paying firms only.[2069]

6.3.2.4 Impact on Firm Value

Table 23 gives the pooled-OLS results of the analysis relating the two aggregate ownership measures and the presence of a blockholder to firm value as proxied by Tobin's q. The specifications 1.4.1-1.4.3 also include a set of control variables as well as industry and time fixed effects.[2070]

Column two reports the effect of cumulative blockholder ownership *[cum_own]* on firm valuation. As can be seen, *[cum_own]* has a positive and strongly significant (at the 1% level) impact on firm value: a one unit increase in the cumulative ownership leads to a 0.3298 unit increase in firm value c.p. The highly significant influence of concentrated ownership structures on firm value is confirmed by the *[h_index]* which has a highly significant influence on firm value as depicted in column three. Finally, also specification 1.4.3 yields a highly significant coefficient of the presence of a blockholder *[bh1_dummy]*: the firm value of firms with a blockholder exceeds the firm value of firms without a blockholder by about 0.1494 units c.p.[2071] The economic size of the relationship is nonnegligible: consider a firm with a Tobin's q of 1.2498 which constitutes the median Tobin's q in the sample. If this firm goes from the median cumulative ownership *[cum_own]* of 55.64% to zero percent, firm value would decrease by 14.68% c.p.[2072] However, it should be noted that this effect does not automatically imply the active creation of firm value. The blockholder (and its portfolio firm) may just profit from a favorable evaluation by outside investors in the form of a greater share valuation. In sum, the highly significant coefficients of all three ownership variables suggest that aggregate measures of ownership are able to detect a systematic influence of blockholder monitoring on firm value. Since these variables are only able to measure the net effect of the diverse blockholder identities and particularities of firms' ownership structures, the results suggest that the effect on firm value across these identities and particularities is an on average favorable for shareholders.

With regard to the variables controlling for firm characteristics used in the specifications 1.4.1-1.4.3, most of the results are not surprising and in line with the expectations formulated in section 5.3.4.[2073] The presence of growth opportunities *[growth]* has a significantly positive (at the 1% level) effect on Tobin's q, in accordance with previous empirical findings e.g. by *Maury/Pajuste* (2005) and *Attig et al.* (2009).[2074] In line with the expectations and previous

---

2069 See Truong/Heaney (2007): 189.

2070 The regression specifications are depicted in appendix 7.

2071 In terms of goodness-of-fit, specification 1.4.1 explains about 20.90% of the sample variation in Tobin's q, relative to 20.74% and 19.64% in specification 1.4.2 and 1.4.3, respectively.

2072 See Cronqvist/Nilsson (2003): 711 for a similar calculation.

2073 All regressions based on firm value as measured by *[tobinq]* presented in the subsequent tables include the same controls. For brevity, in the following analyses, the coefficients of the controls are only mentioned in case they change signs or are substantially affected in terms of magnitude or statistical significance.

2074 See Maury/Pajuste (2005): 1826; Attig et al. (2009): 409f.

findings,[2075] also capital expenditures *[capex]* have a positive and strongly significant (at the 1% level) effect on Tobin's q.[2076] Overall, firms with growth opportunities and higher investments enjoy higher valuations. *[cash_assets]* has a positive effect on Tobin's q as well.[2077] Apparently, the liquidity cushion provided by higher cash levels outweighs any concerns regarding an increased level of blockholder or managerial discretion. Consistent with existing evidence and the expectations, a firm's assets tangibility *[ppe_assets]* has a significant and negative effect on Tobin's q.[2078]

In contrast to the expectations derived from previous empirical evidence,[2079] firm age *[age]* does not have a negative effect on firm value, suggesting that older, more mature firms do not face a value discount relative to younger firms. Firm size *[ln_assets]* has a highly significant and negative coefficient.[2080] Analogous to the explanation of the previous section, the negative coefficient may be in line with the assumption that larger firms, due to their complexity, may provide a blockholder with greater discretion which the stock market incorporates into the firms' value.

The liquidity of a firm's stock is significantly positive related to firm value,[2081] suggesting that it contributes to more effective monitoring rather than a disposal of shares in case of dissatisfactory performance. This is also in line with the decreasing effect of *[liq]* on managerial agency costs as well as the suggested substitution effect with regard to dividend payouts. The issuance of preferred stock *[pfd]* may either aggravate the effective monitoring of firm management or augment agency conflicts between blockholders. As already suggested by the insignificant coefficient of *[pfd]* in specifications 1.1.1-1.1.3 and 1.3.1-1.3.3, as well as by the significantly negative coefficient in specification 1.2.2 and 1.2.3, this expectation, however, is not supported by the estimate which suggests a significant and positive relationship.[2082]

The estimates related to the presence of alternative governance mechanisms are largely insignificant. It has been argued that the level of debt *[debt]* may have a positive (e.g. disciplinary role) or negative (e.g. bankruptcy costs) effect on firm value.[2083] In the present case, the effect on firm value is insignificant.[2084] Similarly, although one-third and parity codetermination have a positive effect on firm value, only *[codet_par]* is significant in specification 1.4.3. Moreover, the presence of a bank has an insignificant effect on Tobin's q, although it is found

2075 See Laeven/Levine (2008): 596; Attig et al. (2009): 409f; Konijn et al. (2011): 1337.

2076 This effect may also be driven by the fact that *[capex]* reduce potential agency costs of debt through their inverse relationship with *[discr_assets]*. See section 6.3.2.2.

2077 See also Trinchera (2012): 147.

2078 See Laeven/Levine (2008): 596; Konijn et al. (2011): 1337. A negative but insignificant relationship is observed by Maury/Pajuste (2005): 1826.

2079 See Ruiz-Mallorquí/Santana-Martín (2011): 125.

2080 Similar results are observed e.g. by Maury/Pajuste (2005): 1826; Attig et al. (2009): 409f; Konijn et al. (2011): 1337; Ruiz-Mallorquí/Santana-Martín (2011): 125.

2081 As positive relationship is also observed by Konijn et al. (2011): 1337.

2082 A reason for this may be provided in section 6.3.3.4.

2083 Please see section 5.3.4.2.

2084 Prior evidence on the effect of the debt level is mixed. No significance is also observed by Maury/Pajuste (2005): 1826; Laeven/Levine (2008): 596. Attig et al. (2009): 409f and Konijn et al. (2011): 1337 find a significantly negative relationship, whereas Ruiz-Mallorquí/Santana-Martín (2011): 125 find a significant and positive relationship.

Table 23
This table presents the stage 1 pooled-OLS results w.r.t. firm value as proxied by *[tobinq]* (specification 1.4.1-1.4.3). The regressions include industry and year fixed effects; standard errors are clustered by firm. T-statistics are reported in parentheses. In case of a directional hypothesis, one-sided p-Values are calculated. *, **, and *** indicates statistical significance at the 10%, 5%, and 1% level, respectively.

	(1.4.1)	(1.4.2)	(1.4.3)
cum own	**0.3298*** **		
	(5.18)		
h_index		**0.3718*** **	
		(4.33)	
bh1_dummy			**0.1494*** **
			(2.67)
growth	0.2064***	0.2076***	0.2053***
	(4.63)	(4.69)	(4.59)
ppe_assets	-0.3942***	-0.3675**	-0.3460**
	(-2.34)	(-2.19)	(-2.03)
capex	2.1758***	2.1937***	2.1825***
	(3.02)	(3.07)	(3.00)
cash_assets	1.0977***	1.1090***	1.1044***
	(5.61)	(5.66)	(5.68)
age	0.0014	0.0013	0.0016*
	(1.24)	(1.17)	(1.45)
ln_assets	-0.1109***	-0.1142***	-0.1133***
	(-4.46)	(-4.58)	(-4.52)
pfd	0.1783**	0.1867**	0.2176**
	(1.71)	(1.81)	(2.06)
liq	0.4404***	0.4454***	0.3695***
	(6.66)	(6.70)	(5.80)
insd_own	-0.2555**	-0.1564	-0.2008
	(-1.97)	(-1.22)	(-1.53)
debt	-0.1331	-0.1284	-0.1563
	(-0.87)	(-0.84)	(-1.01)
codet_third	0.0123	0.0176	0.0440
	(0.21)	(0.30)	(0.74)
codet_par	0.1058	0.1074	0.1417*
	(1.22)	(1.24)	(1.64)
bank	-0.0496	-0.0076	-0.0494
	(-1.12)	(-0.17)	(-1.09)
insolv	-0.0368	-0.0160	-0.0173
	(-0.46)	(-0.19)	(-0.21)
takeover	0.3626***	0.3388**	0.3893***
	(2.67)	(2.48)	(2.81)
segm_chng	-0.2958***	-0.2883***	-0.3063***
	(-3.05)	(-2.93)	(-3.07)
govt	0.0320	0.0625	0.0451
	(0.35)	(0.70)	(0.49)
Constant	1.6023***	1.6896***	1.6038***
	(13.26)	(14.19)	(12.57)
Industry dummies	Yes	Yes	Yes
Year dummies	Yes	Yes	Yes
Adjusted R^2	0.2090	0.2074	0.1964
Number of obs.	2,978	2,978	2,978
Firms	484	484	484

Table 23: Regression results of firm value under the assumption of blockholder homogeneity

to decrease managerial agency costs in section 6.3.2.1. Finally, consistent with the entrenchment and not with the incentive alignment effect, insider ownership *[insd_own]* decreases Tobin's q. However, the effect is significant only in specification 1.4.1 (at the 5% level).[2085]

[2085] Note that convincing evidence for an entrenchment effect would require the *[insd_own]* variable to be significant also in specification 1.1.1-1.1.3.

Overall, the evidence indicates that in the presence of ownership structures that foster blockholder monitoring, alternative governance mechanisms do not contribute to an increased firm value. In line with the deliberations in section 4.3.2, this may suggest that blockholder monitoring and alternative governance mechanisms act as substitutes.

In line with the expectation, firms that left the prime or general standard *[segm_chng]* have a significantly lower firm value than their peers. Surprisingly, firms that went bankrupt during the sample period *[insolv]* are not traded at a discount in the years prior to the bankruptcy. The positive and significant coefficient of the takeover dummy illustrates that primarily successfully performing firms become subject to a takeover.[2086] In contrast to the expectations, the presence of a governmental blockholder *[govt]* does not lower firm value. The (unreported) industry dummies do not provide convincing evidence that firm value is affected by the firms' industry. In specification 1.4.1 (1.4.2), only the diversified (industrial) industry has a weakly significant and negative effect on firm value, relative to the technology industry. In contrast, the year dummies provide evidence of a significant time effect. Relative to the year 2005, the year 2007 has a significantly positive effect on firm value. This effect reverses in the years 2008 and 2009 which coincide with the global financial crisis. Moreover, the years 2011 and 2012 have a significant and negative effect on Tobin's q which might be a result of the European sovereign debt crisis.[2087]

6.3.2.5 Résumé

To recapitulate, the analysis at hand focuses on the estimation of a base case for the analyses that follow. Apart from a set of controls, it disregards any factor that might affect blockholder monitoring and treats blockholders as a homogenous group. It has been argued above that aggregate ownership measures may have a limited ability to explain the variation in the respective dependent variable, since they amalgamate different blockholder types and ownership structures despite their potential effect on the feasibility of monitoring (e.g. the blockholder's power) as well as on the blockholder's ability and incentive to monitor. Hence, the analysis refrains from a hypothesis-based investigation and rather focuses on whether concentrated ownership affects the three agency cost proxies as well as firm value.

With regard to the managerial agency cost proxy, the results indicate insignificant coefficients for all three measures of ownership. As a consequence, concentrated ownership has an insignificant impact on managerial agency costs. However, this insignificance does not necessarily constitute evidence against an effective blockholder monitoring. Since the effects of different blockholder characteristics and interrelationships are averaged, the result only implies that concentrated ownership on average has no effect. In other words, there may be certain ownership structures and blockholder types that result in effective blockholder monitoring and lower managerial agency costs. Their effect, however, may be weakened by ownership structures and blockholder types that lead to higher managerial agency costs. As a consequence, the net effect is insignificant. The results based on agency costs of debt show that at least the cumula-

[2086] Alternatively, the firm value may have already increased in expectation of a future takeover.

[2087] Due to the importance of the year dummies, the stability of the parameters is examined in section 6.3.5.2.

tive blockholder ownership favorably and significantly affects the agency costs of debt proxy. Hence, there appears to be a systematic relationship between blockholder monitoring and agency costs of debt, although this cannot be confirmed by the two remaining ownership variables. Results based on principal-principal agency costs and firm value are uniformly consistent with a favorable effect of blockholder monitoring, despite the aggregation of effects by the ownership variables. This suggests a strong and favorable unidirectional influence of the different blockholder characteristics and interrelationships that are amalgamated in the aggregate ownership measures. The specific effects of these characteristics and interrelationships constitute the focus of the following sections.

6.3.3 Analysis under the Assumption of Blockholder Heterogeneity

The preceding analysis did not control for any blockholder characteristic that might affect the blockholder's monitoring. The key question of the following section therefore is: Do the characteristics of the *largest* blockholder affect agency costs and firm value?

6.3.3.1 Impact on Managerial Agency Costs

Table 24 depicts the pooled-OLS results of regressions of managerial agency costs on the largest blockholders' characteristics, a set of control variables and industry and time fixed effects.[2088]

Column two focuses on the **largest blockholder's ownership** *[bh1_cont]*. Based on agency theoretic arguments, higher *[bh1_cont]* should result in lower managerial agency costs.[2089] While the coefficient of *[bh1_cont]* has the expected negative sign, it is not significantly smaller than zero.[2090] Thus, $H1.1_a$ cannot be supported:[2091] on average, higher ownership of the largest blockholder does not result in lower managerial agency costs c.p. A possible reason for this insignificance may be the fact that the ownership size effect on managerial agency costs is non-linear. To detect a potential non-linear effect, two additional regression models are estimated; their results are depicted in column two and three of table 47 (appendix 9).[2092] Specification 2.1.4 employs the squared ownership of the largest blockholder *[bh1_cont_sq]*. However, the corresponding coefficient is insignificant. Specification 2.1.5 splits the ownership variable in four dummy variables that allow for different slopes for the respective ownership ranges. As can be seen, blockholders with an ownership of 5-25% and 25-50%, respectively, are associated with higher managerial agency costs, relative to firms without a blockholder.[2093] One may argue that the monitoring of the average blockholder is ineffective in re-

2088 The regression specifications are depicted in appendix 7.

2089 See also $H1.1_a$ in section 5.2.

2090 The insignificant and negative coefficient supports the results of Singh/Davidson III (2003): 810 based on large US corporations. Based on a sample of small US corporations, Ang et al. (2000): 98 find a significant negative effect of the largest blockholder's ownership on the ratio of operating expense to annual sales.

2091 More specifically, the coefficient of *[bh1_cont]* does not provide significant evidence against the corresponding null hypothesis. See also FN 1559.

2092 Table 47 reports only selected coefficients, but the specifications include the same statistical controls as in table 24. Their signs, magnitude, and significance remain unchanged.

2093 Both variables are significant at a 10% level. Ownership levels of 50-75% and 75%-100% are insignificant.

Table 24
This table presents the stage 2 pooled-OLS results w.r.t. managerial agency costs as proxied by *[opex_sales]* (specification 2.1.1-2.1.3). The regressions include industry and year fixed effects; standard errors are clustered by firm. T-statistics are reported in parentheses. In case of a directional hypothesis, one-sided p-Values are calculated. *, **, and *** indicates statistical significance at the 10%, 5%, and 1% level, respectively.

	(2.1.1)	**(2.1.2)**	**(2.1.3)**
bh1_cont	**-0.0480**	**-0.0670**	
	(-0.95)	**(-1.23)**	
bh1_supb		**0.0371**	
		(1.33)	
bh1_mgmtb		**-0.0249**	
		(-0.74)	
bh1_pe_cont			**0.0423**
			(0.54)
bh1_fam_cont			**-0.1400****
			(-2.09)
bh1_si_cont			**-0.0615**
			(-1.06)
bh1_insti_cont			**-0.4000****
			(-2.40)
stdev_ni			0.0002
			(0.90)
beta			-0.0453
			(-1.46)
age	0.0017***	0.0017***	0.0017***
	(2.66)	(2.59)	(2.44)
ln_assets	-0.0562***	-0.0588***	-0.0650***
	(-3.60)	(-3.82)	(-3.63)
pfd	0.0295	0.0272	0.0364
	(0.55)	(0.50)	(0.67)
liq	-0.1194***	-0.1190***	-0.1266***
	(-2.74)	(-2.73)	(-2.82)
insd_own	0.0518	0.0498	0.0007
	(0.55)	(0.51)	(0.01)
debt	0.2014***	0.2009***	0.1888**
	(2.42)	(2.40)	(2.21)
codet_third	0.0169	0.0176	0.0419
	(0.42)	(0.44)	(1.01)
codet_par	-0.0538	-0.0523	-0.0103
	(-0.90)	(-0.89)	(-0.17)
bank	-0.0434*	-0.0436*	-0.0446*
	(-1.47)	(-1.51)	(-1.50)
insolv	0.1142**	0.1185**	0.1069**
	(2.09)	(2.16)	(1.95)
takeover	0.0202	0.0122	0.0099
	(0.26)	(0.16)	(0.13)
segm_chng	-0.0607	-0.0563	-0.0485
	(-0.82)	(-0.76)	(-0.66)
govt	0.0306	0.0252	0.0181
	(0.52)	(0.43)	(0.32)
Constant	0.9642***	0.9778***	1.0365***
	(13.42)	(13.45)	(12.52)
Industry dummies	Yes	Yes	Yes
Year dummies	Yes	Yes	Yes
Adjusted R^2	0.1922	0.1950	0.2028
Number of obs.	3,084	3,084	2,971
Firms	489	489	473

Table 24: Regression results of managerial agency costs under the assumption of blockholder heterogeneity

ducing managerial agency costs. However, in this case, one would not expect positive coefficients.

The positive coefficients may be explained by two factors mentioned in the literature.[2094] First, blockholders with lower ownership levels face less costs resulting from the generation of private benefits. Consequently, there might be the risk that management will be willing to pay private benefits to the blockholder in exchange for its abandonment of monitoring and greater discretion for the management.[2095] Second, over-monitoring by a blockholder might lower managerial incentives and effort which negatively affects its cost discipline.[2096] Overall, the results suggest a non-linear ownership size effect on managerial agency costs and thus provide evidence in support of $H1.1_b$.

Specification 2.1.2 of table 24 regresses managerial agency costs on the **largest blockholder's presence on the supervisory board** *[bh1_supb]* and **management board** *[bh1_mgmtb]* in order to investigate $H1.1_c$ and $H1.1_d$, respectively. Since the relationship is theoretically ambiguous, both hypotheses are non-directional and expect a significant effect of the respective variable on managerial agency costs. However, table 24 illustrates that both *[bh1_supb]* and *[bh1_mgmtb]* have an insignificant effect on managerial agency costs, providing no support for both hypotheses. While the results may be surprising at first, the insignificant coefficients are in line with the theoretical reasoning. It has been stated above that board representation on the one hand may result in a more effective blockholder monitoring relative to the monitoring by blockholders without a board representation. On the other hand, board representation may result in a convergence of interest between management and blockholder and/or in a generation of private benefits; both aspects come at the expense of effective monitoring of firm management. Since *[bh1_supb]* and *[bh1_mgmtb]* measure the effect of the average blockholder, there may be some blockholders that utilize their board presence to effectively monitor management whereas there may be some blockholders whose interests converge with those of the management or who are paid private benefits in return for lax monitoring. The sign of the coefficients suggest that the latter aspect slightly dominates for *[bh1_supb]* whereas the former effect slightly dominates for *[bh1_mgmtb]*.

Finally, specification 2.1.3 accounts for the four **blockholder identities** of the largest blockholder. As can be seen, the ownership of all types except private equity investors reduces managerial agency costs. The relationship is significant at the 5% level for family blockholders and institutional investors. Although it has already been indicated by the descriptive analysis, the insignificant (and positive) coefficient of private equity investors is somewhat surprising: Due to their superior information, their experience in the management of portfolio firms, and the governance changes they typically apply to their portfolio firms, they were expected to lower managerial agency costs.[2097] In contrast, institutional investors are successful in mitigating managerial agency costs although they possess the lowest ownership level of the

2094 This is based on the assumption that *[opex_sales]* is an efficient measure of managerial agency costs.

2095 See Bainbridge (2012): 247 for a similar argument. In this case, one should observe greater principal-principal agency costs for these ownership levels. Please refer to section 6.3.3.3 for details.

2096 See Goergen et al. (2008): 179. Please see also the costs of monitoring listed in section 3.1.3.

2097 A possible reason for the insignificance may be the phenomenon of over-monitoring by a blockholder. According to Goergen et al. (2008): 179 this lowers managerial incentives and effort which may negatively affect managerial cost discipline. See also the costs of monitoring listed in section 3.1.3.

four blockholder types.[2098] As expected, the ownership of families significantly decreases managerial agency costs. To investigate if family ownership indeed has the strongest effect (*H1.1$_f$*), the standardized (beta) coefficients are calculated. Based on these coefficients, a one standard deviation increase in the ownership of the family (given it is the largest blockholder) decreases the agency cost proxy by 0.08 standard deviation, relative to a decrease of 0.07 for institutional investors. Hence, of the four blockholder types, the ownership of families has the largest standardized effect.[2099] Overall, specification 2.1.3 provides results in support of hypotheses *H1.1$_e$* and *H1.1$_f$*.[2100]

Table 24 indicates that the **control variables** remain largely unaffected when accounting for blockholder heterogeneity, relative to the results of stage 1. The coefficients of *[age]*, *[debt]*, and *[insolv]* are still associated with higher managerial agency costs. In contrast, *[ln_assets]* and *[liq]* significantly lower managerial agency costs. A bank blockholder contributes to the reduction of managerial agency costs also in the presence of the four major blockholder types (specification 2.1.3) and appears to be more effective than private equity and strategic investors.[2101] Specification 2.1.3 also comprises two proxies for firm-specific risk; both variables are insignificant.

H1.1$_g$ hypothesizes a **non-linear ownership size effect** on managerial agency costs for family and institutional investors. Consistent with this hypothesis, specification 2.1.7 of table 48 (appendix 10) delivers a significant relationship between the squared ownership of both types and *[opex_sales]*.[2102] With regard to institutional investors, the coefficients suggest a greater reduction of managerial agency costs for higher levels of ownership, which is consistent with the theoretical expectations in section 5.2.3.1.[2103] With regard to family blockholders, the coefficients suggest a u-shaped relationship. In particular, family ownership is associated with lower managerial agency costs up to an ownership of 42.54%.[2104] Beyond this level, the ownership is associated with increasing managerial agency costs which may either be due to greater family entrenchment or family altruism.[2105]

Since existing empirical evidence suggests the importance of a **family's representation on a firm's management or supervisory board**, H1.1$_h$ expects the effect of board representation on the ownership size effect to be strongest for family blockholders. To investigate this hypothesis, the blockholder types' ownership is interacted with the largest blockholder's pres-

---

[2098] See section 6.2.3.2.

[2099] Considering all independent variables, firm size has the largest standardized effect (0.34) followed by liquidity (0.15). Note that the significant blockholder type variables have a larger standardized effect than a bank blockholder (0.04).

[2100] Please note that specification 2.1.3 is able to increase the variation in *[opex_sales]* explained by the model to 20.28%, up from 19.21% when simply accounting for the cumulative ownership (specification 1.1.1).

[2101] This conclusion assumes that the reduction of managerial agency costs is a goal of all blockholder types.

[2102] Table 48 reports only selected coefficients, but the specifications include the same statistical controls as in table 24. Their signs, magnitude and significance remain unchanged. Please note that accounting for non-linearity, specification 2.1.7 is able to increase the variation in managerial agency costs explained by the model from 20.28% (specification 2.1.3) to 21.13%.

[2103] The relationship is graphically illustrated in figure 23 (appendix 10).

[2104] This is calculated by building the derivative of: opex_sales $= -0.5421 bh1\_fam\_cont + 0.6372 bh1\_fam\_cont^2$ w.r.t bh1_fam_cont. Figure 24 (appendix 10) graphically illustrates this result.

[2105] This result confirms the result of Leiber (2008): 129, 200-202.

ence on the supervisory and management board, respectively. The results based on *[opex_sales]* are shown in column two of table 49 (appendix 11).[2106] Inconsistent with $H1.1_h$, board representation does not have an effect on the ownership size effect of families on managerial agency costs. In fact, board presence does not affect the relationship between any blockholder type's ownership and managerial agency costs which questions the importance of board representation at least for these four blockholder types. However, while the ownership of families, given their presence on either board, (insignificantly) increases managerial agency costs, it significantly decreases managerial agency costs if the family is present on neither board. This result may suggest that family board representation results in family entrenchment which is consistent with the results based on the squared ownership above.

6.3.3.2 Impact on Agency Costs of Debt

Table 25 provides the results of pooled-OLS estimations that regress agency costs of debt on the largest blockholders' characteristics, a set of control variables, and industry and time fixed effects.[2107]

Specification 2.2.1 focuses on the effect of the **largest blockholder's ownership** *[bh1_cont]*. An analysis of the risk preferences and utility functions of large shareholders and debtholders suggests reconcilable interests of both parties. Since the largest blockholder should further be exposed to significant costs from an unfavorable treatment of debtholders, its ownership should be associated with lower agency costs of debt.[2108] In line with this expectation, *[bh1_cont]* has a negative effect on the blockholders' potential to engage in wealth transfer strategies. However, the one-sided p-Value equals 0.134 and thus does not provide significant evidence in favor of $H1.2_a$.[2109] Nevertheless, the blockholder's incentive to transfer value from debtholders may vary based on the level of its ownership and the resulting exposure to the costs of a value transfer. This potential non-linear effect is investigated in column four and five of table 47 (appendix 9).[2110] As can be seen, *[bh1_cont_sq]* does not significantly affect the agency cost of debt proxy. In contrast, the dummies depicting the four ownership intervals point to significantly lower agency costs of debt for blockholders with an ownership of 25-50% and 50-75%, respectively. Apparently, at these ownership levels, the incentive to signal the absence of agency costs of debt is strongest for the average largest blockholder. The insignificant (and negative) coefficient of *[bh1_5to25]* provides only weak evidence for the fact that smaller blockholders have a greater incentive to transfer value from a firm's debtholders. Overall, the non-linear ownership size effect on *[discr_assets]* provides support for $H1.2_b$.

2106 Table 49 reports only selected coefficients, but the specifications include the same statistical controls as in table 24. Their signs, magnitude and significance remain unchanged. Since there are too few observations for an institutional investor's presence on a firm's boards, the respective variable is not interacted with *[bh1_supb]* and *[bh1_mgmtb]*.

2107 The regression specifications are depicted in appendix 7.

2108 See also $H1.2_a$ in section 5.2.

2109 The insignificance is surprising, since the cumulative ownership measure is significant (see section 6.3.2.2). This points to the importance of additional blockholders beyond the largest blockholder. Evidence on the effect of additional blockholders is provided in section 6.3.4.2.

2110 Table 47 reports only selected coefficients, but the specifications include the same statistical controls as in table 25. Their signs, magnitude, and significance remain unchanged.

Table 25
This table presents the stage 2 pooled-OLS results w.r.t. agency costs of debt as proxied by *[discr_assets]* (specification 2.2.1-2.2.3). The regressions include industry and year fixed effects; standard errors are clustered by firm. T-statistics are reported in parentheses. In case of a directional hypothesis, one-sided p-Values are calculated. *, **, and *** indicates statistical significance at the 10%, 5%, and 1% level, respectively.

	(2.2.1)	**(2.2.2)**	**(2.2.3)**
bh1_cont	**-0.0172**	**-0.0167**	
	(-1.11)	**(-1.00)**	
bh1_supb		**-0.0041**	
		(-0.53)	
bh1_mgmtb		**0.0096**	
		(1.05)	
bh1_pe_cont			**0.0001**
			(0.00)
bh1_fam_cont			**0.0043**
			(0.22)
bh1_si_cont			**-0.0160**
			(-0.83)
bh1_insti_cont			**-0.1140****
			(-2.23)
stdev_ni			0.0000
			(-0.20)
beta			0.0161*
			(1.72)
capex	-2.0395***	-2.0420***	-2.0664***
	(-14.17)	(-14.21)	(-14.14)
age	-0.0007***	-0.0007***	-0.0007***
	(-3.55)	(-3.47)	(-3.23)
ln_assets	0.0051	0.0056	0.0048
	(1.14)	(1.25)	(0.99)
pfd	-0.0282*	-0.0283*	-0.0350**
	(-1.33)	(-1.35)	(-1.67)
liq	0.0389***	0.0385***	0.0340***
	(3.57)	(3.56)	(3.17)
insd_own	-0.0033	-0.0032	-0.0155
	(-0.13)	(-0.13)	(-0.58)
debt	-0.2384***	-0.2382***	-0.2308***
	(-8.46)	(-8.46)	(-8.02)
codet_third	-0.0588***	-0.0589***	-0.0562***
	(-4.50)	(-4.51)	(-4.14)
codet_par	-0.0792***	-0.0793***	-0.0719***
	(-4.00)	(-4.01)	(-3.60)
bank	0.0086	0.0089	0.0092
	(1.08)	(1.13)	(1.15)
insolv	0.0142	0.0142	0.0117
	(0.75)	(0.76)	(0.61)
takeover	-0.0339	-0.0316	-0.0332
	(-1.19)	(-1.10)	(-1.16)
segm_chng	0.0022	0.0007	-0.0005
	(0.12)	(0.04)	(-0.03)
govt	-0.0195*	-0.0185	-0.0235**
	(-1.29)	(-1.23)	(-1.54)
Constant	1.0061***	1.0020***	0.9906***
	(52.02)	(52.13)	(45.18)
Industry dummies	Yes	Yes	Yes
Year dummies	Yes	Yes	Yes
Adjusted R^2	0.5086	0.5092	0.5114
Number of obs.	3,020	3,020	2,907
Firms	487	487	471

Table 25: Regression results of agency costs of debt under the assumption of blockholder heterogeneity

To investigate H1.2_c and H1.2_d, specification 2.2.2 regresses agency costs of debt on the **largest blockholder's presence on the supervisory board** *[bh1_supb]* and **management board** *[bh1_mgmtb]*, respectively. Consistent with H1.2_c, the coefficient of *[bh1_supb]* is negative and suggests that the largest blockholder's presence on the supervisory board is associated with a lower potential of the blockholder to engage in wealth transfer strategies. However, the relationship is insignificant and therefore provides only weak support of H1.2_c. In contrast, *[bh1_mgmtb]* seems to increase the blockholder's potential to engage in wealth transfer strategies. While this relationship is consistent with H1.2_d, the one-sided p-Value of 0.15 indicates statistical insignificance. The insignificance of both variables may be a result of firm-level governance mechanisms that appear to effectively prohibit a firm from offering potential opportunities for the blockholder to transfer wealth from the debtholders or act as substitute for a blockholder signaling an absence of agency costs of debt. As can be seen, both the firm's level of debt and the two codetermination regimes are highly significant. With regard to employee codetermination, one may argue that employee representatives, due to their long-term concern and detailed knowledge of the firm, have the incentive and the ability to evaluate and uncover decisions made to the benefit of the shareholder(s) only.

The fourth column shows the results of specification 2.2.3 which accounts for the ownership of the four **blockholder identities**. In line with H1.2_f, the ownership size effect of families, private equity, and institutional investors on agency costs of debt is non-positive. In particular, all three blockholder types have an insignificant effect on the blockholders' opportunity to transfer wealth from debtholders. This appears to confirm the expectation that these blockholder types, due to their long-term interest, are significantly exposed to the costs of any transfer of wealth and hence have low incentives to do so. In contrast to these investor types, institutional investors are assumed to have a short-term horizon which reduces their exposure to any costs from exploiting debtholders. Consequently, H1.2_e assumes that the agency costs of debt increase with higher ownership of an institutional investor. However, specification 2.2.3 delivers a significantly (at the 5% level) negative coefficient of institutional investor ownership; inconsistent with H1.2_e, the ownership of institutional investors is associated with a lower opportunity to transfer wealth from the debtholders.[2111] This effect may be explained as follows: both the institutional investors and the existing or potential debtholders are aware of the investor's incentive to expropriate debtholders. In order not to lose access to funds, the institutional investor proactively signals the absence of shareholder-debtholder agency conflicts by reducing the amount of discretionary assets. Since the incentive to engage in transfers of wealth is lower for the remaining blockholder types, they do not face pressure to signal an absence of shareholder-debtholder conflicts and therefore have an insignificant effect on *[discr_assets]*.

In terms of standardized effects, a one standard deviation increase in the ownership of an institutional investor decreases the agency costs of debt proxy by 0.05 standard deviation. This effect is small when compared to the standardized effects of the alternative governance mech-

[2111] Note that this has already been indicated by the institutional investors' mean level of discretionary assets as shown in section 6.2.3.3.

anisms: their standardized coefficients amount to -0.24 for *[debt]*, -0.16 for *[codet_third]* and -0.22 for *[codet_par]*.[2112] The presence of a governmental blockholder is associated with a 0.04 standard deviation decrease in discretionary assets. Overall, specification 2.2.3 indicates that the effect of the four blockholder identities on the potential for wealth transfer strategies at the expense of debtholders is negligible.[2113] As argued earlier, the low magnitude of these variables may be a result of effective firm-level governance mechanisms that either prohibit the blockholder from using its monitoring for the transfer of wealth or constitute substitutes for an effective monitoring by the blockholder.

Accounting for blockholder heterogeneity in specifications 2.2.1-2.2.3 hardly affects the **control variables** relative to specifications 1.2.1-1.2.3. The coefficients of *[capex]*, *[age]*, *[pfd]*, *[debt]*, *[codet_third]*, *[codet_par]*, and *[govt]* maintain a significant and negative effect on the amount of discretionary assets. The coefficient of *[liq]* remains significant and positive. In contrast to these variables, *[bank]* turns insignificant. Whereas a bank, due to its superior access to information and signaling effect, enables a firm to hold more intangible (discretionary) assets when presuming blockholder homogeneity, this signaling effect turns insignificant when accounting for blockholder heterogeneity. Either blockholders (despite their insignificant coefficients) act as a substitute for a bank blockholder or the signal sent by the presence of a bank blockholder is ineffective in the presence of a (potentially more powerful) blockholder willing to exploit debtholders.[2114] Of the two variables that control for firm-specific risk in specification 2.2.3, *[beta]* is significantly and positively related to *[discr_assets]*. This seems to suggest that more risky firms hold more discretionary assets; however, also the reverse may be true: a greater amount of discretionary assets increases a firm's risk.

In their study, *Anderson et al.* (2003) find a **non-linear relationship** between family ownership and agency costs of debt, suggesting that families with higher levels of ownership become entrenched.[2115] In line with their finding, also $H1.2_g$ hypothesizes a non-linear relationship between family ownership and *[discr_assets]*. In order to investigate a non-linear effect, specification 2.2.7 in table 48 (appendix 10) regresses *[discr_assets]* on the blockholders' ownership and their squared ownership.[2116] Based on the results, family ownership indeed has a non-linear effect on agency costs of debt: the squared ownership term is significant and positive at the 5% level and suggests a u-shaped relationship. Consistent with family entrenchment, their ownership lowers agency costs of debt up to an ownership of 31.07%.[2117] Beyond

---

2112 As expected, the largest standardized effect is observed for *[capex]*: a one standard deviation increase in this variable results in a 0.40 decrease in discretionary assets.

2113 The negligible effect of the blockholder types' ownership is also confirmed by the adjusted R^2. The variance explained by specification 2.2.3 equals 51.14%, relative to 51.07% in specification 1.2.1.

2114 Note that for the second argument to be truly convincing, *[bhl_cont]* or the blockholder types should have a significant relationship with *[discr_assets]*.

2115 See Anderson et al. (2003): 279-281.

2116 Table 48 reports only selected coefficients, but the specifications include the same statistical controls as in table 25. Their signs, magnitude, and significance remain unchanged. In order to facilitate comparison, also the ownership of the remaining types is squared.

2117 This is calculated by building the derivative of:
$\text{discr\_assets} = -0.0691 bh1\_fam\_cont + 0.1112 bh1\_fam\_cont^2$ w.r.t bh1_fam_cont. Figure 25 (appendix 10) graphically illustrates this result.

this level, agency costs of debt increase with higher family ownership.[2118] However, at the mean family ownership of 40.62% (given it is the largest blockholder), the amount of discretionary assets is still lower in family firms relative to non-family firms.

Due to the presumed importance of **family board representation**, H1.2_h expects the effect of blockholder board representation on the ownership size effect on agency costs of debt to be strongest for family blockholders. Since board presence may provide the family with greater discretion, a negative effect of board presence on the relationship between family ownership and agency costs of debt would provide further evidence for an entrenchment of the family. However, specification 2.2.6 in table 49 (appendix 11) yields insignificant results on the interaction between family ownership and its representation on the supervisory or management board, respectively.[2119] Insignificant coefficients are also reported for the interactions based on the remaining blockholder types. Hence, there is no support for H1.2_h.[2120] Interestingly, the ownership of all blockholder types decreases agency costs of debt if they are represented on neither board.[2121] However, if they are represented on either management or supervisory board, their level of ownership is (insignificantly) associated with higher agency costs of debt. This can be regarded as weak evidence for the fact that board presence increases the blockholders' power and discretion and may therefore be associated with a greater potential to shift value from debtholders to blockholders.

6.3.3.3 Impact on Principal-Principal Agency Costs

In order to investigate whether blockholder characteristics affect principal-principal agency costs, table 26 shows the pooled-OLS results of the specifications 2.3.1-2.3.3.[2122]

Column two provides evidence with regard to the effect of the **largest blockholder's ownership**. It is expected that *[bh1_cont]* has a significant effect on principal-principal agency costs. However, due to opposite effects, agency theoretic propositions fail to make an exact prediction with regard to the sign of the empirical relationship.[2123] The coefficient in specification 2.3.1 suggests a significant effect of the largest blockholder's ownership on dividend payouts, being consistent with H1.3_a. In particular, the coefficient has a positive effect on a firm's dividend payouts. Since there is an inverse relationship between dividend payouts and the likelihood of principal-principal conflicts, the size of the largest blockholder's ownership decreases principal-principal agency costs. Apparently, increasing levels of ownership and the associated greater exposure to the costs reduce the blockholder's incentive to expropriate the remaining shareholders.[2124] H1.3_b suggests a non-linear relationship between *[bh1_cont]* and the size of dividend payouts. In order to investigate potential non-linearities, column six and

2118 These results are consistent with the findings by Anderson et al. (2003): 279-281. However, they observe a minimum level of agency costs of debt at an ownership of 41.87%.

2119 Table 49 reports only selected coefficients, but the specifications include the same statistical controls as in table 25. Their signs, magnitude, and significance remain unchanged.

2120 The results do not support the findings of Anderson et al. (2003): 278, who find that firms in which a family member is the CEO face higher cost of debt financing.

2121 This relationship is significant for institutional investors only.

2122 The regression specifications are depicted in appendix 7.

2123 See also H1.3_a in section 5.2.

2124 Based on a one-sided p-Value, the coefficient is significantly larger than zero at a 5% level.

seven of table 47 in appendix 9 present the results of a regression using the squared ownership term (specification 2.3.4) and ownership interval dummies (specification 2.3.5).[2125] While the squared ownership term is insignificant, the four interval dummies are consistent with the expectation of a non-linear ownership size effect formulated in H1.3$_b$. Specifically, the signs of the coefficients provide some evidence of an intermediate level of ownership that simultaneously provides sufficient power and limits a blockholder's exposure to the costs resulting from its expropriation: ownership levels within the range of 25-50% are associated with (insignificantly) lower dividend payments.[2126] Beyond this intermediate level, *[bh1_cont]* is associated with significantly higher dividend payments.[2127] These results are similar to those observed by *Truong/Heaney* (2007), who find the shareholdings of the largest blockholder to be negatively (positively) related to dividend payouts at low (high) ownership levels.[2128] The results are inconsistent with the assumption that dividends are redundant in the presence of a monitoring blockholder (substitution hypothesis).[2129] Rather than acting as a substitute, the payment of dividends seems to be a device of an effectively monitoring largest blockholder.

Specification 2.3.2 focuses on the relationship between the **largest blockholder's presence on the supervisory or management board** and principal-principal agency costs. Under the

Table 26
This table presents the stage 2 pooled-OLS results w.r.t. principal-principal agency costs as proxied by *[div_payout]* (specification 2.3.1-2.3.3). The regressions include industry and year fixed effects; standard errors are clustered by firm. T-statistics are reported in parentheses. In case of a directional hypothesis, one-sided p-Values are calculated. *, **, and *** indicates statistical significance at the 10%, 5%, and 1% level, respectively.

	(2.3.1)	(2.3.2)	(2.3.3)
bh1_cont	**0.0011****	**0.0014*****	
	(2.07)	**(2.38)**	
bh1_supb		**-0.0004***	
		(-1.34)	
bh1_mgmtb		**-0.0001**	
		(-0.27)	
bh1_pe_cont			**0.0044*****
			(2.93)
bh1_fam_cont			**-0.0002**
			(-0.32)
bh1_si_cont			**0.0000**
			(-0.07)
bh1_insti_cont			**0.0075****
			(1.91)
stdev_ni			0.0000
			(0.20)
beta			-0.0005
			(-1.48)

[2125] Table 47 reports only selected coefficients, but the specifications include the same statistical controls as in table 26. Their signs, magnitude, and significance remain unchanged.

[2126] This result at least cannot convincingly invalidate the assumption that management pays private benefits to blockholders with lower levels of ownership for their abandonment of monitoring (see section 6.3.3.1).

[2127] The magnitude and significance level is strongest for blockholders owning at least 75% of a firm's shares. This is intuitive, since such a level of ownership provides the blockholder with substantial discretion in decision making. See also section 2.2.3.2.

[2128] See Truong/Heaney (2007): 676.

[2129] See e.g. Farinha (2003): 1183; Goergen et al. (2005): 378; Bøhren et al. (2012): 3-5. For a sample of listed Norwegian commercial and savings banks over the time period of 1989-2002, the substitution hypothesis is supported by Bøhren/Ødegaard (2006): 20.

Table 26 cont'd

	(2.3.1)	(2.3.2)	(2.3.3)
growth	-0.0006***	-0.0006***	-0.0005***
	(-3.08)	(-2.97)	(-2.89)
prof	0.0061***	0.0060***	0.0064***
	(4.86)	(4.84)	(5.02)
div_prevy	0.0032***	0.0032***	0.0033***
	(11.81)	(11.96)	(11.93)
age	0.0000**	0.0000**	0.0000**
	(2.13)	(2.15)	(2.13)
ln_assets	-0.0007***	-0.0006***	-0.0006***
	(-4.54)	(-4.44)	(-3.29)
pfd	-0.0000	0.0000	-0.0001
	(-0.02)	(0.01)	(-0.18)
liq	-0.0007	-0.0007	-0.0009
	(-1.41)	(-1.36)	(-1.64)
insd_own	0.0001	0.0003	0.0006
	(0.15)	(0.29)	(0.57)
debt	-0.0028***	-0.0028***	-0.0030***
	(-3.30)	(-3.31)	(-3.63)
codet_third	0.0003	0.0003	0.0004
	(0.85)	(0.84)	(0.99)
codet_par	-0.0001	-0.0001	0.0000
	(-0.22)	(-0.26)	(-0.02)
bank	0.0000	0.0000	-0.0002
	(0.11)	(0.08)	(-0.61)
insolv	0.0004	0.0003	0.0004
	(0.78)	(0.62)	(0.75)
takeover	0.0000	0.0001	0.0002
	(0.06)	(0.10)	(0.31)
segm_chng	-0.0011**	-0.0011**	-0.0008**
	(-2.29)	(-2.26)	(-1.87)
govt	0.0004	0.0005	0.0005
	(0.98)	(1.05)	(1.09)
Constant	0.0037***	0.0037***	0.0041***
	(5.14)	(5.15)	(4.89)
Industry dummies	Yes	Yes	Yes
Year dummies	Yes	Yes	Yes
Adjusted R^2	0.2842	0.2854	0.3072
Number of obs.	2,228	2,228	2,226
Firms	425	425	425

Table 26: Regression results of principal-principal agency costs under the assumption of blockholder heterogeneity

assumption that a blockholder's self-interest differs from the interest of the remaining shareholders, the representation on the supervisory board should strongly increase the blockholder's power and discretion and should result in lower costs of private benefits. Consequently, *[bh1_supb]* is expected to be associated with greater principal-principal agency costs (H1.3_c).

In line with H1.3_c, *[bh1_supb]* significantly (at a 10% level) increases the likelihood of principal-principal agency costs: if the largest blockholder is represented in the supervisory board, it retains its portfolio firm's earnings so that the financial resources remain under its control and can be used for the generation of private benefits. Based on a similar reasoning, also *[bh1_mgmtb]* is expected to have a positive effect on principal-principal agency costs (H1.3_d). While the sign of the coefficient is consistent with H1.3_d, it is not significant, providing only weak evidence in favor of the hypothesis. The insignificance of *[bh1_mgmtb]* may suggest that the payout strategy proposed by the management may meet resistance of a powerful supervisory board, provided that the blockholder is not represented on the supervisory board, either.[2130]

Finally, specification 2.3.3 accounts for the four **blockholder identities** and regresses the dividend payout ratio on the identities' level of ownership. Since private equity and institutional investors should have utility functions and risk preferences reconcilable with those of the remaining (minority) shareholders, $H1.3_e$ presumes higher ownership of these blockholders to reduce principal-principal agency costs. In contrast, families' and strategic investors' self-interests should differ from those of the remaining shareholders; as both should have strong incentives and be well-positioned to extract private benefits, $H1.3_f$ expects higher principal-principal agency costs for these blockholder types. Consistent with $H1.3_e$, the ownership of private equity and institutional investors decreases principal-principal agency costs at a 1% and 5% significance level, respectively.[2131] In terms of standardized coefficients, a one standard deviation increase in the ownership of a private equity (institutional) investor increases the dividend payout ratio by 0.13 (0.11) standard deviation. Hence, private equity investors have a stronger effect on principal-principal agency costs than institutional investors.[2132] Compared to the control variables, the effect of both investor types is meaningful.[2133] While the payment of dividends in the previous year by far has the strongest standardized effect (0.39), the effect of the investor types is comparable to those of a firm's profitability (0.16) and age (0.10). Overall, the results suggest that these blockholders effectively monitor in the interest of the remaining shareholders. Turning to the ownership of families and strategic investors, specification 2.3.3 finds the ownership of both types to insignificantly increase principal-principal agency costs which does not provide sufficient evidence for higher principal-principal agency costs as stated in $H1.3_f$.[2134]

As regards the **control variables**, the coefficients in table 26 point in the same direction as under the assumption of blockholder homogeneity. Hence, a firm's growth opportunities, size,

2130 Also the existing empirical evidence suggests that independent, powerful supervisory boards may limit private benefits of the largest blockholder. Please see section 4.1.2.2.

2131 With regard to institutional investors, the evidence is consistent with Alli/Khan/Ramirez (1993): 525 and Truong/Heaney (2007): 669 who find that firms tend to pay dividends when a financial institution is the largest blockholder. Based on data on 96 hedge fund targets in Germany, also Achleitner et al. (2010): 813, 821f find hedge funds to target firms that exhibit dividend potential in order to increase payouts after the investment. Based on a survey, Brav et al. (2005): 509f, 517 find that more than half of their respondents agreed that institutional investors influence the dividend or repurchase decisions. In addition, nonpayers reported they would start paying dividends following institutional pressure. In contrast, Topalov (2011): 170 observes that institutional investors do not have a significant impact on dividend payments.

2132 However, private equity firms may also use dividends financed by new borrowings to generate additional returns from a portfolio firm. See Cheffins/Armour (2008): 12. These dividends are highly controversial, since they may be paid at the expense of a firm's long-term viability and should therefore not contribute to a reduction of principal-principal agency costs. See also Watt (2008): 555.

2133 In comparison to the 28.43% of the variation explained by specification 1.3.1, accounting for the blockholder types increases the adjusted R^2 to 30.72% which further illustrates the relevance of the blockholder identities when explaining a firm's payout policy.

2134 With regard to strategic investors, Barclay et al. (2009): 2424 find that after a corporation acquires a large block of shares, the payment of dividends remains unchanged or is decreased. However, the authors reject the possibility that this signals an increased agency conflict: using two measures of corporate governance quality, they find that firms with a corporate blockholder do not differ in terms of governance quality relative to other firms. Rather, they find that lower dividend payments are explained by the fact that the new blockholder focuses on the pursuance of operating strategies by increasing capital expenditures.

and level of debt, as well as the change of the stock market segment significantly decrease the dividend payout ratio.[2135] Moreover, a firm's profitability and age as well as the payment of dividends in the previous year significantly increase the dividend payouts of the sample firms. In specification 2.3.3, firm-specific risk as proxied by *[beta]* and *[stdev_ni]* are insignificantly different from zero.

Section 5.2.3.3 argues that the ability of families and strategic investors to extract private benefits should increase with greater levels of ownership. Hence, an expropriation of the remaining shareholders by these investors should be more likely for higher levels of ownership ($H1.3_g$). In order to investigate this **non-linearity** hypothesis, specification 2.3.7 in table 48 of appendix 10 regresses the dividend payouts on the blockholder types' ownership and their squared ownership.[2136] With regard to strategic investors, the coefficients suggest a u-shaped relationship: up to an ownership level of 41.80%, increasing ownership results in lower dividend payouts.[2137] Beyond this level, greater ownership of strategic investors is associated with higher dividend payments. A u-shaped relationship is also observed for families: family ownership decreases dividend payouts up to an ownership of 38.75%; ownership beyond this level increases dividend payouts.[2138] Although the results support the non-linear relationship hypothesized by $H1.3_g$, they are surprising, since greater dividend payouts are associated with lower principal-principal agency costs and hence do not support a generation of private benefits at higher ownership levels. There are two possible explanations. First, the relationship suggests a greater self-dealing of the two types at lower ownership levels which limit the blockholders' exposure to the costs of their private benefits. Above these levels, the blockholders are exposed to a greater portion of the costs and rather pay out the funds to the remaining shareholders. [2139] Second, greater ownership increases the entrenchment of both blockholders and enables them to set their favored payout policy also against (possible) resistance of the remaining shareholders. As a consequence, families and strategic investors may use portfolio firm resources as a source of their individual income[2140] which should be detrimental for the remaining shareholders. Given the non-linear results on managerial agency costs and agency costs of debt, the latter explanation should be more likely than the former at least for family firms.[2141]

2135 However, the liquidity proxy in specification 2.3.3 turns insignificant.

2136 Table 48 reports only selected coefficients, but the specifications include the same statistical controls as in table 26. Their signs, magnitude, and significance remain unchanged. In order to facilitate comparison, also the ownership of the remaining types is squared.

2137 This is calculated by building the derivative of:
div_payout = $-0.0051 bh1\_si\_cont + 0.0061 bh1\_si\_cont^2$ w.r.t bh1_si_cont.

2138 This is calculated by building the derivative of:
div_payout = $-0.0031 bh1\_fam\_cont + 0.0040 bh1\_fam\_cont^2$ w.r.t bh1_fam_cont. Figure 26 (appendix 10) graphically illustrates this result.

2139 Note that portfolio firms of strategic investors make lower dividend payouts relative to firms without a strategic investor until the strategic investor's ownership exceeds ~ 83.61%.

2140 For example, Ellermann (2003): 338 argues that strategic investors may use their portfolio firms' dividend payments to increase their own profits.

2141 Higher dividends may also be a result of minority shareholders using their legal rights to force the payout of cash to impede the inefficient use of cash by blockholders. See La Porta et al. (2000a): 5; Gugler/Yurtoglu (2003): 735. However, minority shareholders' ability to force firms to pay out excess cash may be questioned in the presence of a blockholder. See Renneboog/Szilagyi (2006): 17. Faccio et al. (2001): 58 argue that the difficulty of organizing dispersed shareholders gives blockholders "de facto control".

Existing literature on family blockholders stresses that conflicts with the remaining shareholders are more likely in the case of family **presence on either management or supervisory board**. However, the greater discretion that comes with board presence does not accrue exclusively to family firms but might also affect the monitoring of the remaining blockholder types.[2142] Therefore, specification 2.3.6 in table 49 of appendix 11 interacts the supervisory and management board presence with the blockholder identities' level of ownership.[2143] As can be seen, private equity investors with a management board presence have a significantly stronger (positive) effect on dividend payouts than private equity investors without a board presence. Since private equity investors should have interests compatible with those of the remaining shareholders, the significant interaction term illustrates that the intensity and effectiveness of their monitoring in the interest of all shareholders is facilitated by the board presence.[2144]

It is argued above that the greater discretion that comes with higher ownership may enable strategic investors to use dividends for increasing their own profits. Consistent with this presumption, strategic investors with supervisory board presence have a significantly stronger (positive) effect on dividend payouts than strategic investors without board presence which have a significantly negative effect on the level of dividend payouts. This may suggest that board presence provides strategic investors with sufficient power to pursue their self-interest. Inconsistent with the suggestions of the existing literature, family board presence does not have a significant effect on the relationship between family ownership and principal-principal agency costs. Overall, the significant interaction coefficients of strategic and private equity investors provide some evidence for $H1.3_h$.

6.3.3.4 Impact on Firm Value

Table 27 gives the pooled-OLS results of an analysis relating blockholder characteristics, a set of control variables as well as industry and time fixed effects to firm value as proxied by Tobin's q.[2145]

Specification 2.4.1 regresses firm value on the **largest blockholder's ownership** *[bh1_cont]*. Consistent with $H1.4_a$, *[bh1_cont]* has a highly significant (at the 1% level) and positive influence on firm value: a one unit increase in the largest blockholder's ownership increases firm value by 0.3384 units. In terms of economic significance, if a firm with a median Tobin's q (1.2498) goes from the median ownership of the largest blockholder (31.07%) to zero percent, firm value would decrease by 8.41% c.p.[2146] These results illustrate that existing and prospective shareholders expect the largest blockholder's ownership to decrease overall agency costs and therefore incorporate the expected reduction of agency costs into the firm's val-

2142 See $H1.3_h$ in section 5.2.

2143 Table 49 reports only selected coefficients, but the specifications include the same statistical controls as in table 26. Their signs, magnitude, and significance remain unchanged.

2144 While a one unit increase in private equity investor's ownership increases dividend payouts by 0.0036 units if the investor is present on neither board, the same change increases dividend payouts by 0.0119 (0.0083+0.0036) units if the investor is present on the management board.

2145 The regression specifications are depicted in appendix 7.

2146 See Cronqvist/Nilsson (2003): 711 for a similar calculation.

ue.[2147] The positive effect of the largest blockholder's ownership supports the results of *Ruhwedel* (2003), who finds a similar relationship for a sample of 952 firm-year observations of German firms in 1997-2000.[2148] Since both theory and the empirical evidence in the previous sections suggest that a blockholder's incentive structure changes with increasing equity ownership, table 47 (appendix 9) also presents the results of regressions using the squared ownership term (specification 2.4.4) and ownership interval dummies (specification 2.4.5) to explain the variation in firm value.[2149] While the squared ownership term is insignificant, three of the four interval dummies are significant and positive. Consistent with the insignificant results for *[opex_sales]*, *[discr_assets]*, and *[div_payout]*, the largest blockholder does not increase firm value if the size of its ownership is within 5-25%. Blockholders with an ownership between 25-50% are associated with lower agency costs of debt but higher managerial agency costs. Consequently, the net effect on a firm's overall agency costs is only weakly significant and of low magnitude. In contrast, blockholders with an ownership beyond 50% have strongly significant and positive impact on firm value, being consistent with an incentive alignment of the average blockholder at higher levels of ownership.[2150] In general, the non-linearity of the ownership size effect is in support of $H1.4_b$.

To investigate $H1.4_c$ and $H1.4_d$, specification 2.4.2 regresses firm value on **the largest blockholder's presence on the supervisory board** *[bh1_supb]* **and management board** *[bh1_mgmtb]*, respectively. With regard to the latter, $H1.4_d$ expects a negative effect on firm value. Consistent with the hypothesis, the largest blockholder's representation on a firm's management board is indeed regarded as unfavorable by existing and prospective shareholders, albeit it is insignificant. While the insignificant coefficient provides only weak evidence in favor of $H1.4_d$, it is consistent with the net effect of *[bh1_mgmtb]* suggested by the previous results: *[bh1_mgmtb]* is found to insignificantly (1) lower managerial agency costs, (2) increase agency costs of debt and (3) increase principal-principal agency costs; the net effect on firm value should consequently be insignificantly negative.

With regard to *[bh1_supb]*, $H1.4_c$ proposes a significant effect of the largest blockholder's supervisory board presence on firm value. Consistent with this hypothesis, the coefficient in specification 2.4.2 points to a significant (at the 5% level) and positive influence of *[bh1_supb]* on firm value. However, the significantly positive coefficient is counterintuitive given the previous results: *[bh1_supb]* is found to significantly increase principal-principal agency costs, to insignificantly increase managerial agency costs, and to insignificantly decrease agency costs of debt. Based on these results, the net effect of *[bh1_supb]* on firm value should be negative. There may be two reasons for the significant and positive coefficient. First, the blockholder sitting on the supervisory board is successful in concealing its genera-

2147 Recall that *[bh1_cont]* seems to reduce managerial agency costs, agency costs of debt as well as principal-principal agency costs, albeit the reduction is only significant for principal-principal agency costs.

2148 See Ruhwedel (2003): 242. In contrast, Kehren (2006): 196f finds an insignificant relationship between the largest blockholder's ownership and Tobin's q for a German sample during 1996-2000.

2149 Table 47 reports only selected coefficients, but the specifications include the same statistical controls as in table 27. Their signs, magnitude, and significance remain unchanged.

2150 Ruhwedel (2003): 234f finds a similar relationship for ownership levels above 50%. However, below this threshold, she finds a significantly negative effect of the largest blockholder's ownership. Drobetz et al. (2009): 372f, 378 also find results consistent with greater blockholder incentives for high ownership levels.

tion of private benefits and generating trust among the remaining supervisory board members and shareholders which therefore do not suspect an unfavorable impact of the blockholder. Second, the negative coefficient in specification 2.3.2 does not suggest higher principal-principal agency conflicts but a substitution effect. This is based on the assumption that dividends are redundant in the presence of an effectively monitoring blockholder,[2151] since the blockholder rather relies on supervisory board meetings to monitor corporate management.[2152]

The last column of table 27 presents the results of specification 2.4.3, which accounts for the **identity of the largest blockholder**. Based on agency theoretic arguments, $H1.4_e$ and $H1.4_f$ expect family and private equity investor ownership to decrease a firm's overall agency costs and to increase firm value. Since the influence of strategic and institutional investors on overall agency costs is unknown, $H1.4_g$ and $H1.4_h$ are formulated non-directionally. With regard to the ownership of private equity investors, specification 2.4.3 yields a significant (at the 1% level) and positive coefficient which supports $H1.4_f$ and suggests that existing and prospective

Table 27
This table presents the stage 2 pooled-OLS results w.r.t. firm value as proxied by *[tobinq]* (specification 2.4.1-2.4.3). The regressions include industry and year fixed effects; standard errors are clustered by firm. T-statistics are reported in parentheses. In case of a directional hypothesis, one-sided p-Values are calculated. *, **, and *** indicates statistical significance at the 10%, 5%, and 1% level, respectively.

	(2.4.1)	(2.4.2)	(2.4.3)
bh1_cont	**0.3384*** (4.31)**	**0.2885*** (3.32)**	
bh1_supb		**0.0848** (2.08)**	
bh1_mgmtb		**-0.0270 (-0.50)**	
bh1_pe_cont			**0.7403*** (3.84)**
bh1_fam_cont			**0.2851** (2.24)**
bh1_si_cont			**0.2718*** (3.18)**
bh1_insti_cont			**0.0101 (0.08)**
stdev_ni			0.0001 (0.30)
beta			-0.0483 (-0.93)
growth	0.2086*** (4.74)	0.2094*** (4.77)	0.2021*** (4.67)
ppe_assets	-0.3622** (-2.16)	-0.3800** (-2.27)	-0.3415** (-2.02)
capex	2.1777*** (3.03)	2.2177*** (3.14)	1.9844*** (2.74)
cash_assets	1.1018*** (5.64)	1.1184*** (5.71)	1.1572*** (5.78)
age	0.0013 (1.20)	0.0013 (1.17)	0.0017* (1.58)
ln_assets	-0.1140*** (-4.56)	-0.1191*** (-4.75)	-0.1173*** (-3.90)

2151 See e.g. Farinha (2003): 1183; Goergen et al. (2005): 378; Bøhren et al. (2012): 3-5. For a sample of listed Norwegian commercial and savings banks over the time period of 1989-2002, the substitution hypothesis is supported by Bøhren/Ødegaard (2006): 20.

2152 See Bøhren/Ødegaard (2006): 4; Bøhren et al. (2012): 5.

Table 27 cont'd

	(2.4.1)	(2.4.2)	(2.4.3)
pfd	0.1869**	0.1818**	0.1558*
	(1.81)	(1.77)	(1.54)
liq	0.4395***	0.4379***	0.4281***
	(6.62)	(6.59)	(6.27)
insd_own	-0.1645	-0.1810	0.0213
	(-1.28)	(-1.38)	(0.16)
debt	-0.1358	-0.1261	-0.1593
	(-0.89)	(-0.82)	(-1.02)
codet_third	0.0157	0.0189	0.0232
	(0.27)	(0.32)	(0.38)
codet_par	0.1070	0.1120*	0.1285*
	(1.24)	(1.29)	(1.40)
bank	-0.0074	-0.0074	-0.0136
	(-0.17)	(-0.17)	(-0.30)
insolv	-0.0171	-0.0054	-0.0318
	(-0.20)	(-0.06)	(-0.38)
takeover	0.3512***	0.3371***	0.3306***
	(2.57)	(2.49)	(2.50)
segm_chng	-0.2952***	-0.2888***	-0.2975***
	(-3.01)	(-3.00)	(-3.03)
govt	0.0577	0.0471	0.0765
	(0.65)	(0.53)	(0.83)
Constant	1.6501***	1.6652***	1.7021***
	(13.73)	(13.63)	(12.13)
Industry dummies	Yes	Yes	Yes
Year dummies	Yes	Yes	Yes
Adjusted R^2	0.2073	0.2105	0.2154
Number of obs.	2,978	2,978	2,876
Firms	484	484	469

Table 27: Regression results of firm value under the assumption of blockholder heterogeneity

shareholders regard private equity investors as favorable.[2153] Moreover, the results show a significant (at the 5% level) and positive effect of family ownership on firm value which provides evidence in favor of H1.4_e.[2154]

Significant increases in firm value are also a consequence of greater ownership of strategic investors; the coefficient is significant at the 1% level and in support of H1.4_h. In contrast to these three blockholders, the results do not present a significant effect of institutional investors on firm value which provides no support for H1.4_g. Given the influence of institutional investor ownership on the components of a firm's overall agency costs, the insignificance of the coefficient is surprising: institutional investors constitute the only blockholder type that significantly reduces each component of overall agency costs. In contrast, the effect of strategic investors is insignificant for each component of the overall agency costs; nevertheless, strategic investor ownership significantly increases firm value.[2155] This may suggest that a firm's shareholders account for effects of the blockholder types that go beyond a reduction of a firm's overall agency costs. As argued in section 5.2.1, a blockholder may have a certification effect for its portfolio firm or provide know-how, technology and managerial exper-

[2153] The positive effect of private equity firms is generally consistent with the empirical evidence reviewed in section 4.1.3.2.2.

[2154] This result is in line with Leiber (2008): 200 but inconsistent with empirical evidence that finds significant effects of families only if they are also actively involved in the firm. See section 4.1.3.1.2.

[2155] Also private equity and family blockholders have a significant effect on only a single component of global agency costs.

tise.[2156] As a consequence, strategic investors may have an effect on firm value despite having no significant influence on agency costs.[2157]

Of the four blockholder types, the ownership of the largest blockholder has the greatest effect on firm value if it is a private equity investor: the standardized coefficient of *[bh1_pe_cont]* amounts to 0.13 compared to 0.09 and 0.10 for *[bh1_fam_cont]* and *[bh1_si_cont]*, respectively.[2158] When considering all independent variables, firm size has the largest effect on firm value: a one standard deviation increase in size reduces firm value by 0.33 standard deviation. An increase in the cash level *[cash_assets]* results in an increase in firm value by 0.24 standard deviation. Relative to the control variables, the ownership levels of the three significant blockholder types make a meaningful contribution to firm value which is comparable to the contribution of the growth variable (0.10). The coefficients are also economically significant. If a firm with a median Tobin's q (1.2498) goes from the mean ownership of the largest blockholder, given it is a private equity investor (33.40%), to zero percent, firm value would decrease by 19.78% c.p.[2159] Using a similar calculation, the drop in firm value would amount to 9.65% and 12.46% for family and strategic investors, respectively.

In comparison to stage 1, the sign, magnitude as well as the statistical significance of most **control variables** remain largely unchanged when accounting for blockholder heterogeneity in the specifications 2.4.1-2.4.3. Consequently, *[growth]*, *[capex]*, *[cash_assets]*, *[pfd]*, *[age]*[2160], *[liq]*, and *[takeover]* still lead to significant increases in firm value whereas the variables *[ppe_assets]*, *[ln_assets]*, and *[segm_chng]* result in significant decreases in firm value. Moreover, parity codetermination *[codet_par]* is weakly significant and appears to positively affect firm value in specification 2.4.2 and 2.4.3. In line with the results in stage 1, also the coefficients of *[pfd]* in stage 2 suggest a value increasing effect resulting from the issuance of preferred stock, which is contrary to the expectation in section 5.3.4.1. An analysis of the ownership structure of firms with outstanding preferred stock suggests that in 57% (17%) of these firms, a family (strategic investor) is the largest blockholder. Recalling the highly significant and positive coefficient of these blockholder types mentioned above, the positive coefficient of *[pfd]* may be driven by these results. This would also be in line with the reduced significance of *[pfd]* in specification 2.4.3: here, the effect of preferred stock is partly captured by the family and strategic investor variables. Finally, both *[stdev_ni]* and *[beta]* in specification 2.4.3 are insignificantly different from zero.[2161]

The baseline set of control variables is chosen to control as much as possible for portfolio firm heterogeneity and omitted variables. Nevertheless, the specifics of the sample may require two additional control variables. First, in 233 firm year observations, the respective firm holds own shares, for instance as a result of a repurchase. This increases the voting rights of

2156 See also Douma et al. (2006): 642f.
2157 This issue is investigated in more detail further below.
2158 Also a one-sided Wald test suggests that the coefficient of private equity blockholders is significantly larger than the coefficients of families and institutional investors.
2159 See Cronqvist/Nilsson (2003): 711 for a similar calculation.
2160 Firm age has a significant effect only in specification 2.4.3.
2161 In terms of goodness-of-fit, the adjusted R^2 slightly improves from 20.90% in specification 1.4.1 to 21.54% in specification 2.4.3.

the remaining shareholders, since pursuant to § 16 (3) AktG, the firm itself is not eligible to vote.[2162] Consequently, shares held by the particular firm reduce the voting pool and may affect the results obtained so far. Therefore, the specifications 2.4.1-2.4.3 are reestimated using an additional variable which controls for own shares, *[own_shares]*. Table 50 (appendix 12) presents the results and illustrates that the signs, magnitudes, and significance levels are largely unaffected. *[own_shares]* has a significantly positive effect on firm value only in specification 2.4.3. Second, the sample also comprises 23 SEs. Compared to AGs, SEs differ in a number of points which may affect a blockholder's monitoring. Among others, SEs can choose between a two-tier board model and a one-tier board model.[2163] Moreover, adapted rules with regard to the German codetermination apply to SEs.[2164] Therefore, as a robustness test, the regression specifications 2.4.1-2.4.3 are reestimated using a dummy variable to identify SEs, *[SE_dummy]*. As shown in table 51 (appendix 12), all variables maintain their signs and significance levels. Overall, the inclusion of the *[own_shares]* and *[SE_dummy]* variable, respectively, does not affect the main conclusion derived from the results in table 27.

$H1.4_i$, $H1.4_j$ and $H1.4_k$ expect a **non-linear ownership size effect** of families, institutional and strategic investors on firm value. In order to investigate these hypotheses, specification 2.4.7 in table 48 (appendix 10) regresses firm value on the blockholder types' ownership and their squared ownership.[2165] The specification delivers a significant coefficient of the squared ownership of families and strategic investors, being in support of hypotheses $H1.4_i$ and $H1.4_k$. The squared ownership of institutional investors is insignificant and provides no evidence for $H1.4_j$. With regard to strategic investors, the coefficient suggests a u-shaped relationship: for levels beyond 5.66%, the ownership of strategic investors is associated with increases in firm value.[2166] Given the non-linear effect of strategic investors on principal-principal agency costs

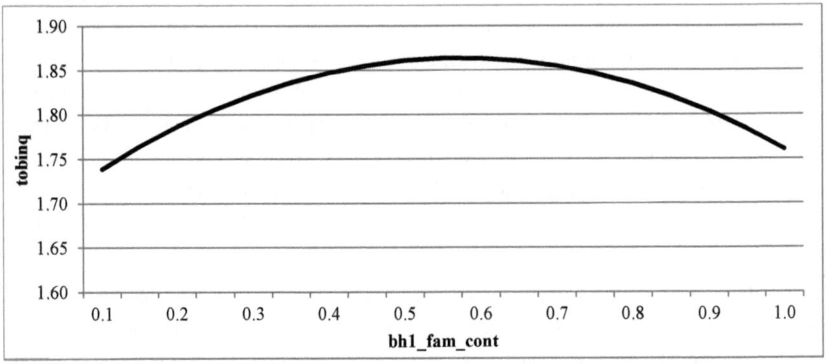

Figure 13: Non-linear relationship between bh1_fam_cont and tobinq

---

2162 See also Leiber (2008): 131.

2163 For further details, please see §§ 15-19 SEAG for the two-tier board model and §§ 20-49 SEAG for the one-tier board model. However, larger SEs typically choose the two-tier model; for instance, all SEs in the DAX employ a two-tier model.

2164 Please see SEBG for further details.

2165 Table 48 reports only selected coefficients, but the specifications include the same statistical controls as in table 27. Their signs, magnitude, and significance remain unchanged.

2166 This is calculated by building the derivative of:
$\text{tobinq} = -0.0502 bh1\_si\_cont + 0.4434 bh1\_si\_cont^2$ w.r.t bh1_si_cont.

suggested in section 6.3.3.3, this is unexpected, however, may be explained by the provision of know-how and expertise which should increase with the strategic investor's level of ownership. The coefficient of the squared family ownership suggests an inverse u-shaped (concave) relationship between family ownership and firm value: As depicted in figure 13, family ownership is associated with higher firm value only up to an ownership of 57.16%.[2167] For ownership beyond this level, family ownership decreases firm value. The concave relationship for family ownership suggests that shareholders are aware of family entrenchment and account for the unfavorable effect of large family ownership on the components of agency costs that has been detected in the preceding sections.[2168]

Since the ownership size effect on firm value may also depend on the **blockholders' presence on the firm's boards** (H1.4$_I$), specification 2.4.6 in table 49 (appendix 11) interacts the supervisory and management board presence with the blockholder identities' level of ownership.[2169] The results illustrate that the ownership of private equity firms that are not present on a firm's bodies significantly (at the 10% level) increases firm value. However, the increase in firm value is stronger if the private equity investor is present on its portfolio firm's supervisory board. Hence, an active involvement by the private equity investor in its portfolio firms is regarded as favorable by the remaining and prospective shareholders.[2170] Share ownership of families that are not present on a firm's boards significantly (at the 1% level) increases firm value. However, the ownership of families that are present on a firm's management board significantly (at the 1% level) decreases firm value.[2171] Apparently, the remaining shareholders account for family entrenchment and a greater "us versus them" mentality in case the family is present on the management board of its portfolio firms. This confirms preliminary evidence of family entrenchment based on the interaction term in the regression on managerial agency costs. Moreover, it is in line with the unfavorable impact of family ownership on the agency cost proxies and firm value once it exceeds a certain threshold. Strategic investor ownership is associated with significantly greater firm value if the investor is present on neither board; this relationship is not significantly affected by its presence on the management or supervisory board. Overall, the results of specification 2.4.6 provide some support for H1.4$_I$.

As outlined in the explanation of the theoretical model in section 5.1.1, the present study aims to clarify whether the **impact of blockholder monitoring on firm value is driven by its effect on agency costs** as presumed by the theory of blockholder monitoring. The relevance of this investigation becomes evident when considering the empirical results. As stated previous-

---

2167 This is calculated by building the derivative of:
$tobinq = 0.6431 bh1\_fam\_cont - 0.5625 bh1\_fam\_cont^2$ w.r.t bh1_fam_cont.

2168 Note that a negative impact on firm value does not automatically imply the destruction of firm value. Rather, the family pays for expected agency costs in the form of lower share valuation by outside investors. See also Cronqvist/Nilsson (2003): 715.

2169 Table 49 reports only selected coefficients, but the specifications include the same statistical controls as in table 27. Their signs, magnitude, and significance remain unchanged. Since there are too few observations for an institutional investor's presence on a firm's boards, the respective variable is not interacted with *[bh1_supb]* and *[bh1_mgmtb]*.

2170 The importance is also illustrated by the fact that 56% of the private equity investors have at least one representative on the supervisory board. See also table 16.

2171 If a family is present on the management board, the effect of its ownership on firm value amounts to -0.602 (0.5007-0.5609).

ly, strategic investors have an insignificant effect on the components of overall agency costs but significantly increase firm value. This may suggest that a blockholder's effect on firm value may not exclusively stem from a reduction of agency costs. If a firm's existing or prospective shareholders value the ownership of a certain blockholder type for reasons that go beyond agency cost reductions, this should imply that blockholder ownership should be able to explain a significant portion of the variation in firm value also when accounting for a firm's agency costs. In contrast, if the effect of the blockholder types on firm value found above stems primarily from its effect on agency costs, one should expect a weaker relationship between the blockholder identities' ownership and firm value, as agency costs already capture the effect of the blockholder identities' ownership. In this case, the influence of the blockholder identities on firm value would be partially mediated by the agency cost proxies.[2172]

In order to investigate this issue, specification 2.4.8 in table 52 (appendix 13) first regresses firm value on the three agency cost proxies and a set of control variables.[2173] It is expected that greater agency costs reduce firm value. Specification 2.4.8 indeed delivers the expected coefficients for the three proxies.[2174] However, only the principal-principal agency cost proxy has a significant effect on firm value. Apparently, a firm's existing and prospective shareholders do not significantly incorporate managerial agency costs and agency costs of debt – at least those accounted for by the proxies used in the case at hand – into the firm's share price.

Specification 2.4.9 then regresses firm value on the agency cost proxies and the four blockholder types' ownership. As shown in table 52 (appendix 13),[2175] the coefficients of private equity and strategic investor ownership remain largely unaffected relative to specification 2.4.3. The coefficient of *[bh1_pe_cont]* decreases slightly from 0.7403 to 0.7305 whereas the coefficient of *[bh1_si_cont]* shows a marginal increase from 0.2718 to 0.2725; both variables remain highly significant at the 1% level. Relative to these variables, *[bh1_fam_cont]* is subject to greater changes: its coefficient increases from 0.2851 to 0.3524 and its significance increases from a 5% to a 1% level.[2176] With regard to the agency cost proxies, the coefficient of *[opex_sales]* remains generally unchanged. In contrast, the proxy for agency costs of debt changes its sign but remains insignificant. The coefficient and significance of *[div_payout]* decreases; however, it is still significant at a 5% level. Moreover, based on standardized coefficients, increases in each of the three significant blockholder identities' ownership have a greater effect than increases in the dividend payout ratio. The results of the regression thus suggest that the three significant blockholders create value for their portfolio firms that goes beyond their effect on agency costs (at least beyond those costs that are accounted for by the agency cost proxies used in the case at hand). As presumed in section 5.2.1, this creation of value can stem from a certification, signaling or from transfers of resources to the portfolio firm.

2172 Mediation is beyond the scope of this paper. For details please see Baron/Kenny (1986).

2173 This constitutes path 4 of the theoretical model in section 5.1.1. The specification includes the same statistical controls as in table 27. Their signs, magnitude, and significance remain unchanged.

2174 Recall that there is an inverse relationship between dividend payouts and principal-principal agency costs.

2175 The signs, magnitude, and significance of the controls in specification 2.4.9 remain unchanged.

2176 Note that the standardized coefficients of the three blockholder types exhibit changes in the same direction.

6.3.3.5 Résumé

The goal of stage 2 was to investigate whether the characteristics of the largest blockholder affect agency costs and firm value. To recapitulate, the following conclusions based on an examination of blockholder characteristics can be drawn:

(1) The influence of blockholder monitoring on agency costs and firm value is highly dependent on the size of the blockholder's ownership. This is the case when accounting for the blockholder's ownership and for the blockholder type's ownership. Moreover, family entrenchment seems to occur already at ownership levels below 50%, at which the blockholder possesses control over the portfolio firm. This may suggest that the low average presence at a firm's AGM, as highlighted in section 2.2.5, allows at least family blockholders to pursue their interests without possessing the simple majority.

(2) Although the importance of board presence is stressed by theoretical and empirical evidence[2177] and suggested by the frequent presence of blockholder types in supervisory or management boards of their portfolio firms,[2178] it is not found to decrease managerial agency costs or agency costs of debt. Moreover, the results do not suggest that board presence consistently and significantly affects the ownership size effect of any blockholder type on agency costs or firm value. In general, this questions the importance of management or supervisory board representation for effective monitoring at least for the blockholders examined in the study at hand.

(3) The effect of the largest blockholder's ownership on agency costs and firm value depends on the identity of the largest blockholder and hence also on the compatibility of the intentions of the blockholder identities and the remaining shareholders. Overall, the differentiation between the types of shareholders in the ownership structure of publicly-listed firms is essential for a full understanding of the role and impact of shareholders on their portfolio firms.

(4) If the presence of a blockholder results in a transfer of wealth from debtholders to the blockholder, the opportunity to do so is not increased by greater investments in discretionary assets. Rather, blockholders whose interests are most likely to differ from those of debtholders (i.e. institutional investors) seem to proactively signal the absence of shareholder-debtholder agency conflicts by reducing the amount of discretionary assets.[2179] Similarly, if there is an expropriation of the remaining shareholders by the largest blockholder, this is not achieved through the retention of capital within the largest blockholder's portfolio firm. However, given their ownership provides them with sufficient discretion, families and strategic investors pay out dividends and may thereby use portfolio firm resources as a source of their individual income.

(5) Blockholder characteristics are unsuccessful in explaining the variation of the agency cost of debt proxy. A potential reason for this insignificance might be the existence of highly effective alternative governance mechanisms (i.e. leverage and codetermination) as well as the

2177 See section 4.1.2.

2178 See also table 13 and 16.

2179 However, for greater levels of ownership, family blockholders are associated with increasing agency costs of debt and thus points to transfers of value from debtholders to the family.

presence of a governmental blockholder which may either act as substitute for blockholder monitoring or limit value shifts by the blockholder. Apart from agency costs of debt, the evidence indicates that when accounting for blockholder monitoring, alternative governance mechanisms only weakly contribute to a reduction of agency costs or an increase in firm value. Referring back to the deliberations in section 4.3.2, this may suggest that blockholder monitoring affects agency costs and firm value independently and beyond the influence of alternative governance mechanisms. One may even consider this as evidence of blockholder monitoring acting as a substitute for alternative governance mechanisms.

(6) The effect of the blockholder types on firm value does not exclusively stem from a reduction of a firm's overall agency costs. First, only principal-principal agency costs have a significantly negative effect on firm value. Second, the ownership size effect of the blockholder types on firm value remains largely unchanged when simultaneously accounting for agency costs. Apparently, the blockholders create value for their portfolio firms that goes beyond their effect on agency costs and, in the case of strategic investors, may be able to outweigh an unfavorable or increasing effect on a firm's overall agency costs through providing alternative benefits for the firm and its shareholders.

Overall, the incorporation of blockholder heterogeneity allows for more differentiated conclusions relative to blockholder homogeneity. The validity of the results on blockholder monitoring should be further enhanced when incorporating blockholder interrelationships.

6.3.4 Analysis under the Assumption of Blockholder Interrelationships

The following sections present the results of the final, third stage of the regression analysis which accounts for blockholder interrelationship and aims to investigate if blockholder interrelationships affect agency costs and firm value as well as the ownership size effect of the four blockholder types on agency costs and firm value.

6.3.4.1 Impact on Managerial Agency Costs

The subsequent sections provide the results of specifications regressing managerial agency costs on the ownership of a second blockholder as well as on the two proxies for a heterogenous ownership structure.

Ownership of a Second Blockholder

Table 28 depicts the pooled-OLS results of regressions of managerial agency costs on the blockholder types' ownership, the ownership of the second largest blockholder as well as on interaction terms comprising both variables.[2180]

Specification 3.1.1 focuses on the ownership size of the second largest blockholder *[bh2_cont]* independent of its type in order to investigate if it has an effect on the relationship

[2180] While the regressions include the same set of control variables and industry and time fixed effects as in specification 2.1.3, they are not depicted here. Please note that their signs, magnitude and significance levels remain largely unaffected by the inclusion of the second largest blockholder's ownership. The regression specifications are depicted in appendix 7.

between the largest blockholder type's ownership and managerial agency costs. With regard to this effect, $H2.1_a$ hypothesizes that the larger the ownership size of the second largest blockholder, the stronger the negative ownership size effect on a firm's managerial agency costs. Consistent with this hypothesis, the interaction of *[bh2_cont]* and the ownership of private equity firms and family blockholders, respectively, exhibit a significantly negative effect on managerial agency costs, suggesting that the effect of the ownership of these blockholder types on managerial agency costs is indeed stronger for higher levels of *[bh2_cont]*.

Concerning private equity firms, their ownership size effect on managerial agency costs is insignificant and positive in the absence of a second blockholder. The interaction of *[bh1_pe_cont]* and *[bh2_cont]*, however, illustrates that the ownership size effect of private equity firms changes sign and is significantly (at the 10% significance level) negative – that is, the larger the ownership size of the second largest blockholder, the stronger the negative ownership size effect of private equity firms on managerial agency costs. This stronger negative ownership size effect is in line with the expectation and therefore consistent with $H2.1_a$.

With regard to family blockholders, the coefficient of *[bh1_fam_cont]* suggests that the ownership of a family blockholder does not significantly reduce managerial agency costs if the ownership of the second largest blockholder is zero. However, the interaction term shows that the effect of the family's ownership on managerial agency costs is greater (by the amount of -1.9728) for each one unit increase in *[bh2_cont]*.[2181] Similar to the effect of private equity ownership, the ownership size effect of families for a larger ownership size of the second largest blockholder provides support for $H2.1_a$.

In terms of standardized coefficients, the effect of a one standard deviation increase in the family's ownership on managerial agency costs increases from -0.0396 standard deviation in case of zero ownership of the second largest blockholder to -0.0806 standard deviation when accounting for the ownership of the second largest blockholder.[2182] The greater effect of family ownership on managerial agency costs for higher levels of *[bh2_cont]* is also illustrated in figure 27 (appendix 14). In contrast, the effect of institutional investor ownership on managerial agency costs is lower for higher levels of *[bh2_cont]*; the interaction term is significantly positive and reduces the (standardized) effect of institutional investors on managerial agency costs from -0.0293 when *[bh2_cont]* is zero to -0.0123 when *[bh2_cont]* is non-zero.[2183] This effect may be explained by the non-linearity of the relationship observed in section 6.3.3.1: the effect of institutional investors on managerial agency costs is found to be stronger for higher levels of institutional ownership. However, higher levels of *[bh2_cont]* most likely result in lower levels of ownership by the institutional investor and thereby reduce the inves-

---

2181 For details on the interpretation of these interactions, see Stock/Watson (2012): 324.

2182 Note that when using interaction terms, standardized (beta) regression coefficients cannot be used. Therefore, all variables that are part of the interaction term have been standardized in advance. See also Aiken/West (1991): 28-48 and Kohler/Kreuter (2005): 197.

2183 See also figure 28 in appendix 14.

Table 28
This table presents the stage 3 pooled-OLS results of managerial agency costs as proxied by *[opex_sales]* on the ownership and type of a second blockholder (specification 3.1.1 & 3.1.2). Although not reported, the regressions include control variables as well as industry and year fixed effects; standard errors are clustered by firm. T-statistics are reported in parentheses. In case of a directional hypothesis, one-sided p-Values are calculated. *, **, and *** indicates statistical significance at the 10%, 5%, and 1% level, respectively.

	(3.1.1)	(3.1.2)
bh1_pe_cont*bh2_cont	**-1.0324***	
	(-1.38)	
bh1_fam_cont*bh2_cont	**-1.9728*****	
	(-3.55)	
bh1_si_cont*bh2_cont	**-0.0668**	
	(-0.12)	
bh1_insti_cont*bh2_cont	**2.3114*****	
	(2.84)	
bh1_pe_cont*bh2_pe_cont		**1.6136**
		(1.64)
bh1_fam_cont*bh2_fam_cont		**1.0449**
		(1.25)
bh1_si_cont*bh2_si_cont		**1.0647****
		(1.78)
bh1_insti_cont*bh2_insti_cont		**1.0493**
		(0.70)
bh2_cont	0.2983*	
	(1.39)	
bh2_pe_cont		-0.4620
		(-1.13)
bh2_fam_cont		-0.6015**
		(-2.25)
bh2_si_cont		-0.0823
		(-0.33)
bh2_insti_cont		0.1760
		(0.73)
bh1_pe_cont	0.1138	0.0537
	(1.19)	(0.69)
bh1_fam_cont	-0.0028	-0.1397**
	(-0.04)	(-2.03)
bh1_si_cont	-0.0615	-0.0791*
	(-0.97)	(-1.36)
bh1_insti_cont	-0.6370***	-0.4492***
	(-6.37)	(-2.68)
Constant	1.0303***	1.0674***
	(12.33)	(12.80)
Control variables	Yes	Yes
Industry dummies	Yes	Yes
Year dummies	Yes	Yes
Adjusted R^2	0.2157	0.2094
Number of obs.	2,971	2,971
Firms	473	473

Table 28: Regression results of managerial agency costs on the ownership of a second blockholder

tor's effect on managerial agency costs. To sum up, the interaction of *[bh2_cont]* and the ownership of private equity firms and families provide some support for $H2.1_a$.[2184]

The presence of another blockholder may also result in collusion if the two blockholders have similar interests and these interests differ from those of the remaining shareholders. Since a collusion of blockholders may result in less effective monitoring, $H2.1_b$ expects that if both blockholders are a family or a strategic investor, then the larger the ownership size of the sec-

[2184] The importance of incorporating the ownership of the second blockholder also becomes evident based on the adjusted R^2, which increases from 20.28% in specification 2.1.3 to 21.57% in specification 3.1.1.

ond largest blockholder, the stronger the positive ownership size effect on a firm's managerial agency costs. In order to investigate this hypothesis, specification 3.1.2 interacts the blockholder type's ownership with the ownership of the second largest blockholder, given it is of the same type as the largest blockholder. The results show that the ownership of both strategic investors and families significantly decreases managerial agency costs when the ownership of the second largest blockholder (which is of the same type) is zero. However, the interaction terms show that the effect of both blockholders' ownership on managerial agency costs changes sign; in particular, both blockholders' ownership increases managerial agency costs for higher ownership of the second largest blockholder (given it is of the same type). This effect is significant (at the 5% level) for strategic investors. Apparently, the monitoring of families and especially strategic investors is less effective when there is a second blockholder of the same type. Consistent with $H2.1_b$, this may suggest that the largest and second largest blockholders collude and allow management to realize some private benefits in order to generate private benefits themselves.[2185] If this is the case, the self dealing should also be reflected in greater principal-principal agency costs which is investigated in section 6.3.4.3.

Heterogenous Ownership Structure

Table 29 presents the pooled-OLS results of regressions of managerial agency costs on two measures of a heterogenous ownership structure[2186] which are expected to lower managerial agency costs ($H2.1_c$).

Consistent with $H2.1_c$, specification 3.1.3 reports a negative coefficient of *[ln_bh_count]*. However, its effect on managerial agency costs is not significantly smaller than zero. In contrast, specification 3.1.4 delivers a negative and significant (at the 10% level) coefficient of *[ln_bhtypes_count]*. In particular, the coefficient shows that a 10% increase in *[ln_bhtypes_count]* decreases managerial agency costs by 0.0035 units. Overall, the results provide support for $H2.1_c$; rather than negatively affecting the feasibility of monitoring and incentive to engage in managerial monitoring, a heterogenous ownership structure seems to increase the monitoring effectiveness by enabling blockholders to benefit from complementarities and facilitating mutual monitoring among blockholders.[2187]

At least with regard to managerial agency costs, *[ln_bhtypes_count]* seems to be a more efficient measure of the complementarities and mutual monitoring resulting from the presence of multiple blockholder types. Furthermore, the results suggest that if a more heterogenous ownership structure results in greater blockholder-blockholder agency conflicts, these do not materialize in less effective monitoring of firm management. Finally, since *[ln_bhtypes_count]* is significant when controlling for *[bh1_cont]*, the heterogeneity of a firm's ownership structure

2185 Please note that a similar effect can be observed for private equity firms: The interaction coefficient is also significant based on the one-sided p-Value. However, since no directional hypothesis on these investors is formulated, the variable is not indicated as being significant.

2186 The regressions are based on specification 2.1.1 and therefore also comprise the largest blockholder's ownership as well as the same set of control variables and industry and time fixed effects. Since the incorporation of the variables measuring a heterogenous ownership structure do not alter the coefficients of the control variables qualitatively, they are not examined at this stage.

2187 This result thus also confirms the evidence on the effect of *[bh2_cont]* found in specification 3.1.1 above.

Table 29
This table presents the stage 3 pooled-OLS results of managerial agency costs as proxied by *[opex_sales]* on the proxies of a heterogenous ownership structure (specification 3.1.3 & 3.1.4). The regressions include industry and year fixed effects; standard errors are clustered by firm. T-statistics are reported in parentheses. In case of a directional hypothesis, one-sided p-Values are calculated. *, **, and *** indicates statistical significance at the 10%, 5%, and 1% level, respectively.

	(3.1.3)	(3.1.4)
ln_bh_count	**-0.0226**	
	(-1.05)	
ln_bhtypes_count		**-0.0346***
		(-1.42)
bh1_cont	-0.0921*	-0.0888*
	(-1.62)	(-1.59)
age	0.0016***	0.0016***
	(2.39)	(2.37)
ln_assets	-0.0525***	-0.0516***
	(-3.36)	(-3.29)
pfd	0.0156	0.0115
	(0.29)	(0.21)
liq	-0.1402***	-0.1416***
	(-3.15)	(-3.19)
insd_own	0.0638	0.0670
	(0.66)	(0.69)
debt	0.1649**	0.1636**
	(1.95)	(1.93)
codet_third	0.0203	0.0166
	(0.50)	(0.41)
codet_par	-0.0379	-0.0438
	(-0.62)	(-0.72)
bank	-0.0423*	-0.0364
	(-1.38)	(-1.17)
insolv	0.1509***	0.1531***
	(2.78)	(2.81)
takeover	0.0202	0.0197
	(0.23)	(0.23)
segm_chng	-0.0573	-0.0588
	(-0.78)	(-0.79)
govt	0.0327	0.0383
	(0.57)	(0.67)
Constant	0.9807***	0.9780***
	(13.08)	(13.23)
Industry dummies	Yes	Yes
Year dummies	Yes	Yes
Adjusted R^2	0.1928	0.1946
Number of obs.	2,899	2,895
Firms	485	485

Table 29: Regression results of managerial agency costs on proxies of a heterogenous ownership structure

affects managerial agency costs independently and beyond the influence of the largest blockholder.[2188]

6.3.4.2 Impact on Agency Costs of Debt

The following sections present the results of specifications regressing agency costs of debt on the ownership of a second blockholder and the proxies for a heterogenous ownership structure.

[2188] The largest blockholder's ownership is also found to significantly decrease managerial agency costs.

Ownership of a Second Blockholder

Table 30 depicts the pooled-OLS results of regressions of agency costs of debt on the blockholder types' ownership, the ownership of the second largest blockholder as well as on interaction terms comprising both variables.[2189]

The theoretical argumentation in section 5.2.4.2 states that the ownership of the second largest blockholder should affect the ownership size effect on agency costs of debt across all blockholder types. However, the effect should be strongest for institutional investors since they are expected to have the greatest incentive to transfer wealth from debtholders (H2.2_a). The results of section 6.3.3.2 already indicate that institutional investors, being aware of their incentive to exploit debtholders, seem to proactively signal the absence of shareholder-debtholder agency conflicts rather than to increase the likelihood of shareholder-debtholder agency conflicts. In line with this finding, the coefficient of *[bh1_insti_cont]* in specification 3.2.1 suggests that institutional investor ownership is associated with significantly lower agency costs of debt if the ownership of a second blockholder is zero. Nevertheless, *[bh2_cont]* still has an effect on this relationship: the interaction term illustrates that the higher *[bh2_cont]*, the greater the decrease in agency costs of debt associated with institutional investor ownership. In terms of the standardized effect, the ownership of the second largest blockholder increases the largest blockholder's effect on *[discr_assets]* from -0.0085 to -0.0147. This result therefore provides support for H2.2_a.

The ownership of the second largest blockholder also affects the relationship between family ownership and agency costs of debt. The results show that the ownership of families significantly increases a firm's discretionary assets in the absence of a second blockholder. However, the interaction term shows that the effect of family ownership on agency costs of debt changes sign; in particular, family ownership decreases agency costs of debt for higher ownership levels of the second largest blockholder. These results suggest that in the absence of a second blockholder with sufficient power to supervise the family's monitoring, families may use discretionary assets to create opportunities for transfers of wealth from debtholders. With higher ownership of the second largest blockholder, the costs from a transfer of wealth increase and the family reduces its investments in discretionary assets. These results are consistent with the findings in section 6.3.3.2 which also point to family entrenchment and a transfer of wealth for higher levels of family ownership.

The family blockholder's discretion and hence also its entrenchment should increase if another member of the family constitutes the second largest blockholder. In line with this, H2.2_b presumes that if both blockholders are of the same type, then for higher levels of ownership of the second largest blockholder, the ownership size effect on a firm's agency costs of debt becomes stronger. Specification 3.2.2 investigates this hypothesis for the four blockholder types and interacts the blockholder types' ownership with the ownership of the second largest blockholder, given it is of the same type as the largest blockholder.

2189 While the regressions include the same set of control variables and industry and time fixed effects as in specification 2.2.3, they are not depicted here. Please note that their signs, magnitude, and significance levels remain largely unaffected by the inclusion of the second largest blockholder's ownership. The regression specifications are depicted in appendix 7.

Table 30
This table presents the stage 3 pooled-OLS results of agency costs of debt as proxied by *[discr_assets]* on the ownership and type of a second blockholder (specification 3.2.1 & 3.2.2). Although not reported, the regressions include control variables as well as industry and year fixed effects; standard errors are clustered by firm. T-statistics are reported in parentheses. In case of a directional hypothesis, one-sided p-Values are calculated. *, **, and *** indicates statistical significance at the 10%, 5%, and 1% level, respectively.

	(3.2.1)	(3.2.2)
bh1_pe_cont*bh2_cont	**-0.1003**	
	(-0.35)	
bh1_fam_cont*bh2_cont	**-0.5110*** **	
	(-2.61)	
bh1_si_cont*bh2_cont	**-0.1731**	
	(-1.06)	
bh1_insti_cont*bh2_cont	**-0.8406*** **	
	(-3.01)	
bh1_pe_cont*bh2_pe_cont		**0.3730**
		(1.47)
bh1_fam_cont*bh2_fam_cont		**-0.2238**
		(-0.71)
bh1_si_cont*bh2_si_cont		**0.0216**
		(0.10)
bh1_insti_cont*bh2_insti_cont		**-1.2342*** **
		(-5.13)
bh2_cont	0.0021	
	(0.03)	
bh2_pe_cont		0.1208*
		(1.63)
bh2_fam_cont		-0.1365**
		(-1.89)
bh2_si_cont		-0.2060***
		(-2.93)
bh2_insti_cont		0.0413
		(0.55)
bh1_pe_cont	0.0023	-0.0094
	(0.05)	(-0.24)
bh1_fam_cont	0.0399**	0.0087
	(1.74)	(0.44)
bh1_si_cont	-0.0124	-0.0206
	(-0.58)	(-1.06)
bh1_insti_cont	-0.0519**	-0.0807**
	(-1.84)	(-2.22)
Constant	0.9914***	0.9971***
	(44.37)	(45.88)
Control variables	Yes	Yes
Industry dummies	Yes	Yes
Year dummies	Yes	Yes
Adjusted R^2	0.5194	0.5243
Number of obs.	2,907	2,907
Firms	471	471

Table 30: Regression results of agency costs of debt on the ownership of a second blockholder

The regression result delivers a significant interaction term only for institutional blockholders. The negative sign suggests that the decrease in *[discr_assets]* associated with higher ownership of the institutional investor is stronger if the second largest blockholder is an institutional investor as well. Hence, an institutional investor's incentive to signal an absence of shareholder-debtholder agency costs is even stronger for higher ownership levels of another institutional blockholder.[2190] The insignificance of the interaction term including the ownership of

[2190] The standardized effect of institutional investor ownership is doubled for higher ownership of the second largest blockholder, provided it is also an institutional investor.

family blockholders does not provide further support for family entrenchment. Overall, the insignificant interactions are in line with the insignificant effects of the largest blockholder types observed in specification 2.2.3.

Heterogenous Ownership Structure

In order to analyze the impact of heterogenous ownership structures on agency costs of debt, table 31 presents the pooled-OLS results of agency costs of debt regressed on two measures of a heterogenous ownership structure[2191] which are expected to lower agency costs of debt ($H2.2_c$).

In line with $H2.2_c$, specification 3.2.3 reports a negative coefficient of *[ln_bh_count]* which is significantly smaller than zero at a 5% significance level. The coefficient suggests that a 10% increase in *[ln_bh_count]* decreases *[discr_assets]* by 0.0012 units and thus the blockholders' potential to engage in wealth transfer strategies. While the coefficient of *[ln_bhtypes_count]* in specification 3.2.4 is negative as well, it does not significantly lower the amount of discre-

Table 31
This table presents the stage 3 pooled-OLS results of agency costs of debt as proxied by *[discr_assets]* on the proxies of a heterogenous ownership structure (specification 3.2.3 & 3.2.4). The regressions include industry and year fixed effects; standard errors are clustered by firm. T-statistics are reported in parentheses. In case of a directional hypothesis, one-sided p-Values are calculated. *, **, and *** indicates statistical significance at the 10%, 5%, and 1% level, respectively.

	(3.2.3)	(3.2.4)
ln_bh_count	**-0.0117****	
	(-1.84)	
ln_bhtypes_count		**-0.0024**
		(-0.35)
bh1_cont	-0.0261*	-0.0173
	(1.54)	(-1.05)
capex	-2.0497***	-2.0511***
	(-14.41)	(-14.29)
age	-0.0007***	-0.0007***
	(-3.36)	(-3.31)
ln_assets	0.0051	0.0053
	(1.13)	(1.18)
pfd	-0.0241	-0.0249
	(-1.13)	(-1.16)
liq	0.0376***	0.0383***
	(3.30)	(3.36)
insd_own	0.0029	-0.0025
	(0.12)	(-0.10)
debt	-0.2414***	-0.2398***
	(-8.30)	(-8.21)
codet_third	-0.0569***	-0.0576***
	(-4.33)	(-4.38)
codet_par	-0.0821***	-0.0827***
	(-4.11)	(-4.12)
bank	0.0137*	0.0100
	(1.56)	(1.14)
insolv	0.0094	0.0081
	(0.50)	(0.43)
takeover	-0.0281	-0.0288
	(-0.91)	(-0.94)

[2191] The regressions are based on specification 2.2.1 and therefore comprise the largest blockholder's ownership and the same set of control variables and industry and time fixed effects. Since their coefficients are not affected qualitatively, they are not examined at this stage.

Table 31 cont'd

	(3.2.3)	(3.2.4)
segm_chng	0.0018	0.0016
	(0.10)	(0.09)
govt	-0.0161	-0.0183
	(-1.04)	(-1.19)
Constant	1.0177***	1.0072***
	(48.93)	(48.81)
Industry dummies	Yes	Yes
Year dummies	Yes	Yes
Adjusted R^2	0.5082	0.5063
Number of obs.	2,843	2,839
Firms	483	483

Table 31: Regression results of agency costs of debt on proxies of a heterogenous ownership structure

tionary assets. Nevertheless, the results are generally consistent with a negative association between a heterogenous ownership structure and the potential to engage in wealth transfer strategies hypothesized in H2.2$_c$.[2192]

The decreasing effect of more heterogenous ownership structures on *[discr_assets]* may stem from a greater probability that there either is a blockholder (1) whose self-interest is in line with the interests of the debtholders or (2) whose exposure to the costs resulting from an exploitation of debtholders is sufficiently high to provide it with an incentive to limit such an exploitation through a supervision of the other blockholder(s). Apparently, this probability is higher when accounting for the number of blockholders rather than for the number of blockholder types. This suggests that concerning agency costs of debt, also blockholders of the same type may differ in terms of incentives or exposure to the costs resulting from a transfer of value and hence limit value transfers also via a supervision of blockholder(s) of the same type. Similar to the findings regarding managerial agency costs, the proxies for a heterogenous ownership structure are significant when controlling for the ownership of the largest blockholder. This illustrates that *[ln_bh_count]* affects agency costs of debt independently and beyond the influence of the largest blockholder.[2193]

6.3.4.3 Impact on Principal-Principal Agency Costs

The following sections present the results of specifications regressing principal-principal agency costs on the ownership of a second blockholder, blockholder incontestability, and the proxies for a heterogenous ownership structure.

Ownership of a Second Blockholder

Table 32 depicts the pooled-OLS results of regressions of principal-principal agency costs on the blockholder types' ownership, the ownership of the second largest blockholder as well as on interaction terms comprising both variables.[2194]

2192 This result thus also confirms the evidence on the effect of *[bh2_cont]* found in specification 3.2.1 above.

2193 The largest blockholder's ownership is also found to significantly decrease agency costs of debt.

2194 While the regressions include the same set of control variables and industry and time fixed effects as in specification 2.3.3, they are not depicted here. Please note that their signs, magnitude, and significance levels remain largely unaffected by the inclusion of the second largest blockholder's ownership. The regression specifications are depicted in appendix 7.

In order to investigate if it has an effect on the relationship between the largest blockholder type's ownership and principal-principal agency costs, specification 3.3.1 focuses on the ownership of the second largest blockholder *[bh2_cont]*. The theoretical argumentation in section 5.2.4.3 states that the ownership of the second largest blockholder is expected to result in reduced self-dealing of the largest blockholder. Since the probability of self-dealing is assumed to be strongest for strategic investors and families, the second largest blockholder's ownership should most likely have an effect on the relationship between the largest blockholder type's ownership and principal-principal agency costs if the largest blockholder is a family or strategic investor. In particular, $H2.3_a$ states that if the largest blockholder is either a family or strategic investor, then the larger the ownership size of the second largest blockholder, the stronger the negative ownership size effect on a firm's principal-principal agency costs.[2195]

However, the results depicted in column two do not support this hypothesis. The interaction terms between the largest blockholder types' ownership and *[bh2_cont]* are all insignificant. Hence, the ownership of the second largest blockholder does not significantly affect the relationship between the largest blockholders' ownership and principal-principal agency costs. A possible explanation for the insignificance of *[bh2_cont]* may be the non-negative effect of the largest blockholder types' ownership on dividend payouts if *[bh2_cont]* is zero. In fact, the ownership of institutional investors significantly reduces principal-principal agency costs

Table 32

This table presents the stage 3 pooled-OLS results of principal-principal agency costs as proxied by *[div_payout]* on the ownership and type of a second blockholder (specification 3.3.1 & 3.3.2). Although not reported, the regressions include control variables as well as industry and year fixed effects; standard errors are clustered by firm. T-statistics are reported in parentheses. In case of a directional hypothesis, one-sided p-Values are calculated. *, **, and *** indicates statistical significance at the 10%, 5%, and 1% level, respectively.

	(3.3.1)	**(3.3.2)**
bh1_pe_cont*bh2_cont	**0.0166** (1.46)	
bh1_fam_cont*bh2_cont	**-0.0047** (-0.77)	
bh1_si_cont*bh2_cont	**-0.0069** (-1.24)	
bh1_insti_cont*bh2_cont	**-0.0049** (-0.21)	
bh1_pe_cont*bh2_pe_cont		**0.0216**** (2.29)
bh1_fam_cont*bh2_fam_cont		**0.0081** (0.83)
bh1_si_cont*bh2_si_cont		**-0.0150***** (-2.33)
bh1_insti_cont*bh2_insti_cont		**0.0924***** (4.81)
bh2_cont	-0.0002 (-0.08)	
bh2_pe_cont		-0.0003 (-0.10)
bh2_fam_cont		-0.0028 (-1.02)

2195 See section 5.2.4.3.

Table 32 cont'd

	(3.3.1)	(3.3.2)
bh2_si_cont		0.0032
		(1.27)
bh2_insti_cont		-0.0002
		(-0.12)
bh1_pe_cont	0.0022	0.0039***
	(1.16)	(2.71)
bh1_fam_cont	0.0001	-0.0003
	(0.14)	(-0.46)
bh1_si_cont	0.0003	0.0001
	(0.37)	(0.17)
bh1_insti_cont	0.0081**	0.0040
	(1.73)	(1.16)
Constant	0.0041***	0.0043
	(4.93)	(5.16)
Control variables	Yes	Yes
Industry dummies	Yes	Yes
Year dummies	Yes	Yes
Adjusted R^2	0.3127	0.3190
Number of obs.	2,226	2,226
Firms	425	425

Table 32: Regression results of principal-principal agency costs on the ownership of a second blockholder

if *[bh2_cont]* is zero. Since the largest blockholder does not seem to generate private benefits, the second largest blockholder may lack the incentive to engage in the costly supervision of the respective largest blockholder type's monitoring. The insignificant interaction also does not suggest blockholder-blockholder agency conflicts arising as a result of the second blockholder's presence.

According to $H2.3_b$, if both blockholders are of the same type, then for higher levels of ownership of the second largest blockholder, the ownership size effect on a firm's principal-principal agency costs should become stronger. Consistent with $H2.3_b$, the ownership of the second largest blockholder (given it is of the same type as the largest blockholder) increases the association between the ownership of private equity, strategic and institutional investors and a firm's principal-principal agency costs. With regard to private equity and institutional investors, the higher the ownership of the second largest blockholder (given it is of the same type as the respective largest blockholder), the stronger the reduction in principal-principal agency costs resulting from increases in the largest blockholder types' ownership. These results confirm the findings of stage 2 and indicate that private equity and institutional investors are associated with lower principal-principal agency costs.[2196] With regard to strategic investors, their positive ownership size effect on principal-principal agency costs is stronger for higher ownership of the second largest blockholder, given it is also a strategic investor; in this case, both blockholders seem to collude and pursue private benefits to the detriment of the remaining shareholders. The pursuance of private benefits by a coalition of strategic investors is also consistent with their less effective monitoring of management observed in specification 3.1.2.[2197]

[2196] See section 6.3.3.3.

[2197] See section 6.3.4.1.

Blockholder Incontestability

If a collusion is motivated by insufficient power of the largest blockholder, a generation of private benefits should also be observable if the largest blockholder individually has sufficient power, i.e. if it is incontestable. Since differential interests are most likely for strategic investors and families, $H2.3_d$ states that if the largest blockholder is a family or strategic investor, then for higher incontestability of the largest blockholder, the positive ownership size effect on a firm's principal-principal agency costs is stronger. In contrast, if the largest blockholder is a private equity or institutional investor, then the relation between the incontestability of the largest blockholder and the ownership size effect on a firm's principal-principal agency costs is expected to be non-positive ($H2.3_e$). To investigate these hypotheses, specifications 3.3.3-3.3.6 interact the four incontestability variables with the blockholder types' ownership, respectively. The results are depicted in table 33.[2198]

As can be seen, the interaction between the incontestability variables and family (strategic investor) ownership has a negative coefficient for all (three) incontestability variables. Moreover, for both families and strategic investors, two (negative) interaction terms are significant (at the 10% level). This illustrates that if the largest blockholder is a family or strategic inves-

Table 33

This table presents the stage 3 pooled-OLS results of principal-principal agency costs as proxied by *[div_payout]* on four incontestability variables interacted with the blockholder identities (specification 3.3.3-3.3.6). Although not reported, the regressions include control variables as well as industry and year fixed effects; standard errors are clustered by firm. T-statistics are reported in parentheses. In case of a directional hypothesis, one-sided p-Values are calculated. *, **, and *** indicates statistical significance at the 10%, 5%, and 1% level, respectively.

	bh1/bh2	**bh1/bh2_bh3**	**diff_bh12345**	**bh1_majority**
bh1_pe_cont*incont	**0.0001**	**0.0002**	**-0.0097*** **	**-0.0028**
	(0.24)	**(0.41)**	**(-2.37)**	**(-1.00)**
bh1_fam_cont*incont	**-0.0004***	**-0.0004***	**-0.0012**	**-0.0019**
	(-1.32)	**(-1.39)**	**(-0.48)**	**(-0.98)**
bh1_si_cont*incont	**-0.0004***	**-0.0004***	**0.0010**	**-0.0003**
	(-1.52)	**(-1.62)**	**(0.40)**	**(-0.18)**
bh1_insti_cont*incont	**0.0019*** **	**0.0021*** **	**-0.0064**	**0.0071**
	(4.41)	**(3.37)**	**(-0.78)**	**(1.26)**
incont	0.0003**	0.0004**	0.0029**	0.0013
	(1.86)	(1.94)	(1.72)	(1.26)
bh1_pe_cont	0.0032**	0.0032**	0.0064***	0.0051***
	(1.86)	(1.87)	(3.15)	(2.63)
bh1_fam_cont	-0.0003	-0.0004	-0.0011	-0.0002
	(-0.31)	(-0.51)	(-1.05)	(-0.26)
bh1_si_cont	0.0003	0.0003	-0.0023**	-0.0011
	(0.46)	(0.36)	(-2.05)	(-1.26)
bh1_insti_cont	0.0009	0.0019	0.0081**	0.0045*
	(0.32)	(0.62)	(1.94)	(1.38)
Constant	0.0041***	0.0037***	0.0037***	0.0036***
	(4.78)	(4.99)	(4.98)	(4.86)
Control variables	Yes	Yes	Yes	Yes
Industry dummies	Yes	Yes	Yes	Yes
Year dummies	Yes	Yes	Yes	Yes
Adjusted R^2	0.3351	0.3340	0.3216	0.3164
Number of obs.	2,109	2,109	2,226	2,226
Firms	421	421	425	425

Table 33: Regression results of principal-principal agency costs on the largest blockholder types' incontestability

2198 While the regressions include the same set of control variables and industry and time fixed effects as in specification 2.3.3, they are not depicted here. Their coefficients are not altered qualitatively.

tor, then for higher incontestability of both blockholder types, their ownership is associated with a stronger increase in their portfolio firm's principal-principal costs.[2199] This is consistent with H2.3$_d$ and suggests that both families and strategic investors exploit higher levels of discretion for the generation of private benefits to the detriment of the remaining shareholders.[2200]

In contrast, the interactions between the incontestability variables and private equity and institutional investors point to a non-positive ownership size effect on a firm's principal-principal agency costs. In particular, the results based on two incontestability variables show that for higher incontestability of institutional investors, their ownership is associated with significantly higher dividend payouts and thus a greater decrease in principal-principal agency costs. With regard to private equity firms, one of the interaction terms is significantly negative, which is contrary to the expectation and illustrates that for greater incontestability, a private equity firm's ownership is associated with a greater increase in principal-principal agency costs. However, the remaining interactions between the incontestability variables and private equity firm ownership are insignificant. Thus, the evidence with regard to institutional and private equity investors is consistent with H2.3$_e$.[2201]

Heterogenous Ownership Structure

In order to analyze the impact of heterogenous ownership structures on principal-principal agency costs, table 34 presents the pooled-OLS results of regressions of principal-principal agency costs on two proxies for a heterogenous ownership structure.[2202]

As argued in section 5.2.4.3, a more heterogenous ownership structure can either decrease principal-principal agency costs through a mitigation of minority shareholder-blockholder conflicts or increase principal-principal agency costs if the mitigation of the minority shareholder-blockholder conflict is outweighed by an emergence of blockholder-blockholder conflicts. Therefore, H2.3$_c$ is formulated non-directionally and states that the heterogeneity of a firm's ownership structure has an effect on its principal-principal agency costs.[2203]

Specification 3.3.7 in table 34 delivers a significant (at the 10% level) and positive coefficient of *[ln_bh_count]*. Hence, a higher number of blockholders is associated with significantly higher dividend payments. Consistent with this effect, also specification 3.3.8 reports a signif-

---

[2199] This may be of particular importance for family firms, since the descriptive analysis in section 6.2.3.3 suggested the highest incontestability in terms of *[bh1/bh2]* and *[bh1/bh2_bh3]* for family blockholders.

[2200] In line with these findings, Jara-Bertin et al. (2008): 152f find the contestability of the family blockholder to be significant for the reduction of the risk of expropriation of the remaining shareholders by family blockholders. Also Maury/Pajuste (2005): 1827f find that the contestability of control is more important for family than for non-family firms. Although they do not differentiate between blockholder types, Attig et al. (2009): 410 find that a lower contestability of the largest blockholder translates into a negative valuation.

[2201] In unreported regressions, a firm's dividend payout ratio is regressed on the incontestability variables without accounting for blockholder heterogeneity. The results show that incontestability in general has a non-negative effect on principal-principal agency costs. This illustrates the importance of accounting for blockholder heterogeneity when aiming at a more differentiated conclusion.

[2202] The regressions are based on specification 2.3.1 and therefore comprise the largest blockholder's ownership and the same set of control variables and industry and time fixed effects. Since their coefficients are not affected qualitatively, they are not examined at this stage.

[2203] See section 5.2.4.3.

icant (at the 5% level) and positive coefficient of *[ln_bhtypes_count]* which illustrates that also a higher number of different blockholder types is associated with significantly higher dividend payments. Since both heterogeneity measures are significant, $H2.3_c$ can be supported. Moreover, the positive effect of both heterogeneity variables on the dividend payout ratio points to lower principal-principal agency costs for increasing heterogeneity of a firm's blockholders. This is in line with the presumption that a more heterogenous ownership structure reduces the blockholders' power and incentive to generate private benefits at the expense of minority shareholders and thereby avoids principal-principal agency costs. At the same time, the reduction in principal-principal agency costs stemming from lower conflicts between minority shareholders and blockholders is not outweighed by greater blockholder-blockholder conflicts, whose likelihood increases with a greater number of blockholders.

To recapitulate, the results illustrate that heterogenous ownership structures mitigate conflicts between minority shareholders and the blockholder(s) while avoiding blockholder-blockholder agency conflicts.[2204] Similar to the previous findings, the heterogeneity variables are significant when controlling for the ownership of the largest blockholder. This illustrates that a heterogenous ownership structure reduces the likelihood of principal-principal agency costs independently and beyond the influence of the largest blockholder.

Table 34

This table presents the stage 3 pooled-OLS results of principal-principal agency costs as proxied by *[div_payout]* on the proxies of a heterogenous ownership structure (specification 3.3.7 & 3.3.8). The regressions include industry and year fixed effects; standard errors are clustered by firm. T-statistics are reported in parentheses. In case of a directional hypothesis, one-sided p-Values are calculated. *, **, and *** indicates statistical significance at the 10%, 5%, and 1% level, respectively.

	(3.3.7)	(3.3.8)
ln_bh_count	**0.0004***	
	(1.88)	
ln_bhtypes_count		**0.0006****
		(2.19)
bh1_cont	0.0015**	0.0014**
	(2.25)	(2.19)
growth	-0.0006***	-0.0006***
	(-3.00)	(-2.96)
prof	0.0063***	0.0062***
	(4.75)	(4.79)
div_prevy	0.0032***	0.0032***
	(11.60)	(11.58)
age	0.0000**	0.0000**
	(2.25)	(2.20)
ln_assets	-0.0007***	-0.0007***
	(-4.29)	(-4.30)
pfd	0.0000	0.0001
	(-0.02)	(0.09)
liq	-0.0007	-0.0007
	(-1.29)	(-1.32)
insd_own	-0.0001	-0.0001
	(-0.08)	(-0.13)

2204 As high levels of ownership are necessary to change a firm's dividend policy, the higher dividend payments imply that multiple blockholders cooperate in order to increase the payout to shareholders.

Table 34 cont'd

	(3.3.7)	(3.3.8)
debt	-0.0027***	-0.0027***
	(-3.08)	(-3.13)
codet_third	0.0003	0.0003
	(0.76)	(0.77)
codet_par	-0.0001	-0.0001
	(-0.23)	(-0.20)
bank	-0.0001	-0.0002
	(-0.42)	(-0.74)
insolv	0.0003	0.0003
	(0.57)	(0.54)
insolv	0.0003	0.0003
	(0.57)	(0.54)
takeover	0.0000	0.0000
	(-0.04)	(-0.04)
segm_chng	-0.0011***	-0.0011**
	(-2.35)	(-2.24)
govt	0.0003	0.0002
	(0.64)	(0.42)
Constant	0.0033***	0.0033***
	(3.81)	(3.98)
Industry dummies	Yes	Yes
Year dummies	Yes	Yes
Adjusted R^2	0.2824	0.2845
Number of obs.	2,111	2,107
Firms	421	421

Table 34: Regression results of principal-principal agency costs on proxies of a heterogenous ownership structure

6.3.4.4 Impact on Firm Value

The following sections present the results of specifications regressing firm value on the ownership of a second blockholder, blockholder incontestability, and the proxies for a heterogenous ownership structure.

Ownership of a Second Blockholder

Table 35 depicts pooled-OLS results of regressions of firm value on the blockholder types' ownership, the second largest blockholder's ownership and on interaction terms comprising both variables.[2205]

The ownership of the second largest blockholder is expected to contribute to a reduction of a firm's overall agency costs. Hence, for higher levels of *[bh2_cont]*, the largest blockholder type's ownership should be associated with a stronger increase in firm value (H2.4_a). Consistent with H2.4_a, specification 3.4.1 shows that the interactions of *[bh2_cont]* and the ownership of private equity firms and families, respectively, exhibit a significantly positive effect on firm value, suggesting that their ownership size effect on firm value is indeed stronger for

2205 While the regressions include the same set of control variables and industry and time fixed effects as in specification 2.4.3, they are not depicted here. Their coefficients are not altered qualitatively. The regression specifications are depicted in appendix 7.

higher levels of *[bh2_cont]*.[2206] The interaction of *[bh2_cont]* and strategic and institutional investor ownership is insignificant. While these results provide only some evidence of $H2.4_a$, they are consistent with the observed effects on the components of a firm's overall agency costs. The results for all three types of agency costs show that the effect of the ownership of strategic investors on the agency costs is unaffected by higher levels of *[bh2_cont]*; this insignificance is reflected in the effect on firm value. With regard to institutional investors, from the shareholder's perspective, higher levels of *[bh2_cont]* unfavorably (favorably) influence the relationship between institutional investor ownership and managerial agency costs (agency costs of debt). Overall, the net effect on firm value should thus be insignificant.[2207] With regard to private equity investors, *[bh2_cont]* has a significant effect on the relationship between private equity ownership and managerial agency costs. This greater reduction in managerial agency costs should also be reflected in the firm's value.[2208] With regard to families, *[bh2_cont]* has a significant effect on the relationship between family ownership and managerial agency costs as well as between family ownership and agency costs of debt which is incorporated into the firm's value.[2209]

Specification 3.4.2 focuses on the effect of the second largest blockholder's ownership, given it is of the same type as the largest blockholder. In this case, $H2.4_b$ presumes that the larger

Table 35

This table presents the stage 3 pooled-OLS results of firm value as proxied by *[tobinq]* on the ownership and type of a second blockholder (specification 3.4.1 & 3.4.2). Although not reported, the regressions include control variables as well as industry and year fixed effects; standard errors are clustered by firm. T-statistics are reported in parentheses. In case of a directional hypothesis, one-sided p-Values are calculated. *, **, and *** indicates statistical significance at the 10%, 5%, and 1% level, respectively.

	(3.4.1)	(3.4.2)
bh1_pe_cont*bh2_cont	**3.5256**** **(2.04)**	
bh1_fam_cont*bh2_cont	**1.8158**** **(1.69)**	
bh1_si_cont*bh2_cont	**0.3615** **(0.43)**	
bh1_insti_cont*bh2_cont	**-0.8390** **(-0.62)**	
bh1_pe_cont*bh2_pe_cont		**5.9316***** **(2.84)**
bh1_fam_cont*bh2_fam_cont		**0.4579** **(0.28)**
bh1_si_cont*bh2_si_cont		**-0.6720** **(-0.67)**
bh1_insti_cont*bh2_insti_cont		**-0.0779** **(-0.05)**
bh2_cont	-0.2119 (-0.61)	

2206 This is consistent with the results of Attig et al. (2009): 409, who find that the control rights of the second largest blockholder are significantly and positively associated with firm value in East Asian firms.

2207 In contrast, Ruiz-Mallorquí/Santana-Martín (2011): 125 find that if the largest blockholder is an institutional investor, increased ownership of a second- and third-largest blockholder is negatively related to Tobin's q. The evidence is based on a sample of 111 Spanish non-financial firms between 1996 and 2009.

2208 The (standardized) effect of private equity investors on firm value increases from 0.0892 when *[bh2_cont]* is zero to 0.1441 when *[bh2_cont]* is not zero.

2209 The impact of *[bh2_cont]* on the effect of family ownership is in line with Jara-Bertin et al. (2008): 147f who state that additional blockholders "play an outstanding role" in family firms as they limit and protect themselves "from the possible excess use of power by the core family shareholders." Also Maury/Pajuste (2005): 1828f find that the size of a second non-family blockholder increases the value of a family firm.

Table 35 cont'd

	(3.4.1)	(3.4.2)
bh2_pe_cont		0.3427
		(0.43)
bh2_fam_cont		-0.1914
		(-0.37)
bh2_si_cont		0.1933
		(0.52)
bh2_insti_cont		0.6837*
		(1.32)
bh1_pe_cont	0.3964*	0.6210***
	(1.48)	(3.25)
bh1_fam_cont	0.1676	0.2990**
	(1.22)	(2.31)
bh1_si_cont	0.2708***	0.2890***
	(3.05)	(3.40)
bh1_insti_cont	0.1393	-0.0157
	(0.87)	(-0.11)
Constant	1.7026***	1.6926***
	(11.82)	(11.90)
Control variables	Yes	Yes
Industry dummies	Yes	Yes
Year dummies	Yes	Yes
Adjusted R^2	0.2217	0.2232
Number of obs.	2,876	2,876
Firms	469	469

Table 35: Regression results of firm value on the ownership of a second blockholder

the ownership size of the second largest blockholder, the stronger the ownership size effect on firm value. The results illustrate that the ownership of families, private equity and strategic investors is associated with a significantly higher firm value, given the ownership of the second blockholder (which is of the same type as the respective largest blockholder) is zero. However, the interaction terms show that the effect of families' and strategic investors' ownership on firm value turns insignificant for higher levels of the second largest blockholder. For these blockholder types, a firm's remaining shareholders do not appreciate the presence of a second blockholder if it is of the same type. This is of particular interest for family firms, since shareholders seem to favorably respond to the presence of another blockholder in general (see specification 3.4.1). The results therefore illustrate that firm's existing or prospective shareholders may fear a collusion of the largest and second largest blockholder if they are of the same type and either a family or strategic investor.[2210]

Concerning strategic investors, the results on managerial agency costs and principal-principal agency costs point to a potential collusion of the two largest blockholders if they are strategic investors. Therefore, one should expect the coefficient of the interaction of the largest and second largest blockholder's ownership to be significantly negative for strategic investors. The fact that this coefficient is insignificant may suggest that shareholders account for additional effects of strategic investors that offset a (possible) increase in a firm's overall agency

[2210] In line with this possible explanation, Maury/Pajuste (2005): 1828f find that the size of a second family blockholder decreases the value of a family firm. Also Jara-Bertin et al. (2008): 153 find that having a family as a second or third largest blockholder when the largest blockholder is also a family negatively impacts firm value. Attig et al. (2008): 736f find the implied cost of equity of both Western European and East Asian firms to increase if the two largest shareholders are families.

costs.[2211] In contrast to families and strategic investors, the ownership of the second largest blockholder (if it is a private equity investor) increases the positive effect of a private equity investor's ownership on firm value. Thus, a firm's shareholders do not expect a collusion if the two largest blockholders are private equity investors.[2212] To recapitulate, the results of specification 3.4.2 are inconsistent with H2.4$_b$.

Blockholder Incontestability

It is expected that a firm's remaining shareholders account for the influence of the largest blockholder type's incontestability on the relationship between the type's ownership and principal-principal agency costs by incorporating the expected agency costs into the firm's value. To determine the effect on firm value, specifications 3.4.3-3.4.6 in table 36 interact the incontestability variables with the blockholder types' ownership, respectively.[2213]

Although greater incontestability of the largest blockholder is found to result in a significantly stronger positive ownership size effect of family and strategic investors on principal-principal agency costs,[2214] the results illustrate that higher agency costs are not incorporated into the

Table 36

This table presents the stage 3 pooled-OLS results of firm value as proxied by *[tobinq]* on four incontestability variables interacted with the blockholder identities (specification 3.4.3-3.4.6). Although not reported, the regressions include control variables as well as industry and year fixed effects; standard errors are clustered by firm. T-statistics are reported in parentheses. In case of a directional hypothesis, one-sided p-Values are calculated. *, **, and *** indicates statistical significance at the 10%, 5%, and 1% level, respectively.

	bh1/bh2	bh1/bh2_bh3	diff_bh12345	bh1_majority
bh1_pe_cont*incont	**-0.0279**	**-0.0365**	**-0.8302**	**-0.7341****
	(-0.71)	**(-0.77)**	**(-1.28)**	**(-1.87)**
bh1_fam_cont*incont	**0.0484****	**0.0411***	**-1.0010*****	**-0.2901**
	(1.77)	**(1.38)**	**(-3.14)**	**(-1.08)**
bh1_si_cont*incont	**-0.0078**	**-0.0158**	**0.0433**	**-0.1957**
	(-0.38)	**(-0.72)**	**(0.16)**	**(-0.93)**
bh1_insti_cont*incont	**-0.0204**	**-0.0230**	**-0.3905**	**-0.3708**
	(-0.61)	**(-0.58)**	**(-1.09)**	**(-1.17)**
incont	0.0046	0.0062	0.2624*	0.1736**
	(0.38)	(0.45)	(1.52)	(1.65)
bh1_pe_cont	0.7690***	0.7732***	0.9822***	1.0943***
	(3.25)	(3.46)	(3.09)	(3.90)
bh1_fam_cont	0.0671	0.1153	0.5598***	0.3624**
	(0.49)	(0.84)	(2.85)	(1.81)
bh1_si_cont	0.2618**	0.2780***	0.1183	0.3001*
	(2.56)	(2.75)	(0.77)	(1.81)
bh1_insti_cont	0.0165	0.0152	0.1277	0.1859
	(0.11)	(0.10)	(0.49)	(0.66)
Constant	1.7221***	1.7186***	1.6631***	1.6805***
	(11.79)	(11.74)	(11.76)	(11.88)
Control variables	Yes	Yes	Yes	Yes
Industry dummies	Yes	Yes	Yes	Yes
Year dummies	Yes	Yes	Yes	Yes
Adjusted R^2	0.2218	0.2204	0.2223	0.2184
Number of obs.	2,709	2,709	2,876	2,876
Firms	464	464	469	469

Table 36: Regression results of firm value on the largest blockholder types' incontestability

[2211] See also section 6.3.3.4.
[2212] This is also suggested by the significant and positive interaction coefficient in specification 3.3.2.
[2213] While the regressions include the same set of control variables and industry and time fixed effects as in specification 2.4.3, they are not depicted here. Their coefficients are not altered qualitatively.
[2214] See section 6.3.4.3.

firm's share price. While the coefficient of the interaction of strategic investor ownership and the respective incontestability variable is negative in three out of four interactions, none of the coefficients is significant. With regard to family blockholders, two interaction terms are significantly associated with higher firm value whereas one interaction term is significantly associated with lower firm value. Hence, also higher incontestability of a family blockholder does not result in a stronger negative ownership size effect of families on firm value. The findings for both strategic investors and families are therefore inconsistent with $H2.4_d$. As argued previously, both shareholder types may provide additional benefits for the firm and its shareholders that offset their increasing effect on principal-principal agency costs for higher levels of incontestability.[2215]

Since private equity and institutional investors should have interests similar to those of the remaining shareholders, the relation between their incontestability and their ownership size effect on firm value should be non-negative.[2216] However, the coefficients of the interaction of institutional and private equity investor ownership and the incontestability variables are negative across all four interactions. Moreover, the interaction of private equity ownership with *[bh1_majority]* is significant at the 5% level. Although only one coefficient is significant, the results are surprising and provide only weak support for $H2.4_e$. Apparently, shareholders seem to be skeptical towards private equity and institutional investor ownership if these blockholder types are highly incontestable. Since (1) private equity ownership in general, (2) private equity ownership interacted with its supervisory board presence, and (3) private equity ownership interacted with the ownership of a second blockholder all have a positive effect on firm value, this skepticism is particularly astonishing for private equity investors.

A final aspect worth mentioning is the effect of *[bh1_majority]*. As can be seen in column five, the ownership of families, private equity and strategic investors has a significant and positive effect on firm value if they (1) are not equipped with the simple majority or (2) possess the simple majority but there is another blockholder which owns a blocking minority.[2217] However, the interaction terms show that the effect of the blockholder types' ownership changes sign; in particular, the blockholder types' ownership decreases firm value in case they possess the simple majority and there is no blockholder with a blocking minority. Although this effect is significant only for private equity investors, the uniform reversion of the relationship still points to the importance of ownership thresholds.[2218]

Heterogenous Ownership Structure

To analyze the impact of heterogenous ownership structures on firm value, table 37 presents the pooled-OLS results of firm value regressed on the proxies for a heterogenous ownership

---

2215 With regard to strategic investors, these benefits may constitute know-how, technologies or expertise. With regard to family firms, the benefits may constitute survivability capital or superior human and social capital.

2216 This is confirmed by a non-positive effect of the two blockholder types' incontestability on their relationship with principal-principal agency costs. See section 6.3.4.3.

2217 These results match those of specification 2.4.3.

2218 This importance has also been suggested by figure 11, which shows that blockholder ownership is highly concentrated around the important control thresholds.

structure.[2219] From the shareholders' perspective, the net effect of heterogenous ownership structures on a firm's overall agency costs should be favorable and hence result in higher firm value.[2220]

Specification 3.4.7 indicates that *[ln_bh_count]* significantly (at the 5% level) increases firm value: a 10% increase in *[ln_bh_count]* results in a 0.0073 unit increase in firm value. A similar effect can be observed for *[ln_bhtypes_count]* which exhibits a significant (at the 5% level) and positive coefficient in specification 3.4.8. Consequently, both measures of heterogenous ownership structures provide support for H2.4$_c$. The results are also in line with the empirical evidence of the previous sections. Since a heterogenous ownership structure is found to reduce all three types of agency costs, rational shareholders account for these reduc-

Table 37

This table presents the stage 3 pooled-OLS results of firm value as proxied by *[tobinq]* on the proxies of a heterogenous ownership structure (specification 3.4.7 & 3.4.8). The regressions include industry and year fixed effects; standard errors are clustered by firm. T-statistics are reported in parentheses. In case of a directional hypothesis, one-sided p-Values are calculated. *, **, and *** indicates statistical significance at the 10%, 5%, and 1% level, respectively.

	(3.4.7)	(3.4.8)
ln_bh_count	**0.0730**** **(2.06)**	
ln_bhtypes_count		**0.0632**** **(1.60)**
bh1_cont	0.3996*** (4.49)	0.3692*** (4.10)
growth	0.2062*** (4.29)	0.2057*** (4.32)
ppe_assets	-0.3847** (-2.21)	-0.3713** (-2.13)
capex	2.1935*** (2.98)	2.1765*** (2.97)
cash_assets	1.1061*** (5.37)	1.1276*** (5.48)
age	0.0015* (1.29)	0.0014 (1.23)
ln_assets	-0.1146*** (-4.40)	-0.1145*** (-4.40)
pfd	0.1947** (1.82)	0.2011** (1.89)
liq	0.4683*** (6.61)	0.4645*** (6.55)
insd_own	-0.2096 (-1.59)	-0.2003 (-1.53)
debt	-0.1234 (-0.79)	-0.1301 (-0.83)
codet_third	0.0054 (0.09)	0.0065 (0.11)
codet_par	0.0862 (0.95)	0.0886 (0.98)
bank	-0.0389 (-0.77)	-0.0388 (-0.79)
insolv	-0.0182 (-0.21)	-0.0157 (-0.17)

2219 The regressions are based on specification 2.4.1 and therefore also comprise the largest blockholder's ownership as well as the same set of control variables and industry and time fixed effects. Since their coefficients are not affected qualitatively, they are not examined at this stage.

2220 See H2.4$_c$ in section 5.2.

Table 37 cont'd

	(3.4.7)	(3.4.8)
takeover	0.3815***	0.3829***
	(2.55)	(2.56)
segm_chng	-0.2961***	-0.2939***
	(-3.06)	(-3.04)
govt	0.0390	0.0363
	(0.43)	(0.40)
Constant	1.5922***	1.6178***
	(12.43)	(12.64)
Industry dummies	Yes	Yes
Year dummies	Yes	Yes
Adjusted R^2	0.2104	0.2097
Number of obs.	2,805	2,801
Firms	479	479

Table 37: Regression results of firm value on proxies of a heterogenous ownership structure

tions in their valuation of the firm. In particular, they do so independent of the effect of the largest blockholder's ownership, whose magnitude and significance does not materially change relative to specification 2.4.1. The results also confirm the sparse empirical evidence on the effect of heterogenous ownership structures. *Attig et al.* (2009) also find that the number of additional blockholders next to the largest blockholder increase firm value as measured by Tobin's q.[2221]

Overall, a firm's shareholders seem to associate more heterogenous ownership structures with more effective monitoring and generally regard them as a benefit.

6.3.4.5 Résumé

The goal of the third stage was to investigate if blockholder interrelationships affect agency costs and firm value as well as the relationship between the four blockholder types and agency costs and firm value. Based on the results, this résumé summarizes the following key findings:

(1) The ownership of the second largest blockholder has a significant effect on the relationship between the ownership of the blockholder types and agency costs and firm value, respectively. Overall, the evidence suggests that the second largest blockholder's ownership translates into improved monitoring by enhancing the largest blockholder type's power and incentive to engage in monitoring and by restraining its discretion and incentives to pursue its self-interest to the detriment of the remaining capital providers. However, this effect cannot be uniformly observed for the blockholder types which suggests that the influence of the second largest blockholder depends on the underlying characteristics specific to the largest blockholder. Moreover, the results on principal-principal agency costs do neither suggest blockholder-blockholder agency conflicts arising due to the second blockholder's presence nor a collusion of the two blockholders against the remaining shareholders.[2222]

(2) Incorporating blockholder interrelationships allows for a more differentiated conclusion regarding the effect of strategic investors on a firm's overall agency costs. In particular, the

[2221] See Attig et al. (2009): 397f. The evidence is based on a 1996-sample of 1,252 publicly-traded firms from Hong Kong, Indonesia, Japan, Korea, Malaysia, Philippines, Singapore, Taiwan, and Thailand.

[2222] Note that the colluding blockholders would hold on average the simple majority. See section 6.2.4.1.

results point to higher managerial and principal-principal agency costs if the two largest blockholders are strategic investors. In this case, the two blockholders seem to collude to increase their discretion and pursue private benefits to the detriment of the remaining shareholders.[2223] However, the pursuance of private benefits by a strategic investor is also observed if it individually has sufficient power to do so. The result on the strategic investor's incontestability illustrates that for higher incontestability, a strategic investor's ownership is associated with a greater increase in its portfolio firm's principal-principal agency costs. In light of these findings, it is astonishing that these higher agency costs are not incorporated in the respective firm's value. Under the presumption that a firm's remaining shareholders are knowledgeable about and able to provide estimates of agency costs possibly inherent in publicly-traded firms, this suggests potential offsetting benefits of strategic investors.[2224]

(3) The recognition of blockholder interrelationships also provides further evidence on the role of family blockholders. The interaction of a family's ownership (given it is the largest type) and the second largest blockholder's ownership significantly decreases managerial agency costs and increases firm value. However, if the second largest blockholder is also a family member, the interaction term comprising both blockholders' ownership unfolds a significant effect on neither managerial agency costs nor firm value. Furthermore, the result on the family's incontestability illustrates that for higher incontestability, a family's ownership is associated with a greater increase in its portfolio firm's principal-principal agency costs. This evidence may hint at potential adverse effects for the remaining shareholders if a family blockholder has an opportunity to collude or excessive power. While this finding may not be convincing on its own, it adds to the existing evidence of stage 2 which already insinuated potential adverse effects for the remaining shareholders if a family blockholder is provided with too much discretion in the form of higher ownership and management board presence.

(4) While the recognition of blockholder interrelationships suggests potential adverse effects of strategic investors and families if they are incontestable or have the opportunity to collude, similar effects are not observed for private equity and institutional investors. Rather, the findings confirm the results of stage 2 which suggested that the ownership of private equity and institutional investors is associated with lower principal-principal agency costs.[2225] This is intuitive, since both types frequently interact with other investors in different firms and are therefore interested in a good reputation which ensures that they are in demand with regard to the formation of coalitions with other investors.[2226] Hence, the types have low incentives to challenge or expropriate the remaining shareholders.

(5) The heterogeneity of a firm's ownership structure consistently reduces the components of a firm's overall agency cost. The benefits of a heterogenous blockholder structure are also recognized by a firm's shareholders who incorporate these benefits into firm value. Moreover,

---

2223 Hence, at least for strategic investors, the preliminary evidence of coalition forming suggested in section 6.2.4.2 seems to be confirmed.

2224 Please also see the results of specification 2.4.9 and the corresponding discussion in section 6.3.3.4.

2225 At least with regard to private equity investors, this is also reflected in the firms' value.

2226 See also Black (1992a): 817. This is also supported by the preliminary evidence of coalition forming in section 6.2.4.2.

it affects agency costs and firm value beyond the influence of the largest blockholder's ownership. Overall, the results are neither consistent with a negative impact of heterogenous ownership structures on the monitoring feasibility and the blockholders' incentive to engage in monitoring nor in support of the argument that a greater number of (different) blockholders results in increased blockholder-blockholder agency conflicts. Instead, the results point to a greater monitoring effectiveness that stems from complementarities realized by the blockholders and a greater mutual monitoring among the blockholders.

6.3.5 Robustness Tests

It is essential to verify that the results of the regression analysis in the previous sections are not vitiated by misspecifications. Therefore, the following sections deal with a battery of robustness tests.

6.3.5.1 Fixed Effects Model

Since the specification tests in section 6.3.1.2 suggest that the fixed effects model is most appropriate for the data at hand, this section summarizes the results of fixed effects regressions in order to test for the impact of time constant firm-specific effects not accounted for in the pooled-OLS regressions.[2227] As explained in section 6.3.1.2, the fixed effects model uses the variation *within* firms rather than the variation *between* firms to explain the variation of the respective dependent variable. Since the descriptive analyses suggest that the ownership structure remains rather stable over time, little variation within firms is expected that can be used to explain the variation in the dependent variables. Hence, the primary explanatory variables are expected to be less significant in the fixed effects regressions relative to the pooled-OLS regressions.

Table 53 (appendix 15) depicts the fixed effects regression results under the assumption of blockholder homogeneity (stage 1). Column two and three show that, similar to pooled-OLS results, the impact of *[cum_own]* and *[h_index]* on managerial agency costs is insignificant.[2228] With regard to agency costs of debt, column four and five report that both variables significantly reduce the potential to engage in wealth transfer strategies; note that in the pooled-OLS regressions, only *[cum_own]* is found to be significant.[2229] Concerning principal-principal agency costs, the two ownership variables in column six and seven maintain their expected relationship, however, decrease in significance since only *[cum_own]* is significant (at the 10% level).[2230] Similar to the results on dividend payouts, also the results on firm value

[2227] Since the use of dummy variables in the fixed effects model is impossible, the estimated regressions differ from those of the pooled-OLS regressions. The fixed effects models are also tested for autocorrelation and heteroscedasticity. The tests indicate the presence of both autocorrelation and heteroscedasticity. Therefore, the regressions use heteroscedasticity- and autocorrelation-consistent (HAC) standard errors.

[2228] With regard to the control variables, firm age and size turn insignificant, whereas the level of insider ownership turns significant and thus is consistent with the convergence-of-interest hypothesis.

[2229] Turning to the control variables, firm age is now insignificant whereas firm size is now significant.

[2230] Of the control variables, firm age and size turn insignificant.

(column eight and nine) show a lower significance of the two ownership variables: only *[cum_own]* is associated with a significantly higher firm value.[2231]

Table 54 and 55 (appendix 15) report the fixed effects results under the assumption of blockholder heterogeneity (stage 2). Table 54 first depicts the results using *[bh1_cont]*. As can be seen, *[bh1_cont]* has a significant effect only on agency costs of debt; the coefficient suggests that it significantly lowers agency costs of debt. Hence, the fixed effects results differ from those of pooled-OLS which report a significant coefficient of *[bh1_cont]* on principal-principal agency costs and firm value.[2232] Table 55 depicts the fixed effects results using the ownership of the four blockholder identities. With regard to managerial agency costs, column two does not show a significant effect of the ownership of any blockholder type.[2233] Column three shows that greater family ownership significantly reduces agency costs of debt. The ownership of institutional investors, significant in pooled-OLS, is insignificant when using fixed effects. Concerning principal-principal agency costs, the fixed effects results are similar to those of pooled-OLS: the ownership of private equity and institutional investors leads to higher dividend payouts and hence lower principal-principal agency costs. Finally, the results on firm value show that the ownership of private equity firms significantly increases firm value. While the pooled-OLS results also report significant coefficients for families and strategic investors, their ownership is insignificant in table 55.[2234]

Table 56-58 (appendix 15) report (selected) fixed effects results under the assumption of blockholder interrelationships (stage 3). Table 56 focuses on the effect of the interaction between the largest and second largest blockholder type's ownership, given both are of the same type. The results based on firm value, for instance, point to significantly lower firm value if the two largest blockholders are private equity, strategic or institutional investors. In contrast, pooled-OLS results suggest that the ownership of the second largest blockholder (if it is a private equity investor) increases the positive ownership size effect of a private equity investor on firm value. Overall, the fixed effects results differ substantially from those of pooled-OLS: the differences refer to the magnitude, sign, and significance of the interaction terms. Table 57 depicts the results of regressions of agency costs and firm value on the proxies for a heterogenous ownership structure. With the exception of regressions on agency costs of debt, the results confirm those obtained from pooled-OLS: heterogenous ownership structures significantly reduce managerial agency costs and principal-principal agency costs which is reflected in a positive effect of heterogenous ownership structures on firm value.[2235] Finally, table 58 reports the regressions focusing on the effect of the largest blockholder identities' incontestability. With regard to principal-principal agency costs, the signs of the interaction coefficients

2231 With the exception of *[debt]* (significant at the 10% level), the control variables remain largely unchanged.

2232 Relative to the stage 1 fixed effects results, the control variables remain unchanged. Only the *[insd_own]* coefficient turns significant in the regression on dividend payouts (column 4) and provides further evidence of the convergence-of-interest hypothesis supported by the *[insd_own]* coefficient in column two.

2233 In contrast, pooled-OLS results in significant and negative coefficients for the ownership of families and institutional investors.

2234 Relative to the stage 1 fixed effects results, the control variables remain unchanged. Only firm size turns insignificant in the regression on agency costs of debt.

2235 In terms of control variables, both size and significance remain largely unaffected relative to the stage 1 fixed effects results. Only the level of debt turns insignificant in regressions based on Tobin's q.

for all types except strategic investors remain unchanged. However, none of the interactions including family ownership are significant. In contrast, the interaction between *[bh1/bh2]* and *[bh1_pe_cont]* is now significant; the interaction with *[diff_bh12345]* remains significant and negative. With regard to institutional investors, the interaction with *[bh1/bh2_bh3]* and *[diff_bh12345]* turns insignificant and significant, respectively. Turning to firm value, the incontestability of a private equity and family blockholder, measured by *[diff_bh12345]* results in a greater decrease in firm value for higher levels of ownership of the two blockholders. While this effect is insignificant for private equity blockholders under pooled-OLS, it is consistent with the pooled-OLS results for family blockholders. Apart from this, the interaction terms between family ownership and the respective incontestability variable change their sign and turn insignificant under fixed effects.

Since the purpose of this section is to highlight that pooled-OLS results are sensitive to the methodology employed, the results of the fixed effects models are not described in further detail. Overall, the sensitivity of the results appears to be strongest for more specific measures of a firm's ownership structure: the more general measures of ownership concentration in stage 1 and heterogenous ownership structures in stage 3 remain largely consistent with those of pooled-OLS. This may be due to the fact that these measures incorporate changes in the total ownership structure of a firm and are hence more likely to vary over time.[2236] Overall, the results confirm *Roberts/Whited* (2013), who state that "if the research question is inherently aimed at understanding cross-sectional variation in a variable, then fixed effects defeat this purpose."[2237] In line with this, fixed effects are unsuccessful in quantifying the determinants of variations in agency costs and firm value.

6.3.5.2 Parameter Stability

A major advantage of panel data is the ability to control for changes (breaks) in the economic environment. The regression analysis so far implicitly assumes parameter stability for the sample period. However, if a break occurs within a sample, regressions that focus on the whole sample and neglect this break may provide a misleading foundation for inference, as the estimated relationships may hold on average but may differ substantially for the period prior and after the break.[2238]

Within the sample at hand, the financial crisis might constitute such a structural change. By mid 2008, the crisis, having its roots in the US subprime market, and the resulting liquidity freeze were having major impact on financial institutions worldwide. At that time, financial institutions were striving to raise additional capital to finance losses realized on their financial assets. The crisis in the financial sector intensified with the collapse and liquidation of Lehman Brothers which resulted in a general loss of investor confidence and an evaporation of

---

2236 Whereas the ownership of the largest blockholder's identity is unaffected by a change in ownership of a fourth blockholder, aggregate ownership measures and the heterogeneity of a firm's ownership structure are affected by this change and hence offer more variation that can be used to explain the variation in the dependent variables.

2237 Roberts/Whited (2013): 559. See also Coles et al. (2012): 165 for a similar view.

2238 See also Stock/Watson (2012): 599.

trust that severely affected financial institutions.[2239] In the face of the uncertainty and economic turmoil, banks were either unwilling or unable to lend and credit dried up. Through its impact on the cost and availability of credit, the financial crisis quickly spilled over to the real economy, causing a massive erosion of shareholder value and a significant drop in GDP.[2240] The importance of the financial crisis is also suggested by the year dummies in regressions based on Tobin's q. As can be seen in table 59 (appendix 16), relative to the year 2005, the dummies are associated with significantly higher levels of Tobin's q in 2006 and 2007. However, apart from 2010, the years following the financial crisis have a significant and negative effect on Tobin's q.[2241]

The stability of the parameters in the regressions conducted in the previous analyses is tested using a **parameter stability test**. The basic idea of this test is to split the sample into two sub-samples, a pre-crisis and a post-crisis period, and then to perform three regressions; one regression for each of the sub-periods as well as one for the complete sample.[2242] The residual sums of squares for the three samples are then compared based on a Chow test,[2243] which constitutes an F-test based on the differences between the residual sums of squares of the restricted and unrestricted regressions:

$$F(k, T-2k) = \frac{RSS_W - (RSS_{Pre} + RSS_{Post})}{RSS_{Pre} + RSS_{Post}} \times \frac{T-2k}{k} \quad (6.11)$$

Here RSS_w = residual sum of squares for the whole sample,

RSS_{Pre} = residual sum of squares for the pre-crisis sample, comprising the years 2005-2007,

RSS_{Post} = residual sum of squares for the post-crisis sample, comprising the years 2008-2012,

T = number of observations of the whole sample,

k = number of regressors in each regression and

2 = number of sub-samples.

Hence, the test measures the difference between the residual sums of squares for the whole sample (RSS_W) and the sum of the residual sums of squares for the two sub-samples ($RSS_{Pre} + RSS_{Post}$). Thus, it tests whether a single regression is more efficient than two separate regressions on two subsamples. If the coefficients are stable over time, this difference will be marginal and the null hypothesis that the parameters are stable over time cannot be rejected.[2244]

2239 For more details on the financial crisis and its origins, please see Kirkpatrick (2009): 4f; Larosière et al. (2009): 7-12.

2240 See also Larosière et al. (2009): 6; Bainbridge (2012): 4f. Figure 29 in appendix 16 depicts the German GDP as well as the average value of Tobin's q for the years 2005-2012. As can be seen, there is a significant drop in Tobin's q in 2008. Since Germany's export driven economy has been fully exposed to the sharply falling export demand, its GDP experienced a large drop in 2009. See also Detzer et al. (2013): 310.

2241 The results are in line with the average Tobin's q depicted in Figure 29 (appendix 16). The decline in Tobin's q for the years 2010 onwards may show the negative effect of the European sovereign debt crisis.

2242 The regression for the whole period is typically called restricted regression, while the regressions on the two sub-periods are called unrestricted regressions. See for example Brooks (2008): 180f.

2243 The test is named for its inventor, Gregory Chow. Please see Chow (1960).

2244 See Brooks (2008): 180f.

Table 38
This table presents the results of the Chow test performed for specification 2.4.1 and 2.4.3.

	(2.4.1)	(2.4.3)
RSS_W	1,154.9597	1,113.4858
RSS_{Pre}	424.7383	406.2363
RSS_{Post}	717.2294	692.1119
k	29	34
T	2876	2876
F statistic	**1.1055**	**1.3345**

Table 38: Results of the Chow test

The Chow test is performed exemplary for specification 2.4.1 and 2.4.3. The respective residual sums of squares are depicted in table 38. With regard to specification 2.4.1, the test statistic is given by $\frac{1,154.9597-(424.7383+717.2294)}{424.7383+717.2294} \times \frac{2,876-2\times 29}{29} = 1.1055$ which should be compared with a 5%, F(29; 2,818) ~ 1.4715. With regard to specification 2.4.3, the test statistic is given by $\frac{1,113.4858-(406.2363+692.1119)}{406.2363+692.1119} \times \frac{2876-2\times 34}{34} = 1.3345$ which should be compared with a 5%, F (34; 2,808) ~ 1.4337. Overall, the test statistics of both specifications are below their respective critical F-values. Consequently, the null hypothesis of parameter stability does not have to be rejected. Hence, the influence of the largest blockholder's ownership (specification 2.4.1) and of the ownership of the largest blockholder types (specification 2.4.3) is stable during both crisis and non-crisis times.

In order to get a better understanding of the stability of the regression parameters, (cross-sectional) **year-by-year regressions** are performed. If there are structural shifts within the sample, these will emerge in the time series of yearly coefficients. Moreover, the regressions are not subject to time series correlation[2245] and enable the investigation of whether the relationships between the ownership and the dependent variables remain constant over time.[2246] This is necessary, since it is conceivable that the importance of blockholder monitoring is dependent on the external market environment. On the one hand, the performance of the overall stock market might affect the incentives of a blockholder to engage in monitoring: In times of increasing stock prices, the incentive for monitoring is low, whereas in times of declining stock prices, blockholders might search for ways to increase the value of their holdings through active monitoring.[2247] Moreover, the falling share prices and the, as a result, undervalued firms should have provided opportunities for investors to buy-up shares and initiate changes within these firms.[2248] Consequently, blockholder monitoring might be more pronounced in case of declining stock markets. On the other hand, *Cheffins* (2009) finds that large shareholders have generally been reluctant to become active and challenge management during the financial crisis and concludes that shareholder activism did not play a central role in the overcoming of the crisis.[2249] Also *Armour/Cheffins* (2012) argue that the resulting mar-

2245 See Bøhren/Ødegaard (2006): 48.
2246 Bott (2002): 161 criticizes that this has been done by only very few studies.
2247 See Halpern (1999): 54.
2248 See also Cheffins (2009): 47-49.
2249 See Cheffins (2009): 2f, 47-49. The evidence is based on an examination of corporate governance practices in a sample of 37 US firms that were removed from the S&P 500 index during the crisis in 2008.

ket turmoil had discouraged shareholder activism “despite shares of potential targets being ‘cheap’ by historical standards.”[2250]

The results of the yearly regressions based on specification 2.4.1 and 2.4.3 are depicted in table 60 and 61 (appendix 17).[2251] With regard to table 60, the ownership of the largest blockholder *[bh1_cont]* has a significant and positive effect on firm value in each year except 2007. Although its significance differs for some years, the yearly coefficients provide strong evidence that the relationship between *[bh1_cont]* and firm value remains constant over time. In terms of the controls, a significant relationship for each year can only be observed for *[cash_assets]*, *[ln_assets]*, and *[liq]*. Although a firm's growth opportunities are highly significant for the whole sample, they are not significant in 2008, 2010 and 2012. The alternative governance mechanisms are significant only occasionally which is in line with their insignificant effect observed for the whole sample.

With regard to table 61, the yearly coefficients of the blockholder types' ownership confirm the expectation based on the whole sample coefficients. The ownership of private equity investors significantly increases portfolio firm value in the years 2007-2011; family blockholders increase the value of their portfolio firms in 2005, 2007-2009 and 2012; the ownership of strategic investors is associated with greater firm value in 2005-2008 and 2011-2012. In contrast to these types, institutional investors have a significant effect on firm value only in one of the eight years: their ownership is associated with significantly lower firm value in 2006. Interestingly, private equity and family blockholder ownership significantly increases firm value also during the peak of the financial crisis and the resulting downturn in economic activity in the years 2008 and 2009.[2252] Turning to the control variables, a significant relationship for each year can only be observed for *[cash_assets]* and *[liq]*. Similar to the results of table 60, *[growth]* results in significantly higher firm value only in 2005-2007 and 2009. In line with a greater investor concern about (firm-specific) risk during the crisis, a firm's beta *[beta]* has a significant and negative effect on firm value in 2008 and 2009.[2253]

Intriguingly, corporate governance variables do not have an effect on firm value during the crisis. In both specifications, none of the governance mechanisms has a significant effect on firm value in 2008 or 2009. Since the ownership variables significantly increase firm value also during the crisis, this provides further evidence that blockholder monitoring either acts as a substitute for alternative governance mechanisms or is more effective than the alternative governance mechanisms controlled for in the analysis. Another aspects worth to be mentioned refers to the variance in Tobin's q that is explained by the two regression specifications. With regard to table 60, the adjusted R^2 amounts to only about 10% in 2008. In contrast, it yields an adjusted R^2 of about 18-21% in 2005-2007, 2009 and 2012; during 2010-2011, roughly 15% of the variation in Tobin's q is explained by the model. Similar results are observed in table 61. These findings illustrate that the firms' fundamentals and characteristics have only a lim-

2250 Armour/Cheffins (2009): 32.

2251 Since these regressions have fewer observations, less significant coefficients are expected. The following deliberations focus on the most remarkable findings only.

2252 The ownership of strategic investors unfolds a significant influence on Tobin's q only in 2008.

2253 Moreover, it has a significant and negative effect on firm value also in 2012.

ited ability to explain the declines in firm value during the peak of the financial crisis in 2008 (and to a lesser extent during the European sovereign debt crisis in 2010 and 2011). Apparently, share prices during the crisis were, to a major extent, driven by a loss of investor confidence and trust.

Overall, neither the parameter stability test nor the year-by-year regressions affect the main conclusions drawn in the three stages of the regression analysis.

6.3.5.3 Sensitivity Analysis

The following section comprises a number of sensitivity tests in order to further illustrate the robustness of the regression results in the sections 6.3.2-6.3.4.

Lagged Variables

The use of lagged ownership variables addresses two issues that may be relevant in the study at hand. First, agency costs and firm value may not be immediately influenced by the blockholders' monitoring. In particular, it is reasonable to assume that a blockholder needs some time in order to fully understand the business of its portfolio firm, develop relationships with management, and get full access to information. Moreover, political dynamics by which the blockholder gains support from or places representatives on the supervisory board and exerts pressure on management may take some time.[2254] In addition, blockholder monitoring may affect the dependent variables with some lag due to decisions that have an influence in the long-run only.[2255] Finally, while the monitoring may be immediately reflected in a firm's market valuation, it might take longer to be reflected in a firm's agency cost proxies.[2256] Therefore, lagged variables ensure that the effect of blockholder monitoring shows up in the dependent variables.[2257] Furthermore, lagged variables also reduce the demands with regard to capital market efficiency. Since the market, in this case, is not required to immediately incorporate the information, the market has to be weak form efficient only.[2258]

Second, the use of lagged ownership variables constitutes a preliminary test for endogeneity.[2259] Specifically, it enables the differentiation between the hypothesis that blockholders, via their monitoring, improve agency costs and firm value versus the hypothesis that blockholders simply invest in firms with lower agency costs and higher firm value: if blockholder monitoring affects agency costs and firm value, it should do so prior to the year showing improvements in these variables. In contrast, if blockholders select firms based on their low agency costs and high value, the ownership structure prior to the year showing improvements should have no effect.[2260]

2254 See also David et al. (2001): 146.
2255 See Thomsen et al. (2006): 254. See also Bhagat et al. (2004): 17.
2256 See Cronqvist/Nilsson (2003): 711.
2257 See Cornett et al. (2007): 1781.
2258 For a discussion of capital market efficiency, please see section 5.1.2 as well as Fama (1970).
2259 See also Dahya et al. (2008): 88. Section 6.3.5.4 focuses on endogeneity in greater detail.
2260 For a similar reasoning, see Cornett et al. (2007): 1781.

Based on these arguments, this approach also questions empirical studies that gather data on dependent variables at an earlier date than data on ownership structures. For instance, *Cable* (1985) measures the financial performance of the sample firms in 1976, whereas he takes the voting rights from reports issued in 1978 and 1980;[2261] his hypothesis that bank involvement impacts firms' financial performance would require exactly the reverse ordering.[2262] Similarly, *Seifert et al.* (2005) gather ownership data from 2000 and collect dependent variables from 1997-1999.[2263]

To test the robustness of the results, the specifications 2.1.1, 2.2.1, 2.3.1, and 2.4.1 and the specifications 2.1.3, 2.2.3, 2.3.3 and 2.4.3 are estimated using ownership variables that are lagged one time period. The lagging of the ownership variables results in a loss of one observation per firm; in the case at hand, 531 firm-year observations are deleted. The results of the lagged regressions are depicted in table 62 (appendix 18) and show that the significance levels, signs and magnitudes of the ownership variables are broadly similar to those of the non-lagged regressions.[2264] This suggests that the insignificance of the ownership variables in the original, non-lagged regressions is unlikely to be a result of more long-term blockholder influences that are not immediately reflected in the dependent variables.[2265] Moreover, the results provide preliminary evidence inconsistent with an endogenous relationship between the (significant) ownership variables and agency costs and firm value.[2266]

Alternative Definition of the Dividend Payout Ratio

Section 5.3.1.3 mentioned a number of alternative variables to measure dividend payouts and hence principal-principal agency costs. In order to test the sensitivity of the results to the use of another dividend payout variable, specification 2.3.1 and 2.3.3 are reestimated using an alternative definition of the dividend payout ratio. *[div_payout_a]* is defined as a firm's regular cash dividend as a percentage of the firm's cash flows and can be regarded as the ratio of cash distributed to cash generated.[2267] Table 63 (appendix 18) summarizes the results of both specifications using *[div_payout_a]*. Column two focuses on the largest blockholder's ownership *[bh1_cont]* and shows that it has an insignificant positive effect on *[div_payout_a]*. Since this effect is significant when using *[div_payout]*, the influence of the largest blockholder's ownership is sensitive to the selection of the dividend variable. Column three focuses on the own-

2261 See Cable (1985): 125.
2262 See Emmons/Schmid (1998): 35 for a similar argumentation.
2263 See Seifert et al. (2005): 180.
2264 While not depicted in table 62, the control variables remain unaffected when using lagged variables.
2265 Note, however, that the ownership of private equity investors now seems to decrease managerial agency costs (column three). Albeit the influence is insignificant, it may point to another reason for the insignificant positive coefficient found in specification 2.1.3: the effect of the governance changes implemented by private equity investors may affect managerial agency costs only in the longer-term.
2266 Note that this evidence also removes any concerns regarding the specific point in time at which the ownership structure is collected and stated by the "Orbis" database. See section 6.1.2.
2267 A firm's cash flow is calculated as the sum of net income, depreciation and amortization, other non-cash adjustments, and changes in non-cash working capital. A similar variable definition is used also by La Porta et al. (2000a): 11; Faccio et al. (2001): 60; Andres et al. (2009): 179. According to La Porta et al. (2000a): 11, this measure has two potential disadvantages. First, it can be easily manipulated by accounting tricks. Second, and more important, the diversion of resources by the blockholder may occur before cash flows are reported, in which case the ratio overestimates the share of true earnings that is paid out as dividends.

ership of the four blockholder types. As can be seen, families and strategic investors have an insignificant and negative influence on the payment of dividends, whereas private equity and institutional investors have a significant and positive influence on the dividend payouts, suggesting that the latter two blockholders are associated with lower principal-principal agency costs. Although the significance of private equity ownership decreases from a 1% to a 5% level, the effect of the largest blockholder type in general is insensitive to the change in the dividend payout variable. Turning to the control variables, their sign and significance remain largely unchanged. The greatest changes are observed for *[codet_third]*, which turns highly significant, and *[segm_chng]*, which turns insignificant when employing *[div_payout_a]*. Moreover, the presence of a governmental blockholder significantly lowers principal-principal agency costs when dividends are measured as a percentage of the firm's cash flows.

Long-term Dependent Variable

A potential cost of blockholder monitoring mentioned in section 3.1.3 constitutes an excessive focus of the portfolio firm on short-term results. In particular, the higher firm value observed for greater ownership of the largest blockholder may come at the expense of a firm's long-term performance. To investigate if blockholder monitoring also creates value in the long-run, three-year averages of Tobin's q are calculated. *[tobinq_3y_avg]* therefore equals a firm's Tobin's q, averaged over the years t, t+1 and t+2.[2268] The long-term variable is then employed as dependent variable in specification 2.4.1 and 2.4.3. Table 64 (appendix 18) depicts the results. Focusing on *[bh1_cont]*, column two shows a significant (at the 1% level) effect on the three-year average Tobin's q. Hence, inconsistent with an excessive short-term focus, the positive effect of the blockholder's monitoring is not limited to the current year but is also reflected in the firm's value in the two consecutive years. Column three reports the results using the largest blockholder identity's ownership. With regard to the ownership of private equity investors, the regression yields a significant (at the 1% level) and positive coefficient. Moreover, the results show a significant (at the 10% level) and positive effect of family ownership on the long-term firm value. Significant increases in *[tobinq_3y_avg]* are also a consequence of greater ownership of strategic investors; the coefficient is significant at the 1% level. The ownership of institutional investors is insignificant. Overall, these findings confirm the results of specification 2.4.3 based on *[tobinq]*, albeit the significance of *[bh1_fam_cont]* slightly decreased.

While the ownership variables are unaffected, some changes in the significance of the control variables can be observed when using *[tobinq_3y_avg]*. In particular, the presence of preferred stock turns insignificant in both regression specifications. In addition, *[codet_par]* turns significantly positive, indicating that the increased supervision in case of parity codetermination increases long-term firm value. Moreover, the presence of a bank blockholder is now significantly associated with lower long-term firm value which might be regarded as evidence that a bank has goals different from the maximization of (long-term) shareholder value. Finally, *[govt]* significantly decreases long-term firm value which is consistent with the hy-

2268 This variable also enables the measurement of the effect of blockholders whose monitoring might not be directly reflected in greater firm value as they focus on measures to improve firm value in the long-run.

pothesis that government-owned firms exhibit a weak performance in terms of conventional performance measures.

To recapitulate, the higher firm value associated with the ownership of the largest blockholder and with the ownership of the four blockholder identities observed in section 6.3.3.4 does not come at the expense of long-term performance.

Firms in Financial Distress

The incentive of a blockholder to engage in monitoring may be dependent on the financial health of its portfolio firm. If the firm is in strong financial shape, monitoring may only result in marginal increases in firm value which do not outweigh the monitoring costs. In contrast, if a firm suffers from financial distress, a blockholder's benefits from monitoring should be substantial, providing it with a greater incentive to engage in monitoring.[2269] With regard to the different blockholder identities, financially distressed firms are especially attractive for private equity and institutional investors, as they are best able to employ their expertise to enhance performance by, for example, efficiency improvements or divestments.[2270] In line with this, *Kahan/Rock* (2007) find that hedge funds target underperforming firms in order to engage in activism.[2271] Overall, professional investors should be more experienced in the monitoring of financially distressed firms. Therefore, it is expected that higher levels of ownership of private equity and institutional investors should result in the greatest increase in firm value for financially distressed firms. With regard to non-financially distressed firms, the results are expected to match those of stage 2 (specification 2.4.3).

To examine these expectations, specification 2.4.1 and 2.4.3 are reestimated on a sample of financially distressed and non-financially distressed firms. In line with *Dyck/Zingales* (2004b), financial distress is proxied by a firm's earnings per share.[2272] In particular, firms with negative or zero earnings per share are classified as financially distressed, whereas firms with positive earnings per share are classified as non-distressed. The results of the regressions are summarized in table 65 of appendix 18. Column two and three show the results of specification 2.4.1 for financially distressed and non-distressed firms, respectively. As can be seen, *[bh1_cont]* significantly increases firm value in both financially distressed and non-distressed firms. However, the effect of *[bh1_cont]* is less significant in the sample comprising financially distressed firms. Column four and five display the results of specification 2.4.3. With regard to financially distressed firms (column four), the ownership of both private equity and institutional investors significantly increases firm value. The ownership of strategic investors is weakly significant whereas family blockholders have an insignificant effect on firm value.

2269 In line with this argumentation, Köke/Renneboog (2005): 505f, 508 find that the presence of strong blockholders causes substantial increases in productivity for UK firms in financial distress. However, the presence of controlling blockholders does not increase productivity in poorly performing German firms. For Germany, the evidence is based on a sample of 1,074 listed and unlisted firms during 1986-1996. For the UK, the evidence is based on a sample of 502 listed firms during 1992-1999.

2270 See also Achleitner et al. (2009): 10. This argument is empirically supported by the authors. See Achleitner et al. (2009): 20 and Achleitner et al. (2010): 809.

2271 See Kahan/Rock (2007): 1069. This is not proven by Klein/Zur (2009): 189, who find that hedge funds targets are more profitable and healthy.

2272 See Dyck/Zingales (2004b): 547.

Concerning non-financially distressed firms (column five), the results mirror those of stage 2: the ownership of private equity investors, families, and strategic investors significantly increases firm value. Of particular interest are the results concerning institutional investors. Apparently, shareholders regard their ownership and the associated monitoring as favorable only for financially distressed firms. This may be a result of a superior expertise in the turnaround of their portfolio firms which may outweigh any unfavorable effects expected by shareholders that dominate their evaluation of institutional investor monitoring in non-distressed firms. The insignificant effect of family ownership on the value of financially distressed firms suggests that families either do not provide survivability capital[2273] in case of economic difficulties or its provision is not accounted for by the remaining shareholders.[2274] Overall, the empirical evidence confirms the expectations formulated above.

Differences between financially and non-financially distressed firms are also observed in terms of the control variables. For instance, *[ppe_assets]* and *[capex]* have a significant effect on the value of non-distressed firms but an insignificant effect on the value of distressed firms.[2275] Moreover, the level of debt has a significantly positive effect on firm value in distressed firms and a significantly negative effect on firm value in non-distressed firms. Since the expected bankruptcy costs associated with higher debt levels should be more relevant for distressed firms, the positive effect is surprising. Apparently, the disciplinary effect of leverage outweighs these costs in financially distressed firms. Furthermore, parity codetermination is significantly associated with higher firm value in distressed firms but not in non-financially distressed firms which suggests an added value of a supervision by employee representatives in a crisis situation. Finally, *[govt]* is associated with a higher value in the distressed sample. While this does not reflect the expectation formulated in section 5.3.4.3, it is conceivable that a governmental blockholder acts as a certification for the distressed firm and lowers its bankruptcy risk relative to distressed firms without a governmental blockholder.

6.3.5.4 Endogeneity

The empirical corporate governance literature is frequently faced with the problem of endogeneity.[2276] In econometric terms, endogeneity can be defined as a correlation of one or more explanatory variable(s) with the error term of a regression model.[2277] In terms of equation 6.3, this can be written as: $Cov(OWN, v) \neq 0$. In case of endogeneity, the OLS results above overstate the actual relationship between the explanatory and the dependent variable and provide misleading results.[2278] Therefore, it is vital to test for the endogeneity of owner-

2273 For a definition of survivability capital please see section 4.1.3.1.1.

2274 The results on the distressed subsample are inconsistent with the findings of Köke/Renneboog (2005). Since their German evidence is based on a sample of 1986-1996, this suggests that the importance of blockholders, in particular of private equity and institutional investors, has increased recently.

2275 Note that less significant coefficients may be due to fewer observations in the financially distressed subsample.

2276 According to Börsch-Supan/Köke (2002): 299, endogeneity is the most serious econometric problem within these studies.

2277 See e.g. Bress (2008): 143; Wooldridge (2010): 54; Wooldridge (2012): 527; Roberts/Whited (2013): 494.

2278 See Beiner et al. (2006): 251.

ship to ensure the robustness and relevance of the results.[2279] The tests carried out in the study at hand are preceded by a description of the endogeneity problem in the context of ownership structure as well as by a discussion of the importance of endogeneity in the present research.

Description of Endogeneity

Endogeneity in the context of ownership structure is inextricably linked with a number of papers published by *Demsetz* (1983, 1985, 2001), who proposes the following: Putting its respective characteristics aside, a firm's ownership structure should maximize firm value and constitutes "an endogenous outcome of competitive selection in which various cost advantages and disadvantages are balanced to arrive at an equilibrium organization of the firm."[2280] Assuming diffuse ownership constitutes the outcome of such a competitive selection, one therefore cannot argue that it fails to result in a maximization of firm value and an efficient resource allocation. Although it may be more difficult to monitor the actions of management in a dispersed ownership structure, this has no implications on the value of the firm: Since the providers of share capital recognize their inability to exert control over the firm and its management prior to their investment, there must be a compensating benefit if they still are to provide equity capital.[2281] This is supported by the persistent presence of diffuse ownership structures. Unless diffuse ownership results in benefits that outweigh its costs, one would not observe diffuse ownership in a rational world.[2282] If such compensating benefits exist for some firms and not for others, firms and their shareholders endogenously trade-off the costs and benefits and choose an ownership structure so as to maximize their performance.[2283] Accordingly, ownership structure and firm profitability should be unrelated.[2284]

The key implication of Demsetz' work for the present thesis is the proposition that endogenous characteristics of a firm determine its ownership structure. In the present case, an investor systematically bases its investment decisions on its preferences regarding endogenous firm characteristics.[2285] Hence, rather than investing into a firm irrespective of its characteristics and changing these characteristics according to its preferences *ex post*, a blockholder selects a particular firm that exhibits its preferred characteristics *ex ante*.[2286] As a result, the direction of causality between a firm's ownership structure and characteristics is unclear: on the one hand, unfavorable characteristics of a firm as perceived by the existing blockholder frequently induce monitoring by this blockholder and substantial increases in firm value. On the other hand, a prospective blockholder may successfully identify firms with favorable characteristics and high firm value and subsequently purchase a stake in these firms.[2287] This is typically re-

---

[2279] Thereby, this section focuses on the effect of *[bh1_cont]* on firm value, that is, specification 2.4.1.

[2280] Demsetz (1983): 384.

[2281] See Demsetz (1983): 384, 386, 390. See also Demsetz/Lehn (1985): 1174 and Gedajlovic (1993): 735.

[2282] See Demsetz/Lehn (1985): 1156. See also Demsetz/Villalonga (2001): 215f.

[2283] See Demsetz/Villalonga (2001): 227, 230f. Thus, "different governance structures are optimal for different firms". Hermalin/Weisbach (1991): 102.

[2284] See Demsetz (1983): 386; Demsetz/Lehn (1985): 1174. See also Gedajlovic (1993): 736f.

[2285] See Gugler/Weigand (2003): 483. See also Gugler/Yurtoglu (2003): 740.

[2286] See Cronqvist/Fahlenbrach (2008): 3947 for an analogical explanation approach. See also Alonso-Bonis/de Andrés-Alonso (2007): 207.

[2287] See Lehmann/Weigand (2000); Börsch-Supan/Köke (2002): 297; Andres (2008): 443; Edmans (2014): 3.

ferred to as reverse causality or simultaneity,[2288] which constitutes one of the three sources of endogeneity.[2289]

Importance of Endogeneity

There are two arguments that question the importance of endogeneity in the case at hand. First, the existing empirical evidence does not find strong support for the presence of endogeneity. *Demsetz/Villalonga* (2001) examine the impact of two aspects of ownership structure, the fraction of shares owned by the five largest blockholders and the fraction of shares owned by corporate management, on Tobin's q. While they find "unequivocal evidence for the endogeneity of ownership structure"[2290] their evidence relates to the fraction owned by management rather than by the five largest blockholders.[2291] Hence, their results do not imply a universal validity of the endogenous nature of blockholdings. In their examination of the relationship between ownership structure and firm value, *Alonso-Bonis/Andrés-Alonso* (2007) provide evidence of an endogenous nature of the ownership structure, which, according to the authors, necessitates the need to complement existing estimation techniques with more sophisticated models that are able to control for endogeneity.[2292] However, the use of more sophisticated models largely provides results comparable to those observed when using more basic methodologies. *Anderson/Reeb* (2003), inter alia, use instrumental variables to control for a potential endogenous relationship between family ownership and firm performance in US firms. They find that the regressions employing instrumental variables produce results consistent with those of OLS.[2293] *Cornett et al.* (2007) examine the relation between institutional investor ownership and firm performance. To control for endogeneity, they use analyst coverage as an instrument for ownership by institutional blockholders. Their results using the instrument depict highly similar coefficients and standard errors compared to the original results. Hence, the authors conclude that endogeneity issues with regard to shareholdings are not severe.[2294] Also *Maury/Pajuste* (2005) find instrumental variable regressions to confirm the results of pooled OLS.[2295]

Empirical studies that employ alternative techniques do not provide support of endogeneity either. *Gutiérrez/Tribó* (2004) estimate multinomial logit models for the likelihood of a firm choosing a particular ownership structure. The results indicate that firm characteristics are weak predictors of ownership structures which are rather determined by exogenous factors

2288 See Kennedy (2008): 139f.

2289 See Wooldridge (2010): 55; Roberts/Whited (2013): 499. Endogeneity can also arise as a result of a measurement error. When either dependent or independent variables are measured imperfectly, the measurement error is contained in the error term. If it is correlated with one of the independent variables, OLS estimates are inconsistent. See Wooldridge (2010): 55; Roberts/Whited (2013): 501f. Moreover, endogeneity can arise as a result of omitted variables. If some characteristics that affect both firm value and the ownership variable are omitted, these appear in the error term. Provided these variables are correlated with the ownership variable, the regression suffers from endogeneity. See Börsch-Supan/Köke (2002): 297; Ruhwedel (2003): 160; Wooldridge (2010): 54f; Roberts/Whited (2013): 498.

2290 Demsetz/Villalonga (2001): 230.

2291 See Demsetz/Villalonga (2001): 228f.

2292 See Alonso-Bonis/de Andrés-Alonso (2007): 206f, 215.

2293 See Anderson/Reeb (2003): 1322.

2294 See Cornett et al. (2007): 1787.

2295 See Maury/Pajuste (2005): 1829, 1832.

important to the potential blockholder.[2296] *Cronqvist/Fahlenbrach* (2008) utilize the predictions with regard to the timing of changes in firm policies to test the potential endogeneity of their results. The authors find that the firm's policies just prior to an engagement of the blockholder are significantly different from the policies after the investment.[2297] Hence, the change in policies occurs after the blockholder's investment in the firm, being in support of an exogenous determination of the blockholder's presence.

With regard to German evidence, empirical results generally suggest an exogenous influence of blockholders on firm performance. *Gugler/Weigand* (2003) employ instrumental variable techniques and find that large shareholders have an impact on firm performance that is exogenous in the German system of corporate governance.[2298] Similarly, the estimation of regression models by instrumental variables as performed by *Edwards/Weichenrieder* (2004) provide no evidence that the results obtained using OLS techniques are affected by an inappropriate use of this estimation method.[2299] With regard to family ownership, *Andres* (2008) shows that even after controlling for endogeneity, the relationship between firm performance and family ownership variables remains unchanged.[2300] In contrast to these studies, *Seifert et al.* (2005) find that ownership is endogenously related to firm performance in Germany and propose the use of 2SLS rather than OLS for estimation.[2301]

The second argument refers to the stability of the largest blockholder's ownership. As outlined in section 6.2.3.1, the ownership of the largest blockholder remains stable during the sample period. This is further illustrated in figure 14 which plots the mean ownership of the largest blockholder per year as well as the mean Tobin's q. If the largest blockholder's ownership was endogenously related to firm value, a drop (increase) in Tobin's q would be followed by a drop (increase) of the largest blockholder's ownership. However, the drop in Tobin's q

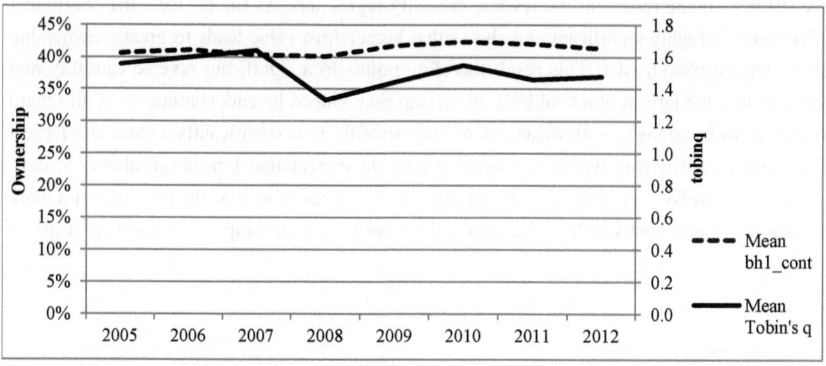

Figure 14: Mean bh1_cont and mean tobinq during 2005-2012

2296 See Gutiérrez/Tribó (2004): 4, 13f.

2297 See Cronqvist/Fahlenbrach (2008): 3967-3969.

2298 The evidence is based on regressions on 167 firms over the time period 1991-1996. See Gugler/Weigand (2003): 484, 486. The results support the evidence provided by Lehmann/Weigand (2000): 181 who find no gain from using instrumental variables and regard ownership concentration as an exogenous variable.

2299 See Edwards/Weichenrieder (2004): 163.

2300 See Andres (2008): 443f.

2301 See Seifert et al. (2005): 186.

from 2007 to 2008 does not affect the ownership of the largest blockholder which remains largely constant (40.28% in 2007 and 40.10% in 2008). Hence, the average largest blockholder apparently sticks to its portfolio firm.[2302] Moreover, one can only observe a slight increase in the ownership as a result of increasing Tobin's q in the years 2008-2010.[2303] Overall, the stable ownership is inconsistent with an endogenous ownership structure.[2304] An exogenous nature of the ownership structure is also suggested by the results on the lagged ownership variables which match those of the non-lagged variables. If blockholder ownership is endogenous, the ownership structure prior to the year showing improvements should be insignificant.

Endogeneity Tests

Despite these arguments, a number of endogeneity tests have been performed. A first, preliminary test constitutes a regression based on **reverse causality**. This involves a regression with the ownership of the largest blockholder as the dependent variable and firm value as primary explanatory variable.[2305] Here, the primary question is whether or not the variation in firm value explains the variation in the largest blockholder's ownership. Hence, the following equation is to be estimated:[2306]

$$\begin{aligned} \text{bh1\_cont}_{it} = {} & \alpha+\beta_1\text{tobinq}_{it}+\beta_2\text{growth}_{it}+\beta_3\text{ppe\_assets}_{it}+\beta_4\text{capex}_{it}+\beta_5\text{cash\_assets}_{it} \\ & +\beta_6\text{beta} + \beta_7\text{stdev\_ni}+\beta_8 \textstyle\sum_{i=1}^{N} \text{CONTROL}'_{it}+\beta_9\text{YEAR}_t+ \beta_{10}\text{INDUSTRY}_i \\ & +\nu_{it} \end{aligned} \tag{6.12}$$

Since the largest blockholder is significantly exposed to firm-specific risk, the risk of a firm may affect the size of the largest blockholder's ownership. Therefore, the two risk measures *[stdev_ni]* and *[beta]* are included as additional regressors. If *[bh1_cont]* is exogenous, the coefficient of firm value (β_1) should not be significantly different from zero. Table 66 (appendix 19) depicts the results of the reverse causality regression. As can be seen, the coefficient of *[tobinq]* is highly significant and shows that higher firm value leads to greater ownership of the largest blockholder. This result therefore points to a significant reverse causality and suggests that the largest blockholder's ownership may indeed be endogenous.[2307] With regard to the control variables, both measures of firm-specific risk significantly reduce the largest blockholder's ownership which is consistent with the expectation formulated above. Moreover, a firm's growth opportunities, the liquidity of its shares as well as the presence of a bank blockholder significantly reduce the largest blockholder's ownership.[2308] In contrast, a firm's

2302 See also Gugler/Yurtoglu (2003): 741; Andres (2008): 443.

2303 During this period, the mean ownership of the largest blockholder increases from 40.10% to 42.33%.

2304 Gugler/Weigand (2003): 483 follow a similar argumentation.

2305 For a similar approach, please see Lehmann/Weigand (2000): 178-181; Ruhwedel (2003): 249-252.

2306 The regression equation is estimated using pooled-OLS with standard errors clustered by firm.

2307 Lehmann/Weigand (2000): 181 find firm performance to be of "little help in explaining the variation of ownership concentration across firms and over time" and conclude that "ownership concentration can be taken as an exogenous variable". The authors measure performance based on the ROA.

2308 The negative effect of a bank blockholder illustrates a general reluctance of investors to invest in firm's with a bank blockholder which may arise as a result of the dual role of banks as shareholder and debtholder and the associated interest conflicts.

age, size, the issuance of preferred stock, and employee codetermination are associated with greater ownership of the largest blockholder.[2309]

In order to verify the preliminary evidence of endogeneity, a **Granger causality** test is performed.[2310] A general precondition for causality is that changes in the cause (independent) variable should precede changes in the effect (dependent) variable.[2311] In the case at hand, if *[bh1_cont]* is an endogenous variable, then changes in firm value should cause changes in the largest blockholder's ownership. Hence, the Granger causality analysis tests this condition by investigating if prior year firm value explains the current ownership of the largest blockholder.[2312] Therefore, it includes the lagged firm value as additional explanatory variable in a regression of *[bh1_cont]* on lagged values of *[bh1_cont]* and control variables.[2313] In particular, the following regression models are estimated:[2314]

$$\text{tobinq}_{it} = \alpha + \beta_{1a}\text{bh1\_cont}_{i(t-1)} + \beta_{2a}\text{tobinq}_{i(t-1)} + \beta_3\text{growth}_{it} + \beta_4\text{ppe\_assets}_{it} + \beta_5\text{capex}_{it} + \beta_6\text{cash\_assets}_{it} + \beta_7\sum_{i=1}^{N}\text{CONTROL}'_{it} + \beta_8\text{YEAR}_t + \beta_9\text{INDUSTRY}_i + \nu_{1,it} \quad (6.13)$$

$$\text{bh1\_cont}_{it} = \alpha + \beta_{1b}\text{bh1\_cont}_{i(t-1)} + \beta_{2b}\text{tobinq}_{i(t-1)} + \beta_3\text{growth}_{it} + \beta_4\text{ppe\_assets}_{it} + \beta_5\text{capex}_{it} + \beta_6\text{cash\_assets}_{it} + \beta_7\sum_{i=1}^{N}\text{CONTROL}'_{it} + \beta_8\text{YEAR}_t + \beta_9\text{INDUSTRY}_i + \nu_{2,it} \quad (6.14)$$

Provided *[bh1_cont]* is exogenous, lagged values of *[tobinq]* in equation 6.14 should add no information with regard to the explanation of the variation in ownership beyond that provided by lagged values of ownership and the remaining regressors.[2315] More formally, if $\beta_{1a} \neq 0$ and $\beta_{2b} = 0$, one can deduce unidirectional Granger causality from *[bh1_cont]* to *[tobinq]* and *[bh1_cont]* is said to be strictly exogenous. If $\beta_{1a} = 0$ and $\beta_{2b} \neq 0$ one can infer unidirectional Granger causality from *[tobinq]* to *[bh1_cont]* and *[bh1_cont]* is said to be endogenous.[2316] The results of the test are presented in table 39. As can be seen, the coefficient of the lagged values of *[bh1_cont]* in equation 6.13 (β_{1a}) is significantly different from zero at the 1% level. In addition, the coefficient of the lagged values of *[tobinq]* in equation 6.14 (β_{2b}) is not significantly different from zero. As a result, one can infer Granger causality from *[bh1_cont]* to *[tobinq]*; *[bh1_cont]* therefore can be regarded as exogenous. Similar results are observed when estimating equation 6.13 and 6.14 using *[bh1_cont]* and *[tobinq]* lagged by two periods.[2317] Overall, the Granger causality test provides evidence inconsistent with an endogenous nature of blockholder ownership.

2309 Despite all the criticism voiced by researchers and practitioners, codetermination does not seem to deter investments by blockholders.

2310 The test goes back to Granger (1969).

2311 See also Börsch-Supan/Köke (2002): 300f; Thomsen et al. (2006): 252.

2312 See also Bhagat/Jefferis Jr. (2002): 19.

2313 See also Dittmann et al. (2010): 49.

2314 The regression equation is estimated using pooled-OLS with standard errors clustered by firm.

2315 See Stock/Watson (2012): 580.

2316 See Granger (1969): 431; Greene (2003): 382, 592f; Thomsen et al. (2006): 253; Wooldridge (2012): 649f.

2317 Please note that Thomsen et al. (2006): 252 point to potential problems of the Granger causality test in case of only a few time series observations per firm, which might be the case in the present study.

Table 39
The following table presents selected results of the Granger causality test. The regressions include control variables as well as industry and year fixed effects; standard errors are clustered by firm. T-statistics are reported in parentheses. *, **, and *** indicates statistical significance at the 10%, 5%, and 1% level, respectively.

	Dependent Variable	
	tobinq	**bh1_cont**
bh1_cont (t-1)	**0.1018***	0.8056***
	(2.57)	(44.60)
tobinq (t-1)	0.6689***	**0.0063**
	(21.64)	**(1.35)**
bh1_cont (t-2)	**0.1213**	0.6880***
	(2.03)	(23.55)
tobinq (t-2)	0.5499***	**0.0071**
	(15.70)	**(1.04)**

Table 39: Results of the Granger causality test

Nevertheless, the **Durbin-Wu-Hausman test** is performed as a final endogeneity test.[2318] Under the assumption that *[bh1_cont]* is the only endogenous variable, the Durbin-Wu-Hausman test involves a two-stage procedure. In the first stage, *[bh1_cont]* is regressed on all exogenous variables of specification 2.4.1 as well as on the risk variables found significant in the reverse causality regression (equation 6.12); the residuals *[resid]* of this regression are obtained.

$$\begin{aligned} \text{bh1\_cont}_{it} = {} & \alpha + \beta_1 \text{growth}_{it} + \beta_2 \text{ppe\_assets}_{it} + \beta_3 \text{capex}_{it} + \beta_4 \text{cash\_assets}_{it} + \beta_5 \text{beta} \\ & + \beta_6 \text{stdev\_ni} + \beta_7 \textstyle\sum_{i=1}^{N} \text{CONTROL}'_{it} + \beta_8 \text{YEAR}_t + \beta_9 \text{INDUSTRY}_i \\ & + \nu_{1,it} \end{aligned} \tag{6.15}$$

In the second stage, the residuals *[resid]* obtained in stage 1 are included as an additional regressor in specification 2.4.1.[2319]

$$\begin{aligned} \text{tobinq}_{it} = {} & \alpha + \beta_1 \text{resid} + \beta_2 \text{bh1\_cont}_{it} + \beta_3 \text{growth}_{it} + \beta_4 \text{ppe\_assets}_{it} + \beta_5 \text{capex}_{it} \\ & + \beta_6 \text{cash\_assets}_{it} + \beta_7 \textstyle\sum_{i=1}^{N} \text{CONTROL}'_{it} + \beta_8 \text{YEAR}_t + \beta_9 \text{INDUSTRY}_i \\ & + \nu_{2,it} \end{aligned} \tag{6.16}$$

The reasoning underlying this procedure is as follows. Since the exogenous variables are uncorrelated with the error term ν_{it} of specification 2.4.1, *[bh1_cont]* is uncorrelated with ν_{it} if and only if $\nu_{1,it}$ is uncorrelated with ν_{it}. As the error term is unobservable, the test employs the regression residuals.[2320] The significance of these residuals is tested using a t-test with the null hypothesis of no endogeneity. If β_1 in equation 6.16 is significant, one has to reject the null hypothesis of no endogeneity. With regard to the coefficient β_1, the results of the regression show a t-statistic of -0.31 and a corresponding p-Value of 0.758. Consequently, the null hypothesis of no endogeneity does not have to be rejected.[2321]

2318 This test is applied by e.g. Ruhwedel (2003): 253f; Beiner et al. (2006): 267; Andreas et al. (2010): 66 and has been derived by Durbin (1954); Wu (1973) and Hausman (1978). It examines the differences between OLS and 2SLS estimates of a potentially endogenous variable and determines the statistical significance of this difference. Due to its easier application, this difference is typically calculated using a regression test. See e.g. Wooldridge (2010): 131; Wooldridge (2012): 527. This is also described in this section.

2319 The regression equation is estimated using pooled-OLS with standard errors clustered by firm. See also Wooldridge (2010): 131f.

2320 See Wooldridge (2012): 527f.

2321 The regression results of equation 6.15 and 6.16 are depicted in table 67 (appendix 19).

2SLS Instrumental Variable Estimation

Although the results of the endogeneity tests provide no support of endogeneity, the instrumental variable technique is employed to illustrate the robustness of the pooled-OLS results. This approach replaces the (potentially) endogenous variable *[bh1_cont]* with a variable (z) that is (1) correlated with the endogenous variable *[bh1_cont]* and (2) uncorrelated with the error term. Furthermore, the variable is not allowed to appear as an explanatory variable in the original regression equation (specification 2.4.1 in the case at hand); that is, the only role z plays in influencing *[tobinq]* is through its effect on *[bh1_cont]*. The variable z is then called the instrumental variable for *[bh1_cont]*.[2322]

The instrumental variable technique is typically estimated using 2SLS which can, as suggested by its name, be divided into two parts.[2323] In the first stage, *[bh1_cont]* is regressed on all exogenous variables of the original regression equation along with the instruments to obtain the predicted values for *[bh1_cont]*, $\widehat{bh1\_cont}_{it}$.[2324]

$$\begin{aligned} bh1\_cont_{it} = {} & \alpha+\beta_1 stdev_{ni}+\beta_2 beta+\beta_2 growth_{it}+\beta_3 ppe\_assets_{it}+\beta_4 capex_{it} \\ & +\beta_5 cash\_assets_{it}+\beta_6 \textstyle\sum_{i=1}^{N} CONTROL'_{it}+\beta_7 YEAR_t+\beta_8 INDUSTRY_i \\ & +v_{1,it} \end{aligned} \quad (6.17)$$

In equation 6.17, the portfolio firm's risk as measured by *[stdev_ni]* and *[beta]* is used as instrumental variable for *[bh1_cont]*. It is intuitive that shareholders choose their level of ownership according to the risk characteristics of the investee firm. If this firm has a high degree of risk, a shareholder should be unwilling to make a large investment, since this reduces its diversification and increases its exposure to the firm's risk. Hence, the higher a firm's risk, the lower the ownership size of the largest blockholder is likely to be.[2325] This has also been indicated by the results of the reverse causality regression above: table 66 shows a significantly negative impact of *[stdev_ni]* and *[beta]* on *[bh1_cont]*.[2326] Since equation 6.17 uses two instruments for one endogenous variable, one may want to test whether the instruments are valid in the sense that they are uncorrelated with the error term. *Wooldridge (2010)* suggests the Sargan test[2327] which tests the absence of correlations between the instruments and the error term under the null hypothesis of no correlation.[2328] Based on the two instruments, the test

---

2322 See Wooldridge (2010): 89f; Wooldridge (2012): 508; Roberts/Whited (2013): 511f. See also Bress (2008): 143; Hochberg (2011): 441.

2323 See Roberts/Whited (2013): 513f.

2324 See Wooldridge (2012): 521f; Roberts/Whited (2013): 513f. For a similar approach, see e.g. Ruhwedel (2003): 254f; Dahya et al. (2008): 92; Faccio et al. (2011): 3625.

2325 See also Edwards/Weichenrieder (2004): 162.

2326 Please note that the existing ownership literature frequently uses the lagged ownership variable as an instrument. See e.g. Januszewski et al. (2002): 317; Gugler/Weigand (2003): 484; Maury/Pajuste (2005): 1829; Bøhren/Ødegaard (2006): 57; Douma et al. (2006): 646; Andres (2008): 443. However, both the Granger causality and the robustness test in section 6.3.5.3 indicate that the lagged *[bh1_cont]* has a direct effect on firm value and therefore cannot be used as an instrument in the case at hand.

2327 For details, please see Sargan (1958).

2328 See Wooldridge (2010): 134-136.

yields a p-Value of 0.2640; consequently, the null hypothesis does not have to be rejected, providing some confidence in the instrumental variables used.[2329]

In the second stage of the 2SLS procedure, the original regression equation is estimated with the endogenous variable *[bh1_cont]* replaced with the predicted values $\widehat{bh1\_cont}_{it}$ from the first stage and all the control variables.[2330]

$$tobinq_{it} = \alpha + \beta_1 \widehat{bh1\_cont}_{it} + \beta_2 growth_{it} + \beta_3 ppe\_assets_{it} + \beta_4 capex_{it} + \beta_5 cash\_assets_{it} + \beta_6 \sum_{i=1}^{N} CONTROL'_{it} + \beta_7 YEAR_t + \beta_8 INDUSTRY_i + \nu_{2,it} \quad (6.18)$$

Having estimated the instrumental variable procedure, the results are compared with those of the pooled-OLS regression. If the results are similar in terms of signs and significance, there is no evidence of an endogenous relationship; causality in this case runs in one direction only.[2331]

Table 68 (appendix 19) presents the results.[2332] The regression delivers a significant (at the 5% level) and positive coefficient of $\widehat{bh1\_cont}_{it}$, suggesting that the largest blockholder's ownership significantly increases firm value also when estimated using instrumental variables. Although the significance of the coefficient is lower relative to pooled-OLS, the result does not provide evidence of an endogenous relationship. With regard to the control variables, the signs, magnitude, and significance remain unchanged for most variables. Only age, the ownership of insiders, and parity codetermination turn significant when using the 2SLS procedure. Overall, the near-equivalency of the results of the instrumental variable estimation technique, in particular with regard to the largest blockholder's ownership, confirms the validity of the pooled-OLS results. As suggested by the endogeneity tests, the ownership of the largest blockholder, at least in the present sample, is exogenously determined.

The use of instrumental variable techniques to counter endogeneity has met with substantial criticism in the academic literature. The major disadvantage of this approach is the difficulty to find a valid instrument.[2333] While the first condition of the instrument – its correlation with the endogenous variable – is testable, the absence of a correlation of the instrument with the error term is not testable.[2334] Moreover, the results of the instrumental variable regression highly depend on the quality of the instrument. Without an adequate theoretical underpinning for the selection of the instruments, the specification of simultaneous equation models is nontrivial.[2335] Therefore, *Dittmann et al.* (2010), *Konijn et al.* (2011), and *Drees et al.* (2013) abstain from using 2SLS techniques as they are unable to construct convincing instruments.[2336]

2329 This test is also applied by Januszewski et al. (2002): 317; Beiner et al. (2006): 273; Alonso-Bonis/de Andrés-Alonso (2007): 212. For criticism on this test, please see Roberts/Whited (2013): 515.

2330 See e.g. Ruhwedel (2003): 254f; Dahya et al. (2008): 92; Wooldridge (2010): 96f; Wooldridge (2012): 521-524; Roberts/Whited (2013): 513. As recommended by Wooldridge (2010): 98, the 2SLS model is estimated with heteroscedasticity-robust standard errors.

2331 See also Dahya et al. (2008): 92.

2332 In order to facilitate the comparison with the pooled-OLS regression, the regression output of the pooled-OLS is also depicted in column two.

2333 See Wooldridge (2010): 94; Coles et al. (2012): 165.

2334 See Bress (2008): 143, 146.

2335 See Leiber (2008): 198.

2336 See Dittmann et al. (2010): 50; Konijn et al. (2011): 1334; Drees et al. (2013): 295.

Laeven/Levine (2008) argue that they are unable to resolve questions about the direction of causality due to an insufficient number of valid instruments in the governance literature.[2337] *Bøhren/Ødegaard* (2006) find their empirical results to change when using 2SLS models. However, they argue that these results are sensitive to the choice of instruments and doubt that simultaneous equation models "can offer deeper insight than single-equation models into how corporate governance and economic performance interact."[2338] Based on these problems, the instrumental variable procedure can hardly be viewed as panacea for an investigation of the relationship between ownership and firm value. Therefore, any conclusions from this analysis should be drawn tentatively.

6.4 Limitations of the Study

The previous section illustrates the general robustness of the empirical results based on several additional tests. Nevertheless, the empirical analysis as well as the theoretical foundation might be subject to some limitations which are pointed out in the following.

Although the problem of **endogeneity** has been addressed by a number of robustness tests in section 6.3.5.4, they cannot eliminate all doubt due to concerns regarding the instrumental variable estimation technique. These concerns are primarily a result of an insufficient number of (valid) instruments for ownership concentration to be used in instrumental variable regressions, which has been criticized by a number of empirical researchers.[2339] Therefore, this does not constitute a limitation of the present thesis only, but applies to all empirical studies employing instrumental variable regressions as a robustness test for the endogeneity of ownership structures. Nevertheless, based on the available empirical methodologies, the present study addressed the endogeneity problem inherent in studies on firms' ownership structures to the highest possible extent. Future studies may employ a different empirical approach and use an event study methodology to address the endogeneity problem. This involves the identification of external events such as the acquisition of a share block and the subsequent analysis of the impact of these events on firm characteristics.[2340]

In addition to the agency-theoretic explanations for dividend payments, a firm may also adapt its dividend payments to match the blockholder's **tax preferences**. In general, the tax treatment of dividends and capital gains in Germany depends on the legal structure of the respective blockholder and the country of residence. An analysis of the blockholders' legal structure revealed that differences in terms of legal structure between the blockholder types are marginal: a majority of blockholders across the four blockholder types is organized as corporate bodies[2341]. If the blockholder is a German corporate body, dividends and capital gains (realized upon disposal of the shares) from equity investments are exempt from taxation.[2342] In the

2337 See Laeven/Levine (2008): 595.

2338 Bøhren/Ødegaard (2006): 62-64.

2339 See e.g. Laeven/Levine (2008): 595; Leiber (2008): 198; Dittmann et al. (2010): 50; Konijn et al. (2011): 1334; Drees et al. (2013): 295.

2340 See Börsch-Supan/Köke (2002): 305.

2341 In German: "Körperschaften".

2342 See § 8b (1) Sentence 1 KStG and § 8b (2) Sentence 1 KStG. Note that dividends, at the level of the issuing firm, are subject to a deduction of the capital gains tax pursuant to § 43 (1) Sentence 3 EStG, § 43 (1) No. 1

shareholder's tax assessment, only 5% of the income from dividends or capital gains are regarded as non-deductible costs.[2343] Hence, a tax consequence for a blockholder organized as a German corporate body only arises as a result of the non-deductible operating expenses to the amount of 5% of the income. Since this applies to capital gains and dividends alike, there should be no reason for a preference for dividends or capital gains at least at the level of the corporate body that has made the equity investment. However, this general tax exemption applies only as long as the income from dividends and capital gains remains within the corporate body. Tax consequences hence arise if it distributes this income to its own shareholder(s)[2344] which may for instance be the founding family. In general, the possibility of a tax-driven payout policy by a blockholder should be subject to a different investigation.

Moreover, the empirical results depend on the quality of the data. **Measurement errors** may occur in the measurement of ownership structures. As described in section 2.2.3.1, investors are required to publish information on the size of their voting rights whenever their holdings exceed or fall below certain thresholds. However, this requirement implies no reporting obligation for a shareholder that increases its ownership from 31% of the voting rights to 48%, although this might have a substantial effect on the shareholder's power, given the low shareholder presence on firms' AGMs.[2345] Therefore, an effective and efficient depiction of the sample firm's actual ownership structure is highly dependent on the quality of the database "Orbis". However, through the use of plausibility checks based on alternative data sources, measurement errors should be minimized. Besides, the study abstained from a focus on the ultimate owner, since a consistent identification of the ultimate owner could not be guaranteed. Therefore, it only researched the ultimate owner in the case of investment vehicles and family firms. In general, the thesis at hand may understate influences that result from a pyramidal ownership structure. Finally, measurement errors may result from the definition of blockholder types which involves a trade-off: while a more narrow definition of blockholder types improves the comparability, it also decreases the respective sample size and hence the statistical validity. With regard to this trade-off, the present thesis attached more weight to the statistical validity at the expense of a more narrow classification of, for example, the institutional investor group.

Measurement errors may also occur in the measurement of agency costs which have been indirectly approximated by variables that represent circumstances that most likely lead to agency costs as well as by aggregate outcome measures that proxy for specific components of agency costs. Therefore, the employed variables are imperfect in that they are unable to measure all manifestations of the agency costs. For instance, the proxy for managerial agency costs *[opex_sales]* measures the costs arising from shirking and perquisite consumption by the corporate management. However, an effectively monitoring blockholder may also foster a long-term focus, prevent value-reducing diversification strategies or mitigate the free cash

EStG in conjunction with § 32 (3) Sentence 3 KStG. These taxes, however, can be offset against the corporate income tax of the corporate body that receives the dividend. See § 43 (1) Sentence 3 EStG.

2343 See § 8b (5) Sentence 1 KStG.

2344 Tax consequences only arise, if this shareholder is not another corporate body.

2345 See section 2.2.5.

flow problem. These aspects are not captured by the managerial agency cost proxy which might subsequently understate the total effect of blockholder monitoring on managerial agency costs. Nevertheless, one may argue that a blockholder whose monitoring effectively reduces managerial shirking and perquisite consumption may also limit other forms of managerial malfeasance. Hence, *[opex_sales]* may be regarded as proxy for a general endeavor of the blockholder to monitor corporate management. Similarly, also the firm's payout policy, proxying for principal-principal agency costs, constitutes only one of several mechanisms blockholders can use to pursue private benefits at the expense of the remaining shareholders. With regard to shareholder-debtholder agency costs, *[discr_assets]* does not measure actual agency costs but rather the blockholder's potential to engage in wealth transfer strategies. By focusing on opportunities for the blockholder to transfer wealth, it constitutes an indirect measure of agency costs of debt which should be kept in mind when interpreting the corresponding evidence.

Moreover, the model and methodology might be limited due to an **inability to capture all forms of monitoring**. The influence of blockholders on a firm's management is frequently exerted in private and informal meetings or phone calls between blockholder representatives and management and is thus imperceptible.[2346] Moreover, blockholder monitoring, or the mere presence of a blockholder, may indirectly and hence unverifiably deter corporate or managerial malfeasance.[2347] While the benefits of a successful deterrence of managerial malfeasances and behind-the-scenes negotiations redound to the benefit of the remaining shareholders, it is questionable whether they are accounted for in the shareholders' assessment of firm value. An analysis of the impact of a firm's ownership structure on its value may thus underestimate the benefits of blockholder monitoring.[2348] However, note that the inability to observe the blockholder's monitoring activities understates the effect of blockholder monitoring to the extent that the remaining shareholders are not aware of this monitoring and hence do not reflect this in the firm's stock price. In contrast, the inability to observe the blockholder's monitoring should have no influence on the three agency cost proxies, since they measure the outcome of the activism and hence comprise all forms of activism that lead to the respective outcome. Overall, the inability to comprehend all forms of (private) monitoring does not question the validity of the results. Rather, it illustrates that, when incorporated, unobservable forms of monitoring should further increase the significance of the results.

The empirical analysis is based on three important theoretical assumptions. Although the **drawbacks of the theoretical assumptions** have been knowingly accepted, they constitute limitations of the present thesis. A primary assumption is that a firm's existing or future shareholders formulate rational expectations, are knowledgeable about and able to provide estimates of a firm's overall agency costs, and are subsequently able to include these estimates into their assessment of firm value. Although this assumption accredits significant capabilities

---

2346 See e.g. Black (1998): 8; Gillan/Starks (1998): 20; Gillan/Starks (2003): 11f; Becht et al. (2008): 3095f; van der Elst/Vermeulen (2011): 14f.

2347 See Barber (2006): 10. In line with this, Bottazzi et al. (2008): 489 state that the measurement of monitoring constitutes a major empirical challenge, as the blockholder's activities are non-contractible and thus not reported in contracts, difficult to observe, and consequently also unavailable in standard data sources.

2348 See Barber (2006): 10.

to the shareholders, *Core et al.* (2006) find that both analysts and investors are able to incorporate superior governance in the firms' stock prices.[2349] The derivation of the hypotheses regarding firm value further assumes that shareholders attach equal weight to the overall agency cost components. While this serves the purpose of simplification, it may not be a truly adequate picture of reality, since shareholders may give different weights to the agency cost types when valuing a firm's shares. Finally, it is assumed that the blockholder's impact on firm value reflects its net effect on the firm's overall agency costs. However, the effect on firm value may stem from additional aspects that cannot be explained by agency theoretic propositions. These may comprise certification and reputation effects of the blockholder or expected transfers of resources from the investor to the investee firm. Thus, a positive relationship between blockholder ownership and firm value might not necessarily imply reduced overall agency costs through monitoring but may result from the signaling effect which is associated with a large block acquisition. In this case, there is a correlation between blockholder monitoring and firm value, however, no actual causal relationship.

Overall, these limitations are not expected to seriously challenge the main conclusions drawn in the empirical analysis. However, in line with the (post)positivist worldview, one has to acknowledge that "evidence established in research is always imperfect and fallible." [2350] Therefore, "absolute truth can never be found."[2351]

2349 See Core et al. (2006): 659, 684f.
2350 Creswell (2009): 7. See also Phillips/Burbules (2000): 3.
2351 Creswell (2009): 7. See also Phillips/Burbules (2000): 77.

7 Conclusion

The following chapter aims at a conclusion of the present research. Therefore, section 7.1 first outlines the selected approach. Section 7.2 then presents the key findings of the analysis as well as their implications for the current corporate governance debate. Finally, section 7.3 highlights some opportunities for future research in the context of blockholder monitoring.

7.1 Approach

Shareholder engagement and monitoring is currently high on the agenda of policymakers, both on a global and a European level. In its review on corporate governance in both financial and non-financial institutions, the European Commission concluded that shareholders did not engage in an active monitoring of their portfolio firms to contribute to their long-term viability. Therefore, the Commission questioned the effectiveness of corporate governance rules that presuppose effective shareholder monitoring. Moreover, the Commission implemented a new regulation with regard to AIFMs which had not been regulated before. This regulation seeks to increase the transparency and accountability of, inter alia, private equity firms with regard to their motives underlying their investments in public or private companies.

In light of these developments, the present thesis aimed to provide a clearer understanding of the nature and effect of shareholder monitoring. In particular, the purpose of the thesis was to *determine the influence of blockholders on agency costs and firm value* for a sample of publicly-held German firms during the time period of 2005-2012. Thereby, it aspired to move away from a one-size-fits-all approach by accounting for the specific institutional and organizational settings, blockholder heterogeneity, and blockholder interrelationships.

In order to achieve this purpose, the thesis adopted a positive scientific approach and thus primarily focused on drawing theoretically-guided causal inferences. Founded on an extension of agency theoretic propositions, it developed a revised definition of blockholder monitoring. According to the traditional corporate governance view, a blockholder's large ownership provides it with the incentive and power to monitor corporate management, thereby solving the problem of rational apathy faced by small shareholders. The blockholder's monitoring mitigates managerial agency problems and the resulting agency costs which is ultimately reflected in an increased firm value to the benefit of all shareholders. However, this understanding of blockholder monitoring suffers from a number of deficiencies, since some of its assumptions may not be applicable in the case of a single (or multiple) blockholder(s). Therefore, the revised definition of blockholder monitoring acknowledges that (1) the maximization of shareholder value is complemented by private benefits of control within a blockholder's utility function; (2) opportunistic behavior can also be exerted by shareholders; (3) next to the manager-shareholder agency relationship, a blockholder's monitoring also affects the remaining agency relationships within a firm since it simultaneously acts as agent to the firm's debtholders and remaining shareholders, and (4) blockholder monitoring does not per se result in increased firm value. Moreover, it was argued that a blockholder's monitoring may be affected by some determinants that have frequently been disregarded in existing empirical studies, namely blockholder characteristics, blockholder interrelationships, the legal environment, the presence of alternative governance mechanisms, and the characteristics of the blockholder's portfolio firm.[2352]

On the basis of the revised definition of blockholder monitoring, these determinants were incorporated in a model of blockholder monitoring. According to the model, the size of its ownership provides the blockholder both with the incentive and the power to engage in active and continuous monitoring of corporate management. This managerial monitoring does not only affect the manager-shareholder agency conflict but also the shareholder-debtholder and principal-principal agency conflicts. As a consequence, the blockholder's impact on firm value does not only depend on its effect on managerial agency costs but on its net effect on a firm's overall agency costs. This net effect is reflected in the blockholder's influence on firm value. The model therefore envisages the effect of blockholder monitoring on a firm's overall agency costs and firm value to be examined in separate analyses. Moreover, it allows for an assessment of whether or not an effect on a firm's agency costs is indeed reflected in firm value and whether or not blockholders have an effect on firm value that goes beyond their effect on a firm's overall agency costs.

In order to determine the influence of blockholders on agency costs and firm value, the model was estimated in three stages which reflect the three research questions the thesis aims to answer. Based on the assumption of blockholder homogeneity, the first stage investigated *if concentrated ownership affects agency costs and firm value*. Thereby, this stage disregarded any factor that might affect blockholder monitoring apart from alternative governance mechanisms and firm characteristics as well as additional controls. Based on the assumption of blockholder heterogeneity, the second stage investigated *if the characteristics of the largest blockholder affect agency costs and firm value*. Hence, this stage accounted for blockholder heterogeneity in terms of the ownership size, presence on the portfolio firm's management or supervisory board, and identity[2353]. Based on the assumption of blockholder interrelationships, the third stage investigated *if blockholder interrelationships affect agency costs and firm value as well the relationship between the four blockholder types and agency costs and firm value*. Therefore, the third stage accounted for the heterogeneity of a firm's ownership structure, the largest blockholder's incontestability, and the presence of a second blockholder. Simultaneously, it accounted for blockholder heterogeneity in terms of the blockholder identities.

Based primarily on agency theoretic propositions, the thesis deducted hypotheses with regard to the expected relationship between these variables and agency costs and firm value for each of the three research questions. In line with a deductive procedure, the causal relationships specified within the hypotheses were subsequently tested empirically. Thereby, the empirical analysis employed an advanced version of the pooled-OLS which incorporated industry and year fixed effects that account for unobserved effects across industries and time. The key results of this empirical analysis are summarized in the following section.

[2352] Due to a focus on German firms, the impact of the legal environment could not be investigated.

[2353] The identities accounted for are: families, strategic investors, institutional investors, and private equity investors.

7.2 Key Findings and Implications

Before turning to the results of the regression analysis and their implications, this part provides a brief summary of the descriptive results to highlight the most important characteristics of the German ownership pattern during the years 2005-2012.

Summary of the Descriptive Results

As illustrated by previous studies,[2354] the ownership structure of German publicly-held firms decreased as a result of significant changes in the financial system in the early-2000s. However, the evidence provided for the years 2005-2012 shows that the alteration of the ownership structure, at least on an aggregated level, may have been concluded. In particular, the cumulative ownership of blockholders within a particular firm remains largely stable within a range of 51.73% (2005) and 54.04% (2012), respectively, and is thus still highly concentrated. The presence of blockholders is pervasive – roughly 96.16% of the sample firms have a blockholder in 2012. With regard to the largest blockholder, its average equity ownership exceeds 40% in every year of the sample. In more than 60% of the sample firms, the largest blockholder owns a blocking minority and in more than one-third of the firms it owns the simple majority. The results further suggest that blockholders consciously acquire their stakes with due regard to important ownership thresholds and the associated ownership rights. Overall, the average largest blockholder possesses sufficient power to effectively monitor management but also substantial discretion – all the more if one accounts for the low shareholder presence at the firms' AGMs. The four blockholder types investigated within this thesis, together with banks and insider blockholders, represent the largest blockholder in about 87% of the sample firms. Hence, the present thesis covers the most important blockholder types within German ownership structures. Of these blockholder types, families most frequently constitute the largest blockholder, followed by strategic investors, private equity investors, and institutional investors. If they are the largest blockholder, strategic investors hold the greatest equity ownership of all blockholder types.

Extending the scope beyond the largest blockholder, the analysis illustrates that, of the sample firms with a blockholder, the number of firms with more than one blockholder increases from 61.69% in 2005 to 68.09% in 2012. In addition, more than one-third of the firms have more than two blockholders. In general, the average number of blockholders across all firms equals 2.43 in 2012, the largest number of blockholders within a single firm equals ten. The analysis further showed that the average ownership of the second largest blockholder amounts to about 13-15% of the voting rights and is thus substantially smaller than the average ownership of the largest blockholder. With regard to the blockholder identities, institutional investors most frequently constitute the second or third largest blockholder, followed by families, strategic investors, and private equity investors. The second largest blockholder thereby seems to favor investments in firms whose largest blockholder is of the same type as itself. Overall, the findings highlight the importance of incorporating additional blockholders and likely blockholder

2354 See section 2.2.4.

interrelationships when studying blockholder monitoring within the German corporate landscape.

Summary of the Regression Results

The summary of the regression results is structured according to the research questions and the corresponding assumptions of blockholder homogeneity, heterogeneity, and interrelationships. With regard to the assumption of **blockholder homogeneity**, it has been assumed that aggregate ownership measures may have a limited ability to explain the variation in the respective dependent variable, since they amalgamate various blockholder particularities and ownership structures despite their potential effect on the blockholder's power, ability, and incentive to monitor. Consistent with this assumption, none of the aggregate ownership measures has a statistically significant impact on managerial agency costs. Moreover, only one of the ownership measures is found to significantly reduce agency costs of debt. In contrast, from the perspective of the remaining shareholders, the evidence with regard to principal-principal agency costs and firm value is uniformly consistent with a favorable effect of blockholder monitoring: all aggregate ownership variables are significantly associated with lower principal-principal agency costs and higher firm value, despite the aggregation of effects by these ownership variables. This suggests that the favorable influence of blockholder monitoring on principal-principal agency costs and firm value on average predominates across the diverse particularities of blockholders and ownership structures. Nevertheless, the results under the assumption of blockholder homogeneity show that concentrated ownership has a limited effect at least on managerial agency costs and agency costs of debt. Moreover, the results are limited in that they do not allow a conclusion on whether the insignificant relationships stem from intentional blockholder passivity or ineffective blockholder monitoring on the one hand, or from aggregating potentially opposing effects across different blockholder particularities and ownership structures on the other hand. In conclusion, the evidence on measures of ownership concentration highlights the importance of employing more advanced variables which are able to account for the particularities of blockholders and of a firm's ownership structure.

With regard to particularities of blockholders, the following key findings emerge under the assumption of **blockholder heterogeneity**. The largest blockholder's monitoring and hence its effect on agency costs and firm value strongly depends on its *ownership size*. Apart from managerial agency costs, the blockholder's monitoring associated with its ownership size decreases all components of a firm's overall agency costs which is also reflected in a higher firm value.

The evidence with regard to the *blockholder's presence on its portfolio firm's supervisory or management board* does not support the importance of board presence as a determinant of blockholder monitoring stressed by theoretical arguments. A blockholder's representation on the firm's management board does not unfold a significant influence on any agency cost variable or firm value. A blockholder's representation on the firm's supervisory board, however, is associated with lower dividend payments and a higher firm value. Due to its effect on firm value, the negative impact of the blockholder's supervisory broad presence on dividend payments is not regarded as evidence of a greater likelihood of principal-principal agency conflicts but of a substitution effect. In contrast to principal-principal agency costs and firm value, supervisory board presence of the largest blockholder has no effect on managerial agency costs and agency costs of debt.

The empirical analysis further highlights that the effect of the largest blockholder's ownership on agency costs and firm value differs between the *four blockholder types* investigated. The ownership of institutional investors significantly decreases managerial agency costs, agency costs of debt, and principal-principal agency costs. However, this reduction of all components of a firm's overall agency costs is not reflected in a higher firm value. Share ownership of family blockholders significantly lowers managerial agency costs; these reductions are also reflected in a higher firm value. Private equity investors significantly decrease principal-principal agency costs and increase firm value. Higher firm values are also observed for strategic investors, although they do not have a significant effect on any component of a firm's overall agency costs. Of the family blockholders, private equity and strategic investors, the largest increase in firm value can be observed for private equity investors. This increase is also economically significant: If a firm with a median firm value goes from the private equity blockholder's mean ownership to zero percent, firm value would decrease by about 20% c.p. Overall, these results do not provide evidence of potential adverse effects of these blockholders on their portfolio firm's stakeholders. If any of the four blockholder types engages in the transfer of wealth from debtholders or in an expropriation of the remaining shareholders, this is not achieved through greater investments in discretionary assets or the retention of capital within the blockholder's portfolio firm, respectively. Accounting for non-linear effects, this conclusion, however, has to be qualified at least for family blockholders. The corresponding results show that beyond a certain level of ownership, the family blockholder is associated with greater managerial agency costs and agency costs of debt. Furthermore, the results on principal-principal agency costs point to family entrenchment at higher levels of ownership. The adverse effect of family blockholders is recognized by a firm's remaining shareholders: family ownership decreases firm value if it exceeds a level of about 57%.

Board presence also does not consistently affect the ownership size effect of any blockholder type on agency costs or firm value. Two exceptions constitute private equity and family blockholders: The evidence indicates that the increase in firm value resulting from *private equity* ownership is stronger if the private equity investor is present on its portfolio firm's supervisory board. In contrast, the ownership of *families* that are present on a firm's management board significantly decreases firm value which is particularly striking since families *not* present on the management board significantly increase firm value. Thus, the remaining shareholders seem to account for family entrenchment and a greater "us versus them" mentality. Altogether, the weak evidence with regard to board presence questions the importance of management or supervisory board representation for effective monitoring, at least for the blockholder types examined in the study at hand. All in all, the evidence on the four blockholder types illustrates that a differentiation between blockholder types is essential for a better understanding of shareholders' impact on their portfolio firms.

The model of blockholder monitoring also allows for an assessment of whether or not the blockholder identities have an effect on firm value beyond their effect on a firm's overall agency costs. In this regard, the results indeed show that the effect of the blockholder types on firm value does not exclusively stem from their effect on a firm's overall agency costs. Thus, with the exception of institutional investors, the blockholders create value for their portfolio firms and the firms' shareholders that goes beyond their influence on agency costs. This value may stem from the blockholders' reputation and the associated signaling effect or from expected knowledge transfers.

The analysis based on the assumption of **blockholder interrelationships** shows that the *second largest blockholder* has a significant effect on the relationship between the largest blockholder type and agency costs and firm value. However, a significant effect cannot be observed for all four blockholder types which suggests that the influence of the second largest blockholder depends on the respective blockholder identity. In particular, the second largest blockholder's ownership amplifies the reduction in managerial agency costs associated with the ownership of private equity firms and families. Moreover, the second largest blockholder's ownership augments the decrease in agency costs of debt associated with institutional investor and family ownership. This effect is of particular interest for family blockholders, since they, in the absence of a second blockholder, are associated with higher agency costs of debt which suggests that the second blockholder effectively supervises the family and limits transfers of wealth. With regard to principal-principal agency costs, the ownership of the second largest blockholder does not significantly influence the effect of any blockholder identity's ownership. However, it does not suggest greater blockholder-blockholder agency conflicts arising as a result of the second blockholder's presence either. Except for institutional investors, the effect of the second largest blockholder's ownership on firm value reflects its effect on the components of a firm's overall agency costs: its ownership amplifies the increase in firm value associated with the ownership of private equity firms and families. Overall, the evidence suggests that, from the perspective of the remaining shareholders, the second largest blockholder's ownership is favorable at least if the largest blockholder is a family or private equity investor and neither results in greater principal-principal agency conflicts nor in a collusion of the two blockholders against the remaining shareholders.

Accounting for the *identity of the second largest blockholder* provides further evidence with regard to the monitoring performed by the blockholder types. If the two largest blockholders are strategic investors, the empirical results point to higher managerial agency costs which suggests that the two blockholders collude and allow management to realize some private benefits in order to generate private benefits themselves. This is supported by their increasing effect on principal-principal agency costs which is higher for higher ownership of the second largest blockholder, given it is also a strategic investor. With regard to firm value, the strategic investor's ownership has a significant positive effect in the absence of a second blockholder of the same type. However, if the two largest blockholders are strategic investors, they negatively affect firm value, albeit not significantly so. Overall, this evidence suggests that if they are the two largest blockholders, strategic investors seem to collude and pursue private benefits to the detriment of the remaining shareholders. With regard to family blockholders, previous evidence illustrates that their ownership significantly decreases managerial agency costs and increases firm value and that these effects are amplified by the presence of a second blockholder. However, if the second largest blockholder is a family member as well, the influences change sign and point to higher managerial agency costs and lower firm value. Although these effects are not significant, they raise concerns about potential adverse effects for the remaining shareholders if a family blockholder has an opportunity to collude. Similar effects are not observed for private equity and institutional investors which both decrease principal-principal agency costs and in the case of private equity investors, increase firm value also in the presence of a second blockholder of the same type.[2355] Apparently, these types have lower incentives to expropriate the remaining stakeholders since they frequently interact with other investors in different firms and are therefore interested in a good reputation.

Similar results are found for the *incontestability of the blockholder identities*. The results on both the strategic investors' and families' incontestability illustrate that for higher incontestability, a strategic investor's or family's positive ownership size effect on their portfolio firms' principal-principal agency costs turns stronger. For both types, the higher principal-principal agency costs are not reflected in firm value, which is astonishing, but can possibly be explained by offsetting benefits of both investors accounted for by the remaining shareholders. With regard to the incontestability of private equity and institutional investors, the results are mixed. Although a firm's shareholders seem to be skeptical towards their incontestability, these investors generally are not found to increase agency costs or to lower firm value.

The evidence with regard to the *heterogeneity of a firm's ownership structure* unidirectionally points to a reduction of all components of a firm's overall agency costs. In particular, greater heterogeneity appears to enhance the effectiveness and intensity of managerial monitoring by enabling blockholders to benefit from complementarities and facilitating mutual monitoring among blockholders. Moreover, it contributes to a reduction of agency costs of debt, since it increases the likelihood of the presence of a blockholder that either shares the same self-interest as a firm's debtholders or faces substantial costs as a result of an exploitation of debtholders. Finally, a more heterogenous ownership structure results in lower principal-principal agency costs due to a reduction of minority shareholder-blockholder agency costs which apparently is not outweighed by greater blockholder-blockholder agency costs arising from the simultaneous presence of different blockholders. The net effect of heterogenous ownership structures on a firm's overall agency costs is also reflected in firm value which increases with greater heterogeneity of the respective firm's ownership structure. Overall, a more heterogenous ownership structure seems to provide benefits for both the firm's debtholders and shareholders.

The regression results are robust to including a wide array of firm-specific characteristics, alternative governance mechanisms specific to the German institutional environment, and other control variables that may either be associated with agency costs and firm value or ownership structure variables. The results are not driven by an endogeneity of blockholder ownership

[2355] Institutional investors decrease agency costs of debt also in the presence of a second blockholder of the same type.

and are statistically significant over a range of model specifications and **robustness tests**. Additional year-by-year regressions largely confirm the results of the whole sample with regard to the influence of the blockholder types' ownership. During the peak of the financial crisis in 2008 and 2009, private equity and family blockholders still had a positive effect on firm value. In contrast, none of the alternative governance mechanisms had a significant positive effect on firm value, suggesting that at least blockholder monitoring exerted by families and private equity investors is either more effective than, or acts as a substitute for, alternative governance mechanisms. Reestimating the model on a sample split into financially distressed and non-distressed firms further highlights that the effect of a blockholder's monitoring and hence its impact on firm value depends on the financial condition of the respective firm. In financially distressed firms, the more experienced private equity and institutional investors have the greatest effect on firm value, possibly due to their superior expertise in improving firm performance through efficiency improvements or divestments. Their positive effect on firm value illustrates that monitoring performed by institutional investors is not per se ineffective in increasing firm value, as suggested by the evidence on the whole sample.

Implications

The subsequent section deals with the implications of the aforementioned empirical results, uses these results to address the key issues raised by the current corporate governance debate and formulates recommendations or suggestions.[2356] From a scientific perspective, it thereby goes beyond the positive scientific approach of detecting causal relationships and adopts a normative approach.

Overall, the empirical results illustrate that blockholder monitoring is effective in improving firm value. Yearly regressions further suggest that the largest blockholder's ownership has been effective in improving the value of German publicly-held firms also during the peak of the financial crisis in 2008 and 2009. Hence, in terms of firm value, this evidence does not provide support for the Commission's statement that shareholders have not lived up to their role of responsible owners. Nevertheless, the effect of blockholder monitoring is found to differ between the four blockholder types investigated, their respective level of ownership, and their incontestability. As a result, any endeavor to encourage shareholder monitoring by the European Commission needs to abandon a one-size-fits-all approach. While it is certainly not feasible to differentiate all particularities of ownership structures, the Commission should recognize that the blockholders' monitoring, inter alia, depends on their identity, ownership, and interrelationships with other blockholders within the same firm. Therefore, it is recommended that the design of an eventual regulation is accompanied by empirical research and subject to scientific monitoring in order to avoid adverse consequences for certain blockholders.

One of the proposals made by the Commission comprised initiatives to improve the visibility of shareholdings and the identification of shareholders' identities to allow firms to better cooperate with their shareholders. Due to the substantial distinctions in the monitoring effec-

[2356] For the key issues, please see section 1.1 as well as section 2.3.1 and 2.3.2.

tiveness or intensity exerted by the four different blockholder types, the Commission's aim is understandable. Based on the results of this research, the identification of shareholders might enable companies and their management to overcome their concerns regarding blockholder monitoring and to understand the impact of different investor types and the structure of ownership in general. In light of the better understanding of blockholder monitoring, it might be recommendable for firm management to develop and foster ownership structures that result in a certain degree of monitoring and thereby signal their determination to maximize shareholder value.[2357]

The Commission further aims at a facilitation and simplification of shareholder cooperation. In this respect, the empirical evidence suggests that, from the perspective of the remaining shareholders, the second largest blockholder's ownership has a favorable effect and does not result in a collusion of the two blockholders against the remaining shareholders. However, this effect depends on the type of the largest and second largest blockholder. If both blockholders are of the same type, the presence of a second blockholder may precisely have the contrary effect: Evidence on strategic investors and, to a lesser extent, on family blockholders, suggests that if the two largest blockholders are strategic investors or members of the same family, this increases managerial and principal-principal agency costs. The results also highlight substantial benefits to be gained from a more heterogenous ownership structure which seems to enable the blockholders to benefit from complementarities and reduces their incentives to act opportunistically. In light of these findings, it is to be welcomed that the Commission seeks to increase shareholder cooperation, as long as it is conscious of potential collusive agreements in case of reconcilable blockholder interests. Moreover, the Commission should aim at facilitating diverse ownership structures.

The European Commission also raised the issue of minority shareholder protection. On an aggregated level, the evidence provided by the present study does not suggest a need for minority shareholder protection. However, this statement does not uniformly apply to all peculiarities of blockholders or of the firms' ownership structures. With regard to *family blockholders*, the ownership of a founding family beyond a certain level seems to result in family entrenchment and an unfavorable effect of family ownership from the perspective of shareholders. A similar unfavorable effect on firm value is observed if the family is represented on its portfolio firm's management board. In addition, a family's ownership is associated with greater principal-principal agency costs for higher levels of incontestability. Taken as a whole, this evidence may hint at potential adverse effects for the remaining shareholders if a family blockholder is provided with excessive power. Similar results are found for *strategic investors* which seem to collude and pursue private benefits if they constitute the two largest blockholders. Moreover, a greater incontestability of a strategic investor results in higher principal-principal agency costs. Although these effects are not reflected in a lower firm value, they most likely have detrimental effects for the remaining shareholders. As shown by these examples, minority shareholder protection may indeed prove necessary in case of specific owner-

2357 Pagano/Röell (1998): 189 argue that the right ownership structure acts as a "precommitment device" for the limitation of agency costs.

ship set-ups. While a more specific protection of minority shareholders in each of these cases is impracticable, the European Commission should focus its endeavors on raising public and especially (minority) shareholders' awareness of the possible adverse effects inherent in these ownership set-ups.

Both the European Commission and the OECD criticized the role of institutional investors in the monitoring of their portfolio firms. With regard to their effect on a firm's overall agency costs, this criticism is not justifiable, since institutional investors decrease each component of overall agency costs and are thus unlikely to be subject to interest conflicts. However, their favorable effect on agency costs is only reflected in a higher firm value for firms in financial distress. The evidence for all sample firms as well as for the years of the financial crisis suggests that a firm's shareholders seem to account for additional (adverse) aspects of institutional investors that are not captured by agency theoretic explanations. Consequently, the Commission should further inquire into the inability of institutional investors to increase firm value.

Based on evidence provided by the present thesis, the strict regulation with regard to private equity investments in publicly-held firms cannot be justified. Although their portfolio firms indeed pay out dividends, the simultaneous positive effect on firm value does not provide evidence consistent with asset stripping at the expense of the remaining shareholders. More likely, the average private equity investor effectively monitors in the interest of the remaining shareholders by paying out any excess cash and thereby signaling an absence of principal-principal agency conflicts. With regard to its effect on firm value, private equity investors' ownership is associated with the greatest increase of all investor types. Moreover, this increase is amplified by its presence on the supervisory board, the ownership of a second blockholder, and by the ownership of a second blockholder that is a private equity investor as well. Only the results on the incontestability of private equity investors may suggest some concern of the remaining shareholders.

7.3 Opportunities for Future Research

The present research contributes to an advancement of the current state of academic knowledge in a number of aspects. First, based on agency theoretic propositions, it developed sound theoretical reasoning for the influence of blockholders on agency costs and firm value that provides a more complete (theoretical) understanding of the functioning of blockholder monitoring. Second, it addressed the existing research gap with regard to the effect of certain particularities of the blockholder and the firms' ownership structure which have not or only insufficiently been investigated by previous empirical evidence. Third, by combining measures of agency costs and firm value within a single study, the present research was able to examine if the effect of blockholder monitoring on firm value is indeed attributable to its effect on a firm's agency costs and thereby presented new evidence on the functioning of blockholder monitoring. Finally, the present thesis provided a detailed description of the newly formed ownership patterns as a result of the changes in Germany's financial system. Nevertheless, the research at hand could not address all existing research gaps and simultaneously uncovered new opportunities for future research.

As previously stated, the model and methodology of the present thesis are limited by an inability to capture all forms and manifestations of blockholder monitoring. While this does not question the validity of the results, it would be interesting to delineate the specific means blockholders use to monitor and influence their portfolio firms. For instance, *Becht et al.* (2008) conduct a clinical study of active monitoring by the Hermes UK Fund and find that private and informal influences are predominantly used for active monitoring.[2358] While this study already provides interesting insights, similar surveys might be conducted with additional blockholder types to compare the respective mechanisms used. Alternatively, these surveys may address the management of firms with blockholders in order to get an insight on the non-public monitoring mechanism used by blockholders.

The theoretical foundation of the model of blockholder monitoring and the derivation of the hypotheses has been based primarily on agency theoretic propositions. Although the present thesis extended the traditional view of blockholder monitoring and provided a revised definition, agency theory has been limited in explaining all observed effects. For instance, it is astonishing that the reduction of a firm's agency costs by institutional investors is not reflected in a higher firm value. Apparently, a firm's remaining shareholders account for some additional (adverse) aspects of institutional investors. In search for potential explanations, future studies may generate further insights by complementing agency theory with propositions of additional theories.

Another limitation of the present thesis constitutes its focus on the German environment which has been regarded as an interesting research area for several reasons. The highly concentrated ownership structures as well as the prevalence of ownership structures with multiple blockholders enable the investigation of blockholder monitoring and the effect of blockholder interrelationships in the first place. However, similar ownership structures are also observed for other continental European countries, such as Spain and Italy.[2359] In light of the key issues raised by the European Commission, it might be necessary to empirically assess the research questions and corresponding hypotheses formulated in the present thesis also in the context of alternative environments.

The results on a sample split between financially distressed and non-distressed firms illustrate that the effect of the blockholder identities' monitoring depends on the financial condition of the respective firm.[2360] On the one hand, this reflects differential skills and experience of blockholders in the management and turn-around of distressed firms. On the other hand, blockholder monitoring in distressed firms should also offer greater possibilities to raise firm value through effective monitoring and thus provides blockholders with greater incentives to

2358 Please see Becht et al. (2008) for further evidence.

2359 With regard to Spain, see Ruiz-Mallorquí/Santana-Martín (2011): 123. With regard to Italy, see De Cesari (2012): 209.

2360 Using a similar approach, Bhojraj/Sengupta (2003): 467-469 find that institutional ownership has a stronger favorable impact on bond yields and ratings for firms with a lower credit rating and argue that the monitoring role of governance mechanisms should be more critical for firms with poor credit ratings.

engage in monitoring in the first place. Based on similar reasoning, monitoring by blockholders might result in a greater value increase for firms with weak governance structures than for firms with strong governance structures. Future studies might therefore investigate if blockholder monitoring is more likely in – and has a greater effect on – firms with weak governance structures relative to those with strong governance structures.

The present thesis highlights a number of determinants that affect a blockholder's monitoring. With regard to blockholder characteristics, these comprise the size of the blockholder's ownership, its presence on the firm's boards as well as its identity. However, other determinants are conceivable. For instance, a recent study by *Chhaochharia et al.* (2012) investigates the impact of institutional investors' geographical proximity to their portfolio firms on the corporate behavior of their portfolio firms. The authors find, inter alia, that firms with high local institutional investor ownership are more profitable and less likely to engage in undesirable corporate activities, suggesting that local blockholders are more effective monitors.[2361] Future research may thus focus on additional blockholder characteristics that affect blockholder monitoring and thereby further contribute to a better understanding of blockholder monitoring.

[2361] See Chhaochharia et al. (2012): 63.

Appendix

Appendix 1 – New Institutional Economics

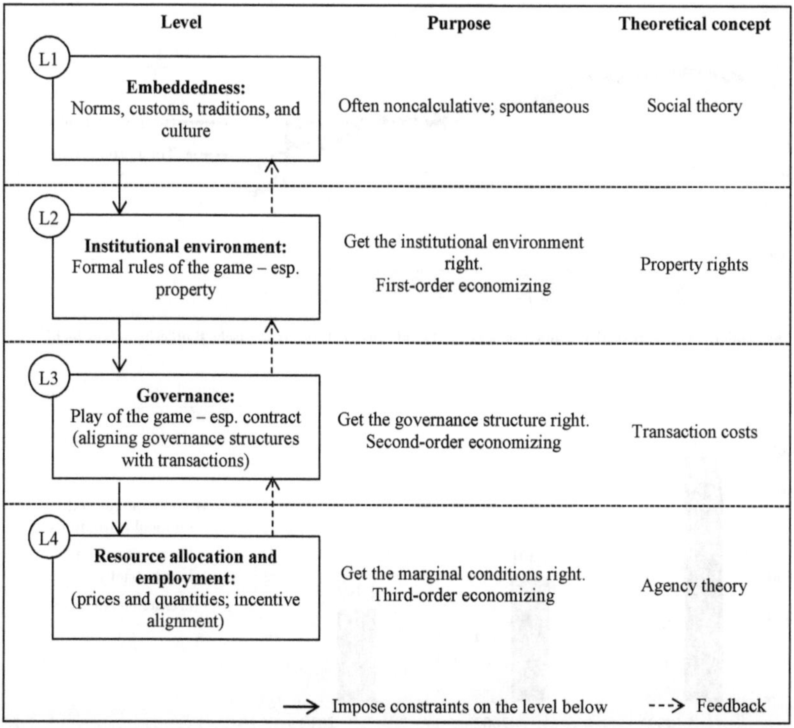

Figure 15: Levels of social analysis within the new institutional economics [own illustration based on Williamson (1998): 26]

Appendix 2 – German Financial System

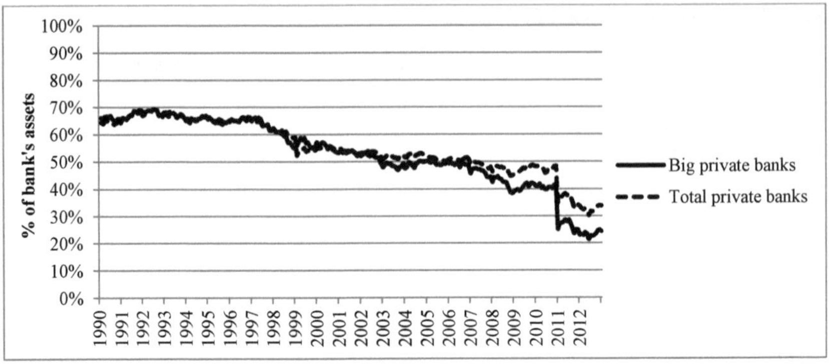

Figure 16: Lending by private banks to non-banks as % of bank's assets [source: Deutsche Bundesbank (2014a, b][2362]

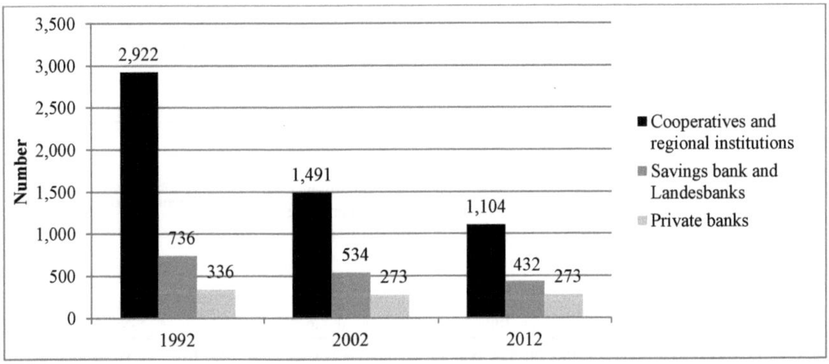

Figure 17: Number of banks by banking group (at calendar year end) [source: Deutsche Bundesbank (2014c)]

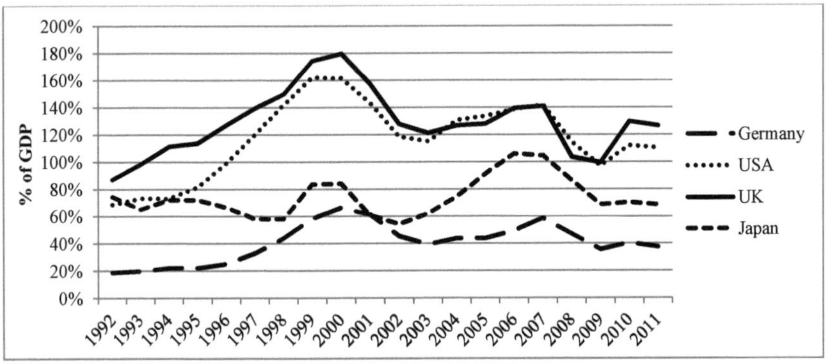

Figure 18: Stock market capitalization as % of GDP [source: Beck, Thorsten et al. (2013)]

2362 Big private banks constitute the largest private banks, e.g. Deutsche Bank AG, Commerzbank AG and Unicredit Bank AG.

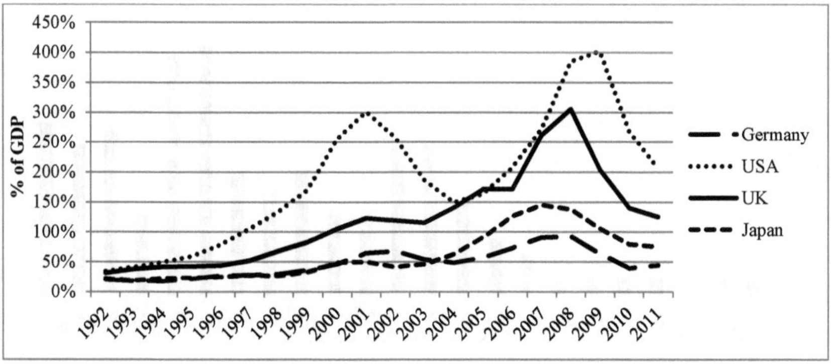

Figure 19: Total value traded on the stock market exchange as % of GDP [source: Beck, Thorsten et al. (2013)]

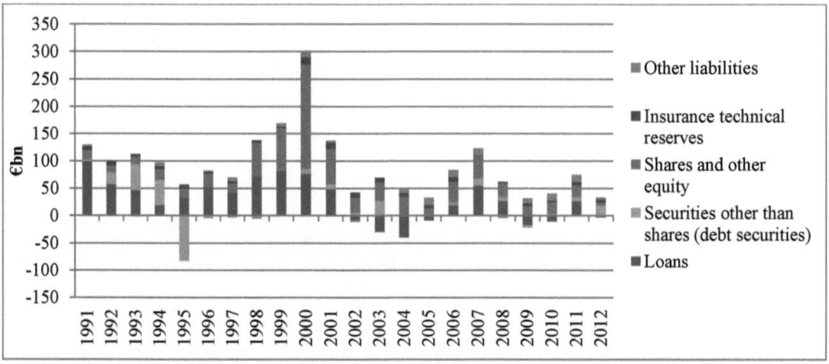

Figure 20: External financing of German non-financial firms (in €bn) [source: Deutsche Bundesbank (2014d)]

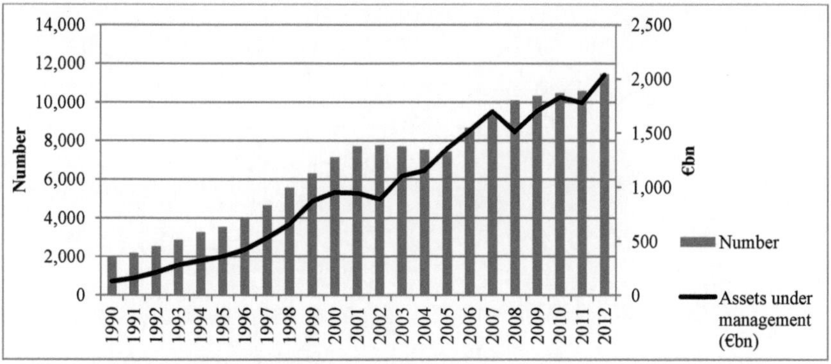

Figure 21: Number and assets under management of open-end investment funds in Germany [source: Bundesverband Investment und Asset Management e.V. (2013)]

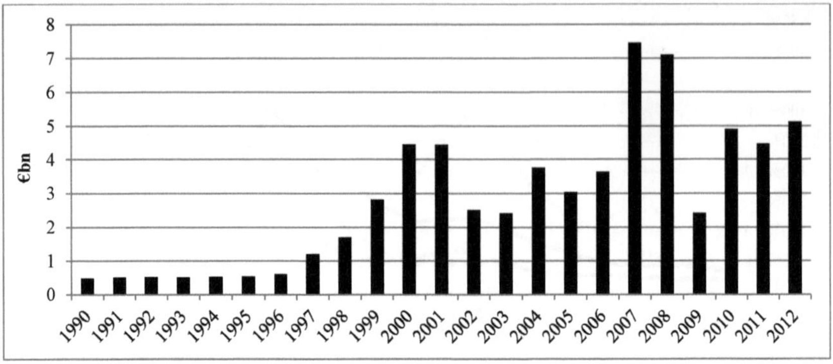

Figure 22: Private equity investments in Germany by private equity firms based in Germany (in €bn) [source: Bundesverband Deutscher Kapitalbeteiligungsgesellschaften (2014)]

Appendix 3 – German Corporate Governance Code

Table 40
The table shows the number of recommendations/suggestions complied with and the rate of compliance. The data is based on 140 questionnaires comprising 27 firms in the DAX, 12 in the TecDax, 28 in the MDAX, 17 in the SDAX, 27 in the remaining Prime Standard, and 29 in the General Standard. The questionnaires were received within the period October 2012 - March 2013.

	DAX	TecDAX	MDAX	SDAX	Prime Standard	General Standard	Total
Recommendations							
Number	91.9	84.3	83.3	77.7	69.6	68.4	**78.6**
Rate of compliance in %	95.8	87.8	86.8	80.9	72.5	71.2	**81.9**
Suggestions							
Number	5.4	5.3	4.8	4.2	4.3	3.4	**4.5**
Rate of compliance in %	76.7	75.0	68.4	60.5	61.4	48.3	**64.1**
Total							
Number	97.3	89.5	88.1	81.9	73.9	71.8	**83.1**
Rate of compliance in %	94.5	86.9	85.5	79.6	71.7	69.7	**80.7**

Table 40: Number and rate of followed German Corporate Governance Code provisions [source: own illustration based on v. Werder/Bartz (2013): 886]

Appendix 4 – Shareholder Rights

Table 41
The table below contains a - by no means exhaustive - list of rights guaranteed by law to certain shareholdings and those that can be amended only in favor of minority shareholdings by the firms' articles of incorporation. It does not contain those rights suspect to amendments of the firms' articles of incorporation that can be amended in favor of majority shareholdings. Thus, it displays the minimum rights to certain aggregated shareholdings.

Required aggregated shareholdings	Content	§§
1% of total share capital or €0.1m	Right to make motion to the court for a special audit based on the suspicion that items on the balance sheet are materially undervalued	§ 258 (2) (with reference to § 142 (2)) AktG
	Right to make motion to the court for a special audit or for the substitution of a special auditor in order to audit processes of founding and managing the company and to audit business relations of the firm with its controlling enterprise	§ 142 (2), (4) AktG; § 315 AktG
5% of total share capital or €0.5m	Right to decide on items on the agenda of the AGM	§ 122 (2) AktG
	Right to claim a judicial decision on the conclusive findings of a special auditor according to § 258 AktG	§ 260 (1) AktG
	Right to make motion to the court to appoint or remove liquidators	§ 265 (3) AktG
	Right to make the motion to the court to appoint a different auditor for important reasons	§ 318 (3) HGB
5% of total share capital*	Right to call an (extraordinary) AGM	§ 122 (1) AktG
more than 5 % of total share capital	Right to block the integration into another stock corporation with domicile in Germany	§ 320 (1) AktG
10% of total share capital or €1m	Right to make a motion to the court to remove an appointed (not elected) member of the supervisory board	§ 103 (3) AktG
	Right to vote on the ratification of the acts of an individual member of the management or supervisory board	§ 120 (1) AktG
	Right to make motion to the court to appoint persons other than those appointed to represent the company to assert the claims for damages	§ 147 (2) AktG
10% of share capital represented at the AGM	Right to vote on a nomination for the election of members of the supervisory board made by shareholders prior to acting on the proposal of the supervisory board	§ 137 AktG
	Right to block the waiver or compromise of any assumption of losses	§ 302 (3) AktG
	Right to block the waiver or compromise of any right of indemnity in relation to *control agreements* (§ 309 (3) AktG, § 310 (4) AktG); against the legal representatives of the controlling enterprise *in case of the absence of a control agreement* (§ 317 (4) AktG, (§ 309 (3) AktG)); against the members of the management and supervisory board *because of faulty dependent company reports* (§ 318 (4) AktG, (§ 309 (3) AktG)); resulting from inadmissible instructions to an integrated company (§ 323 (1) AktG, (§ 309 (3) AktG))	§ 309 (3) AktG and others
10% of total share capital	Right to block the waiver or compromise of any right of indemnity against members of the *management board* (§ 93 (4) AktG) or *supervisory board* (§ 116 AktG, (§ 93 (4) AktG)) *resulting from professional negligence,* against third parties resulting from *improper exertion of their influence* (§ 117 AktG, (§ 93 (4) AktG))	§ 93 (4) AktG and others

Table 41 cont'd

Required aggregated shareholdings	Content	§§
more than 25 % of share capital represented at the AGM*	Right to block the amendment of the firm's articles of incorporation	§ 179 (2) AktG
	Right to block the issue of preferred stock	§ 182 (1) AktG
	Right to block the exclusion of subscription rights in the case of capital increases against (cash) contributions	§ 186 (3) AktG
	Right to block conditional capital increases	§ 193 (1) AktG
	Right to block the issuance of convertible bonds	§ 221 (1) AktG
	Right to block the increase of the share capital up to a specified par value (authorized capital) by issuing new shares against contributions	§ 202 (2) AktG
	Right to block the exclusion of subscription rights if issuing authorized capital or if issuing convertibles, participating bonds or participating rights	§ 203 (1) AktG, § 221 (4) AktG, § 186 (3) AktG
	Right to block the reduction of the share capital as long as it does not occur through the cancellation of shares (§ 237 (4) AktG)	§ 222 (1) AktG, (§ 229 (3) AktG)
more than 25 % of share capital represented at the AGM	Right to block specific types of transactions if the supervisory board refuses to grant consent for these transactions and the management requests the shareholders to approve the transactions	§ 111 (4) AktG
more than 25 % of share capital represented at the AGM*	Right to block the resolution of the AGM to dissolve the company	§ 262 (1) No. 2 AktG
	Right to block the continuation of a dissolved company	§ 274 (1) AktG
	Right to block the conclusion of the enterprise agreements (§ 293 (1), (2) AktG) or its amendment (§ 295 (1) AktG (§ 293 (1), (2) AktG))	§ 293 (1), (2) AktG
	Right to block the integration into another company	§ 319 (2) AktG, § 320 (1) AktG

* or less if stated in the firm's articles of incorporation

Table 41: List of ownership rights granted by German law from the perspective of minority shareholders

Appendix 5 – Ownership Structure

Table 42
Focusing on firms with a blockholder, the following table presents the number and percentage (in italics) of firms that have a second blockholder with an ownership above the important control thresholds 5%, 10%, and 25% for the years 2005-2012.

	2005	**2006**	**2007**	**2008**	**2009**	**2010**	**2011**	**2012**
5%	248	248	305	300	266	258	248	239
	0.6169	*0.6703*	*0.7193*	*0.7317*	*0.6909*	*0.6880*	*0.6631*	*0.6809*
10%	158	149	176	171	155	154	136	128
	0.3930	*0.4027*	*0.4151*	*0.4171*	*0.4026*	*0.4107*	*0.3636*	*0.3647*
25%	37	33	47	40	31	32	26	29
	0.0920	*0.0892*	*0.1108*	*0.0976*	*0.0805*	*0.0853*	*0.0695*	*0.0826*
N	402	370	424	410	385	375	374	351

Table 42: Number and percentage of firms with a second blockholder

Table 43
The following table depicts the number of firm years and their relative frequency (in italics) with a second blockholder (BH2) owning less than 10%, between 10 and 25%, and between 25 and 50% of a firm's equity, given the largest blockholder (BH1) owns less than 10%, between 10 and 25%, between 25 and 50%, between 50 and 75%, and between 75 and 100%.

	BH1 <0.1	**0.1<BH1 <0.25**	**0.25<BH1<0.5**	**0.5<BH1<0.75**	**0.75<BH1<1.0**
BH2 <0.1	**209**	214	214	179	69
	0.6023	*0.3257*	*0.2311*	*0.2579*	*0.1478*
0.1<BH2 <0.25	0	**361**	391	161	39
	-	***0.5495***	*0.4222*	*0.2320*	*0.0835*
0.25<BH2<0.5	0	0	**174**	**98**	3
	-	-	***0.1879***	***0.1412***	*0.0064*
Firm years	347	657	926	694	467

Table 43: Number and ownership of the second largest blockholders for ownership levels of the largest blockholder

Appendix 6 – Applicability of Regression Models

Table 44
The following table presents the results of the specification tests for each stage and the most important primary explanatory variables as shown in column three. Since the F-test and Hausman test cannot be used with dummy variables, no results are reported for *[bh1_dummy]* and *[bh1_supb]/[bh1_mgmtb]*. A p-Value smaller than 0.1 leads to the rejection of the respective null hypothesis.

			F-test for fixed effects		Breusch-Pagan LM test		Robust Hausman test	
Stage	Dependent variable	Explanatory variable	F-statistic	p-Value	χ^2	p-Value	χ^2	p-Value
1	opex_sales	cum_own	31.010	0.000	5,866.950	0.000	24.851	0.000
1	opex_sales	h_index	30.960	0.000	5,858.770	0.000	25.292	0.000
1	opex_sales	bh1_dummy	-	-	5,858.280	0.000	-	-
1	discr_assets	cum_own	17.840	0.000	3,246.740	0.000	196.914	0.000
1	discr_assets	h_index	17.800	0.000	3,252.220	0.000	189.857	0.000
1	discr_assets	bh1_dummy	-	-	3,246.650	0.000	-	-
1	div_payout	cum_own	8.190	0.000	1,628.830	0.000	23.504	0.001
1	div_payout	h_index	8.080	0.000	1,599.990	0.000	24.476	0.001
1	div_payout	bh1_dummy	-	-	1,634.250	0.000	-	-
1	tobinq	cum_own	9.650	0.000	2,219.380	0.000	68.764	0.000
1	tobinq	h_index	9.660	0.000	2,197.830	0.000	67.116	0.000
1	tobinq	bh1_dummy	-	-	2,294.280	0.000	-	-
2	opex_sales	bh1_cont	30.970	0.000	5,860.680	0.000	25.225	0.000
2	opex_sales	bh1_supb, bh1_mgmtb	-	-	5,864.410	0.000	-	-
2	opex_sales	identities	31.230	0.000	5,619.800	0.000	36.687	0.000
2	discr_assets	bh1_cont	17.930	0.000	3,257.020	0.000	188.637	0.000
2	discr_assets	bh1_supb, bh1_mgmtb	-	-	3,241.290	0.000	-	-
2	discr_assets	identities	17.590	0.000	2,968.250	0.000	200.132	0.000
2	div_payout	bh1_cont	8.110	0.000	1,612.360	0.000	25.829	0.001
2	div_payout	bh1_supb, bh1_mgmtb	-	-	1,639.170	0.000	-	-
2	div_payout	identities	8.010	0.000	1,562.140	0.000	48.293	0.000
2	tobinq	bh1_cont	9.650	0.000	2,197.380	0.000	67.743	0.000
2	tobinq	bh1_supb, bh1_mgmtb	-	-	2,307.150	0.000	-	-
2	tobinq	identities	9.550	0.000	2,139.620	0.000	78.785	0.000
3	opex_sales	bh2_cont	31.100	0.000	5,865.260	0.000	26.008	0.000
3	opex_sales	diff_bh12345	31.190	0.000	5,860.830	0.000	27.182	0.000
3	opex_sales	ln_bh_count	29.420	0.000	5,227.380	0.000	25.088	0.000
3	discr_assets	bh2_cont	17.820	0.000	3,244.380	0.000	194.096	0.000
3	discr_assets	diff_bh12345	17.930	0.000	3,268.490	0.000	189.742	0.000
3	discr_assets	ln_bh_count	16.580	0.000	2,863.700	0.000	193.242	0.000
3	div_payout	bh2_cont	8.220	0.000	1,620.210	0.000	28.103	0.001
3	div_payout	diff_bh12345	8.150	0.000	1,608.260	0.000	27.137	0.001
3	div_payout	ln_bh_count	8.000	0.000	1,529.620	0.000	23.846	0.002
3	tobinq	bh2_cont	9.690	0.000	2,209.120	0.000	67.300	0.000
3	tobinq	diff_bh12345	9.680	0.000	2,207.100	0.000	67.955	0.000
3	tobinq	ln_bh_count	9.640	0.000	2,173.220	0.000	62.417	0.000

Table 44: Results of the specification tests

Appendix 7 – Regression Specifications

Stage 1

1.1.1 $opex\_sales_{it} = \alpha+\beta_1 cum\_own_{it}+\beta_2 \sum_{i=1}^{N} CONTROL'_{it}+\beta_3 YEAR_t+\beta_4 INDUSTRY_i+\nu_{it}$

1.1.2 $opex\_sales_{it} = \alpha+\beta_1 h\_index_{it}+\beta_2 \sum_{i=1}^{N} CONTROL'_{it}+\beta_3 YEAR_t+\beta_4 INDUSTRY_i+\nu_{it}$

1.1.3 $opex\_sales_{it} = \alpha+\beta_1 bh1\_dummy_{it}+\beta_2 \sum_{i=1}^{N} CONTROL'_{it}+\beta_3 YEAR_t+\beta_4 INDUSTRY_i+\nu_{it}$

1.2.1 $discr\_assets_{it}= \alpha+\beta_1 cum\_own_{it}+\beta_2 capex_{it}+\beta_3 \sum_{i=1}^{N} CONTROL'_{it} +\beta_4 YEAR_t + \beta_5 INDUSTRY_i+\nu_{it}$

1.2.2 $discr\_assets_{it} = \alpha+\beta_1 h\_index_{it}+\beta_2 capex_{it}+\beta_3 \sum_{i=1}^{N} CONTROL'_{it} +\beta_4 YEAR_t + \beta_5 INDUSTRY_i+\nu_{it}$

1.2.3 $discr\_assets_{it} = \alpha + \beta_1 bh1\_dummy_{it} + \beta_2 capex_{it} + \beta_3 \sum_{i=1}^{N} CONTROL'_{it} + \beta_4 YEAR_t + \beta_5 INDUSTRY_i + \nu_{it}$

1.3.1 $div\_payout_{it}= \alpha+\beta_1 cum\_own_{it}+\beta_2 growth_{it}+\beta_3 prof_{it}+\beta_4 div\_prevy_{it} +\beta_5 \sum_{i=1}^{N} CONTROL'_{it} +\beta_6 YEAR_t + \beta_7 INDUSTRY_i+\nu_{it}$

1.3.2 $div\_payout_{it}= \alpha+\beta_1 h\_index_{it}+\beta_2 growth_{it}+\beta_3 prof_{it}+\beta_4 div\_prevy_{it}+\beta_5 \sum_{i=1}^{N} CONTROL'_{it} +\beta_6 YEAR_t + \beta_7 INDUSTRY_i+\nu_{it}$

1.3.3 $div\_payout_{it}= \alpha+\beta_1 bh1\_dummy_{it}+\beta_2 growth_{it}+\beta_3 prof_{it}+\beta_4 div\_prevy_{it} +\beta_5 \sum_{i=1}^{N} CONTROL'_{it} +\beta_6 YEAR_t + \beta_7 INDUSTRY_i+\nu_{it}$

1.4.1 $tobin_{it}= \alpha+\beta_1 cum\_own_{it}+\beta_2 growth_{it}+\beta_3 ppe\_assets_{it}+\beta_4 capex_{it}+\beta_5 cash\_assets_{it} +\beta_6 \sum_{i=1}^{N} CONTROL'_{it} +\beta_7 YEAR_t+ \beta_8 INDUSTRY_i+\nu_{it}$

1.4.2 $tobin_{it}= \alpha+\beta_1 h\_index_{it}+\beta_2 growth_{it}+\beta_3 ppe\_assets_{it}+\beta_4 capex_{it}+\beta_5 cash\_assets_{it} +\beta_6 \sum_{i=1}^{N} CONTROL'_{it} +\beta_7 YEAR_t+ \beta_8 INDUSTRY_i+\nu_{it}$

1.4.3 $tobin_{it}= \alpha+\beta_1 bh1\_dummy_{it}+\beta_2 growth_{it}+\beta_3 ppe\_assets_{it}+\beta_4 capex_{it}+\beta_5 cash\_assets_{it} +\beta_6 \sum_{i=1}^{N} CONTROL'_{it} +\beta_7 YEAR_t+ \beta_8 INDUSTRY_i+\nu_{it}$

Stage 2

2.1.1 $opex\_sales_{it}= \alpha+\beta_1 bh1\_cont_{it}+\beta_2 \sum_{i=1}^{N} CONTROL'_{it}+\beta_3 YEAR_t+\beta_4 INDUSTRY_i+\nu_{it}$

2.1.2 $opex\_sales_{it}= \alpha+\beta_1 bh1\_cont_{it}+\beta_2 bh1\_supb_{it}+\beta_3 bh1\_mgmtb_{it}+\beta_4 \sum_{i=1}^{N} CONTROL'_{it} +\beta_5 YEAR_t+ \beta_6 INDUSTRY_i+\nu_{it}$

2.1.3 $opex\_sales_{it}= \alpha+\beta_1 bh1\_pe\_cont_{it}+\beta_2 bh1\_fam\_cont_{it}+\beta_3 bh1\_si\_cont_{it} +\beta_4 bh1\_insti\_cont_{it}+\beta_5 stdev\_ni_{it}+\beta_6 beta_{it}+\beta_7 \sum_{i=1}^{N} CONTROL'_{it} +\beta_8 YEAR_t+ \beta_9 INDUSTRY_i+\nu_{it}$

2.1.4 $opex\_sales_{it}= \alpha+\beta_1 bh1\_cont_{it}+\beta_2 bh1\_cont\_sq_{it}+\beta_3 \sum_{i=1}^{N} CONTROL'_{it} +\beta_4 YEAR_t + \beta_5 INDUSTRY_i+\nu_{it}$

2.1.5 $opex\_sales_{it}= \alpha+\beta_1 bh1\_5to25_{it}+\beta_2 bh1\_25to50_{it}+\beta_3 bh1\_50to75_{it}+\beta_4 bh1\_75to100_{it} +\beta_5 \sum_{i=1}^{N} CONTROL'_{it} +\beta_6 YEAR_t+ \beta_7 INDUSTRY_i+\nu_{it}$

2.1.6 $$\text{opex\_sales}_{it} = \alpha + \beta_1 \text{bh1\_supb}_{it} + \beta_2 \text{bh1\_mgmtb}_{it} + \beta_3 \text{bh1\_pe\_cont}_{it} + \beta_4 \text{bh1\_fam\_cont}_{it} + \beta_5 \text{bh1\_si\_cont}_{it} + \beta_6 \text{bh1\_insti\_cont}_{it} + \beta_7 \text{bh1\_pe\_cont}_{it} {*} \text{bh1\_supb}_{it} + \beta_8 \text{bh1\_pe\_cont}_{it} {*} \text{bh1\_mgmtb}_{it} + \beta_9 \text{bh1\_fam\_cont}_{it} {*} \text{bh1\_supb}_{it} + \beta_{10} \text{bh1\_fam\_cont}_{it} {*} \text{bh1\_mgmtb}_{it} + \beta_{11} \text{bh1\_si\_cont}_{it} {*} \text{bh1\_supb}_{it} + \beta_{12} \text{bh1\_si\_cont}_{it} {*} \text{bh1\_mgmtb}_{it} + \beta_{13} \text{stdev\_ni}_{it} + \beta_{14} \text{beta}_{it} + \beta_{15} \sum_{i=1}^{N} \text{CONTROL}'_{it} + \beta_{16} \text{YEAR}_t + \beta_{17} \text{INDUSTRY}_i + \nu_{it}$$

2.1.7 $$\text{opex\_sales}_{it} = \alpha + \beta_1 \text{bh1\_pe\_cont}_{it} + \beta_2 \text{bh1\_pe\_cont\_sq}_{it} + \beta_3 \text{bh1\_fam\_cont}_{it} + \beta_4 \text{bh1\_fam\_cont\_sq}_{it} + \beta_5 \text{bh1\_si\_cont}_{it} + \beta_6 \text{bh1\_si\_cont\_sq}_{it} + \beta_7 \text{bh1\_insti\_cont}_{it} + \beta_8 \text{bh1\_insti\_cont\_sq}_{it} + \beta_9 \text{stdev\_ni}_{it} + \beta_{10} \text{beta}_{it} + \beta_{11} \sum_{i=1}^{N} \text{CONTROL}'_{it} + \beta_{12} \text{YEAR}_t + \beta_{13} \text{INDUSTRY}_i + \nu_{it}$$

2.2.1 $$\text{discr\_assets}_{it} = \alpha + \beta_1 \text{bh1\_cont}_{it} + \beta_2 \text{capex}_{it} + \beta_3 \sum_{i=1}^{N} \text{CONTROL}'_{it} + \beta_4 \text{YEAR}_t + \beta_5 \text{INDUSTRY}_i + \nu_{it}$$

2.2.2 $$\text{discr\_assets}_{it} = \alpha + \beta_1 \text{bh1\_cont}_{it} + \beta_2 \text{bh1\_supb}_{it} + \beta_3 \text{bh1\_mgmtb}_{it} + \beta_4 \text{capex}_{it} + \beta_5 \sum_{i=1}^{N} \text{CONTROL}'_{it} + \beta_6 \text{YEAR}_t + \beta_7 \text{INDUSTRY}_i + \nu_{it}$$

2.2.3 $$\text{discr\_assets}_{it} = \alpha + \beta_1 \text{bh1\_pe\_cont}_{it} + \beta_2 \text{bh1\_fam\_cont}_{it} + \beta_3 \text{bh1\_si\_cont}_{it} + \beta_4 \text{bh1\_insti\_cont}_{it} + \beta_5 \text{stdev\_ni}_{it} + \beta_6 \text{beta}_{it} + \beta_7 \text{capex}_{it} + \beta_8 \sum_{i=1}^{N} \text{CONTROL}'_{it} + \beta_9 \text{YEAR}_t + \beta_{10} \text{INDUSTRY}_i + \nu_{it}$$

2.2.4 $$\text{discr\_assets}_{it} = \alpha + \beta_1 \text{bh1\_cont}_{it} + \beta_2 \text{bh1\_cont\_sq}_{it} + \beta_3 \text{capex}_{it} + \beta_4 \sum_{i=1}^{N} \text{CONTROL}'_{it} + \beta_5 \text{YEAR}_t + \beta_6 \text{INDUSTRY}_i + \nu_{it}$$

2.2.5 $$\text{discr\_assets}_{it} = \alpha + \beta_1 \text{bh1\_5to25}_{it} + \beta_2 \text{bh1\_25to50}_{it} + \beta_3 \text{bh1\_50to75}_{it} + \beta_4 \text{bh1\_75to100}_{it} + \beta_5 \text{capex}_{it} + \beta_6 \sum_{i=1}^{N} \text{CONTROL}'_{it} + \beta_7 \text{YEAR}_t + \beta_8 \text{INDUSTRY}_i + \nu_{it}$$

2.2.6 $$\text{discr\_assets}_{it} = \alpha + \beta_1 \text{bh1\_supb}_{it} + \beta_2 \text{bh1\_mgmtb}_{it} + \beta_3 \text{bh1\_pe\_cont}_{it} + \beta_4 \text{bh1\_fam\_cont}_{it} + \beta_5 \text{bh1\_si\_cont}_{it} + \beta_6 \text{bh1\_insti\_cont}_{it} + \beta_7 \text{bh1\_pe\_cont}_{it} {*} \text{bh1\_supb}_{it} + \beta_8 \text{bh1\_pe\_cont}_{it} {*} \text{bh1\_mgmtb}_{it} + \beta_9 \text{bh1\_fam\_cont}_{it} {*} \text{bh1\_supb}_{it} + \beta_{10} \text{bh1\_fam\_cont}_{it} {*} \text{bh1\_mgmtb}_{it} + \beta_{11} \text{bh1\_si\_cont}_{it} {*} \text{bh1\_supb}_{it} + \beta_{12} \text{bh1\_si\_cont}_{it} {*} \text{bh1\_mgmtb}_{it} + \beta_{13} \text{stdev\_ni}_{it} + \beta_{14} \text{beta}_{it} + \beta_{15} \text{capex}_{it} + \beta_{16} \sum_{i=1}^{N} \text{CONTROL}'_{it} + \beta_{17} \text{YEAR}_t + \beta_{18} \text{INDUSTRY}_i + \nu_{it}$$

2.2.7 $$\text{discr\_assets}_{it} = \alpha + \beta_1 \text{bh1\_pe\_cont}_{it} + \beta_2 \text{bh1\_pe\_cont\_sq}_{it} + \beta_3 \text{bh1\_fam\_cont}_{it} + \beta_4 \text{bh1\_fam\_cont\_sq}_{it} + \beta_5 \text{bh1\_si\_cont}_{it} + \beta_6 \text{bh1\_si\_cont\_sq}_{it} + \beta_7 \text{bh1\_insti\_cont}_{it} + \beta_8 \text{bh1\_insti\_cont\_sq}_{it} + \beta_9 \text{stdev\_ni}_{it} + \beta_{10} \text{beta}_{it} + \beta_{11} \text{capex}_{it} + \beta_{12} \sum_{i=1}^{N} \text{CONTROL}'_{it} + \beta_{13} \text{YEAR}_t + \beta_{14} \text{INDUSTRY}_i + \nu_{it}$$

2.3.1 $$\text{div\_payout}_{it} = \alpha + \beta_1 \text{bh1\_cont}_{it} + \beta_2 \text{growth}_{it} + \beta_3 \text{prof}_{it} + \beta_4 \text{div\_prevy}_{it} + \beta_5 \sum_{i=1}^{N} \text{CONTROL}'_{it} + \beta_6 \text{YEAR}_t + \beta_7 \text{INDUSTRY}_i + \nu_{it}$$

2.3.2 $$\text{div\_payout}_{it} = \alpha + \beta_1 \text{bh1\_cont}_{it} + \beta_2 \text{bh1\_supb}_{it} + \beta_3 \text{bh1\_mgmtb}_{it} + \beta_4 \text{growth}_{it} + \beta_5 \text{prof}_{it} + \beta_6 \text{div\_prevy}_{it} + \beta_7 \sum_{i=1}^{N} \text{CONTROL}'_{it} + \beta_8 \text{YEAR}_t + \beta_9 \text{INDUSTRY}_i + \nu_{it}$$

2.3.3 $$\text{div\_payout}_{it} = \alpha + \beta_1 \text{bh1\_pe\_cont}_{it} + \beta_2 \text{bh1\_fam\_cont}_{it} + \beta_3 \text{bh1\_si\_cont}_{it} + \beta_4 \text{bh1\_insti\_cont}_{it} + \beta_5 \text{stdev\_ni}_{it} + \beta_6 \text{beta}_{it} + \beta_7 \text{growth}_{it} + \beta_8 \text{prof}_{it} + \beta_9 \text{div\_prevy}_{it} + \beta_{10} \sum_{i=1}^{N} \text{CONTROL}'_{it} + \beta_{11} \text{YEAR}_t + \beta_{12} \text{INDUSTRY}_i + \nu_{it}$$

2.3.4 $div\_payout_{it} = \alpha + \beta_1 bh1\_cont_{it} + \beta_2 bh1\_cont\_sq_{it} + \beta_3 growth_{it} + \beta_4 prof_{it} + \beta_5 div\_prevy_{it} + \beta_6 \sum_{i=1}^{N} CONTROL'_{it} + \beta_7 YEAR_t + \beta_8 INDUSTRY_i + v_{it}$

2.3.5 $div\_payout_{it} = \alpha + \beta_1 bh1\_5to25_{it} + \beta_2 bh1\_25to50_{it} + \beta_3 bh1\_50to75_{it} + \beta_4 bh1\_75to100_{it} + \beta_5 growth_{it} + \beta_6 prof_{it} + \beta_7 div\_prevy_{it} + \beta_8 \sum_{i=1}^{N} CONTROL'_{it} + \beta_9 YEAR_t + \beta_{10} INDUSTRY_i + v_{it}$

2.3.6 $div\_payout_{it} = \alpha + \beta_1 bh1\_supb_{it} + \beta_2 bh1\_mgmtb_{it} + \beta_3 bh1\_pe\_cont_{it} + \beta_4 bh1\_fam\_cont_{it} + \beta_5 bh1\_si\_cont_{it} + \beta_6 bh1\_insti\_cont_{it} + \beta_7 bh1\_pe\_cont_{it} * bh1\_supb_{it} + \beta_8 bh1\_pe\_cont_{it} * bh1\_mgmtb_{it} + \beta_9 bh1\_fam\_cont_{it} * bh1\_supb_{it} + \beta_{10} bh1\_fam\_cont_{it} * bh1\_mgmtb_{it} + \beta_{11} bh1\_si\_cont_{it} * bh1\_supb_{it} + \beta_{12} bh1\_si\_cont_{it} * bh1\_mgmtb_{it} + \beta_{13} stdev\_ni_{it} + \beta_{14} beta_{it} + \beta_{15} growth_{it} + \beta_{16} prof_{it} + \beta_{17} div\_prevy_{it} + \beta_{18} \sum_{i=1}^{N} CONTROL'_{it} + \beta_{19} YEAR_t + \beta_{20} INDUSTRY_i + v_{it}$

2.3.7 $div\_payout_{it} = \alpha + \beta_1 bh1\_pe\_cont_{it} + \beta_2 bh1\_pe\_cont\_sq_{it} + \beta_3 bh1\_fam\_cont_{it} + \beta_4 bh1\_fam\_cont\_sq_{it} + \beta_5 bh1\_si\_cont_{it} + \beta_6 bh1\_si\_cont\_sq_{it} + \beta_7 bh1\_insti\_cont_{it} + \beta_8 bh1\_insti\_cont\_sq_{it} + \beta_9 stdev\_ni_{it} + \beta_{10} beta_{it} + \beta_{11} growth_{it} + \beta_{12} prof_{it} + \beta_{13} div\_prevy_{it} + \beta_{14} \sum_{i=1}^{N} CONTROL'_{it} + \beta_{15} YEAR_t + \beta_{16} INDUSTRY_i + v_{it}$

2.4.1 $tobinq_{it} = \alpha + \beta_1 bh1\_cont_{it} + \beta_2 growth_{it} + \beta_3 ppe\_assets_{it} + \beta_4 capex_{it} + \beta_5 cash\_assets_{it} + \beta_6 \sum_{i=1}^{N} CONTROL'_{it} + \beta_7 YEAR_t + \beta_8 INDUSTRY_i + v_{it}$

2.4.2 $tobinq_{it} = \alpha + \beta_1 bh1\_cont_{it} + \beta_2 bh1\_supb_{it} + \beta_3 bh1\_mgmtb_{it} + \beta_4 growth_{it} + \beta_5 ppe\_assets_{it} + \beta_6 capex_{it} + \beta_7 cash\_assets_{it} + \beta_8 \sum_{i=1}^{N} CONTROL'_{it} + \beta_9 YEAR_t + \beta_{10} INDUSTRY_i + v_{it}$

2.4.3 $tobinq_{it} = \alpha + \beta_1 bh1\_pe\_cont_{it} + \beta_2 bh1\_fam\_cont_{it} + \beta_3 bh1\_si\_cont_{it} + \beta_4 bh1\_insti\_cont_{it} + \beta_5 stdev\_ni_{it} + \beta_6 beta_{it} + \beta_7 growth_{it} + \beta_8 ppe\_assets_{it} + \beta_9 capex_{it} + \beta_{10} cash\_assets_{it} + \beta_{11} \sum_{i=1}^{N} CONTROL'_{it} + \beta_{12} YEAR_t + \beta_{13} INDUSTRY_i + v_{it}$

2.4.4 $tobinq_{it} = \alpha + \beta_1 bh1\_cont_{it} + \beta_2 bh1\_cont\_sq_{it} + \beta_3 growth_{it} + \beta_4 ppe\_assets_{it} + \beta_5 capex_{it} + \beta_6 cash\_assets_{it} + \beta_7 \sum_{i=1}^{N} CONTROL'_{it} + \beta_8 YEAR_t + \beta_9 INDUSTRY_i + v_{it}$

2.4.5 $tobinq_{it} = \alpha + \beta_1 bh1\_5to25_{it} + \beta_2 bh1\_25to50_{it} + \beta_3 bh1\_50to75_{it} + \beta_4 bh1\_75to100_{it} + \beta_5 growth_{it} + \beta_6 ppe\_assets_{it} + \beta_7 capex_{it} + \beta_8 cash\_assets_{it} + \beta_9 \sum_{i=1}^{N} CONTROL'_{it} + \beta_{10} YEAR_t + \beta_{11} INDUSTRY_i + v_{it}$

2.4.6 $tobinq_{it} = \alpha + \beta_1 bh1\_supb_{it} + \beta_2 bh1\_mgmtb_{it} + \beta_3 bh1\_pe\_cont_{it} + \beta_4 bh1\_fam\_cont_{it} + \beta_5 bh1\_si\_cont_{it} + \beta_6 bh1\_insti\_cont_{it} + \beta_7 bh1\_pe\_cont_{it} * bh1\_supb_{it} + \beta_8 bh1\_pe\_cont_{it} * bh1\_mgmtb_{it} + \beta_9 bh1\_fam\_cont_{it} * bh1\_supb_{it} + \beta_{10} bh1\_fam\_cont_{it} * bh1\_mgmtb_{it} + \beta_{11} bh1\_si\_cont_{it} * bh1\_supb_{it} + \beta_{12} bh1\_si\_cont_{it} * bh1\_mgmtb_{it} + \beta_{13} stdev\_ni_{it} + \beta_{14} beta_{it} + \beta_{15} growth_{it} + \beta_{16} ppe\_assets_{it} + \beta_{17} capex_{it} + \beta_{18} cash\_assets_{it} + \beta_{19} \sum_{i=1}^{N} CONTROL'_{it} + \beta_{20} YEAR_t + \beta_{21} INDUSTRY_i + v_{it}$

2.4.7 $tobinq_{it} = \alpha + \beta_1 bh1\_pe\_cont_{it} + \beta_2 bh1\_pe\_cont\_sq_{it} + \beta_3 bh1\_fam\_cont_{it} + \beta_4 bh1\_fam\_cont\_sq_{it} + \beta_5 bh1\_si\_cont_{it} + \beta_6 bh1\_si\_cont\_sq_{it} + \beta_7 bh1\_insti\_cont_{it} + \beta_8 bh1\_insti\_cont\_sq_{it} + \beta_9 stdev\_ni_{it} + \beta_{10} beta_{it} + \beta_{11} growth_{it} + \beta_{12} ppe\_assets_{it} + \beta_{13} capex_{it} + \beta_{14} cash\_assets_{it} + \beta_{15} \sum_{i=1}^{N} CONTROL'_{it} + \beta_{16} YEAR_t + \beta_{17} INDUSTRY_i + v_{it}$

2.4.8 $tobinq_{it} = \alpha + \beta_1 opex\_sales_{it} + \beta_2 discr\_assets_{it} + \beta_3 div\_payout_{it} + \beta_4 growth_{it} + \beta_5 ppe\_assets_{it} + \beta_6 capex_{it} + \beta_7 cash\_assets_{it} + \beta_8 \sum_{i=1}^{N} CONTROL'_{it} + \beta_9 YEAR_t + \beta_{10} INDUSTRY_i + \nu_{it}$

2.4.9 $tobinq_{it} = \alpha + \beta_1 opex\_sales_{it} + \beta_2 discr\_assets_{it} + \beta_3 div\_payout_{it} + \beta_4 bh1\_pe\_cont_{it} + \beta_5 bh1\_fam\_cont_{it} + \beta_6 bh1\_si\_cont_{it} + \beta_7 bh1\_insti\_cont_{it} + \beta_8 stdev\_ni_{it} + \beta_9 beta_{it} + \beta_{10} growth_{it} + \beta_{11} ppe\_assets_{it} + \beta_{12} capex_{it} + \beta_{13} cash\_assets_{it} + \beta_{14} \sum_{i=1}^{N} CONTROL'_{it} + \beta_{15} YEAR_t + \beta_{16} INDUSTRY_i + \nu_{it}$

Stage 3

3.1.1 $opex\_sales_{it} = \alpha + \beta_1 bh2\_cont_{it} + \beta_2 bh1\_pe\_cont_{it} + \beta_3 bh1\_fam\_cont_{it} + \beta_4 bh1\_si\_cont_{it} + \beta_5 bh1\_insti\_cont_{it} + \beta_6 bh1\_pe\_cont_{it} * bh2\_cont_{it} + \beta_7 bh1\_fam\_cont_{it} * bh2\_cont_{it} + \beta_8 bh1\_si\_cont_{it} * bh2\_cont_{it} + \beta_9 bh1\_insti\_cont_{it} * bh2\_cont_{it} + \beta_{10} stdev\_ni_{it} + \beta_{11} beta_{it} + \beta_{12} \sum_{i=1}^{N} CONTROL'_{it} + \beta_{13} YEAR_t + \beta_{14} INDUSTRY_i + \nu_{it}$

3.1.2 $opex\_sales_{it} = \alpha + \beta_1 bh2\_pe\_cont_{it} + \beta_2 bh2\_fam\_cont_{it} + \beta_3 bh2\_si\_cont_{it} + \beta_4 bh2\_insti\_cont_{it} + \beta_5 bh1\_pe\_cont_{it} + \beta_6 bh1\_fam\_cont_{it} + \beta_7 bh1\_si\_cont_{it} + \beta_8 bh1\_insti\_cont_{it} + \beta_9 bh1\_pe\_cont_{it} * bh2\_pe\_cont_{it} + \beta_{10} bh1\_fam\_cont_{it} * bh2\_fam\_cont_{it} + \beta_{11} bh1\_si\_cont_{it} * bh2\_si\_cont_{it} + \beta_{12} bh1\_insti\_cont_{it} * bh2\_insti\_cont_{it} + \beta_{13} stdev\_ni_{it} + \beta_{14} beta_{it} + \beta_{15} \sum_{i=1}^{N} CONTROL'_{it} + \beta_{16} YEAR_t + \beta_{17} INDUSTRY_i + \nu_{it}$

3.1.3 $opex\_sales_{it} = \alpha + \beta_1 ln\_bh\_count_{it} + \beta_2 bh1\_cont_{it} + \beta_3 \sum_{i=1}^{N} CONTROL'_{it} + \beta_4 YEAR_t + \beta_5 INDUSTRY_i + \nu_{it}$

3.1.4 $opex\_sales_{it} = \alpha + \beta_1 ln\_bhtypes\_count_{it} + \beta_2 bh1\_cont_{it} + \beta_3 \sum_{i=1}^{N} CONTROL'_{it} + \beta_4 YEAR_t + \beta_5 INDUSTRY_i + \nu_{it}$

3.2.1 $discr\_assets_{it} = \alpha + \beta_1 bh2\_cont_{it} + \beta_2 bh1\_pe\_cont_{it} + \beta_3 bh1\_fam\_cont_{it} + \beta_4 bh1\_si\_cont_{it} + \beta_5 bh1\_insti\_cont_{it} + \beta_6 bh1\_pe\_cont_{it} * bh2\_cont_{it} + \beta_7 bh1\_fam\_cont_{it} * bh2\_cont_{it} + \beta_8 bh1\_si\_cont_{it} * bh2\_cont_{it} + \beta_9 bh1\_insti\_cont_{it} * bh2\_cont_{it} + \beta_{10} stdev\_ni_{it} + \beta_{11} beta_{it} + \beta_{12} capex_{it} + \beta_{13} \sum_{i=1}^{N} CONTROL'_{it} + \beta_{14} YEAR_t + \beta_{15} INDUSTRY_i + \nu_{it}$

3.2.2 $discr\_assets_{it} = \alpha + \beta_1 bh2\_pe\_cont_{it} + \beta_2 bh2\_fam\_cont_{it} + \beta_3 bh2\_si\_cont_{it} + \beta_4 bh2\_insti\_cont_{it} + \beta_5 bh1\_pe\_cont_{it} + \beta_6 bh1\_fam\_cont_{it} + \beta_7 bh1\_si\_cont_{it} + \beta_8 bh1\_insti\_cont_{it} + \beta_9 bh1\_pe\_cont_{it} * bh2\_pe\_cont_{it} + \beta_{10} bh1\_fam\_cont_{it} * bh2\_fam\_cont_{it} + \beta_{11} bh1\_si\_cont_{it} * bh2\_si\_cont_{it} + \beta_{12} bh1\_insti\_cont_{it} * bh2\_insti\_cont_{it} + \beta_{13} stdev\_ni_{it} + \beta_{14} beta_{it} + \beta_{15} capex_{it} + \beta_{16} \sum_{i=1}^{N} CONTROL'_{it} + \beta_{17} YEAR_t + \beta_{18} INDUSTRY_i + \nu_{it}$

3.2.3 $discr\_assets_{it} = \alpha + \beta_1 ln\_bh\_count_{it} + \beta_2 bh1\_cont_{it} + \beta_3 capex_{it} + \beta_4 \sum_{i=1}^{N} CONTROL'_{it} + \beta_5 YEAR_t + \beta_6 INDUSTRY_i + \nu_{it}$

3.2.4 $discr\_assets_{it} = \alpha + \beta_1 ln\_bhtypes\_count_{it} + \beta_2 bh1\_cont_{it} + \beta_3 capex_{it} + \beta_4 \sum_{i=1}^{N} CONTROL'_{it} + \beta_5 YEAR_t + \beta_6 INDUSTRY_i + \nu_{it}$

3.3.1 $div\_payout_{it} = \alpha + \beta_1 bh2\_cont_{it} + \beta_2 bh1\_pe\_cont_{it} + \beta_3 bh1\_fam\_cont_{it} + \beta_4 bh1\_si\_cont_{it} + \beta_5 bh1\_insti\_cont_{it} + \beta_6 bh1\_pe\_cont_{it} * bh2\_cont_{it} + \beta_7 bh1\_fam\_cont_{it} * bh2\_cont_{it} + \beta_8 bh1\_si\_cont_{it} * bh2\_cont_{it} + \beta_9 bh1\_insti\_cont_{it} * bh2\_cont_{it} + \beta_{10} stdev\_ni_{it} + \beta_{11} beta_{it} + \beta_{12} growth_{it} + \beta_{13} prof_{it} + \beta_{14} div\_prevy_{it} + \beta_{15} \sum_{i=1}^{N} CONTROL'_{it} + \beta_{16} YEAR_t + \beta_{17} INDUSTRY_i + \nu_{it}$

3.3.2 $div\_payout_{it} = \alpha + \beta_1 bh2\_pe\_cont_{it} + \beta_2 bh2\_fam\_cont_{it} + \beta_3 bh2\_si\_cont_{it} + \beta_4 bh2\_insti\_cont_{it} + \beta_5 bh1\_pe\_cont_{it} + \beta_6 bh1\_fam\_cont_{it} + \beta_7 bh1\_si\_cont_{it} + \beta_8 bh1\_insti\_cont_{it} + \beta_9 bh1\_pe\_cont_{it} * bh2\_pe\_cont_{it} + \beta_{10} bh1\_fam\_cont_{it} * bh2\_fam\_cont_{it} + \beta_{11} bh1\_si\_cont_{it} * bh2\_si\_cont_{it} + \beta_{12} bh1\_insti\_cont_{it} * bh2\_insti\_cont_{it} + \beta_{13} stdev\_ni_{it} + \beta_{14} beta_{it} + \beta_{15} growth_{it} + \beta_{16} prof_{it} + \beta_{17} div\_prevy_{it} + \beta_{18} \sum_{i=1}^{N} CONTROL'_{it} + \beta_{19} YEAR_t + \beta_{20} INDUSTRY_i + \nu_{it}$

3.3.3-3.3.6 $div\_payout_{it} = \alpha + \beta_1 incont_{it} + \beta_2 bh1\_pe\_cont_{it} + \beta_3 bh1\_fam\_cont_{it} + \beta_4 bh1\_si\_cont_{it} + \beta_5 bh1\_insti\_cont_{it} + \beta_6 bh1\_pe\_cont_{it} * incont_{it} + \beta_7 bh1\_fam\_cont_{it} * incont_{it} + \beta_8 bh1\_si\_cont_{it} * incont_{it} + \beta_9 bh1\_insti\_cont_{it} * incont_{it} + \beta_{10} stdev\_ni_{it} + \beta_{11} beta_{it} + \beta_{12} growth_{it} + \beta_{13} prof_{it} + \beta_{14} div\_prevy_{it} + \beta_{15} \sum_{i=1}^{N} CONTROL'_{it} + \beta_{16} YEAR_t + \beta_{17} INDUSTRY_i + \nu_{it}$

$incont_{it}$ measured separately as:	- bh1/bh2	(3.3.3)
	- bh1/bh2_bh3	(3.3.4)
	- diff_bh12345	(3.3.5)
	- bh1_majority	(3.3.6)

3.3.7 $div\_payout_{it} = \alpha + \beta_1 ln\_bh\_count_{it} + \beta_2 bh1\_cont_{it} + \beta_3 growth_{it} + \beta_4 prof_{it} + \beta_5 div\_prevy_{it} + \beta_6 \sum_{i=1}^{N} CONTROL'_{it} + \beta_7 YEAR_t + \beta_8 INDUSTRY_i + \nu_{it}$

3.3.8 $div\_payout_{it} = \alpha + \beta_1 ln\_bhtypes\_count_{it} + \beta_2 bh1\_cont_{it} + \beta_3 growth_{it} + \beta_4 prof_{it} + \beta_5 div\_prevy_{it} + \beta_6 \sum_{i=1}^{N} CONTROL'_{it} + \beta_7 YEAR_t + \beta_8 INDUSTRY_i + \nu_{it}$

3.4.1 $tobinq_{it} = \alpha + \beta_1 bh2\_cont_{it} + \beta_2 bh1\_pe\_cont_{it} + \beta_3 bh1\_fam\_cont_{it} + \beta_4 bh1\_si\_cont_{it} + \beta_5 bh1\_insti\_cont_{it} + \beta_6 bh1\_pe\_cont_{it} * bh2\_cont_{it} + \beta_7 bh1\_fam\_cont_{it} * bh2\_cont_{it} + \beta_8 bh1\_si\_cont_{it} * bh2\_cont_{it} + \beta_9 bh1\_insti\_cont_{it} * bh2\_cont_{it} + \beta_{10} stdev\_ni_{it} + \beta_{11} beta_{it} + \beta_{12} growth_{it} + \beta_{13} ppe\_assets_{it} + \beta_{14} capex_{it} + \beta_{15} cash\_assets_{it} + \beta_{16} \sum_{i=1}^{N} CONTROL'_{it} + \beta_{17} YEAR_t + \beta_{18} INDUSTRY_i + \nu_{it}$

3.4.2 $tobinq_{it} = \alpha + \beta_1 bh2\_pe\_cont_{it} + \beta_2 bh2\_fam\_cont_{it} + \beta_3 bh2\_si\_cont_{it} + \beta_4 bh2\_insti\_cont_{it} + \beta_5 bh1\_pe\_cont_{it} + \beta_6 bh1\_fam\_cont_{it} + \beta_7 bh1\_si\_cont_{it} + \beta_8 bh1\_insti\_cont_{it} + \beta_9 bh1\_pe\_cont_{it} * bh2\_pe\_cont_{it} + \beta_{10} bh1\_fam\_cont_{it} * bh2\_fam\_cont_{it} + \beta_{11} bh1\_si\_cont_{it} * bh2\_si\_cont_{it} + \beta_{12} bh1\_insti\_cont_{it} * bh2\_insti\_cont_{it} + \beta_{13} stdev\_ni_{it} + \beta_{14} beta_{it} + \beta_{15} growth_{it} + \beta_{16} ppe\_assets_{it} + \beta_{17} capex_{it} + \beta_{18} cash\_assets_{it} + \beta_{19} \sum_{i=1}^{N} CONTROL'_{it} + \beta_{20} YEAR_t + \beta_{21} INDUSTRY_i + \nu_{it}$

3.4.3-3.4.6 $tobin_{it} = \alpha + \beta_1 incont_{it} + \beta_2 bh1\_pe\_cont_{it} + \beta_3 bh1\_fam\_cont_{it} + \beta_4 bh1\_si\_cont_{it} + \beta_5 bh1\_insti\_cont_{it} + \beta_6 bh1\_pe\_cont_{it} * incont_{it} + \beta_7 bh1\_fam\_cont_{it} * incont_{it} + \beta_8 bh1\_si\_cont_{it} * incont_{it}$

$$+\beta_9 bh1\_insti\_cont_{it}{*}incont_{it}+\beta_{10}stdev\_ni_{it}+\beta_{11}beta_{it}+\beta_{12}growth_{it}$$
$$+\beta_{13}ppe\_assets_{it}+\beta_{14}capex_{it}+\beta_{15}cash\_assets_{it}+\beta_{16}\sum_{i=1}^{N}CONTROL'_{it}$$
$$+\beta_{17}YEAR_t+\beta_{18}INDUSTRY_i+\nu_{it}$$

$incont_{it}$ measured separately as:
- bh1/bh2 (3.4.3)
- bh1/bh2_bh3 (3.4.4)
- diff_bh12345 (3.4.5)
- bh1_majority (3.4.6)

3.4.7 $tobinq_{it}=\alpha+\beta_1 ln\_bh\_count_{it}+\beta_2 bh1\_cont_{it}+\beta_3 growth_{it}+\beta_4 ppe\_assets_{it}+\beta_5 capex_{it}+\beta_6 cash\_assets_{it}+\beta_7\sum_{i=1}^{N}CONTROL'_{it}+\beta_8 YEAR_t+\beta_9 INDUSTRY_i+\nu_{it}$

3.4.8 $tobinq_{it}=\alpha+\beta_1 ln\_bhtypes\_count_{it}+\beta_2 bh1\_cont_{it}+\beta_3 growth_{it}+\beta_4 ppe\_assets_{it}+\beta_5 capex_{it}+\beta_6 cash\_assets_{it}+\beta_7\sum_{i=1}^{N}CONTROL'_{it}+\beta_8 YEAR_t+\beta_9 INDUSTRY_i+\nu_{it}$

Appendix 8 – Diagnostic Tests

Table 45
The following table presents the results of the diagnostic tests using pooled-OLS. A p-Value smaller than 0.1 leads to the rejection of the respective null hypothesis.

			Heteroscedasticity				Autocorrelation	
			White-test		Breusch-Pagan-test			
Stage	Dependent variable	Explanatory variable	χ^2	p-Value	χ^2	p-Value	F-statistic	p-Value
1	opex_sales	cum_own	904.010	0.000	0.290	0.589	22.798	0.000
1	opex_sales	h_index	930.740	0.000	0.550	0.458	23.005	0.000
1	opex_sales	bh1_dummy	878.120	0.000	0.140	0.707	22.468	0.000
1	discr_assets	cum_own	1165.440	0.000	305.290	0.000	6.450	0.011
1	discr_assets	h_index	1197.090	0.000	314.000	0.000	6.589	0.011
1	discr_assets	bh1_dummy	1155.880	0.000	311.120	0.000	6.572	0.011
1	div_payout	cum_own	741.680	0.000	384.060	0.000	5.066	0.025
1	div_payout	h_index	758.680	0.000	387.130	0.000	5.099	0.025
1	div_payout	bh1_dummy	682.120	0.000	341.540	0.000	5.155	0.024
1	tobinq	cum_own	1029.640	0.000	391.260	0.000	8.366	0.004
1	tobinq	h_index	1028.350	0.000	368.630	0.000	8.410	0.004
1	tobinq	bh1_dummy	990.120	0.000	342.380	0.000	8.483	0.004
2	opex_sales	bh1_cont	933.550	0.000	0.480	0.488	23.167	0.000
2	opex_sales	bh1_supb, bh1_mgmtb	903.430	0.000	0.170	0.676	22.394	0.000
2	opex_sales	identities	1143.130	0.000	1.740	0.187	18.858	0.000
2	discr_assets	bh1_cont	1186.760	0.000	313.260	0.000	6.626	0.010
2	discr_assets	bh1_supb, bh1_mgmtb	1229.890	0.000	320.920	0.000	6.583	0.011
2	discr_assets	identities	1489.640	0.000	308.870	0.000	5.728	0.017
2	div_payout	bh1_cont	753.420	0.000	376.960	0.000	5.142	0.024
2	div_payout	bh1_supb, bh1_mgmtb	756.460	0.000	330.510	0.000	5.191	0.023
2	div_payout	identities	1094.920	0.000	533.680	0.000	4.534	0.034
2	tobinq	bh1_cont	1023.570	0.000	368.280	0.000	8.370	0.004
2	tobinq	bh1_supb, bh1_mgmtb	1064.850	0.000	369.340	0.000	8.456	0.004
2	tobinq	identities	1189.670	0.000	366.140	0.000	8.551	0.004
3	opex_sales	bh2_cont	977.760	0.000	0.360	0.550	22.877	0.000
3	opex_sales	diff_bh12345	970.170	0.000	0.480	0.489	22.724	0.000
3	opex_sales	ln_bh_count	980.850	0.000	1.380	0.240	22.680	0.000
3	discr_assets	bh2_cont	1198.500	0.000	302.060	0.000	6.366	0.012
3	discr_assets	diff_bh12345	1208.050	0.000	306.610	0.000	6.600	0.011
3	discr_assets	ln_bh_count	1154.870	0.000	284.370	0.000	9.268	0.003
3	div_payout	bh2_cont	799.310	0.000	383.390	0.000	5.096	0.025
3	div_payout	diff_bh12345	827.620	0.000	376.120	0.000	5.191	0.023
3	div_payout	ln_bh_count	798.810	0.000	346.910	0.000	4.539	0.034
3	tobinq	bh2_cont	1071.880	0.000	391.000	0.000	8.384	0.004
3	tobinq	diff_bh12345	1049.830	0.000	378.930	0.000	8.953	0.003
3	tobinq	ln_bh_count	1029.610	0.000	339.360	0.000	5.643	0.018

Table 45: Results of the tests for heteroscedasticity and autocorrelation

Table 46
The following table presents the VIF of the variables included in each of the regression specifications estimated in the regression analysis. To save space, for each dependent variable of the respective stage, the table only depicts the VIFs of those specifications that have the highest mean VIF. The highest VIF for each specification is shaded in grey. VIFs that are larger than 10 are considered as a sign of multicollinearity.

	Stage 1				Stage 2				Stage 3			
Variable	opex_sales	discr_assets	div_payout	tobinq	opex_sales	discr_assets	div_payout	tobinq	opex_sales	discr_assets	div_payout	tobinq
ln_assets	4.54	4.51	4.73	4.55	6.55	6.56	7.05	6.59	4.55	4.51	4.74	4.56
codet_par	4.00	4.03	4.23	4.17	4.32	4.36	4.47	4.47	4.00	4.03	4.22	4.17
liq	2.28	2.28	2.41	2.28	2.29	2.29	2.41	2.33	2.25	2.25	2.39	2.30
bics_ind	2.24	2.25	2.40	2.32	2.21	2.22	2.42	2.30	2.25	2.26	2.41	2.34
bics_con_c	1.97	1.99	2.11	2.05	1.96	1.98	2.12	2.04	1.97	1.99	2.12	2.05
bics_con_nonc	1.96	1.96	2.04	2.00	1.94	1.94	2.06	1.99	1.96	1.96	2.04	2.01
year_07	1.82	1.82	2.08	1.83	1.83	1.83	2.12	1.84	1.82	1.82	2.08	1.82
year_08	1.80	1.81	2.30	1.82	1.83	1.84	2.36	1.86	1.80	1.81	2.30	1.82
year_11	1.79	1.80	2.36	1.80	1.79	1.80	2.37	1.81	1.79	1.80	2.36	1.80
year_10	1.79	1.79	2.35	1.79	1.80	1.80	2.39	1.80	1.79	1.79	2.35	1.79
year_09	1.78	1.79	2.38	1.82	1.79	1.80	2.42	1.83	1.78	1.78	2.38	1.81
year_12	1.75	1.77	2.30	1.77	1.76	1.78	2.32	1.78	1.75	1.76	2.30	1.77
year_06	1.72	1.73	1.94	1.74	1.74	1.74	1.96	1.76	1.72	1.73	1.94	1.74
codet_third	1.72	1.73	1.78	1.82	1.85	1.87	1.92	1.92	1.72	1.74	1.78	1.82
bics_comm	1.69	1.68	1.72	1.67	1.69	1.68	1.73	1.68	1.69	1.69	1.72	1.68
bics_ut	1.41	1.42	1.57	1.48	1.41	1.41	1.55	1.50	1.42	1.43	1.57	1.52
bics_bm	1.40	1.41	1.54	1.51	1.42	1.43	1.55	1.53	1.41	1.42	1.55	1.53
h_index	1.27	1.28	1.31									
pfd	1.20	1.20	1.14	1.21	1.28	1.28	1.18	1.28	1.20	1.20	1.14	1.20
govt	1.20	1.20	1.25	1.21	1.22	1.22	1.26	1.22	1.21	1.21	1.26	1.22
debt	1.18	1.18	1.26	1.54	1.18	1.18	1.28	1.54	1.18	1.18	1.27	1.54
bics_enrgy	1.18	1.19	1.25	1.22	1.20	1.20	1.27	1.24	1.18	1.19	1.25	1.22
age	1.16	1.16	1.17	1.19	1.18	1.18	1.17	1.20	1.16	1.16	1.17	1.19
insolv	1.09	1.09	1.09	1.10	1.11	1.11	1.09	1.11	1.10	1.10	1.09	1.10
segm_chng	1.07	1.07	1.07	1.07	1.07	1.08	1.07	1.08	1.07	1.08	1.07	1.08
bank	1.07	1.07	1.08	1.06	1.08	1.08	1.09	1.08	1.08	1.09	1.09	1.09
insd_own	1.06	1.06	1.08	1.08	1.18	1.18	1.21	1.18	1.07	1.07	1.09	1.08
takeover	1.05	1.05	1.06	1.05	1.07	1.07	1.06	1.07	1.06	1.06	1.06	1.06
bics_div	1.05	1.05	1.06	1.05	1.05	1.05	1.07	1.05	1.05	1.05	1.06	1.05
stdev_ni					2.28	2.29	2.36	2.29				
prof			1.38				1.43				1.38	
ppe_assets				2.22				2.23				2.21
growth			1.10	1.06			1.10	1.07			1.10	1.06
div_prevy			1.52				1.56				1.53	
diff_bh12345									6.64	6.60	6.75	6.55
cum_own				1.25								
cash_assets				1.47				1.48				1.47
capex		1.10		1.46		1.11		1.48		1.10		1.46
bh1_si_cont					1.46	1.47	1.49	1.46				
bh1_pe_cont					1.18	1.18	1.20	1.18				
bh1_insti_cont					1.11	1.11	1.11	1.11				
bh1_fam_cont					1.43	1.43	1.40	1.43				
bh1_cont									6.58	6.53	6.75	6.51
beta					1.27	1.27	1.37	1.28				

Table 46: Variance inflation factors for selected regression specifications

Appendix 9 – Non-linearity of the Largest Blockholder's Ownership

Table 47
This table presents the stage 2 pooled-OLS results focusing on the non-linearity of the relationship between *[bhl_cont]* and *[opex_sales]* (specification 2.1.4 & 2.1.5), *[discr_assets]* (specification 2.2.4 & 2.2.5), *[div_payout]* (specification 2.3.4 & 2.3.5), and *[tobinq]* (specification 2.4.4 & 2.4.5). Although not reported, the regressions include control variables as well as industry and year fixed effects; standard errors are clustered by firm. T-statistics are reported in parentheses. In case of a directional hypothesis, one-sided p-Values are calculated. *, **, and *** indicates statistical significance at the 10%, 5%, and 1% level, respectively.

	(2.1.4)	**(2.1.5)**	**(2.2.4)**	**(2.2.5)**	**(2.3.4)**	**(2.3.5)**	**(2.4.4)**	**(2.4.5)**
bh1_cont	**-0.0206**		**-0.0493**		**-0.0005**		**0.4163***	
	(-0.12)		**(-1.03)**		**(-0.28)**		**(1.55)**	
bh1_cont_sq	**-0.0309**		**0.0362**		**0.0018**		**-0.0881**	
	(-0.17)		**(0.69)**		**(0.92)**		**(-0.30)**	
bh1_5to25		**0.0599***		**-0.0125**		**0.0003**		**0.0283**
		(1.31)		**(-1.01)**		**(1.19)**		**(0.47)**
bh1_25to50		**0.0694***		**-0.0205***		**-0.0001**		**0.0864***
		(1.42)		**(-1.46)**		**(-0.45)**		**(1.30)**
bh1_50to75		**0.0002**		**-0.0211***		**0.0006***		**0.2425*****
		(0.00)		**(-1.37)**		**(1.48)**		**(3.45)**
bh1_75to100		**0.0186**		**-0.0213**		**0.0014****		**0.2639*****
		(0.722)		**(-1.10)**		**(2.42)**		**(3.33)**
Constant	0.9603***	0.9031***	1.0106***	1.0169***	0.0039***	0.0038***	1.6396***	1.6630***
	(12.84)	(11.19)	(49.42)	(46.56)	(5.42)	(5.26)	(13.22)	(13.33)
Control variables	Yes	Yes	Yes	Yes	Yes	Yes	Yes	Yes
Industry dummies	Yes	Yes	Yes	Yes	Yes	Yes	Yes	Yes
Year dummies	Yes	Yes	Yes	Yes	Yes	Yes	Yes	Yes
Adjusted R^2	0.1920	0.1957	0.5087	0.5088	0.2848	0.2895	0.2071	0.2096
Number of obs.	3,084	3,084	3,020	3,020	2,228	2,228	2,978	2,978
Firms	489	489	487	487	425	425	484	484

Table 47: Regression results focusing on the non-linearity of the largest blockholder's ownership

Appendix 10 – Non-linearity of the Largest Blockholder Types' Ownership

Table 48

This table presents the stage 2 pooled-OLS results focusing on the non-linearity of the relationship between the largest blockholder types' ownership and *[opex_sales]* (specification 2.1.7), *[discr_assets]* (specification 2.2.7), *[div_payout]* (specification 2.3.7), and *[tobinq]* (specification 2.4.7). Although not reported, the regressions include control variables as well as industry and year fixed effects; standard errors are clustered by firm. T-statistics are reported in parentheses. In case of a directional hypothesis, one-sided p-Values are calculated. *, **, and *** indicates statistical significance at the 10%, 5%, and 1% level, respectively.

	(2.1.7)	**(2.2.7)**	**(2.3.7)**	**(2.4.7)**
bh1_pe_cont_sq	**-0.0214**	**-0.1431**	**-0.0012**	**-0.4594**
	(-0.07)	**(-1.08)**	**(-0.24)**	**(-0.62)**
bh1_fam_cont_sq	**0.6472*****	**0.1112****	**0.0040***	**-0.5625***
	(2.83)	**(1.42)**	**(1.30)**	**(-1.32)**
bh1_si_cont_sq	**-0.2022**	**0.0491**	**0.0061****	**0.4434***
	(-0.83)	**(0.64)**	**(2.38)**	**(1.40)**
bh1_insti_cont_sq	**-0.6719****	**0.1117**	**0.0093**	**-0.1880**
	(-1.91)	**(1.11)**	**(0.58)**	**(-0.37)**
bh1_pe_cont	0.0426	0.0804	0.0045*	1.0421**
	(0.18)	(0.98)	(1.32)	(2.00)
bh1_fam_cont	-0.5421***	-0.0691	-0.0031*	0.6431**
	(-3.00)	(-1.28)	(-1.50)	(1.98)
bh1_si_cont	0.0842	-0.0586	-0.0051***	-0.0502
	(0.42)	(-0.91)	(-2.43)	(-0.19)
bh1_insti_cont	-0.0211	-0.1878***	0.0026	0.1433
	(-0.07)	(-2.06)	(0.42)	(0.33)
Constant	1.0594***	0.9940***	0.0044***	1.6801***
	(12.60)	(44.37)	(5.35)	(11.79)
Control variables	Yes	Yes	Yes	Yes
Industry dummies	Yes	Yes	Yes	Yes
Year dummies	Yes	Yes	Yes	Yes
Adjusted R^2	0.2113	0.5132	0.3137	0.2174
Number of obs.	2,971	2,907	2,226	2,876
Firms	473	471	425	469

Table 48: Regression results focusing on the non-linearity of the largest blockholder types' ownership

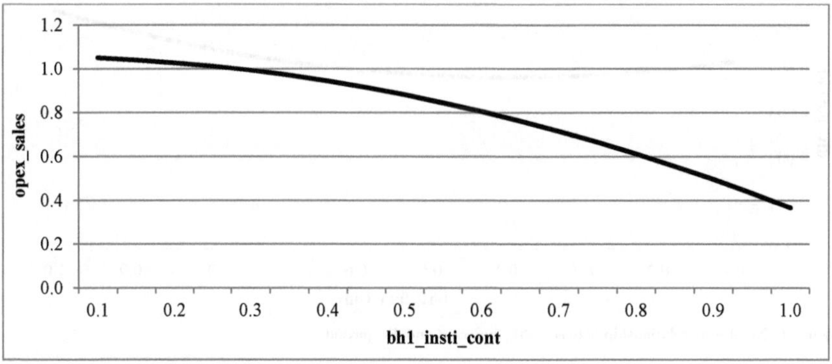

Figure 23: Non-linear relationship between bh1_insti_cont and opex_sales

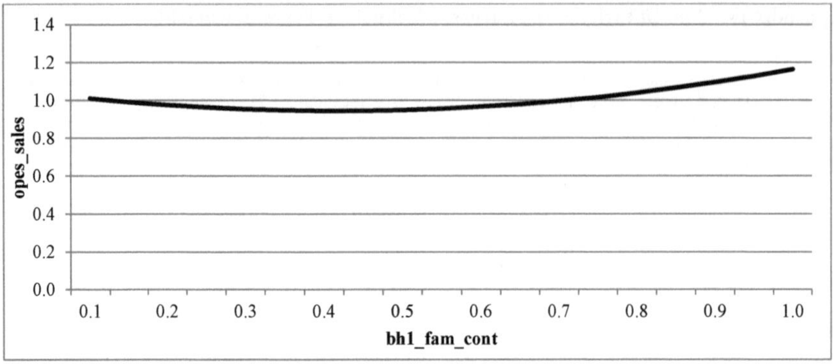

Figure 24: Non-linear relationship between bh1_fam_cont and opex_sales

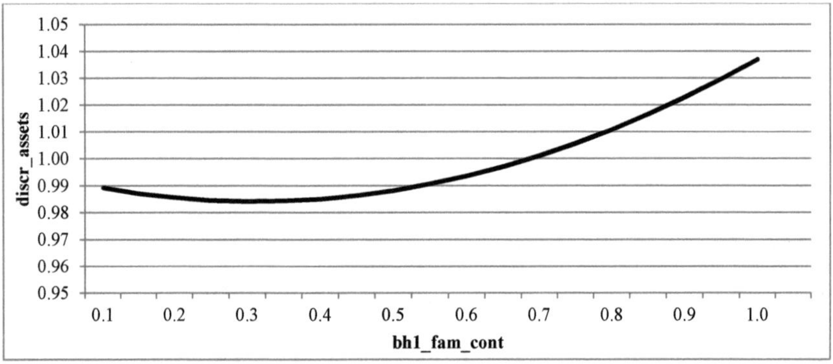

Figure 25: Non-linear relationship between bh1_fam_cont and discr_assets

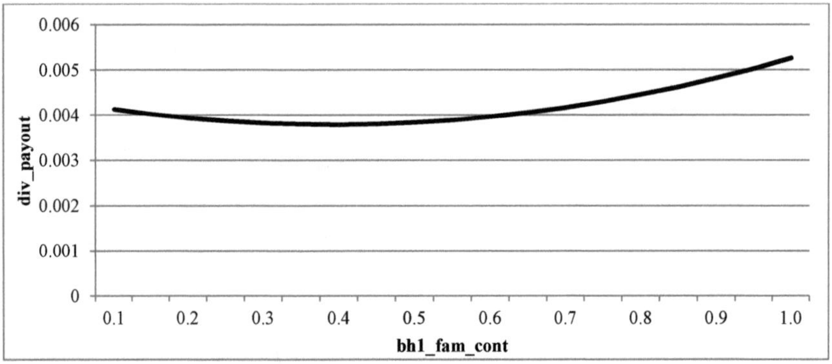

Figure 26: Non-linear relationship between bh1_fam_cont and div_payout

Appendix 11 – Largest Blockholder Types' Presence on the Management or Supervisory Board

Table 49

This table presents the stage 2 pooled-OLS results focusing on the influence of the largest blockholder types' presence on the management or supervisory board based on specification 2.1.6, 2.2.6, 2.3.6, and 2.4.6. Because of too few observations, bh1_insti_cont is not interacted with bh1_supb and bh1_mgmtb. Although not reported, the regressions include control variables as well as industry and year fixed effects; standard errors are clustered by firm. T-statistics are reported in parentheses. In case of a directional hypothesis, one-sided p-Values are calculated. *, **, and *** indicates statistical significance at the 10%, 5%, and 1% level, respectively.

	(2.1.6)	(2.2.6)	(2.3.6)	(2.4.6)
bh1_pe_cont*bh1_supb	**-0.1206**	**0.0044**	**-0.0004**	**0.5987****
	(-0.69)	**(0.06)**	**(-0.12)**	**(1.73)**
bh1_pe_cont*bh1_mgmtb	**-0.0913**	**0.0636**	**0.0083*****	**-0.7536**
	(-0.43)	**(0.77)**	**(2.37)**	**(-1.11)**
bh1_fam_cont*bh1_supb	**0.1313**	**0.0370**	**-0.0012**	**0.0124**
	(0.95)	**(0.85)**	**(-0.86)**	**(0.07)**
bh1_fam_cont*bh1_mgmtb	**0.1337**	**0.0167**	**0.0001**	**-0.5607*****
	(0.89)	**(0.34)**	**(0.03)**	**(-2.52)**
bh1_si_cont*bh1_supb	**-0.0434**	**0.0218**	**0.0019****	**0.0427**
	(-0.42)	**(0.72)**	**(1.77)**	**(0.29)**
bh1_si_cont*bh1_mgmtb	**-0.0877**	**0.0511**	**0.0011**	**-0.1587**
	(-0.56)	**(1.22)**	**(0.43)**	**(-0.69)**
bh1_supb	0.0319	-0.0119	-0.0001	0.0338
	(0.88)	(-1.17)	(-0.19)	(0.67)
bh1_mgmtb	-0.0065	0.0029	0.0000	0.1025
	(-0.13)	(-0.19)	(-0.01)	(1.26)
bh1_pe_cont	0.1151	-0.0007	0.0036*	0.3497*
	(0.74)	(-0.01)	(1.39)	(1.34)
bh1_fam_cont	-0.2823**	-0.0234	0.0003	0.5007***
	(-1.99)	(-0.56)	(0.26)	(2.59)
bh1_si_cont	-0.0436	-0.0290	-0.0016**	0.2386*
	(-0.49)	(-1.09)	(-2.15)	(1.82)
bh1_insti_cont	-0.3877**	-0.1192**	0.0073**	0.0183
	(-2.29)	(-2.28)	(1.86)	(0.13)
Constant	1.0367***	0.9935***	0.0041***	1.7149***
	(12.21)	(44.17)	(4.60)	(12.28)
Control variables	Yes	Yes	Yes	Yes
Industry dummies	Yes	Yes	Yes	Yes
Year dummies	Yes	Yes	Yes	Yes
Adjusted R^2	0.2040	0.5119	0.3171	0.2257
Number of obs.	2,971	2,907	2,226	2,876
Firms	473	471	425	469

Table 49: Regression results based on the largest blockholder types' presence on the supervisory or management board

Appendix 12 – Controlling the Stage 2 Pooled-OLS Results for Own Shares and SEs

Table 50

This table presents the stage 2 pooled-OLS results w.r.t. firm value as proxied by *[tobinq]* (specification 2.4.1-2.4.3), complemented with *[own_shares]* as additional control variable. The regressions include industry and year fixed effects; standard errors are clustered by firm. T-statistics are reported in parentheses. In case of a directional hypothesis, one-sided p-Values are calculated. *, **, and *** indicates statistical significance at the 10%, 5%, and 1% level, respectively.

	(2.4.1)	(2.4.2)	(2.4.3)
bh1_cont	**0.3386*** **	**0.2895*** **	
	(4.31)	**(3.33)**	
bh1_supb		**0.0844** **	
		(2.07)	
bh1_mgmtb		**-0.0290**	
		(-0.54)	
bh1_pe_cont			**0.7577*** **
			(3.94)
bh1_fam_cont			**0.2915** **
			(2.31)
bh1_si_cont			**0.2884*** **
			(3.39)
bh1_insti_cont			**0.0320**
			(0.24)
stdev_ni			0.0001
			(0.37)
beta			-0.0456
			(-0.88)
growth	0.2096***	0.2105***	0.2040***
	(4.76)	(4.80)	(4.73)
ppe_assets	-0.3616**	-0.3798**	-0.3402**
	(-2.16)	(-2.27)	(-2.02)
capex	2.1978***	2.2403***	2.0113***
	(3.05)	(3.16)	(2.77)
cash_assets	1.1024***	1.1196***	1.1576***
	(5.65)	(5.72)	(5.80)
age	0.0013	0.0013	0.0017*
	(1.20)	(1.17)	(1.59)
ln_assets	-0.1150***	-0.1202***	-0.1200***
	(-4.60)	(-4.78)	(-3.97)
pfd	0.1873**	0.1824**	0.1563*
	(1.81)	(1.78)	(1.55)
liq	0.4416***	0.4402***	0.4337***
	(6.63)	(6.60)	(6.33)
insd_own	-0.1633	-0.1795	0.0310
	(-1.27)	(-1.37)	(0.23)
debt	-0.1274	-0.1171	-0.1452
	(-0.83)	(-0.76)	(-0.93)
codet_third	0.0182	0.0215	0.0274
	(0.31)	(0.37)	(0.45)
codet_par	0.1081	0.1132*	0.1303*
	(1.25)	(1.30)	(1.41)
bank	-0.0058	-0.0057	-0.0102
	(-0.13)	(-0.13)	(-0.22)
insolv	-0.0165	-0.0049	-0.0321
	(-0.20)	(-0.06)	(-0.38)
takeover	0.3551***	0.3408***	0.3345***
	(2.59)	(2.52)	(2.53)

Table 50 cont'd

	(2.4.1)	(2.4.2)	(2.4.3)
segm_chng	-0.2958***	-0.2892***	-0.2989***
	(-3.01)	(-3.00)	(-3.06)
govt	0.0560	0.0452	0.0753
	(0.62)	(0.51)	(0.81)
own_shares	*0.0642*	*0.0672*	*0.1070**
	(0.82)	*(0.86)*	*(1.31)*
Constant	1.6463***	1.6617***	1.6947***
	(13.69)	(13.58)	(12.12)
Industry dummies	Yes	Yes	Yes
Year dummies	Yes	Yes	Yes
Adjusted R^2	0.2076	0.2108	0.2166
Number of obs.	2,978	2,978	2,876
Firms	484	484	469

Table 50: Regression results of specification 2.4.1-2.4.3 controlling for own shares

Table 51

This table presents the stage 2 pooled-OLS results w.r.t. firm value as proxied by *[tobinq]* (specification 2.4.1-2.4.3), complemented with *[SE_dummy]* as additional control variable. The regressions include industry and year fixed effects; standard errors are clustered by firm. T-statistics are reported in parentheses. In case of a directional hypothesis, one-sided p-Values are calculated. *, **, and *** indicates statistical significance at the 10%, 5%, and 1% level, respectively.

	(2.4.1)	(2.4.2)	(2.4.3)
bh1_cont	**0.3385*** **	**0.2886*** **	
	(4.31)	**(3.32)**	
bh1_supb		**0.0846** **	
		(2.08)	
bh1_mgmtb		**-0.0268**	
		(-0.50)	
bh1_pe_cont			**0.7405*** **
			(3.84)
bh1_fam_cont			**0.2878** **
			(2.26)
bh1_si_cont			**0.2723*** **
			(3.19)
bh1_insti_cont			**0.0126**
			(0.09)
stdev_ni			0.0001
			(0.32)
beta			-0.0490
			(-0.94)
growth	0.2083***	0.2092***	0.2016***
	(4.73)	(4.77)	(4.66)
ppe_assets	-0.3590**	-0.3783**	-0.3358**
	(-2.14)	(-2.26)	(-1.98)
capex	2.1686***	2.2128***	1.9682***
	(3.02)	(3.14)	(2.72)
cash_assets	1.1007***	1.1178***	1.1550***
	(5.63)	(5.69)	(5.77)
age	0.0014	0.0013	0.0018*
	(1.20)	(1.16)	(1.61)
ln_assets	-0.1146***	-0.1194***	-0.1184***
	(-4.53)	(-4.70)	(-3.90)
pfd	0.1873**	0.1820**	0.1560*
	(1.81)	(1.77)	(1.55)

Table 51 cont'd

	(2.4.1)	(2.4.2)	(2.4.3)
liq	0.4397***	0.4380***	0.4286***
	(6.62)	(6.59)	(6.28)
insd_own	-0.1641	-0.1808	0.0225
	(-1.28)	(-1.38)	(0.17)
debt	-0.1365	-0.1265	-0.1606
	(-0.89)	(-0.83)	(-1.03)
codet_third	0.0151	0.0185	0.0223
	(0.26)	(0.32)	(0.37)
codet_par	0.1065	0.1118*	0.1279*
	(1.23)	(1.29)	(1.39)
bank	-0.0071	-0.0072	-0.0130
	(-0.16)	(-0.16)	(-0.28)
insolv	-0.0179	-0.0058	-0.0329
	(-0.21)	(-0.07)	(-0.39)
takeover	0.3521***	0.3376***	0.3323***
	(2.57)	(2.49)	(2.52)
segm_chng	-0.2974***	-0.2900***	-0.3011***
	(-3.03)	(-3.01)	(-3.08)
govt	0.0585	0.0476	0.0778
	(0.66)	(0.54)	(0.85)
SE_dummy	*0.0185*	*0.0098*	*0.0303*
	(0.25)	*(0.13)*	*(0.40)*
Constant	1.6520***	1.6652***	1.7062***
	(13.69)	(13.59)	(12.12)
Industry dummies	Yes	Yes	Yes
Year dummies	Yes	Yes	Yes
Adjusted R^2	0.2070	0.2102	0.2152
Number of obs.	2,978	2,978	2,876
Firms	484	484	469

Table 51: Regression results of specification 2.4.1-2.4.3 controlling for SEs

Appendix 13 – Regressions of Firm Value on Agency Costs and Blockholder Identities

Table 52
This table presents the stage 2 pooled-OLS results w.r.t. firm value as proxied by *[tobinq]* based on specification 2.4.8 and 2.4.9. To facilitate comparison, the table also comprises the results of specification 2.4.3. The regressions include industry and year fixed effects; standard errors are clustered by firm. T-statistics are reported in parentheses. In case of a directional hypothesis, one-sided p-Values are calculated. *, **, and *** indicates statistical significance at the 10%, 5%, and 1% level, respectively.

	(2.4.8)	(2.4.3)	(2.4.9)
bh1_pe_cont		**0.7403*** **	**0.7305*** **
		(3.84)	**(3.06)**
bh1_fam_cont		**0.2851** **	**0.3524*** **
		(2.24)	**(2.53)**
bh1_si_cont		**0.2718*** **	**0.2725*** **
		(3.18)	**(3.02)**
bh1_insti_cont		**0.0101**	**-0.1027**
		(0.08)	**(-0.51)**
opex_sales	**-0.0671**		**-0.0686**
	(-0.95)		**(-1.00)**
discr_assets	**-0.0274**		**0.0260**
	(-0.19)		**(0.16)**
div_payout	**16.3592*** **		**13.8455** **
	(2.39)		**(2.06)**
stdev_ni		0.0001	0.0002
		(0.30)	(0.65)
beta		-0.0483	-0.0356
		(-0.93)	(-0.60)
growth	0.1917***	0.2021***	0.2026***
	(3.42)	(4.67)	(3.59)
ppe_assets	-0.4529***	-0.3415**	-0.3605**
	(-2.78)	(-2.02)	(-2.07)
capex	1.8978***	1.9844***	1.7586***
	(2.49)	(2.74)	(2.37)
cash_assets	1.0450***	1.1572***	1.0850***
	(4.62)	(5.78)	(4.70)
age	0.0016*	0.0017*	0.0017*
	(1.39)	(1.58)	(1.58)
ln_assets	-0.1186***	-0.1173***	-0.1219***
	(-4.11)	(-3.90)	(-3.65)
pfd	0.2539**	0.1558*	0.1743*
	(1.83)	(1.54)	(1.38)
liq	0.3778***	0.4281***	0.4420***
	(5.35)	(6.27)	(6.12)
insd_own	-0.2838*	0.0213	-0.0655
	(-1.98)	(0.16)	(-0.45)
debt	-0.0805	-0.1593	-0.0679
	(-0.48)	(-1.02)	(-0.41)
codet_third	0.0463	0.0232	0.0302
	(0.71)	(0.38)	(0.46)
codet_par	0.1482*	0.1285*	0.1264
	(1.53)	(1.40)	(1.26)
bank	-0.0479	-0.0136	-0.0155
	(-1.01)	(-0.30)	(-0.34)
insolv	-0.0559	-0.0318	-0.0598
	(-0.51)	(-0.38)	(-0.55)
takeover	0.4027**	0.3306***	0.3570**
	(2.28)	(2.50)	(2.06)

Table 52 cont'd

	(2.4.8)	(2.4.3)	(2.4.9)
segm_chng	-0.2749***	-0.2975***	-0.2581**
	(-2.33)	(-3.03)	(-2.26)
govt	0.0429	0.0765	0.0654
	(0.42)	(0.83)	(0.65)
Constant	1.8695***	1.7021***	1.7511***
	(8.89)	(12.13)	(7.76)
Industry dummies	Yes	Yes	Yes
Year dummies	Yes	Yes	Yes
Adjusted R^2	0.2078	0.2154	0.2275
Number of obs.	2,450	2,876	2,447
Firms	446	469	446

Table 52: Regression results of firm value on agency costs and the largest blockholder identities

Appendix 14 – Interaction Between the Ownership of the Second Largest Blockholder and the Ownership of Family Blockholders and Institutional Investors

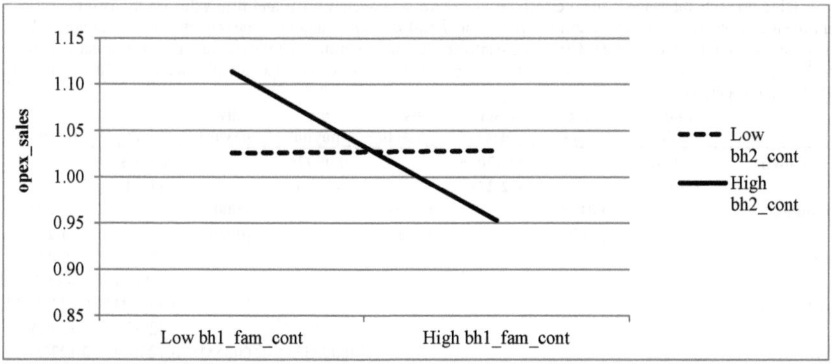

Figure 27: Interaction between bh2_cont and bh1_fam_cont

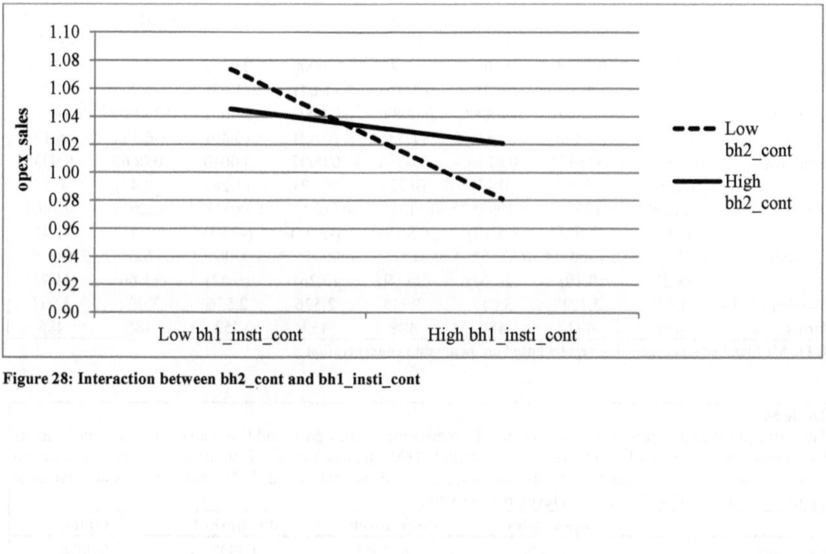

Figure 28: Interaction between bh2_cont and bh1_insti_cont

Appendix 15 – Fixed Effects Regressions

Table 53

This table presents the stage 1 fixed effects results regressing agency costs and firm value on the two time variant measures of ownership concentration *[cum_own]* and *[h_index]* and the time variant control variables. The regressions include HAC standard errors. T-statistics are reported in parentheses. In case of a directional hypothesis, one-sided p-Values are calculated. *, **, and *** indicates statistical significance at the 10%, 5%, and 1% level, respectively.

	opex sales	opex sales	discr assets	discr assets	div payout	div payout	tobinq	tobinq
cum_own	**-0.0243**		**-0.0170****		**0.0007***		**0.1103***	
	(-1.08)		**(-2.24)**		**(1.71)**		**(1.84)**	
h_index		**0.0195**		**-0.0208****		**0.0004**		**0.1007**
		(0.62)		**(-2.24)**		**(0.69)**		**(1.26)**
ppe_assets							-0.5999**	-0.6060**
							(-2.05)	(-2.06)
cash_assets							0.4801***	0.4773***
							(2.82)	(2.81)
growth					-0.0005***	-0.0005***	0.1236***	0.1236***
					(-3.41)	(-3.44)	(3.43)	(3.43)
prof					0.0043***	0.0043***		
					(4.01)	(4.02)		
capex			-0.5235***	-0.5265***			1.7017***	1.7251***
			(-5.13)	(-5.15)			(3.33)	(3.37)
age	0.0018	0.0014	-0.0002	-0.0001	0.0000	0.0000	-0.0075	-0.0076
	(0.86)	(0.70)	(-0.23)	(-0.16)	(1.02)	(1.03)	(-1.26)	(-1.27)
ln_assets	-0.0089	-0.0086	0.0088*	0.0089*	0.0002	0.0002	-0.3398***	-0.3403***
	(-0.52)	(-0.51)	(1.54)	(1.55)	(0.52)	(0.49)	(-6.11)	(-6.12)
insd_own	-0.1567***	-0.1761***	0.0156	0.0068	0.0007	0.0010	-0.0663	-0.0039
	(-2.52)	(-2.91)	(0.47)	(0.22)	(0.77)	(1.28)	(-0.44)	(-0.03)
debt	0.1189**	0.1217**	-0.1097***	-0.1101***	-0.0031***	-0.0031***	-0.2657	-0.2664
	(1.91)	(1.94)	(-5.19)	(-5.18)	(-2.91)	(-2.93)	(-1.47)	(-1.47)
Constant	0.7442***	0.7300***	0.8156***	0.8111***	0.0005***	0.0008***	3.4205***	3.4577***
	(8.27)	(8.10)	(26.60)	(26.69)	(0.26)	(0.42)	(11.60)	(11.71)
Number of obs.	3,121	3,121	3,045	3,045	2,526	2,526	3,002	3,002
Firms	492	492	488	488	452	452	485	485

Table 53: Fixed effects regression results based on ownership concentration

Table 54

This table presents the stage 2 fixed effects results regressing agency costs and firm value on *[bh1_cont]* and the time variant control variables. The regressions include HAC standard errors. T-statistics are reported in parentheses. In case of a directional hypothesis, one-sided p-Values are calculated. *, **, and *** indicates statistical significance at the 10%, 5%, and 1% level, respectively.

	opex_sales	discr_assets	div_payout	tobinq
bh1_cont	**0.0070**	**-0.0170****	**0.0002**	**0.0896**
	(0.24)	**(-2.08)**	**(0.41)**	**(1.17)**
ppe_assets				-0.6043**
				(-2.05)
cash_assets				0.4761***
				(2.81)
growth			-0.0005***	0.1234***
			(-3.46)	(3.43)
prof			0.0043***	
			(4.00)	
capex		-0.5278***		1.7311***
		(-5.16)		(3.38)
age	0.0015	-0.0001	0.0000	-0.0076
	(0.74)	(-0.18)	(1.05)	(-1.27)

Table 54 cont'd

	opex_sales	discr_assets	div_payout	tobinq
ln_assets	-0.0088	0.0090*	0.0002	-0.3409***
	(-0.52)	(1.57)	(0.48)	(-6.12)
insd_own	-0.1745***	0.0068	0.0011	-0.0056
	(-2.88)	(0.21)	(1.32)	(-0.04)
debt	0.1210**	-0.1100***	-0.0031***	-0.2663
	(1.93)	(-5.17)	(-2.94)	(-1.47)
Constant	0.7315***	0.8121***	0.0008	3.4507***
	(8.06)	(26.83)	(0.42)	(11.73)
Number of obs.	3,121	3,045	2,526	3,002
Firms	492	488	452	485

Table 54: Fixed effects regression results based on the largest blockholder's ownership

Table 55

This table presents the stage 2 fixed effects results regressing agency costs and firm value on the largest blockholder types' ownership and the time variant control variables. The regressions include HAC standard errors. T-statistics are reported in parentheses. In case of a directional hypothesis, one-sided p-Values are calculated. *, **, and *** indicates statistical significance at the 10%, 5%, and 1% level, respectively.

	opex_sales	discr_assets	div_payout	tobinq
bh1_pe_cont	**-0.0058**	**-0.0067**	**0.0037*** **	**0.2694***
	(-0.12)	**(-0.33)**	**(3.02)**	**(1.55)**
bh1_fam_cont	**-0.0530**	**-0.0230***	**-0.0001**	**-0.0103**
	(-1.02)	**(-1.30)**	**(-0.18)**	**(-0.07)**
bh1_si_cont	**0.0438**	**-0.0124**	**0.0001**	**0.0939**
	(1.24)	**(-0.96)**	**(0.11)**	**(1.08)**
bh1_insti_cont	**-0.2461**	**-0.0416**	**0.0066** **	**-0.0877**
	(-1.23)	**(-1.03)**	**(1.75)**	**(-0.46)**
stdev_ni	0.0001	0.0000	0.0000*	-0.0002
	(0.50)	(0.62)	(1.85)	(-0.93)
beta	0.0002	0.0019	-0.0001	-0.0103
	(0.01)	(0.35)	(-0.27)	(-0.28)
ppe_assets				-0.5699**
				(-1.87)
cash_assets				0.4732***
				(2.74)
growth			-0.0005***	0.1325***
			(-3.44)	(3.59)
prof			0.0044***	
			(4.12)	
capex		-0.4969***		1.7167***
		(-4.91)		(3.31)
age	-0.0001	-0.0000	0.0001	-0.0055
	(-0.06)	(-0.06)	(1.11)	(-0.91)
ln_assets	-0.0079	0.0074	0.0002	-0.3442***
	(-0.46)	(1.26)	(0.48)	(-6.12)
insd_own	-0.1475**	-0.0116	0.0018*	0.0679
	(-2.49)	(-0.46)	(1.65)	(0.43)
debt	0.1099*	-0.1086***	-0.0032***	-0.2524
	(1.77)	(-4.97)	(-3.05)	(-1.38)
Constant	0.7525***	0.8156***	0.0006	3.4727***
	(8.30)	(26.06)	(0.29)	(11.68)
Number of obs.	3,008	2,931	2,523	2,900
Firms	476	472	452	470

Table 55: Fixed effects regression results based on the largest blockholder identities' ownership

Table 56
This table presents the stage 3 fixed effects results regressing agency costs and firm value on the interaction between the largest and second largest blockholders' ownership, given both are of the same type, as well as on the time variant control variables. The regressions include HAC standard errors. T-statistics are reported in parentheses. In case of a directional hypothesis, one-sided p-Values are calculated. *, **, and *** indicates statistical significance at the 10%, 5%, and 1% level, respectively.

	opex_sales	discr_assets	div_payout	tobinq
bh1_pe_cont*bh2_pe_cont	**-0.0559**	**0.0923**	**-0.0042**	**-2.5932****
	(-0.13)	**(0.87)**	**(-0.53)**	**(-2.17)**
bh1_fam_cont*bh2_fam_cont	**-1.0394***	**-0.3205***	**-0.0122****	**-0.9441**
	(-1.50)	**(-1.30)**	**(-1.86)**	**(-0.95)**
bh1_si_cont*bh2_si_cont	**0.0001**	**0.0756**	**0.0241****	**-2.4667****
	(0.00)	**(0.32)**	**(2.47)**	**(-1.77)**
bh1_insti_cont*bh2_insti_cont	**-1.4651**	**0.6379**	**0.0354***	**-6.3567***
	(-0.65)	**(1.04)**	**(1.31)**	**(-1.32)**
bh2_pe_cont	-0.2755*	0.1367**	-0.0028	0.0144
	(-1.29)	(1.94)	(-0.80)	(0.03)
bh2_fam_cont	-0.2552**	-0.0080	0.0025	0.3212
	(-1.97)	(-0.21)	(1.23)	(1.01)
bh2_si_cont	0.0478	-0.0442*	0.0034*	0.2926
	(0.30)	(-1.35)	(1.59)	(1.17)
bh2_insti_cont	0.0788	-0.0349	0.0007	0.6851**
	(0.66)	(-0.85)	(0.38)	(2.00)
bh1_pe_cont	-0.0388	0.0111	0.0038***	0.1898
	(-0.77)	(0.69)	(2.97)	(0.99)
bh1_fam_cont	-0.0551	-0.0365**	0.0002	-0.0454
	(-0.94)	(-2.11)	(0.30)	(-0.27)
bh1_si_cont	0.0620*	-0.0098	0.0001	0.0650
	(1.58)	(-0.96)	(0.14)	(0.66)
bh1_insti_cont	-0.2214	-0.0552	0.0107***	-0.2513
	(-0.83)	(-1.08)	(2.61)	(-1.03)
Constant	0.7153***	0.8187***	-0.0000	3.4851
	(6.40)	(18.14)	(-0.01)	(11.90)
Control variables	Yes	Yes	Yes	Yes
Number of obs.	2,549	2,484	2,229	2,464
Firms	457	452	439	451

Table 56: Fixed effects regression results based on the interaction between the largest and second largest blockholder types' ownership

Table 57
This table presents the stage 3 fixed effects results regressing agency costs and firm value on the two measures of the heterogeneity of a firm's ownership structure and the time variant control variables. The regressions include HAC standard errors. T-statistics are reported in parentheses. In case of a directional hypothesis, one-sided p-Values are calculated. *, **, and *** indicates statistical significance at the 10%, 5%, and 1% level, respectively.

	opex sales	opex sales	discr assets	discr assets	div payout	div payout	tobinq	tobinq
ln_bh	**-0.0318*****		**-0.0024**		**0.0004*****		**0.0368***	
_count	**(-2.95)**		**(-0.64)**		**(2.77)**		**(1.45)**	
ln_bhtypes		**-0.0323*****		**-0.0016**		**0.0005*****		**0.0542****
_count		**(-2.64)**		**(-0.45)**		**(2.85)**		**(1.91)**
bh1_cont	-0.0034	0.0046	-0.0197**	-0.0189**	0.0003	0.0002	0.1124	0.1094
	(-0.10)	(0.13)	(-1.90)	(-1.86)	(0.43)	(0.29)	(1.26)	(1.24)
ppe_assets							-0.5135**	-0.5142*
							(-1.74)	(-1.75)
cash_assets							0.5387***	0.5380***
							(3.01)	(3.01)

Table 57 cont'd

	opex _sales	opex _sales	discr _assets	discr _assets	div _payout	div _payout	tobinq	tobinq
growth					-0.0005***	-0.0005***	0.1244***	0.1264***
					(-3.00)	(-2.93)	(3.16)	(3.21)
prof					0.0044***	0.0043***		
					(3.72)	(3.68)		
capex			-0.5365***	-0.5361***			1.7264***	1.7244***
			(-5.14)	(-5.14)			(3.29)	(3.30)
age	0.0015	0.0016	-0.0001	-0.0001	0.0001	0.0001	-0.0056	-0.0057
	(0.72)	(0.74)	(-0.17)	(-0.17)	(1.10)	(1.10)	(-0.92)	(-0.94)
ln_assets	-0.0124	-0.0117	0.0103**	0.0103**	0.0001	0.0000	-0.3482***	-0.3498***
	(-0.69)	(-0.64)	(1.66)	(1.66)	(0.16)	(0.11)	(-5.86)	(-5.90)
insd_own	-0.1847***	-0.1987***	0.0152	0.0135	0.0008	0.0010	0.0138	0.0158
	(-2.60)	(-2.87)	(0.44)	(0.39)	(0.82)	(0.96)	(0.09)	(0.11)
debt	0.0934*	0.0903*	-0.1072***	-0.1076***	-0.0031***	-0.0031***	-0.2247	-0.2229
	(1.41)	(1.35)	(-4.83)	(-4.84)	(-2.78)	(-2.76)	(-1.16)	(-1.15)
Constant	0.7856***	0.7739***	0.8067***	0.8053***	0.0011	0.0013	3.3953***	3.4034***
	(8.42)	(8.17)	(25.36)	(25.74)	(0.53)	(0.61)	(10.92)	(10.95)
Number of obs.	2,928	2,924	2,863	2,859	2,378	2,374	2,824	2,820
Firms	488	488	484	484	446	446	480	480

Table 57: Fixed effects regression results based on the heterogeneity of a firm's ownership structure

Table 58

This table presents the stage 3 fixed effects results regressing principal-principal agency costs, proxied by *[div_payout]*, and firm value, proxied by *[tobinq]*, on the interaction between the largest blockholder types' ownership and the incontestability proxies as well as on the time variant control variables. The regressions include HAC standard errors. T-statistics are reported in parentheses. In case of a directional hypothesis, one-sided p-Values are calculated. *, **, and *** indicates statistical significance at the 10%, 5%, and 1% level, respectively.

	dependent variable: div_payout			dependent variable: tobinq		
	bh1/bh2	bh1/bh2_bh3	diff_bh12345	bh1/bh2	bh1/bh2_bh3	diff_bh12345
bh1_pe_cont*incont	**0.0004***	**0.0003**	**-0.0107*****	**0.0314**	**0.0252**	**-1.7343*****
	(1.51)	**(1.01)**	**(-2.96)**	**(1.08)**	**(0.61)**	**(-3.62)**
bh1_fam_cont*incont	**-0.0001**	**-0.0002**	**-0.0005**	**-0.0078**	**-0.0190**	**-0.8466****
	(-0.50)	**(-1.10)**	**(-0.33)**	**(-0.29)**	**(-0.66)**	**(-2.46)**
bh1_si_cont*incont	**0.0002**	**0.0001**	**0.0015**	**-0.0087**	**-0.0132**	**-0.1193**
	(1.16)	**(0.57)**	**(0.65)**	**(-0.46)**	**(-0.65)**	**(-0.57)**
bh1_insti_cont*incont	**0.0014***	**0.0010**	**-0.0155***	**-0.0652***	**-0.0628**	**-0.1379**
	(1.56)	**(0.84)**	**(-1.43)**	**(-1.38)**	**(-1.14)**	**(-0.60)**
incont	0.0001	0.0001	-0.0009	0.0136	0.0168*	0.1428
	(0.65)	(1.25)	(-0.76)	(1.19)	(1.35)	(1.14)
bh1_pe_cont	0.0017	0.0021*	0.0081***	0.0529	0.0927	0.9395***
	(1.03)	(1.36)	(3.97)	(0.24)	(0.41)	(3.24)
bh1_fam_cont	-0.0003	-0.0002	0.0008	-0.0456	-0.0121	0.3290*
	(-0.52)	(-0.26)	(0.95)	(-0.25)	(-0.07)	(1.62)
bh1_si_cont	-0.0010	-0.0007	-0.0001	0.0589	0.0683	0.0996
	(-1.15)	(-0.82)	(-0.08)	(0.60)	(0.70)	(0.62)
bh1_insti_cont	0.0022	0.0045	0.0088**	0.0102	-0.0400	0.0482
	(0.57)	(1.26)	(2.36)	(0.05)	(-0.20)	(0.21)
Constant	0.0013	0.0013	0.0003	3.4622***	3.4602***	3.4290***
	(0.66)	(0.66)	(0.14)	(10.93)	(10.93)	(11.63)
Control variables	Yes	Yes	Yes	Yes	Yes	Yes
Number of obs.	2,375	2,375	2,523	2,728	2,728	2,900
Firms	446	446	452	465	465	470

Table 58: Fixed effects regression results based on the largest blockholder types' incontestability

Appendix 16 – Parameter Stability

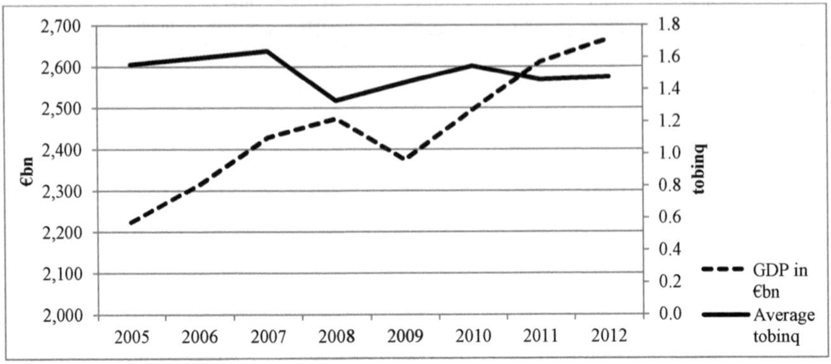

Figure 29: German GDP and sample firms' average tobinq during 2005-2012 [source: own calculation and Statistisches Bundesamt (2014)]

Table 59
The table presents the coefficients of the year dummies used in specification 2.4.1. The year 2005 constitutes the base case. Standard errors are clustered by firm. T-statistics are reported in parentheses. *, **, and *** indicates statistical significance at the 10%, 5%, and 1% level, respectively.

year_06	0.0398*
	(1.49)
year_07	0.0707**
	(2.18)
year_08	-0.2258***
	(-5.78)
year_09	-0.0770**
	(-1.87)
year_10	-0.0004
	(-0.01)
year_11	-0.1078***
	(-2.62)
year_12	-0.0719**
	(-1.76)
Control variables	Yes
Industry dummies	Yes

Table 59: Year dummy coefficients of specification 2.4.1

Appendix 17 – Year-by-year Regressions

Table 60

This table presents the results of the yearly (cross-sectional) OLS regressions on firm value proxied by *[tobinq]* based on specification 2.4.1. The regressions include industry fixed effects; standard errors are heteroscedasticity consistent. T-statistics are reported in parentheses. In case of a directional hypothesis, one-sided p-Values are calculated. *, **, and *** indicates statistical significance at the 10%, 5%, and 1% level, respectively.

	2005	**2006**	**2007**	**2008**	**2009**	**2010**	**2011**	**2012**
bh1_cont	**0.3654***	**0.3271**	**0.1582**	**0.3601***	**0.2746**	**0.2254***	**0.4247***	**0.4775***
	(2.78)	**(2.22)**	**(1.24)**	**(2.88)**	**(2.06)**	**(1.49)**	**(2.84)**	**(3.28)**
growth	0.2514***	0.1923**	0.2835**	0.0787	0.3282***	0.1755	0.2811*	0.1085
	(2.89)	(1.80)	(2.25)	(0.77)	(2.36)	(1.27)	(1.45)	(0.61)
ppe_assets	-0.3321*	-0.4766*	-0.5478**	-0.2742	-0.0246	-0.5244**	-0.2313	-0.4610**
	(-1.31)	(-1.58)	(-2.09)	(-1.01)	(-0.09)	(-1.68)	(-0.73)	(-1.73)
capex	2.3323**	3.0601**	3.4318***	2.2423**	1.1397	1.7254	0.9214	1.2765
	(1.71)	(2.09)	(2.78)	(1.81)	(0.83)	(1.17)	(0.72)	(0.97)
cash_assets	1.2011***	1.2494***	1.1053***	0.8456***	1.5488***	1.3053***	0.9656***	0.6657**
	(3.79)	(3.73)	(3.61)	(2.94)	(4.58)	(3.70)	(2.77)	(1.89)
age	-0.0006	0.0017	0.0008	0.0017	0.0033**	0.0017	0.0021	-0.0002
	(-0.50)	(1.01)	(0.57)	(1.16)	(2.04)	(1.22)	(1.22)	(-0.16)
ln_assets	-0.1362***	-0.1036***	-0.0762**	-0.0791***	-0.0709**	-0.1605***	-0.1269***	-0.1746***
	(-4.35)	(-3.10)	(-2.06)	(-2.39)	(-1.76)	(-4.22)	(-3.13)	(-4.09)
pfd	0.0915	0.1550	0.1495	0.2006*	0.2859**	0.1588	0.3239**	0.0895
	(0.70)	(1.12)	(1.06)	(1.32)	(1.77)	(1.11)	(2.00)	(0.68)
liq	0.4816***	0.3881***	0.3858***	0.2858***	0.4460***	0.3015***	0.5315***	0.7089***
	(5.02)	(3.60)	(3.72)	(2.65)	(4.57)	(2.82)	(4.51)	(5.76)
insd_own	0.0381	-0.1324	-0.4512**	-0.1490	0.2772	-0.1861	-0.4929**	-0.2297
	(0.21)	(-0.59)	(-2.21)	(-0.70)	(0.84)	(-0.59)	(-2.38)	(-0.98)
debt	-0.0009	-0.4314*	-0.5545**	0.0317	-0.0870	0.0340	0.0838	-0.1626
	(-0.00)	(-1.72)	(-2.21)	(0.15)	(-0.33)	(0.11)	(0.33)	(-0.57)
codet_third	0.0899	0.1453*	0.0924	0.0007	-0.0902	0.0530	-0.1485*	0.0069
	(0.93)	(1.57)	(1.02)	(0.01)	(-0.90)	(0.54)	(-1.34)	(0.06)
codet_par	0.1682*	0.2409**	0.1657*	0.0655	-0.0727	0.3386***	-0.0909	0.1340
	(1.29)	(1.71)	(1.28)	(0.47)	(-0.47)	(2.34)	(-0.61)	(0.86)
bank	0.0557	0.1798**	0.0522	0.0333	-0.0838	-0.0165	-0.0663	-0.1569**
	(0.57)	(1.68)	(0.61)	(0.38)	(-1.03)	(-0.16)	(-0.68)	(-1.65)
insolv	-0.0502	0.1045	0.0277	-0.0093	-0.1053	0.0855	-0.4969***	-
	(-0.43)	(0.75)	(0.22)	(-0.06)	(-0.73)	(0.27)	(-2.62)	
takeover	0.1211	0.2314*	0.3229**	0.5376***	0.7629***	0.6274	0.2496	-
	(0.96)	(1.84)	(2.08)	(2.52)	(2.93)	(0.88)	(1.27)	
segm_chng	-0.2604**	-0.2536***	-0.3290**	-0.1277	-0.3130**	-0.3066*	-0.1692	-
	(-2.16)	(-2.41)	(-2.03)	(-0.94)	(-2.30)	(-1.47)	(-0.64)	
govt	0.1905	0.1607	0.0294	0.0868	-0.1010	-0.1205	0.0541	0.1712
	(1.13)	(0.17)	(0.93)	(0.73)	(-0.96)	(-1.02)	(0.38)	(1.14)
Constant	1.6602***	1.5951***	1.5719***	1.2243***	1.3295***	1.8863***	1.7390***	1.9702***
	(8.67)	(9.57)	(8.19)	(7.80)	(6.50)	(8.26)	(7.41)	(8.21)
Industry dummies	Yes	Yes	Yes	Yes	Yes	Yes	Yes	Yes
Year dummies	No	No	No	No	No	No	No	No
Adjusted R^2	0.1816	0.2162	0.2042	0.0969	0.2273	0.1479	0.1454	0.1866
Number of obs.	369	358	404	399	373	364	367	344

Table 60: Yearly (cross-sectional) regression results based on the largest blockholder's ownership

Table 61
This table presents the results of the yearly (cross-sectional) OLS regressions on firm value proxied by *[tobinq]* based on specification 2.4.3. The regressions include industry fixed effects; standard errors are heteroscedasticity consistent. T-statistics are reported in parentheses. In case of a directional hypothesis, one-sided p-Values are calculated. *, **, and *** indicates statistical significance at the 10%, 5%, and 1% level, respectively.

	2005	2006	2007	2008	2009	2010	2011	2012
bh1_pe	**0.3379**	**0.3037**	**0.8637*** **	**0.7008** **	**0.8461*** **	**1.0103*** **	**1.2487*** **	**0.3221**
_cont	**(1.01)**	**(0.96)**	**(2.55)**	**(2.23)**	**(2.76)**	**(2.68)**	**(3.58)**	**(0.84)**
bh1_fam	**0.3030** **	**0.1304**	**0.3226** **	**0.4056** **	**0.3341* **	**0.1204**	**0.2992**	**0.3473* **
_cont	**(1.77)**	**(0.69)**	**(1.83)**	**(2.00)**	**(1.59)**	**(0.58)**	**(1.25)**	**(1.50)**
bh1_si	**0.1994* **	**0.4069** **	**0.1761* **	**0.1968* **	**0.1175**	**0.1090**	**0.3282** **	**0.4010*** **
_cont	**(1.33)**	**(2.41)**	**(1.32)**	**(1.41)**	**(0.76)**	**(0.69)**	**(2.25)**	**(2.75)**
bh1_insti	**0.3777**	**-0.4543* **	**-0.1744**	**0.2134**	**0.3414**	**-0.2539**	**0.0672**	**0.2406**
_cont	**(0.88)**	**(-1.42)**	**(-0.61)**	**(0.96)**	**(1.20)**	**(-1.09)**	**(0.26)**	**(0.81)**
stdev_ni	-0.0000	-0.0002	-0.0002	0.0001	0.0001	-0.0002	0.0005	0.0008*
	(-0.01)	(-0.45)	(-0.54)	(0.10)	(0.16)	(-0.37)	(0.97)	(1.57)
beta	-0.0570	0.0720	0.1211	-0.1961*	-0.1885*	-0.1071	-0.1567	-0.3024*
	(-0.63)	(0.73)	(1.24)	(-1.81)	(-1.81)	(-0.83)	(-1.18)	(-1.81)
growth	0.2194***	0.2040**	0.2360**	0.0720	0.3314**	0.1804	0.2444	0.1920
	(2.51)	(1.82)	(2.03)	(0.66)	(2.16)	(1.28)	(1.11)	(0.96)
ppe_assets	-0.3589*	-0.4249*	-0.5227**	-0.3252	0.0189	-0.5152*	-0.2041	-0.3429
	(-1.39)	(-1.39)	(-1.93)	(-1.10)	(0.07)	(-1.57)	(-0.62)	(-1.14)
capex	2.3355**	2.2646*	3.4025***	2.6589**	1.1241	1.4058	0.1716	0.8739
	(1.69)	(1.56)	(2.63)	(1.94)	(0.78)	(0.93)	(0.13)	(0.57)
cash_assets	1.2227***	1.3590***	1.0630***	0.9205***	1.6183***	1.3726***	1.0894***	0.7527**
	(3.82)	(3.97)	(3.42)	(3.12)	(4.70)	(3.89)	(3.13)	(2.13)
age	0.0002	0.0025*	0.0014	0.0017	0.0035**	0.0021*	0.0026*	0.0001
	(0.13)	(1.49)	(0.96)	(1.13)	(2.16)	(1.53)	(1.49)	(0.07)
ln_assets	-0.1409***	-0.1092***	-0.0659*	-0.0762**	-0.0661	-0.1527***	-0.1497***	-0.2033***
	(-3.48)	(-2.54)	(-1.43)	(-1.70)	(-1.27)	(-2.97)	(-3.02)	(-4.09)
pfd	0.0894	0.1785	0.1109	0.1194	0.2123*	0.0978	0.2613**	0.0824
	(0.69)	(1.28)	(0.78)	(0.76)	(1.32)	(0.67)	(1.74)	(0.58)
liq	0.4432***	0.3631***	0.3535***	0.2875***	0.4721***	0.3226***	0.5146***	0.7664***
	(4.62)	(3.13)	(3.31)	(2.65)	(64.77)	(2.96)	(4.43)	(5.88)
insd_own	0.2044	0.0203	-0.2885	0.0680	0.4930	-0.0454	-0.2227	-0.0500
	(1.02)	(0.08)	(-1.22)	(0.29)	(1.38)	(-0.14)	(-1.03)	(-0.20)
debt	-0.0168	-0.4005	-0.6327***	0.0377	-0.1388	-0.0149	0.0988	-0.1985
	(-0.07)	(-1.59)	(-2.46)	(0.17)	(-0.50)	(-0.05)	(0.38)	(-0.63)
codet_third	0.0808	0.1528*	0.0530	0.0555	-0.0505	0.0972	-0.0968	0.0392
	(0.79)	(1.48)	(0.53)	(0.54)	(-0.48)	(0.91)	(-0.79)	(0.34)
codet_par	0.2006*	0.2583**	0.1498	0.1111	-0.0618	0.3514**	0.0201	0.1913
	(1.46)	(1.68)	(1.09)	(0.74)	(-0.36)	(2.19)	(0.12)	(1.14)
bank	0.0532	0.1681*	0.0333	0.0347	-0.1037	-0.0240	-0.0670	-0.1535*
	(0.54)	(1.54)	(0.39)	(0.40)	(-1.21)	(-0.23)	(-0.66)	(-1.57)
insolv	-0.0474	0.0707	-0.0028	0.0181	-0.1047	0.0204	-0.7525***	-
	(-0.38)	(0.52)	(-0.02)	(0.11)	(-0.69)	(0.06)	(-3.04)	
takeover	0.1186	0.1684	0.3325**	0.4888**	0.7713***	0.5437	0.0060	-
	(0.92)	(1.34)	(2.13)	(2.28)	(3.16)	(0.90)	(0.02)	
segm_chng	-0.2492**	-0.3721***	-0.2505**	-0.1410	-0.2943**	-0.2804*	-0.1349	-
	(-2.07)	(-2.63)	(-2.00)	(-0.96)	(-2.07)	(-1.38)	(-0.54)	
govt	0.2144	0.0733	0.1946	0.0587	-0.0938	-0.1131	0.0825	0.1962
	(1.24)	(0.41)	(1.11)	(0.49)	(-0.83)	(-0.89)	(0.54)	(1.26)
Constant	1.7504***	1.5637***	1.4331***	1.3647***	1.4493***	1.9460***	1.8958***	2.2780***
	(7.62)	(7.52)	(6.42)	(6.88)	(5.70)	(6.80)	(6.78)	(7.88)

Table 61 cont'd

	2005	2006	2007	2008	2009	2010	2011	2012
Industry dummies	Yes	Yes	Yes	Yes	Yes	Yes	Yes	Yes
Year dummies	No	No	No	No	No	No	No	No
Adjusted R^2	0.1645	0.2279	0.2182	0.0969	0.2328	0.1677	0.1645	0.1805
Number of obs.	356	347	391	386	359	351	354	332

Table 61: Yearly (cross-sectional) regression results based on the largest blockholder types' ownership

Appendix 18 – Sensitivity Analysis

Table 62

This table presents the pooled-OLS regression results of the agency costs and firm value variables on the lagged ownership of the largest blockholder (based on specifications 2.1.1, 2.2.1, 2.3.1, and 2.4.1) and the lagged ownership of the largest blockholder types (based on specifications 2.1.3, 2.2.3, 2.3.3, and 2.4.3), respectively. Although not reported, the regressions include control variables as well as industry and year fixed effects; standard errors are clustered by firm. T-statistics are reported in parentheses. In case of a directional hypothesis, one-sided p-Values are calculated. *, **, and *** indicates statistical significance at the 10%, 5%, and 1% level, respectively.

	(2.1.1)	(2.1.3)	(2.2.1)	(2.2.3)	(2.3.1)	(2.3.3)	(2.4.1)	(2.4.3)
bh1_cont (t-1)	**-0.0399**		**-0.0109**		**0.0014*** **		**0.3209*** **	
	(-0.73)		**(-0.67)**		**(2.51)**		**(3.82)**	
bh1_pe_cont (t-1)		**-0.0723**		**0.0220**		**0.0040*** **		**0.8680*** **
		(-0.81)		**(0.51)**		**(2.76)**		**(4.15)**
bh1_fam_cont (t-1)		**-0.1209** **		**0.0039**		**0.0004**		**0.2681** **
		(-1.75)		**(0.19)**		**(0.53)**		**(2.12)**
bh1_si_cont (t-1)		**-0.0553**		**-0.0127**		**0.0005**		**0.2385*** **
		(-0.81)		**(-0.64)**		**(0.63)**		**(2.60)**
bh1_insti_cont (t-1)		**-0.3212** **		**-0.1140** **		**0.0074** **		**0.0195**
		(-1.78)		**(-2.28)**		**(1.90)**		**(0.14)**
Constant	0.9251***	0.9430***	1.0155***	1.0113***	0.0038***	0.0039***	1.6086***	1.7804***
	(12.36)	(12.05)	(51.26)	(51.52)	(5.08)	(5.45)	(12.00)	(11.80)
Control variables	Yes	Yes	Yes	Yes	Yes	Yes	Yes	Yes
Industry dummies	Yes	Yes	Yes	Yes	Yes	Yes	Yes	Yes
Year dummies	Yes	Yes	Yes	Yes	Yes	Yes	Yes	Yes
Adjusted R^2	0.1967	0.2049	0.5049	0.5076	0.2876	0.2992	0.2009	0.2133
Number of obs.	2,608	2,150	2,555	2,555	2,008	2,008	2,532	2,445
Firms	471	449	467	467	413	413	465	451

Table 62: Regression results based on lagged ownership variables

Table 63

This table presents the pooled-OLS regression results w.r.t. principal-principal agency costs as proxied by *[div_payout_a]* based on specification 2.3.1 and 2.3.3. The regressions include industry and year fixed effects; standard errors are clustered by firm. T-statistics are reported in parentheses. In case of a directional hypothesis, one-sided p-Values are calculated. *, **, and *** indicates statistical significance at the 10%, 5%, and 1% level, respectively.

	(2.3.1)	(2.3.3)
bh1_cont	**0.0042**	
	(0.89)	
bh1_pe_cont		**0.0260** **
		(1.91)
bh1_fam_cont		**-0.0027**
		(-0.48)
bh1_si_cont		**-0.0048**
		(-0.85)
bh1_insti_cont		**0.0584** **
		(1.66)
stdev_ni		0.0000
		(1.30)
beta		-0.0065**
		(-2.23)
growth	-0.0032**	-0.0029*
	(-1.70)	(-1.54)
prof	0.0503***	0.0536***
	(5.46)	(5.41)
div_prevy	0.0334***	0.0339***
	(13.34)	(13.20)

Table 63 cont'd

	(2.3.1)	(2.3.3)
age	0.0002***	0.0002***
	(2.70)	(2.76)
ln_assets	-0.0078***	-0.0084***
	(-6.88)	(-5.61)
pfd	0.0046	0.0042
	(0.83)	(0.86)
liq	-0.0083**	-0.0088**
	(-2.15)	(-2.29)
insd_own	0.0080	0.0084
	(0.81)	(0.83)
debt	-0.0203***	-0.0219***
	(-2.82)	(-3.17)
codet_third	0.0088***	0.0101***
	(2.56)	(3.06)
codet_par	0.0008	0.0026
	(0.17)	(0.56)
bank	0.0010	-0.0006
	(0.36)	(-0.22)
insolv	0.0058	0.0058
	(1.06)	(1.13)
takeover	0.0031	0.0047
	(0.54)	(0.86)
segm_chng	-0.0060	-0.0042
	(-0.97)	(-0.72)
govt	0.0058*	0.0055*
	(1.52)	(1.48)
Constant	0.0397***	0.0469***
	(6.68)	(6.65)
Industry dummies	Yes	Yes
Year dummies	Yes	Yes
Adjusted R²	0.3289	0.3463
Number of obs.	2,209	2,207
Firms	423	423

Table 63: Regression results on the alternative definition of the dividend payout ratio

Table 64

This table presents the pooled-OLS regression results of specification 2.4.1 and 2.4.3 using the three-year average Tobin's q *[tobinq_3y_avg]*. The regressions include industry and year fixed effects (year fixed effects exclude the year 2012); standard errors are clustered by firm. T-statistics are reported in parentheses. In case of a directional hypothesis, one-sided p-Values are calculated. *, **, and *** indicates statistical significance at the 10%, 5%, and 1% level, respectively.

	(2.4.1)	(2.4.3)
bh1_cont	**0.2748*** **	
	(3.35)	
bh1_pe_cont		**0.6406*** **
		(2.72)
bh1_fam_cont		**0.1630* **
		(1.31)
bh1_si_cont		**0.2613*** **
		(2.81)
bh1_insti_cont		**0.0116**
		(0.09)
stdev_ni		0.0002
		(0.58)

Table 64 cont'd

	(2.4.1)	(2.4.3)
beta		0.0207
		(0.37)
growth	0.1788***	0.1828***
	(4.25)	(4.35)
ppe_assets	-0.3094**	-0.2844*
	(-1.79)	(-1.63)
capex	1.2917**	1.1438*
	(1.72)	(1.49)
cash_assets	1.1604***	1.1839***
	(5.73)	(5.59)
age	0.0008	0.0012
	(1.00)	(1.27)
ln_assets	-0.1202***	-0.1273***
	(-4.70)	(-3.93)
pfd	0.0361	0.0273
	(0.43)	(0.32)
liq	0.4121***	0.4042***
	(5.86)	(5.55)
insd_own	-0.1230	0.0262
	(-0.94)	(0.19)
debt	-0.1214	-0.1400
	(-0.76)	(-0.86)
codet_third	0.0228	0.0354
	(0.37)	(0.54)
codet_par	0.1581**	0.1752**
	(1.85)	(1.88)
bank	-0.0555*	-0.0706**
	(-1.39)	(-1.73)
insolv	-0.0893	-0.1132
	(-0.85)	(-1.12)
takeover	0.2241**	0.2077*
	(2.09)	(1.94)
segm_chng	-0.3015***	-0.2956***
	(-2.91)	(-2.90)
govt	-0.0896**	-0.0735*
	(-1.88)	(-1.44)
Constant	1.7688***	1.7889***
	(15.40)	(12.78)
Industry dummies	Yes	Yes
Year dummies	Yes	Yes
Adjusted R^2	0.2359	0.2421
Number of obs.	2,383	2,302
Firms	454	440

Table 64: Regression results on the three-year average tobinq

Table 65
This table presents the pooled-OLS regression results of specification 2.4.1 and 2.4.3 estimated based on a sample of financially distressed and non-distressed firms, respectively. Financially distressed firms constitute those with negative earnings per share, non-distressed firms those with positive earnings per share. The regressions include industry and year fixed effects; standard errors are clustered by firm. T-statistics are reported in parentheses. In case of a directional hypothesis, one-sided p-Values are calculated. *, **, and *** indicates statistical significance at the 10%, 5%, and 1% level, respectively.

	Financially distressed	**Non-financially distressed**	**Financially distressed**	**Non-financially distressed**
bh1_cont	**0.2782****	**0.3503*****		
	(1.94)	**(4.31)**		
bh1_pe_cont			**0.6814*****	**0.7587*****
			(3.02)	**(2.89)**
bh1_fam_cont			**0.1544**	**0.3236*****
			(0.73)	**(2.38)**
bh1_si_cont			**0.2396***	**0.2568*****
			(1.52)	**(2.92)**
bh1_insti_cont			**0.4456****	**-0.0462**
			(1.71)	**(-0.32)**
stdev_ni			0.0023***	-0.0004
			(3.76)	(-1.36)
beta			-0.0084	-0.0553
			(-0.10)	(-0.96)
growth	0.2406***	0.2027***	0.2409***	0.1943***
	(3.12)	(3.63)	(3.38)	(3.41)
ppe_assets	-0.0219	-0.4640***	-0.0345	-0.4396**
	(-0.10)	(-2.35)	(-0.16)	(-2.25)
capex	0.6585	2.6532***	0.4536	2.5860***
	(0.63)	(3.29)	(0.46)	(3.19)
cash_assets	1.2239***	1.0182***	1.2268***	1.0826***
	(3.88)	(4.74)	(4.01)	(4.92)
age	-0.0004	0.0014	-0.0005	0.0018*
	(-0.32)	(1.18)	(-0.44)	(1.50)
ln_assets	-0.2121***	-0.0773***	-0.2778***	-0.0580**
	(-4.66)	(-3.05)	(-5.19)	(-1.91)
pfd	0.1978	0.1525*	0.2062	0.1143
	(0.69)	(1.37)	(0.68)	(1.08)
liq	0.4547***	0.4266***	0.3607***	0.4160***
	(3.93)	(6.08)	(3.24)	(5.81)
insd_own	-0.3964	-0.1230	-0.2048	0.0930
	(-1.38)	(-0.89)	(-0.66)	(0.67)
debt	0.4182*	-0.5035***	0.4084*	-0.5559***
	(1.95)	(-2.87)	(1.96)	(-3.02)
codet_third	0.0820	0.0160	0.1432**	0.0039
	(0.99)	(0.24)	(1.70)	(0.06)
codet_par	0.2208*	0.0793	0.2352*	0.0652
	(1.42)	(0.82)	(1.51)	(0.64)
bank	-0.0524	0.0110	-0.0590	0.0081
	(-0.69)	(0.22)	(-0.78)	(0.16)
insolv	-0.0382	-0.0075	-0.0695	-0.0275
	(-0.36)	(-0.09)	(-0.64)	(-0.32)
takeover	0.5683**	0.2299*	0.5892***	0.2174*
	(2.33)	(1.91)	(2.49)	(1.82)
segm_chng	-0.2814***	-0.2506**	-0.2766***	-0.2473**
	(-2.54)	(-2.04)	(-2.45)	(-1.95)
govt	0.2534*	0.0277	0.2684*	0.0579
	(1.38)	(0.26)	(1.56)	(0.55)

Table 65 cont'd

	Financially distressed	**Non-financially distressed**	**Financially distressed**	**Non-financially distressed**
Constant	1.7982***	1.5883***	2.0274***	1.5572***
	(8.09)	(12.96)	(8.85)	(10.46)
Industry dummies	Yes	Yes	Yes	Yes
Year dummies	Yes	Yes	Yes	Yes
Adjusted R^2	0.2691	0.2126	0.2904	0.2207
Number of obs.	721	2,257	720	2,156
Firms	290	444	290	429

Table 65: Regression results based on a sample split into financially and non-financially distressed firms

Appendix 19 – Endogeneity

Table 66
This table presents the pooled-OLS reverse causality regression results on *[bh1_cont]*. The regression includes industry and year fixed effects; standard errors are clustered by firm. T-statistics are reported in parentheses. *, **, and *** indicates statistical significance at the 10%, 5%, and 1% level, respectively.

tobinq	**0.0456*** **
	(3.91)
stdev_ni	-0.0004**
	(-2.50)
beta	-0.1193***
	(-5.70)
growth	-0.0317**
	(-2.15)
ppe_assets	0.0615
	(0.70)
capex	0.1074
	(0.33)
cash_assets	-0.0103
	(-0.16)
age	0.0008*
	(1.73)
ln_assets	0.0272**
	(2.52)
pfd	0.0932**
	(2.35)
liq	-0.2101***
	(-7.91)
insd_own	-0.0270
	(-0.33)
debt	-0.0780
	(-1.30)
codet_third	0.0727***
	(2.77)
codet_par	0.0703**
	(2.03)
bank	-0.0831***
	(-5.02)
insolv	0.0251
	(0.71)
takeover	0.0698
	(1.59)
segm_chng	-0.0084
	(-0.23)
govt	-0.0039
	(-0.14)
Constant	0.2021***
	(3.50)
Industry dummies	Yes
Year dummies	Yes
Adjusted R^2	0.2299
Number of obs.	2,876
Firms	469

Table 66: Results of the reverse causality regression

Table 67
This table presents the regression results of the Durbin-Wu-Hausman test. *[bh1_cont]* constitutes the dependent variable in stage 1, *[tobinq]* the dependent variable in stage 2. Both regressions include industry and year fixed effects; standard errors are clustered by firm. T-statistics are reported in parentheses. *, **, and *** indicates statistical significance at the 10%, 5%, and 1% level, respectively.

	Stage 1	**Stage 2**
resid		**-0.1148**
		(-0.31)
bh1_cont		0.4422
		(1.22)
stdev_ni	-0.0004**	
	(-2.52)	
beta	-0.1232***	
	(-5.85)	
growth	-0.0233	0.2087***
	(-1.58)	(4.63)
ppe_assets	0.0489	-0.3817**
	(0.55)	(-2.26)
capex	0.2003	2.1055***
	(0.61)	(2.84)
cash_assets	0.0379	1.1298***
	(0.59)	(5.71)
age	0.0009*	0.0014
	(1.85)	(1.11)
ln_assets	0.0227**	-0.1202***
	(2.15)	(-4.79)
pfd	0.1012**	0.1730
	(2.53)	(1.56)
liq	-0.1953***	0.4588***
	(-7.39)	(4.24)
insd_own	-0.0181	-0.1722
	(-0.21)	(-1.32)
debt	-0.0924	-0.1377
	(-1.52)	(-0.87)
codet_third	0.0753***	0.0089
	(2.81)	(0.13)
codet_par	0.0779**	0.1129
	(2.24)	(1.13)
bank	-0.0851***	-0.0041
	(-5.08)	(-0.07)
insolv	0.0147	-0.0226
	(0.42)	(-0.27)
takeover	0.0830*	0.3340**
	(1.92)	(2.36)
segm_chng	-0.0235	-0.2967***
	(-0.63)	(-3.00)
govt	-0.0029	0.0533
	(-0.10)	(0.59)
Constant	0.2846***	1.6433***
	(5.21)	(10.08)
Industry dummies	Yes	Yes
Year dummies	Yes	Yes
Adjusted R^2	0.2196	0.2091
Number of obs.	2,890	2,876
Firms	471	469

Table 67: Results of the Durbin-Wu-Hausman test

Table 68

This table presents the 2SLS regression results. $\widehat{bh1\_cont}$ is instrumented with *[stdev_ni]* and *[beta]*.The regressions include industry and year fixed effects; standard errors are clustered by firm. T-statistics are reported in parentheses. In case of a directional hypothesis, one-sided p-Values are calculated. To facilitate the comparison, column two depicts the original pooled-OLS regression model. *, **, and *** indicates statistical significance at the 10%, 5%, and 1% level, respectively.

	Regression model stage 2 (pooled-OLS)	**Instrumental variable regression (2SLS)**
bh1_cont/ $\widehat{bh1\_cont}$	**0.3384*** **	**0.4447** **
	(4.31)	**(1.80)**
growth	0.2086***	0.2087***
	(4.74)	(4.72)
ppe_assets	-0.3622**	-0.3814***
	(-2.16)	(-3.83)
capex	2.1777***	2.1042***
	(3.03)	(4.54)
cash_assets	1.1018***	1.1293***
	(5.64)	(9.82)
age	0.0013	0.0014**
	(1.20)	(2.27)
ln_assets	-0.1140***	-0.1202***
	(-4.56)	(-9.26)
pfd	0.1869**	0.1725***
	(1.81)	(3.08)
liq	0.4395***	0.4590***
	(6.62)	(7.00)
insd_own	-0.1645	-0.1700**
	(-1.28)	(-1.96)
debt	-0.1358	-0.1382
	(-0.89)	(-1.44)
codet_third	0.0157	0.0088
	(0.27)	(0.21)
codet_par	0.1070	0.1127**
	(1.24)	(1.94)
bank	-0.0074	-0.0039
	(-0.17)	(-0.10)
insolv	-0.0171	-0.0237
	(-0.20)	(-0.39)
takeover	0.3512***	0.3333***
	(2.57)	(4.21)
segm_chng	-0.2952***	-0.2968***
	(-3.01)	(-5.60)
govt	0.0577	0.0532
	(0.65)	(1.06)
Constant	1.6501***	1.6428***
	(13.73)	(15.89)
Test statistic (p-Value) of the Sargan test		1.2477 (0.2640)
Industry dummies	Yes	Yes
Year dummies	Yes	Yes
Adjusted R^2	0.2073	0.2079
Number of obs.	2,978	2,876
Firms	484	469

Table 68: Results of the 2SLS instrumental variable regression

References

Achleitner, Ann-Kristin et al. (2009): Economic consequences of private equity investments on the German stock market. Working paper. URL: http://papers.ssrn.com /sol3/papers.cfm?abstract_id=1086598, accessed on October 14, 2014.

Achleitner, Ann-Kristin/Betzer, André/Gider, Jasmin (2010): Do Corporate Governance Motives Drive Hedge Fund and Private Equity Fund Activities? In: European Financial Management, 16 (5): 805–828.

Admati, Anat R./Pfleiderer, Paul (2009): The "Wall Street Walk" and Shareholder Activism: Exit as a Form of Voice. In: The Review of Financial Studies, 22 (7): 2645–2685.

Admati, Anat R./Pfleiderer, Paul/Zechner, Josef (1994): Large Shareholder Activism, Risk Sharing, and Financial Market Equilibrium. In: Journal of Political Economy, 102 (6): 1097–1130.

Agarwal, Rajshree/Elston, Julie A. (2001): Bank–firm relationships, financing and firm performance in Germany. In: Economics Letters, 72 (2): 225–232.

Agrawal, Anup/Knoeber, Charles R. (1996): Firm performance and mechanisms to control agency problems between managers and shareholders. In: Journal of Financial and Quantitative Analysis, 31 (3): 377–397.

Agrawal, Anup/Mandelker, Gershon N. (1990): Large shareholders and the monitoring of managers: The case of antitakeover charter amendments. In: Journal of Financial and Quantitative Analysis, 25 (2): 143–161.

Aiken, Leona S./West, Stephen G. (1991): Multiple Regression: Testing and Interpreting Interactions. Newbury Park: Sage Publications, Inc.

Akerlof, George A. (1970): The Market for "Lemons": Quality Uncertainty and the Market Mechanism. In: The Quarterly Journal of Economics, 84 (3): 488–500.

Alchian, Armen A./Demsetz, Harold (1972): Production, Information Costs, and Economic Organization. In: The American Economic Review, 62 (5): 777–795.

Alchian, Armen A./Demsetz, Harold (1973): The Property Right Paradigm. In: The Journal of Economic History, 33 (1): 16–27.

Allen, Franklin/Bernardo, Antonio E./Welch, Ivo (2000): A Theory of Dividends Based on Tax Clienteles. In: The Journal of Finance, 55 (6): 2499–2536.

Allen, Franklin/Gale, Douglas (1995): A welfare comparison of intermediaries and financial markets in Germany and the US. In: European Economic Review, 39 (2): 179–209.

Allen, Jeffrey W./Phillips, Gordon M. (2000): Corporate equity ownership, strategic alliances, and product market relationships. In: Journal of Finance, 55 (6): 2791–2815.

Alli, Kasim L./Khan, A. Qayyum/Ramirez, Gabriel G. (1993): Determinants of Corporate Dividend Policy: A Factorial Analysis. In: The Financial Review, 28 (4): 523–547.

Al-Malkawi, Husam-Aldin N./Rafferty, Michael/Pillai, Rekha (2010): Dividend Policy : A Review of Theories and Empirical Evidence. In: International Bulletin of Business Administration, 9 (9): 171–200.

Almazan, Andres/Hartzell, Jay C./Starks, Laura T. (2005): Active institutional shareholders and costs of monitoring: Evidence from executive compensation. In: Financial Management, 34 (4): 5–34.

Alonso-Bonis, Susana/de Andrés-Alonso, Pablo (2007): Ownership Structure and Performance in Large Spanish Companies: Empirical Evidence in the Context of an Endogenous Relation. In: Corporate Ownership & Control, 4 (4): 206–216.

Altenhain, Karsten (2002): Die Neuregelung der Marktpreismanipulation durch das Vierte Finanzmarktförderungsgesetz. In: Betriebs-Berater, 57 (37): 1874–1879.

Amihud, Yakov/Lev, Baruch (1981): Risk Reduction as a Managerial Motive for Conglomerate Mergers. In: The Bell Journal of Economics, 12 (2): 605–617.

Amihud, Yakov/Murgia, Maurizio (1997): Dividends, Taxes, and Signaling: Evidence from Germany. In: The Journal of Finance, 52 (1): 397–408.

Ampenberger, Markus (2010): Unternehmenspolitik in börsennotierten Familienunternehmen. Wiesbaden: Gabler Verlag.

Anderson, Ronald C./Mansi, Sattar A./Reeb, David M. (2003): Founding family ownership and the agency cost of debt. In: Journal of Financial Economics, 68 (2): 263–285.

Anderson, Ronald C./Reeb, David M. (2003): Founding-Family ownership and firm performance: evidence from the S&P 500. In: The Journal of Finance, 58 (3): 1301–1328.

Andreas, Jörn M./Rapp, Marc S./Wolff, Michael (2010): Determinants of director compensation in two-tier systems: evidence from German panel data. In: Review of Managerial Science, 6 (1): 33–79.

Andres, Christian (2008): Large shareholders and firm performance - An empirical examination of founding-family ownership. In: Journal of Corporate Finance, 14 (4): 431–445.

Andres, Christian et al. (2009): Dividend policy of German firms - A panel data analysis of partial adjustment models. In: Journal of Empirical Finance, 16 (2): 175–187.

Ang, James S./Cole, Rebel A./Lin, James W. (2000): Agency Costs and Ownership Structure. In: The Journal of Finance, 55 (1): 81–106.

Armour, John/Cheffins, Brian (2009): The Rise and Fall (?) of Shareholder Activism by Hedge Funds. ECGI - Law Working Paper No. 136/2009. URL: http://papers.ssrn.com/sol3/papers.cfm?abstract_id=1489336, accessed on October 15, 2014.

Armstrong, Christopher S./Gow, Ian D./Larcker, David F. (2013): The Efficacy of Shareholder Voting: Evidence from Equity Compensation Plans. In: Journal of Accounting Research, 51 (5): 909–950.

Arnold, Michael/Wenninger, Thomas G. (2010): Maßnahmen zur Abwehr feindlicher Übernahmeangebote. In: Corporate Finance law, 1 (1): 79–89.

Arrow, Kenneth J. (1969): The Organization of Economic Activity: Issues Pertinent to the Choice of Market versus Non-market Allocation. Published by the Joint Economic Committee of Congress in 1969. URL: http://msuweb.montclair.edu/~lebelp/arrownonmktactivity1969.pdf, accessed on October 14, 2014.

Arrow, Kenneth J. (1974): The Limits of Organization. New York: W. W. Norton & Company.

Arrow, Kenneth J. (1985): Informational Structure of the Firm. In: The American Economic Review, 75 (2): 303–307.

Arrow, Kenneth J. (1991): The Economics of Agency. In: Pratt, John W./Zeckhauser, Richard J. (Editors): Principals and Agents: The Structure of Business. Boston: Harvard Business School Press: 37–51.

Assmann, Hans-Dieter/Lange, Barbara/Sethe, Rolf (2005): The Law of Business Associations. In: Reimann, Mathias/Zekoll, Joachim (Editors): Introduction to German Law, 2nd ed. The Hague: Kluwer Law International: 143–178.

Atanasov, Vladimir (2005): How much value can blockholders tunnel? Evidence from the Bulgarian mass privatization auctions. In: Journal of Financial Economics, 76 (1): 191–234.

Attig, Najah/El Ghoul, Sadok/Guedhami, Omrane (2009): Do Multiple Large Shareholders Play a Corporate Governance Role? Evidence from East Asia. In: The Journal of Financial Research, 32 (4): 395–422.

Attig, Najah/Guedhami, Omrane/Mishra, Dev (2008): Multiple Large Shareholders, Control Contests, and Implied Cost of Equity. In: Journal of Corporate Finance, 14 (5): 721–737.

Back, Kerry/Li, Tao/Ljungqvist, Alexander (2013): Liquidity and Governance. ECGI - Finance Working Paper No. 388. URL: http://papers.ssrn.com/sol3/papers.cfm?abstract_id=2350362, accessed on October 14, 2014.

Bainbridge, Stephen M. (2005): Shareholder Activism and Institutional Investors. UCLA School of Law, Law & Economics Research Paper No. 05-20. URL: http://papers.ssrn.com/sol3/papers.cfm?abstract_id=796227, accessed on October 14, 2014.

Bainbridge, Stephen M. (2012): Corporate Governance after the Financial Crisis. New York: Oxford University Press.

Bak, Jacek (2002): Aktienrecht zwischen Markt und Staat - Eine ökonomische Kritik der Satzungsstrenge. Wiesbaden: Deutscher Universitäts-Verlag.

Ballwieser, Wolfgang/Dobler, Michael (2003): Bilanzdelikte: Konsequenzen, Ursachen und Massnahmen zu ihrer Vermeidung. In: Die Unternehmung, 57 (6): 449–469.

Baltagi, Badi H. (2008): Econometric Analysis of Panel Data, 4th ed. Sussex: John Wiley & Sons, Ltd.

Barber, Brad M. (2006): Monitoring the Monitor: Evaluating CalPERS' Shareholder Activism. Working Paper. URL: http://papers.ssrn.com/sol3/papers.cfm?abstract_id=890321, accessed on October 14, 2014.

Barclay, Michael J./Holderness, Clifford G. (1989): Private Benefits from Control of Public Corporations. In: Journal of Financial Economics, 25 (2): 371–395.

Barclay, Michael J./Holderness, Clifford G./Sheehan, Dennis P. (2009): Dividends and Corporate Shareholders. In: The Review of Financial Studies, 22 (6): 2423–2455.

Barnea, Amir/Haugen, Robert A./Senbet, Lemma W. (1981): Agency Imperfections, Problems and Capital Structure: A Review. In: Financial Management, 10 (3): 7–22.

Barnea, Amir/Haugen, Robert A./Senbet, Lemma W. (1985): Agency Problems and Financial Contracting. New Jersey: Prentice Hall.

Barnea, Amir/Rubin, Amir (2010): Corporate Social Responsibility as a Conflict Between Shareholders. In: Journal of Business Ethics, 97 (1): 71–86.

Barney, Jay (1991): Firm Resources and Sustained Competitive Advantage. In: Journal of Management, 17 (1): 99–120.

Baron, Reuben M./Kenny, David A. (1986): The moderator-mediator variable distinction in social psychological research: conceptual, strategic, and statistical considerations. In: Journal of Personality and Social Psychology, 51 (6): 1173–1182.

Barontini, Roberto/Caprio, Lorenzo (2006): The Effect of Family Control on Firm Value and Performance: Evidence from Continental Europe. In: European Financial Management, 12 (5): 689–723.

Barthelmess, Philipp (2010): Einfluss einer Private Equity Beteiligung auf den Erfolg von Unternehmen. Online-Publikation. URL: http://rosdok.uni-rostock.de/file/rosdok_disshab_0000000397/rosdok_derivate_0000004207/Dissertation_Barthelmess_2010.pdf, accessed on October 14, 2014.

Baumol, William J. (1967): Business Behavior, Value and Growth. New York: Harcourt, Brace & World Inc.

Baums, Theodor (2001): Bericht der Regierungskommission Corporate Governance. Köln: Dr. Otto Schmidt.

Baums, Theodor (2002): Company Law Reform in Germany. Working Paper. URL: http://papers.ssrn.com/sol3/papers.cfm?abstract_id=329962, accessed on October 14, 2014.

Baums, Theodor/Scott, Kenneth E. (2005): Taking Shareholder Protection Seriously? Corporate Governance in the United States and Germany. In: The American Journal of Comparative Law, 53 (1): 31–75.

Bebchuk, Lucian A. (2013): The Myth that Insulating Boards Serves Long-Term Value. In: Columbia Law Review, 113 (6): 1637–1694.

Bebchuk, Lucian A./Roe, Mark J. (1999): A Theory of Path Dependence in Corporate Ownership and Governance. In: Stanford Law Review, 52 (1): 127–170.

Bebchuk, Lucian A./Kahan, Marcel (1990): A Framework for Analyzing Legal Policy Towards Proxy Contests. In: California Law Review, 78 (5): 1071–1135.

Becht, Marco et al. (2008): Returns to Shareholder Activism: Evidence from a Clinical Study of the Hermes UK Focus Fund. In: Review of Financial Studies, 22 (8): 3093–3129.

Becht, Marco/Boehmer, Ekkehart (2003): Voting Control in German Corporations. In: International Review of Law and Economics, 23 (1): 1–29.

Becht, Marco/Bolton, Patrick/Röell, Alisa (2005): Corporate Governance and Control. ECGI - Finance Working Paper No. 02/2002, updated August 2005. URL: http://papers.ssrn.com/sol3/papers.cfm?abstract_id=343461, accessed on October 14, 2014.

Becht, Marco/Röell, Ailsa (1999): Blockholdings in Europe: An international comparison. In: European Economic Review, 43 (4-6): 1049–1056.

Beiner, Stefan et al. (2006): An Integrated Framework of Corporate Governance and Firm Valuation. In: European Financial Management, 12 (2): 249–283.

Benartzi, Shlomo/Michaely, Roni/Thaler, Richard (1997): Do Changes in Dividends Signal the Future or the Past? In: The Journal of Finance, 52 (3): 1007–1034.

Bennedsen, Morten/Wolfenzon, Daniel (2000): The balance of power in closely held corporations. In: Journal of Financial Economics, 58 (1-2): 113–139.

Berglöf, Erik (1994): A Control Theory of Venture Capital Finance. In: Journal of Law, Economics & Organization, 10 (2): 247–267.

Bergstrom, Theodore C. (1995): On the Evolution of Altruistic Ethical Rules for Siblings. In: The American Economic Review, 85 (1): 58–81.

Berle, Adolf A. (1931): Corporate Powers as Powers in Trust. In: Harvard Law Review, 44 (7): 1049–1074.

Berle, Adolf A./Means, Gardiner C. (2010): The Modern Corporation & Private Property, 11th ed. New Brunswick: Transaction Publishers.

Bernhardt, Wolfgang (2002): Der Deutsche Corporate Governance Kodex: Zuwahl (comply) oder Abwahl (explain)? In: Der Betrieb, 55 (36): 1841–1846.

Bernhardt, Wolfgang (2007): Unternehmensmitbestimmung nach Biedenkopf. In: Betriebs-Berater, 62 (7): 381–383.

Bernhardt, Wolfgang (2008): Sechs Jahre Deutscher Corporate Governance Kodex - Eine Erfolgsgeschichte? In: Betriebs-Berater, 63 (32): 1686–1692.

Bernheim, Bert D./Wanzt, Adam (1995): A Tax-Based Test of the Dividend Signaling Hypothesis. In: The American Economic Review, 85 (3): 532–551.

Bernheim, Bert D./Whinston, Michael D. (1986): Common Agency. In: Econometrica, 54 (4): 923–942.

Bertrand, Marianne/Mullainathan, Sendhil (2001): Are CEOS Rewarded for Luck? The Ones Without Principals Are. In: The Quarterly Journal of Economics, 116 (3): 901–932.

Bertrand, Marianne/Mullainathan, Sendhil (2003): Enjoying the Quiet Life? Corporate Governance and Managerial Preferences. In: Journal of Political Economy, 111 (5): 1043–1075.

Bessler, Wolfgang/Drobetz, Wolfgang/Holler, Julian (2008): Capital Markets and Corporate Control: Empirical Evidence from Hedge Fund Activism in Germany. Working Paper. URL: http://www.fma.org/Turin/Papers/FMATurinCorporateGovernanceHedgeFunds2009.pdf, accessed on October 14, 2014.

Bester, Helmut/Hellwig, Martin (1987): Moral Hazard and Equilibrium Credit Rationing: An Overview of the Issues. In: Bamberg, Günter/Spremann, Klaus (Editors): Agency Theory, Information, and Incentives Berlin: Springer: 135–166.

Bevilacqua, Jonathan (2006): Convergence and Divergence: Blurring the Lines Between Hedge Funds and Private Equity Funds. In: Buffalo Law Review, 54: 101–127.

Bhagat, Sanjai/Black, Bernard/Blair, Margaret (2004): Relational Investing and Firm Performance. In: The Journal of Financial Research, 27 (1): 1–30.

Bhagat, Sanjai/Jefferis Jr., Richard H. (2002): The Econometrics of Corporate Governance Studies. Cambridge: The MIT Press.

Bhattacharya, Sudipto (1979): Imperfect Information, Dividend Policy, and "The Bird in the Hand" Fallacy. In: The Bell Journal of Economics, 10 (1): 259–270.

Bhide, Amar (1993): The hidden costs of stock market liquidity. In: Journal of Financial Economics, 34 (1): 31–51.

Bhojraj, Sanjeev/Sengupta, Partha (2003): Effect of Corporate Governance on Bond Ratings and Yields: The Role of Institutional Investors and Outside Directors. In: Journal of Business, 76 (3): 455–475.

Black, Bernard S. (1990): Shareholder Passivity Reexamined. In: Michigan Law Review, 89 (3): 520–608.

Black, Bernard S. (1992a): Agents Watching Agents: The Promise of Institutional Investor Voice. In: UCLA Law Review, 39 (4): 811–893.

Black, Bernard S. (1992b): Institutional Investors and Corporate Governance: The Case for Institutional Voice. In: Journal of Applied Corporate Finance, 5 (3): 19–32.

Black, Bernard S. (1998): Shareholder Activism and Corporate Governance in the United States. In: Newman, Peter (Editor): The New Palgrave Dictionary of Economics and the Law. London: Palgrave Macmillan: 1–20.

Black, Stanley W./Moersch, Mathias (1998): Competition and Convergence in Financial Markets. Amsterdam: Elsevier Science B.V.

Blickle, Marina (1987): Information Systems and the Design of Optimal Contracts. In: Bamberg, Günter/Spremann, Klaus (Editors): Agency Theory, Information, and Incentives. Berlin: Springer: 93–103.

Bloch, Francis/Hege, Ulrich (2001): Multiple Shareholders and Control Contests. Working Paper. URL: http://papers.ssrn.com/sol3/papers.cfm?abstract_id=2273211, accessed on October 14, 2014.

Böcking, Hans-Joachim/Orth, Christian (1998a): Kann das "Gesetz zur Kontrolle und Transparenz im Unternehmensbereich (KonTraG)" einen Beitrag zur Verringerung der Erwartungslücke leisten? - Eine Würdigung auf Basis von Rechnungslegung und Kapitalmarkt. In: Die Wirtschaftsprüfung, 51 (8): 351–364.

Böcking, Hans-Joachim/Orth, Christian (1998b): Neue Vorschriften zur Rechnungslegung und Prüfung durch das KonTraG und das KapAEG. In: Der Betrieb, 51 (25): 1241–1246.

Boecker, Corinna (2010): Accounting Fraud aufdecken und vorbeugen. Berlin: Erich Schmidt.

Boehmer, Ekkehart (1998): Who controls Germany? An exploratory analysis. Working Paper. URL: http://www.jura.uni-frankfurt.de/43029818/paper71.pdf, accessed on October 14, 2014.

Boehmer, Ekkehart (2000): Business Groups, Bank Control, and Large Shareholders: An Analysis of German Takeovers. In: Journal of Financial Intermediation, 9 (2): 117–148.

Bøhren, Øyvind/Josefsen, Morten G./Steen, Pål E. (2012): Stakeholder conflicts and dividend policy. In: Journal of Banking & Finance, 36 (10): 1–33.

Bøhren, Øyvind/Norli, Øyvind (1997): Determinants of Intercorporate Shareholdings. In: European Finance Review, 1 (2): 265–287.

Bøhren, Øyvind/Ødegaard, Bernt A. (2006): Governance and Performance Revisited. In: Ali, Paul U./Gregoriou, Greg N. (Editors): International Corporate Governance After Sarbanes-Oxley. Hoboken, New Jersey: John Wiley & Sons, Inc.: 27–64.

Bolton, Patrick/Von Thadden, Ernst-Ludwig (1998): Blocks, Liquidity, and Corporate Control. In: The Journal of Finance, 53 (1): 1–25.

Bonini, Stefano/Alkan, Senem/Salvi, Antonio (2012): The Effects of Venture Capitalists on the Governance of Firms. In: Corporate Governance: An International Review, 20 (1): 21–45.

Borokhovich, Kenneth A. et al. (2006): Variation in the Monitoring Incentives of Outside Stockholders. In: Journal of Law and Economics, 49 (2): 651–680.

Börsch-Supan, Axel/Köke, Jens (2002): An Applied Econometricians' View of Empirical Corporate Governance Studies. In: German Economic Review, 3 (3): 295–326.

Bott, Claudia (2002): Aktionärsstruktur, Kontrolle und Erfolg von Unternehmen. Wiesbaden: Deutscher Universitäts-Verlag.

Bottazzi, Laura/Rin, Marco da/Hellmann, Thomas (2008): Who are the active investors? Evidence from venture capital. In: Journal of Financial Economics, 89 (3): 488–512.

Boyson, Nicole M./Mooradian, Robert M. (2011): Corporate governance and hedge fund activism. In: Review of Derivatives Research, 14 (2): 169–204.

Braendle, Udo C. (2006): Shareholder Protection in the USA and Germany - "Law and Finance" Revisited. In: German Law Review, 7 (3): 257–278.

Brailsford, Timothy J./Oliver, Barry R./Pua, Sandra L. (2002): On the relation between ownership structure and capital structure. In: Accounting and Finance, 42 (1): 1–26.

Brav, Alon et al. (2005): Payout policy in the 21st century. In: Journal of Financial Economics, 77 (3): 483–527.

Brav, Alon et al. (2008): Hedge Fund Activism, Corporate Governance, and Firm Performance. In: The Journal of Finance, 63 (4): 1729–1775.

Brennan, Michael J./Cao, Huining H. (1997): International Portfolio Investment Flows. In: The Journal of Finance, 52 (5): 1851–1880.

Brennan, Michael J./Thakor, Anjan V. (1990): Shareholder Preferences and Dividend Policy. In: The Journal of Finance, 45 (4): 993–1018.

Bress, Stefan (2008): Corporate Governance in Deutschland. Köln: Josef Eul Verlag GmbH.

Breusch, Trevor S./Godfrey, Adrian R. (1980): Lagrange Multiplier Test and to Model Applications Specification in Econometrics. In: Review of Economic Studies, 47 (1): 239–253.

Brickley, James A./Lease, Ronald C./Smith Jr., Clifford W. (1988): Ownership Structure and Voting on Antitakeover Amendments. In: Journal of Financial Economics, 20 (1-2): 267–291.

Brooks, Chris (2008): Introductory Econometrics for Finance, 2nd ed. Cambridge: Cambridge University Press.

Burkart, Mike/Gromb, Denis/Panunzi, Fausto (1997): Large shareholders, monitoring, and the value of the firm. In: Quarterly Journal of Economics, 112 (3): 693–728.

Burkart, Mike/Panunzi, Fausto/Shleifer, Andrei (2003): Family Firms. In: The Journal of Finance, 58 (5): 2167–2201.

Bushee, Brian J. (2004): Identifying and Attracting the "Right" Investors - Evidence on the Behavior of Institutional Investors. In: Journal of Applied Corporate Finance, 16 (4). 28–35.

Busse v. Colbe, Walther (1999): Der befreiende Konzernabschluß nach international anerkannten Rechnungslegungsgrundsätzen. In: Dörner, Dietrich/Menhold, Dieter/Pfitzer, Norbert (Editors): Reform des Aktienrechts, der Rechnungslegung und Prüfung. Stuttgart: Schäffer-Poeschel: 401–420.

Cable, John (1985): Capital Market Information and Industrial Performance: The Role of West German Banks. In: The Economic Journal, 95 (377): 118–132.

Cameron, A. Colin/Trivedi, Pravin K. (2009): Microeconometrics Using Stata. College Station: Stata Press.

Chan, Ann L.-C./Hsu, Audrey W. (2013): Corporate Pyramids, Conservatism and Cost of Debt: Evidence from Taiwan. In: The International Journal of Accounting, 48 (3): 390–413.

Cheffins, Brian R. (2006): Dividends as a Substitute for Corporate Law: The Separation of Ownership and Control in the United Kingdom. In: Washington and Lee Law Review, 63 (4): 1273–1338.

Cheffins, Brian R. (2009): Did Corporate Governance "Fail" During the 2008 Stock Market Meltdown? The Case of the S&P 500. In: The Business Lawyer, 65 (1): 1–61.

Cheffins, Brian R./Armour, John (2008): The Eclipse of Private Equity. In: Delaware Journal of Corporate Law, 33 (1): 1–109.

Chen, Xia/Harford, Jarrad/Li, Kai (2007): Monitoring: Which institutions matter? In: Journal of Financial Economics, 86 (2): 279–305.

Chen, Xia/Qiang, Cheng/Dai, Zhonglan (2013): Family Ownership and CEO Turnovers. In: Contemporary Accounting Research, 30 (3): 1166–1190.

Chen, Xiaoying C./Yur-Austin, Jasmine (2007): Re-measuring agency costs: The effectiveness of blockholders. In: The Quarterly Review of Economics and Finance, 47 (5): 588–601.

Chhaochharia, Vidhi/Kumar, Alok/Niessen-Ruenzi, Alexandra (2012): Local investors and corporate governance. In: Journal of Accounting and Economics, 54 (1): 42–67.

Chirinko, Robert S./Elston, Julie A. (2006): Finance, control and profitability: the influence of German banks. In: Journal of Economic Behavior & Organization, 59 (1): 69–88.

Chow, Gregory C. (1960): Tests of Equality Between Sets of Coefficients in Two Linear Regressions. In: Econometrica, 28 (3): 591–605.

Chrisman, James J./Chua, Jess H./Litz, Reginald (2003): A unified systems perspective of family firm performance: an extension and integration. In: Journal of Business Venturing, 18 (4): 467–472.

Chung, Kee H./Pruitt, Stephen W. (1994): A Simple Approximation of Tobin's q. In: Financial Management, 23 (3): 70–74.

Claessens, Stijn et al. (2002): Disentangling the incentive and entrenchment effects of large shareholdings. In: The Journal of Finance, 57 (6): 2741–2771.

Claessens, Stijn/Djankov, Simeon/Lang, Larry H. (2000): The separation of ownership and control in East Asian Corporations. In: Journal of Financial Economics, 58 (1-2): 81–112.

Claessens, Stijn/Fan, Joseph P. (2002): Corporate Governance in Asia: A Survey. In: International Review of Finance, 3 (2): 71–103.

Claussen, Carsten P. (1998): Wie ändert das KonTraG das Aktiengesetz? In: Der Betrieb, 51 (4): 177–186.

Clifford, Christopher P. (2008): Value creation or destruction? Hedge funds as shareholder activists. In: Journal of Corporate Finance, 14 (4): 323–336.

Coase, Ronald H. (1937): The Nature of the Firm. In: Economica, 4 (16): 386–405.

Coase, Ronald H. (1960): The Problem of Social Cost. In: Journal of Law and Economics, 3: 1–44.

Coffee, John C. (1986): Shareholders versus Managers: The Strain in the Corporate Web. In: Michigan Law Review, 85 (1): 1–109.

Coffee, John C. (1991): Liquidity versus Control: The Institutional Investor as Corporate Monitor. In: Columbia Law Review, 91 (6): 1277–1368.

Coleman, James S. (1988): Social Capital in the Creation of Human Capital. In: American Journal of Sociology, 94: 95–120.

Coles, Jeffrey L./Lemmon, Michael L./Meschke, Felix J. (2012): Structural models and endogeneity in corporate finance: The link between managerial ownership and corporate performance. In: Journal of Financial Economics, 103 (1): 149–168.

Connelly, Brian L. et al. (2010): Ownership as a Form of Corporate Governance. In: Journal of Management Studies, 47 (8): 1561–1589.

Core, John E./Guay, Wayne R./Rusticus, Tjomme O. (2006): Does Weak Governance Cause Weak Stock Returns? An Examination of Firm Operating Performance and Investors' Expectations. In: The Journal of Finance, 61 (2): 655–687.

Cornett, Marcia M. et al. (2007): The impact of institutional ownership on corporate operating performance. In: Journal of Banking & Finance, 31 (6): 1771–1794.

Correia da Silva, Luis/Georgen, Marc/Renneboog, Luc (2004): Dividend Policy and Corporate Governance. Oxford: Oxford University Press.

Cotter, James F./Peck, Sarah W. (2001): The structure of debt and active equity investors: The case of the buyout specialist. In: Journal of Financial Economics, 59 (1): 101–147.

Crespi-Cladera, Rafel/Renneboog, Luc (2003): Corporate monitoring by shareholder coalitions in the UK. ECGI - Finance Working Paper No. 12/2003. URL: http://papers.ssrn.com/sol3/papers.cfm?abstract_id=379124, accessed on October 14, 2014.

Creswell, John W. (2009): Research Design, 3rd. ed. Thousand Oaks: Sage Publications, Inc.

Cromme, Gerhard (2005): Corporate Governance in Germany and the German Corporate Governance Code. In: Corporate Governance: An International Review, 13 (3): 362–367.

Cronqvist, H./Fahlenbrach, R. (2008): Large Shareholders and Corporate Policies. In: Review of Financial Studies, 22 (10): 3941–3976.

Cronqvist, Henrik/Nilsson, Mattias (2003): Agency Costs of Controlling Minority Shareholders. In: The Journal of Financial and Quantitative Analysis, 38 (4): 695–719.

Cumming, Douglas/Siegel, Donald S./Wright, Mike (2007): Private equity, leveraged buyouts and governance. In: Journal of Corporate Finance, 13 (4): 439–460.

Cziraki, Peter/Renneboog, Luc/Szilagyi, Peter G. (2010): Shareholder Activism through Proxy Proposals: The European Perspective. In: European Financial Management, 16 (5): 738–777.

Dahya, Jay/Dimitrov, Orlin/McConnell, John J. (2008): Dominant shareholders, corporate boards, and corporate value: A cross-country analysis. In: Journal of Financial Economics, 87 (1): 73–100.

Dai, Na (2007): Does investor identity matter? An empirical examination of investments by venture capital funds and hedge funds in PIPEs. In: Journal of Corporate Finance, 13 (4): 538–563.

Dalton, Dan R. et al. (2003): Meta-Analyses of Financial Performance and Equity: Fusion or Confusion? In: The Academy of Management Journal, 46 (1): 13–26.

Dalziel, Thomas/White, Robert E./Arthurs, Jonathan D. (2011): Principal Costs in Initial Public Offerings. In: Journal of Management Studies, 48 (6): 1346–1364.

David, Parthiban/Hitt, Michael A./Gimeno, Javier (2001): The influence of Activism by Institutional Investors on R&D. In: The Academy of Management Journal, 44 (1): 144–157.

Davis, James H./Schoorman, F. David/Donaldson, Lex (1997): Toward a Stewardship Theory of Management. In: The Academy of Management Review, 22 (1): 20–47.

De Alessi, Louis (1991): Development of the Property Rights Approach. In: Furubotn, Eirik G./Richter, Rudolf (Editors): The New Institutional Economics: A Collection of Articles from the Journal of Institutional and Theoretical Economics. Tübingen: Mohr Siebeck: 46–53.

De Cesari, Amedeo (2012): Expropriation of minority shareholders and payout policy. In: The British Accounting Review, 44 (4): 207–220.

DeAngelo, Harry/DeAngelo, Linda/Skinner, Douglas J. (1996): Reversal of fortune: Dividend signaling and the disappearance of sustained earnings growth. In: Journal of Financial Economics, 40 (3): 341–371.

Deilmann, Barabra/Otte, Sabine (2010): "Say on Pay" - erste Erfahrungen der Hauptversammlungspraxis. In: Der Betrieb, 63 (10): 545–547.

DeMott, Deborah A. (1998): Agency Principles and Large Block Shareholders. In: Cardozo Law Review, 19 (1): 321–340.

Demsetz, Harold (1967): Toward a Theory of Property Rights. In: The American Economic Review, 57 (2): 347–359.

Demsetz, Harold (1983): The Structure of Ownership and the Theory of the Firm. In: Journal of Law and Economics, 26 (2): 375–390.

Demsetz, Harold/Lehn, Kenneth (1985): The Structure of Corporate Ownership: Causes and Consequences. In: Journal of Political Economy, 93 (6): 1155–1177.

Demsetz, Harold/Villalonga, Belen (2001): Ownership Structure and Corporate Performance. In: Journal of Corporate Finance, 7 (3): 209–233.

Denis, David J./Denis, Diane K./Sarin, Atulya (1997): Agency Problems, Equity Ownership, and Corporate Diversification. In: The Journal of Finance, 52 (1): 135–160.

Denis, David J./Osobov, Igor (2008): Why do firms pay dividends? International evidence on the determinants of dividend policy. In: Journal of Financial Economics, 89 (1): 62–82.

Denis, David J./Sarin, Atulya (1999): Ownership and board structures in publicly traded corporations. In: Journal of Financial Economics, 52 (2): 187–223.

Dharwadkar, Ravi/George, Gerard/Brandes, Pamela (2000): Privatization in emerging economies: An agency theory perspective. In: The Academy of Management Review, 25 (3): 650–669.

Dhillon, Amrita/Rossetto, Silvia (2009): Corporate Control and Multiple Large Shareholders. Warwick Economic Research Paper Number 891. URL: http://www2.warwick.ac.uk/fac/soc/economics/research/workingpapers/2009/twerp_891.pdf, accessed on October 14, 2014.

Dietrich, Benjamin H. (2009): German Banking Structure, Pricing and Competition. Frankfurt: Peter Lang.

Dittmann, Ingolf/Maug, Ernst/Schneider, Christoph (2010): Bankers on the Boards of German Firms: What They Do, What They Are Worth, and Why They Are (Still) There. In: Review of Finance, 14 (1): 35–71.

Dixit, Avinash/Grossman, Gene M./Helpman, Elhanan (1997): Common Agency and Coordination: General Theory and Application to Government Policy Making. In: Journal of Political Economy, 105 (4): 752–769.

Döll, Matthias (2009): Say on Pay: Ein Blick ins Ausland und auf die neue Deutsche Regelung. Institute for Law and Finance Working Paper Series No. 107. URL: http://www.ilf-frankfurt.de/uploads/media/ILF_WP_107.pdf, accessed on October 14, 2014.

Donaldson, Gordon (1963): Financial Goals: Management vs. Stockholders. In: Harvard Business Review, 41 (3): 116–129.

Donaldson, L./Davis, James. H. (1991): Stewardship Theory or Agency Theory: CEO Governance and Shareholder Returns. In: Australian Journal of Management, 16 (1): 49–64.

Dooley, Michael P. (1992): Two Models of Corporate Governance. In: The Business Lawyer, 47 (2): 461–527.

Dougherty, Christopher (2007): Introduction to Econometrics, 3rd ed. Oxford: Oxford University Press.

Douma, Sytse/George, Rejie/Kabir, Rezaul (2006): Foreign and domestic ownership, business groups, and firm performance: evidence from a large emerging market. In: Strategic Management Journal, 27 (7): 637–657.

Drees, Friedel/Mietzner, Mark/Schiereck, Dirk (2013): Effects of corporate equity ownership on firm value. In: Review of Managerial Science, 7 (3): 277–308.

Drobetz, Wolfgang/Gugler, Klaus/Hirschvogl, Simone (2009): The Determinants of the German Corporate Governance Rating. In: Bjuggren, Per-Olof/Mueller, Dennis C. (Editors): The Modern Firm, Corporate Governance and Investment. Northampton: Edward Elgar: 361–379.

Drobetz, Wolfgang/Schillhofer, Andreas/Zimmermann, Heinz (2004): Corporate Governance and Expected Stock Returns: Evidence from Germany. In: European Financial Management, 10 (2): 267–293.

Drucker, David M. (2003): Testing for serial correlation in linear panel-data models. In: The Stata Journal, 3 (2): 168–177.

Drukarczyk, Jochen (1993): Theorie und Politik der Finanzierung, 2nd ed. München: Vahlen.

Du Plessis, Jean J. et al. (2012): German Corporate Governance in International and European Context, 2nd ed. Heidelberg: Springer.

Durbin, James (1954): Errors in Variables. In: Review of the International Statistical Institute, 22 (1): 23–32.

Dushnitsky, Gary/Lenox, Michael J. (2006): When does corporate venture capital investment create firm value? In: Journal of Business Venturing, 21 (6): 753–772.

Dybvig, Philip H./Warachka, Mitch (2010): Tobin 's Q Does Not Measure Performance: Theory, Empirics, and Alternative Measures. Working Paper. URL: http://papers.ssrn.com/sol3/papers.cfm?abstract_id=1562444, accessed on October 14, 2014.

Dyck, Alexander/Zingales, Luigi (2004a): Control Premiums and the Effectiveness of Corporate Governance Systems. In: Journal of Applied Corporate Finance, 16 (2-3): 51–72.

Dyck, Alexander/Zingales, Luigi (2004b): Private Benefits of Control: An International Comparison. In: The Journal of Finance, 59 (2): 537–600.

Easterbrook, Frank H. (1984): Two Agency-Cost Explanations of Dividends. In: The American Economic Review, 74 (4): 650–659.

Easterbrook, Frank H./Fischel, Daniel R. (1981): The Proper Role of Target's Management in Responding to a Tender Offer. In: Harvard Law Review, 94 (6): 1161–1204.

Edmans, Alex (2009): Blockholder Trading, Market Efficiency, and Managerial Myopia. In: The Journal of Finance, 64 (6): 2481–2513.

Edmans, Alex (2014): Blockholders and Corporate Governance. ECGI - Finance Working Paper No. 385. URL: http://papers.ssrn.com/sol3/papers.cfm?abstract_id=2285781, accessed on October 14, 2014.

Edmans, Alex/Fang, Vivian W./Zur, Emanuel (2013): The Effect of Liquidity on Governance. In: Review of Financial Studies, 26 (6): 1443–1482.

Edwards, Jeremy S./Nibler, Marcus (2000): Corporate governance in Germany: the role of banks and ownership concentration. In: Economic Policy, 15 (31): 237–267.

Edwards, Jeremy S./Weichenrieder, Alfons J. (2004): Ownership concentration and Share Valuation. In: German Economic Review, 5 (2): 143–171.

Edwards, Jeremy S./Weichenrieder, Alfons J. (2009): Control rights, pyramids, and the measurement of ownership concentration. In: Journal of Economic Behavior & Organization, 72 (1): 489–508.

Eggers, Thies/Reiß, Christian/Schichold, Bernd (2009): Der Sachverstand des Financial Expert – Praxisfragen nach BilMoG. In: Der Aufsichtsrat, 6 (11): 157–159.

Ehrhardt, Olaf/Nowak, Eric (2003): The Effect of IPOs on German Family-Owned Firms: Governance Changes, Ownership Structure, and Performance. In: Journal of Small Business Management, 41 (2): 222–232.

Eisenhardt, Kathleen M. (1989): Agency Theory: An Assessment and Review. In: The Academy of Management Review, 14 (1): 57–74.

Ellermann, Hans-Heinrich (2003): Dividendenpolitik und Long-Run Performance in Deutschland. Wiesbaden: Deutscher Universitäts-Verlag.

Ellul, Andrew/Guntay, Levent/Lel, Ugur (2007): External Governance and Debt Agency Costs of Family Firms. International Finance Discussion Paper Number 908. URL: http://www.federalreserve.gov/pubs/ifdp/2007/908/ifdp908.pdf, accessed on October 14, 2014.

Elsas, Ralf/Krahnen, Jan P. (1998): Is relationship lending special? Evidence from credit-file data in Germany. In: Journal of Banking & Finance, 22 (10): 1283–1316.

Elsas, Ralf/Krahnen, Jan P. (2004): Universal Banks and Relationships with Firms. In: Krahnen, Jan P./Schmidt, Reinhard H. (Editors): The German Financial System. Oxford: Oxford University Press: 197–232.

Emmons, William R./Schmid, Frank A. (1998): Universal Banking, Control Rights, and Corporate Finance in Germany. In: Federal Reserve Bank of St. Louis Review, 80 (4): 19–42.

Epstein, Richard A. (1991): Agency Costs, Employment Contracts, and Labor Unions. In: Pratt, John W./Zeckhauser, Richard J. (Editors): Principals and Agents: The Structure of Business. Boston: Harvard Business School Press: 127–148.

Ernst, Edgar/Gassen, Joachim/Pellens, Bernhard (2005): Verhalten und Präferenzen deutscher Aktionäre: Eine Befragung privater und institutioneller Anleger zu Informationsverhalten, Dividendenpräferenz und Wahrnehmung von Stimmrechten. Frankfurt am Main: Deutsches Aktieninstitut e.V.

Eulerich, Marc/Rapp, Marc S./Wolff, Michael (2012): Ausgewählte Aspekte der Vorstandsvergütung: „Say-on- Pay“-Abstimmungen während der Hauptversammlung. In: Zeitschrift für Corporate Governance, 7 (2): 69–73.

Ewert, Ralf (1987): The Financial Theory of Agency as a Tool for an Analysis of Problems in External Accounting. In: Bamberg, Günter/Spremann, Klaus (Editors): Agency Theory, Information, and Incentives. Berlin: Springer: 281–309.

Faccio, Mara/Lang, Larry H. (2002): The ultimate ownership of Western European corporations. In: Journal of Financial Economics, 65 (3): 365–395.

Faccio, Mara/Lang, Larry H./Young, Leslie (2001): Dividends and Expropriation. In: The American Economic Review, 91 (1): 54–78.

Faccio, Mara/Lasfer, M. Ameziane (2000): Do occupational pension funds monitor companies in which they hold large stakes? In: Journal of Corporate Finance, 6 (1): 71–110.

Faccio, Mara/Marchica, Maria-Teresa/Mura, Roberto (2011): Large Shareholder Diversification and Corporate Risk-Taking. In: Review of Financial Studies, 24 (11): 3601–3641.

Fallgatter, Michael J. (2006): Zum Vorstandsvergütungs-Offenlegungsgesetz. In: Zeitschrift Führung und Organisation, 75 (4): 207–210.

Fama, Eugene F. (1970): Efficient Capital Markets: A Review of Theory and Empirical Work. In: The Journal of Finance, 25 (2): 383–417.

Fama, Eugene F. (1980): Agency Problems and the Theory of the Firm. In: Journal of Political Economy, 88 (2): 288–307.

Fama, Eugene F./Jensen, Michael C. (1983a): Agency Problems and Residual Claims. In: Journal of Law and Economics, 26 (2): 327–349.

Fama, Eugene F./Jensen, Michael C. (1983b): Separation of Ownership and Control. In: Journal of Law and Economics, 26 (2): 301–325.

Farinha, Jorge (2003): Dividend Policy, Corporate Governance and the Managerial Entrenchment Hypothesis: An Empirical Analysis. In: Journal of Business Finance & Accounting, 30 (9-10): 1173–1209.

Faust, Michael/Bahnmüller, Reinhard/Fisecker, Christiane (2011): Das kapitalmarktorientierte Unternehmen. Berlin: Edition Sigma.

Fauver, Larry/Fuerst, Michael E. (2006): Does good corporate governance include employee representation? Evidence from German corporate boards. In: Journal of Financial Economics, 82 (3): 673–710.

Fee, C. Edward/Hadlock, Charles J./Thomas, Shawn (2006): Corporate Equity Ownership and the Governance of Product Market Relationships. In: The Journal of Finance, 61 (3): 1217–1251.

Filatotchev, Igor/Mickiewicz, Tomasz M. (2006): Ownership Concentration, Private Benefits of Control and Debt Financing. In: Mickiewicz, Tomasz M. (Editor): Corporate Governance and Finance in Poland and Russia. Houndmills: Palgrave Macmillan: 159–176.

Fleischer, Holger (2005): Das Vorstandsvergütungs-Offenlegungsgesetz. In: Der Betrieb, 58 (30): 1611–1617.

Fleming, Grant/Heaney, Richard/McCosker, Rochelle (2005): Agency costs and ownership structure in Australia. In: Pacific-Basin Finance Journal, 13 (1): 29–52.

Florackis, Chrisostomos (2008): Agency costs and corporate governance mechanisms: evidence for UK firms. In: International Journal of Managerial Finance, 4 (1): 37–59.

Flören, Roberto H. (2002): Crown princes in the clay: An empirical study on the tackling of succession challenges in Dutch family farms. Assen: Koninklijke Van Gorcum.

Fohlin, Caroline (1998): Relationship Banking, Liquidity, and Investment in the German Industrialization. In: The Journal of Finance, 53 (5): 1737–1758.

Förschle, Gerhart/Glaum, Martin/Mandler, Udo (1998): Internationale Rechnungslegung und Kapitalaufnahmeerleichterungsgesetz - Meinungswandel bei Führungskräften deutscher Unternehmungen? In: Der Betrieb, 51 (46): 2281–2288.

Frankfurter, George M./Wood, Bob G. (2002): Dividend policy theories and their empirical tests. In: International Review of Financial Analysis, 11 (2): 111–138.

Franks, Julian/Mayer, Colin (2001): Ownership and Control of German Corporations. In: The Review of Financial Studies, 14 (4): 943–977.

Freeman, R. Edward (2010): Strategic Management: A Stakeholder Approach. Cambridge: Cambridge University Press.

Furubotn, Eirik G./Pejovich, Svetozar (1972): Property Rights and Economic Theory: A Survey of Recent Literature. In: Journal of Economic Literature, 10 (4): 1137–1162.

Furubotn, Eirik G./Richter, Rudolf (1991): New Institutional Economics: An Assessment. In: Furubotn, Eirik G./Richter, Rudolf (Editors): The New Institutional Economics: A Collection of Articles from the Journal of Institutional and Theoretical Economics. Tübingen: Mohr: 1–31.

Gantchev, Nickolay (2013): The costs of shareholder activism: Evidence from a sequential decision model. In: Journal of Financial Economics, 107 (3): 610–631.

Gantenberg, Philipp (2005): Die Reform der Hauptversammlung durch den Regierungsentwurf eines Gesetzes zur Unternehmensintegrität und Modernisierung des Anfechtungsrechts - UMAG. In: Der Betrieb, 58 (4): 207–212.

Gao, Yu/Gao, Yuan/Smith, Abbie (2009): Bondholder Activism and Delay in Financial Reporting. Working Paper. URL: http://assets.csom.umn.edu/assets/142807.pdf, accessed on October 14, 2014.

Gedajlovic, Eric R. (1993): Ownership, Strategy and Performance: Is the Dichotomy Sufficient? In: Organization Studies, 14 (5): 731–752.

Gedajlovic, Eric R./Shapiro, Daniel M. (1998): Management and Ownership Effects: Evidence from Five Countries. In: Strategic Management Journal, 19 (6): 533–553.

Geib, Gerd (1999): Gesetz zur Kontrolle und Transparenz im Unternehmensbereich. In: Wagner, Fred/Koch, Gottfried (Editors): Aktuelle Fragen in der Versicherungswirtschaft. Karlsruhe: Verlag Versicherungswirtschaft: 19–51.

Gerke, Wolfgang/Oerke, Marc/Sentner, Arnd (1997): Der Informationsgehalt von Dividendenänderungen auf dem deutschen Aktienmarkt. In: Die Betriebswirtschaft, 57 (6): 810–822.

Ghosh, Dhiren/Vogt, Andrew (2012): Outliers: An Evaluation of Methodologies. Paper prepared for the Joint Statistical Meeting 2012. URL: http://www.amstat.org/sections/SRMS/proceedings/y2012/Files/304068_72402.pdf; accessed on October 14, 2014.

Gillan, Stuart L. (2006): Recent Developments in Corporate Governance: An Overview. In: Journal of Corporate Finance, 12 (3): 381–402.

Gillan, Stuart L./Starks, Laura T. (1998): A Survey of Shareholder Activism : Motivation and Empirical Evidence. In: Contemporary Finance Digest, 2 (3): 10–34.

Gillan, Stuart L./Starks, Laura T. (2000): Corporate governance proposals and shareholder activism: the role of institutional investors. In: Journal of Financial Economics, 57 (2): 275–305.

Gillan, Stuart L./Starks, Laura T. (2003): Corporate Governance, Corporate Ownership, and the Role of Institutional Investors: A Global Perspective. In: Journal of Applied Finance, 13 (2): 4–22.

Giroud, Xavier/Mueller, Holger M. (2010): Does corporate governance matter in competitive industries? In: Journal of Financial Economics, 95 (3): 312–331.

Goergen, Marc/Manjon, Miguel C./Renneboog, Luc (2008): Recent developments in German corporate governance. In: International Review of Law and Economics, 28 (3): 175–193.

Goergen, Marc/Renneboog, Luc/Correia da Silva, Luis (2005): When do German firms change their dividends? In: Journal of Corporate Finance, 11 (1-2): 375–399.

Gomes, Armando/Novaes, Walter (2005): Sharing of Control versus Monitoring as Corporate Governance Mechanisms. Institute for Law and Economics Research Paper No. 01-12, Penn Institute for Economic Research Working Paper No. 01-029. URL: http://papers.ssrn.com/sol3/papers.cfm?abstract_id=277111, accessed on October 14, 2014.

Gomez-Mejia, Luis R./Nunez-Nickel, Manuel/Gutierrez, Isabel (2001): The Role of Family Ties in Agency Contracts. In: The Academy of Management Journal, 44 (1): 81–95.

Gompers, Paul A./Metrick, Andrew (1998): How are Large Institutions Different from Other Investors? Why do these Differences Matter? Harvard Institute of Economic Research Working Papers No. 1830. URL: https://ideas.repec.org/p/fth/harver/1830.html, accessed on October 14, 2014.

Goncharov, Igor/Werner, Joerg Richard/Zimmermann, Jochen (2006): Does Compliance with the German Corporate Governance Code Have an Impact on Stock Valuation? An empirical analysis. In: Corporate Governance: An International Review, 14 (5): 432–445.

Gordon, Lilli A./Pound, John (1993): Information, Ownership Structure, and Shareholder Voting: Evidence from Shareholder-Sponsored Corporate Governance Proposals. In: The Journal of Finance, 48 (2): 697–718.

Gordon, Myron J. (1959): Dividends, Earnings, and Stock Prices. In: The Review of Economics and Statistics, 41 (2): 99–105.

Gordon, Myron J. (1963): Optimal Investment and Financing Policy. In: The Journal of Finance, 18 (2): 264–272.

Gordon, Robert A. (1961): Business Leadership in the Large Corporation, 5th ed. Los Angeles: University of California Press.

Gorton, Gary/Schmid, Frank A. (2002): Class Struggle inside the Firm: A Study of German Codetermination. Federal Reserve Bank of St. Louis Working Paper 2000-025B. URL: http://research.stlouisfed.org/wp/2000/2000-025.pdf, accessed on October 14, 2014.

Gorton, Gary/Schmid, Frank A. (2000): Universal banking and the performance of German firms. In: Journal of Financial Economics, 58 (1-2): 29–80.

Gottschlich, Klaus J. (1996): Die Eigentümerkontrolle in der modernen Publikumsgesellschaft. Dissertation Universität Freiburg in der Schweiz.

Granger, Clive W. (1969): Investigating Causal Relations by Econometric Models and Cross-spectral Methods. In: Econometrica, 37 (3): 424–438.

Gräwe, Daniel (2013): Die historische Entwicklung der Corporate Governance. In: Zeitschrift für Corporate Governance, 8 (1): 24–30.

Greene, William H. (2003): Econometric Analysis, 5th ed. New Jersey: Pearson Education Inc.

Greenwood, Robin/Schor, Michael (2009): Investor activism and takeovers. In: Journal of Financial Economics, 92 (3): 362–375.

Grinstein, Yaniv/Michaely, Roni (2005): Institutional Holdings and Payout Policy. In: The Journal of Finance, 60 (3): 1389–1426.

Grossman, Sanford J./Hart, Oliver D. (1980): Takeover Bids, The Free-Rider Problem, and the Theory of the Corporation. In: The Bell Journal of Economics, 11 (1): 42–64.

Grossmann, Sanford J./Hart, Oliver D. (1983): An Analysis of the Principal-Agent Problem. In: Econometrica, 51 (1): 7–45.

Groß, Kerstin (2007): Equity Ownership and Performance. Heidelberg: Physica-Verlag.

Guedhami, Omrane/Mishra, Dev (2009): Excess Control, Corporate Governance and Implied Cost of Equity: International Evidence. In: The Financial Review, 44 (4): 489–524.

Guercio, Diane del/Hawkins, Jennifer (1999): The motivation and impact of pension fund activism. In: Journal of Financial Economics, 52 (3): 293–340.

Gugler, Klaus (2003): Corporate governance, dividend payout policy, and the interrelation between dividends, R&D, and capital investment. In: Journal of Banking & Finance, 27 (7): 1297–1321.

Gugler, Klaus/Weigand, Jürgen (2003): Is ownership really endogenous? In: Applied Economics Letters, 10 (8): 483–486.

Gugler, Klaus/Yurtoglu, B. Burcin (2003): Corporate governance and dividend pay-out policy in Germany. In: European Economic Review, 47 (4): 731–758.

Gutiérrez, María/Tribó, Josep A. (2004): Private benefits extraction in closely-held corporations: The case for multiple large shareholders. Universidad Carlos III de Madrid Working Paper 04-43 Business Economics Series 15. URL: https://ideas.repec.org/p/cte/wbrepe/wb044315.html, accessed on October 14, 2014.

Haas, Tillmann (2010): Die Bundesanstalt für Finanzdienstleistungsaufsicht. In: Grieser, Simon G./Heemann, Manfred (Editors): Bankenaufsichtsrecht: Entwicklungen und Perspektiven. Frankfurt: Frankfurt School: 59–69.

Habbershon, Timothy G./Williams, Mary L. (1999): A Resource-Based Framework for Assessing the Strategic Advantages of Family Firms. In: Family Business Review, 12 (1): 1–25.

Hackethal, Andreas (2004): German Banks and Banking Structure. In: Krahnen, Jan P./Schmidt, Reinhard H. (Editors): The German Financial System. Oxford: Oxford University Press.

Hackethal, Andreas/Schmidt, Reinhard H./Tyrell, Marcel (2005): Banks and German Corporate Governance: on the way to a capital market-based system? In: Corporate Governance: An International Review, 13 (3): 397–407.

Halpern, Paul (1999): Systemic perspectives on corporate governance Systems. Conference and Symposium on Corporate Governance and Globalization.

Hamdani, Assaf/Yafeh, Yishay (2012): Institutional Investors as Minority Shareholders. In: Review of Finance, 17 (2): 691–725.

Hamzah, Ahmad H./Zulkafli, Abdul H. (2014): Multiple Shareholders Structure (MSS) and Corporate Financial Policy In: Journal of Finance and Bank Management, 2 (1): 107–134.

Hansch, Julia (2012): Die Kosten der Unternehmenskontrolle in Deutschland und den USA. Köln: Kölner Wissenschaftsverlag.

Hansmann, Henry (1988): Ownership of the Firm. In: Journal of Law, Economics & Organization, 4 (2): 267–304.

Harris, Milton/Raviv, Artur (1991): The Theory of Capital Structure. In: The Journal of Finance, 46 (1): 297–355.

Hartmann-Wendels, Thomas (1987): Dividend Policy under Asymmetric Information. In: Bamberg, Günter/Spremann, Klaus (Editors): Agency Theory, Information, and Incentives Berlin: Springer: 229–253.

Hartmann-Wendels, Thomas (1991): Rechnungslegung der Unternehmen und Kapitalmarkt aus informationsökonomischer Sicht. Heidelberg: Physica-Verlag Heidelberg.

Hartmann-Wendels, Thomas (2001): Finanzierung. In: Jost, Peter J. (Editor): Die Prinzipal-Agenten-Theorie in der Betriebswirtschaftslehre. Stuttgart: Schäffer-Poeschel Verlag: 117–146.

Hausman, Jerry A. (1978): Specification Tests in Econometrics. In: Econometrica, 46 (6): 1251–1271.

Hellmann, Thomas/Puri, Manju (2000): The Interaction Between Product Market and Financing Strategy: The Role of Venture Capital. In: The Review of Financial Studies, 13 (4): 959–984.

Hellmann, Thomas/Puri, Manju (2002): Venture Capital and the Professionalization of Start-Up Firms: Empirical Evidence. In: The Journal of Finance, 57 (1): 169–197.

Hellwig, Martin (2000): On the Economics and Politics of Corporate Finance and Corporate Control. In: Vives, Xavier (Editor): Corporate governance: theoretical and empirical perspectives. Cambridge: Cambridge University Press: 95–136.

Helwege, Jean/Pirinsky, Christo/Stulz, René M. (2007): Why Do Firms Become Widely Held? An Analysis of the Dynamics of Corporate Ownership. In: The Journal of Finance, 62 (3): 995–1028.

Herfindahl, Orric C. (1950): Concentration in the U. S. Steel Industry. Columbia University: Unpublished doctoral dissertation.

Hermalin, Benjamin E./Weisbach, Michael S. (1991): The Effects of Board Composition and Direct Incentives on Firm Performance. In: Financial Management, 20 (4): 101–112.

Himmelberg, Charles P./Hubbard, R. Glenn/Palia, Darius (1999): Understanding the determinants of managerial ownership and the link between ownership and Performance. In: Journal of Financial Economics, 53 (3): 353–384.

Hirte, Heribert et al. (2003): Das Transparenz- und Publizitätsgesetz. München: C.H. Beck.

Hochberg, Yael V. (2011): Venture Capital and Corporate Governance in the Newly Public Firm. In: Review of Finance, 16 (2): 429–480.

Holderness, Clifford G./Sheehan, Dennis P. (1988): The Role of Majority Shareholders in Publicly Held Corporations - An Exploratory Analysis. In: Journal of Financial Economics, 20 (1-2): 317–346.

Holmstrom, Bengt (1982): Moral hazard in teams. In: The Bell Journal of Economics, 13 (2): 324–340.

Holmström, Bengt (1979): Moral hazard and observability. In: The Bell Journal of Economics, 10 (1): 74–91.

Höpner, Martin (2003): Wer beherrscht die Unternehmen? Shareholder Value, Managerherrschaft und Mitbestimmung in Deutschland. Frankfurt: Campus Verlag.

Huddart, Steven (1993): The Effect of a Large Shareholder on Corporate Value. In: Management Science, 39 (11): 1407–1421.

Hussey, Jill/Hussey, Roger (1997): Business Research. A practical guide for undergraduate and postgraduate students. London: MacMillan Press Ltd.

Hwang, LeeSeok/Kim, Yong O. (1998): Does the Ownership Structure of Debt and Equity Affect the Agency Costs of Debt? Japanese Evidence. In: Journal of Accounting, Auditing & Finance, 13 (1): 37–66.

Ihrig, Hans-Christoph/Wagner, Jens (2002): Die Reform geht weiter: Das Transparenz- und Publizitätsgesetz kommt. In: Betriebs-Berater, 57 (16): 789–797.

Jahn, Daniel F. et al. (2002): Die Wirkungen des Deutschen Corporate Governance Kodex aus Investorenperspektive : Ergebnisse einer Studie. In: Zeitschrift für Corporate Governance, 2 (11): 64–68.

Januszewski, Silke I./Köke, Jens/Winter, Joachim K. (2002): Product market competition, corporate governance and firm performance: an empirical analysis for Germany. In: Research in Economics, 56 (3): 299–332.

Jara-Bertin, Mauricio/López-Iturriaga, Félix J./López-de-Foronda, Óscar (2008): The Contest to the Control in European Family Firms: How Other Shareholders Affect Firm Value. In: Corporate Governance: An International Review, 16 (3): 146–159.

Jenkinson, Tim/Ljungqvist, Alexander (2001): The role of hostile stakes in German corporate governance. In: Journal of Corporate Finance, 7 (4): 397–446.

Jensen, Gerald R./Solberg, Donald P./Zorn, Thomas S. (1992): Simultaneous Determination of Insider Ownership, Debt, and Dividend Policies. In: The Journal of Financial and Quantitative Analysis, 27 (2): 247–263.

Jensen, Michael C. (1983): Organization Theory and Methodology. In: The Accounting Review, 58 (2): 319–339.

Jensen, Michael C. (1986): Agency Costs of Free Cash Flow, Corporate Finance, and Takeovers. In: The American Economic Review, 76 (2): 323–329.

Jensen, Michael C. (1993): The Modern Industrial Revolution, Exit, and the Failure of Internal Control Systems. In: The Journal of Finance, 48 (3): 831–880.

Jensen, Michael C. (1994): Self-Interest, Altruism, Incentives, and Agency Theory. In: Journal of Applied Corporate Finance, 7 (2): 1–15.

Jensen, Michael C./Meckling, William H. (1976): Theory of the Firm: Managerial Behavior, Agency Costs and Ownership Structure. In: Journal of Financial Economics, 3 (4): 305–360.

Jensen, Michael C./Meckling, William H. (1979): Rights and Production Functions: An Application to Labor-Managed Firms and Codetermination. In: The Journal of Business, 52 (4): 469–506.

Jensen, Michael C./Warner, Jerold B. (1988): The Distribution of Power Among Corporate Managers, Shareholders, and Directors. In: Journal of Financial Economics, 20 (2): 3–24.

Jilg, Thomas (1996): Die Treuepflicht des Aktionärs. Frankfurt: Europäische Hochschulschriften: Reihe 2, Rechtswissenschaft. Bd. 2005.

John, Kose/Litov, Lubomir/Yeung, Bernard (2008): Corporate Governance and Risk-Taking. In: The Journal of Finance, 63 (4): 1679–1728.

John, Kose/Williams, Joseph (1985): Dividends, Dilution, and Taxes: A Signalling Equilibrium. In: The Journal of Finance, 40 (4): 1053–1070.

Johnson, Simon et al. (2000): Tunneling. In: AEA Papers and Proceedings, 90 (2): 22–27.

Jost, Peter-Jürgen (1996): On the Role of Commitment in a Principal Agent Relationship with an Informed Principal. In: Journal of Economic Theory, 68 (2): 510–530.

Jost, Peter-Jürgen (2001): Die Prinzpal-Agenten-Theorie in der Betriebswirtschaftslehre. Stuttgart: Schäffer-Poeschel.

Kahan, Marcel/Rock, Edward B. (2007): Hedge Funds in Corporate Governance and Corporate Control. In: University of Pennsylvania Law Review, 155 (5): 1021–1093.

Kahn, Charles/Winton, Andrew (1998): Ownership Structure, Speculation, and Shareholder Intervention. In: The Journal of Finance, 53 (1): 99–129.

Kalay, Avner (1980): Signaling, Information Content, and the Reluctance to Cut Dividends. In: The Journal of Financial and Quantitative Analysis, 15 (4): 855–869.

Kang, Jun-Koo/Stulz, René M. (1997): Why is there a home bias? An analysis of foreign portfolio equity ownership in Japan. In: Journal of Financial Economics, 46 (1): 3–28.

Kaplan, Steven N. (1989): The Effects of Management Buyouts on Operating Performance and Value. In: Journal of Financial Economics, 24 (2): 217–254.

Kaplan, Steven N. (1994): Top Executives, Turnover, and Firm Performance in Germany. In: Journal of Law, Economics & Organization, 10 (1): 142–159.

Kaplan, Steven N./Strömberg, Per (2009): Leveraged Buyouts and Private Equity. In: Journal of Economic Perspectives, 23 (1): 121–146.

Karpoff, Jonathan M./Malatesta, Paul H./Walkling, Ralph A. (1996): Corporate governance and shareholder initiatives: Empirical evidence. In: Journal of Financial Economics, 42 (3): 365–395.

Kaserer, Christoph/Moldenhauer, Benjamin (2008): Insider ownership and corporate performance: evidence from Germany. In: Review of Managerial Science, 2 (1): 1–35.

Kaulmann, Thomas (1987): Managerialism versus the Property Rights Theory of the Firm. In: Bamberg, Günter/Spremann, Klaus (Editors): Agency Theory, Information, and Incentives. Berlin: Springer: 439–459.

Kehren, Sven (2006): Paketaktionäre, Macht und Unternehmenserfolg. Wiesbaden: Deutscher Universitäts-Verlag.

Kengelbach, Jens/Roos, Alexander (2006): Entflechtung der Deutschland AG. In: M&A Review, 17 (1): 12–21.

Kennedy, Peter (2008): A Guide to Econometrics, 6th ed. Malden: Blackwell Publishing.

Khan, Tehmina (2006): Company Dividends and Ownership Structure: Evidence from UK Panel Data. In: The Economic Journal, 116 (510): 172–189.

Kim, Kenneth A./Kitsabunnarat-Chatjuthamard, P./Nofsinger, John R. (2007): Large shareholders, board independence, and minority shareholder rights: Evidence from Europe. In: Journal of Corporate Finance, 13 (5): 859–880.

Kirsch, Hans-Jürgen (2002): Vom Bilanzrichtlinien-Gesetz zum Transparenz- und Publizitätsgesetz. In: Die Wirtschaftsprüfung, 55 (14): 743–755.

Klein, April/Zur, Emanuel (2009): Entrepreneurial Shareholder Activism: Hedge Funds and Other Private Investors. In: The Journal of Finance, 64 (1): 187–229.

Klein, April/Zur, Emanuel (2011): The Impact of Hedge Fund Activism on the Target Firm's Existing Bondholders. In: Review of Financial Studies, 24 (5): 1735–1771.

Klein, Benjamin/Crawford, Robert G./Alchian, Armen A. (1978): Vertical Integration, Appropriable Rents, and the Competitive Contracting Process. In: Journal of Law and Economics, 21 (2): 297–326.

Koch, Jens (2006): Das Gesetz zur Unternehmensintegrität und Modernisierung des Anfechtungsrechts (UMAG). In: Zeitschrift für Unternehmens- und Gesellschaftsrecht, 35 (6): 769–804.

Koch, Rosemarie/Stadtmann, Georg (2010): Das Gesetz zur Angemessenheit der Vorstandsvergütung. European University Viadrina Frankfurt (Oder) Department of Business Administration and Economics Discussion Paper No. 288. URL: http://www.wiwi.europa-uni.de/de/forschung/publikationen-projekte/dp/_dokumente/288_Koch_Stadtmann.pdf, accessed on October 14, 2014.

Koch, Stefan (2005): Neuerungen im Insiderrecht und der Ad-hoc-Publizität. In: Der Betrieb, 58 (5): 267–274.

Kohler, Ulrich/Kreuter, Frauke (2005): Data Analysis Using Stata. College Station: Stata Press.

Köhler, Annette G. (2005): Audit Committees in Germany – Theoretical Reasoning and Empirical Evidence. In: Schmalenbach Business Review, 57 (3): 229-252.

Köke, Jens (2001): New evidence on ownership structures in Germany. In: Kredit und Kapital, 34 (2): 257–292.

Köke, Jens/Renneboog, Luc (2005): Do Corporate Control and Product Market Competition Lead to Stronger Productivity Growth? Evidence from Market-Oriented and Blockholder-Based Governance Regimes. In: Journal of Law and Economics, 48 (2): 475–516.

Konijn, Sander J./Kräussl, Roman/Lucas, Andre (2011): Blockholder dispersion and firm value. In: Journal of Corporate Finance, 17 (5): 1330–1339.

Kornmeier, Martin (2007): Wissenschaftstheorie und wissenschaftliches Arbeiten. Heidelberg: Physica-Verlag.

Kramer, Robert (2011): Die AIFM-Richtlinie - Neuer Rechtsrahmen für die Verwaltung alternativer Investmentfonds. In: Der Betrieb, 64 (37): 2077–2084.

Kroker, Matthias/Rapp, Marc S./Wolff, Michael (2010): Are Private Equity Investors Governance Champions or Simply Stock Picking Specialists? Working Paper. URL: http://www.researchgate.net/publication/228419326_ARE_PRIVATE_EQUITY_INVESTORS_GOVERNANCE_CHAMPIONS_OR_SIMPLY_STOCK_PICKING_SPECIALISTS, accessed on October 14, 2014.

Kugler, Stefan (2002): Viertes Finanzmarktförderungsgesetz - Aufbruch zu neuen Ufern im Investmentrecht? In: Betriebs-Berater, 57 (20): 1001–1006.

Künkele, Kai P./Zwirner, Christian (2009): BilMoG: Handelsrechtliche Reform mit steuerlichen Konsequenzen? Übersicht über die Änderungen durch das BilMoG und die steuerlichen Folgen. In: Deutsches Steuerrecht, 47 (25): 1277–1283.

La Porta, Rafael et al. (1997): Legal Determinants of External Finance. In: The Journal of Finance, 52 (3): 1131–1150.

La Porta, Rafael et al. (2000a): Agency Problems and Dividend Policies around the World. In: The Journal of Finance, 55 (1): 1–33.

La Porta, Rafael et al. (2000b): Investor protection and corporate governance. In: Journal of Financial Economics, 58 (1-2): 3–27.

La Porta, Rafael et al. (2002): Investor Protection and Corporate Valuation. In: The Journal of Finance, 58 (3): 1147–1170.

La Porta, Rafael/Silanes, Florencia López de/Shleifer, Andrei (1999): Corporate ownership around the world. In: Journal of Finance, 54 (2): 471–517.

Laeven, Luc/Levine, Ross (2008): Complex ownership structures and corporate valuations. In: Review of Financial Studies, 21 (2): 579–604.

Lane, Peter J./Cannella Jr., Albert A./Lubatkin, Michael H. (1998): Agency Problems as Antecedents to Unrelated Mergers and Diversification: Amihud and Lev Reconsidered. In: Strategic Management Journal, 19 (6): 555–578.

Laruelle, Annick/Valenciano, Federico (2001): Shapley-Shubik and Banzhaf Indices Revisited. In: Mathematics of Operations Research, 26 (1): 89–104.

Leech, Dennis (2001): Shareholder Voting Power and Corporate Governance: A Study of Large British Companies. In: Nordic Journal of Political Economy, 27 (1): 33–54.

Leech, Dennis/Leahy, John (1991): Ownership structure, control type classifications and the performance of large British companies. In: The Economic Journal, 101 (409): 1418–1437.

Lehmann, Erik/Frick, Bernd (2005): Corporate governance in Germany: ownership, codetermination, and firm performance in a stakeholder economy. In: Gospel, Howard/Pendleton, Andrew (Editors): Corporate governance and labour management: an international comparison. Oxford: Oxford University Press: 122–147.

Lehmann, Erik/Weigand, Jürgen (2000): Does the Governed Corporation Perform Better? Governance Structures and Corporate Performance in Germany. In: European Finance Review, 4 (2): 157–195.

Leiber, Marietta K. (2008): Performance-Studie deutscher Familienunternehmen. Augsburg.

Levinthal, Daniel (1988): A survey of agency models of organizations. In: Journal of Economic Behavior & Organization, 9 (2): 153–185.

Lewellen, Wilbur G./Badrinath, Swaminathan G. (1997): On the measurement of Tobin's q. In: Journal of Financial Economics, 44 (1): 77–122.

Lins, Karl V. (2003): Equity Ownership and Firm Value in Emerging Markets. In: The Journal of Financial and Quantitative Analysis, 38 (1): 159.

Lintner, John (1956): Distribution of Incomes of Corporations Among Dividends, Retained Earnings, and Taxes. In: The American Economic Review, 46 (2): 97–113.

Lintner, John (1962): Dividends, Earnings, Leverage, Stock Prices and the Supply of Capital to Corporations. In: The Review of Economics and Statistics, 44 (3): 243–269.

Long, Michael S./Malitz, Ileen B. (1985): Investment Patterns and Financial Leverage. In: Friedman, Benjamin M. (Editor): Corporate capital structures in the United States. Chicago: University of Chicago Press: 325–351.

Lopatta, Kerstin et al. (2013): The Effect of the German Accounting Law Modernization Act (BilMoG) on the Earnings Quality of Private Firms. In: Corporate Finance law, 4 (5): 234–242.

Louven, Christoph/Ingwersen, Malte (2013): Wie nachhaltig muss die Vorstandsvergütung sein? In: Betriebs-Berater, 68 (21): 1219–1222.

Lucas, Deborah J./McDonald, Robert L. (1998): Shareholder Heterogeneity, Adverse Selection, and Payout Policy. In: The Journal of Financial and Quantitative Analysis, 33 (2): 233–253.

Lück, Wolfgang (1999): Betriebswirtschaftliche Aspekte der Einrichtung eines Überwachungssystems und eines Risikomanagementsystems. In: Dörner, Dietrich/Menhold, Dieter/Pfitzer, Norbert (Editors): Reform des Aktienrechts, der Rechnungslegung und Prüfung. Stuttgart: Schäffer-Poeschel: 139–176.

MacNeil, Iain (2010): Activism and collaboration among shareholders in UK listed companies. In: Capital Markets Law Journal, 5 (4): 419–438.

Manne, Henry G. (1965): Mergers and the Market for Corporate Control. In: Journal of Political Economy, 73 (2): 110–120.

Marris, Robin (1967): The economic theory of managerial capitalism. London: MacMillan and Company Ltd.

Marsch, Rüdiger (1974): Die rechtliche Problematik der Verwendung von Jahresüberschüssen deutscher Aktiengesellschaften unter besonderer Berücksichtigung der Kleinaktionärsinteressen. Göttingen: Goltze.

Marsch-Barner, Reinhard (1999): Die Abschaffung von Mehrstimmrechten und Stimmrechtsbeschränkung. In: Dörner, Dietrich/Menhold, Dieter/Pfitzer, Norbert (Editors): Reform des Aktienrechts, der Rechnungslegung und Prüfung. Stuttgart: Schäffer-Poeschel: 283–296.

Maskin, Eric/Tirole, Jean (1990): The Principal-Agent Relationship with an Informed Principal: The Case of Private Values. In: Econometrica, 58 (2): 379–409.

Matthews, Robin C. (1986): The Economics of Institutions and the Sources of Growth. In: The Economic Journal, 96 (384): 903–918.

Maug, Ernst (1998): Large Shareholders as Monitors: Is There a Trade-Off between Liquidity and Control? In: The Journal of Finance, 53 (1): 65–98.

Maurer, Raimond (2004): Institutional Investors in Germany: Insurance Companies and Investment Funds. In: Krahnen, Jan P./Schmidt, Reinhard H. (Editors): The German Financial System. Oxford: Oxford University Press.

Maury, Benjamin (2006): Family ownership and firm performance: Empirical evidence from Western European corporations. In: Journal of Corporate Finance, 12 (2): 321–341.

Maury, Benjamin/Pajuste, Anete (2005): Multiple large shareholders and firm value. In: Journal of Banking & Finance, 29 (7): 1813–1834.

Mazzi, Chiara (2011): Family business and financial performance: Current state of knowledge and future research challenges. In: Journal of Family Business Strategy, 2 (3): 166–181.

McConnell, John J./Servaes, Henri (1990): Additional evidence on equity ownership and corporate value. In: Journal of Financial Economics, 27 (2): 595–612.

Meinhövel, Harald (1999): Defizite der Principal-Agent-Theorie. Lohmar: Josef Eul Verlag GmbH.

Mello, Antonio S./Parsons, John E. (1992): Measuring the Agency Cost of Debt. In: The Journal of Finance, 47 (5): 1887–1904.

Mezzetti, Claudio (1997): Common Agency with Horizontally Differentiated Principals. In: RAND Journal of Economics, 28 (2): 323–345.

Mietzner, Mark/Schweizer, Denis (2011): Hedge Funds versus Private Equity Funds as Shareholder Activists in Germany - Differences in Value Creation. In: Journal of Economics and Finance, 28 (2): 181–208.

Mietzner, Mark/Schweizer, Denis/Tyrell, Marcel (2011): Intra-Industry Effects of Shareholder Activism in Germany–Is There a Difference between Hedge Fund and Private Equity Investments? In: Schmalenbach Business Review, 63: 151–185.

Milde, Hellmuth (1987): Managerial Contracting with Public and Private Information. In: Bamberg, Günter/Spremann, Klaus (Editors): Agency Theory, Information, and Incentives. Berlin: Springer: 39–59.

Miller, Merton H./Modigliani, Franco (1961): Dividend Policy, Growth, and the Valuation of Shares. In: The Journal of Business, 34 (4): 411–433.

Miller, Merton H./Rock, Kevin (1985): Dividend Policy under Asymmetric Information. In: The Journal of Finance, 40 (4): 1031–1051.

Milnor, John W./Shapley, Lloyd S. (1978): Value of Large Games II: Oceanic Games. In: Mathematics of Operations Research, 3 (4): 290–307.

Mínguez-Vera, Antonio/Martín-Ugedo, Juan F. (2007): Does ownership structure affect value? A panel data analysis for the Spanish market. In: International Review of Financial Analysis, 16 (1): 81–98.

Mintz, Steven M. (2005): Corporate Governance in an International Context: legal systems, financing patterns and cultural variables. In: Corporate Governance: An International Review, 13 (5): 582–597.

Molho, Ian (1997): The Economics of Information - Lying and Cheating in Markets and Organizations. Oxford: Blackwell Publishers Ltd.

Molz, Rick (1995): The Theory of Pluralism in Corporate Governance: A Conceptual Framework and Empirical Test. In: Journal of Business Ethics, 14 (10): 789–804.

Morck, Randall/Shleifer, Andrei/Vishny, Robert W. (1988): Management Ownership and Market Valuation. In: Journal of Financial Economics, 20 (1-2): 293–315.

Morck, Randall/Wolfenzon, Daniel/Yeung, Bernard (2005): Corporate Governance, Economic Entrenchment, and Growth. In: Journal of Economic Literature, 43 (3): 655–720.

Mülbert, Peter O. (1996): Empfehlen sich gesetzliche Regelungen zur Einschränkung des Einflusses der Kreditinstitute auf Aktiengesellschaften? München: Beck.

Myers, Stewart C. (1977): Determinants of Corporate Borrowing. In: Journal of Financial Economics, 5 (2): 147–175.

Myers, Stewart C. (2001): Capital Structure. In: The Journal of Economic Perspectives, 15 (2): 81–102.

Narayanan, M. P. (1985): Managerial Incentives for Short-term Results. In: The Journal of Finance, 40 (5): 1469–1484.

Narayanaswamy, C. R./Shukla, Ravi (2001): Application Of Binomial Option Pricing Methodology to Explain Stockholder-Bondholder Conflict. In: Journal of Applied Finance, 11 (1): 35–40.

Nash, Robert C./Netter, Jeffry M./Poulsen, Annette B. (2003): Determinants of contractual relations between shareholders and bondholders: investment opportunities and restrictive covenants. In: Journal of Corporate Finance, 9 (2): 201–232.

Neus, Werner (1989): Ökonomische Agency-Theorie und Kapitalmarktgleichgewicht. Wiesbaden: Betriebswirtschaftlicher Verlag Dr. Th. Gabler GmbH.

Nix, Petra/Chen, Jean J. (2013): The Role of Institutional Investors in Corporate Governance. New York: Palgrave Macmillan.

Noack, Ulrich (2002): Neuerungen im Recht der Hauptversammlung durch das Transparenz- und Publizitätsgesetz und den Deutschen Corporate Governance Kodex. In: Der Betrieb, 55 (12): 620–626.

Noe, Thomas H. (2002): Investor Activism and Financial Market Structure. In: The Review of Financial Studies, 15 (1): 289–318.

Nonnenmacher, Rolf/Pohle, Klaus/v. Werder, Axel (2009): Aktuelle Anforderungen an Prüfungsausschüsse. In: Der Betrieb, 62 (27): 1447–1454.

North, Douglass C. (1991): Institutions. In: The Journal of Economic Perspectives, 5 (1): 97–112.

Nowak, Eric (2001): Recent Developments in German Capital Markets and Corporate Governance. In: Journal of Applied Corporate Finance, 14 (3): 35–48.

Nowak, Eric (2004): Investor Protection and Capital Market Regulation in Germany. In: Krahnen, Jan P./Schmidt, Reinhard H. (Editors): The German Financial System. Oxford: Oxford University Press: 425–449.

Nowak, Eric/Ehrhardt, Olaf/Weber, Felix-Michael (2006): "Running in the Family": The Evolution of Ownership, Control, and Performance in German Family-owned Firms, 1903-2003. Swiss Finance Institute Research Paper No. 06-13. URL: http://papers.ssrn.com/sol3/papers.cfm?abstract_id=891255, accessed on October 14, 2014.

Nowak, Eric/Rott, Roland/Mahr, Till G. (2005): Wer den Kodex nicht einhält, den bestraft der Kapitalmarkt? Eine empirische Analyse der Selbstregulierung und Kapitalmarktrelevanz des Deutschen Corporate Governance Kodex. In: Zeitschrift für Unternehmens- und Gesellschaftsrecht, 34 (2): 252–279.

Opler, Tim/Titman, Sheridan (1993): The Determinants of Leveraged Buyout Activity: Free Cash Flow vs. Financial Distress Costs. In: The Journal of Finance, 48 (5): 1985–1999.

Opper, Sonja (2001): Der Stand der Neuen Institutionenökonomik. In: Wirtschaftsdienst, 81 (10): 601–608.

Pagano, Marco/Röell, Alisa (1998): The choice of stock ownership structure: agency costs, monitoring, and the decision to go public. In: The Quarterly Journal of Economics, 113 (1): 187–225.

Park, Tido (2003): Kapitalmarktstrafrechtliche Neuerungen des Vierten Finanzmarktförderungsgesetzes. In: Betriebs-Berater, 58 (30): 1513–1517.

Parrino, Robert/Sias, Richard W./Starks, Laura T. (2003): Voting with their feet: institutional ownership changes around forced CEO turnover. In: Journal of Financial Economics, 68 (1): 3–46.

Peemöller, Volker H./Hofmann, Stefan (2005): Bilanzskandale - Delikte und Gegenmaßnahmen Berlin: Erich Schmidt.

Pellens, Bernhard et al. (2003): Ausschüttungspolitik börsennotierter Unternehmen in Deutschland. In: Die Betriebswirtschaft, 63 (3): 309–332.

Peng, Mike W. (2003): Institutional Transitions and Strategic Choices. In: The Academy of Management Review, 28 (2): 275–296.

Pérez-González, Francisco (2003): Large Shareholders and Dividends: Evidence From U.S. Tax Reforms. Working Paper. URL: http://web.stanford.edu/~fperezg/lgsh.pdf, accessed on October 14, 2014.

Perfect, Steven B./Wiles, Kenneth W. (1994): Alternative constructions of Tobin's q: An empirical comparison. In: Journal of Empirical Finance, 1 (3-4): 313–341.

Perrow, Charles (1986): Economic Theories of Organization. In: Theory and Society, 15 (1-2): 11–45.

Phillips, Denis C./Burbules, Nicholas C. (2000): Postpositivism and Educational Research Lanham: Rowman & Littlefield Publishers, Inc.

Pindado, Julio/de la Torre, Chabela (2006): The Role of Investment, Financing and Dividend Decisions in Explaining Corporate Ownership Structure: Empirical Evidence from Spain. In: European Financial Management, 12 (5): 661–687.

Pluskat, Sorika (2005): Die Neuregelung der Directors' Dealings in der Fassung des Anlegerschutzverbesserungsgesetzes. In: Der Betrieb, 58 (20): 1097–1101.

Pound, John (1988): Proxy contests and the efficiency of shareholder oversight. In: Journal of Financial Economics, 20 (1-2): 237–265.

Pozen, Robert C. (1994): Institutional Investors: The Reluctant Activists. In: Harvard Business Review, 73 (1-2): 140–149.

Pratt, John W./Zeckhauser, Richard J. (1991): Principals and Agents: An Overview. In: Pratt, John W./Zeckhauser, Richard J. (Editors): Principals and Agents: The Structure of Business. Boston: Harvard Business School Press: 1–35.

Prevost, Andrew K./Rao, Ramesh P. (2000): Of What Value Are Shareholder Proposals Sponsored by Public Pension Funds? In: The Journal of Business, 73 (2): 177–204.

Prokot, Alexander (2006): Strategische Ausschüttungspolitik deutscher Aktiengesellschaften - Dividendenstrategien im Kapitalmarktkontext. Wiesbaden: Deutscher Universitäts-Verlag.

Prowse, Stephen D. (1990): Institutional investment patterns and corporate financial behavior in the United States and Japan. In: Journal of Financial Economics, 27 (1): 43–66.

Prowse, Stephen D. (1994): Corporate Governance in an International Perspective: a survey of corporate control mechanisms among large firms in the United States, the United Kingdom, Japan and Germany. Bank for International Settlements Economic Papers No. 41 – July 1994. URL: http://www.bis.org/publ/econ41.htm, accessed on October 14, 2014.

Qandil, Johanna S. (2014): Wahrnehmung der Qualität der Abschlussprüfung: Eine theoretische und empirische Analyse für den deutschen Kapitalmarkt. Wiesbaden: Springer Gabler.

Rappaport, Alfred (1981): Selecting strategies that create shareholder value. In: Harvard Business Review, 59 (5-6): 139–150.

Rees, Ray (1985a): The Theory of Principal and Agent Part I. In: Bulletin of Economic Research, 37 (1): 3–26.

Rees, Ray (1985b): The Theory of Principal and Agent Part II. In: Bulletin of Economic Research, 37 (2): 75–97.

Reilly, Frank K./Brown, Keith C. (2011): Investment Analysis and Portfolio Management, 10th ed. Mason: South Western Cengage Learning.

Renders, Annelies/Gaeremynck, Ann (2012): Corporate Governance, Principal-Principal Agency Conflicts, and Firm Value in European Listed Companies. In: Corporate Governance: An International Review, 20 (2): 125–143.

Renneboog, Luc/Simons, Tomas/Wright, Mike (2007): Why do public firms go private in the UK? The impact of private equity investors, incentive realignment and undervaluation. In: Journal of Corporate Finance, 13 (4): 591–628.

Renneboog, Luc/Szilagyi, Peter G. (2006): How relevant is dividend policy under low shareholder protection? CentER Discussion Paper No. 2006-73. URL: https://pure.uvt.nl/portal/files/779221/73.pdf, accessed on October 14, 2014.

Renneboog, Luc/Trojanowski, Grzegorz (2007): Control structures and payout policy. In: Managerial Finance, 33 (1): 43–64.

Richter, Rudolf (1994): Institutionen ökonomisch analysiert. Tübingen: Mohr Siebeck.

Rieckers, Oliver/Spindler, Gerald (2004): Corporate Governance: Legal Aspects. In: Krahnen, Jan P./Schmidt, Reinhard H. (Editors): The German Financial System. Oxford: Oxford University Press: 350–385.

Ringe, Wolf-Georg (2014): Changing Law and Ownership Patterns in Germany: Corporate Governance and the Erosion of Deutschland AG. Oxford Legal Studies Research Paper No. 42/2014. URL: http://papers.ssrn.com/sol3/papers.cfm?abstract_id=2457431, accessed on October 15, 2014.

Ringleb, Henrik-Michael et al. (2008): Deutscher Corporate Governance Kodex - Kommentar, 3rd ed. München: C.H. Beck.

Roberts, Michael R./Whited, Toni M. (2013): Endogeneity in Empirical Corporate Finance. In: Constantinides, George M./Harris, Milton/Stulz, René M. (Editors): Handbook of the Economics of Finance, 2nd ed. Oxford: Elsevier B.V.: 493–572.

Rose, Paul/Sharfman, Bernard (2013): Shareholder Activism as a Corrective Mechanism in Corporate Governance. Ohio State Public Law Working Paper No. 225. URL: http://papers.ssrn.com/sol3/papers.cfm?abstract_id=2324151, accessed on October 14, 2014.

Ross, Stephen A. (1973): The Economic Theory of Agency : The Principal's Problem In: The American Economic Review, 63: 134–139.

Rozeff, Michael S. (1982): Growth, beta and agency costs as determinants of dividend payout ratios. In: The Journal of Financial Research, 5 (3): 249–259.

Rudolph, Bernd (2002): Viertes Finanzmarktförderungsgesetz - ist der Name Programm? In: Betriebs-Berater, 57 (20): 1036–1041.

Ruhwedel, Franca (2003): Eigentümerstruktur und Unternehmenserfolg – Eine theoretische und empirische Analyse deutscher börsennotierter Unternehmen. Frankfurt: Peter Lang.

Ruiz-Mallorquí, María V./Santana-Martín, Domingo J. (2009): Ultimate Institutional Owner and Takeover Defenses in the Controlling versus Minority Shareholders Context. In: Corporate Governance: An International Review, 17 (2): 238–254.

Ruiz-Mallorquí, María V./Santana-Martín, Domingo J. (2011): Dominant institutional owners and firm value. In: Journal of Banking & Finance, 35 (1): 118–129.

Ryan, Lori V./Schneider, Marguerite (2002): The Antecedents of Institutional Investor Activism. In: Academy of Management Review, 27 (4): 554–573.

Rydqvist, Kristian (1987): The Pricing of Shares with Different Voting Power and the Theory of Oceanic Games. Stockholm: Economic Research Institute, Stockholm School of Economics.

Saam, Nicole J. (2002): Prinzipale, Agenten und Macht. Tübingen: Mohr Siebeck.

Sánchez-Ballesta, Juan P./García-Meca, Emma (2011): Ownership Structure and the Cost of Debt. In: European Accounting Review, 20 (2): 389–416.

Sappington, David E. (1991): Incentives in Principal-Agent Relationships. In: The Journal of Economic Perspectives, 5 (2): 45–66.

Sargan, John D. (1958): The Estimation of Economic Relationships using Instrumental Variables. In: Econometrica, 26 (3): 393–415.

Sauter, Maike (2008): Der Referentenentwurf eines Gesetzes zur Umsetzung der Aktionärsrechterichtlinie (ARUG). Institute for Law and Finance Working Paper Series No. 85. URL: http://www.ilf-frankfurt.de/uploads/media/ILF_WP_085.pdf, accessed on October 14, 2014.

Schanze, Erich (1987): Contract, Agency, and the Delegation of Decision Making. In: Bamberg, Günter/Spremann, Klaus (Editors): Agency Theory, Information, and Incentives. Berlin: Springer: 461–471.

Scharfstein, David (1988): The disciplinary role of takeovers. In: The Review of Economic Studies, 55 (2): 185–199.

Schichold, Bernd/Kruse, Jens (2011): Der Financial Expert im Spannungsfeld zwischen Finanzvorstand und Abschlussprüfer. In: Der Aufsichtsrat, 8 (1): 2–3.

Schira, Josef (2005): Statistische Methoden der VWL und BWL. Theorie und Praxis, 2nd ed. München: Pearson Studium.

Schmid, Frank A./Wahrenburg, Mark (2004): Mergers and Acquisitions. In: Krahnen, Jan P./Schmidt, Reinhard H. (Editors): The German Financial System. Oxford: Oxford University Press: 261–288.

Schmid, Stefan/Kretschmer, Katharina (2004): The German Corporate Governance System and the German "Mitbestimmung" - An Overview. European School of Management Working Paper No. 8. URL: http://www.escpeurope.eu/uploads/media/Schmid-Kretschmer_2004_The_German_Corporate_Governance_System.pdf, accessed on October 14, 2014.

Schmidt, Reinhard H. (1987): Agency Costs are not a "Flop"! In: Bamberg, Günter/Spremann, Klaus (Editors): Agency Theory, Information, and Incentives. Berlin: Springer: 495–509.

Schmidt, Reinhard H. (2004): Corporate Governance in Germany: An Economic Perspective. In: Krahnen, Jan P./Schmidt, Reinhard H. (Editors): The German Financial System. Oxford: Oxford University Press: 386–424.

Schmidt, Reinhard H./Tyrell, Marcel (2004): What Constitutes a Financial System in General and the German Financial System in Particular? In: Krahnen, Jan P./Schmidt, Reinhard H. (Editors): The German Financial System. Oxford: Oxford University Press: 19–68.

Schneider, Dieter (1987): Agency Costs and Transaction Costs: Flops in the Principal-Agent Theory of Financial Markets. In: Bamberg, Günter/Spremann, Klaus (Editors): Agency Theory, Information, and Incentives. Berlin: Springer: 481–494.

Schröder, Ulrich/Schrader, Alexander (1998): The changing role of banks and corporate governance in Germany: evolution towards the market? In: Black, Stanley W./Moersch, Mathias (Editors): Competition and Convergence in Financial Markets Amsterdam: Elsevier Science B.V.: 17–39.

Schulze, William S. et al. (2001): Agency Relationships in Family Firms: Theory and Evidence. In: Organization Science, 12 (2): 99–116.

Schwintowski, David (2007): Räuberische Aktionäre: Konsequenzen der empirischen Forschung. In: Der Betrieb, 60 (49): 2695–2700.

Seger, Frank (1997): Banken, Erfolg und Finanzierung: Eine Analyse für deutsche Industrieunternehmen. Wiesbaden: Gabler Verlag.

Seibert, Ulrich (1999): Das Gesetz zur Kontrolle und Transparenz im Unternehmensbereich - Die aktienrechtlichen Regelungen im Überblick. In: Dörner, Dietrich/Menhold, Dieter/Pfitzer, Norbert (Editors): Reform des Aktienrechts, der Rechnungslegung und Prüfung. Stuttgart: Schäffer-Poeschel Verlag: 1–26.

Seifert, Bruce/Gonenc, Halit/Wright, Jim (2005): The international evidence on performance and equity ownership by insiders, blockholders, and institutions. In: Journal of Multinational Financial Management, 15 (2): 171–191.

Seifert, Werner G. et al. (2002): Performance ist kein Schicksal. Frankfurt: Campus Verlag GmbH.

Setia-Atmaja, Lukas Y. (2009): Governance Mechanisms and Firm Value: The Impact of Ownership Concentration and Dividends. In: Corporate Governance: An International Review, 17 (6): 694–709.

Shapiro, Susan P. (2005): Agency Theory. In: Annual Review of Sociology, 31 (1): 263–284.

Shapley, Lloyd S./Shubik, Martin (1954): A Method for Evaluating the Distribution of Power in a Committee System. In: The American Political Science Review, 48 (3): 787–792.

Sharma, Pramodita (2004): An Overview of the Field of Family Business Studies: Current Status and Directions for the Future. In: Family Business Review, 17 (1): 1–36.

Shavell, Steven (1979): Risk sharing and incentives in the principal and agent relationship. In: The Bell Journal of Economics, 10 (1): 55–73.

Sherman, Hugh/Beldona, Sam/Joshi, Maheshkumar P. (1998): Institutional investor heterogeneity : implications for strategic decisions. In: Corporate Governance, 6 (3): 166–173.

Shleifer, Andrei/Vishny, Robert W. (1986): Large Shareholders and Corporate Control. In: Journal of Political Economy, 94 (3): 461–488.

Shleifer, Andrei/Vishny, Robert W. (1997): A Survey of Corporate Governance. In: The Journal of Finance, 52 (2): 737.

Shome, Dilip K./Singh, Sudhir (1995): Firm value and external blockholdings. In: Financial management, 24 (4): 3–14.

Short, Helen/Zhang, Hao/Keasey, Kevin (2002): The link between dividend policy and institutional ownership. In: Journal of Corporate Finance, 8 (2): 105–122.

Simon, Stefan/Zetzsche, Dirk (2010): Das Vollmachtstimmrecht von Banken und geschäftsmäßigen Vertretern (§ 135 AktG nF) im Spannungsfeld von Corporate Governance, Präsenzsicherung und prozeduraler Effizienz. In: Zeitschrift für Unternehmens- und Gesellschaftsrecht, 39 (5): 918–957.

Singh, Manohar/Davidson III, Wallace N. (2003): Agency costs, ownership structure and corporate governance mechanisms. In: Journal of Banking & Finance, 27 (5): 793–816.

Sirmon, David G./Hitt, Michael A. (2003): Managing Resources: Linking Unique Resources, Management, and Wealth Creation in Family Firms. In: Entrepreneurship Theory and Practice, 27 (4): 339–358.

Smith, Adam (1789): An inquiry into the nature and causes of the wealth of nations. Philadelphia: Thomas Dobson.

Smith Jr., Clifford W./Warner, Jerold B. (1979): On Financial Contracting. In: Journal of Financial Economics, 7 (2): 117–161.

Smith, Michael P. (1996): Shareholder Activism by Institutional Investors: Evidence from CalPERS. In: The Journal of Finance, 51 (1): 227–252.

Spence, Michael (1973): Job Market Signaling. In: The Quarterly Journal of Economics, 87 (3): 355–374.

Spremann, Klaus (1987): Agent and Principal. In: Bamberg, Günter/Spremann, Klaus (Editors): Agency Theory, Information, and Incentives. Berlin: Springer Verlag: 3–37.

Stadler, Maximilian (2010): Shareholder-Aktivismus durch Hedge Fonds: Empirische Untersuchung für Deutschland. Berlin.

Steck, Kai-Uwe/Schmitz, Rainer (2005): Das Kapitalmarktrecht nach dem Anlegerschutzverbesserungsgesetz. In: Finanz Betrieb, 7 (3): 187–196.

Stein, Jeremy C. (1989): Efficient Capital Markets, Inefficient Firms: A Model of Myopic Corporate Behavior. In: The Quarterly Journal of Economics, 104 (4): 655–669.

Stelzig, Peter (2000): Zur Treuepflicht des Aktionärs unter besonderer Berücksichtigung ihrer geschichtlichen Entwicklung. Dissertation Universität Münster.

Stock, James H./Watson, Mark M. (2012): Introduction to Econometrics, 3rd ed. Essex: Pearson Education Ltd.

Streeck, Wolfgang/Hassel, Anke (2003): "Germany Ltd." is passé. In: MaxPlanckResearch, 2: 72–79.

Streeck, Wolfgang/Höpner, Martin (2003): Alle Macht dem Markt? Frankfurt/New York: Campus Verlag GmbH.

Strunk, Günther et al. (2003): TransPuG und Corporate Governance Kodex - Neue gesellschafts-, bilanz- und steuerrechtliche Anforderungen für die Unternehmenspraxis. Berlin: Erich Schmidt Verlag.

Stulz, René M. (1990): Managerial discretion and optimal financing policies. In: Journal of Financial Economics, 26 (1): 3–27.

Sunder, Jayanthi/Sunder, Shyam V./Wongsunwai, Wan (2011): Debtholder Responses to Shareholder Activism: Evidence from Hedge Fund Interventions. Working Paper. URL: https://www.stern.nyu.edu/sites/default/files/assets/documents/con_031697.pdf, accessed on October 14, 2014.

Swoboda, Peter (1987): The Liquidation Decision as a Principal-Agent Problem. In: Bamberg, Günter/Spremann, Klaus (Editors): Agency Theory, Information, and Incentives Berlin: Springer Verlag: 167–177.

Talaulicar, Till/v. Werder, Axel (2008): Patterns of Compliance with the German Corporate Governance Code. In: Corporate Governance: An International Review, 16 (4): 255–273.

Thamm, Christian/Schiereck, Dirk (2014): Shareholder Activism in Deutschland - Eine Bestandsaufnahme. In: Corporate Finance, 1 (1): 17–27.

Theis, Jochen C. (2014): Kommunikation zwischen Unternehmen und Kapitalmarkt. Wiesbaden: Springer Gabler.

Theisen, Manuel R. (1999): Zur Reform des Aufsichtsrats - Eine betriebswirtschaftliche Bestandsanalyse und Perspektive. In: Dörner, Dietrich/Menhold, Dieter/Pfitzer, Norbert

(Editors): Reform des Aktienrechts, der Rechnungslegung und Prüfung Stuttgart: Schäffer-Poeschel Verlag: 293–252.

Theissen, Erik (2004): Organized Equity Markets. In: Krahnen, Jan P./Schmidt, Reinhard H (Editors): The German Financial System. Oxford: Oxford University Press.

Thomsen, Steen/Pedersen, Torben (2000): Ownership structure and economic performance in the largest European companies. In: Strategic Management Journal, 21 (6): 689–705.

Thomsen, Steen/Pedersen, Torben/Kvist, Hans K. (2006): Blockholder ownership: effects on firm value in market and control based governance systems. In: Journal of Corporate Finance, 12 (2): 246–269.

Thüsing, Gregor (2009): Das Gesetz zur Angemessenheit der Vorstandsvergütung. In: Die Aktiengesellschaft, 54 (15): 517–528.

Tielmann, Jörgen/Heppe, Hans-Jörg (2003): Germany's Fourth Financial Markets Promotion Act. In: The International Lawyer, 37 (1): 191–210.

Titman, Sheridan/Wessels, Roberto (1988): The Determinants of Capital Structure Choice. In: The Journal of Finance, 43 (1): 1–19.

Tobin, James (1969): A General Equilibrium Approach To Monetary Theory. In: Journal of Money, Credit and Banking, 1 (1): 15–29.

Topalov, Mihail (2011): Die Wahrnehmung von Dividenden durch Finanzvorstände - Eine empirische Untersuchung zu den Determinanten der Dividendenpolitik in der Bundesrepublik Deutschland. Wiesbaden: Springer Gabler.

Tranfield, David/Denyer, David/Smart, Palminder (2003): Towards a Methodology for Developing Evidence-Informed Management Knowledge by Means of Systematic Review. In: British Journal of Management, 14 (3): 207–222.

Travlos, Nickolaos G./Cornett, Marcia M. (1993): Going Private Buyouts and Determinants of Shareholders' Returns. In: Journal of Accounting, Auditing & Finance, 8 (1): 1–25.

Trinchera, Oliver (2012): Large Blockholders, Shareholder Protection and Taxes: Their Impact on Firm Performance and Payout Policy. München: Universitätsbibliothek der TU München.

Truong, Thanh/Heaney, Richard (2007): Largest shareholder and dividend policy around the world. In: The Quarterly Review of Economics and Finance, 47 (5): 667–687.

V. Werder, Axel/Bartz, Jenny (2013): Corporate Governance Report 2013: Abweichungskultur und Unabhängigkeit im Lichte der Akzeptanz und Anwendung des aktuellen DCGK. In: Der Betrieb, 66 (17): 885–895.

Van der Elst, Christoph (2011): Revisiting Shareholder Activism at AGMs: Voting Determinants of Large and Small Shareholders. ECGI Finance Working Paper No. 311/2011, Tilburg Law School Legal Studies Research Paper No. 019/2011. URL:

http://papers.ssrn.com/sol3/papers.cfm?abstract_id=1886865, accessed on October 14, 2014.

Van der Elst, Christoph/Vermeulen, Erik (2011): Europe's Corporate Governance Green Paper: Do Institutional Investors Matter? Tilburg Law School Research Paper No. 014/2011 URL: http://papers.ssrn.com/sol3/papers.cfm?abstract_id=1860144, accessed on October 14, 2014.

Velte, Patrich (2010): Der deutsche Prüfungsausschuss nach dem BilMoG und dem VorstAG. In: Zeitschrift für internationale und kapitalmarktorientierte Rechnungslegung, 10 (9): 429–433.

Vesper-Gräske, Marvin (2013): Articles " Say On Pay " In Germany : The Regulatory Framework And Empirical Evidence. In: German Law Journal, 14 (7): 749–795.

Viciano-Gofferje, Martin (2013): Neue Transparenzanforderungen für Private Equity Fonds nach dem Kapitalanlagegesetzbuch. In: Betriebs-Berater, 30 (42): 2506–2511.

Villalonga, Belen/Amit, Raphael (2006): How do family ownership, control and management affect firm value? In: Journal of Financial Economics, 80 (2): 385–417.

Vitols, Sigurt (2005): Changes in Germany's Bank-Based Financial System: implications for corporate governance. In: Corporate Governance: An International Review, 13 (3): 386–396.

Volhard, Patricia/El-Qalqili, Joel (2013): Private Equity und AIFM-Richtlinie. In: Corporate Finance law, (4): 202–206.

Wahal, Sunil (1996): Pension Fund Activism and Firm Performance. In: The Journal of Financial and Quantitative Analysis, 31 (1): 1–23.

Walsh, Carl E. (2010): Monetary Theory and Policy, 3rd ed. Cambridge: The MIT Press.

Walsh, James P./Seward, James K. (1990): On the Efficiency of Internal and External Corporate Control Mechanisms. In: The Academy of Management Review, 15 (3): 421–458.

Watt, Andrew (2008): The impact of private equity on European companies and workers: key issues and a review of the evidence. In: Industrial Relations Journal, 39 (6): 548–568.

Wenger, Ekkehard/Kaserer, Christoph (1998): The German system of corporate governance - A model which should not be imitated. In: Black, Stanley W./Moersch, Mathias (Editors): Competition and Convergence in Financial Markets. Amsterdam: Elsevier Science B.V.: 41–78.

Werner, Steve/Tosi, Henry L./Gomez-Mejia, Luis (2005): Organizational governance and employee pay: How ownership structure affects the firm's compensation strategy. In: Strategic Management Journal, 26 (4): 377–384.

Widmann, Tobias (2009): Das Fehlen des Finanzexperten nach dem BilMoG - Worst-Case-Szenario für den Aufsichtsrat? In: Betriebs-Berater, 64 (49): 2602–2606.

Wilhelm, Jochen E. (1987): On Stakeholders' Unanimity. In: Bamberg, Günter/Spremann, Klaus (Editors): Agency Theory, Information, and Incentives. Berlin: Springer Verlag: 179–204.

Williamson, Oliver E. (1971): The Vertical Integration of Production: Market Failure Considerations. In: The American Economic Review, 61 (2): 112–123.

Williamson, Oliver E. (1973): Markets and Hierarchies: Some Elementary Considerations. In: The American Economic Review, 63 (2): 316–325.

Williamson, Oliver E. (1974): The Economics of Discretionary Behaviour: Managerial Objectives in a Theory of the Firm. London: Kershaw Publishing Company Ltd.

Williamson, Oliver E. (1976): Franchise Bidding for Natural Monopolies-in General and with Respect to CATV. In: The Bell Journal of Economics, 7 (1): 73–104.

Williamson, Oliver E. (1981): The Economics of Organization: The Transaction Cost Approach. In: American Journal of Sociology, 87 (3): 548–577.

Williamson, Oliver E. (1998): Transaction Cost Economics: How It Works; Where It Is Headed. In: De Economist, 146 (1): 23–58.

Williamson, Oliver E. (2000): The New Institutional Economics: Taking Stock, Looking Ahead. In: Journal of Economic Literature, 38 (3): 595–613.

Witt, Peter (2001): Corporate Governance. In: Jost, Peter-Jürgen (Editor): Die Prinzipal-Agenten-Theorie in der Betriebswirtschaftslehre, Stuttgart: Schäffer-Poeschel Verlag: 85–115.

Witt, Peter (2003): Corporate Governance Systeme im Wettbewerb. Wiesbaden: Deutscher Universitäts-Verlag.

Woidtke, Tracie (2002): Agents watching agents? Evidence from pension fund ownership and firm value. In: Journal of Financial Economics, 63 (1): 99–131.

Wolf, J. Benedict (1999): The Effects of Agency Problems on the Financial Behavior, Performance, and Efficiency of German Industrial Stock Corporations. Frankfurt: Peter Lang.

Wollenhaupt, Markus/Beck, Rocco (2013): Das neue Kapitalanlagegesetzbuch (KAGB): Überblick über die Neuregelung des deutschen Investmentrechts nach der Umsetzung der AIFM-RL. In: Der Betrieb, 66 (35): 1950–1959.

Wooldridge, Jeffrey M. (2010): Econometric Analysis of Cross Section and Panel Data, 2nd ed. Cambridge: The MIT Press.

Wooldridge, Jeffrey M. (2012): Introductory Econometrics – A Modern Approach, 5th ed. Mason: South Western Cengage Learning.

Wright, Mike/Robbie, Ken (1998): Venture Capital and Private Equity: A Review and Synthesis. In: Journal of Business & Accounting, 25 (5): 521–570.

Wruck, Karen H. (1989): Equity Ownership Concentration and firm value - Evidence from Private Equity Financings. In: Journal of Financial Economics, 23 (1): 3–28.

Wu, De-Min (1973): Alternative Tests of Independence between Stochastic Regressors and Disturbances. In: Econometrica, 41 (4): 733–750.

Yafeh, Yishay/Yosha, Oved (2003): Large Shareholders and Banks: Who Monitors and How? In: The Economic Journal, 113 (484): 128–146.

Yoon, Pyung Sig/Starks, Laura T. (1995): Signaling, Investment Opportunities, and Dividend Announcements. In: The Review of Financial Studies, 8 (4): 995–1018.

Young, Michael N. et al. (2003): Principal-Principal Agency. In: Chinese Management Review, 6 (1): 17–45.

Young, Michael N. et al. (2008): Corporate governance in emerging economies: A review of the principal–principal perspective. In: Journal of Management Studies, 45 (1): 196–220.

Zeckhauser, Richard J./Pound, John (1990): Are Large Shareholders Effective Monitors? An Investigation of Share Ownership and Corporate Performance. In: Hubbard, R. Glenn (Editor): Asymmetric Information, Corporate Finance, and Investment. Chicago: University of Chicago Press: 149–180.

Zhou, Xianming (2001): Understanding the determinants of managerial ownership and the link between ownership and performance: comment. In: Journal of Financial Economics, 62 (3): 559–571.

Zülch, Henning/Hoffmann, Sebastian (2009): Die Modernisierung des deutschen Handelsbilanzrechts durch das BilMoG: Wesentliche Alt- und Neuregelungen im Überblick. In: Der Betrieb, 62 (15): 745–752.

Zwiebel, Jeffrey (1995): Block investment and partial benefits of corporate control. In: The Review of Economic Studies, 62 (2): 161–185.

List of Laws and Other Standards

AktG (2013): Aktiengesetz of September 6, 1965 (BGBl. I: 1089) including all subsequent amendments in the version of July 23, 2013. In: BGBl. I: 2586.

AnlSVG (2011): Gesetz zur Stärkung des Anlegerschutzes und Verbesserung der Funktionsfähigkeit des Kapitalmarkts (Anlegerschutz- und Funktionsverbesserungsgesetz) of April 5, 2011 (BGBl. I: 538) including all subsequent amendments in the version of December 6, 2011. In: BGBl. I: 2481.

AnSVG (2005): Gesetz zur Verbesserung des Anlegerschutzes (Anlegerschutzverbesserungsgesetz – AnSVG) of October 28, 2004 (BGBl. I: 2630) including all subsequent amendments in the version of June 22, 2005. In: BGBl. I: 1698.

ARUG (2009): Gesetz zur Umsetzung der Aktionärsrechterichtlinie of July 30, 2009. In: BGBl. I: 2479.

BilKoG (2004): Gesetz zur Kontrolle von Unternehmensabschlüssen (Bilanzkontrollgesetz - BilKoG) of December 15, 2004. In BGBl. I: 3408.

BilMoG (2009): Gesetz zur Modernisierung des Bilanzrechts of May 25, 2009. In: BGBl. I: 1102.

BilReG (2004): Gesetz zur Einführung internationaler Rechnungslegungsstandards und zur Sicherung der Qualität der Abschlussprüfung (Bilanzrechtsreformgesetz - BilReG) of December 9, 2004. In: BGBl. I: 3166.

BörsG (2014): Börsengesetz of July 16, 2007 (BGBl. I: 1330, 1351) including all subsequent amendments in the version of July 15, 2014. In: BGBl. I: 934.

DrittelbG (2011): Gesetz über die Drittelbeteiligung der Arbeitnehmer im Aufsichtsrat (Drittelbeteiligungsgesetz – DrittelbG) of May 18, 2004 (BGBl. I: 974) including all subsequent amendments in the version of December 22, 2011. In BGBl. I: 3044.

EstG (2014): Einkommensteuergesetz (EStG) of October 16, 1934 (RGBl.: 1005) including all subsequent amendments in the version of July 25, 2014. In BGBl. I: 1266.

European Commission (2009a): Directive 2009/65/EC of the European Parliament and of the Council of 13 July 2009 on the coordination of laws, regulations and administrative provisions relating to undertakings for collective investment in transferable securities (UCITS). In: Official Journal of the European Union (L302): 32-96.

European Commission (2011b): Directive 2011/61/EU of the European Parliament and of the Council of 8 June 2011 on Alternative Investment Fund Managers and amending Directives 2003/41/EC and 2009/65/EC and Regulations (EC) No 1060/2009 and (EU) No 1095/2010. In: Official Journal of the European Union (L174): 1-73.

FinDAG (2013): Gesetz über die Bundesanstalt für Finanzdienstleistungsaufsicht (Finanzdienstleistungsaufsichtsgesetz - FinDAG) of April 22, 2002 (BGBl. I: 1310) including all subsequent amendments in the version of February 13, 2013. In BGBl. I: 174, 185.

FMFG (2002): Gesetz zur weiteren Fortentwicklung des Finanzplatzes Deutschland (Viertes Finanzmarktförderungsgesetz) of June 21, 2002. In: BGBl. I: 2010.

GCGC (2013): German Corporate Governance Code as amended on May 13, 2013 with proposals from the plenary meeting of May 13, 2013. URL: http://dcgk.de//files/dcgk/usercontent/en/download/code/D_CorGov_final_2013.pdf, accessed on September 22, 2014.

GWB (2014): Gesetz gegen Wettbewerbsbeschränkungen (GWB) of August 26, 1998 (BGBl. I: 2521) including all subsequent amendments in the version of July 21, 2014. In: BGBl. I: 1066.

HGB (2014): Handelsgesetzbuch of May 10, 1897 (RGBl.: 2019) including all subsequent amendments in the version of July 15, 2014. In: BGBl. I: 934.

IASB (2014): International Financial Reporting Standards. London: International Accounting Standards Board.

InvÄndG (2007): Gesetz zur Änderung des Investmentgesetzes und zur Anpassung anderer Vorschriften (Investmentänderungsgesetz) of December 21, 2007. In BGBl. I: 3089.

KAGB (2014): Kapitalanlagegesetzbuch (KAGB) of July 4, 2013 (BGBl. I: 1981) including all subsequent amendments in the version of July 15, 2014. In BGBl. I: 934.

KAGG (2013): Gesetz über Kapitalanlagegesellschaften of September 9, 1998 (BGBl. I: 2726) including all subsequent amendments in the version of December 17, 2013. In: BGBl. I: 255.

KapAEG (2004): Gesetz zur Verbesserung der Wettbewerbsfähigkeit deutscher Konzerne an Kapitalmärkten und zur Erleichterung der Aufnahme von Gesellschafterdarlehen (Kapitalaufnahmeerleichterungsgesetz - KapAEG) of April 20, 1998 (BGBl. I: 707) including all subsequent amendments in the version of December 4, 2004. In: BGBl. I: 3166.

KonTraG (1998): Gesetz zur Kontrolle und Transparenz im Unternehmensbereich of April 27, 1998. In: BGBl. I: 786.

KStG (2014): Körperschaftsteuergesetz (KStG) of August 31, 1976 (BGBl. I: 2597) including all subsequent amendments in the version of July 25, 2014. In BGBl. I: 1266.

KWG (2014): Gesetz über das Kreditwesen (Kreditwesengesetz - KWG) of 9 September, 1998 (BGBl. I: 2776) including all subsequent amendments in the version of July 15, 2014. In: BGBl. I: 934.

MitbestG (2011): Gesetz über die Mitbestimmung der Arbeitnehmer (Mitbestimmungsgesetz - MitbestG) of May 4, 1976 (BGBl. I: 1153) including all subsequent amendments in the version of December 22, 2011. In BGBl. I: 3044.

Montan-MitbestG (2006): Gesetz über die Mitbestimmung der Arbeitnehmer in den Aufsichtsräten und Vorständen der Unternehmen des Bergbaus und der Eisen und Stahl erzeugenden Industrie of May 21, 1951 (BGBl. I: 347) including all subsequent amendments in the version of October 31, 2006. In BGBl. I: 2407.

SEAG (2009): Gesetz zur Ausführung der Verordnung (EG) Nr. 2157/2001 des Rates vom 8. Oktober 2001 über das Statut der Europäischen Gesellschaft (SE) (SE-Ausführungsgesetz - SEAG) of December 22, 2004 (BGBl. I: 3675) including all subsequent amendments in the version of July 30, 2009. In BGBl. I: 2479.

SEBG (2004): Gesetz über die Beteiligung der Arbeitnehmer in einer Europäischen Gesellschaft (SE-Beteiligungsgesetz - SEBG) of December 22, 2004. In BGBl. I: 3675, 3686.

TransPuG (2002): Gesetz zur weiteren Reform des Aktien- und Bilanzrechts, zu Transparenz und Publizität (Transparenz- und Publizitätsgesetz - TransPuG) of July 19, 2002. In: BGBl. I: 2681.

UMAG (2005): Gesetz zur Unternehmensintegrität und Modernisierung des Anfechtungsrechts of September 22, 2005. In: BGBl. I: 2802.

VorstAG (2009): Gesetz zur Angemessenheit der Vorstandsvergütung of July 31, 2009. In: BGBl. I: 2509.

VorstOG (2005): Gesetz über die Offenlegung der Vorstandsvergütungen of August 3, 2005. In: BGBl. I: 2267.

WpHG (2014): Gesetz über den Wertpapierhandel (Wertpapierhandelsgesetz - WpHG) of September 9, 1998 (BGBl. I: 2708) including all subsequent amendments in the version of July 15, 2014. In: BGBl. I: 934.

WpÜG (2013): Wertpapiererwerbs- und Übernahmegesetz (WpÜG) of December 20, 2001 (BGBl. I: 3822) including all subsequent amendments in the version of August 7, 2013. In BGBl. I: 3154.

List of Other Sources

Bain & Company (2013): Global Private Equity Report 2013. URL: http://www.bain.com/Images/BAIN_REPORT_Global_Private_Equity_Report_2013.pdf, accessed on October 13, 2014.

Beck, Thorsten et al. (2013): Financial Development and Structure Dataset (updated Nov. 2013). URL: http://go.worldbank.org/X23UD9QUX0, accessed on October 13, 2014.

BGH (1988): BGH judgment of February 1, 1988 II ZR 75/87. In: Neue Juristische Wochenschrift, 25: 1579-1583.

BGH (1995): BGH judgment of March 20, 1995 II ZR 205/94. In: Neue Juristische Wochenschrift, 27: 1739-1750.

Bundesverband Deutscher Kapitalbeteiligungsgesellschaften (2014): Jährliche Private Equity-Investitionen seit 1990. URL: http://www.bvkap.de/privateequity.php/cat/172/title/Interaktive_Charts, accessed on October 13, 2014.

Bundesverband Investment und Asset Management e.V. (2013): Investmentstatistik. URL: http://www.bvi.de/fileadmin/user_upload/Statistik/ZeitreihenStatistik2013.pdf, accessed on October 13, 2014.

Bureau van Dijk (2013): Orbis: Company information around the globe. URL: http://www.bvdinfo. com/de-de/about-bvd/brochure-library/brochures/orbis, accessed on October 13, 2014.

Clifford Chance (2011): Restricting stealth takeover strategies – The German Investor Protection Improvement Act. URL: http://www.cliffordchance.com/briefings/2011/04/restricting_stealthtakeoverstrategies-th.html, accessed on October 13, 2014.

Commission of the European Communities (2009): Communication for the Spring European Council - Driving European recovery. In: COM(2009) 114 final.

Detzer, Daniel et al. (2013): The German Financial System. Financialisation, Economy, Society and Sustainable Development Studies in Financial Systems No 3. URL: http://www.fessud.eu/wp-content/uploads/PDF/German%20Financial%20System%20-%20Final%2015.05.2013.pdf, accessed on October 14, 2014.

Deutsche Börse AG (2010): General Standard und Prime Standard - Zugang zum europäischen Kapitalmarkt. URL: http://xetra.com/xetra/dispatch/de/binary/gdb_content_pool/imported_files/public_files/10_downloads/33_going_being_public/40_stock_market_segmentation/sm_rcm_broschuere.pdf, accessed on December 17, 2011.

Deutsche Börse AG (2012a): Prime Standard and General Standard – the markets for excellence. URL: http://xetra.com/xetra/dispatch/en/binary/gdb_content_pool/imported_files/public_files/10_downloads/33_going_being_public/10_products/245_prime_general_standard/fact_sheet_ps_gs.pdf, accessed on October 13, 2014.

Deutsche Börse AG (2012b): Entry Standard for shares. URL: http://deutsche-berse.com/dbg/dispatch/en/binary/gdb_content_pool/imported_files/public_files/10_do wnloads/33_going_being_public/10_products/transparency_factsheets/FS_ES_shares.pdf, accessed on October 13, 2014.

Deutsche Börse AG (2013): Guide to the Equity Indices of Deutsche Börse. URL: http://www.dax-indices.com/DE/MediaLibrary/Document/Equity_L_6_19_e.pdf, accessed on October 13, 2014.

Deutsche Bundesbank (2014a): Lending to non-banks (non-MFIs), total. URL: http://www.bundesbank.de/Navigation/EN/Statistics/Time_series_databases/Macro_economic_time_series/its_list_node.html?listId=www_s100_mb3031_01_01, accessed on October 13, 2014.

Deutsche Bundesbank (2014b): Balance sheet total (up to December 1998 Volume of business). URL: http://www.bundesbank.de/Navigation/EN/Statistics/Time_series_databases/Macro_economic_time_series/its_list_node.html?listId=www_s100_mb2425_1_02, accessed on October 13, 2014.

Deutsche Bundesbank (2014c): Number of reporting credit institutions. URL: http://www.bundesbank.de/Navigation/EN/Statistics/Time_series_databases/Macro_economic_time_series/its_list_node.html?listId=www_s100_mb2425_1_01, accessed on October 13, 2014.

Deutsche Bundesbank (2014d): External financing consolidated. URL: http://www.bundesbank.de/Navigation/EN/Statistics/Time_series_databases/Macro_economic_time_series/its_list_node.html?listId=www_v39_nuaf, accessed on October 13, 2014.

Deutsche Telekom (2006): Annual Report 2006. URL: http://www.telekom.com/investor-relations/publications/Financial-results/204382, accessed on October 16, 2014.

European Commission (2009b): Proposal for a Directive of the European Parliament and of the Council on Alternative Investment Fund Managers and amending Directives 2004/39/EC and 2009/…/EC. In: COM(2009) 207 final.

European Commission (2009c): Commission Staff Working Document Accompanying the Proposal for a Directive of the European Parliament and of the Council on Alternative Investment Fund Managers and amending Directives 2004/39/EC and 2009/…/EC. In: SEC(2009) 576.

European Commission (2010a): Commission Staff Working Document Corporate Governance in Financial Institutions: Lessons to be drawn from the current financial crisis, best practices. Accompanying document to the Green Paper Corporate governance in financial institutions and remuneration policies. In: SEC(2010) 669.

European Commission (2010b): Green Paper - Corporate governance in financial institutions and remuneration policies. In: COM(2010) 284 final.

European Commission (2010c): Feedback Statement - Summary of Responses to Commission Green Paper on Corporate Governance in Financial Institutions. URL:

http://ec.europa.eu/internal_market/consultations/docs/2010/governance/feedback_statement_en.pdf, accessed on October 13, 2014.

European Commission (2010d): European Commission Green Paper on corporate governance in financial institutions and report on remunerations - frequently asked questions. In: MEMO/10/229.

European Commission (2011a): Green Paper - The EU corporate governance framework. In COM(2011) 164 final.

European Commission (2011c): Feedback Statement - Summary of Responses to the Commission Green Paper on the EU Corporate Governance Framework. URL: http://ec.europa.eu/internal_market/company/docs/modern/20111115-feedback-statement_en.pdf, accessed on October 13, 2014.

European Commission (2012): Communication from the Commission to the European Parliament, the Council, the European and Social Committee and the Committee of the Regions. Action Plan: European company law and corporate governance - a modern legal framework for more engaged shareholders and sustainable companies. In: COM(2012) 740/2.

Hans-Böckler-Stiftung (2007): Results of the "Biedenkopf Commission" – the Government Commission on the modernisation of employee board-level representation in Germany. URL: http://www.boeckler.de/pdf/bb_zusammenfassung_BiKo_engl.pdf, accessed on February 6, 2014.

Kirkpatrick, Grant (2009): The Corporate Governance Lessons from the Financial Crisis. Financial Market Trends, OECD. URL: http://www.oecd.org/finance/financial-markets/42229620.pdf, accessed on October 14, 2014.

Kommission zur Modernisierung der deutschen Unternehmensmitbestimmung (2006): Bericht der wissenschaftlichen Mitglieder der Kommission mit Stellungnahmen der Vertreter der Unternehmen und der Vertreter der Arbeitnehmer. URL: http://kohte.jura.uni-halle.de/recht/Kommissionsbericht_Endfassung.pdf, accessed on October 13, 2014.

Larosière, Jacques de et al. (2009): Report on financial supervision in the EU (De Larosière report). URL: http://ec.europa.eu/internal_market/finances/docs/de_larosiere_report_en.pdf, accessed on October 13, 2014.

Lazette, Michelle P. (2013): Who's in control? Private equity firms don't have to be. In: Crain's Cleveland Business, August 25, 2013. URL: http://www.crainscleveland.com/article/20130825/SUB1/308259995/whos-in-control-private-equity-firms-dont-have-to-be, accessed on October 14, 2014.

Maisch, Michael (2005): Hans Eichel löst die Deutschland AG auf. In: Handelsblatt, August 31, 2005. URL: http://www.handelsblatt.com/unternehmen/industrie/steuerbefreiung-fuer-beteiligungsverkaeufe-hans-eichel-loest-die-deutschland-ag-auf/2545460.html, accessed on October 14, 2014.

OECD (2004): OECD Principles of Corporate Governance. URL: http://www.oecd.org/corporate/ca/corporategovernanceprinciples/31557724.pdf, accessed on October 13, 2014.

OECD (2009): Corporate Governance and the Financial Crisis: Key Findings and Main Messages. URL: http://www.oecd.org/corporate/ca/corporategovernanceprinciples/43056196.pdf, accessed on October 13, 2014.

Schutzgemeinschaft der Kapitalanleger e.V. (2012a): Statistiken – Hauptversammlungspräsenzen DAX. URL: http://www.sdk.org/assets/Statistiken/HV-Praesenzen/praesenz-dax12.pdf, accessed on October 13, 2014.

Schutzgemeinschaft der Kapitalanleger e.V. (2012b): Statistiken – Hauptversammlungspräsenzen MDAX. URL: http://www.sdk.org/assets/Statistiken/HV-Praesenzen/praesenz-mdax12.pdf, accessed on October 13, 2014.

Schutzgemeinschaft der Kapitalanleger e.V. (2012c): Statistiken – Hauptversammlungspräsenzen SDAX. URL: http://www.sdk.org/assets/Statistiken/HV-Praesenzen/praesenz-sdax12.pdf, accessed on October 13, 2014.

Schutzgemeinschaft der Kapitalanleger e.V. (2012d): Statistiken – Hauptversammlungspräsenzen TecDAX. URL: http://www.sdk.org/assets/Statistiken/HV-Praesenzen/praesenz-tecdax12.pdf, accessed on October 13, 2014.

Statistisches Bundesamt (2014): Volkswirtschaftliche Gesamtrechnungen des Bundes – Brutto-wertschöpfung, Bruttoinlandsprodukt (nominal/preisbereinigt): Deutschland, Jahre. URL: https://offenedaten.de/dataset/destatis-statistik-81000/resource/f11853e4-e7f4-409b-a4c8-9b4e1dc6b1c3, accessed on February 19, 2014.

ThyssenKrupp AG (2014): Supervisory Board. URL: http://www.thyssenkrupp.com/en/investor/aufsichtsrat.html, accessed on October 16, 2014.

MIX
Papier aus verantwortungsvollen Quellen
Paper from responsible sources
FSC® C105338

If you have any concerns about our products,
you can contact us on
ProductSafety@springernature.com

In case Publisher is established outside the EU,
the EU authorized representative is:
Springer Nature Customer Service Center GmbH
Europaplatz 3, 69115 Heidelberg, Germany

Printed by Libri Plureos GmbH
in Hamburg, Germany